The Oxford Latin Mini Dictionary

Edited by
James Morwood

D0401929

OXFORD
UNIVERSITY PRESS

OXFORD
UNIVERSITY PRESS

Great Clarendon Street, Oxford OX2 6DP

Oxford University Press is a department of the University of Oxford.
It furthers the University's objective of excellence in research, scholarship,
and education by publishing worldwide in

Oxford New York

Auckland Cape Town Dar es Salaam Hong Kong Karachi
Kuala Lumpur Madrid Melbourne Mexico City Nairobi
New Delhi Shanghai Taipei Toronto

With offices in

Argentina Austria Brazil Chile Czech Republic France Greece
Guatemala Hungary Italy Japan Poland Portugal Singapore
South Korea Switzerland Thailand Turkey Ukraine Vietnam

Oxford is a registered trade mark of Oxford University Press
in the UK and in certain other countries

Published in the United States
by Oxford University Press Inc., New York

© Oxford University Press 2008

The moral rights of the authors have been asserted
Database right Oxford University Press (maker)

First published 1995 as the Pocket Oxford Latin Dictionary
Based on original content published by Routledge & Kegan Paul Ltd. 1913

British Library Cataloguing in Publication Data

Data available

Library of Congress Cataloging in Publication Dat

Data available

Typeset by Asiatype, Inc
Printed and bound in Italy
by L.E.G.O. S.p.A.

ISBN 978-0-19-953438-8

10 9 8 7 6 5 4 3

Preface

When it first appeared in 1995, the *Pocket Oxford Latin Dictionary* was in part a response to the completion in 1982 of the monumental *Oxford Latin Dictionary*. There was clearly a need for a shorter, more accessible and considerably less expensive dictionary to take account of the important philological advances which that work had made. Within its modest compass, the *Pocket Oxford Latin Dictionary* presented a Latin language cleansed of suspect accretions and an English language cleansed of Victorian usage. Now, thirteen years later, it appears in a new, improved edition: the *Oxford Latin Mini Dictionary*.

OLMD is based on S.C. Woodhouse's Latin Dictionary, first published by Routledge and Kegan Paul in 1913 and subsequently reprinted many times. In the English into Latin section, the spirit of Woodhouse has been allowed some free play, even though the pruning knife, if not the axe, had to be much at work on his inventive and lively luxuriance. Save for the tidying up of of typographical conventions, this section is unchanged from the first edition.

In a modern dictionary, the Latin into English section is of the greater importance. It is in this section of this dictionary that the *Oxford Latin Dictionary* makes itself especially felt. In the first edition, the section was centred on the Latin of the so-called Golden Age (from 100 BC to the death of Livy). In the new edition many words have been added, thus broadening the scope of the dictionary to include Plautus and Terence

Preface

(third and second centuries BC) and Pliny the Younger and Tacitus (late first and second centuries AD). Furthermore, many words from late and medieval Latin have been included

In redesigning the grammar section we have taken a conscious decision to employ the order of cases that Latin learners in the UK are generally taught; this order may surpris readers outside the UK who have been brought up on the traditional ordering of the cases of nouns, adjectives, and pronouns. The accusative case thus appears in our tables immediately below the nominative (the overall order being nom., acc., gen., dat., and abl.). The traditional ordering, where the genitive directly follows the nominative, dates bac to classical times, and it was indeed used in the British Isles until the advent of Kennedy's *Latin Primer* in 1866. The fact that this order is no longer the norm in the UK is due almost entirely to the overwhelming use of Kennedy's primer in Latir teaching in British schools since the late 19th century. There are sound pedagogical reasons for Kennedy's ordering—mo notably, it emphasises the fact that all neuters have identical nom. and acc.—, and since a dictionary should provide only handy reference summary of word inflections, we feel justifie in our choice of the UK order for this Oxford volume.

JAMES MORWOO
Wadham Colleg
Oxford

Guide to Pronunciation

ne English sounds referred to are those of standard southern
itish English.

onsonants

onsonants are pronounced as in modern English, but note
e following:

c   is always hard, as in <u>c</u>at (never soft as in ni<u>c</u>e).

g   is always hard, as in <u>G</u>od (except when it is followed
       by **n**: **gn** is sounded 'ngn' as in ha<u>ngn</u>ail, so magnus is
       pronounced **'mangnus'**).

h   is always sounded, as in <u>h</u>ope.

i   is used as a consonant as well as a vowel; as a consonant
       it sounds like English 'y', so Latin **iam** is pronounced
       'yam'.

q   occurs, as in English, only before **u**; **qu** is sounded as in
       English <u>qu</u>ick.

r   is rolled as in Scots English, and is always sounded; so in
       Latin **sors** both **r** and **s** are sounded.

s   is always soft, as in <u>s</u>it (never like 'z', as in ro<u>s</u>e).

v   in Classical Latin was pronounced like English 'w';
       so **vīdī** sounds 'weedee'. This sound is often written
       u (and thus not distinguished in print from the
       vowel **u**), and indeed the Romans themselves made
       no distinction in writing. There was no 'v' sound in
       Classical Latin.

Guide to Pronunciation

Where double consonants occur, as in English 'sitting', both consonants are pronounced; so **ille** is pronounced 'ille' (the **l** is sounded long as in English 'hall-light').

☑ Note that in words containing consonantal **i** between two vowels, this **i** was pronounced as a double consonant (though written single); so the first syllable of **maior** is heavy although the **a** is short, because the consonantal **i** is double.

Vowels

Latin had five different simple vowel sounds, each of which could be short or long:

a short, as in English c**u**p (*not* as in c**a**p).

ā long, as in English f**a**ther.

e short, as in English p**e**t.

ē long, as in English **ai**m (or, more accurately, French g**ai**).

i short, as in English d**i**p.

ī long, as in English d**ee**p.

o short, as in English p**o**t.

ō long, as in English m**o**bile (or, more accurately, French b**eau**).

u short, as in English p**u**t.

ū long, as in English c**oo**l.

☑ Throughout this dictionary, except in the English–Latin section and in words marked as **LM** (i.e. Late/Medieval), all naturally long vowels are marked with a macron: all vowels not so marked are short.

Latin also had six diphthongs. A diphthong can be defined as a vowel (**a**, **e**, or **o**) followed by a glide (**i**, **e**, or **u**).

Guide to Pronunciation

ae as in English high.

au as in English how.

ei as in English eight.

eu e-u (as in Cockney English tell, *not* as in English yew).

oe as in English boy (only shorter).

ui u-i (as in French oui).

☑ In 'Church Latin' (the Latin used in the Roman Catholic Church), it is conventional to pronounce sounds in an 'Italian' way; e.g. **c** and **g** are pronounced 'ch' and 'j'/'dg' (as in church and judge) before **e**, **i** and **ae**, **gn** is pronounced 'ny' (as in vineyard), **v** is pronounced like English 'v' (as in level), and **ae** is pronounced 'ay' (as in day).

Number of syllables and stress

1 Except in obvious diphthongs (**ae**, **au**, **oe**, and often **eu**), every single vowel signals a separate syllable, as in English 'recipe' (three syllables). Thus Latin **dēsine** is three syllables and **diem** is two.

2 The stress in words with two syllables almost always falls on the first syllable.

3 The stress in words of more than two syllables falls on the penultimate syllable if this is metrically 'heavy' (i.e. contains a long vowel, a diphthong, or a vowel followed by two consonants), e.g. **festína**, **agénda**. It falls on the antepenultimate (third from last) syllable when the penultimate is metrically 'light' (i.e. contains a short vowel before either another vowel or a single consonant), e.g. **dóminus**. This pair of rules is natural for English speakers.

4 For the purposes of syllable weight, **x** always counts as
   two consonants ('ks') while **qu** always counts as a single
   consonant ('kʷ'). Strictly speaking, a syllable can be light
   even where it contains a short vowel that is followed by
   two consonants, provided that those two consonants are
   one of the following pairs (so-called 'mute plus liquid'
   combinations): br, bl, cr, cl, dr, gr, gl, pr, pl, tr.

☑ The distinction observed here between syllable *weight* and *vowel*
   length, i.e. between metrically heavy and light syllables and
   naturally long and short vowels, is relatively recent. Older books use
   'long' and 'short' indifferently for both syllables and vowels, thereby
   encouraging mispronunciation. See also the section on Some
   Common Metres of Latin Verse.

List of Abbreviations

bl.	ablative	**int.**	interjection
cc.	accusative	**ir.**	irregular
ct.	active	**LM**	Late/Medieval Latin
(dj).	adjective	**m(asc).**	masculine
d(v).	adverb	**med.**	medical
	with nouns common (i.e. m. or f.)	**mil.**	military
	with dates *circa* ('around')	**mus.**	musical
		n.	noun
f.	*cónfer* ('compare')	**NB**	*notā bene* ('note well')
L	Classical Latin		
omp.	comparative	**neg.**	negative
onj.	conjunction	**nom.**	nominative
at.	dative	**n(t).**	neuter
ecl.	declension	**num.**	numeral
ep.	deponent	**pass.**	passive
.g.	*exemplī grātiā* ('for example')	**perf.**	perfect
		pl.	plural
tc.	*et cētera* ('and so on')	**plpf.**	pluperfect
em).	feminine	**pple.**	participle
g.	figurative	**prep.**	preposition
	flōruit ('flourished, was in his prime')	**pres.**	present
ut.	future	**pron.**	pronoun
en.	genitive	**rel.**	relative
e	*id est* ('that is')	**sing., sg.**	singular
npers.	impersonal	**subj.**	subjunctive
npf.	imperfect	**sup.**	superlative
npv.	imperative	**usu.**	usually
decl.	indeclinable	**v. (i./t.)**	verb (intransitive/transitive)
d(ic).	indicative	**viz.**	*vidēlicet* ('namely')
fin.	infinitive	**voc.**	vocative

Aa

ab (also **abs**) *prep with abl* from; by (of the agent); away from; since, starting with; at □ ~ **tergō** from behind

bacus, **ī** *m* counting-board; side-board; square stone on the top of columns

baliēnātiō, **ōnis** *f* legal transfer of property

baliēnō ① *v* transfer by sale or contract; remove

bavus, **ī** *m* great-great-grandfather, ancestor

bbas, **atis** *m* [LM] abbot

bbatia, **ae** *f* [LM] monastery, abbey

bbatissa, **ae** *f* [LM] abbess

bdicātiō, **ōnis** *f* renunciation; disowning (of a son)

bdicō ① *v* resign; abolish; disinherit

bdō, **didī**, **ditum** ③ *v* hide, conceal; plunge; remove

bdōmen, **inis** *nt* lower part of the belly, paunch; gluttony

bdūcō, **ūxī**, **uctum** ③ *v* lead away, carry off; abduct, seduce

beō, **īre**, **iī/īvī**, **itum** *v ir* go away, depart; vanish; escape; be hanged □ **ē mediō** ~ die

berrātiō, **ōnis** *f* diversion, relief

berrō ① *v* go astray, deviate (from); disagree (with)

bhinc *adv* from this time, since, ago; from this place

abhorreō ② *v usu with* **ab** *and abl* be averse (to), shudder at; be inconsistent (with)

abiciō, **lēcī**, **lectum** ③ *v* throw away; slight, give up; humble, debase

abiectē *adv* in a spiritless manner; in humble circumstances; negligently

abiectus, **a**, **um** *adj* downcast, mean, abject, base

abiēgnus, **a**, **um** *adj* made of fir

abiēs, **etis** *f* white fir; ship; spear

abigō, **ēgī**, **āctum** ③ *v* drive or send away

abitus, **ūs** *m* going away; departure; way out, exit

abiūdicō ① *v* deprive by judicial verdict

abiungō, **ūnxī**, **ūnctum** ③ *v* unyoke, remove, separate

abiūrō ① *v* deny on oath, repudiate

ablēgātiō, **ōnis** *f* sending away, dispatch

ablēgō ① *v* send away, remove

abluō, **uī**, **ūtum** ③ *v* wash away, blot out, purify; quench; remove

abnegō ① *v* deny, refuse; keep back

abnuō, **uī**, **ūtum** ③ *v* deny, refuse, reject

aboleō, **ēvī** ② *v* abolish, destroy

abolēscō, **ēvī** ③ *v* cease, be extinct, fall into disuse

abolitiō, **ōnis** *f* abolition,

a

cancellation, annulment

abōminor ① *v dep* (seek to) avert (by prayer); detest

aborior, abortus sum ④ *v dep* pass away, disappear; miscarry

abortiō, ōnis *f* abortion, miscarriage

abortīvus, a, um *adj* abortive; addled

abortus, ūs *m* miscarriage

abrādō, āsī, āsum ③ *v* scratch off, shave; 'knock off', rob

abripiō, ripuī, reptum ③ *v* drag away by force; abduct, kidnap

abrogātiō, ōnis *f* repeal of a law

abrogō ① *v* repeal wholly, abolish

abrumpō, ūpī, uptum ③ *v* break off, tear asunder, cut through

abruptiō, ōnis *f* breaking, breaking off

abruptus, a, um *adj* precipitous, steep; hasty, rash

abs ▸ ā

abscēdō, essī, essum ③ *v* go away, depart; desist

abscessus, ūs *m* going away, absence

abscīdō, īdī, īsum ③ *v* cut off, remove

abscindō, idī, issum ③ *v* cut off, tear away; put an end to

abscīsus, a, um *adj* steep, abrupt

abscondō, (di)dī ③ *v* hide; keep secret

absēns, ntis *adj* absent

absentia, ae *f* absence

absiliō, liī/luī ④ *v* leap away; fly apart

absimilis, e *adj* unlike

absistō, stitī ③ *v* stand off, go away; desist from, leave off

absolūtē *adv* completely, perfectly

absolūtiō, ōnis *f* finishing, acquittal, perfection

absolūtus, a, um *adj* free, complete, unconditional

absolvō, lvī, lūtum ③ *v* absolve (from), discharge, dismiss, release; finish; pay, satisfy

absonus, a, um *adj* out of tune, discordant, incongruous

absorbeō, buī/psī, ptum ② *v* absorb, suck in

absque *prep with abl* without, except

abstēmius, a, um *adj* sober, temperate; fasting

abstergeō, rsī, rsum ② *v* wipe off or dry or clean; remove

absterreō ② *v* frighten away

abstinēns, ntis *adj* abstinent, temperate

abstinenter *adv* abstinently

abstinentia, ae *f* abstinence; fasting; moderation

abstineō, tentum ② *v* restrain, keep away; abstain, forbear

abstō, stitī, stitum ① *v* stand at a distance

abstrahō, āxī, actum ③ *v* drag away from; separate

abstrūdō, ūsī, ūsum ③ *v* thrust away, conceal

abstrūsus, a, um *adj* secret, reserved

abstulī *pf of* ▸ **auferō**

absum, abesse, āfuī *v ir* be absent *or* away (from) *or* distant; be wanting

absūmō, mpsī, mptum ③ *v* spend, use up, waste, squander, ruin

absurdus, a, um *adj* of a harsh sound; absurd; nonsensical

abundanter *adv* abundantly, copiously

abundantia, ae *f* abundance, plenty, riches

abundē *adv* abundantly

abundō ① *v* abound (in), be rich

abusque *prep with abl* all the way from

abūsus, ūs *m* misuse, wasting

abūtor, abūsus sum ③ *v dep* use up, waste; misuse

ac *conj* and, and besides; than

acadēmīa, ae *f* academy, university

acadēmicus, a, um *adj* academic

acalanthis, idis *f* a small song-bird

acanthus, ī *m* bear's-foot; the gum arabic tree

accēdō, essī, essum ③ *v* go or come to or near, approach; attack; fall to one's share, be added, come over to; be like, enter upon

accelerō ① *v* accelerate, hasten; make haste

accendō, ndī, ēnsum ③ *v* set on fire, light, illuminate; inflame

accēnseō, ēnsum ② *v* attach as an attendant to

accēnsus, ī *m* supernumerary soldier; attendant; orderly

accentus, ūs *m* accent, intonation

acceptiō, ōnis *f* taking, accepting; meaning, sense

acceptum, ī *nt* (financial) credit

acceptus, a, um *adj* welcome, well-liked; (of money) received

accersō¹, īvī/iī, ītum ③ *v* send for, call; procure; summon, accuse

accersō² ▶ **accessō**

accessiō, ōnis *f* approach; increase, addition; (med) fit

accessus, ūs *m* approach, admittance, attack

accidentia, ium *npl* ⓛⓜ accidents (Aristotelian qualities)

accīdō, īdī, īsum ③ *v* cut short, weaken

accidō, idī ③ *v* fall at or near; happen

accingō, īnxī, īnctum ③ *v* gird on or about; provide (with), prepare (for)

acciō ④ *v* send for, summon

accipiō, cēpī, ceptum ③ *v* accept, collect, take, receive; undertake; hear, learn, find; get; sustain; obey; treat

  □ **sat ~** take or exact security

accipiter, tris *m* hawk

accītus, ūs *m* summons, call

acclāmātiō, ōnis *f* acclamation, shout; crying against

acclāmō ① *v* shout (at), cry out against

acclārō ① *v* make clear, reveal

acclīnis, e *adj* leaning (on), sloping; inclined, disposed (to)

acclīnō ① *v* lay down, rest (on), lean against, incline (to)

acclīvis, e *adj*, **acclīvus, a, um** *adj* sloping upwards

accola, ae *m/f* neighbour

accolō, luī, ultum ③ *v* dwell near

accommodātiō, ōnis *f*

a

adjustment, willingness to oblige

accommodātus, a, um *adj* fit, suitable

accommodō ① *v* adjust, fit, suit; apply; synchronize

accommodus, a, um *adj* fit, convenient

accrēdō, didī ③ *v with dat* give credence to, believe

accrēscō, ēvī, ētum ③ *v* grow on, increase, swell, be annexed to

accrētiō, ōnis *f* increasing, increment

accubitiō, ōnis *f* reclining (at meals)

accubō, buī, itum ① *v* lie near or by; recline at table; sit down

accumbō, buī ③ *v* lie down, recline at table

accumulātor, ōris *m* heaper up

accumulō ① *v* accumulate, heap up

accūrātiō, ōnis *f* carefulness, painstakingness

accūrātus, a, um *adj* accurate, with care, meticulous

accūrō ① *v* take care of, attend to; do carefully

accurrō, (cu)currī, ursum ③ *v* run *or* hasten to

accursus, ūs *m* rushing up; attack

accūsābilis, e *adj* blameable, reprehensible

accūsātiō, ōnis *f* accusation

accūsātor, ōris *m* accuser, plaintiff; informer

accūsātōrius, a, um *adj* accusatory

accūsitō ① *v with acc of person and crime* accuse repeatedly

accūsō ① *v* accuse, blame,

reprimand

acer, eris *nt* maple-tree

ācer, cris, cre *adj* sharp, sour, pungent, piercing; violent; keen, furious, swift, active, ardent, courageous; drastic, critical; bracing, of keen intellect

acerbitās, ātis *f* acerbity, sourness; severity, bitterness; anguish, hardship

acerbō ① *v* embitter; aggravate

acerbus, a, um *adj* unripe, sour, bitter; crude; shrill, rough, violent; severe; grievous

acernus, a, um *adj* of maple

acerra, ae *f* box or casket for incense

acervātim *adv* in heaps, summarily, without any order

acervō ① *v* heap up

acervus, ī *m* heap

acēscō, cuī ③ *v* turn sour

acētāria, ōrum *ntpl* salad prepared with vinegar

acētum, ī *nt* vinegar; sourness of disposition; sharpness of wit

acidus, a, um *adj* acid, sour

aciēs, iēī *f* edge, point; battle-array, line of battle; the sight of the eyes; pupil of the eye; quickness of apprehension

acināces, ācis *m* scimitar

acinum, ī *nt*, **acinus, ī** *m* grape ivy-berry; pip, seed

acipēnser, eris *m* sturgeon

aclys, ydis *f* javelin

aconītum, ī *nt* wolf's-bane, aconite

acquiēscō, ēvī, ētum ③ *v* lie down to rest; acquiesce (in), assent; subside

cquīrō, īsīvī, īsītum ③ *v*
acquire, get, obtain

cquīsītiō, ōnis *f* acquisition

criculus, a, um *adj* shrewd,
acute

crimōnia, ae *f* acrimony,
sharpness, briskness

criter *adv* sharply, vehemently,
severely, steadfastly

croāma, atis *nt* item in an
entertainment, act, 'turn'

croāsis, is *f* lecture

cta, ōrum *ntpl* acts, exploits;
chronicles, record

cta, ae *f* sea-shore

ctiō, ōnis *f* action; plot (of a
play); legal process

ctitō ① *v* act or plead frequently

ctīvus, a, um *adj* active

ctor, ōris *m* plaintiff, advocate;
agent; player, actor; herdsman

ctuārius¹, (i)ī *m* short-hand
writer, clerk, book-keeper,
secretary

ctuārius², a, um *adj* swift,
nimble, light

ctum, ī *nt* deed, exploit

ctuōsus, a, um *adj* active, busy

ctus, ūs *m* act, performance,
action; delivery

ctūtum *adv* forthwith, instantly,
n no time at all

culeātus, a, um *adj* prickly;
stinging, sharp, subtle

culeus, ī *m* sting, prickle; point;
sarcasm

cūmen, inis *nt* sharpened point,
sting, sharpness, cunning, fraud

cuō, uī, ūtum ③ *v* whet,
sharpen; spur on, provoke

acus, ūs *f* needle, pin

acūtē *adv* acutely

acūtulus, a, um *adj* subtle, clever

acūtus, a, um *adj* sharp, pointed;
violent, severe; glaring; acute,
quick-witted; high-pitched

ad *prep with acc* to, towards, near by,
at, before, up to, until, about; in
comparison with, according to; in
addition to, after, concerning; *with
gerund(ive)* in order to

adaequē *adv* equally, so much; in
like manner, so also

adaequō ① *v* equalize, level,
compare (to); be equal

adamantēus, a, um *adj*
adamantine

adamantinus, a, um *adj* hard as
the hardest iron

adamās, ntis *m* the hardest iron;
diamond

adamō ① *v* love passionately

adaperiō, ruī, rtum ④ *v* throw
open, uncover

adapertilis, e *adj* that may be
opened

adaptō ① *v* adjust, fit

adaquō ① *v* water

adauctus, ūs *m* increase, growth

adaugeō, xī, ctum ② *v* increase,
intensify

adbibō, bibī ③ *v* drink, drink in

addecet ② *v impers* it is fitting

addēnseō ② *v* make more dense,
close up (the ranks)

addīcō, īxī, ictum ③ *v* be
propitious; adjudge; confiscate;
knock down to, award; consecrate;
sacrifice

addictiō, ōnis *f* adjudication,
assignment

a

addictus, ī m a person enslaved for debt or theft

addiscō, didicī ③ v learn besides

additāmentum, ī nt addition

addō, didī ③ v add, give, bring to, say in addition; attach, annex □ ~ **gradum** gather pace, speed up

addubitō ① v doubt, hesitate

addūcō, ūxī, uctum ③ v bring or lead to or along; lead on, induce, contract, tighten

adedō, ēsse, ēdī, ēsum v ir eat up, eat into, squander

adēmptiō, ōnis f taking away

adeō² adv so much, to such a degree, so, so far, just, even, much more, much less, 'you know'

adeō², īre, iī/īvī, itum v ir go to or approach, address, accost, visit; attack; undergo, take a part in; enter on (an inheritance)

adeps, ipis m/f fat, lard, grease; corpulence; bombast

adeptiō, ōnis f obtaining, attainment

adeptus ▶ pple from **adipīscor**

adequitō ① v ride up to

adf- ▶ aff-

adg- ▶ agg-

adhaereō, haesī, haesum ② v, **adhaerēscō ③** v adhere, stick, cling to

adhaesiō, ōnis f adhesion, linkage

adhibeō ② v apply, hold (to); use; invite, admit

adhinniō ④ v whinny (to)

adhortātiō, ōnis f exhortation

adhortātor, ōris m encourager

adhortor ① v dep exhort, encourage

adhūc adv to this point, until now, yet, still; besides

adiaceō ② v with dat lie beside or near to

adiciō, iēcī, iectum v throw to, add to

adiectiō, ōnis f addition

adigō, ēgī, āctum ③ v drive, bring, drive in, bind by oath

adimō, ēmī, emptum ③ v take away, rescue, deprive

adipīscor, adeptus sum ③ v dep reach, get, obtain, arrive (at), overtake

aditus, ūs m access, way, means, opportunity

adiūdicō ① v adjudge, impute

adiūmentum, ī nt help, assistance

adiūnctiō, ōnis f union, addition

adiūnctum, ī nt quality, characteristic

adiungō, ūnxī, ūnctum ③ v join to, yoke, add to

adiūrō ① v swear solemnly, confirm by oath

adiūtō ① v help

adiūtor, ōris m assistant, helper, supporter

adiūtōrium, (i)ī nt help, assistance

adiūtrīx, īcis f female assistant, helper

adiuvō, iūvī, iūtum ① v assist, help, cherish, favour, mitigate

adl- ▶ all-

admētior, mēnsus sum ④ v dep measure out

adminiculum, ī nt prop, support, stay, means, aid,

assistance

administer, **trī** *m* servant, assistant, supporter

administrātiō, **ōnis** *f* administration; aid, assistance; execution, management, care of affairs

administrātor, **ōris** *m* director, manager

administrō ① *v* administer, manage, serve

admīrābilis, **e** *adj* admirable, wonderful, strange

admīrābilitās, **ātis** *f* wonderful character, remarkableness

admīrābiliter *adv* admirably, astonishingly

admīrātiō, **ōnis** *f* admiration, wondering

admīrātor, **ōris** *m* admirer

admīror ① *v dep* admire, wonder at

admisceō, **ixtum** ② *v* mix, mingle with; mix up with, involve

admissārius, **(i)ī** *m* stallion; sodomite

admissiō, **ōnis** *f* letting in, admission

admissum, **ī** *nt* crime, offence

admittō, **īsī**, **issum** ③ *v* let in, admit, grant, permit, commit, let go, give rein to

admixtiō, **ōnis** *f* (ad)mixture

admodum *adv* quite, very, excessively; altogether, entirely; just so; certainly

admōlior ④ *v dep* make an effort

admoneō ② *v* admonish, warn; remind; persuade

admonitiō, **ōnis** *f* reminding; warning, advice; rebuke

admonitor, **ōris** *m* one who

reminds

admonitus, **ūs** *m* admonition, warning

admoveō, **mōvī**, **mōtum** ② *v* move or bring to, apply, use, direct; lay on

admurmurō ① *v* murmur in protest or approval

adnatō ① *v* swim toward

adnectō, **exum** ③ *v* tie on, annex

adnexus, **ūs** *m* tie, connection

adnītor, **nīxus/nīsus sum** ③ *v dep* lean upon, strive

adnō ① *v* swim to, sail to or toward

adnotō ① *v* note down, notice

adnumerō ① *v* count out, pay, count (in)

adnūntiō ① *v* announce

adnuō, **uī**, **ūtum** ③ *v* nod at or to, assent, promise, grant, indicate by a nod

adoleō, **ultum** ② *v* burn; honour by burnt offering

adolēscō, **ēvī**, **ultum** ③ *v* grow up, increase

adopertus, **a**, **um** *adj* covered

adoptīvus, **a**, **um** *adj* adoptive

adoptō ① *v* select, adopt

ador, **ōris** *nt* coarse grain

adorior, **ortus sum** ④ *v dep* attack, undertake, try

adornō ① *v* equip, set off, prepare, adorn

adōrō ① *v* adore, worship; beg

adp- ▶ **app-**

adpōtus, **a**, **um** *adj* intoxicated, drunk

adprīmē *adv* to the highest degree, extremely

adr- ▶ **arr-**

adrādō, āsī, āsum ③ v scrape, shave, prune

ads- ▶ **ass-**

adscēnsus ▶ **ascēnsus**

adsum, esse, fuī v ir be near, be present, arrive; with dat aid

adūlātiō, ōnis f fawning, flattery

adūlātor, ōris m flatterer

adūlātōrius, a, um adj flattering, adulatory

adulēscēns, ntis m/f young man or girl

adulēscentia, ae f youth (time of life)

adulēscentula, ae f young woman

adulēscentulus, ī m young man, mere youth

adūlor ① v dep fawn upon (as a dog); flatter

adulter¹, erī m, **adultera, ae** f adulterer

adulter², era, erum adj adulterous; counterfeit

adulterīnus, a, um adj counterfeit, false

adulterium, (i)ī nt adultery

adulterō ① v commit adultery (with); falsify, corrupt

adultus, a, um adj full grown, adult

adumbrātiō, ōnis f sketch

adumbrō ① v shadow out, sketch in outline; represent

aduncitās, ātis f hookedness, curvature

aduncus, a, um adj crooked, hooked

adurgeō, ursī ② v press hard, pursue

adūrō, ussī, ustum ③ v burn, scorch; consume

adusque prep with acc right up to, as far as; adv wholly

advectīcius, a, um adj imported, foreign

advectus, a, um adj imported; immigrant

advehō, ēxī, ectum ③ v carry, bring, convey (to)
□ **advehor** arrive by travel, ride to

advena, ae m/f foreigner, stranger, interloper; adj alien, foreign

adveniō, vēnī, ventum ④ v come to, arrive at; develop

adventīcius, a, um adj coming from abroad, foreign, unusual

adventō ① v approach, arrive

adventor, ōris m visitor, customer

adventus, ūs m arrival, approach, attack; LM Advent

adversārius, a, um adj opposite
■ **adversārius, (i)ī** m opponent, enemy
■ **adversāria, ōrum** ntpl memorandum-book

adversātor, ōris m antagonist

adversātrīx, īcis f female antagonist

adversor ① v dep with dat be against, oppose, withstand

adversum, adversus adv opposite, against; prep with acc towards, opposite to, against

adversus, a, um adj opposite, directly facing; adverse, evil, hostile; unfavourable
■ **rēs adversae** fpl adverse circumstances

adversō flūmine against the stream

dvertō, rtī, rsum ▣ v turn or irect to, apply

animum advertō notice, ▶ **nimadvertō**

dvesperāscit, āvit ▣ v impers vening approaches

dvigilō ▣ v watch by, take care

dvocātiō, ōnis f legal support; elay; pleading in the law courts

dvocātus, ī m counsellor, dvocate, witness

dvocō ▣ v call for, summon, call as counsel

dvolō ▣ v fly to, hasten towards

dvolvō, lvī, lūtum ▣ v roll to r towards

genibus advolvor fall at the nees (of anyone)

vor- ▶ **adver-**

lytum, ī nt innermost part of a emple, sanctuary

dēs, dis f (also **aedis**) sg emple; pl house, room

dicula, ae f small house, hapel, niche, closet

dificātiō, ōnis f house-uilding; building; ⓛ instruction, ducation

dificātor, ōris m builder, architect

dificium, (i)ī nt building

dificō ▣ v build, make, create

dilicius, a, um adj of an aedile

dilis, is m aedile

dilitās, ātis f aedileship

ditu(m)us, ī m one who has harge of a temple, sacristan

ger, gra, grum adj sick, infirm, ad, sorrowful, painful, grievous

aegis, idis f the aegis (Minerva's shield); shield, defence

aegrē adv uncomfortably, reluctantly, with difficulty, scarcely □ ~ **est** with dat be disagreeable or displeasing to

aegrēscō ▣ v become sick, grow worse, grieve

aegrimōnia, ae f sorrow, anxiety, melancholy

aegritūdō, inis f sickness, disease, grief, sorrow

aegrōtātiō, ōnis f sickness, disease, morbid desire

aegrōtō ▣ v be sick, be mentally ill

aegrōtus, a, um adj sick, diseased

aemulātiō, ōnis f emulation, rivalry

aemulātor, ōris m imitator, rival

aemulātus, ūs m emulation, envy

aemulor ▣ v dep emulate; be envious, jealous of

aemulus, a, um adj emulous, envious, grudging, (of things) comparable (with); m/f rival

aenigma, atis nt enigma, riddle, obscure saying

aequābilis, e adj equal, alike, uniform, steady, equable

aequābilitās, ātis f equality, fairness, uniformity

aequābiliter adv uniformly, equally

aequaevus, a, um adj of the same age

aequālis, e adj even, equal, of the same age, coeval; m/f contemporary

aequālitās, ātis f evenness;

equality

aequāliter adv equally, evenly

aequanimitās, ātis f evenness of mind, patience, calmness

aequātiō, ōnis f equal distribution

aequē adv equally, in the same manner as, justly

aequinoctiālis, e adj equinoctial

aequinoctium, (i)ī nt equinox

aequiperō [] v compare, liken; with dat become equal (with)

aequitās, ātis f evenness, conformity, symmetry, equanimity, fairness, impartiality

aequō [] v level; equal; compare; reach as high or deep as

aequor, oris nt level surface, plain, surface of the sea, sea

aequoreus, a, um adj of the sea, bordering on the sea

aequus, a, um adj level, even, equal, like, just, kind, favourable, impartial, fair, patient, contented
□ **aequō animō** calmly
■ **aequum,** ī nt plain, flat ground
□ **ex aequō** from the same level

āēr, eris m air, atmosphere; cloud, mist

aerārium, (i)ī nt treasury

aerārius, a, um adj pertaining to copper, brass, etc.; m/f a citizen of the lowest class

aerātus, a, um adj covered with or made of copper or brass

aereus, a, um adj made of copper, bronze or brass

aeripēs, edis adj brazen-footed

āerius, a, um adj aerial, towering, airy

aerūgō, inis f rust of copper,

verdigris; canker of the mind, envy, ill-will, avarice

aerumna, ae f toil, hardship, calamity

aerumnōsus, a, um adj full of trouble, wretched, calamitous

aes, aeris nt copper ore, copper, bronze; money, pay, wages, bronze statue, etc.
□ **aliēnum** debt

aesculus, ī f a variety of oak tree, perhaps either durmast or Hungarian oak

aestās, ātis f summer; a year

aestifer, era, erum adj producing heat, sultry

aestimābilis, e adj having wor or value

aestimātiō, ōnis f valuation, value, price

aestimātor, ōris m valuer, appraiser; judge

aestimō [] v value; estimate; consider

aestīva, ōrum ntpl summer-quarters; the campaigning seaso

aestīvō [] v pass the summer

aestīvus, a, um adj summer-lik summer...

aestuārium, (i)ī nt estuary, inl tidal opening

aestuō [] v boil, foam, billow, seethe; rage, waver, be undecide

aestuōsus, a, um adj hot, sultr billowy

aestus, ūs m heat, fire, tide, swe of the sea; passion; hesitation, anxiety

aetās, ātis f life-time, age, perio generation

aetātula, ae f the tender age o

childhood

aeternitās, ātis f eternity, immortality

aeternō v immortalize

aeternus, a, um adj eternal, everlasting, imperishable
■ **aeternum** adv for ever

aethēr, eris m upper air, heaven, sky

aetherius, a, um adj ethereal, heavenly

aethra, ae f brightness, splendour; clear sky

aevum, ī nt time, life, time of life, age, old age, generation

affābilis, e adj easy of access, affable, friendly

affatim adv sufficiently, amply

affātus, ūs m address, speech, converse

affectātiō, ōnis f seeking after; affectation

affectiō, ōnis f mental condition, feeling, disposition, affection, love

affectō v try to accomplish, aim at, desire, aspire, lay claim to, pretend

affectus¹, ūs m disposition, state (of body and mind), affection, passion, love

affectus², a, um adj endowed with; disposed; impaired, sick

afferō, afferre, attulī, allātum ir bring to, deliver, bring word, allege, produce, contribute, cause

afficiō, fēcī, fectum v affect, move, influence

affīgō, īxī, īxum v with dat fasten to, fix on; impress on

affingō, īnxī, īctum v add (to), embellish, counterfeit,

attribute (wrongly)

affinis, e adj neighbouring, adjacent, related by marriage, connected (with)

affinitās, ātis f neighbourhood; relationship (by marriage)

affirmātiō, ōnis f affirmation, assertion

affirmō v affirm, assert, confirm

afflātus, ūs m breathing on, breeze, blast, breath; inspiration

afflictātiō, ōnis f grievous suffering, torment, affliction

afflictō v strike repeatedly, damage, vex

afflīgō, īxī, īctum v afflict, throw down, crush, grieve, humble, weaken, damage

afflō v blow or breathe on; inspire

affluenter adv abundantly, copiously, lavishly

affluentia, ae f abundance, profusion, superfluity

affluō, ūxī, ūxum v flow on; flock together, abound

affor v dep speak to, address

affulgeō, lsī v with dat shine on; smile upon

affundō, ūdī, ūsum v pour upon (into)
□ **affundor** prostrate oneself

agāsō, ōnis m driver, groom, stable-boy; lackey

age int fossilized imperative from **agō** come! well! all right!

agedum int fossilized imperative from **agō** and **dum** come! well! all right!

agellus, ī m little field, farm

ager, grī m field, ground, territory,

a

country, farm

agger, eris *m* heap, mound, dam; mudwall; rampart; causeway

aggerō¹, essī, estum ③ *v* carry to, bring, add, heap up, on or into

aggerō² ① *v* heap up, fill up, increase

aggestus, ūs *m* piling up

agglomerō ① *v* gather into a body

agglūtinō ① *v* glue to, fasten to

aggravō ① *v* aggravate, weigh down, oppress

aggredior, gressus sum ③ *v dep* approach, attack, undertake

aggregō ① *v* join together, attach
□ **sē aggregāre** ally oneself to

agilis, e *adj* agile, nimble, quick, busy

agilitās, ātis *f* activity, quickness

agitātiō, ōnis *f* agitation, exercise; violent motion

agitātor, ōris *m* driver, charioteer

agitō ① *v* agitate, drive or shake or move about, revolve; consider, pursue, exercise, manage; keep, celebrate, disturb, distress

agmen, inis *nt* herd, flock, troop, swarm, army (on the march)
□ **prīmum ~** the vanguard
□ **novissimum ~** the rear(guard)

agna, ae *f* female lamb

agnātus, ī *m* relation on the father's side; one born after a father has made his will

agnīna, ae *f* flesh of a lamb

agnōmen, inis *nt* an additional name denoting an achievement, a nickname

agnōscō, nōvī, nitum ③ *v*

recognize, acknowledge

agnus, ī *m* lamb

agō, ēgī, āctum ③ *v* drive, act, do, transact, carry off, steal, apply, rouse, cause to bring forth, urge, deal, think, manage, exercise, accuse, deliver (a speech), play (as an actor), behave (as), pass, spend, disturb
□ **grātiās ~ with** *dat* thank
□ **~ dē with** *abl* discuss
□ **āctum est dē with** *abl* it's all up with ...!

agrārius, a, um *adj* agrarian

agrestis, e *adj* rustic, rude, wild, savage
■ **agrestis, is** *m* countryman, peasant

agricola, ae *m* farmer, cultivator

ai *int* ah! alas!

aiō *v ir* say; say yes, assent, affirm

āla, ae *f* wing; upper arm, arm-pit
□ **an army's wing**

alacer, cris, cre *adj* cheerful, brisk, active, courageous, eager, ready

alacritās, ātis *f* cheerfulness, eagerness, liveliness

ālāris, e *adj*, **ālārius, a, um** *adj* pertaining to an army's wing, of the auxiliary cavalry

ālātus, a, um *adj* winged

alauda, ae *f* lark

albātus, a, um *adj* clothed in white

albeō ② *v* be or grow white

albēscō ③ *v* become white

albicō ① *v* be white

albidus, a, um *adj* whitish, pale

albulus, a, um *adj* white, pale

album, ī *nt* white (the colour);

white tablet, list of names, register

lbus, a, um *adj* white, pale, hoary, bright, clear, favourable, fortunate

lcēdō, inis *f*, **alcyōn, onis** *f* kingfisher

lcēdonia, ōrum *ntpl* halcyon days

lea, ae *f* die, dice-play, gambling, chance, venture, risk

leātor, ōris *m* dice-player, gambler

leātōrius, a, um *adj* of dice □ **āleātōria damna** losses at gambling

leō, ōnis *m* gambler

les, itis *m/f* bird, fowl; augury; *adj* winged, swift

lga, ae *f* sea-weed; rubbish

lgeō, lsī ② *v* be cold, feel chilly, endure cold

lgor, ōris *m*, **algus, ūs** *m* coldness

liā *adv* by another way

liātum, ī *nt* food seasoned with garlic

liās *adv* at another time, elsewhere, otherwise

libī *adv* elsewhere, in another place

licubī *adv* somewhere, anywhere

licunde *adv* from some place, from some source or other

liēnātiō, ōnis *f* transference, aversion, dislike

liēnigena, ae *m* stranger, foreigner

liēnō ① *v* alienate, transfer by sale, estrange; *in passive* avoid (with antipathy); be insane

liēnus, a, um *adj* another's, foreign; contrary, averse, hostile; unfavourable, insane □ **aes aliēnum** debt

āliger, era, erum *adj* winged

alimentum, ī *nt* nourishment, food

aliō *adv* to another place; to another subject; to another purpose

ālipēs, edis *adj* wing-footed, swift

aliptēs, ae *m* one who anoints (athletes), trainer of gymnasts

aliquā *adv* somehow

aliquamdiū *adv* for some time

aliquandō *adv* sometimes, at length, formerly, hereafter

aliquantō, aliquantum *adv* somewhat, to some (considerable) extent

aliquantus, a, um *adj* a certain quantity or amount or number of

aliquī, aliquae, aliquod *adj* some, any

aliquis, quid *pn* someone, somewhat, something

aliquō *adv* to some place or other

aliquot *adj indec* some, a number of

aliter *adv* otherwise, else; in a different way

ālium, (i)ī *nt* garlic

aliunde *adv* from another person or place

alius, alia, aliud *adj* another, different, changed □ **alius ... alius** one ... another

allābor, lapsus sum ③ *v dep* glide towards, move forwards

allābōrō ① *v* make a special effort

allāpsus, ūs *m* gliding approach; flowing towards or near

a

allātrō ☐ v bark at; rail at

allectō ☐ v allure, entice

allēgātiō, ōnis f intercession; allegation

allēgō, ēgī, ēctum ☐ v choose, admit

allēgō ☐ v depute, commission

allevō ☐ v lift up, raise; alleviate, diminish, weaken, console

alli- ▸ **āli-**

alliciō, xī, ectum ☐ v draw gently to, entice, attract

allīdō, īsī, īsum ☐ v dash against; shipwreck

alligō ☐ v bind to, bind, impede, entangle; bind by an obligation

allinō, lēvī, litum ☐ v smear over

allocūtiō, ōnis f address, consolation, harangue

alloquium, (i)ī nt address, encouragement

alloquor, locūtus sum ☐ v dep speak to, address, harangue

allūdō, ūsī, ūsum ☐ v frolic around, play with, jest

alluō, uī ☐ v wash against, bathe

alluviēs, iēī f flood-land by a river

almus, a, um adj nourishing, kind, propitious

alnus, ī f alder; plank, bridge, boat

alō, aluī, al(i)tum ☐ v nurse, nourish, maintain; promote; cherish

Alpīnus, a, um adj of the Alps

alsius, a, um adj liable to injury from cold

alsus, a, um adj cool

altāria, ium ntpl altar

altē adv on high, highly, deeply, far back

alter, era, erum adj another, the other, any other, the former, the latter
□ **unus et ~** one or two, a few

alterās ▸ **aliās**

altercātiō, ōnis f contention, dispute, debate

altercor ☐ v dep bicker, dispute, quarrel; dispute in the law-courts

alternō ☐ v do by turns, vary; alternate, waver

alternus, a, um adj alternate, one after the other, by turns, mutual
□ **alternīs vicibus** alternately, by turns

alteruter, tra, trum adj either, one of two

altisonus, a, um adj high-sounding, lofty; sublime

altitonāns, ntis adj thundering from on high

altitūdō, inis f height, depth; (fig) loftiness, profundity, noblemindedness, secrecy

altivolāns, ntis adj high-flying

altor, ōris m nourisher, foster-father

altrīnsecus adv on the other side

altrīx, īcis f female nourisher, wet-nurse

altum, ī nt the deep, the sea; a height

altus, a, um adj high, deep, shrill, lofty, noble; deeply rooted; far-fetched

ālūcinor ☐ v dep wander in mind, talk idly, dream

alumnus, a, um adj nourished, brought up; m nursling, foster-child, disciple

lūta, **ae** f a piece of soft leather; a beauty patch

lveus, **ī** m cavity; tub; tray; hold of a ship, boat; gaming-board; bee-hive; bathing-tub; river-bed

lvus, **ī** f belly, paunch, womb, stomach; bee-hive

ma ▸ hama

mābilis, **e** adj amiable, pleasant

mābiliter adv lovingly, amicably, pleasantly

mandō ① v send away, dismiss

māns, **ntis** m/f lover, sweetheart, mistress

manter adv lovingly, affectionately

māracus, **ī** m/f, **amāracum**, **ī** nt marjoram

māritiēs, **iēī** f bitterness, harshness

māritūdō, **inis** f bitterness, sharpness, disagreeableness

mārus, **a**, **um** adj bitter, harsh, shrill, sad, calamitous; ill-natured

mātiō, **ōnis** f love-making, petting

mātor, **ōris** m lover, devotee

mātōrius, **a**, **um** adj loving, amorous, procuring love

mātrix, **īcis** f sweetheart, mistress

mbāgēs, **gis** f, **ambāgēs**, **um** fpl round-about way, shifting, shuffling, prevarication; long-winded story; obscurity, ambiguity

mbedō, **ēsse**, **ēdī**, **ēsum** v ir gnaw round the edge, consume

mbigō ③ v hesitate, be in doubt, argue, wrangle

mbiguitās, **ātis** f ambiguity

ambiguus, **a**, **um** adj changeable, varying, doubtful, dark, ambiguous, wavering, fickle

ambiō ④ v surround, solicit, ask, aspire to; canvass

ambitiō, **ōnis** f ambition; currying favour, vain display; effort, canvassing

ambitiōsus, **a**, **um** adj ambitious, eager to please; importunate; showy

ambitus, **ūs** m circuit; canvass, bribery; circumlocution; ostentation

ambō, **ae**, **ō** adj both (two together)

ambrosia, **ae** f food of the gods

ambrosius, **a**, **um** adj immortal, divine

ambulācrum, **ī** nt walkway planted with trees, promenade, park

ambulātiō, **ōnis** f walking about; place for promenading

ambulātiuncula, **ae** f little walk; small place for walking

ambulō ① v go about, take a walk, travel

ambūrō, **ussī**, **ustum** ③ v burn around, scorch, burn wholly up; make frost-bitten

ambustulātus, **a**, **um** adj scorched, toasted

amen int Hebrew 'truth' ⟨LM⟩ truly; so be it, amen

āmēns, **ntis** adj mad, frantic

āmentia, **ae** f madness, stupidity

ames, **itis** m pole for supporting bird-nets

amethystus, **ī** f amethyst

amīca, **ae** f female friend,

sweetheart, mistress, courtesan

amiciō, cuī/xī, ctum 4 v clothe, wrap about; veil

amīcitia, ae f friendship, alliance, affinity

amictus, ūs m upper garment, cloak, dress, clothing

amīcula, ae f mistress, lady-friend

amiculum, ī nt mantle, cloak

amīculus, ī m little friend, dear friend, humble friend

amīcus, ī m friend, ally, lover, patron; counsellor, courtier
■ ~, **a, um** adj friendly, fond of

āmissiō, ōnis f loss

amita, ae f father's sister, aunt

āmittō, īsī, issum 3 v lose, dismiss, let fall, let slip

ammirālius, (i)ī m LM emir, governor

amnis, is m stream, river

amō 1 v love, like, be fond of, make love; have a tendency to
□ **amābō (tē)** used as int please

amoenitās, ātis f pleasantness, delight, charm

amoenus, a, um adj pleasant, agreeable, charming

āmōlior 4 v dep remove, obliterate; avert, refute

amōmum, ī nt Eastern spice-plant; spice from this plant

amor, ōris m love; the beloved; Cupid; eager desire
■ **amōrēs, um** mpl girlfriend

āmoveō, mōvī, mōtum 2 v remove, move away, steal; banish

amphisbaena, ae f a species of serpent supposed to have a head at both ends of its body

amphitheātrum, ī nt amphitheatre

amphora, ae f large earthenware jar, usually two-handled

amplectō 3 v, **amplector, amplexus sum** 3 v dep embrace, lay hold of; surround, contain; cherish; understand

amplexor 1 v dep love, esteem

amplexus, ūs m embracing, embrace, surrounding

amplificātiō, ōnis f enlargement, amplification

amplificē adv magnificently, splendidly

amplificō 1 v amplify, enlarge, praise loudly

ampliō 1 v make wider, enlarge, adjourn

amplitūdō, inis f width, breadth, size, bulk; importance; fulness of expression

amplius adv more, further

ampliusculē adv rather more

amplus, a, um adj ample, large, wide; distinguished

ampulla, ae f bottle or flask for holding liquids; pl inflated expressions, bombast

amputātiō, ōnis f pruning, lopping off

amputō 1 v lop off, prune, shorten

amulētum, ī nt charm

amygdalum, ī nt almond tree

an conj whether? or, either

anadēma, atis nt band for the hair

anapaestus, ī m anapaest, metrical foot, two shorts followed by a long

nas, atis *f* duck

nathema, atis *nt* [LM] cursing, nathema

naticula, ae *f* duckling

natocismus, ī *m* compound nterest

nceps, itis *adj* two-edged, wo-headed; dangerous, doubtful; ouble, undecided

ncīle, is *nt* small figure-of-eight hield

ncilla, ae *f* maid-servant, female lave

ncillula, ae *f* little serving-maid, oung female slave

ncora, ae *f* anchor

ncorāle, is *nt* anchor cable

ndabata, ae *m* a gladiator who ought blindfolded

ndrogynus, ī *m* hermaphrodite

ndrōn, nis *m* the men's partment in a house

nē(t)um, ī *nt* dill, anise

netīnus, a, um *adj* of a duck, uck's

nfrāctus, ūs *m* curving, ending, circuit, windings; ircumlocution

ngelus, ī *m* [LM] angel, messenger

ngina, ae *f* a suffocating bstruction, quinsy

ngiportus, ūs *m*,

ngiportum, ī *nt* narrow street r alley

ngō, ānxī, ānctum ③ *v* press ght, throttle; cause pain, vex, rouble

ngor, ōris *m* suffocation, hoking, anguish, vexation

nguicomus, a, um *adj* with naky hair

anguifer, era, erum *adj* snake-bearing

anguilla, ae *f* eel

anguīnus, a, um *adj* of a snake, snaky

anguis, is *m/f* snake, serpent; (constellation) the Dragon

angulus, ī *m* angle, corner, nook, out-of-the-way spot

angustiae, ārum *fpl* strait, defile, narrowness; want, perplexity, trouble; narrow-mindedness

angustō ① *v* make narrow, constrict, crowd together

angustus, a, um *adj* narrow, confined; scanty, poor, needy, low, mean; narrow-minded

anhēlitus, ūs *m* panting, puffing, breathing, breath, exhalation

anhēlō ① *v* pant, gasp, breathe out

anhēlus, a, um *adj* panting, puffing

anicula, ae *f* little old woman

anīlis, e *adj* old-womanish

anīlitās, ātis *f* old age (in women)

anima, ae *f* air, breeze, breath, soul, life

animadversiō, ōnis *f* observation, attention, reproach, punishment

animadvertō, rtī, rsum ③ *v* observe, attend to, remark, notice, understand, perceive; avenge, punish, blame

animal, ālis *nt* animal

animālis, e *adj* made of air, animal

animāns, ntis *adj* living; *m/f/nt*

a

being, animal

animō 🔲 *v* animate, encourage, give life to, revive

animōsus, a, um *adj* courageous, bold, strong, ardent, energetic, stormy

animula, ae *f* little life

animus, ī *m* (rational) soul, mind, will, purpose, desire, character; courage; anger; pride; pleasure, inclination; memory, judgment, consciousness, opinion; vital power, life

□ **bonō animō esse** be of good heart

□ **ex animō** from the heart, with sincerity

□ **aequō animō** with equanimity, calmly

ann- ▶ **adn-**

annālēs, ium *mpl* annals, year-books

annālis, e *adj* relating to the year, chronicle, history

annatō 🔲 *v* swim towards

anniversārius, a, um *adj* annual, yearly

annōn *conj* or not?

annōna, ae *f* year's produce, provision, victuals, price of grain or other food

annōsus, a, um *adj* aged, old

annōtinus, a, um *adj* of last year

annus, ī *m* year, season, year's produce; age

annuus, a, um *adj* yearly, lasting a year

anquīrō, sīvī, sītum 🔲 *v* search diligently after, inquire into, examine judicially

ānsa, ae *f* handle; opportunity

ānser, eris *m/f* goose

ante *prep with acc* before, in front of; *adv* in front, before (of time), forwards

anteā *adv* before this, formerly

antecapiō, cēpī, ceptum 🔲 *v* take beforehand, anticipate

antecēdēns, ntis *adj* previously existent

antecēdō, essi, essum 🔲 *v* go before, precede; excel, surpass

antecellō 🔲 *v* surpass, excel

antecessiō, ōnis *f* going before, antecedent cause

antecursor, ōris *m usu in pl* leading troops, vanguard

anteeō, īre, īī/īvī *v ir* go before; surpass; anticipate; prevent

anteferō, ferre, tulī, lātum *v* carry before; prefer

antegredior, gressus sum 🔲 *dep* go before, precede

antehāc *adv* before this time; earlier

antelūcānus, a, um *adj* before daybreak

antemerīdiānus, a, um *adj* before noon

antenna, ae *f* sail-yard; sail

antepīlānī, ōrum *mpl* men who fought in the first or second line

antepōnō, posuī, positum 🔲 *v* place before; prefer

antequam *conj* before

antēs, ium *mpl* rows (of plants)

antesignānus, ī *m* leader; *pl* troops who fought in the front rank of a legion

antestō, stitī 🔲 *v with dat* surpass

antestor 🔲 *v dep* call as a witness

anteveniō, vēnī, ventum ④ *v* come before; anticipate, forestall

antevertō, tī, ersum ③ *v* act first, precede; give priority to

anticipātiō, ōnis *f* preconception

anticipō ① *v* occupy beforehand; anticipate

antidotum, ī *nt* antidote, remedy

antiphona, ae *f* [LM] antiphon, psalm (sung responsively/ alternately)

antīquārius, (i)ī *m* antiquarian, student of the past

antīquē *adv* in the old way, in an old-fashioned manner

antīquitās, ātis *f* antiquity, the ancients; virtue of olden time

antīquitus *adv* in former times

antīquō ① *v* reject (a bill)

antīquus, a, um *adj* old, ancient; aged; of the old stamp, simple, honest, venerable

antistes, itis *m/f* high-priest; chief priestess; *with gen* master (in); [LM] bishop

antistita, ae *f* chief priestess

antlia, ae *f* a mechanism for raising water, treadmill

antrum, ī *nt* cave, cavern

anulārius, (i)ī *m* ring-maker

anulus, ī *m* ring; signet-ring

anus, ī *m* ring, anus

anus, ūs *f* old woman; sibyl; *f adj* aged, old

anxietās, ātis *f* anxiety; carefulness

anxius, a, um *adj* anxious, uneasy; disturbed; concerned; careful

apage *int* be off! get away with (you)!

aper, prī *m* wild boar

aperiō, ruī, rtum ④ *v* open; discover; show, explain

apertus, a, um *adj* open; public; exposed; wide, extended; cloudless; clear; frank

apex, icis *m* point, top, summit; cap, crown; conical cap of a priest; highest honour; [LM] *pl* letters

aphractum, ī *nt*, **aphractus, ī** *f* undecked boat

apis, is *f* bee

apīscor, aptus sum ③ *v dep* reach, obtain

apium, (i)ī *nt* wild celery or parsley

aplustre, is *nt* ornamented stern-port of a ship

apodȳtērium, (i)ī *nt* undressing-room in a bathing-house

apologus, ī *m* narrative; fable

apostolicus, a, um *adj* [LM] apostolic
  ■ **apostolicus, i** *m* pope

apostolus, ī *m* [LM] apostle

apothēca, ae *f* store-house, store-room, wine-cellar

apparātus¹, ūs *m* preparation; provision; equipment; splendour, pomp

apparātus², a, um *adj* prepared, ready; splendid, sumptuous

appāreō ② *v* appear; be evident; *with dat* attend *or* serve
  □ **appāret** it is clear

appārītiō, ōnis *f* service, attendance; servants

appārītor, ōris *m* (public) servant; lictor, clerk

apparō ① *v* prepare, fit out,

provide; attempt

appellātiō, ōnis f appeal; calling by name; name, title; pronunciation

appellātor, ōris m appellant

appellitō 🔲 v call or name frequently

appellō¹ 🔲 v call upon; address; dun; appeal (to); bring into court; accuse; name, entitle, pronounce

appellō², pulī, pulsum 🔲 v drive to; bring to land; come ashore

appendix, cis f appendage; supplement

appendō, ndī, ēnsum 🔲 v weigh out

appetēns, ntis adj with gen eager for; avaricious

appetentia, ae f longing after, appetite

appetītiō, ōnis f desire; grasping (at)

appetītus, ūs m desire, appetite

appetō, īvī/iī, ītum 🔲 v seek or grasp after; assail; strive eagerly after, long for; approach

appingō 🔲 v paint upon; add in writing

applaudō, sī, sum 🔲 v strike together; clap; applaud

applicātiō, ōnis f application, inclination

applicātus, a, um adj situated close (to); devoted (to)

applicō, cāvī/cuī, cātum/ citum 🔲 v join to, place near; apply (to); devote (to); connect

appōnō, posuī, positum 🔲 v put or lay to; apply to; add to; serve up

apportō 🔲 v carry, convey, bring

to; cause

appositus, a, um adj adjacent, near; fit, appropriate

apprehendō, ndī, ēnsum 🔲 v seize, lay hold of

approbātiō, ōnis f approbation; proof; decision

approbō 🔲 v approve; prove; confirm; justify; allow; make good

approperō 🔲 v hasten, hurry

appropinquātiō, ōnis f approach, drawing near

appropinquō 🔲 v approach, draw near

appugnō 🔲 v attack, assault

appulsus, ūs m driving to; landing; approach; influence

aprīcātiō, ōnis f a basking in the sun

aprīcor 🔲 v dep sun oneself

aprīcus, a, um adj exposed to the sun; sunny

Aprīlis, is m April

aps- ▶ **abs-**

aptē adv closely, snugly; fitly, suitably

aptō 🔲 v fit, apply, put on; adjust; prepare, furnish

aptus, a, um adj attached to; connected, suitable, adapted; with **ex** and **abl** dependent (upon)

apud prep with acc at the house of, at, by, near, with; among; in; before; in the time of; in the works of

aput ▶ **apud**

aqua, ae f water; rain; sea; lake; river

aquaeductus, ūs m aqueduct

aquārius, a, um adj relating to water

a ~, **(i)ī** m water-carrier; overseer of the public water supply; Water-bearer (as a constellation)

quāticus, **a**, **um** adj aquatic; watery, rainy

quātiō, **ōnis** f fetching of water

quātor, **ōris** m water-carrier

quila, **ae** f eagle; standard of a Roman legion

quilifer, **erī** m standard-bearer

quilō, **ōnis** m north wind; north

quilōnius, **a**, **um** adj northern

quor [1] v dep fetch water

quōsus, **a**, **um** adj abounding in water, humid, rainy

ra, **ae** f altar; sanctuary; home; refuge, shelter

rabarchēs, **ae** m Egyptian tax-gatherer

rānea, **ae** f spider; cobweb

rāneōsus, **a**, **um** adj covered with spiders' webs

rāneus, **ī** m spider

rātiō, **ōnis** f ploughing; tilled ground

rātor, **ōris** m ploughman, farmer

rātrum, **ī** nt plough

rbiter, **trī** m eye-witness; umpire, arbiter, lord, master, governor

rbitrātus, **ūs** m arbitration; choice; pleasure, will

rbitrium, **(i)ī** nt judgment of an arbitrator; sentence; will, mastery, authority

rbitror [1] v dep observe, perceive, pass sentence; believe, think, be of an opinion

rbor, **oris** f tree; mast; oar; ship

rboreus, **a**, **um** adj of or belonging to trees

arbuscula, **ae** f shrub; sapling

arbustum, **ī** nt copse, plantation, grove of trees; shrub

arbuteus, **a**, **um** adj of the strawberry tree

arbutum, **ī** nt wild strawberry; wild strawberry tree

arbutus, **ī** f wild strawberry tree

arca, **ae** f chest, strong-box, coffer; purse; coffin; prison-cell, ark

arcānum, **ī** nt secret, mystery

arcānus, **a**, **um** adj secret, hidden, mysterious

arceō, **ī** [2] v keep off, prevent; protect

accessō, **īvī/iī**, **ītum** [3] v send for, call; procure; summon, accuse

archiepiscopus, **ī** m [LM] archbishop

architectōn, **nis** m architect, builder

architectūra, **ae** f architecture

architectus, **ī** m architect; inventor, designer

arcitenēns, **ntis** adj holding a bow (epithet of Apollo); (constellation) the Archer

arct- ▸ **art-**

arctē adv (also **artē**) closely, tightly, briefly, in a confined space

arctō [1] v (also **artō**) compress, contract; abridge; limit

Arctos, **ī** f the Great Bear or the Little Bear; the north

Arctōus, **a**, **um** adj northern

Arctūrus, **ī** m brightest star in the constellation Bo

arctus, **a**, **um** adj (also **artus**) close, thick, narrow; short; strict;

scanty, brief

arcula, **ae** f small box, casket

arcus, **ūs** m arch; bow; rainbow; anything arched or curved

ardaliō, **ōnis** m busybody, fusspot

ardea, **ae** f heron

ardēns, **ntis** adj burning; glowing, fiery; eager, ardent, passionate

ardeō, **arsī**, **(arsum)** ② v burn, blaze; flash; glow, sparkle; be inflamed; be in a turmoil

ardēscō, **arsī** ③ v take fire, kindle; be inflamed

ardor, **ōris** m fire, flame, heat; brightness; ardour, love, intensity

arduus, **a**, **um** adj steep, high; difficult, arduous

ārea, **ae** f open space; building site; threshing-floor; granary; courtyard; field of action

ārefaciō, **fēcī**, **factum** ③ v dry up

arēna, **ae** f sand; sandy land or desert; seashore; place of contest, amphitheatre

arēnāria, **ae** f sand-pit

arēnōsus, **a**, **um** adj sandy

āreō ② v be dry; be thirsty

ārēscō ③ v become dry

argentāria, **ae** f banking-house, banking business; silver-mine

argentārius, **(i)ī** m banker, financial agent
  ■ ~, **a**, **um** adj pertaining to silver or money

argentātus, **a**, **um** adj silvered

argenteus, **a**, **um** adj, **argenteolus**, **a**, **um** adj of silver; silvery

argentum, **ī** nt silver; silver plate; money

argilla, **ae** f white clay, potter's earth

argūmentātiō, **ōnis** f argumentation; proof

argūmentor ① v dep support or prove by argument, reason

argūmentum, **ī** nt argument, proof; subject, plot (of a play)

arguō, **uī**, **ūtum** ③ v prove, assert, accuse; convict; condemn

argūtātiō, **ōnis** f creaking

argūtiae, **ārum** fpl clever use of words; verbal trickery; wit

argūtus, **a**, **um** adj melodious; distinct, clear; sagacious, witty; cunning, sly; talkative, rustling, rattling

āridulus, **a**, **um** adj dry, parched

āridum, **ī** nt dry land

āridus, **a**, **um** adj dry, parched; barren; thirsty; poor; shrivelled

ariēs, **etis** m ram; battering-ram; the Ram (in the zodiac)

arietō ① v butt like a ram; strike violently

arista, **ae** f beard of an ear of grain; ear of corn; grain crop

arithmētica, **ōrum** ntpl arithmetic

āritūdō, **inis** f dryness, drought

arma, **ōrum** ntpl arms, weapons; tools; tackling; shield; soldiers; army; war; battle
  □ **vī et armīs** by force of arms

armāmenta, **ōrum** ntpl tackle of a ship

armāmentārium, **(i)ī** nt arsenal, armoury

armārium, **(i)ī** nt cabinet, cupboard; book-case

armātūra, **ae** f armour, harness;

armed soldiers

armentālis, e *adj* of cattle

armentum, ī *nt* herd (of large cattle); a head of cattle

armifer, armiger, era, erum *adj* armed, warlike

■ ~, **erī** *m* armour-bearer, squire

armilla, ae *f* bracelet

armipotēns, ntis *adj* powerful in arms, valiant, warlike

armisonus, a, um *adj* sounding with the clash of arms

armō ① *v* equip; arm; kindle; incite to war; rig (a ship)

armus, ī *m* forequarter (of an animal), shoulder

arō ① *v* plough, till; furrow, wrinkle; produce by ploughing

arrabō, ōnis *m* down-payment, deposit, pledge

arrēpō, psī, ptum ③ *v* creep towards

arrīdeō, rīsī, rīsum ② *v* smile upon; please

arrigō, ēxī, ēctum ③ *v* set upright, raise; animate, rouse

arripiō, uī, eptum ③ *v* snatch away; take hold of; pick up (knowledge); appropriate; arrest; assail

arrōdō, ōsī, ōsum ③ *v* gnaw or nibble at

arrogāns, ntis *adj* arrogant

arrogantia, ae *f* arrogance, conceit

arrogō ① *v* ask, question; arrogate to one's self, claim; confer (upon)

ars, tis *f* skill; art; work of art; profession; theory; manner of acting; cunning, artifice

artē *adv* closely, tightly, briefly, in a

confined space

□ ~ **dormiō** sleep soundly

artēria, ae *f* windpipe; artery

arthrīticus, a, um *adj* affected with rheumatism

articulus, ī *m* joint; part; moment of time, critical moment

artifex, icis *m* artist, artificer; maker, author; *adj* skilful; artful

artificiōsus, a, um *adj* skilful; ingenious; artificial, unnatural

artificium, (i)ī *nt* handicraft, art, trade; skill; theory, system; cunning

artō ① *v* compress, contract; abridge, limit

artus¹, ūs *mpl* joints; limbs

artus², a, um *adj* close, thick, narrow; short; strict; scanty, brief

ārula, ae *f* small altar

arundineus, a, um *adj* of reeds; reedy

arundō, inis *f* reed; fishing rod; arrow-shaft; arrow; pen; shepherd's pipe

arvīna, ae *f* fat, lard

arvum, ī *nt* arable field; country; dry land; stretch of plain

arvus, a, um *adj* arable

arx, cis *f* stronghold, citadel; the Capitoline hill at Rome; defence, refuge

ās, assis *m* a copper coin of small value

ascendō, ndī, ēnsum ③ *v* mount up, ascend

ascēnsiō, ōnis *f* ascent; progress; advancement

ascēnsus, ūs *m* ascending, ascent; approach; a stage in advancement

asciō 4 *v* take to, associate, admit, take on as staff

ascīscō, scīvī, scītum 3 *v* receive, admit, approve of, associate; appropriate, adopt

ascrībō, psī, ptum 3 *v* add in writing; ascribe, impute; appoint; enrol; reckon, number

asella, ae *f* she-ass

asellus, ī *m* ass, donkey

asīlus, ī *m* gadfly

asinus, ī *m* ass; blockhead

asōtus, ī *m* debauchee

aspectō 1 *v* look or gaze at; observe; (of places) look towards

aspectus, ūs *m* looking at, glance, view; sight; horizon; appearance; aspect, mien

asper, era, erum *adj* rough; uneven; harsh, sour; bitter; rude, violent, unkind, savage; wayward, austere; wild, fierce; critical, adverse

aspergō¹, rsī, rsum 3 *v* besprinkle; defile, stain

aspergō², inis *f* besprinkling; spray

asperitās, ātis *f* roughness; severity; harshness; tartness; shrillness; fierceness

aspernor 1 *v dep* despise

asperō 1 *v* make rough; sharpen; make fierce, violent

aspersiō, ōnis *f* sprinkling

aspiciō, xī, ectum 3 *v* look at, behold; (of places) look towards; consider, contemplate

aspīrātiō, ōnis *f* exhalation; aspiration; sounding an 'h'

aspīrō 1 *v* breathe or blow upon; infuse; be favourable to; assist;

aspire to

aspis, idis *f* asp

asportātiō, ōnis *f* carrying away

asportō 1 *v* carry away, remove

asprētum, ī *nt* rough ground

assa, ōrum *ntpl* sweating bath

assecla ▶ assecula

assectātiō, ōnis *f* waiting on, attendance

assectātor, ōris *m* follower, companion; disciple

assector 1 *v dep* accompany, attend; support

assec(u)la, ae *m* attendant, servant; hanger-on, sycophant

assēnsiō, ōnis *f* assent, applause

assēnsor, ōris *m* one who agrees or approves

assēnsus, ūs *m* assent, approbation, applause

assentātiō, ōnis *f* flattering agreement, toadyism

assentātor, ōris *m* flatterer, 'yes-man'

assentātrīx, īcis *f* female flatterer

assentior, sēnsus sum 4 *v dep* assent to, approve, comply with

assentor 1 *v dep* agree completely with; flatter

assequor, secūtus sum 3 *v dep* follow on, pursue; overtake; gain, attain to; equal, rival; understand

asser, eris *m* pole, post, stake

asserō, ruī, rtum 3 *v* assert; free; claim

assertor, ōris *m* restorer of liberty; protector, advocate; champion

asservō 1 *v* keep, preserve,

watch, observe

assessor, ōris *m* assessor, counsellor

assevēranter *adv* earnestly, emphatically

assevērātiō, ōnis *f* affirmation, asseveration; seriousness

assevērō ① *v* act with earnestness; assert strongly

assideō, sēdī, sessum ② *v* sit by; be an assessor; besiege; *with dat* resemble

assīdō, sēdī ③ *v* sit down

assiduē *adv* continually, constantly

assiduitās, ātis *f* attendance; assiduity, care; recurrence, repetition

assiduē ▶ assiduē

assiduus, a, um *adj* assiduous; continual, unremitting

assignātiō, ōnis *f* distribution or allotment of land; plot of land

assignō ① *v* assign; impute

assiliō, siluī, sultum ④ *v* leap up, rush (at)

assimilis, e *adj* similar, like

assimulō ① *v* make like; compare; counterfeit, pretend, feign

assistō, stitī ③ *v* stand at or by, attend; be present at; make a stand

assoleō ② *v* be accustomed or in the habit of

assuēfaciō, fēcī, factum ③ *v* accustom (to)

assuēscō, ēvī, ētum ③ *v* accustom (to); become accustomed

assuētūdō, inis *f* custom, habit; intimacy

assuētus, a, um *adj* accustomed, customary, usual

assula, ae *f* splinter, chip (of wood or stone)

assultō ① *v* jump at; attack

assultus, ūs *m* attack, assault

assūmō, mpsī, mptum ③ *v* take up, adopt, receive; add to; usurp, arrogate

assūmptiō, ōnis *f* adoption; minor premiss

assuō ③ *v* sew or patch on

assurgō, surrēxī, surrēctum ③ *v* claim, rise or stand up; rise, soar

assus, a, um *adj* roasted; dry

ast ▶ at

asternō ③ *v* prostrate oneself, lie prone (on)

astō, stitī ① *v* stand at or by; assist; stand upright

astrepō, puī ③ *v* make a noise at, shout in support

astrictus, a, um *adj* bound by rules; terse, brief; parsimonious

astringō, īnxī, ictum ③ *v* tighten, bind, fasten; oblige, contract

astrologia, ae *f* astronomy, astrology

astrologus, ī *m* astronomer, astrologer

astrum, ī *nt* star, constellation; sky

astruō, ūxī, ūctum ③ *v* build on; add to; ᴸᴹ affirm, declare

astupeō ② *v* be stunned or astonished (at)

āstus, ūs *m* craft, cunning, trick

āstūtia, ae *f* cunning, slyness, trick

āstūtus, a, um *adj* clever, expert;

sly, cunning

asȳlum, ī *nt* place of refuge, sanctuary

asymbolus, **a**, **um** *adj* making no contribution; scot-free

at *conj* (also **ast**) but, yet; but then; on the contrary; at least

atat *int* ah!

atavus, ī *m* great-great-great-grandfather; ancestor

āter, **tra**, **trum** *adj* black; gloomy, dismal, unlucky

āthlēta, **ae** *m* wrestler, athlete

atomus, ī *f* atom

atque *conj* and, and also, and even, and too; yet; nevertheless; *after words expressing comparison* as, than

atquī *conj* but, yet, notwithstanding, however, rather, but now; and yet; well now

ātrāmentum, ī *nt* writing-ink; blacking

ātrātus, **a**, **um** *adj* darkened; wearing mourning

ātriēnsis, **is** *m* steward

ātriolum, ī *nt* small ante-room

ātrium, **(i)ī** *nt* hall in a Roman house; palace; 〔LM〕 graveyard

atrōcitās, **ātis** *f* fierceness; savageness, cruelty; severity

atrōciter *adv* savagely, cruelly, fiercely, severely

atrōx, **ōcis** *adj* savage, cruel, fierce, severe

attāctus, **ūs** *m* touch

attamen *adv* but yet, but however, nevertheless

attat ▸ **atat**

attendō, **ndī**, **ntum** ③ *v* turn towards; apply; attend to, listen carefully

attentē *adv* diligently, carefully

attentiō, **ōnis** *f* attention

attentō ① *v* try, attempt; assail, attack

attentus, **a**, **um** *adj* attentive; careful

attenuō ① *v* thin, weaken, lessen, diminish

atterō, **trīvī**, **trītum** ③ *v* rub against; wear out, impair

Atticē *adv* in the Attic manner; elegantly

Atticus, **a**, **um** *adj* Attic, Athenian; classic, elegant

attineō, **tentum** ② *v* hold on or fast; delay; belong (to), concern, relate to

attingō, **tigī**, **tāctum** ③ *v* touch; arrive at; border upon; affect; mention in passing; achieve, win; relate to; treat in hostile manner

attollō ③ *v* lift up; erect, build; exalt; extol

attondeō, **ndī**, **ōnsum** ② *v* clip, prune

attonitus, **a**, **um** *adj* thunder-struck; stupefied, amazed; inspired, frenzied

attonō, **nuī**, **nitum** ① *v* strike with lightning; drive crazy

attorqueō ② *v* whirl at

attrahō, **āxī**, **actum** ③ *v* attract; drag on

attrectō ① *v* touch, handle; deal with

attribuō, **uī**, **ūtum** ③ *v* assign; attribute or impute to

attribūtiō, **ōnis** *f* assignment of a debt; attribution of a quality

au *int* oh! ow! oh dear!

auceps, **cupis** *m* bird-catcher;

bird-seller

auctificus, a, um adj giving increase

auctiō, ōnis f public sale, auction

auctiōnārius, a, um adj pertaining to an auction

auctiōnor ① v dep put up to public sale

auctō ① v increase

auctor, ōris m/f creator, maker, inventor; father; teacher; leader; founder, author; promoter; adviser; protector; witness; vendor; bail; guardian, champion

auctōrāmentum, ī nt wages, pay; reward

auctōritās, ātis f authority, power; reputation, credit; opinion, judgment; command; influence, importance; credibility

auctōror ① v dep bind oneself, hire oneself

auctus, ūs m growth, increase, bulk

aucupium, (i)ī nt bird-catching; game birds

aucupor ① v dep go bird-catching; lie in wait for

audācia, ae f boldness; courage, valour; audacity

audāc(i)ter adv boldly, courageously

audāx, ācis adj bold, courageous, audacious; foolhardy, rash; desperate

audēns, ntis adj daring, bold

audentia, ae f boldness, courage

audeō, audēre, ausus sum ② v semi-dep dare, venture

audientia, ae f hearing; audience, attention

audiō ④ v hear; listen, hearken; regard; grant; obey

audītiō, ōnis f hearing; report, hearsay

audītor, ōris m hearer, auditor; disciple

audītōrium, (i)ī nt lecture-room, audience

audītus, ūs m hearing; listening; sense of hearing; hearsay

auferō, auferre, abstulī, ablātum v ir bear away; snatch away; carry off; obtain; destroy

aufugiō, fūgī ③ v flee away or from

augeō, auxī, auctum ② v increase, augment; make a lot of

augēscō ③ v grow, become greater

augmen, inis nt growth, increase, bulk

augur, uris m/f augur; soothsayer

augurālis, e adj pertaining to augurs, relating to soothsaying ■ **augurāle, is** nt place of augury, commander's hut

augurātiō, ōnis f prediction by means of augury

augurātō adv after taking the auguries

augurātus, ūs m office of an augur; augury

augurium, (i)ī nt profession of an augur, soothsaying, prediction

auguror ① v dep act as augur; foretell; conjecture, speculate

Augustus¹, ī m August (month)

augustus², a, um adj sacred, venerable; majestic, august

aula, ae f inner court of a house; hall; palace; royal court; courtiers

a

aulaeum, **ī** *nt* curtain of a theatre; canopy; tapestry

aura, **ae** *f* air, gentle breeze; breath; wind; gleam, glittering; odour, exhalation
□ **~ populāris** the breath of popular favour

aurātus, **a**, **um** *adj* gilt, golden

aureolus, **a**, **um** *adj* golden, splendid

aureus, **a**, **um** *adj* golden; gilded; shining like gold; beautiful
□ **mīliārium aureum** golden milestone erected by Augustus at the head of the forum in Rome, from which all distances were reckoned

auricomus, **a**, **um** *adj* golden-haired

auricula, **ae** *f* ear

aurifer, **era**, **erum** *adj* gold-bearing

aurifex, **icis** *m* goldsmith

aurīga, **ae** *m* charioteer; helmsman; (constellation) the Wagoner; groom

auris, **is** *f* ear; hearing

aurītus, **a**, **um** *adj* hearing well; long-eared

aurōra, **ae** *f* dawn, daybreak

aurum, **ī** *nt* gold

auscultō ① *v* listen to; overhear; obey

ausim ▶ *subj* from **audeō**

auspex, **icis** *m* diviner by birds; soothsayer; patron, supporter

auspicātō *adv* after taking the auspices; auspiciously

auspicātus, **a**, **um** *adj* consecrated by auguries; favourable, auspicious

auspicium, **(i)ī** *nt* auspices; the right of taking auspices; leadership, authority; sign, omen

auspicor ① *v dep* take the auspice

auster, **trī** *m* south wind; south

austēritās, **ātis** *f* harshness; gloominess; severity

austērus, **a**, **um** *adj* austere; harsh; sour; sharp; rough, dark, stern; unornamented

austrālis, **e** *adj* southern

austrīnus, **a**, **um** *adj* southern

ausum, **ī** *nt* daring attempt, enterprise; crime, outrage

ausus *pple* from ▶ **audeō**

aut *conj* or; or else, either

autem *conj* but; however; indeed; on the contrary

autumnālis, **e** *adj* autumnal

autumnus, **ī** *m* autumn

autumō ① *v* say yes, affirm; say, mention

auxiliāris, **e** *adj* help-bringing, auxiliary

auxiliārius, **a**, **um** *adj* helping, auxiliary

auxilior ① *v dep* give aid; *with dat* assist

auxilium, **(i)ī** *nt* help, aid, assistance
■ **auxilia**, **ōrum** *ntpl* auxiliary contingents

avāritia, **ae** *f* avarice, rapacity, miserliness

avārus, **a**, **um** *adj* avaricious, covetous, stingy

avē *int* greetings!

āvehō, **ēxī**, **ectum** ③ *v* carry away
□ **avehor** ride away, go away

āvellō, **vellī/vulsī**, **vulsum** ③

v pluck away, tear off; separate
by force

vēna, ae f oats; wild oats; stem,
stalk, straw; oaten pipe, pan pipes

veō ② v be eager or anxious;
desire

verruncō ① v avert (something
bad)

versor¹ ① v dep turn oneself
away in disgust or horror; avoid,
refuse; reject

versor², **ōris** m embezzler

versus, a, um adj turned away;
averse; hostile

vertō, rtī, rsum ③ v turn
away from or aside; steal,
misappropriate; divert, estrange

via, ae f grandmother

viārium, (i)ī nt haunt of wild
birds; aviary

viditās, ātis f covetousness,
greed; ardent desire, lust

vidus, a, um adj eager, greedy;
avaricious; lustful

vis, is f bird; omen, portent

vītus, a, um adj ancestral; of a
grandfather

vius, a, um adj out of the way;
pathless; straying

■ **āvia, ōrum** ntpl remote places

vocō ① v call away; remove;
divert the mind

volō ① v fly away; hasten away

vunculus, ī m (maternal) uncle
or great-uncle

vus, ī m grandfather; ancestor

xis, is m axle; chariot; axis (of the
earth); north pole; heaven; sky;
region, clime; board, plank

xulus, ī m plank, board

babae int hey!

bāca, ae f (also **bacca**) berry;
olive-berry; pearl

bācātus, a, um adj set with pearls

baccar, aris nt an aromatic root

Baccha, ae f (also **Bacchē**) a
votary of Bacchus

Bacchānālia, ium ntpl
Bacchanalian orgies, feast of
Bacchus

Bacchantēs, ntum fpl votaries
of Bacchus

Bacchēus, a, um adj,
Bacchicus, a, um adj Bacchic

bacchor ① v dep celebrate the
rites of Bacchus; revel, rave; riot,
run wild

bācifer, era, erum adj berry-
bearing

bacillum, ī nt little staff; lictor's
staff

baculum, ī nt stick, walking-stick,
lictor's staff

bāiulus, ī m porter, carrier

bālaena, ae f whale

balanus, ī f acorn; balsam;
shell-fish

balatrō, ōnis m buffoon, joker

bālātus, ūs m bleating of sheep

balbus, a, um adj stammering,
stuttering

balbūtiō ④ v stammer, stutter;
speak obscurely, babble

ballaena ▶ bālaena

bal(i)neārius, a, um adj

pertaining to baths

bal(i)neātor, **ōris** *m* bath-attendant

bālō □ *v* bleat, baa

balsamum, **ī** *nt* balsam-tree, balm

balteus, **ī** *m* belt, sword-belt, baldric; woman's girdle

baptisma, **atis** *nt* LM baptism

barathrum, **ī** *nt* abyss, chasm; the infernal region

barba, **ae** *f* beard

barbaria, **ae** *f*, **barbariēs**, **iēī** *f* foreign country; barbarousness; barbarism (in language); brutality

barbaricus, **a**, **um** *adj* outlandish; barbarous

barbarus, **a**, **um** *adj* foreign, barbarous; uncivilized; cruel, savage

■ ~, **ī** *m* foreigner, barbarian

barbātulus, **a**, **um** *adj* having a small beard

barbātus, **a**, **um** *adj* bearded; adult

■ ~, **ī** *m* ancient Roman, philosopher

barbitos, **ī** (*acc* **ton**, *voc* **te**) *m/f* lyre

barbula, **ae** *f* little beard

bārō, **ōnis** *m* block-head, lout

barrus, **ī** *m* elephant

bāsiātiō, **ōnis** *f* a kiss

basilica, **ae** *f* oblong hall with double colonnade used for a law-court and as an exchange; LM church

basiliscus, **ī** *m* basilisk

bāsiō □ *v* kiss

basis, **is** *f* pedestal; base; foundation

bāsium, **(i)ī** *nt* a kiss

beātitās, **ātis** *f*, **beātitūdō**, **inis** *f* supreme happiness, blessedness

beātus, **a**, **um** *adj* happy, blessed; wealthy; abundant

bellātor, **ōris** *m* warrior; *adj* warlike

bellātrīx, **īcis** *f* female warrior

belliātus, **a**, **um** *adj* pretty, beautiful

bellicōsus, **a**, **um** *adj* fond of war, warlike

bellicus, **a**, **um** *adj* of or belonging to war, military; warlike

belliger, **era**, **erum** *adj* waging war, martial

belligerō □ *v* wage or carry on war

bellipotēns, **ntis** *adj* powerful in war

bellō □ *v*, **bellor** □ *v dep* wage war, fight

bellum, **ī** *nt* war; combat, fight
□ **bellī** *loc* used as *adv* at the wars

bellus, **a**, **um** *adj* handsome, pretty, neat, agreeable, polite

bēlua, **ae** *f* beast; monster; brute, fool, idiot

bēluōsus, **a**, **um** *adj* abounding in beasts *or* monsters

bene *adv* well, rightly, beautifully, pleasantly; opportunely

benedīcō, **īxī**, **ictum** □ *v with dat* speak well of; speak kindly to; LM *with acc or dat* bless

benedictiō, **ōnis** *f* LM blessing, benediction

benedictum, **ī** *nt* kind word

benefactum, **ī** *nt* good deed

beneficentia, **ae** *f* beneficence,

kindness

beneficiāriī, ōrum *mpl* soldiers exempted from certain military services

beneficium, (i)ī *nt* benefit, kindness; favour, help; 🔲 benefice

beneficus, a, um *adj* beneficent, kind

benevolēns, ntis *adj* benevolent, well-wishing, kind-hearted

benevolentia, ae *f* benevolence, goodwill, kindness, favour

benevolus, a, um *adj* well-wishing, kind, friendly, devoted

benignitās, ātis *f* good-heartedness, kindness, liberality, bounty

benignus, a, um *adj* kind-hearted, mild, affable; liberal, bounteous; fruitful

beō 🔲 *v* make happy, bless

bēs, bessis *m* two-thirds of any whole

bēstia, ae *f* beast; wild beast

bēstiārius, (i)ī *m* fighter with wild beasts at public shows

bēstiola, ae *f* little creature, insect

bēta, ae *f* beet; beetroot

betulla, ae *f* birch tree

bibliothēca, ae *f* library

biblus, ī *m* 🔲 book

bibō, bibī, — 🔲 *v* drink; imbibe; absorb, suck up; drink in; get drunk

bibulus, a, um *adj* fond of drinking, ever thirsty; soaking, spongy

biceps, itis *adj* two-headed; with

two summits

bicolor, ōris *adj* of two colours

bicorniger, ī *adj* the two-horned (god), epithet of Bacchus

bicornis, e *adj* two-horned; two-pronged

bidēns¹, ntis *m* two-pronged

bidēns², ntis *m/f* sheep; two-pronged hoe

bīduum, ī *nt* period of two days

biennium, (i)ī *nt* period of two years

bifāriam *adv* in two parts; in two ways

bifer, era, erum *adj* bearing fruit or flowers twice a year

bifidus, a, um *adj* cloven, forked

biforis, e *adj* having two leaves or casements; from a double pipe

biförmis, e *adj* two-shaped

bifröns, ntis *adj* with two faces

bifurcus, a, um *adj* two-forked

bīga, ae *f* often pl in form two-horsed chariot; pair of horses

bīgātus, ī *m* a piece of money stamped with a representation of the bigae

biiugis, e *adj*, **biiugus, a, um** *adj* two-horsed

bilibris, bre *adj* weighing two pounds

bilinguis, e *adj* two-tongued; speaking two languages; double-tongued, treacherous

bīlis, is *f* gall, bile; wrath, anger; madness, folly

bilūstris, tre *adj* lasting two lustres, lasting ten years

bimaris, e *adj* situated between two seas

bimembris, bre adj having limbs of two kinds, part man part beast

bimestris, tre adj two months old; lasting two months

bīmus, a, um adj two years old; for two years

bīnī, ae, a adj two by two; two each

bipatēns, ntis adj opening two ways; wide open

bipedālis, e adj two feet long, wide or thick

bipennifer, era, erum adj bearing a two-edged axe

bipennis, e adj two-edged ■ ~, is f two-edged axe

bipertītō adv in two parts or divisions

bipēs, edis adj two-footed

birēmis, is f ship with two banks of oars

bis adv twice

bisanteus, ei m **LM** bezant, gold coin

bisulcus, a, um adj forked; cloven-footed

bitūmen, inis nt bitumen, pitch, asphalt

bivium, (i)ī nt a meeting-place of two roads

bivius, a, um adj traversable both ways

blaesus, a, um adj mispronouncing one's words through a speech defect, drunkenness, etc., stammering

blandīmentum, ī nt blandishment, flattery, charms

blandior ④ v dep flatter, coax; allure; please

blanditia, ae f flattering,

compliment; pl flatteries, courtship, blandishment

blandus, a, um adj flattering; pleasant, alluring, charming, gentle

blatta, ae f cockroach; moth

boārius, a, um adj of oxen ◻ **forum boārium** the cattle market at Rome

bōlētus, ī m mushroom

bolus, ī m a throw at dice; what is caught in a fishing net, a haul; profit, gain

bombus, ī m buzzing, booming

bonitās, ātis f goodness; kindness, benevolence

bonum, ī nt good; wealth, goods; benefit; advantage; profit; endowment, virtue ◻ **summum** ~ the supreme good (philosophical term)

bonus, a, um adj good; kind; beautiful; pleasant; right; useful; considerable; rich; virtuous; promising, happy; favourable; high, honourable

boō ① v cry aloud, roar; call loudly upon

boreās, ae m north wind

boreus, a, um adj northern

bōs, bovis m/f ox, bull; cow

bovārius ▸ boārius

brācae, ārum fpl trousers, breeches

brācātus, a, um adj breeched

bracchium, brāchium, (i)ī nt arm; fore-arm; claw; branch, shoot; earthwork connecting fortified points; yard-arm

bracchiolum, brāchiolum, ī nt a little arm

3

bractea | cadō

●**ractea**, **brattea**, ae f thin sheet of gold metal

●**ravium, (i)ī** nt LM prize

●**revi** adv briefly, in a few words

●**reviloquentia**, ae f brevity of speech

●**revis**, e adj short, little, brief; small; concise; shallow
□ **(in) brevī** soon

●**revitās**, **ātis** f shortness; smallness; brevity

●**reviter** adv shortly, briefly

●**rūma**, ae f winter solstice; winter

●**rūmālis**, e adj wintry

●**rūtus**, a, um adj heavy, unwieldy; dull, stupid

●**ūbō**, **ōnis** m horned or eagle owl

●**ubulcitō** ① v, **bubulcitor** ① v dep take care of or drive cattle; be a farm labourer

●**ubulcus**, **ī** m ploughman, farm-labourer

●**ūbulus**, a, um adj of cattle or oxen; rawhide, oxhide

●**ūbus** dat/abl pl of ▶ **bōs**

●**ūcaeda**, ae m ox-slaughterer; one beaten with oxhide whips

●**ucca**, ae f cheek

●**uccula**, ae f little cheek; cheek-piece of a helmet

●**ūcerus**, a, um adj ox-horned

●**ūcina**, ae f trumpet; war-trumpet; watch-horn

●**ūcinātor**, **ōris** m trumpeter; proclaimer

●**ūcolicus**, a, um adj pastoral, bucolic

●**ūcula**, ae f heifer

●**ūfō**, **ōnis** m toad

bulbus, **ī** m bulb; onion

bulla, ae f bubble; boss, knob, stud; locket hung round the necks of children

burgenses, **ium** mpl LM townspeople

bustum, **ī** nt pyre, tomb

būteō, **ōnis** m a species of hawk

būtyrum, **ī** nt butter

buxifer, **era**, **erum** adj bearing box-trees

buxum, **ī** nt box-wood; top; flute

buxus, **ī** f evergreen box-tree; box-wood; (poet) flute

Cc

caballus, **ī** m horse, riding horse, pack-horse

cacabus, **ī** m cooking-pot

cacātus, a, um nt fouled

cac(c)hin(n)ātiō, **ōnis** f immoderate or boisterous laughter, guffawing

cac(c)hin(n)ō ① v laugh loudly or boisterously, guffaw; laugh loudly at

cac(c)hin(n)us, **ī** m laugh, guffaw

cacūmen, **inis** nt tip, end; peak, summit

cacūminō ① v make pointed or tapered

cadāver, **eris** nt dead body, corpse

cadō, **cecidī**, **cāsum** ③ v fall (down, from); be slain; abate, decay; happen; end, close; fall through, fail

cădūceum, **ī** *nt*, **cădūceus**, **ī** *m* herald's staff; wand of Mercury

cădūcifer, **era**, **erum** *adj* staff-bearer

■ ~, **erī** *m* Mercury

cădūcus, **a**, **um** *adj* ready to fall; tottering, falling, fallen; frail, perishable, vain

cadus, **ī** *m* large jar for wine, jar; funeral urn

caecĭtās, **ātis** *f* blindness

caecō 🔲 *v* blind; obscure; make morally blind

caecus, **a**, **um** *adj* blind; obscure; hidden, secret; confused; rash; vain, uncertain; dark, gloomy

caedēs, **dis** *f* felling; slaughter; murder; persons slain; blood, gore

caedō, **cecĭdī**, **caesum** 🔲 *v* fell, hew; cut; slaughter; murder

caelātor, **ōris** *m* engraver, worker in bas-relief

caelātūra, **ae** *f* engraving

caelebs, **ibis** *adj* unmarried, single, widowed

caeles, **itis** *adj* heavenly

■ ~, **itis** *m* a god

caelestis, **e** *adj* heavenly; divine; god-like

■ **caelestēs**, **um** *m/pl* the gods

caelicola, **ae** *m/f* inhabitant of heaven

caelifer, **era**, **erum** *adj* supporting the sky

caelō 🔲 *v* engrave, chase

caelum[1], **ī** *nt* heaven; sky; climate, weather

caelum[2], **ī** *nt* graving-tool, chisel

caementārius, **(i)ī** *m* LM mason

caementum, **ī** *nt* small stones,

rubble (used in concrete)

caenum, **ī** *nt* mud, filth; (of persons) scum

caepa, **ae** *f*, **caepe**, **is** *nt* onion

caerimōnia, **ae** *f* ritual; reverence, worship; sanctity

caesariēs, **iēī** *f* long, flowing or luxuriant hair

caesim *adv* by cutting; with the edge of the sword; in short clauses

caesiō, **ōnis** *f* hewing or cutting down of trees

caespes, **itis** *m* turf, sod, grassy ground; altar

caestus, **ūs** *m* boxing-glove

calamister, **trī** *m* curling-tongs

calamistrātus, **a**, **um** *adj* curled with the curling-iron

calamĭtās, **ātis** *f* disaster, ruin, misfortune; defeat

calamĭtōsus, **a**, **um** *adj* calamitous; miserable; ruinous; damaged

calamus, **ī** *m* reed, cane; reed-pen; reed-pipe; arrow; angling-rod; stalk

calathus, **ī** *m* wicker basket, flower basket; wine-cup; vessel for cheese or curdled milk

calātor, **ōris** *m* servant, attendant

calcar, **āris** *nt* spur

calceō 🔲 *v* put shoes on

calceus, **ī** *m* shoe

calciō ▶ **calceō**

calcitrātus, **ūs** *m* kicking with the heels

calcitrō 🔲 *v* kick with the heels; be refractory

calcō 🔲 *v* tread under foot; trample upon, spurn, despise

calculus, **ī** *m* pebble, stone used for reckoning; reckoning, calculation

caldārium, **(i)ī** *nt* hot-bath

calefaciō, **fēcī**, **factum** ③ *v* warm, heat; excite

caleō ② *v* be warm or hot, be flushed; be in love; be excited

calēscō ③ *v* grow warm or hot; become inflamed

caliga, **ae** *f* soldier's boot

cālīginōsus, **a**, **um** *adj* foggy, misty

cālīgō¹ ① *v* be dark

cālīgō², **inis** *f* mist; darkness, gloom; moral or intellectual darkness

calix, **cis** *m* cup, goblet; LM chalice

calleō ② *v* have experience or skill in, know; know how to

calliditās, **ātis** *f* shrewdness, skilfulness; slyness

callidus, **a**, **um** *adj* expert, skilful; crafty, sly

callis, **is** *m* rough track, path; pasturage

callum, **ī** *nt* hardened skin, hide; callousness; lack of feeling

cālō, **ōnis** *m* soldier's servant

calor, **ōris** *m* warmth, heat; passion, zeal, ardour; love

calt(h)a, **ae** *f* marigold

calumnia, **ae** *f* sophistry; false accusation, false claim

calumniātor, **ōris** *m* false accuser, pettifogger

calumnior ① *v dep* contrive false accusations; depreciate, find fault with

calvitium, **(i)ī** *nt* baldness

calvus, **a**, **um** *adj* bald

calx¹, **cis** *f* heel

calx², **cis** *f* chalk, limestone, goal (because the goal-line was marked with chalk)

camēlus, **ī** *m* camel, dromedary

Camēna, **ae** *f* Muse; poetry

camera, **ae** *f* LM room, chamber

camīnus, **ī** *m* smelting furnace, forge; domestic stove

campānum, **ī** *nt* LM bell

campester, **tris**, **tre** *adj* flat, level, open; of the Campus Martius

campestre, **is** *nt* loin-cloth worn by athletes

campus, **ī** *m* plain, field; field of battle; level surface; place for games, exercise, *etc.*; field of action; expanse of water, sea □ **Campus Martius** an open space by the side of the Tiber at Rome

canālis, **is** *m/f* channel, conduit, canal

cancellārius, **(i)ī** *m* LM chancellor

cancellī, **ōrum** *mpl* railing, lattice; barrier; boundaries, limits

cancer, **crī** *m* crab; Cancer, the sign of the zodiac; cancer

candefaciō, **fēcī**, **factum** ③ *v* make white; make hot

candēla, **ae** *f* candle; waxed cord

candēlābrum, **ī** *nt* stand for candles, candelabrum

candeō ② *v* be of brilliant whiteness, shine; become or be hot

candēscō, **duī** ③ *v* grow light; grow white; become hot

candidātus, **ī** *m* candidate; aspirant

candidus, a, um *adj* dazzling white, clear, bright; clean, spotless; candid, frank; lucky; fair-skinned

candor, ōris *m* dazzling whiteness, brightness; beauty; candour; kindness, moral purity

cāneō ② *v* be hoary, be white

cānēscō ③ *v* grow hoary; grow old, be white

canīcula, ae *f* bitch; dog-star, dog-days

canīnus, a, um *adj* canine; abusive, snarling

canis, is *m/f* dog; hound; subordinate, 'jackal'; dog-star; the lowest throw at dice

canistrum, ī *nt* wicker basket

cānitiēs, iēī *f* white or grey colouring; grey hair; old age

canna, ae *f* reed, cane; reed-pipe

canō, cecinī, cantum ③ *v* sing; crow; sound, play (an instrument); recite; celebrate in song or poetry; prophesy; blow (signals); sound (for a retreat)

canor, ōris *m* song, music, tune

canōrus, a, um *adj* melodious, harmonious

cantharis, idis *f* blister-beetle; Spanish fly (used in medicine and as a poison)

cantharus, ī *m* large drinking vessel with handles

cant(h)ērius, (i)ī *m* poor-quality horse, gelding

canticum, ī *nt* song; passage in a comedy chanted or sung; LM canticle

cantilēna, ae *f* refrain; little song, ditty

cantiō, ōnis *f* incantation, spell

cantitō ① *v* sing over and over

cantō ① *v* sing; play, recite; praise; forewarn; enchant; bewitch

cantor, ōris *m* singer; poet; eulogist

cantus, ūs *m* song, poem; singing; melody; prophecy; incantation

cānus, a, um *adj* white, hoary, grey; foamy; old, aged

capācitās, ātis *f* capacity, largeness

capāx, ācis *adj* spacious, roomy; capable

capella, ae *f* she-goat; kid

caper, prī *m* he-goat

capessō, īvī/iī, ītum ③ *v* seize eagerly; manage; undertake; pursue with zeal

capillātus, a, um *adj* having long hair

capillus, ī *m* hair of the head; hair

capiō, cēpī, captum ③ *v* take, seize; capture, occupy; get, obtain; captivate, win over; make choice of; find out; understand; choose, select; undertake
□ **cōnsilium** ∼ decide, resolve, have an idea; deliberate, take counsel

capistrum, ī *nt* halter

capitāl, is *nt* (also **capitāle**) capital crime or the punishment due to it

capitālis, e *adj* belonging to the head or life; deadly, mortal; dangerous; excellent, first-rate

Capitōlium, (i)ī *nt* the Capitoline hill at Rome

capitulāre, is *nt* LM order,

rescript

capra, ae *f* she-goat

caprea, ae *f* roe-deer

capreolus, ī *m* a young roebuck; rafter

caprigenus, a, um *adj* of goats

caprimulgus, ī *m* country bumpkin; nightjar

capripēs, edis *adj* goat-footed

capsa, ae *f* cylindrical case (for books)

capsula, ae *f* small box for books; chest

captātor, ōris *m* legacy hunter; one who strives to obtain

captiō, ōnis *f* deception, fraud; disadvantage; a piece of sophistry

captiōsus, a, um *adj* harmful, disadvantageous, captious

captīvitās, ātis *f* captivity; capture

captīvus, a, um *adj* taken prisoner (in war, as booty); of captives

■ **~, ī** *m* prisoner, captive

captō ① *v* snatch, endeavour to catch; strive after; hunt legacies; ensnare

captus, ūs *m* capacity, ability, potentiality

capulus, ī *m* handle; sword-hilt

caput, itis *nt* head; top; end; source; beginning; principal point; mouth (of a river); article, chapter; life; person; civil rights; intelligence; author, leader, chief; capital city; capital as opposed to interest

arbasus, ī *f.* (in pl **carbasa, ōrum** *nt*) linen; sail; linen garment; awning

carbaseus, a, um *adj* made of linen

carbō, ōnis *m* charcoal; glowing coal

carbunculus, ī *m* (live) coal

carcer, eris *m* prison, jail; barriers at the beginning of a race-course; starting-point; beginning

carchēsium, (i)ī *nt* drinking-cup

cardiacus, a, um *adj* of the heart or stomach; suffering from stomach

cardō, inis *m* door-hinge; pole, axis; chief point or circumstance

carduus, ī *m* thistle

cārectum, ī *nt* bed of sedge

careō ② *v* with *abl* be without, want; be absent from; miss, lose, be free from

cārex, icis *f* reed-grass; sedge

carīna, ae *f* bottom of a ship, keel; ship

cariōsus, a, um *adj* rotten

cāritās, ātis *f* dearness; high price; love

carmen, inis *nt* song, strain; poem; oracle, prophecy; magic formula; instrumental music

carnifex, icis *m* executioner, murderer, butcher, torturer; scoundrel

carnificīna, ae *f* work or trade of an executioner; torture

carnificius, a, um *adj* of a hangman

carnificō ① *v* execute, butcher

carnuf- ▶ **carnif-**

carō, carnis *f* flesh; meat

carpatinus, a, um *adj* made of hide

carpentarius, (i)ī *m* LM

carpenter

carpentum, ī *nt* two-wheeled carriage

carpō, rpsī, ptum ③ *v* pluck (off); gather; browse; tear off; rob, plunder; enjoy, use; slander; weaken; consume; harass
□ **~ viam/iter** proceed on a journey

carptim *adv* in detached parts

carrus, ī *m* Gallic wagon

cārus, a, um *adj* dear, costly; precious, loved

casa, ae *f* hut, cottage; shop, booth

cāseus, ī *m* cheese

casia, ae *f* cinnamon

cassida, ae *f*, **cassis, idis** *f* helmet (usu. of metal)

cassis, is *m* often in pl hunting-net

cassus, a, um *adj* empty; lacking, deprived of; vain, fruitless
□ **in cassum** in vain

castanea, ae *f* chestnut-tree; chestnut

castellānī, ōrum *mpl* garrison of a fort

castellum, ī *nt* fortified settlement, garrison; refuge, stronghold

castīgātiō, ōnis *f* punishment, reprimanding

castīgātor, ōris *m* corrector, reprover

castīgō ① *v* chastise, punish, correct, mend

castimōnia, ae *f* chastity, abstinence; purity of morals

castitās, ātis *f* chastity

castoreum, ī *nt* aromatic secretion obtained from the

beaver

castrēnsis, e *adj* of or connected with the camp or active military service

castrō ① *v* castrate; impair, weaken

castrum, ī *nt* fortified post, settlement
■ **castra, ōrum** *ntpl* military camp; war-service; day's march; field of activity
□ **pōnō ~** pitch camp
□ **moveō ~** break camp

castus, a, um *adj* pure; spotless; chaste; pious; sacred

casula, ae *f* chasuble (vestment of a priest)

cāsus, ūs *m* fall, overthrow; error; accident, chance, event; occasion; misfortune; danger, risk; death; (grammar) case
□ **cāsū** by chance, by accident

catafracta, ae *m*, **catafractēs, ae** *m* coat of mail

catafractus, ī *m* soldier armed in mail

catagraphus, a, um *adj* (of material) figured

catapulta, ae *f* machine for discharging bolts or other missiles; catapult

catasta, ae *f* platform where slaves were exhibited for sale

catella, ae *f* little chain

catellus, ī *m* little dog, puppy

catēna, ae *f* chain; fetter; bond, restraint

catēnātus, a, um *adj* chained, fettered

caterva, ae *f* crowd; troop, company; flock

catervātim *adv* in troops; in

cathedra | celebrātiō

disordered masses

cathedra, ae f farm-chair, easy chair; chair of a teacher; [LM] bishop's chair

catulus, ī m young dog, puppy, whelp

catus, a, um adj knowing, shrewd, wise, prudent

cauda, ae f tail

caudex ▸ cōdex

caulae, ārum fpl railing, lattice barrier; holes, pores

caulis, is m stalk; cabbage

caupō, ōnis m shopkeeper; innkeeper

caupōna, ae f inn, tavern, lodging-house

caurus ▸ cōrus

causa, ae f (formerly **caussa**) cause, reason, motive; occasion; pretence; excuse; matter, subject; affair, business; process, suit; (political) party; blame, fault; connection, friendship; condition, state
□ **causā** with gen on account of, because of
□ **causam dīcō** plead a case

causidicus, ī m advocate, barrister

causor ① v dep allege as an excuse; plead a cause, bring an action

causula, ae f speech in a petty lawsuit

cautēs, tis f rough pointed rock; cliff, reef

cautiō, ōnis f caution, heedfulness; stipulation; pledge

cautus, a, um adj cautious, heedful; made safe, secured

cavaedium nt [from **cavum** and

aedium] inner court in a house

cavea, ae f enclosure, cage, coop; audience's part of a theatre; theatre

caveō, cāvī, cautum ② v be on one's guard, take care; beware of; give security; get security; order or stipulate (by will, in writing)
□ **cavē** with (nē/ut and) subj (mind that you) don't … !

caverna, ae f cavern, grotto, cave, hole; vault of the sky

cavillātiō, ōnis f quibbling, banter, jeering

cavillātor, ōris m jester, banterer, captious critic

cavillor ① v dep cavil at; scoff, jeer, satirize

cavō ① v hollow out; pierce through; make by hollowing out

cavum, ī nt, **cavus, ī** m hole, cavity, cave, burrow

cavus, a, um adj hollow, concave; deep-channelled

cecidī ▸ cadō

cecidī ▸ caedō

cecinī ▸ canō

cēdō, cessī, cessum ③ v go, walk; turn out, come to pass; fall to, devolve; yield, give way; withdraw; go off; succeed; allow, grant; give up

cedo (pl **cette**) impv give here! pray! let us hear, tell! suppose, what if?

cedrus, ī f cedar; cedar-oil

celeber, bris, bre adj much frequented, populous; renowned, famous

celebrātiō, ōnis f throng; celebrating of a festival

celebrātus, a, um *adj* crowded; festive; current, popular

celebritās, ātis *f* crowded conditions; crowding; renown

celebrō ② *v* frequent, crowd; inhabit; practise, perform; celebrate; make known

celer, eris, ere *adj* swift, quick; lively; hurried; rash, hasty

celerēs, um *mpl* bodyguard of the Roman kings

celeritās, ātis *f* swiftness, quickness

celeriter *adv* quickly

celerō ① *v* quicken, accelerate; make haste

celēs, ētis *m* small fast boat

celeuma, atis *nt* call of the boatswain giving the time to rowers

cella, ae *f* cell; cellar; storehouse; larder; principal *or* subsidiary chamber in a temple; slave's room, 'garret'

cellārium, (i)i *nt* LM pantry

cellārius, (i)i *m* butler, storekeeper

cellula, ae *f* little room

cēlō ① *v* hide, conceal; keep in ignorance; keep dark

celōx, ōcis *f* cutter, yacht

celsus, a, um *adj* high, lofty; great, sublime; haughty

cementarius, (i)i *m* LM mason

cēna, ae *f* dinner, supper, course for dinner

cēnāculum, ī *nt* upper-room, attic

cēnātiō, ōnis *f* dining-room

cēnitō ① *v* dine often

cēnō ① *v* dine, sup, dine on

cēnseō, cēnsum ② *v* count, reckon; tax, assess; estimate, value; think, be of the opinion; decree; vote to

cēnsitor, ōris *m* census-taker, registration official

cēnsor, ōris *m* censor; censurer, critic

cēnsōrius, a, um *adj* of or belonging to a censor; austere, moral

cēnsūra, ae *f* censorship; judgment, control

cēnsus, ūs *m* valuation of every Roman citizen's estate; registering of a man (his age, family, profession, *etc.*); sum assessed; property

centaurēum, ēi *nt* centaury (a herb)

centēnī, ae, a *adj* a hundred each; a hundred

centē(n)sima, ae *f* hundredth part

centē(n)simus, a, um *adj* the hundredth

centiceps, itis *adj* hundred-headed

centimanus, a, um *adj* hundred-handed

centum *adj indec* a hundred

centumvirī, ōrum *mpl* a panel of judges chosen annually to decide civil suits

centuria, ae *f* century
 □ **~ comitiāta** a political unit for voting

centuriātim *adv* by centuries

centuriō¹ ① *v* arrange (recruits, *etc.*) in military centuries

◻ **comitia centuriāta** the assembly in which the Romans voted by centuries

centuriō², **ōnis** *m* commander of a century, captain, centurion

cēpī ▸ **capiō**

cēra, **ae** *f* wax; wax-covered writing-tablet; letter; seal of wax; waxen image

cerasus, **ī** *f* cherry-tree; cherry

cērātus, **a**, **um** *adj* provided, coated, fastened *or* caulked with wax

Cereālis, **e** *adj* of Ceres, of corn
■ **Cereālia**, **ium** *ntpl* the festival of Ceres

cerebrum, **ī** *nt* brain; understanding, anger

cēreus, **a**, **um** *adj* waxen; wax-coloured; pliant, soft
■ **∼**, **ī** *m* wax taper

cernō, **crēvī**, **crētum** ③ *v* sift; discern, perceive; decide; determine; make formal acceptance of an inheritance

cernuus, **a**, **um** *adj* head foremost

cerrītus, **a**, **um** *adj* possessed by Ceres, frantic, mad

certāmen, **inis** *nt* contest, struggle; battle, rivalry, combat; point of contention

certātim *adv* with rivalry, in competition; eagerly

certātiō, **ōnis** *f* striving, contention

certē *adv* certainly, surely; really; yet indeed, at least

certō¹ *adv* certainly, surely; in fact

certō² ① *v* fight, contend; strive; contend at law

certus, **a**, **um** *adj* certain; sure;

safe; distinct; fixed, agreed upon; steady, resolute; constant, faithful; unerring

◻ **certiōrem faciō** inform

◻ **prō certō sciō/habeō** know for certain

cērula, **ae** *f* red pencil

cērussa, **ae** *f* white powder used as a cosmetic; white lead

cerva, **ae** *f* hind, doe; deer

cervīcal, **ālis** *nt* pillow

cervīnus, **a**, **um** *adj* pertaining to a deer or stag

cervīx, **īcis** *f* neck

cervus, **ī** *m* hart, stag
■ **cervī** *pl* defensive palisade, stakes stuck into the ground, chevaux-de-frise

cessātiō, **ōnis** *f* relaxation, respite; idleness

cessātor, **ōris** *m* idler, sluggard

cessō ① *v* hold back, leave off, delay, loiter; cease (from); idle; be wanting; go wrong

cētārium, **(i)ī** *nt* fish-pond

cētārius, **(i)ī** *m* fishmonger

cēterōquī *adv* in other respects, otherwise

cēterum *adv* for the rest; but; besides

cēterus, **a**, **um** *adj* the other
■ **cēterī** *pl* the others, the rest

cette *pl* from ▸ **cedo**

cētus, **ī** *m* whale; porpoise; dolphin; sea-monster

ceu *adv* as, just as; as if

chalybēius, **a**, **um** *adj* of steel

chalybs, **bis** *m* steel, iron

Chaos *nt* formless state of primordial matter; pit of the Lower World

charta, ae f (leaf of) paper; writing

Chēlae, ārum fpl the claws of Scorpio which extended into the sign Libra

chelydrus, ī m venomous water-snake

chelys, acc yn f lyre

chīrographum, ī nt handwriting; manuscript; bond

chīrūrgia, ae f surgery

chīrūrgus, ī m surgeon

chlamydatus, a, um adj wearing a chlamys

chlamys, ydis f a Greek cloak or cape frequently for military use

chorda, ae f string of a musical instrument

chorēa, ae f dance

chorus, ī m dance with singing; chorus, choir; band, group

chrisma, atis nt LM consecrated oil, chrism

chrÿsolithos, ī m/f topaz

cibus, ī m food; fare

cicāda, ae f cricket, cicada

cicātrīx, īcis f scar, cicatrice

ciccum, ī nt a proverbially worthless object

cicer, eris nt chick-pea

cicindēla, ae f firefly; candle

cicōnia, ae f stork

cicūta, ae f hemlock; shepherd's pipe

cieō, cīvī, citum ② v move; shake; rouse; disturb; provoke; call on, invoke; produce

cimentarius LM ▶ **caementarius**

cīmex, icis m bed-bug

cinaedus, ī m catamite

cincinnātus, a, um adj with curled hair

cincinnus, ī m ringlet; (fig) rhetorical flourish

cīnctūtus, a, um adj wearing a girdle or loin-cloth

cinerārius, (i)ī m hair-curler, hair-dresser

cingō, cīnxī, cīnctum ③ v gird; surround; beleaguer; crown

cingulum, ī nt band, belt; sword-belt

cinis, eris m/f ashes; ruins

cinnamum, ī nt the cinnamon shrub

circā adv (all) around; prep with acc about, near to; concerning

circēnsēs, ium mpl games and exercises of wrestling, running, fighting, etc., in the circus

circiter adv/prep with acc about, near; towards

circueō, īre, īvī/iī, itum v ir go or march around; encompass; go about canvassing; circumvent

circuitiō, ōnis f a going round; patrol; circumlocution

circuitus, ūs m going round, circuit; way round; circumference; circumlocution

circulor ⓘ v dep form groups round oneself

circulus, ī m circle; orbit; ring, hoop; company

circum adv (all) around, about; prep with acc around, about, among; at, near

circumagō, ēgī, āctum ③ v drive in a circle, turn round; wheel

circumcīdō, cīdī, cīsum ③ v cut

around, clip; diminish; remove

circumclūdō, ūsī, ūsum ③ *v* enclose on all sides

circumcolō ③ *v* dwell round about

circumcursō ① *v* run about over; run around (a person)

circumdō, dedī, datum ① *v* put round; surround; enclose

circumdūcō, dūxī, ductum ③ *v* lead or draw around; lead out of the way; cheat; cancel

circumeō ▸ **circueō**

circumferō, ferre, tulī, lātum *v ir* carry about or round; spread round, divulge; purify; turn (eyes, face, hands, *etc.*) to a new direction

circumfluō, flūxī ③ *v* flow round; be rich in

circumfluus, a, um *adj* circumfluent, surrounding; surrounded with water

circumforāneus, a, um *adj* connected with (the business of) the forum; itinerant

circumfundō, ūdī, ūsum ③ *v* pour around
□ **circumfundor** flow round; surround

circumgredior, gressus sum ③ *v dep* go round behind by a flanking movement

circumiaceō ② *v* lie round about

circumiciō, iēcī, iectum ③ *v* cast or place around; encompass with

circumiectus[1], ūs *m* encompassing, embrace

circumiectus[2], a, um *adj* surrounding

circumit- ▸ **circuit-**

circumitiō, ōnis *f* (also **circuitiō**) a going round; patrol; circumlocution

circumitus, ūs *m* (also **circuitus**) going round, circuit; way round; circumference; circumlocution

circumligō ① *v* bind round or to; encircle

circumliniō ④ *v*, **circumlinō, lēvī, litum** ③ *v* smear or anoint round, decorate

circumluō ③ *v* wash or flow around

circummittō, mīsī, missum ③ *v* send around

circummūniō ④ *v* wall around, fortify

circummūnītiō, ōnis *f* circumvallation

circumplector, plexus sum ③ *v dep* embrace, surround, circumvallate

circumplicō ① *v* coil round

circumpōnō, posuī, positum ③ *v* put or place around

circumrētiō ④ *v* encircle with a net

circumrōdō, rōsī ③ *v* gnaw all round; slander

circumsaepiō, psī, ptum *v* fence round, enclose

circumscrībō, psī, ptum *v* draw a line around; circumscribe; hem in; cheat; circumvent

circumscrīptē *adv* concisely; in periodic style

circumscrīptiō, ōnis *f* encircling; circle; boundary; outline; deceiving; periodic sentence

circumscrīptor, ōris *m* cheat;

defrauder

circumsedeō, **sēdī**, **sessum** ② v sit around; besiege

circumsīdō ③ v besiege, surround

circumsiliō ④ v leap around

circumsistō, **stetī** ③ v stand round

circumsonō ① v resound on every side, ring again with; echo round

circumspectiō, **ōnis** f careful consideration

circumspectō ① v look about searchingly

circumspectus, **a**, **um** adj circumspect, cautious; wary; carefully considered

circumspiciō, **spexī**, **spectum** ③ v look about; take heed; survey; seek for

circumstō, **stetī** ① v stand round; surround

circumstrepō ③ v make a noise around

circumvādō, **vāsī** ③ v form a ring round, surround

circumvagus, **a**, **um** adj moving round, encircling

circumvallō ① v surround with siege works

circumvectiō, **ōnis** f circular course; transport

circumvector ① v dep sail round, travel round

circumvehor, **vectus sum** ③ v dep make the round of; travel round; sail around

circumveniō, **vēnī**, **ventum** ④ v come round; surround; beat; oppress; circumvent

circumvinciō, **vīnxī**, **vīnctum** ④ v tie round

circumvolitō ① v fly around about

circumvolō ① v fly around

circumvolvō, **volūtum** ③ v roll round, twine around

circus, **ī** m circle; circus (at Rome)

cirrus, **ī** m lock of curly hair; tuft

cis prep with acc on this side (of); within

Cisalpīnus, **a**, **um** adj lying on the south side of the Alps

cisium, **(i)ī** nt two-wheeled carriage

cista, **ae** f chest, box

cisterna, **ae** f cistern

cistophorus, **ī** m an Asiatic coin

citātus, **a**, **um** adj quick, rapid □ **equō citātō** at full gallop

citerior, **ius** adj on this side, hithermost; nearer

cithara, **ae** f lyre

citharista, **ae** m lyre-player

citharistria, **ae** f femal lyre-player

citharoedus, **ī** m one who sings to the lyre

citimus, **a**, **um** adj nearest, next

cito, comp **citius**, sup **citissimē** adv soon; quickly

citō ① v cite; summon; excite; encourage

citrā prep with acc on this side; within, short of; without, apart from

citreus, **a**, **um** adj of citron

citrō adv to this side, hither □ **ultrō citrōque** to and fro; in and out; on both sides

citrum, **ī** *nt* wood of the citron-tree; table made of citron-wood

citus, **a**, **um** *adj* quick, swift, rapid

cīvicus, **a**, **um** *adj* civic, civil; legal □ **cīvica corōna** a crown of oak leaves presented to one who had saved a fellow-countryman in war

cīvīlis, **e** *adj* civic, civil; political, public, polite, courteous

cīvīliter *adv* in a civil sphere; in a manner suited to citizens

cīvis, **is** *m/f* citizen; countryman or woman

cīvitās, **ātis** *f* citizenship; citizens; city; state

clādēs, **dis** *f* defeat; destruction; ruin; plague; slaughter; calamity

clam *adv/prep with acc* secretly; unknown to

clāmātor, **ōris** *m* shouter

clāmitātiō, **ōnis** *f* shouting, bawling

clāmitō ① *v* shout repeatedly; proclaim

clāmō ① *v* shout; shout the name of

clāmor, **ōris** *m* shout, cry, clamour; applause; noise, din

clanculum *adv* secretly

clandestīnus, **a**, **um** *adj* secret, hidden, clandestine

clangor, **ōris** *m* clang, noise

clārē *adv* brightly; clearly; aloud; lucidly

clāreō ② *v* shine; be famous

clārēscō, **ruī** ③ *v* begin to shine; become clear or evident; become famous

clārisonus, **a**, **um** *adj* loud- or clear-sounding

clāritās, **ātis** *f* clearness,

brightness; distinctness; celebrity; renown

clāritūdō, **inis** *f* clearness, brightness; distinctness; celebrity; renown

clārō ① *v* make visible, brighten, make illustrious

clārus, **a**, **um** *adj* clear, bright; loud, distinct; evident; illustrious, famous

classiārius, **(i)ī** *m* mariner; sailor, seaman; *pl* naval forces

classicum, **ī** *nt* military trumpet-call

classicus, **a**, **um** *adj* belonging to the fleet; belonging to the highest class of citizen

classis, **is** *f* class of the Roman people; army; fleet

claudeō ② *v*, **claudō**, **clausum** ③ *v* limp, halt; be weak, be imperfect

claudicō ① *v* limp, be lame; waver, be defective

claudō, **clausī**, **clausum** ③ *v* shut, close; conclude, finish; enclose; imprison; surround; besiege

claudus, **a**, **um** *adj* limping, lame; defective, wavering, uncertain

claustra, **ōrum** *ntpl* bolts, bars; enclosure; barrier; door, gate; bulwark; dam

claustrum, **ī** *nt* [LM] cloister

clausula, **ae** *f* conclusion, end; close of a periodic sentence

clāva, **ae** *f* cudgel, club

clāviger, **erī** *m* club-bearer; key-bearer

clāvis, **is** *f* door-key

clāvus, **ī** *m* nail; tiller, helm, helm

of the ship of state; rudder
□ **lātus ~** a broad purple stripe

clēmēns, ntis *adj* merciful, gentle, mild; quiet, peaceable; courteous; moderate

clēmentia, ae *f* clemency, mercy; mildness; calmness

clepō, psī, ptum 3 *v* steal

clepsydra, ae *f* water-clock

clēricus, ī *m*, **clerus, ī** *m* LM cleric, clergy

cliēns, ntis *m* client; vassal; dependent

clientēla, ae *f* clientship; vassalage; patronage; clients; vassals

clima, atis *nt* LM region

clīmactēricus, a, um *adj* critical

clipeātus, a, um *adj* furnished with a shield

clipeus, ī *m* round, usually bronze shield; disc of the sun

clītellae, ārum *fpl* pack-saddle

clītellārius, a, um *adj* bearing a pack-saddle

clīvōsus, a, um *adj* hilly, steep

clīvus, ī *m* sloping ground, slope

cloāca, ae *f* sewer, drain

clueō 2 *v* be called, be named, be reputed

clūnis, is *m/f* buttocks, haunches

coacervātiō, ōnis *f* heaping together or up

coacervō 1 *v* heap together or up; amass

coacēscō, ī 3 *v* become sour

coāctor, ōris *m* collector (of money, taxes, *etc*.)

coāctū *adv* by force

coāctum ▶ cōgō

coaequō 1 *v* make level, regard as equal

coāgmentō 1 *v* join, connect; construct

coāgmentum, ī *nt* joint

coalēscō, aluī, alitum 3 *v* grow together, close; become unified or strong

coarguō, uī 3 *v* prove, make manifest; refute; convict

coccum, ī *nt* scarlet colour; scarlet cloth

cochlea, ae *f* snail; LM *pl* spiral staircase

coctilis, e *adj* (of bricks) baked; built of baked bricks

cocus ▶ coquus

cōdex, icis *m* trunk of a tree; piece of wood; (bound) book; account-book

cōdicillus, ī *m* rescript of the Emperor, petition to the Emperor; codicil; *pl* set of writing tablets

coēgī ▶ cōgō

coemō, ēmī, ēmptum 3 *v* buy up

coēmptiō, ōnis *f* (fictitious) sale of a woman to a man (legal term)

coeō, īre, īvī/iī, itum *v* go or come together, meet, clash; assemble; conspire; curdle; heal; unite

coepī, isse, coeptum *v* begin

coeptō 1 *v* begin, attempt

coeptum, ī *nt* beginning, undertaking

coerceō 2 *v* enclose; limit; correct, keep in order; punish; restrain

coercitiō, ōnis *f* coercion, restraint; punishment

coetus, ūs *m* meeting, assembly, company

cōgitābundus, a, um *adj* wrapped in thought, thoughtful, pensive

cōgitātiō, ōnis *f* thinking, meditation; thought; intention; plan; opinion; reasoning power

cōgitō 🔲 *v* consider, ponder, think; meditate; intend; look forward to; imagine

cōgnātiō, ōnis *f* relationship by birth; relatives, family; affinity

cōgnātus, a, um *adj* related by birth; related; similar; having affinity with

▪ cognātus, ī *m* relation, relative

cognitiō, ōnis *f* getting to know; idea, notion; examination, inquiry

cognitor, ōris *m* attorney; guarantor of identity

cognōmen, inis *nt* family name; sobriquet

cognōmentum, ī *nt* surname; name

cognōscō, nōvī, nitum 🔳 *v* learn, get to know; inform oneself of; understand; investigate; observe, perceive; identify

cōgō, coēgī, coāctum 🔳 *v* drive together; collect; curdle; force, compel; prove conclusively

cohaereō, haesī, haesum 🔲 *v* adhere (to); stick together; be consistent

cohaerēscō, haesī 🔳 *v* cohere, stick, adhere

cohērēs, ēdis *m/f* co-heir, joint-heir

cohibeō 🔲 *v* hold together; restrain; curb; hinder; confine

cohonestō 🔲 *v* honour, grace;

make respectable

cohorrēscō, ruī 🔳 *v* shudder

cohors, rtis *f* farmyard; cohort; bodyguard; attendants

cohortātiō, ōnis *f* exhortation, encouragement

cohortor 🔲 *v dep* cheer up, encourage; exhort

coitiō, ōnis *f* meeting; conspiracy, combination

coitus, ūs *m* meeting; sexual intercourse

colaphus, ī *m* blow, buffet

collabefīō, fierī, factus sum *v ir semi-dep* collapse, break up; be overthrown politically

collābor, lāpsus sum 🔳 *v dep* collapse, fall in ruins; fall in a swoon *or* in death

collacrimō 🔲 *v* weep together, weep over

collātiō, ōnis *f* placing together; payment of tribute; tax; comparison

collaudātiō, ōnis *f* high praise

collaudō 🔲 *v* praise very much

collectiō, ōnis *f* collection; recapitulation

collēga, ae *m* colleague

collēgium, (i)ī *nt* college, corporation; brotherhood; colleagueship

collibet 🔳 *v impers*, **collibuit, isse, libitum est** 🔳 *v impers with dat* it pleases

collīdō, īsī, īsum 🔳 *v* strike *or* dash together; crush; bring into conflict with each other

colligō¹, ēgī, ēctum 🔳 *v* collect, assemble; acquire; pick up; infer; reckon; sum up

colligō | comes

□ **sē/animum colligere**
recover oneself or one's spirits

colligō² ① *v* bind together, connect; fetter

collinō, lēvī, litum ③ *v* besmear; pollute

collis, is *m* hill

collocātiō, ōnis *f* placing together; arrangement; marrying

collocō ① *v* put in a particular place together, arrange; bestow; employ; lay out; give in marriage

collocūtiō, ōnis *f* conversation, conference; discussion

colloquium, (i)ī *nt* conversation, discourse, interview

colloquor, locūtus sum ③ *v dep* talk together, converse

collubet ▶ collibet

collūceō ② *v* shine brightly

collūdō, ūsī, ūsum ③ *v* play together; act in collusion

collum, ī *nt* neck

colluō, uī, ūtum ③ *v* wash, rinse out

collūsiō, ōnis *f* secret understanding

collūsor, ōris *m* playmate, fellow gambler

collūstrō ① *v* lighten up; survey on all sides

colluviēs, iēī *f*, **colluviō, ōnis** *f* filth, offscouring; 'cesspool'; turmoil

collybus, ī *m* cost of exchange

collȳrium, (i)ī *nt* eye-salve

colō, coluī, cultum ③ *v* cultivate; take care of; dwell, inhabit; honour, pay court to, revere; worship; adorn; exercise; practise

colocāsia, ae *f* the Egyptian bean

colōnia, ae *f* colony

colōnus, ī *m* farmer

color, ōris *m* colour, complexion; outward show; excuse

colōrātus, a, um *adj* variegated; sunburnt

colōrō ① *v* colour, paint; dye; tan

colōs ▶ color

coluber, brī *m*, **colubra, ae** *f* serpent, snake

colubrifer, era, erum *adj* snake-bearing

colubrifer, era, erum *adj* snake-haired

cōlum, ī *nt* strainer, filter, sieve

columba, ae *f* dove, pigeon

columbus, ī *m* male pigeon

columella, ae *f* small column, pillar

columen, inis *nt* height, peak; roof, gable; summit, head, chief; the highest embodiment or peak

columna, ae *f* column, pillar

columnārium, (i)ī *nt* a pillar-tax

colurnus, a, um *adj* made of hazel

colus, ī *m*, **colus, ūs** *f* distaff

coma, ae *f* hair of the head; wool; foliage

comāns, ntis *adj* hairy; long-haired; leafy

comātus, a, um *adj* long-haired, leafy

□ **Gallia Comāta** Transalpine Gaul

combibō, bibī ③ *v* drink up, absorb

combūrō, ussī, ustum ③ *v* burn, burn up

comedō, ēsse, ēdī, ēs(t)um *v* eat up, consume; waste, squander

comes, itis *m*/*f* companion,

comrade, partner; attendant; ⊡ count

comētēs, ae m comet

cōmicus, a, um adj comic ■ ~, ī m comic actor; writer of comedy

cōmis, e adj courteous, kind, friendly; elegant

cōmitās, ātis f courteousness, kindness, friendliness; good taste

comitātus, ūs m escort, train, retinue; company; ⊡ county

cōmiter adv courteously, kindly, civilly, readily

comitiālis, e adj pertaining to the comitia

comitium, (i)ī nt a place in the forum, where the comitia were held

■ **comitia, ōrum** ntpl elections

comitō ⊡ v, **comitor** ⊡ v dep accompany, attend

commaculō ⊡ v stain deeply, pollute, defile; sully

commeātus, ūs m passage; leave; merchandise; convoy, provisions

commeminī, isse v ir recollect thoroughly, remember

commemorātiō, ōnis f reminding, recalling, citation

commemorō ⊡ v recall; mention

commendābilis, e adj praiseworthy

commendātiō, ōnis f entrusting; recommendation; excellence; approval

commendō ⊡ v commend to; recommend; entrust

commentāriolum, ī nt notebook; treatise

commentārius, (i)ī m, **commentārium, (i)ī** nt notebook, memorandum; commentary; notes, jottings

commentātiō, ōnis f thinking out, mental preparation

commenticius, a, um adj invented, devised; imaginary; forged, false

commentor ⊡ v dep think about; study beforehand; imagine

commentum, ī nt invention, fiction, fabrication; scheme

commentus ▶ pf pple of **comminiscor**

commeō ⊡ v go to and fro; pass; travel

commercium, (i)ī nt commercial intercourse, trade, dealings; relationship

commereō ⊡ v, **commereor** ⊡ v dep merit fully, deserve; be guilty of

commētior, mēnsus sum ⊡ v dep measure

commīlitium, (i)ī nt companionship in military service; comradeship

commīlitō, ōnis m fellow-soldier

comminātiō, ōnis f threatening

comminīscor, mentus sum ⊡ v dep devise, invent; forge; fabricate; state falsely

comminuō, uī, ūtum ⊡ v break into pieces; break up; crush

comminus adv hand to hand; at hand, near

commisceō, mixtum ⊡ v mix together

commiseror ⊡ v dep pity; excite compassion

commissum, ī *nt* enterprise, trust, secret; crime

commissūra, ae *f* joint, seam

committō, **mīsī**, **missum** ③ *v* join, unite; commit, entrust; match (one against another); compare; venture; begin; perpetrate; engage in
□ ~ **proelium** join battle

commoditās, **ātis** *f* fitness, convenience; advantage; obligingness

commodō ① *v* oblige, lend, provide, give

commodum, ī *nt* convenience; profit; wages; advantage

commodus, **a**, **um** *adj* suitable, convenient, fit; advantageous; lucky; obliging, pleasant
■ **commodē** *adv* properly, neatly

commonefaciō, **fēcī**, **factum** ③ *v* remind; impress upon

commoneō ② *v* remind

commōnstrō ① *v* point out

commorātiō, **ōnis** *f* stay (at a place); delay; (fig) dwelling on a point

commorior, **morī**, **mortuus sum** ③ *v dep* die together

commoror ① *v dep* sojourn, stay; stay long, be inactive; dwell upon

commōtiō, **ōnis** *f* agitation; the arousing of emotion

commoveō, **mōvī**, **mōtum** ② *v* move vigorously; stir up; excite; disturb; astonish; affect

commūnicātiō, **ōnis** *f* communication, an imparting

commūnicō ① *v* communicate; impart; share with; receive a share of; [LM] take communion

commūniō⁴ ④ *v* fortify;

strengthen, reinforce, entrench

commūniō², **ōnis** *f* mutual participation, association, sharing; [LM] company; Eucharist, communion

commūnis, **e** *adj* shared by, joint, common, general, ordinary; affable; public

commūnitās, **ātis** *f* joint possession, partnership; fellowship, kinship

commūniter *adv* in common, commonly, generally

commūtābilis, **e** *adj* changeable, variable

commūtātiō, **ōnis** *f* change; exchange

commūtō ① *v* change entirely, alter; exchange, barter

cōmō, **mpsī**, **mptum** ③ *v* arrange, 'do' (hair); dress, adorn

cōmoedia, **ae** *f* comedy

cōmoedus, ī *m* comedian, comic actor

compāctus, **a**, **um** *adj* joined together, sturdy

compāgēs, **gis** *f*, **compāgō**, **inis** *f* the action of binding together; joint, structure, framework

compar, **aris** *adj* like, equal (to); equal, comrade; partner

comparābilis, **e** *adj* comparable

comparātiō, **ōnis** *f* preparation; acquirement

compāreō ② *v* appear, be visible; be present; be in existence

comparō ① *v* unite; compare; prepare; provide (for); acquire; raise (a force); appoint

compellō¹, **pulī**, **pulsum** ③ *v*

drive together or along; collect; impel; force

compellō² ① v accost, address; chide, rebuke, tell off, call to account; abuse

compendium, (i)ī nt abridgement; a short cut; profit; savings
□ ~ **faciō** gain

compēnsō ① v balance, compensate

comperendinō ① v adjourn the trial of

comperiō, rī, rtum ④ v find out, learn, know for certain

compēs, edis f shackle (for the feet); fetter

compescō, ī ③ v confine, curb, restrain

competēns, ntis m/f LM catechumen

competītor, ōris m rival, competitor

competō, īvī/iī, ītum ③ v meet; happen; coincide; suit, agree; correspond; be sound or capable

compīlātiō, ōnis f burglary

compīlō ① v rob, pillage

compingō, pēgī, pāctum ③ v join; fasten up; shut up

Compitālia, ium ntpl festival celebrated at cross-roads in honour of the rural gods

compitum, ī nt cross-roads

complaceō ② v with dat please

complector, plexus sum ③ v dep clasp around; encompass, embrace; lay hold of; contain; comprehend (mentally); comprise

complēmentum, ī nt something that fills out or completes

compleō, ēvī, ētum ② v fill up; fill; complete; fulfil; perfect; supply; recruit; make good

complētorium, (i)ī nt LM compline

complex, icis m LM ally

complexiō, ōnis f combination, connection; summary; dilemma

complexus, ūs m embrace; sexual intercourse

complicō ① v fold up

complōrātiō, ōnis f, complōrātus, ūs m lamentation, (vocal) mourning

complōrō ① v bewail

complūrēs, a adj several, many

compluvium, (i)ī nt a quadrangular, inward-sloping, central portion of roof, designed to guide rain-water into the **impluvium**

compōnō, posuī, positum ③ v put or lay together; arrange, compose; adjust; compare; match; construct, build; compose (books, etc.); soothe, appease, settle; bury

comportō ① v carry, transport, collect

compos, ōtis adj usu with gen in possession of; participating, guilty of
□ ~ **mentis** in full possession of one's faculties

compositiō, ōnis f arrangement; matching

compositō adv by arrangement, concertedly

compositor, ōris m writer, composer

compositus, a, um adj well-arranged; calm

compotiō ④ *v with acc of recipient and gen or abl of object* put someone in possession of

compōtor, **ōris** *m* drinking-companion

comprānsor, **ōris** *m* table-companion

comprecātiō, **ōnis** *f* public supplication *or* prayers

comprecor ① *v dep* supplicate, implore, pray that

comprehendō, **ndī**, **ēnsum** ③ *v* seize *or* grasp; comprise; include; attack; embrace; describe; express; arrest *or* lay hold of; understand

comprehēnsiō, **ōnis** *f* arrest; comprehension, idea; dilemma

comprimō, **essī**, **essum** ③ *v* press *or* squeeze together; keep *or* hold back *or* in; suppress; seduce

comprobātiō, **ōnis** *f* approval

comprobō ① *v* approve; attest, confirm

cōmptus, **a**, **um** *adj* adorned; elegant, neat, polished

compungō, **ūnxī**, **ūnctum** ③ *v* prick, puncture

computatio, **onis** *f* ⚇ reckoning (esp. of the dates of religious festivals)

computō ① *v* calculate, count up, reckon, estimate

cōnāmen, **inis** *nt* attempt; effort, exertion

cōnātum, **ī** *nt* attempted action

cōnātus, **ūs** *m* attempt, undertaking; effort; impulse

concaedēs, **ium** *fpl* barricade

concalefaciō, **fēcī**, **factum** ③ *v* make warm, heat

concalēscō, **luī** ③ *v* become warm, warm up

concallēscō, **luī** ③ *v* become hard *or* callous; become insensible

concamerō ① *v* cover with an arch; vault over

concavus, **a**, **um** *adj* hollowed out, concave; hollow

concēdō, **essī**, **essum** ③ *v* go away, depart, withdraw; yield to, submit; allow, grant; forgive

concelebrō ① *v* go to a place often *or* in large numbers, haunt; celebrate; publish

concentus, **ūs** *m* singing together, harmony, melody; concord

concerpō, **psī**, **ptum** ③ *v* tear in pieces, tear up; pluck off; abuse

concertātiō, **ōnis** *f* dispute, controversy

concertō ① *v* dispute, fight, argue over

concessiō, **ōnis** *f* permission, grant, plea of excuse; the act of yielding

concessus, **ūs** *m* concession; permission

concha, **ae** *f* shell-fish, cockle; pearl; mussel-shell; oyster-shell; Triton's trumpet

  ◻ ~ **persica** mother of pearl

conchȳliātus, **a**, **um** *adj* purple-dyed

conchȳlium, **(i)ī** *nt* shell-fish; purple, purple dye

concidō, **cidī** ③ *v* fall down *or* into decay; fail; faint; be slain; die

concīdō, **cīdī**, **cīsum** ③ *v* cut to pieces; break up; beat, thrash; cut down, kill; weaken; destroy

concieō, **cīvī**, **citum** ② *v* move,

stir up; excite, incite

conciliābulum, **ī** *nt* place of assembly

conciliātiō, **ōnis** *f* union; winning over

conciliātor, **ōris** *m* mediator, agent

conciliō [1] *v* call together; unite, reconcile; mediate; procure; win over; obtain; recommend; bring about, cause

concilium, **(i)ī** *nt* assembly; council

concinnitās, **ātis** *f* neatness, elegance

concinnō [1] *v* fix, put right

concinnus, **a**, **um** *adj* neat, pretty, elegant, pleasing

concinō, **cinuī** [3] *v* sing together; celebrate in song; sound together

concipiō, **cēpī**, **ceptum** [3] *v* take up; conceive; devise; understand; take in; produce, form

concitātiō, **ōnis** *f* rapid motion; passion; excitement, disturbance

concitātus, **a**, **um** *adj* rapid; passionate, energetic

concitō [1] *v* rouse, spur, excite; disturb; pursue; cause

conclāmātiō, **ōnis** *f* shouting together; acclamation

conclāmō [1] *v* cry (out) together, shout; bewail (the dead); proclaim

conclāve, **is** *nt* room; public lavatory

conclūdō, **ūsī**, **ūsum** [3] *v* enclose together; conclude, end; comprise; infer; stop; close

conclūsiō, **ōnis** *f* conclusion, end; siege; peroration; logical conclusion from premises

concolor, **ōris** *adj* of the same colour

concoquō, **coxī**, **coctum** [3] *v* heat thoroughly; digest; mature; put up with; consider well; devise

concordia, **ae** *f* harmony, concord

concordō *v* harmonize, be in agreement

concors, **rdis** *adj* agreeing, harmonious

concrēdō, **didī**, **ditum** [3] *v* entrust for safe keeping, confide

concremō [1] *v* burn up entirely

concrepō, **puī**, **pitum** [1] *v* rattle, clash; snap (one's fingers)

concrēscō, **ēvī**, **ētum** [3] *v* grow together; curdle; congeal; clot

concrētiō, **ōnis** *f* formation into solid matter

concrētus, **a**, **um** *adj* clotted, stiff, frozen; constructed, formed

concubīna, **ae** *f* concubine

concubitus, **ūs** *m* lying together; sexual intercourse

concubius, **a**, **um** *adj*
□ **concubiā nocte** in the early part of the night

conculcō [1] *v* trample upon; oppress; despise

concumbō, **ubuī**, **ubitum** [3] *v* lie with

concupīscō, **īvī/īī**, **ītum** [3] *v* long much for, covet, desire ardently

concurrō, **(cu)currī**, **cursum** [3] *v* run *or* assemble together; join battle; be in conflict; meet; happen simultaneously

concursātiō, **ōnis** *f* running together; skirmish

concursātor, **ōris** m skirmisher

concursiō, **ōnis** f concourse, meeting; repetition

concursō ① v run hither and thither; run together, clash; run to visit

concursus, **ūs** m concourse, crowd; encounter; combination

concutiō, **ussī**, **ussum** ③ v shake violently, brandish; weaken; harass; rouse

condemnō ① v condemn, doom; convict; prosecute a law suit against

condēnseō ② v compress

condēnsus, **a**, **um** adj dense, thick; wedged together

condiciō, **ōnis** f condition, situation, rank; stipulation; term, agreement; marriage; married person
□ **condiciōnem ferō** reach terms

condīcō, **īxī**, **ictum** ③ v agree (upon), declare; promise; undertake; give notice, engage oneself

condīmentum, **ī** nt spice, seasoning

condiō ④ v preserve, pickle; embalm; spice; season, flavour; render pleasant

condiscipulus, **ī** m schoolfellow, fellow-pupil

condiscō, **didicī** ③ v learn thoroughly

conditor, **ōris** m builder, founder, author

condītōrium, **(i)ī** nt tomb

condītus, **a**, **um** adj seasoned, flavoured

condō, **didī**, **ditum** ③ v build,

found; compose, write; make; hide; sheathe; lay or treasure up; preserve, pickle; bury; thrust (into)

condolēscō, **luī** ③ v be painful, ache; feel grief

condōnō ① v give as a present; forgive; remit; devote or sacrifice

condormiō ④ v sleep soundly

condormiscō, **īvī** ③ v fall asleep

condūcō, **dūxī**, **ductum** ③ v lead together, assemble; hire; undertake; contract for; be of use; profit

conductor, **ōris** m hirer; contractor; lessee

conduplicō ① v double, make twofold

cōne- ▶ **conne-**

cōnectō, **exum** ③ v (also **connectō**) tie, fasten or join together, connect; implicate

cōnfarreātiō, **ōnis** f marriage ceremony

cōnfectiō, **ōnis** f making ready, preparation; compiling; mastication

cōnfector, **ōris** m finisher; slayer

cōnfectus, **a**, **um** adj exhausted

cōnferciō, **rsī**, **rtum** ③ v stuff together, press close together

cōnferō, **cōnferre**, **contulī**, **collātum** v ir bring or carry together, collect; contribute, add; join; bestow; lay out; apply; discourse or talk together; match; compare; put off; refer; transfer; impute; compress; betake oneself, go
□ **signa ~** join battle

cōnfertim adv in a compact body or bunch

cōnfertus, **a**, **um** adj close-packed, filled

cōnfessiō, ōnis f confession; acknowledgement; admission; admission of guilt

cōnfestim adv immediately, speedily

cōnficiō, fēcī, fectum ③ v do, accomplish; finish; effect; arrange; produce, cause; conquer; kill; use up; consume, weaken, overwhelm; spend

cōnfidēns, ntis adj bold, daring; over-confident, presumptuous

cōnfidentia, ae f confidence; boldness; impudence, audacity

cōnfidō, fidere, fisus sum v semi-dep with dat trust to, have confidence in

cōnfigō, ixī, ixum ③ v fasten together; pierce through, strike down

cōnfingō, īnxī, ictum ③ v fashion, fabricate, invent, feign

cōnfinis, e adj adjoining, contiguous, allied, akin

cōnfinium, (i)ī nt common boundary; border

cōnfirmātiō, ōnis f confirmation, encouragement

cōnfirmō ① v confirm; strengthen; encourage; prove; say boldly

cōnfiteor, fessus sum ② v dep confess, admit; reveal

cōnflagrō ① v be burnt down; be utterly destroyed

cōnflictō ① v harass, torment; strike frequently, buffet

cōnflīgō, īxī, īctum ③ v strike together, collide, clash; strive; fight; dispute

cōnflō ① v blow on, ignite; melt;

inflame; raise, bring about; arouse

cōnfluō, ūxī ③ v flow together; flock together

cōnfodiō, ōdī, ossum ③ v dig up; wound fatally; pierce

cōnfōrmātiō, ōnis f shape, form; idea, notion; figure of speech

cōnfōrmō ① v shape, fashion; train, educate

cōnfragōsus, a, um adj, **confragus, a, um** adj rough, uneven; hard

cōnfremō, muī ③ v murmur, echo

cōnfricō ① v rub

cōnfringō, ēgī, āctum ③ v break in pieces; ruin, subvert

cōnfugiō, fūgī ③ v flee to, have recourse to

cōnfundō, ūdī, ūsum ③ v pour or mix together; upset, confuse; bewilder

cōnfūsiō, ōnis f mingling; confusion, disorder, trouble

cōnfūtō ① v check, repress; silence; disprove

cōnfutuō, uī, ūtum ③ v fuck violently

congelō ① v congeal; curdle; freeze; grow hard

congeminō ① v redouble

congemō, muī ③ v utter a cry of grief or pain; bewail

congeriēs, iēī f heap, pile, mass; accumulation

congerō, essī, estum ③ v heap up, get together; build; compile; confer

congerrō, ōnis m boon-companion

congestus | cōnor

congestus, **ūs** *m* bringing together, assembling; heap, pile, mass

congiārium, **(i)ī** *nt* largess for soldiers; gift in corn, oil, wine, *etc.*

conglobō ① *v* make into a ball; crowd together

conglūtinō ① *v* glue together

congrātulor ① *v dep* congratulate

congredior, **gressus sum** ③ *v dep* meet; join battle

congregātiō, **ōnis** *f* society, association

congregō ① *v* collect (into a flock); unite

congressiō, **ōnis** *f* meeting, visit, interview; conflict, attack; sexual intercourse

congressus, **ūs** *m* conference, interview; encounter, fight; sexual intercourse

congruēns, **ntis** *adj* consistent; harmonious, fitting

congruō, **ruī** ③ *v* come together; agree, accord; suit

cōni- ▶ **conī-**

coniciō, **lēcī**, **iectum** ③ *v* throw together; cast, fling; drive; direct; conjecture; interpret

coniectō ① *v* conjecture; interpret; think *or* imagine

coniectūra, **ae** *f* conjecture; inference; interpretation; prophecy

coniectus, **ūs** *m* throwing; directing; shot; glance; hail

cōnifer, **cōniger**, **era**, **erum** *adj* coniferous, cone-bearing

cōnitor, **nīxus/nīsus sum** ③ *v dep* endeavour eagerly; struggle;

strain, strive

coniugālis, **e** *adj* conjugal, matrimonial

coniugātor, **ōris** *m* one who unites (in a pair)

coniugium, **(i)ī** *nt* marriage, wedlock; wife; husband

coniūnctim *adv* in combination jointly

coniūnctiō, **ōnis** *f* union, conjunction; agreement; mutual love; familiarity; match; fellowshi

coniungō, **ūnxī**, **ūnctum** ③ *v* yoke together; connect; couple; ally; associate

coniūnx, **ugis** *m/f* (also **coniu**. husband, wife, spouse, mate

coniūrātiō, **ōnis** *f* conspiracy, plot; band of conspirators; takin an oath

coniūrātus, **a**, **um** *adj* leagued ■ **coniūrātī**, **ōrum** *mpl* conspirators

coniūrō ① *v* swear together; conjure, conspire

cōnīveō, **nīvī/nīxī** ② *v* (also **connīveō**) close the eyes; win at, overlook, turn a blind eye

conl- ▶ **coll-**

conm- ▶ **comm-**

connectō, **exuī**, **exum** ③ *v* tie fasten *or* join together, connect; implicate

connītor, **nīxus/nīsus sum** *v dep* endeavour eagerly; struggl strain, strive

connīveō, **nīvī/nīxī** ② *v* close the eyes; wink at, overlook, turn a blind eye

cōnōpēum, **ī** *nt* mosquito-net

cōnor ① *v dep* try, venture,

undertake

onp- ▶ **comp-**

onquassō ① *v* shake violently; unsettle

onqueror, questus sum ③ *v dep* complain of, bewail

onquiēscō, ēvī, ētum ③ *v* repose, rest; be inactive; go to sleep; find rest

onquīrō, īsīvī/īsiī, īsītum ③ *v* search for diligently; rake up; hunt down

onquīsītiō, ōnis *f* levying

ōnsaepiō, psī, ptum ④ *v* enclose, fence

ōnsalūtātiō, ōnis *f* greeting, exchange of greetings

ōnsalūtō ① *v* greet, hail; salute as

ōnsanguineus, a, um *adj* related by blood; brotherly, sisterly **cōnsanguineī, ōrum** *mpl* relatives

ōnsanguinitās, ātis *f* blood-relationship, kinship

ōnscelerātus, a, um *adj* wicked, depraved; criminal

ōnscelerō ① *v* stain with crime, pollute

ōnscendō, ndī, ēnsum ③ *v* mount, ascend; embark

ōnscientia, ae *f* conscience, consciousness; knowledge; remorse

ōnscindō, idī, issum ③ *v* rend in pieces; slaughter

ōnscīscō, īvī/iī, ītum ③ *v* decree **mortem sibi cōnscīscere** commit suicide

ōnscius, a, um *adj* conscious; knowing; guilty; witnessing; self-conscious

cōnscrībillō ① *v* scrawl over, cover with scribbling

cōnscrībō, psī, ptum ③ *v* enlist or enrol; compose, write □ **patrēs cōnscrīptī** the title by which senators were addressed

cōnsecrātiō, ōnis *f* consecration; deification

cōnsecrō ① *v* consecrate; dedicate; hallow; deify

cōnsector ① *v dep* go towards; seek after; imitate; pursue, hunt down; attack

cōnsecūtiō, ōnis *f* consequence; order, sequence; logical consequence

cōnsenēscō, nuī ③ *v* grow old; become weak; lose consideration or respect; fall into disuse

cōnsēnsiō, ōnis *f* agreement, unanimity; conspiracy

cōnsēnsus, ūs *m* unanimity, concord

cōnsentāneus, a, um *adj* agreeable; consistent, fitting

cōnsentiō, ēnsī, ēnsum ④ *v* consent; agree; decree; conspire; be consistent with

cōnsequēns, ntis *adj* following; following as a logical consequence; consistent

cōnsequor, secūtus sum ③ *v dep* follow after; overtake; get or obtain; procure; imitate; reach, come up to; befall; bring about, achieve

cōnserō¹, ēvī, situm ③ *v* sow, plant

cōnserō², ruī, rtum ③ *v* join; link; engage

□ **manum ~** engage in
hostilities

cōnserva, ae f fellow-slave
(female)

cōnservātiō, ōnis f keeping,
preservation

cōnservātor, ōris m keeper;
defender; saviour

cōnservō, ī v preserve, keep from
danger; maintain

cōnservus, ī m fellow-slave

cōnsessor, ōris m assessor

cōnsessus, ūs m assembly;
audience; court

cōnsiderātus, a, um adj
thought out, cautious, deliberate

cōnsiderō, ī v inspect; consider,
contemplate

cōnsīdō, sēdī, sessum ③ v sit
down; settle; sink down; encamp;
take up one's residence; hold a
session; abate; cease

cōnsignō, ī v seal up; attest

cōnsilior, ī v dep take counsel;
advise

cōnsilium, (i)ī nt counsel, advice;
reason; purpose, plan; stratagem;
resolution, will; judgment;
prudence

□ **~ capiō** decide, resolve, have
an idea; deliberate, take counsel

cōnsimilis, e adj similar, like

cōnsistō, stitī, stitum ③ v
stand (together or fast); be frozen;
make a stand; be steadfast; be in
existence; consist (of); halt; cease

cōnsitor, ōris m sower, planter

cōnsociātiō, ōnis f association,
uniting

cōnsociō, ī v associate, unite;
share

cōnsōlātiō, ōnis f consolation,
comfort; encouragement

cōnsōlātor, ōris m comforter

cōnsōlātōrius, a, um adj
consolatory, consoling

cōnsōlor, ī v dep console, solace;
alleviate, allay

cōnsonō, ī v make a noise
together, resound; agree;
harmonize

cōnsonus, a, um adj sounding
together; harmonious

cōnsōpiō ④ v lull to sleep, make
unconscious

cōnsors, rtis adj partaking of;
brotherly, sisterly; m/f colleague,
partner; fellow

cōnsortiō, ōnis f fellowship;
partnership; association

cōnsortium, (i)ī nt fellowship,
participation

cōnspectus¹, ūs m look, sight,
view; presence; contemplation;
range of view

cōnspectus², a, um adj visible;
remarkable

cōnspergō, rsī, rsum ③ v
besprinkle, sprinkle

cōnspiciō, spexī, spectum ③
catch sight of, see; observe; des…

cōnspicor, ī v dep get a sight
of, see

cōnspicuus, a, um adj in sight
visible; illustrious, remarkable

cōnspīrātiō, ōnis f concord,
harmony; unanimity; conspiracy

cōnspīrō, ī v harmonize, agree
conspire

cōnspurcō, ī v befoul, pollute

cōnstāns, ntis adj steadfast, fi…
immovable, constant; secure;

nsistent; sure, steady

nstantia, ae f steadfastness, rmness, constancy, perseverance; resolution; agreement

nsternātiō, ōnis f confusion, smay; mutiny; sedition; sturbance, disorder

nsternō[1], strāvī, strātum [] v estrew; throw down; pave

nsternō[2] [] v terrify, confuse

nstīpō [] v crowd together

nstituō, uī, ūtum [] v put, t, place; constitute, appoint; cree, decide, determine; fix, tablish; range; build; establish; ree (upon); manage; dispose; tend; settle

nstitūtiō, ōnis f constitution, sposition; ordering; rangement; ordinance

nstitūtum, ī nt institution, v; agreement, compact

nstō, stetī [] v stand still; last; settled or certain or known; st; agree (with); exist or be; nsist (of); stand firm

cōnstat [] v impers it is agreed

nstringō, īnxī, īctum [] v nd fast or tight; compress

nstrūctiō, ōnis f building, nstruction

nstruō, ūxī, ūctum [] v heap ; make, build

nstuprō [] v ravish, rape

nsuēfaciō, fēcī, factum [] ccustom

nsuēscō, ēvī, ētum [] v ccustom; become accustomed; accustomed; have intercourse th

nsuētūdō, inis f stom, habit, use; manner;

companionship, familiarity, conversation

cōnsul, lis m consul, one of the chief Roman magistrates

cōnsulāris, e adj consular; of or proper to a consul; ex-consular

cōnsulātus, ūs m consulship

cōnsulō, luī, ltum [] v take counsel; consider; consult (someone); take steps; with dat consult the interest of; take care of; provide for

cōnsultātiō, ōnis f consultation, deliberation

cōnsultē, cōnsultō adv deliberately, on purpose

cōnsultō [] v consult, to take counsel

cōnsultor, ōris m adviser; consulter; lawyer

cōnsultum, ī nt decision; decree

cōnsultus, a, um adj well-considered; knowing, experienced

cōnsummō [] v add up, finish

cōnsūmō, mpsī, mptum [] v use up; eat; consume; squander, destroy; employ

cōnsurgō, surrēxī, surrēctum [] v rise, stand; arise

contabulō [] v board over; cover

contāctus, ūs m touch, contact; contagion

contāgēs, gis f contact; infection

contāgiō, ōnis f, **contāgium, (i)ī** nt contagion, contact, touch; influence; infection

contāminō [] v contaminate, pollute, debase, spoil

contegō, ēxī, ēctum [] v cover (up); hide

contemerō [] v defile, pollute

contemnō, mpsī, mptum 3 v
scorn, contemn

contemplātiō, ōnis f view,
survey, contemplation; meditation

contemplātus, ūs m
contemplation

contemplor 1 v dep,
contemplō 1 v survey, observe;
contemplate

contemptim adv
contemptuously; fearlessly

contemptiō, ōnis f contempt,
scorn, disdain

contemptor, ōris m contemner,
despiser

contemptus¹, ūs m contempt,
scorn

contemptus², a, um adj
contemptible, vile

contendō, ndī, ntum 3 v
stretch, strain; hurl; contend;
fight; dispute; strive, exert; labour;
demand; urge; state emphatically;
go, march; hasten; compare

contentē adv with great exertion

contentiō, ōnis f exertion;
contest, fight; dispute;
comparison; contrast; antithesis

contentus¹, a, um adj tense,
tight; energetic, vigorous

contentus², a, um adj
contented, satisfied

conterminus, a, um adj
bordering upon

conterō, trīvī, trītum 3 v grind,
bruise, crumble; waste; spend;
exhaust

conterreō 2 v frighten
thoroughly

contestor 1 v dep call to witness

contexō, xuī, xtum 3 v

entwine, twist together; conne
compose

contextus, ūs m connection,
coherence; series

conticēscō, cuī 3 v cease to t
fall silent

contignātiō, ōnis f raftering:
storey, floor

contignō 1 v rafter, floor

contiguus, a, um adj adjoinin
bordering upon

continēns, ntis adj contiguou
adjacent; uninterrupted;
temperate, restrained, self-
disciplined
■ ~, **ntis** f mainland

continenter adv without
interruption; temperately

continentia, ae f
abstemiousness, continence,
self-control

contineō, tentum 2 v hold
together; bind; contain; retain;
comprise; confine; keep secret;
hinder, prevent; stop

contingō, tigī, tāctum 3
v touch; seize; border upon;
reach; influence; affect; stain;
befall; come to pass; be akin; b
connected with

continuātiō, ōnis f
continuation, prolongation

continuō¹ adv immediately,
forthwith

continuō² 1 v put in a line; joi
deal with successively, prolong

continuus, a, um adj
continuous; successive

cōntiō, ōnis f assembly, meet
oration

cōntiōnābundus, a, um adj
delivering a public speech

cōntiōnālis, e *adj* belonging to a public assembly

cōntiōnātor, ōris *m* haranguer of the people; demagogue

cōntiōnor [1] *v dep* deliver an oration to a public assembly

cōntiuncula, ae *f* small or negligible meeting

contorqueō, rsī, rtum [2] *v* brandish; fling; twist round

contrā *prep with acc* against; opposite to; contrary to; face to face; *adv* against; opposite to; contrary to; on the contrary; otherwise; mutually; face to face

ex contrāriō on the contrary

contractiō, ōnis *f* contraction; abridgement

contractus, a, um *adj* close; abridged; stinted

contrādīcō, īxī, ictum [3] *v* speak against, contradict, oppose

contrādictiō, ōnis *f* objection, contradiction

contrahō, āxī, actum [3] *v* draw together; gather; tighten; abridge; check; incur; get; cause

contrārius, a, um *adj* opposite, contrary; inimical; harmful

contrectō [1] *v* touch repeatedly, handle

contremīscō, muī [3] *v* tremble all over; tremble at

contribuō, buī, būtum [3] *v* incorporate; contribute

contrīstō [1] *v* make sad, afflict; darken

contrītiō, onis *f* [LM] grief, contrition

contrōversia, ae *f* controversy; dispute

contrōversiōsus, a, um *adj* much disputed, debatable

contrōvors- ▶ **controvers-**

contrucīdō [1] *v* cut down, slaughter

contrūdō, ūsī, ūsum [3] *v* thrust, press in

contubernālis, is *m/f* tent-companion; comrade; mate

contubernium, (i)ī *nt* companionship in a tent; attendance on a superior; common war tent

contueor [2] *v dep* look at, behold, see

contumācia, ae *f* stubbornness

contumāx, ācis *adj* stubborn, defiant

contumēlia, ae *f* insult, affront, ignominy; damage

contumēliōsus, a, um *adj* insolent, abusive

contumulō [1] *v* bury

contundō, udī, ūsum [3] *v* bruise, crush; subdue utterly

conturbātiō, ōnis *f* confusion, panic

conturbātus, a, um *adj* disturbed, perplexed

conturbō [1] *v* upset, throw into confusion; disquiet; go bankrupt

contus, ī *m* long pole, pike

cōnūbium, (i)ī *nt* intermarriage; marriage

cōnus, ī *m* cone; apex of a helmet

convalēscō, luī [3] *v* recover, get better, grow strong

convallis, is *f* a valley (much shut in)

convāsō [1] *v* pack up (baggage)

convectō [1] *v*, **convehō, ēxī,**

ectum ③ v carry together, gather

convellō, llī, ulsum ③ v pull or pluck up; wrench; shatter; overthrow

convenae, ārum mpl refugees, immigrants

conveniēns, ntis adj fitting; appropriate

convenientia, ae f agreement, harmony; fitness

conveniō, vēnī, ventum ④ v come together, assemble; meet; agree; fit, suit; be due; visit, prosecute

conventiculum, ī nt small assemblage; place of assembly

conventiō, ōnis f, **conventum, ī** nt agreement, compact

conventus, ūs m meeting, assembly; provincial court; district

converrō ③ v sweep together, sweep up

conversō ① v turn, turn over in the mind
□ **conversor** ① v dep be a constant visitor (to)

convertō, rtī, rsum ③ v turn round; convert; change, transform; translate

convestiō ④ v clothe, dress, cover

convexus, a, um adj convex, arched, vaulted

convīcium, (i)ī nt cry, clamour; bawling; reproach, abuse

convīctiō, ōnis f companionship, intimacy

convīctor, ōris m messmate, friend

convīctus, ūs m living together, intimacy; banquet, feast

convincō, īcī, ictum ③ v convi prove clearly

convīva, ae m/f table companio guest

convīvālis, e adj convivial

convīvātor, ōris m host

convīvium, (i)ī nt feast, entertainment, banquet

convocō ① v call together, convoke, assemble

convolō ① v fly together; (fig) ru together

convolvō, lvī, lūtum ③ v roll together or round, writhe

convorrō ▶ converrō

cooperiō, ruī, rtum ④ v cover wholly, overwhelm

cooptātiō, ōnis f co-option, adoption

cooptō ① v choose, elect, admit

coorior, coortus sum ④ v dep arise; break forth

cophinus, ī m large basket, hamper

cōpia, ae f abundance, plenty; riches; store; provisions; ability; power; opportunity, means; access to a person

cōpiae, ārum fpl (mil) forces

cōpiōsus, a, um adj plentiful, rich, wealthy; eloquent

cōpō ▶ caupō

cōpula, ae f bond, tie

cōpulātiō, ōnis f connecting, uniting

cōpulō ① v couple, bind or tie together, connect, unite

coquō, coxī, coctum ③ v cook, boil, fry, bake; burn; parch; ripen digest; mature, cherish, stir up

coquus, ī m cook

, rdis nt heart; mind, judgment

cordī esse be pleasing

allium, (i)ī nt coral

am prep with abl in the presence
face to face; adv face to face;
rsonally

bis, is m/f basket

cillum, ī nt, **corculum, ī** nt
le heart

ium, (i)ī nt skin, leather, hide

neus¹, a, um adj of horn,
embling horn

neus², a, um adj of the
nel-tree

nicen, inis m trumpeter,
gler

niger, era, erum adj horn-
aring, horned

nipēs, edis adj horn-footed,
ofed

nix, īcis f crow

nū, ūs nt horn; hoof; bill of
ird; horn of the moon; end,
; peak, cone of a helmet; bow;
mpet; wing of an army; funnel

num, ī nt cornel-berry

nus, ī f cornel-cherry-tree,
nel wood

ōlla, ae f small garland

ōna, ae f garland, wreath,
own; circle (of men); cordon of
ops thrown round an enemy
sition

ōnō v crown, wreathe;
round

poreus, a, um adj corporeal;
shy

pus, oris nt body; flesh;
pse; trunk; frame; corporation

pusculum, ī nt little body,
m

corrēctiō, ōnis f improvement,
correction

corrēctor, ōris m corrector,
improver, reformer

corrēpō, psī v creep, move
stealthily

corrigō, ēxī, ēctum v
straighten, set right; correct

corripiō, puī, eptum v snatch
up, lay hold of; rebuke, chastise;
shorten; hasten; seize unlawfully
□ ~ **viam** hasten on one's way

corrōborō v strengthen,
corroborate

corrogō v collect money by
begging

corrūgō v make wrinkled

corrumpō, ūpī, uptum v
spoil, destroy, deface; falsify;
bribe; corrupt, seduce

corruō, ruī v break down, fall to
the ground

corruptēla, ae f corruption,
enticement to sexual misconduct,
bribery; corrupting influence

corruptiō, ōnis f corruption;
bribery

corruptor, ōris m corrupter,
seducer, briber

cortex, icis m bark, rind; cork

cortīna, ae f cauldron, cauldron
on oracular tripod (at Delphi)

cōrus, ī m north-west wind

coruscō v brandish, shake;
flash, coruscate

coruscus, a, um adj vibrating,
tremulous; flashing

corvus, ī m raven; military engine

corylētum, ī nt copse of hazel-
trees

corylus, ī f hazel-tree

corymbus, ī m cluster of ivy-berries or flowers or fruit

cōs, ōtis f flint-stone; whetstone ■ cōtēs pl rocks

costa, ae f rib; side

costos, ī f, **costum**, ī nt an aromatic plant or its powdered root

cothurnātus, a, um adj wearing the buskin; in lofty style

cothurnus, ī m high boot worn by Greek tragic actors; elevated style, tragic poetry

cōtīdiānus, a, um adj daily

cōtīdiē adv every day, daily

cott- ▸ cōt-

coturnix, īcis f quail

covinnārius, (i)ī m charioteer

coxa, ae f hip

crābrō, ōnis m wasp, hornet □ irritō crābrōnēs disturb a hornets' nest

crāpula, ae f drunkenness; next day's sickness

crās adv tomorrow; in the future

crassitūdō, inis f thickness, density

crassus, a, um adj thick, dense, fat, gross, stupid, crass

crastino ① v LM put off

crāstīnus, a, um adj of tomorrow

crātēr, ēris m, **crātēra**, ae f mixing-bowl; crater of a volcano, basin of fountain; Cup (constellation)

crātis, is f wicker-work; harrow; frame-work

creātor, ōris m creator, author, founder; father

creātrix, īcis f creatress, mother

creatura, ae f LM creature

crēber, bra, **brum** adj thick, close, pressed together, freque numerous; abundant

crēbrēscō, ③ v become frequent, increase

crēbritās, ātis f frequency, closeness in succession

crēbrō adv frequently; in many places

crēdibilis, e adj trustworthy, credible

crēditor, ōris m lender, credit

crēditum, ī nt loan

crēdō, didī, **ditum** ③ v with da believe, trust; entrust; think, be the opinion

crēdulitās, ātis f credulity, trustfulness

crēdulus, a, um adj credulous

cremō ① v burn, consume by f

creō ① v create, make, produce choose; elect; cause; establish

crepida, ae f slipper, sandal

crepīdō, inis f pedestal; brink pier, bank, sidewalk

crepitāculum, ī nt rattle

crepitō ① v rattle, clatter, rustl

crepitus, ūs m rattling, clashi rustling; (of thunder) crash; (of the teeth) chattering; fart

crepō, puī, **pitum** ① v rattle, rustle, clatter; snap the fingers jingle; harp on, grumble at the way that

crepundia, ōrum ntpl child's rattle; cymbals

crepusculum, ī nt twilight, d

crēscō, crēvī, **crētum** ③ v grow; arise, spring; appear; get advantage; increase; attain

5

5

honour, be advanced, be
strengthened

crēta, ae f chalk; clay; paint;
clayey soil

crētātus, a, um adj marked with
chalk; powdered

crētiō, ōnis f declaration
respecting the acceptance of an
inheritance

crētōsus, a, um adj abounding in
chalk or clay

crēvī ▸ crēscō

crībrum, ī nt sieve

crīmen, inis nt crime, offence,
fault; scandal; reproach;
accusation

crīminātiō, ōnis f accusation,
indictment

crīminor 🔟 v dep accuse; charge
(with)

crīminōsus, a, um adj
accusatory; reproachful,
vituperative

crīnālis, e adj worn in the hair;
covered with hair-like filaments

crīnis, is m hair; tail of a comet

crīnītus, a, um adj hairy; having
long locks

  stella crīnīta comet

crispō 🔟 v curl, crisp; shake,
brandish

crispus, a, um adj curled; curly-
headed; quivering

crista, ae f crest; cock's comb;
plume (of a helmet)

cristātus, a, um adj tufted,
crested; plumed

criticus, ī m literary critic

croceus, a, um adj of saffron;
saffron-coloured; yellow

crocinum, ī nt saffron oil used as

a perfume

crocinus, a, um adj of saffron,
yellow

crocodīlus, ī m crocodile

crocum, ī nt, **crocus, ī** m crocus;
saffron; saffron-colour

cruciāmentum, ī nt torture,
torment

cruciātus, ūs m torture; severe
physical or mental pain

cruciō 🔟 v torture; grieve

crūdēlis, e adj cruel, bloodthirsty

crūdēlitās, ātis f cruelty,
barbarity

crūdēscō, duī 🗟 v become fierce
or savage

crūdus, a, um adj raw; bloody;
undigested; unripe, sour; fresh;
immature; vigorous; harsh; cruel

cruentō 🔟 v stain with blood

cruentus, a, um adj gory,
bloody; blood-thirsty; blood-red

crumēna, ae f purse; supply of
money, resources

cruor, ōris m gore, blood; murder

crūs, ris nt leg, shank, shin

crusta, ae f rind, shell, crust, bark

crustulārius, (i)ī m seller of
cakes

crustum, ī nt pastry, cake

crux, cis f cross; torture, trouble,
misery, destruction; gallows, rack

cryptoporticus, ūs f covered
portico

cubiculārius, (i)ī m valet-de-
chambre

cubiculum, ī nt bedroom

cubīle, is nt couch, bed; marriage-
bed; lair

cubitō 🔟 v lie down

cubitum, ī *nt* elbow; forearm; cubit

cubō, buī, bitum [ ] *v* lie down; lie asleep; recline at table

cucumis, eris *m* cucumber

cucurbita, ae *f* gourd

cucurrī ▶ currō

cūdō [ ] *v* strike, stamp; mint coin

cūiās, ātis *adj* of what country or town?

culcitula, ae *f* small mattress

culex, icis *m* gnat, midge

culīna, ae *f* kitchen; fare, victuals

culmen, inis *nt* top, summit; gable; acme, eminence

culmus, ī *m* stalk, stem; thatch

culpa, ae *f* fault, crime, blame; negligence

culpō [ ] *v* blame, find fault with; accuse, censure

culta, ōrum *ntpl* tilled land

culter, trī *m* knife

cultor, ōris *m* husbandman; cultivator, inhabitant; supporter; worshipper

cultrix, īcis *f* female inhabitant

cultūra, ae *f* agriculture; care, culture, cultivation

cultus¹, ūs *m* worship, reverence; culture; refinement; adorning; splendour, smartness; livelihood

cultus², a, um *adj* cultivated, polished, elegant, civilized

culullus, ī *m* a drinking vessel *or* its contents

cūlus, ī *m* anus

cum¹ *prep with abl* with; along with; amid; *with words expressing strife, contention, etc.* against

cum² *conj* when; since; although; as soon as

cumba, ae *f* small boat, skiff

cumulātus, a, um *adj* heaped, abundant, great

cumulō [ ] *v* heap up; accumulate; fill full

cumulus, ī *m* heap, pile; surplus, increase; summit, crown

cūnābula, ōrum *ntpl* cradle; earliest dwelling-place; earliest childhood

cūnae, ārum *fpl* cradle; one's earliest years

cūnctābundus, a, um *adj* lingering, loitering

cūnctāns, ntis *adj* hesitant, clinging; stubborn

cūnctātiō, ōnis *f* delay, hesitation

cūnctātor, ōris *m* delayer

cūnctor [ ] *v dep* tarry, linger, hesitate

cūnctus, a, um *adj* all together, total, complete

cuneātim *adv* in a closely packed formation

cuneātus, a, um *adj* wedge-shaped

cuneus, ī *m* wedge; battalion, e drawn up in the form of a wedge; rows of seats in a theatre

cunīculōsus, a, um *adj* abounding in rabbits

cunīculus, ī *m* rabbit; underground passage; mine; channel

cunnus, ī *m* the female pudend

cupiditās, ātis *f* longing, desi passion; avarice; ambition

cupīdō¹, inis *f* desire, greedine appetite; love; desire of materia gain

pīdō², **inis** m the god of love

pidus, a, um adj longing for, ⸱siring, eager; loving; greedy, ⸱ssionate

piēns, ntis adj desirous, eager ⸱r, anxious

piō, īvī/iī, ītum ③ v long for, ⸱sire; covet

pītor, ōris m one who seeks ⸱ter

ppēdia¹, ae f gourmandism

ppēdia², ōrum ntpl delicacies

presseus, a, um adj of cypress

pressifer, era, erum adj ⸱press-bearing

pressus, ī f cypress-tree; spear ⸱ cypress-wood

r adv why?

ra, ae f attention, care; ⸱ministration; office; written ⸱ork; task, responsibility; sorrow; ⸱xiety, concern; trouble; love; ⸱ject of love

rātiō, ōnis f administration, ⸱anagement; treatment, charge

rātor, ōris m manager, ⸱perintendent; guardian

rculiō, ōnis m corn-weevil

ria, ae f division of the Roman ⸱ople, senate-house, senate

riātus, a, um adj pertaining ⸱ **cūriae**

  comitia cūriāta ntpl the ⸱sembly in which people voted ⸱cording to **cūriae**

  lēx cūriāta f law passed by the ⸱sembly of the thirty divisions of ⸱e Roman people

riō, ōnis m chief priest of a ⸱ria

riōsus, a, um adj careful,

diligent; curious, inquisitive

cūrō ① v take care of, mind; worry or care about; order; attend to; heal; cure

curriculum, ī nt race; race-track; chariot; course of action
  ■ **curriculō** at full speed

currō, cucurrī, cursum ③ v run, hasten

currus, ūs m chariot; triumphal chariot; triumph

cursim adv swiftly, hastily

cursitō ① v, **cursō** ① v run to and fro

cursor, ōris m runner; chariot-racer; courier

cursūra, ae f running

cursus, ūs m running; course, voyage, journey; race; direction; march; career

curtus, a, um adj mutilated; incomplete

curūlis, e adj of curule rank, i.e. of consuls, praetors or curule aediles

curvāmen, inis nt curvature; curved form, arc

curvō ① v make curved, bend; make (a person) stoop

curvus, a, um adj crooked, bent, curved, stooping

cuspis, idis f point, spike; spear; trident (of Neptune); scorpion's sting

custōdēla, ae f charge, custody (of a person or thing)

custōdia, ae f watch, guard; care; watch-house; guard-post; confinement; prison

custōdiō ④ v watch, guard; preserve; take heed; retain

custōs, ōdis m/f keeper; guardian;

protector; watchman; jailer; container

cutis, is f skin

cyathus, ī m wine-ladle, wine-measure

cycnēus, a, um adj of a swan; swan-like

cycnus, cygnus, ī m swan

cylindrus, ī m cylinder; roller (for levelling the ground)

cymbalum, ī nt cymbal

cymbium, (i)ī nt small cup, especially for wine

Cynosūra, ae f (constellation) the Lesser Bear

cyparissus ▶ cupressus

cytisus, ī m/f a fodder plant, tree-medick

Dd

daedalus, a, um adj skilful; skilfully made

daemōn, nis m a supernatural being or spirit

dalmatica, ae f [LM] sleeved tunic, dalmatic (vestment of a deacon)

damma, ae f fallow-deer, doe, small member of deer family

damnātiō, ōnis f condemnation

damnō ① v condemn, sentence; discredit

damnōsus, a, um adj detrimental, injurious, destructive; prodigal

damnum, ī nt damage, injury, loss; hurt, fine

danīsta, ae m money-lender

danīsticus, a, um adj of money-lending, of usury

danunt = dant ▶ dō

dapifer, erī m [LM] waiter

daps, pis f sacrificial feast; banquet

dapsilis, e adj abundant, plent

datiō, ōnis f giving, transfer, assigning

datō ① v make a practice of givi

dator, ōris m giver

dē prep with abl down from; from; away from, out of; about; (made concerning; for; by reason of; af from the time of, according to

☐ **~ imprōvīsō** unexpectedly

dea, ae f goddess

dealbō ① v whitewash, whiten

dēbacchor ① v dep rage, rave

dēbellātor, ōris m conqueror

dēbellō ① v bring a battle or wa to an end; vanquish

dēbeō ② v owe, be in debt; be obliged or bound or destined

dēbilis, e adj weak, feeble; crippled

dēbilitās, ātis f weakness, debility

dēbilitō ① v weaken; maim

dēbitor, ōris m debtor

dēbitum, ī nt debt; duty

dēcantō ① v reel off, chant; rep

dēcēdō, essī, essum ③ v go away, depart; retire, yield; ceas die; disappear; decrease

decem adj indec ten

December, bris m December

decempeda, ae f ten-foot

...easuring rod

decemvirālis, e *adj* belonging to the **decemvirī**

decemvirātus, ūs *m* office of decemvir

decemvirī, ōrum *mpl* commission of ten (magistrates at Rome)

decēns, ntis *adj* fitting; becoming, decent; symmetrical, well-proportioned

decernō, crēvī, crētum ③ *v* distinguish; judge; decide; settle; propose

decerpō, psī, ptum ③ *v* pluck or pull off; destroy; catch, snatch, reap

decertō ① *v* fight out; dispute

decessiō, ōnis *f* going away, departure; retirement; diminution; abatement

decessor, ōris *m* magistrate retiring from his post

decessus, ūs *m* departure; retirement; decrease; ebb; death

decet ② *v impers* it is becoming or right or proper

decidō, idī ③ *v* fall down; pass away; die

decīdō, īdī, īsum ③ *v* cut off; determine, put an end to

deciē(n)s *adv* ten times

decima, ae *f* tenth part; tithe

decimānus, a, um related to the tenth, belonging to the tenth legion or cohort

porta decimāna the rear gate of a Roman camp

decimō ① *v* choose by lot every tenth man (for punishment)

decimus, a, um *adj* tenth

dēcipiō, cēpī, ceptum ③ *v* deceive, cheat

dēclāmātiō, ōnis *f* delivering of a set speech

dēclāmō ① *v* declaim, make speeches

dēclārō ① *v* declare; prove; mean

dēclīnō ① *v* turn aside; avoid; deviate

dēclīvis, e *adj* sloping downwards, declining

■ **declive, is** *nt* slope, declivity

dēclīvitās, ātis *f* falling gradient

dēcoctor, ōris *m* insolvent person, defaulting debtor

dēcolor, ōris *adj* discoloured, faded; degenerate

dēcoquō, coxī, coctum ③ *v* boil down; waste away; become bankrupt

decor, ōris *m* beauty, grace; charm

decorō ① *v* adorn, grace; glorify

decōrus, a, um *adj* decorous; proper; suitable; graceful; handsome; noble

dēcrēscō, ēvī, ētum ③ *v* decrease; diminish; dwindle

dēcrētum, ī *nt* decree, decision; principle, doctrine

decum- ▶ decim-

dēcumbō, ubuī ③ *v* recline at the dinner table; lie ill

decuria,¹ ae *f* group of ten, group

decuriō¹ ① *v* divide into companies of ten

decuriō², ōnis *m* the head of a decuria

dēcurrō, (cu)currī, ursum ③ *v* run down; sail shorewards or downstream; have recourse

d

to; drill

dēcursus, ūs *m* downward course; declivity; charge downhill

dēcurtātus, a, um *adj* mutilated, cut short

decus, oris *nt* grace, ornament; glory; beauty; virtue, decorum; honour, respectability, dignity

dēcutiō, ussī, ussum ③ *v* shake down or off

dēdecet ② *v impers* it is unsuitable for or unbecoming to

dēdecorō ① *v* disgrace

dēdecōrus, a, um *adj* dishonourable

dēdecus, oris *nt* disgrace, infamy; shame; dishonour

dedī ▶ dō

dēdicātiō, ōnis *f* dedication, consecration

dēdicō ① *v* dedicate, devote

dēdignor ① *v dep* disdain; refuse, reject with scorn

dēdiscō, didicī ③ *v* unlearn, forget

dēditīcius, a, um *adj* having surrendered

dēditiō, ōnis *f* surrender

dēditus, a, um *adj* devoted to, fond of

dēdō, dēdidī, dēditum ③ *v* surrender; abandon; yield

dēdoleō ② *v* cease to grieve

dēdūcō, dūxī, ductum ③ *v* lead or draw down; bring away or off; establish (a colony); launch; conduct; escort; derive; compose; withdraw; subtract

dēductiō, ōnis *f* transportation, deduction

deerrō ① *v* go astray

dēfaecō ▶ dēficō

dēfatīgātiō, ōnis *f* weariness, fatigue

dēfatīgō ① *v* tire, exhaust; lose heart

dēfectiō, ōnis *f* failure, deficiency; defection, revolt

dēfector, ōris *m* rebel, renegade

dēfectus, ūs *m* failure; eclipse

dēfendō, ndī, ēnsum ③ *v* defend, guard; preserve; keep off; affirm, maintain

dēfēnsiō, ōnis *f* defence

dēfēnsō ① *v* protect

dēfēnsor, ōris *m* defender, guardian, protector

dēferō, ferre, tulī, lātum *v ir* bring or carry down or off; convey; bring word; bestow; present; tell; transfer; accuse, indict

dēfessus, a, um *adj* tired, worn out

dēfetīgō ▶ dēfatīgō

dēfetīscor, fessus sum ③ *v de[p]* grow weary or faint

dēficiō, fēcī, fectum ③ *v* fail; cease; faint; be discouraged; sink under; be wanting or defective; decay; die; desert, forsake

dēficō ① *v* cleanse, clean

dēfīgō, īxī, īxum ③ *v* fix down, fasten; thrust into; astound, bewitch

dēfīniō ④ *v* limit; define; determine; end

dēfīnītiō, ōnis *f* definition

dēfīnītus, a, um *adj* definite, precise, limited

dēfīō, fierī *v ir semi-dep* be lacking

dēfīxiō, ōnis *f* binding with a

ll, putting a spell on

flagrō v be burnt down;
urn out'; burn down; destroy

flectō, xī, xum v bend or
rn aside or off; divert, modify

fleō, ēvī, ētum v weep
undantly for, mourn the loss of

flōrēscō, ruī v fade, wither

fluō, ūxī, ūxum v flow
wn; glide down; fade; disappear;
ended

fluum, i nt LM downpour

fodiō, ōdī, ossum v dig;
ry

fōrmis, e adj ill-formed, ugly;
apeless; odious; base

formitās, ātis f deformity,
liness, degradation; lack of
od taste

fōrmō¹ v shape, fashion;
lineate, describe

fōrmō² v disfigure; spoil,
pair

fraudō v cheat, defraud

frēnātus, a, um adj unbridled

fricō, cuī, c(ā)tum v rub
rd

fringō, ēgī, āctum v
eak off

frūdō ▸ dēfraudō

frūstror v dep foil or thwart
mpletely

fugiō, ūgī v avoid, run away
om), escape

fundō, ūdī, ūsum v pour
wn or out

fungor, fūnctus sum v dep
n abl discharge, finish; have done
th; have died

gener, eris adj degenerate;
v-born; base

dēflagrō | dēlēnīmentum

dēgenerō v degenerate;
deteriorate, decline

dēgō, gī v spend, pass; live

dēgravō v weigh down;
overpower

dēgredior, gressus sum
v dep march down, descend;
dismount

dēgustō v taste, take a taste
of; try; test

dehinc adv after this; hence;
henceforth; next; since then

dehīscō v gape, split open

dehonestāmentum, ī nt
disfigurement, disgrace

dehonestō v disgrace

dehortor v dep dissuade

dēiciō, iēcī, iectum v throw
down; dislodge; fell; kill; rob of;
dispossess

dēiectus, ūs m throwing down;
fall; declivity; slope

dein, deinde adv afterward;
then; next

deinceps adv in succession; in
a series

dēlābor, lāpsus sum v dep slip
or fall down; descend; sink

dēlātiō, ōnis f accusation,
denunciation

dēlātor, ōris m accuser, informer

dēlectābilis, e adj delightful,
agreeable

dēlectātiō, ōnis f delight,
pleasure, amusement

dēlectō v entice; delight;
amuse; charm

dēlectus ▸ dīlectus

dēlēgō v assign; delegate,
depute; transfer; attribute

dēlēnīmentum, ī nt charm,

allurement

dēlēniō [4] v mitigate, smooth down; soften; bewitch; mollify

dēleō, lēvī, lētum [2] v efface; suppress; destroy; kill; annul

dēlīberābundus, a, um adj deep in thought

dēlīberātiō, ōnis f deliberation, consideration

dēlīberō [1] v consult, deliberate; resolve

dēlībō [1] v taste (of), touch on (a subject) lightly; diminish, detract (from)

dēlībūtus, a, um adj smeared, covered; overflowing (with feeling)

dēlicātus, a, um adj charming, elegant; delicate, tender; voluptuous; luxurious; effeminate

dēliciae, ārum fpl delight, pleasures; dalliance; airs and graces; darling, sweetheart

dēlictum, ī nt fault, offence, crime

dēligō¹, lēgī, lectum [3] v choose out, select, cull, pick off

dēligō² [1] v tie up, fasten

dēlinquō, liquī, lictum [3] v fail (in duty); offend, do wrong

dēliquēscō, licuī [3] v melt away; dissipate one's energy

dēlīrō [1] v be crazy, speak deliriously

dēlīrus, a, um adj crazy, insane; senseless

dēlitēscō, tuī [3] v go into hiding; withdraw

delphīnus, ī m, delphīn, nis m dolphin

dēlūbrum, ī nt shrine, temple

dēlūdificō [1] v dep make a

complete fool of

dēlūdō, ūsī, ūsum [3] v deceive, dupe

dēmānō [1] v run down, percol...

dēmēns, ntis adj senseless; m... foolish

dēmentia, ae f madness, folly

dēmereō [2] v oblige, win the favour of

dēmergō, rsī, rsum [3] v plun... (into), sink; conceal

dēmētior, mēnsus sum [4] v measure out

dēmetō, essuī, essum [3] v mow, reap, cut off

dēmigrō [1] v go away

dēminuō, uī, ūtum [3] v lesse... diminish

dēminūtiō, ōnis f diminutio... decrease

dēmīror [1] v dep wonder, be amazed

dēmissiō, ōnis f letting dow... low spirits, dejection

dēmissus, a, um adj low-lying, hanging down; downcast; hum... unassuming; (of the voice) low

dēmittō, mīsī, missum [3] v sink, lower; send down; dismiss... thrust (into); plunge; sink; dep... demote

dēmō, mpsī, mptum [3] v tak... away; subtract

dēmōlior [4] v dep pull down, demolish; destroy

dēmōnstrātiō, ōnis f demonstration, clear proof

dēmōnstrō [1] v point at; prov... demonstrate; describe; represe...

dēmorior, morī, mortuus sum [3] v dep die off

dēmoror ① *v dep* keep back, delay; linger, stay

dēmorsicō ① *v* bite pieces off, nibble at

dēmoveō, mōvī, mōtum ② *v* move away, put away, remove

dēmulceō, lsī, lctum ② *v* stroke, entrance

dēmum *adv* at length, at last **tum ~** only then

dēnārius, a, um *adj* containing ten

~, (i)ī *m* Roman silver coin originally worth ten *assēs*

dēnārrō ① *v* relate fully

dēnegō ① *v* refuse, deny

dēnī, ae, a *adj* ten each, by tens

dēnique *adv* at last, finally, in fact; in short

dēnōminātus, a, um *adj* named

dēnotō ① *v* specify, point out; brand

dēns, ntis *m* tooth; tusk; ivory

dēnseō, ētum ② *v*, **dēnsō** ① *v* thicken; press close together

dēnsus, a, um *adj* thick, dense; thickly planted with; frequent; concise

dentāle, is *nt* the share-beam of a ploughshare

dentātus, a, um *adj* toothed; having prominent teeth

dēnūbō, ūpsī, ūptum ③ *v* marry (away from her paternal home)

dēnūdō ① *v* make naked, uncover; reveal; rob, despoil

dēnumerō ① *v* pay (money) in full, pay down

dēnūntiātiō, ōnis *f* denunciation, declaration; threat; summons

dēnūntiō ① *v* announce, declare; foretell; threaten; summon (a witness)

dēnuō *adv* anew, afresh, again

deonerō ① *v* unload

deorsum, deorsus *adv* downwards, beneath, below

dēpacīscor, pactus sum ③ *v dep* bargain for, agree upon

dēpāscō, āvī, āstum ③ *v* pasture; eat up, waste, consume

dēpecīscor ▶ dēpacīscor

dēpellō, pulī, pulsum ③ *v* expel; dislodge; avert

dēpendeō ② *v* hang down, from or on; depend upon

dēpendō, ndī, ēnsum ③ *v* pay, expend

dēperdō, didī, ditum ③ *v* ruin; lose

dēpereō, īre, īī *v ir* perish; be lost; be hopelessly in love with

dēpingō, īnxī, īctum ③ *v* paint, depict, portray; describe

dēplangō, ānxī ③ *v* mourn by beating the breast

dēplōrō ① *v* lament, mourn for; give up for lost

dēpōnō, posuī, positum ③ *v* lay down or aside; deposit; commit; entrust; resign; fix, set, plant

dēpopulō ① *v*, **dēpopulor** ① *v dep* lay waste, plunder

dēportō ① *v* carry, convey

dēposcō, poposcī ③ *v* ask for earnestly, require

dēpositum, ī *nt* deposit, trust

dēprāvō ① *v* distort; deprave, corrupt

dēprecābundus, a, um *adj* entreating earnestly

dēprecātor | dēsipiō

dēprecātor, ōris *m* intercessor; one who pleads for the removal (of)

dēprecor ① *v dep* pray against; beg off; beg pardon; avert by prayer

dēpre(he)ndō, ndī, ēnsum ③ *v* catch, find out; discern, perceive; reach, overtake; catch in the act; surprise

dēprimō, essī, essum ③ *v* depress; keep down; sink; humble

dēprōmō, mpsī, mptum ③ *v* bring out

dēpugnō ① *v* fight it out or hard

dēputō ① *v* reckon

dērelicta, ae *f* [M] widow

dērelinquō, liquī, lictum ③ *v* leave behind, abandon, neglect

dērepente *adv* suddenly

dērīdeō, rīsī, rīsum ② *v* laugh at, deride

dērīdiculum, ī *nt* laughing-stock, ridiculousness

dērigēscō, guī ③ *v* grow stiff or rigid

dēripiō, puī, reptum ③ *v* tear off, remove

dērīsor, ōris *m* mocker, scoffer

dērīsus, ūs *m* ridicule, scorn

dērīvātiō, ōnis *f* turning off (into another channel)

dērīvō ① *v* divert, turn or draw off

dērogō ① *v* make or propose (modifications to a law); take away, diminish

dēruptus, a, um *adj* craggy, steep, precipitous

dēsaeviō ④ *v* work off or vent one's rage

dēscendō, ndī, ēnsum ③ *v* descend; fall; alight; slope;

penetrate; stoop, demean oneself

dēscēnsus, ūs *m* climbing down

dēscīscō, īvī/iī, ītum ③ *v* desert defect

dēscrībō, psī, ptum ③ *v* copy; describe; establish

dēscriptiō, ōnis *f* delineation; description

dēsecō, cuī, ctum ① *v* cut off

dēserō, ruī, rtum ③ *v* forsake; desert; give up; fail

dēserta, ōrum *ntpl* wilderness

dēsertor, ōris *m* abandoner; deserter; fugitive

dēsertus, a, um *adj* desert, lonely, waste

dēserviō ④ *v with dat* serve diligently, be devoted to

dēsīderābilis, e *adj* desirable; missed

dēsīderium, (i)ī *nt* desire, wishing, longing for; regret for what is absent; petition; request favourite, darling

dēsīderō ① *v* wish for, desire; need, want; require; miss

dēsidia, ae *f* idleness, sloth

dēsidiōsus, a, um *adj* indolent lazy

dēsīdō, sēdī ③ *v* sink, settle do

dēsignātiō, ōnis *f* appointme designation

dēsignō ① *v* mark out, designa denote; appoint; choose; perpetrate

dēsiliō, siluī, sultum ④ *v* leap down, alight

dēsinō, sīvī/iī, situm ③ *v* leav off, cease, desist

dēsipiō ③ *v* be out of one's min lose one's reason

d

...sistō, stitī, stitum 3 v leave , cease, desist from; stand art, be away

...sōlō 1 v abandon, desert; ...pty

...spectō 1 v look down at; ...erlook; despise

...spectus, ūs m prospect, ...norama; contempt

...spēranter adv despairingly

...spērātiō, ōnis f despair

...spērātus, a, um adj ...sperate; despaired of

...spērō 1 v despair (of)

...spicientia, ae f contempt ...r)

...spiciō, spexī, spectum 3 v ...ok down upon; despise

...spoliō 1 v rob, plunder

...spondeō, ndī, ōnsum 2 v ...omise (in marriage)

...animum ~ despair

...spūmō 1 v skim off

...spuō 3 v spit (out), reject

...stillō ▸ distillō

...stinātiō, ōnis f designation; ...solution, determination

...stinō 1 v fix, determine, ...sign; destine

...stituō, uī, ūtum 3 v leave, ...sert, abandon; give up; ...appoint

...stringō, īnxī, ictum 3 v strip ; draw (a sword); graze (gently); ...nsure

...struō, ūxī, ūctum 3 v pull ...wn; destroy, ruin

...subitō adv suddenly

...suētūdō, inis f ...continuance, disuse

...sultor, ōris m a rider in the

circus who jumped from one horse to another

dēsum, esse, fuī v ir with dat be wanting, fail

dēsūmō, mpsī 3 v pick out, choose

dēsuper adv from above

dētegō, ēxī, ēctum 3 v uncover, lay bare; reveal

dētendō, ndī, ēnsum 3 v strike (tents), let down

dētergeō, rsī, rsum 2 v wipe off; strip off, rub clean

dēterior, ius adj inferior; worse, meaner

dēterminō 1 v set bounds to, limit, determine

dēterō, trīvī, trītum 3 v wear away

dēterreō 2 v deter, discourage

dētestābilis, e adj abominable, detestable

dētestātiō, ōnis f solemn curse

dētestor 1 v dep call down a solemn curse on; detest; avert

dētexō, xuī, xtum 3 v finish weaving, complete

dētineō, tentum 2 v hold down or off, detain; occupy; delay the end of

dētondeō, (to)tondī, tōnsum 2 v shear off, strip off; LM give the tonsure

dētonō, tonuī 1 v expend one's thunder

dētorqueō, rsī, rtum 2 v turn or twist away; distort; divert

dētractor, ōris m detractor, defamer

dētrahō, āxī, actum 3 v draw off; remove; lessen; take away;

detract from; impair

dētrectātiō, ōnis f refusal

dētrectō v refuse; disparage, belittle

dētrīmentum, ī nt detriment, loss, damage; defeat

dētrūdō, ūsī, ūsum v thrust down or from; expel; dispossess; reduce; postpone

dētruncō v lop off; behead; mutilate

dēturbō v dislodge; pull down; upset; topple

deūrō, ussī, ustum v burn down; (of cold) wither

deus, ī m god

dēvāstō v lay waste

dēvehō, ēxī, ectum v carry away, convey
□ **dēvehor** travel downstream

dēveniō, vēnī, ventum v arrive (at); land, turn (to)

dēverberō v whip hard

dēversor v dep put up at an inn; lodge

dēversōrium, (i)ī nt inn, lodging-house

dēverticulum, ī nt by-road; digression; port of call

dēvertō, rtī, rsum v turn aside; lodge; digress

dēvexitās, ātis f downward slope, incline

dēvexus, a, um adj sloping, shelving

dēvinciō, vīnxī, vīnctum v bind fast, tie up; oblige

dēvincō, īcī, ictum v conquer entirely, subdue

dēvītō v avoid

dēvius, a, um adj out-of-the-way,

devious; straying

dēvocō v call down or away, summon

dēvolō v fly down or away; hasten down, hasten away

dēvolvō, lvī, lūtum v roll down

dēvorō v devour; absorb; gul down; check; drink in; use up

dēvōtiō, ōnis f devoting; vow; curse

dēvoveō, vōvī, vōtum v vo devote; curse; bewitch

dexterē adv skilfully

dextrōvorsum adv to the righ

diabolicus, a, um adj [LM] of the Devil

diabolus, ī m [LM] the Devil

diāconus, ī m, **diacon, nis** m [LM] deacon

diadēma, atis nt diadem, ornamental headband

diaeta, ae f course of medical treatment; room; cabin (on a sh

dialectica, ae f [LM] logic

Diālis, e adj of Jupiter

dica, ae f lawsuit, legal action

dicācitās, ātis f mordant or caustic raillery

dicāx, ācis adj witty, smart, sarcastic

diciō, ōnis f sway; dominion; authority

dīcō[1], dīxī, dictum v say, te order; call; declare; express; plea designate

dīcō[2] v dedicate, consecrate; apart; devote (oneself); assign

dicrotum, ī nt a light galley, perhaps propelled by two bank of oars

ctamnum, ī *nt*, dictamnus, *f* dittany

ctāta, ōrum *ntpl* dictated ssons or exercises

ctātor, ōris *m* dictator; chief agistrate

ctātōrius, a, um *adj* of a ctator

ctātūra, ae *f* dictatorship

ctiō, ōnis *f* saying, delivery; eech; oracular utterance

ctitō □ *v* say often; plead often

ctō □ *v* say often; dictate (for riting); compose

ctum, ī *nt* saying, word; maxim; on mot, witticism; order

dicī ▸ discō

dō, dīdidī, dīditum ③ *v* stribute, spread

dūcō, dūxī, ductum ③ *v* draw r lead aside; separate; divide; catter; open out

ērectus *int* go and be hanged! he sense of this uncertain word is one of eremptory dismissal)

ēs, diēī *m* day; daylight; festival; d letter day; lifetime

in diem each day

ffāmō □ *v* spread the news of; ander

fferō, ferre, distulī, dīlātum *v* put off, delay; disperse; spread; ublish; differ; disagree

ffertus, a, um *adj* filled, rowded

fficilis, e *adj* difficult; obstinate, norose, intractable

fficultās, ātis *f* difficulty; rouble; intractability

ffidentia, ae *f* mistrust, strust

diffīdō, fīsus sum ③ *v semi-dep with dat* lack confidence (in); despair

diffindō, idī, issum ③ *v* split; put off

diffingō ③ *v* remodel

diffiteor ② *v dep* disavow, deny

diffluō, ūxī ③ *v* flow away in all directions; melt away; waste away

diffugiō, ūgī ③ *v* flee in different directions; scatter, disperse

diffundō, ūdī, ūsum ③ *v* pour forth; diffuse, spread; cheer

diffutuō, uī, ūtum ③ *v* indulge in promiscuous sexual intercourse

dīgerō, essī, estum ③ *v* distribute, spread over; arrange, dispose

digitus, ī *m* finger; toe; a finger's-breadth

dignātiō, ōnis *f* esteem; repute; rank

dignitās, ātis *f* worthiness; merit; dignity; authority; office; grace; value, honour

dignor □ *v dep* consider worthy

dignus, a, um *adj* worthy, deserving; deserved

dīgredior, gressus sum ③ *v dep* depart, go away; leave (a subject of discussion)

dīgressiō, ōnis *f* going away; digression

dīgressus, ūs *m* departure; digression

dīiūdicō □ *v* decide, judge, determine; distinguish

dīiungō, ūnxī, ūnctum ③ *v* unyoke; separate; disjoin

dīlābor, lāpsus sum ③ *v dep* fall apart or to pieces; disperse; melt away; decay

d

dīlacerō 1 v, **dīlaniō** 1 v tear to pieces

dīlapidō 1 v bring into a state of partial ruin or collapse

dīlargior 4 v dep give away freely

dīlātiō, ōnis f delaying; interval of space

dīlātō 1 v make wider, enlarge, extend, dilate

dīlector, oris m/f LM worshipper

dīlectus, ūs m recruitment, levy; choice

dīligēns, ntis adj careful, diligent, frugal, thrifty

dīligentia, ae f carefulness, attentiveness; economy, frugality

dīligō, ēxī, ēctum 3 v esteem highly, hold dear

dīlūcēscō, cuī 3 v dawn, become light

dīlūcidus, a, um adj plain, distinct, lucid

dīluō, uī, ūtum 3 v wash (off); temper; dilute; dissolve; weaken; refute

dīluviēs, iēī f inundation, flood

dīluvium, (i)ī nt inundation, flood

dīmētior, mēnsus sum 4 v dep measure out

dīmicātiō, ōnis f fight, combat; struggle

dīmicō, micāvī/micuī 1 v fight; struggle, strive

dīmidium, (i)ī nt a half

dīmidius, a, um adj half

dīmittō, īsī, issum 3 v send out or forth; dismiss; disband; release; divorce; break up; detach; let slip; give up, renounce

dimminu- ▶ **dēminu-**

dīmoveō, mōvī, mōtum 2 v separate; put aside; remove

dīnumerō 1 v count, enumerat(e)

dio(e)cēsis, is f LM diocese

dīōta, ae f two-handled wine-ja(r)

dīplōma, atis nt letter of recommendation

dīrēctus, a, um adj straight, vertical; steep; direct, simple

dīrigō, ēxī, ēctum 3 v direct, guide; steer; set in order

direptiō, ōnis f plundering

direptor, ōris m plunderer

dīrimō, ēmī, ēmptum 3 v pu(t) apart; separate; break up, dissol(ve)

dīripiō, puī, eptum 3 v snatch away; tear to pieces; rob, loot

dīrumpō, ūpī, uptum 3 v bre(ak) apart, shatter, burst

dīruō, ruī, rutum 3 v demolish; destroy

dīrus, a, um adj fearful, awful; horrible

dīs, ītis adj (contracted form of) **dīves** rich

discēdō, essī, essum 3 v go o(ff) in different directions; march off; be divided; cease; die; depart fro(m)

disceptātiō, ōnis f debate

disceptātor, ōris m arbitrator

disceptō 1 v dispute; debate; arbitrate

discernō, crēvī, crētum 3 v separate; distinguish

discerpō, psī, ptum 3 v pluck tear in pieces; mangle

discessiō, ōnis f withdrawal, dispersal

discessus, ūs m going apart; separation; departure; marching off

cidium, (i)ī *nt* separation, orce, discord

cīnctus, a, um *adj* wearing se clothes; easy-going

cindō, idī, issum ③ *v* cut in); divide

cingō, īnxī, īnctum ③ *v* gird, strip

ciplīna, ae *f* instruction; owledge; discipline; system; thod

cipula, ae *f* female pupil

cipulus, ī *m* pupil, disciple, nee

clūdō, ūsī, ūsum ③ *v* arate; keep apart

cō, didicī ③ *v* learn, acquire owledge of

color, ōris *adj* of another our; of various colours; iegated

conveniō ④ *v* be inconsistent, different

cordia, ae *f* disagreement, cord

cordō ① *v* be at variance, arrel; be different

cors, rdis *adj* discordant, agreeing; different

crepō, puī ① *v* be out of tune; agree, differ

crībō, īpsī, īptum ③ *v* divide, ign, distribute

crīmen, inis *nt* separating ; division; distinction; erence; crisis; risk

crīminō ① *v* divide up, arate

crīptiō, ōnis *f* assignment, Ision

crūciō ① *v* torture

discumbō, cubuī, cubitum ③ *v* lie down; recline at table; go to bed

discurrō, (cu)currī, cursum ③ *v* run about

discursus, ūs *m* running about; separation, dispersal

discus, ī *m* discus, quoit

discutiō, ussī, ussum ③ *v* shatter, shake violently; dissipate; bring to nothing

disertus, a, um *adj* eloquent; skilfully expressed

disiciō, iēcī, iectum ③ *v* scatter; disperse; squander; frustrate

disiungō, ūnxī, ūnctum ③ *v* (also **dīiungō**) unyoke; separate; disjoin

dispār, aris *adj* unequal, unlike

disparō ① *v* separate, divide

dispellō, pulī, pulsum ③ *v* drive apart *or* away; disperse

dispendium, (i)ī *nt* expense, cost; loss

dispēnsātiō, ōnis *f* management; stewardship

dispēnsātor, ōris *m* steward; treasurer

dispēnsō ① *v* manage; dispense, distribute; pay out; arrange

disperdō, didī, ditum ③ *v* destroy *or* ruin utterly

dispereō, īre, iī *v ir* perish, be destroyed

dispergō, rsī, rsum ③ *v* scatter about, disperse

dispertiō ④ *v* distribute, divide; assign

dispiciō, spexī, spectum ③ *v* look about (for); discover; espy; consider

d

displiceō 2 v displease

displōdō, ōsum 3 v burst apart

dispōnō, posuī, positum 3 v distribute, set in order; post, station; arrange

dispudet 2 v impers be deeply ashamed

disputātiō, ōnis f discussion, argument, debate

disputō 1 v argue, debate

disquīsītiō, ōnis f inquiry

disr- ▸ **diss-, dīr-**

dissecō, cuī, ctum 1 v cut apart or in pieces

dissēminō 1 v broadcast, disseminate

dissēnsiō, ōnis f dissension, disagreement

dissentiō, ēnsī, ēnsum 4 v dissent, disagree; differ

disserō¹, ruī, rtum 3 v discuss, set out in words

disserō², sēvī, situm 3 v sow

dissertō 1 v discuss

dissideō, sēdī, sessum 2 v be at variance; disagree; be separated

dissignō ▸ **dēsignō**

dissiliō, siluī 4 v leap or burst apart

dissimilis, e adj unlike, dissimilar

dissimilitūdō, inis f unlikeness, difference

dissimulanter adv dissemblingly

dissimulātiō, ōnis f dissimulation, dissembling

dissimulātor, ōris m dissembler

dissimulō 1 v dissemble, disguise; hide; ignore

dissipātiō, ōnis f squandering; scattering

dissipō 1 v disperse; squande destroy completely; circulate

dissociābilis, e adj incompati discordant

dissociō 1 v separate, part; se at variance

dissolūtiō, ōnis f disintegrat dissolution; destruction; disconnection; refutation

dissolūtus, a, um adj loose; l negligent; dissolute

dissolvō, lvī, lūtum 3 v unloose; dissolve, destroy; mel pay; refute; annul

dissonus, a, um adj dissonan discordant; different

dissuādeō, āsī, āsum 2 v dissuade, advise against

dissuāsor, ōris m discourage one who advises against

dissultō 1 v fly or burst apart; bounce off

distaedet 2 v impers it wearie is distasteful

distantia, ae f distance; difference

distendō, ndī, ntum 3 v str in different directions, stretch extend; swell out; fill

distillō 1 v trickle down

distinctiō, ōnis f distinction; difference

distinctus, a, um adj separat distinct; definite, lucid

distineō, tentum 2 v keep apart; separate; prevent, distra hold up

distinguō, īnxī, īnctum 3 v divide, part; distinguish; decor

distō 1 v stand apart, be dista be different

'istorqueō, rsī, rtum 2 v twist this way and that

istrahō, āxī, actum 3 v pull or draw apart; wrench; separate; sell; distract; set at variance; estrange

istribuō, uī, ūtum 3 v divide, distribute

istribūtiō, ōnis f division, distribution

istringō, īnxī, ictum 3 v stretch out; detain; distract; pull in different directions

'sturbō 1 v disturb; demolish; upset

tēscō 3 v grow rich

thyrambus, ī m a form of verse used especially for choral singing

tō 1 v enrich

ū adv a long while; long since
diūtius longer
diūtissimē very long

urnus, a, um adj daily

us, a, um adj daylit, divine

ūtinus, a, um adj lasting, long

īturnitās, ātis f long duration

īturnus, a, um adj lasting long

va, ae f goddess

vellō, vellī, vulsum 3 v tear pieces; tear away; estrange; break up

vendō, didī, ditum 3 v sell in mall lots; sell up

verberō 1 v split; strike silently

versitās, ātis f difference

versus, a, um adj opposite; barate, apart; unlike, different; stile; contrary; distant; distinct

es, itis adj rich; talented

idō, īsī, īsum 3 v separate,

divide; distribute; distinguish; break up

dīviduus, a, um adj divisible; divided; half; parted

dīvīnātiō, ōnis f prophecy, prognostication

dīvīnitus adv by divine agency or inspiration; divinely, excellently

dīvīnō 1 v divine; prophesy; guess

dīvīnus, a, um adj divine; prophetic; blessed; excellent
■ ~, ī m prophet

dīvīsiō, ōnis f division; distribution

dīvīsor, ōris m distributor; a candidate's agent hired to distribute bribes

dīvīsus, ūs m division

dīvitiae, ārum fpl riches, wealth

dīvortium, (i)ī nt separation; divorce; point of separation; watershed; by-way, roundabout route

dīvulgō 1 v publish, disseminate news of

dīvum, ī nt sky, open air
□ **sub dīvō** in the open air

dīvus, ī m god

dō, dare, dedī, datum 1 v give; ascribe; grant, permit; furnish, offer; lend; tell of; enable, cause

doceō, doctum 2 v teach; tell; show

docilis, e adj teachable, responsive

doctor, ōris m teacher, instructor, trainer

doctrīna, ae f teaching, instruction; science, learning; system of rules

doctus, a, um adj learned, wise,

expert

documentum, **ī** *nt* example; warning; instruction; proof

dōdrāns, **ntis** *m* three-quarters

dogma, **atis** *nt* doctrine, dogma, teaching

doleō ② *v* feel or suffer pain; grieve for

dōlium, **(i)ī** *nt* large earthenware vessel for storing liquids, grain, *etc.*

dolor, **ōris** *m* pain; grief; anguish; sorrow; resentment

dolōsus, **a**, **um** *adj* crafty, deceitful

dolus, **ī** *m* fraud, deceit; treachery, cunning

domābilis, **e** *adj* able to be tamed

domesticus, **a**, **um** *adj* domestic, familiar; native; private, personal

domicilium, **(i)ī** *nt* dwelling, abode, home

domina, **ae** *f* mistress of a family; lady; wife; lady-love

dominātiō, **ōnis** *f* dominion; despotism

dominātus, **ūs** *m* absolute rule, dominion

dominica, **ae** *f* [LM] Sunday

dominor ① *v dep* act as a despot, rule; be in control

dominus, **ī** *m* master of the house; owner; lord, ruler; host; lover

domitō ① *v* tame, break in

domitor, **ōris** *m* tamer; conqueror

domō, **muī**, **mitum** ① *v* tame; conquer

domus, **ūs/ī** *f* house; home; household; family; native country
□ **domī** at home

dōnābilis, **e** *adj* worthy to be the recipient (of)

dōnārium, **(i)ī** *nt* part of temple where votive offerings were received and stored; treasure chamber

dōnātiō, **ōnis** *f* donation, gift

dōnātīvum, **ī** *nt* gratuity, bount

dōnec *conj* as long as, until

dōnicum *conj* until

dōnō ① *v* present (with), bestow; forgive; give up

dōnum, **ī** *nt* gift, present; offerin

dormiō ④ *v* sleep; rest; go to bed (with)

dormītō ① *v* feel sleepy, drowsy; do nothing

dorsum, **ī** *nt* back; slope of a hill, ridge

dōs, **ōtis** *f* dowry; talent, quality

dōtālis, **e** *adj* forming part of a dowry, relating to a dowry

dōtātus, **a**, **um** *adj* provided w a (good) dowry

drachma, **ae** *f* a Greek silver cc

dracō, **ōnis** *m* snake

dromas, **ados** *m* dromedary

Druidae, **ārum** *mpl*, **Druidēs**...**um** *mpl* druids

dubitanter *adv* doubtingly; hesitatingly

dubitātiō, **ōnis** *f* doubt; hesitation; irresolution

dubitō ① *v* doubt; be uncertain irresolute; hesitate over

dubium, **(i)ī** *nt* doubt

dubius, **a**, **um** *adj* doubtful; variable; uncertain; dangerous; critical

ducatus, **us** *m* [LM] duchy

cēnī, ae, a adj two hundred ch; two hundred

centēsimus, a, um adj two-ndredth

centī, ae, a adj two hundred

cō, dūxī, ductum ③ v lead, nduct, draw, bring; run (a wall, ;.); derive; guide; persuade; ceive; prolong; think, esteem; ckon; pass; spend

uxōrem ~ marry (a woman), ke as wife

ctō ① v lead; deceive, beguile

ctor, ōris m leader, mmander

ctus, ūs m conducting; neralship

dum adv a little while ago; merly

iam ~ long ago

ellum ▶ bellum

im old subj of ▶ **dō**

lcēdō, inis f sweetness; charm

lcis, e adj sweet; pleasant, arming; dear, beloved

m conj while, as long as; until; ovided that

mētum, ī nt thicket

mmodo conj provided that

mōsus, a, um adj overgrown th thorn, briar or the like

mtaxat adv only, at least; so far

mus, ī m thorn or briar bush

o, duae, duo adj two

odecim adj indec twelve

odecimus, a, um adj twelfth

odēnī, ae, a adj twelve each, twelves

odēvīcēnī, ae, a adj eighteen ch

duodēvīcēsimus, a, um adj eighteenth

duodēvīgintī adj indec eighteen

duovirī, ōrum mpl board of two men

duplex, icis adj twofold, double; divided; 'two-faced'

duplicō v double; enlarge; bend double

dūritia, ae f, **dūritiēs, iēī** f hardness; austerity; rigour

dūrō ① v make hard; dry; harden, 'steel'; become hard or stern, etc.; endure; last out; survive

dūrus, a, um adj hard; harsh; hardy, vigorous; stern; unfeeling; inflexible; burdensome, difficult

dux, cis m/f leader, guide; commander, general; LM duke

d
e

· ·

Ee

· ·

eā adv along that path, that way

eādem adv by the same route

eātenus adv so far, to such a degree; int well, that's it

ēbibō, bibī ③ v drink up, drain; absorb; squander

ēblandior ④ v dep obtain by flattery

ēbrietās, ātis f drunkenness

ēbriōsus, a, um adj addicted to drink

ēbrius, a, um adj drunk; intoxicated

ebulum, ī nt, **ebulus, ī** m danewort

ebur, oris nt ivory; ivory statue

ēcastor *int* interjection used by women by Castor!

ecce *int* look! see! behold! here!

eccerē *int* see there!

ecclēsia, ae *f* the assembly of the people; a meeting of the assembly; 𝗟𝗠 church

eccōs *int* here they (m.) are!

eccum *int* here he is!

ecf- ▸ **eff-**

echidna, ae *f* serpent, viper

echīnus, ī *m* sea-urchin

echō, ūs *f* echo

ecloga, ae *f* a short poem

ecqui, quae/qua, quod *pn* is there any?

ecquid *adv* is it true that … ? at all?

ecquis, quid *pn* is there anyone who?

eculeus, ī *m* young or small horse, pony

edāx, ācis *adj* voracious, gluttonous; devouring

ēdentō ⑪ *v* knock the teeth from

ēdentulus, a, um *adj* toothless

edepol *int* by Pollux!

ēdīcō, īxī, ictum ③ *v* publish, declare

ēdictum, ī *nt* proclamation, edict

ēdiscō, didicī ③ *v* learn by heart; study; get to know

ēdisserō, ruī, rtum ③ *v*, **ēdissertō** ⑪ *v* relate, expound

ēditiō, ōnis *f* publishing; edition; statement

ēditus, a, um *adj* high, lofty

edō, ēsse, ēdī, ēsum *v ir* eat; devour; spend (money) on food

ēdō, didī, ditum ③ *v* put forth; emit; publish; relate; bring forth;

beget; proclaim; bring about; cause

ēdoceō, ctum ② *v* teach or inform thoroughly

ēdomō, muī, mitum ⑪ *v* tame completely, conquer

ēdormiō ④ *v* sleep; sleep off

ēducātiō, ōnis *f* bringing up; rearing

ēducātor, ōris *m* bringer up, tutor; foster-father

ēducātrīx, īcis *f* nurse, foster-mother

ēdūcō, dūxī, ductum ③ *v* lead or draw out; bring away; rear; educate; raise, produce

ēducō ⑪ *v* bring up, rear

edūlis, e *adj* eatable

ēdūrus, a, um *adj* very hard

effarciō ▸ **efferciō**

effectus, ūs *m* execution, performance; effect

effēminātus, a, um *adj* womanish, effeminate

effēminō ⑪ *v* emasculate; unman, enervate

efferciō, rsī, rtum ④ *v* stuff, cram, fill out

efferō[1], ferre, extulī, ēlātum *v ir* bring or carry out; produce; utter; raise, advance; proclaim; carry out for burial

efferō[2] ⑪ *v* make savage

efferus, era, erum *adj* savage, cruel, barbarous

effervēscō, vī ③ *v* boil up, seethe; become greatly excited

effētus, a, um *adj* exhausted, worn out

efficāx, ācis *adj* efficacious, effectual

...iciō, fēcī, fectum 3 v effect, ...ecute, accomplish, make; ...oduce; prove; make up

...igiēs, iēī f, effigia, ae f ...rtrait, image, effigy, statue; ...ost

...ingō, īnxī, ictum 3 v form, ...ould; represent, portray; stroke

...lāgitātiō, ōnis f urgent ...mand

...lāgitō 1 v demand or ask ...gently

...lō 1 v blow or breathe out; ...eathe one's last

...luō, ūxī 3 v flow out; escape; ...nish; be forgotten

...odiō, ōdī, ossum 3 v dig out; ...ouge out

...or 1 v dep utter; declare; speak

...rēnō 1 v unbridle, let loose

...rēnus, a, um adj unbridled; ...restrained, unruly

...ringō, frēgī, frāctum 3 v ...eak open

...ugiō, fūgī 3 v escape; flee ...m, avoid; be unnoticed; escape ...e knowledge of

...ugium, (i)ī nt flight; way of ...cape

...ulgeō, lsī 2 v shine forth, ...tter; be or become conspicuous

...ultus, a, um adj propped up, ...pported (by)

...undō, ūdī, ūsum 3 v pour ...t, shed; send out; bring forth ...mbers; discharge; let fall; give ...; waste, squander; bring forth

...ūsē adv over a wide area; in a ...sorderly manner; immoderately

...ūsiō, ōnis f pouring forth; ...odigality, excess

effūsus, a, um adj vast, wide; dishevelled; disorderly; extravagant

effūtiō 4 v blurt out

effutuō, ūtum 3 v wear out with sexual intercourse

ēgelidus, a, um adj lukewarm, tepid

egēns, ntis adj needy, very poor; destitute of

egēnus, a, um adj in want of, destitute of

egeō 2 v with gen or abl want; need; require, be without

ēgerō, essī, estum 3 v carry or bear out; discharge; utter

egestās, ātis f extreme poverty, want

ēgī ▸ agō

ego pn I; I myself

egomet pn I myself; I for my part

ēgredior, gressus sum 3 v dep march or come out; set sail; land; go beyond; ascend; overstep

ēgregius, a, um adj excellent, eminent; illustrious

ēgressus, ūs m departure; flight; landing; place of egress, mouth (of a river); digression

ehem int hah! what! an exclamation expressing gratified surprise, recollection, etc.

ēheu int alas!

eho int here, you! hey! hi!

ei int exclamation expressing anguish or similar

eia int exclamation expressing deprecation, concession, astonishment, urgency

ēiaculor 1 v dep shoot out; discharge

ēiciō, iēcī, iectum 3 v throw or cast out; thrust out; expel; banish; vomit; dislocate; cast ashore; reject

ēiectō 1 v cast out

ēiulātus, ūs m wailing, shrieking

ēiūrō 1 v abjure; resign; reject on oath (of a judge); forswear; disown

eiusmodī gen used as adj of the kind

ēlābor, lāpsus sum 3 v dep escape; slip away

ēlabōrō 1 v take pains, exert oneself; bestow care on

ēlanguēscō, guī 3 v begin to lose one's vigour; slacken, relax

elatio, onis f 🔲 pride

ēlēctilis, e adj choice, dainty

ēlēctiō, ōnis f choice, selection

ēlectrum, ī nt amber; alloy of gold and silver

ēlegāns, ntis adj elegant, fine, handsome; tasteful; fastidious, critical; discriminating, polite

ēlegantia, ae f elegance; niceness; taste; politeness

elegī, ōrum mpl elegiac verses, elegy

elegīa, ae f, **elegeia, ae** f elegy

elementa, ōrum ntpl elements; rudiments; beginnings

elephā(n)s, ntis m, **elephantus, ī** m elephant; ivory

ēlevō 1 v lift up, raise; alleviate; lessen; make light of

ēlicēs, um mpl trench, drain

ēliciō, cuī 3 v entice, coax; call forth; draw forth

ēlīdō, īsī, īsum 3 v strike or dash out; expel; shatter; crush out; strangle; destroy

ēligō, lēgī, lēctum 3 v pick out,

choose

ēlixus, a, um adj thoroughly boiled

elleborōsus, a, um adj in need of hellebore, out of one's mind

elleborum, ī nt one of several acrid and poisonous plans muc used medicinally, especially as a cure for insanity

ēlluō ▸ hēlluō

ēloquēns, ntis adj eloquent, articulate

ēloquentia, ae f, **ēloquiun (i)ī** nt eloquence, articulateness the art of public speaking

ēloquor, locūtus sum 3 v de speak out, utter

ēlūceō, xī 2 v shine forth; show itself; be manifest

ēluctor 1 v dep force a way through; surmount a difficulty

ēlūcubrō 1 v, **ēlūcubror** 1 dep compose at night; burn the midnight oil over

ēlūdificor 1 v dep fool comple

ēlūdō, ūsī, ūsum 3 v elude, escape from; parry; baffle; chea frustrate; mock, make fun of

ēluō, uī, ūtum 3 v wash clean; wash away, clear oneself (of)

ēluviēs, lēī f overflow, flood; washing away (of dirt); scouring (of dirt)

em int there!

ēmancipō 1 v emancipate (a son from his father's authority) alienate; make subservient

ēmānō 1 v flow out; arise, emanate from; become known

emāx, ācis adj fond of buying

ēmendātiō, ōnis f correction

ēmendō ① v correct; repair

ēmentior ④ v dep falsify, invent; feign

ēmereō ② v, **ēmereor** ② v dep earn; serve out one's time

ēmergō, rsī, rsum ③ v rise up out of the water, emerge; escape; appear; arrive

ēmeritus, ī m veteran

ēmētior, mēnsus sum ④ v dep measure out; pass through

ēmicō, micuī ① v spring forth, shine forth, appear suddenly

ēmigrō ① v move, depart

ēminēns, ntis adj lofty; prominent; eminent

ēmineō ② v project; stand out; be pre-eminent; excel

ēminus adv at long range

ēmittō, mīsī, missum ③ v send out or forth; set free; fling; let fall; publish; empty; drain off

emō, ēmī, ēmptum ③ v buy; gain

ēmolliō ④ v soften; enervate, mellow

ēmolumentum, ī nt advantage; benefit

ēmorior, morī, mortuus sum ③ v dep die away; die; perish

ēmoveō, mōvī, mōtum ② v remove; dislodge

emporium, (i)ī nt centre of trade, mart

ēmptiō, ōnis f the act of buying, purchase

ēmptor, ōris m buyer, purchaser

ēmungō, ūnxī, ūnctum ③ v wipe the nose; trick, swindle

ēmūniō ④ v fortify; make roads through

ēn int behold! see!

ēnārrābilis, e adj that may be described or explained

ēnārrō ① v explain or relate in detail

ēnatō ① v escape by swimming

ēnecō, cuī, c(ā)tum ① v kill, deprive of life

ēnervō ① v weaken, enervate

ēnicō ▶ ēnecō

enim conj indeed, for, yes indeed; certainly
   □ ~ **vērō** positively! well, of course; certainly

ēniteō ② v shine forth; be outstanding

ēnitēscō, tuī ③ v become bright; stand out

ēnītor, nīsus/nīxus sum ③ v dep force one's way up; strive; give birth to

ēnō ① v swim out

ēnōdis, e adj without knots; smooth

ēnormis, e adj irregular; immense, enormous

ēns, entis nt Ⓜ thing, being

ēnsis, is m sword

ēnūbō, psī ③ v marry out of one's rank or outside one's community

ēnumerō ① v count up; pay out; specify, enumerate

ēnumquam adv at any time at all? ever?

ēnūntiō ① v speak out, say, express, declare; disclose

eō¹ adv to that place, thither; there, in that place; so far; therefore; so much (more or less)

eō², īre, īī/īvī, itum v i go; walk; march; flow; come in; ride, sail;

turn out

□ ~ **īnfitiās** deny

eōdem *adv* to the same place or purpose

Ēous, a, um *adj* eastern; of the dawn

ephippium, (i)ī *nt* cloth on which the rider of a horse sits

epigramma, atis *nt* epigram; inscription

episcopus, ī *m* LM bishop

epistula, ae *f*, **epistola, ae** *f* letter, dispatch

epos *nt* (*only in nom and acc sg*) epic poem

ēpōtō, ōtum ③ *v* drink down; absorb; swallow up

epulae, ārum *fpl* food, dishes; banquet, feast

epulor ① *v dep* dine sumptuously, feast

epulum, ī *nt* banquet, feast

equa, ae *f* mare

eques, itis *m* horseman, rider; horse-soldier

■ **equitēs** *pl* cavalry; order of knights

equester, tris, tre *adj* equestrian; of, belonging to, or connected with cavalry; belonging to the order of knights

equidem *adv* I for my part; truly, indeed

equīnus, a, um *adj* concerning horses

equitātus, ūs *m* cavalry

equitō ① *v* ride

equus, ī *m* horse

era, ae *f* (*also* **hera**) mistress; lady of the house

ērādīcō ① *v* scrape away, scrape

clean; root out; erase, delete

ergā *prep with acc* opposite to; against, towards

ergastulum, ī *nt* prison on large estate to which refractory slaves were sent for work in chain-gangs; *in pl* convicts

ergō *adv* therefore; then; now

ēricius, (i)ī *m* some kind of spiked barrier

erifuga, ae *m* one who runs away from his master

ērigō, rēxī, rēctum ③ *v* erect; raise; build; rouse, excite, stimulate

erilis, e *adj* of a master or mistress

ērīnāceus, ī *m* hedgehog

ēripiō, puī, reptum ③ *v* snatch away, take by force; rescue

ērogātiō, ōnis *f* paying out, distribution

ērogō ① *v* pay out, expend

errābundus, a, um *adj* wandering

errāticus, a, um *adj* roving, erratic; wild

errātum, ī *nt* error, mistake; lapse

errō[1] ① *v* wander or stray about; go astray; err, mistake; vacillate

errō[2]**, ōnis** *m* truant

error, ōris *m* straying about; winding; maze; uncertainty; error; deception; derangement of the mind

ērubēscō, buī ③ *v* redden; blush for shame

ēructō ① *v* bring up noisily; discharge violently

ērudiō ④ *v* educate, instruct, teach

ērudītiō, ōnis *f* learning

ērudītulus, a, um *adj* learned

ērudītus, a, um *adj* learned, skilled

ērumpō, rūpī, ruptum ③ *v* break out; sally forth, break out of

ēruō, ruī, rutum ③ *v* pluck or dig or root up; overthrow; destroy; elicit

ēruptiō, ōnis *f* sally, sudden rush of troops from a position

erus, ī *m* master; owner

ervum, ī *nt* vetch; fodder, feed

ēsca, ae *f* food; bait; dish, meal

ēscendō, ndī, ēnsum ③ *v* ascend, go up, mount

essedārius, (i)ī *m* fighter in a war-chariot

essedum, ī *nt*, **esseda, ae** *f* war-chariot; light travelling carriage

essentia, ae *f* ⓛⓜ essence

ēste *impv pl of* ▶ **edō**

ēsuriō ④ *v* be hungry; desire eagerly

ēsurītiō, ōnis *f* state of hunger

et *conj* and; also; even; moreover
    ☐ **et ... et** both ... and

etenim *conj* and indeed, the fact is, for

etēsiae, ārum *mpl* etesian winds

ethnicus, ī *m* ⓛⓜ pagan

etiam *conj* and also, too, besides; even now; yes indeed, yes
    ☐ **atque ∼** more and more

etiamnum, etiamnunc *conj* even now, still, yet

etiamsī *conj* even if, although

etiamtum *conj* even then; yet

etsī *conj* although, even if

eu *int* well done! bravo!

euge *int* oh, good! fine!

euhāns, ntis *adj* uttering the name Euhan (Bacchus)

Euhius, (i)ī *m* title given to Bacchus

euhoe *int* cry of joy used by the votaries of Bacchus

eunūchus, ī *m* eunuch

euouae ⓛⓜ abbreviation standing for and consisting of the final six vowels of the phrase **in saecula saeculorum, amen**

eurīpus, ī *m* narrow channel of the sea, straight; canal

eurōus, a, um *adj* eastern

eurus, ī *m* east (or south east) wind; the east

ēvādō, āsī, āsum ③ *v* go or come out; escape, avoid; turn out

ēvagor ① *v dep* wander off; spread; overflow

ēvalēscō, luī ③ *v* increase in strength; prevail, have sufficient strength (to)

ēvānēscō, nuī ③ *v* pass away, disappear, die out

evangelia, ae *f*, **evangelium, (i)ī** *nt* ⓛⓜ gospel

ēvānidus, a, um *adj* vanishing, passing away

ēvāstō ① *v* devastate

ēvehō, ēxī, ectum ③ *v* carry away, convey out; carry up; exalt
    ☐ **ēvehor** ride out out

ēvellō, vellī, vulsum ③ *v* pluck or tear out; root out

ēveniō, vēnī, ventum ④ *v* come out; come about, happen

ēventum, ī *nt* occurrence, event; issue, outcome

ēventus, ūs *m* occurrence, event; result; success

ēverberō 🔟 v beat violently

ēversiō, ōnis f overthrowing; destruction

ēversor, ōris m one who destroys or overthrows

ēvertō, tī, rsum 🔟 v turn upside down; churn up; ruin, overthrow

ēvidēns, ntis adj apparent, evident

ēvigilō 🔟 v be wakeful; watch throughout the night; devise or study with careful attention

ēvinciō, vīnxī, vīnctum 🔟 v bind or wreathe round

ēvincō, vīcī, victum 🔟 v defeat utterly; prevail; persuade

ēviscerō 🔟 v disembowel; eviscerate

ēvītābilis, e adj avoidable

ēvītō 🔟 v shun, avoid

ēvocātī, ōrum mpl veterans again called to service

ēvocātor, ōris m one who orders out troops

ēvocō 🔟 v call out; summon; lure or entice out

ēvolō 🔟 v fly out; rush forth

ēvolvō, lvī, lūtum 🔟 v unroll, unfold; extricate; peruse; explain; roll out or away; wrench out, eject

ēvomō, muī 🔟 v vomit out

ēvulgō 🔟 v make public, divulge

ex (ē used before consonants) prep with abl out of, from; down from, off; by; after; on account of; in accordance with

　□ ~ **aequō** from the same level

　□ ~ **imprōvīsō/īnspērātō** unexpectedly

　□ ~ **itinere** out of the way, away from the road

　□ ~ **pauxillō** little by little

　□ ~ **mediō abeō** die

ex- ▸ also **exs-**

exāctiō, ōnis f method of levying taxes

exāctor, ōris m expeller; exactor; collector of taxes

exāctus, a, um adj exact, accurate

exacuō, cuī, ūtum 🔟 v make sharp or pointed; stimulate

exadvorsum adv opposite

exaedificō 🔟 v complete the building of, construct

exaequō 🔟 v equalize, make equal; regard as equal; be equal (to)

exaestuō 🔟 v boil up; seethe, rage

exaggerō 🔟 v heap up, accumulate; magnify

exagitō 🔟 v drive out; stir up; disturb continually; attack, scold; discuss

exāmen, inis nt swarm (of bees); crowd; apparatus or process of weighing, balance

exāminō 🔟 v weigh; consider, examine

examussim adv perfectly, exactly

exanimis, e adj, **exanimus, a, um** adj lifeless, dead

exanimō 🔟 v deprive of life; kill; alarm greatly; exhaust

exardēscō, arsī, arsum 🔟 v catch fire; blaze, flare up

exārēscō, ruī 🔟 v dry up

exarō 🔟 v plough or dig up; plough; note down (by scratching the wax on the tablets)

exasperō ① *v* roughen; irritate

exatiō ② *v* (also **exsatiō**) satisfy, satiate; glut

exauctōrō ① *v* release or dismiss from military service

exaudiō ④ *v* hear; comply with, heed

excēdō, essī, essum *v* go out or away; withdraw; digress; go beyond; die; leave; surpass; exceed

excellēns, ntis *adj* distinguished, excellent

excellentia, ae *f* superiority, excellence

excellō, luī, lsum ③ *v* be pre-eminent, excel

excelsus, a, um *adj* lofty; high; sublime

exceptiō, ōnis *f* exception, qualification

exceptō ① *v* take out, take up; inhale, take (to oneself)

excerpō, psī, ptum ③ *v* pick out; select

excessus, ūs *m* departure; death; digression

excidium, (i)ī *nt* military destruction

excidō, dī ③ *v* fall out; escape; be deprived of; lose control of one's senses; fall away, disappear

excīdō, īdī, īsum ③ *v* cut out or off, cut down; raze; destroy

excieō, cīvī, cītum ② *v*, **exciō** ④ *v* rouse; call out, send for; summon; evoke

excindō, idī, issum ③ *v* (also **exscindō**) demolish, destroy

excipiō, cēpī, ceptum ③ *v* exempt; take out; except; catch; receive; listen to; follow after

excitō ① *v* rouse up, wake up; raise, erect; arouse

exclāmātiō, ōnis *f* exclamation, saying

exclāmō ① *v* call or cry out; exclaim

exclūdō, ūsī, ūsum ③ *v* shut out, exclude; hatch; prevent

excōgitō ① *v* think out, devise

excolō, luī, ultum ③ *v* improve; develop; honour

excommunicatio, onis *f* [LM] excommunication

excoquō, coxī, coctum ③ *v* boil; temper (by heat); boil away; dry up, parch

excors, rdis *adj* silly, stupid

excrēmentum, ī *nt* excrement; spittle, mucus

excrēscō, ēvī, ētum ③ *v* grow out or up; grow

excruciō ① *v* torture; torment

excubiae, ārum *fpl* watching; watch, guard

excubitor, ōris *m* watchman, sentinel

excubō, buī, bitum ① *v* sleep in the open; keep watch; be attentive

excūdō, ūdī, ūsum ③ *v* strike out; forge; fashion

excurrō, (cu)currī, cursum ③ *v* run out; make an excursion; sally; extend; project

excursiō, ōnis *f* running forth; sally

excursus, ūs *m* running out; excursion; sally, sudden raid

excūsābilis, e *adj* excusable

excūsātiō, ōnis *f* excuse

excūsō ① *v* excuse; plead as an excuse; absolve

excutiō, ussī, ussum 3 *v* shake out or off; cast out; search, examine

execō, ectum 1 *v* (also **exsecō**) cut out or away; castrate

execrābilis, e *adj* (also **exsecrābilis**) accursed, detestable

execrātiō, ōnis *f* (also **exsecrātiō**) imprecation, curse

execror 1 *v dep* (also **exsecror**) curse; detest

exedō, ēsse, ēdī, ēsum *v ir* eat up, consume; hollow

exemplar, āris *nt* model, pattern, example; copy

exemplum, ī *nt* sample; example; precedent; warning; punishment; portrait; copy

exenterō 1 *v* disembowel

exeō, īre, īī, itum *v ir* go out or away; march out; escape; die; perish; rise; exceed

exequiae, ārum *fpl* (also **exsequiae**) funeral procession

exequor, execūtus sum 3 *v dep* (also **exsequor**) follow (to the grave); pursue; accomplish; relate; pursue with vengeance or punishment

exerceō 2 *v* drill, exercise, train; employ; practise; administer; cultivate; harass

exercitātiō, ōnis *f* exercise, practice

exercitātus, a, um *adj* practised, skilled; troubled

exercitium, (i)ī *nt* exercise

exercitō 1 *v* practise

exercitus, ūs *m* army; swarm, flock

exerō, rtum 3 *v* (also **exserō**) stretch forth; thrust out, lay bare

exēsus, a, um *adj* porous

exhālō 1 *v* breathe out; evaporate; die

exhauriō, hausī, haustum 4 *v* drain; empty; drink up; exhaust; see through to the end

exhērēs, ēdis *adj* disinherited

exhibeō 2 *v* present; furnish; exhibit; produce

exhorrēscō, ruī 3 *v* be terrified; tremble at

exhortor 1 *v dep* exhort, encourage, incite

exiccō 1 *v* (also **exsiccō**) dry up; empty (a vessel)

exigō, ēgī, āctum 3 *v* drive out; thrust; exact; finish; examine, weigh; make to conform with

exiguitās, ātis *f* scarcity, smallness of size

exiguus, a, um *adj* scanty, small, petty, short, poor

exiliō, luī 4 *v* (also **exsiliō**) spring forth, leap up

exilis, e *adj* small, thin; poor

exilium, (i)ī *nt* (also **exsilium**) exile

eximius, a, um *adj* select, extraordinary, excellent, fine

eximō, ēmī, ēmptum 3 *v* take out, remove; free, release

exinde, exim, exin *adv* thence; after that; then

existimātiō, ōnis *f* judgment; opinion; reputation; credit

existimō, existumō 1 *v* judge, value, esteem, think

existō, tī, itum 3 *v* (also **exsistō**) step forth, appear;

arise; become; prove to be

exitiābilis, **exitiālis**, **e** *adj* destructive, deadly

exitiōsus, **a**, **um** *adj* destructive, pernicious, deadly

exitium, **(i)ī** *nt* ruin, mischief; death

exitus, **ūs** *m* egress, departure; end; outlet; result; death

exoculō ① *v* knock the eyes out from

exolēscō, **ēvī**, **ētum** ③ *v* grow up; grow out of use; die out

exolvō, **lvī**, **lūtum** ③ *v* (also **exsolvō**) set free; pay; throw off; release; perform

exonerō ① *v* unload, disburden, discharge

exoptō ① *v* long for

exōrābilis, **e** *adj* capable of being moved by entreaty

exōrdior, **ōrsus sum** ④ *v dep* begin, commence

exōrdium, **(i)ī** *nt* beginning, introduction, preface

exorior, **ortus sum** ④ *v dep* arise; begin; spring up; cheer up

exōrnō ① *v* furnish with, adorn, embellish; dress up

exōrō ① *v* obtain by entreaty; win over by entreaty

exors, **rtis** *adj* (also **exsors**) without share in, exempt from lottery

exōsculor ① *v dep* kiss fondly

exōsus, **a**, **um** *adj* hating

exōticus, **a**, **um** *adj* foreign, exotic

expallēscō, **luī** ③ *v* turn very pale

expandō, **ndī**, **passum/ pānsum** ③ *v* spread out, expand;

expound

expatior ① *v dep* (also **exspatior**) wander from the course; spread out

expatrō ① *v* waste in dissoluteness, squander

expavēscō, **ī** ③ *v* become frightened

expectātiō, **ōnis** *f* (also **exspectātiō**) expectation, expectancy

expectō ① *v* (also **exspectō**) await, expect; anticipate; hope for

expediō ④ *v* extricate; make ready; free

◻ **expedit** ④ *v impers* it is profitable *or* expedient

expedītiō, **ōnis** *f* expedition, campaign

expedītus, **a**, **um** *adj* free, easy; ready; ready for action; without baggage; unencumbered; dealt with, cleared up

expellō, **pulī**, **pulsum** ③ *v* expel; banish; reject

expendō, **ndī**, **ēnsum** ③ *v* pay; pay out; weigh, judge; pay a penalty

expergēfaciō, **fēcī**, **factum** ③ *v* arouse, awake

expergīscor, **rrēctus sum** ③ *v dep* awake; bestir oneself

experiēns, **ntis** *adj* active, enterprising

experientia, **ae** *f*, **experīmentum**, **ī** *nt* trial, experiment; experience

experior, **pertus sum** ④ *v dep* make trial of, put to the test, experience, find; attempt

expers, **rtis** *adj with gen* destitute of, without; lacking experience;

e

immune (from)

expertus, a, um *adj* well-proved, tested

expēs *adj* (also **exspēs**) nom. sg. only hopeless

expetō, īvī/iī, ītum ③ *v* ask for; desire; aspire to; demand; happen; fall on (a person)

expiātiō, ōnis *f* atonement, expiation, purification

expīlō ① *v* plunder, rob, despoil

expiō ① *v* atone for, expiate; make amends for; avert by expiatory rites

expīrō ① *v* (also **exspīrō**) breathe out; exhale; expire; die; cease

expiscor ① *v dep* try to fish out (information)

explānō ① *v* explain

expleō, ēvī, ētum ② *v* fill out or up, complete; finish; satisfy; satiate; fulfil, discharge

explicō, cāvī/cuī, cātum/ citum ① *v* unfold; display; disentangle; exhibit; spread out

explōdō, ōsī, ōsum ③ *v* drive (an actor) off the stage; reject

explōrātor, ōris *m* spy, scout

explōrō ① *v* reconnoitre; test, try out; investigate

expoliō¹ ④ *v* polish; refine

expoliō² ① *v* (also **exspoliō**) plunder

expōnō, posuī, positum ③ *v* set out; expose; disembark; publish; exhibit, explain

exportō ① *v* export, carry out

exposcō, poposcī ③ *v* ask for, demand, request; demand the surrender of

expostulātiō, ōnis *f* complaint,

protest

expostulō ① *v* demand, call for; remonstrate, complain about

exprimō, pressī, pressum ③ *v* squeeze, squeeze out; copy, portray; express; extort

exprobrātiō, ōnis *f* reproaching, reproach

exprobrō ① *v* bring up as a reproach

exprōmō, mpsī, mptum ③ *v* bring out; disclose, reveal

expugnābilis, e *adj* open to assault

expugnātiō, ōnis *f* taking by storm

expugnātor, ōris *m* conqueror

expugnāx, ācis *adj* effectual in overcoming resistance

expugnō ① *v* take by assault, storm; conquer; plunder; achieve; persuade

expuō, ūtum ③ *v* (also **exspuō**) spit out; eject; rid oneself of

expurgō ① *v* cleanse, purify; exculpate

exquīrō, īsīvī, īsītum ③ *v* inquire into; look for

exquīsītus, a, um *adj* meticulous; recherché, choice, special

exrādīcitus *adv* from the very roots, utterly and completely

exs- ▸ **ex-** without the 's'

exsanguis, e *adj* bloodless; pale, wan; feeble

exsatiō ① *v* satisfy, satiate; glut

exsaturābilis, e *adj* capable of being satiated

exsaturō ① *v* satisfy, sate, glut

exscindō, idī, issum ③ *v* demolish, destroy

exscrībō, psī, ptum ③ *v* copy, write out

exsecō, secuī, sectum ① *v* cut out *or* away; castrate

exsecrābilis, e *adj* accursed, detestable

exsecrātiō, ōnis *f* imprecation, curse

exsecror ① *v dep* curse; detest

exsequiae, ārum *fpl* funeral procession

exsequor, secūtus sum ③ *v dep* follow (to the grave); pursue; accomplish; relate; pursue with vengeance *or* punishment

exserō, ruī, rtum ③ *v* stretch forth; thrust out, lay bare

exsiccō ① *v* dry up; empty (a vessel)

exsiliō, luī ④ *v* (also **exiliō**) spring forth, leap up

exsilium, (i)ī *nt* exile

exsistō, stitī, stitum *v* step forth, appear; arise; become; prove to be

exsolvō, lvī, lūtum ③ *v* set free; pay; throw off; release; perform

exsomnis, e *adj* wakeful, vigilant

exsors, rtis *adj* without share in, exempt from lottery

exspatior ① *v dep* wander from the course; spread out

exspectātiō, ōnis *f* expectation, expectancy

exspectō ① *v* await, expect; anticipate; hope for

exspēs *adj* (*nom. sg. only*) hopeless

exspīrō ① *v* breathe out; exhale; expire; die; cease

exspoliō ① *v* plunder

exspuō, puī, ūtum ③ *v* spit out; eject; rid oneself of

externō ① *v* terrify, madden

exstillō ① *v* trickle away, dissolve; fall in drops

exstimulō ① *v* goad; stimulate

exstīnctiō, ōnis *f* extinction

exstinguō, īnxī, īnctum ③ *v* quench, extinguish; kill; destroy

exstō ① *v* stand out *or* forth; project; be visible; exist, be on record

exstruō, ūxī, ūctum ③ *v* pile up; build up, raise

exsūdō ① *v* exude; sweat out

exsul, lis *m/f* exile

exsulō ① *v* be an exile

exsultātiō, ōnis *f* exultation, joy

exsultō ① *v* jump about; let oneself go; exult

exsuperābilis, e *adj* able to be overcome

exsuperō ① *v* excel; overtop; surpass; overpower

exsurgō, surrēxī ③ *v* rise, stand up; take action

exsuscitō ① *v* awaken; kindle; (fig) stir up, excite

exta, ōrum *ntpl* bowels, entrails

extemplō *adv* immediately, forthwith

extendō, ndī, entum/ēnsum ③ *v* stretch out, extend; enlarge; prolong; continue

extenuō ① *v* make thin; diminish

extergeō, rsī, rsum ② *v* wipe clean

exterminō ① *v* banish, expel; dismiss

externō ① v (also **exsternō**)
terrify, madden

externus, a, um adj external;
foreign, strange

exterreō ② v strike with terror,
scare

exter(us), era, erum adj outer,
external, foreign
■ **exterior** comp
■ **extrēmus, extimus** sup

extimēscō, muī ③ v take fright,
be alarmed; dread

extimulō ① v (also **exstimulō**)
goad; stimulate

extimus, a, um adj [sup of
exter] uttermost, utmost,
extreme, last

extinguō, īnxī, īnctum ③
v (also **exstinguō**) quench,
extinguish; kill; destroy

extō ① v (also **exstō**) stand out
or forth; project; be visible; exist,
be on record

extollō ③ v raise; lift up; extol,
praise, advance

extorqueō, rsī, rtum ② v twist
or wrench out; extort

extorris, e adj exiled

extortor, ōris m robber

extrā prep with acc outside, without;
out of, beyond; except; adv outside,
without; out of, beyond; except

extrahō, āxī, actum ③ v draw
out, extract; prolong

extrāneus, a, um adj external,
extraneous, foreign; not belonging
to one's family or household

extraordinārius, a, um
adj supplementary; special;
immoderate

extrārius, a, um adj situated
outside; extraneous; not
belonging to one's household,
strange

extrēmum, ī nt limit, outside;
end

extrēmus, a, um adj [sup of
exter] uttermost, utmost,
extreme, last

extrīcō ① v disentangle, extricate,
free

extrīnsecus adv from without;
on the outside

extrūdō, ūsī, ūsum ③ v thrust
out; drive out

extruō, ūxī, ūctum ③ v (also
exstruō) pile up; build up, raise

extundō, udī, ūsum v beat
or strike out; produce with effort;
extort

exturbō ① v thrust out; divorce;
disturb

exūberō ① v surge or gush up; be
abundant, be fruitful

exūdō ① v (also **exsūdō**) exude;
sweat out

exul, lis m/f (also **exsul**) exile

exulcerō ① v make sore or raw;
exasperate, aggravate

exulō ① v (also **exsulō**) be an
exile

exultātiō, ōnis f (also
exsultātiō) exultation, joy

exultō ① v (also **exsultō**) jump
about; let oneself go; exult

exululō ① v invoke with howls

exundātiō, ōnis f overflowing

exundō ① v gush forth; overflow
with

exuō, uī, ūtum ③ v put off; doff;
strip; deprive of; lay aside; cast off

exuperābilis, e *adj* (also **exsuperābilis**) able to be overcome

exuperō ⬚ *v* (also **exsuperō**) excel; overtop; surpass; overpower

exurgeō, rsī ② *v* squeeze out

exurgō, ī ③ *v* (also **exsurgō**) rise, stand up; take action

exūrō, ussī, ustum ③ *v* burn up; destroy; parch, dry up

exuviae, ārum *fpl* things stripped off; spoils, booty; something belonging to a person, serving as a memento

Ff

faba, ae *f* bean

fābella, ae *f* story, fable; play

faber¹, brī *m* artisan, workman; smith; carpenter

faber², bra, brum *adj* of the craftsman or his work

fabrica, ae *f* art, craft

fabricātor, ōris *m* maker, fashioner

fabricō ⬚ *v* (also **fabricor**) fashion, forge, shape; build, construct

fabrīlis, e *adj* of or belonging to a workman; of a metal-worker, carpenter or builder

fābula, ae *f* story; tale; fable; drama, play
 □ **fābulae!** rubbish!

fābulor ⬚ *v dep* talk, converse, chat; invent a story

fābulōsus, a, um *adj* storied, fabulous; celebrated in story

facessō, s(īv)ī/sīī, ītum ③ *v* do; perpetrate; go away

facētiae, ārum *fpl* wit, joke

facētus, a, um *adj* witty, humorous; clever, adept; elegant, fine

faciēs, iēī *f* face, look, pretence; appearance, beauty

facilis, e *adj* easy; pliable; gentle; courteous; good-natured, affable

facilitās, ātis *f* easiness, facility; readiness; good nature, courteousness, affability

facinorōsus, a, um *adj* doing wrong, criminal, wicked

facinus, oris *nt* deed, crime, outrage

faciō, fēcī, factum ③ *v* make; do; fashion; cause; compose; practise; commit; render; value
 □ ~ **lucrī** make a profit
 □ ~ **minoris** consider of less importance
 ■ **fac ut** *with subj* see to it that ... ! please ... !

factiō, ōnis *f* faction, party

factiōsus, a, um *adj* factious, seditious, turbulent

factitō ⬚ *v* do frequently; practise

factum, ī *nt* deed, exploit

facultās, ātis *f* capability; possibility; means; opportunity; skill; quantity available; means

fācundia, ae *f* eloquence

fācundus, a, um *adj* eloquent

faecula, ae *f* lees of wine (used as a condiment or medicine)

faenebris, bre *adj* pertaining to usury; lent at interest

faenerātiō, ōnis f usury, money-lending

faenerātor, ōris m usurer, money-lender

faeniculum, ī nt fennel, especially used as a condiment or medicament

faenīlia, ium ntpl place for storing hay, barn

faenisex, cis m man who cuts hay, mower

faenum, ī nt hay

faenus, eris/oris nt interest; profit; gain
□ **faenore** on loan, at interest

faex, cis f sediment, dregs; dregs of the people

fāgus, ī f beech-tree

fala, ae f wooden siege-tower

falārica, ae f a heavy missile (thrown generally by a catapult)

falcārius, (i)ī m scythe-maker

falcātus, a, um adj armed with scythes; sickle-shaped, curved

falcifer, era, erum adj carrying a scythe; scythed

Falernum, ī nt Falernian wine

fallācia, ae f deceit, trick, stratagem

fallāx, ācis adj deceitful, fallacious; spurious

fallō, fefellī, falsum ③ v cheat, deceive; disappoint; escape notice

falsiparēns, ntis adj having a pretended father

falsus, a, um adj false; deceiving; deceived; spurious
□ **falsō** wrongly, mistakenly; lyingly

falx, cis f sickle; scythe; curved blade

fāma, ae f rumour; fame; renown; ill repute; news

famēlicus, a, um adj starved, famished, hungry

famēs, mis f hunger; famine; craving

familia, ae f household, all persons under the control of one man, whether relations, freedmen, or slaves; family; servants or slaves belonging to one master; estate

familiāris, e adj of the household; familiar; intimate; very friendly; as noun m/f acquaintance, friend

familiāritās, ātis f familiarity, intimacy, close friendship

fāmōsus, a, um adj famed, renowned; infamous, notorious; slanderous, libellous

famulāris, e adj of slaves, servile

famulātus, ūs m state of being a slave, servitude

famulor ① v dep be a servant, attend

famulus, a, um adj servile, subject
■ **famula, ae** f female slave; maid-servant
■ **famulus, ī** m slave, servant; attendant

fānāticus, a, um adj fanatic, frantic; belonging to a temple

fandus, a, um adj that may be spoken; proper, lawful

fānum, ī nt sanctuary, temple

fār, farris nt husked wheat, grain

farciō, rsī, rtum ④ v stuff, cram

farctum, ī nt stuffing, filling, insides

farrāgō, inis f mixed fodder; a hotch-potch

farreus, **a**, **um** *adj* made from grain
■ **farreum**, **ī** *nt* cake made from grain

fars, **tis** *f* stuffing, filling, insides

fās *nt indec* divine law; right; obligation

fascia, **ae** *f* band; puttees

fasciculus, **ī** *m* bundle, packet; bunch (of flowers)

fascinō ① *v* cast a spell on, bewitch

fascis, **is** *m* bundle, parcel
■ **fascēs** *pl* bundles of rods, carried before the highest magistrates of Rome, usually with an axe bound up in the middle of them; the power or office of a magistrate

fāstī, **ōrum** *mpl* list of festivals; calendar; list of consuls who gave their names to the year

fastīdiō ④ *v* disdain; be scornful; feel aversion to, be squeaming

fastīdiōsus, **a**, **um** *adj* squeamish; exacting, fussy; disdainful; nauseating

fastīdium, **(i)ī** *nt* squeamishness, loathing; scornful contempt; pride; fastidiousness

fastīgium, **(i)ī** *nt* slope, declivity; gable, roof; sharp point, tip; summit; height; depth; highest rank, dignity

fastus, **ūs** *m* contempt; haughtiness

fāstus, **a**, **um** *adj*
□ **diēs ~** day on which the courts could sit

fātālis, **e** *adj* destined, fated; fatal
■ **fātāliter** *adv* by destiny or fate

fateor, **fassus sum** ② *v dep* confess; acknowledge

fātidicus, **a**, **um** *adj* prophetic

fātifer, **era**, **erum** *adj* deadly; fatal

fatīgō ① *v* weary, tire, fatigue; harass; importune; overcome

fātiloquus, **a**, **um** *adj* prophetic

fatīscō ③ *v*, **fatīscor** ③ *v dep* gape, crack; grow weak or exhausted

fātum, **ī** *nt* fate, destiny; doom; ill-fate; death

fatuus, **a**, **um** *adj* foolish, silly; idiotic

faucēs, **ium** *fpl* throat; narrow entrance; defile; gulf, abyss

Faunus, **ī** *m* a rustic god

faustus, **a**, **um** *adj* favourable; auspicious; lucky, prosperous

fautor, **ōris** *m* patron; admirer; supporter

faveō, **fāvī**, **fautum** ② *v with dat* favour, befriend; back up

favilla, **ae** *f* ashes, embers

Favōnius, **(i)ī** *m* west wind

favor, **ōris** *m* favour, good-will; bias, applause

favus, **ī** *m* honey-comb

fax, **facis** *f* torch; firebrand; love-flame; fire, torment

faxim *old pf subj of* ▶ **faciō**

faxō *old fut pf of* ▶ **faciō**

febrīculōsus, **a**, **um** *adj* prone to fever, fever-ridden

febris, **is** *f* fever, attack of fever

Februārius, **(i)ī** *m* February

fēcī ▶ **faciō**

fēcunditās, **ātis** *f* fertility, fecundity

fēcundus, **a**, **um** *adj* fruitful,

fertile; abundant

fel, fellis nt gall, bile; poison; bitterness, venom

fēlīcitās, ātis f good fortune, felicity

fēlīx, īcis adj fruitful; lucky, happy, fortunate; successful

fellō ▣ v suck

fēmella, ae f woman, girl

fēmina, ae f female, woman

fēmineus, a, um adj womanly, feminine, womanish, effeminate

femur, feminis/femoris nt thigh

fēn- ▸ **faen-**

fenestra, ae f window; loop-hole

fera, ae f wild beast

fērālis, e adj funereal; deadly, fatal ■ **Fērālia, ium** ntpl festival of the dead

ferāx, ācis adj fruitful, fertile

ferculum, ī nt frame or stretcher for carrying things; dish; course (at dinner)

ferē adv nearly, almost; about; in general; with negatives hardly ever

ferentārius, (i)ī m light-armed soldier, skirmisher

feretrum, ī nt bier

fēriae, ārum fpl holiday

fēriātus, a, um adj keeping holiday, at leisure

ferīna, ae f game, flesh of wild animals

ferīnus, a, um adj of wild beasts

feriō ▣ v strike, knock; hit; slay, kill; strike (a bargain); enter into or conclude (a treaty)

feritās, ātis f wildness, savageness

fermē ▸ **ferē**

ferō, ferre, tulī, lātum v ir carry; bring; bear away; plunder; bear with; lead; produce, bring forth; endure; receive; propose; exhibit □ **ferunt** they say □ **fertur** it is said

ferōcia, ae f fierceness, ferocity; insolence

ferōcitās, ātis f fierceness, savageness; excessive spirits; aggressiveness

ferōx, ōcis adj wild, bold; warlike; cruel; defiant, arrogant

ferrāmentum, ī nt iron tool

ferrāria, ae f iron mine

ferrātilis, e adj clad in chains

ferrātus, a, um adj bound or covered with iron; with iron points or studs

ferreus, a, um adj of iron, iron; hard, cruel; firm

ferriterium, (i)ī nt place of those put in irons

ferritrībāx, ācis adj wearing out fetters

ferrūgineus, a, um adj of the colour of iron-rust, sombre

ferrūgō, inis f iron-rust; colour of iron-rust; dusky colour

ferrum, ī nt iron; sword; any tool of iron; weapon

fertilis, e adj fruitful, fertile; abundant

fertilitās, ātis f fruitfulness, fertility

ferus, a, um adj wild, savage; cruel ■ **∼, ī** m wild beast

fervefaciō, fēcī, factum ▣ v make intensely hot, heat, boil

fervēns, ntis adj boiling hot,

burning; inflamed, impetuous

ferveō, rbuī ② *v* be intensely hot; boil; seethe, be roused

fervēscō ③ *v* grow hot

fervidus, a, um *adj* boiling hot, fiery; torrid; roused; hot-blooded

fervor, ōris *m* heat; ardour, passion

fessus, a, um *adj* wearied, tired; feeble

festīnātiō, ōnis *f* haste, speed, hurry

festīnō ① *v* hasten; hurry

festīvus, a, um *adj* lively, festive

fēstum, ī *nt* holiday, festival; feast-day

fēstus, a, um *adj* festal; solemn, merry

fētiālēs, ium *mpl* Roman college of priests who represented the Roman people in their dealings with other nations

fētidus, a, um *adj* foul-smelling, stinking

fētūra, ae *f* bearing, breeding; young off-spring, brood

fētus¹, ūs *m* birth; offspring; produce

fētus², a, um *adj* pregnant with; fertile; full (of); having newly brought forth

fibra, ae *f* fibre, filament; entrails; leaf, blade (of grasses, *etc.*)

fībula, ae *f* clasp, buckle, brooch

fictilis, e *adj* made of earthenware ■ **fictile, is** *nt* earthenware vessel or statue

fictor, ōris *m* one who devises or makes

fictus, a, um *adj* feigned, false; counterfeit

fīculneus, a, um *f* of a fig-tree
■ **fīculnea, ae** *f* [LM] fig-tree

fīcus, ī/ūs *f* fig-tree

fidēlis, e *adj* faithful; loyal; trustworthy; dependable

fidēlitās, ātis *f* faithfulness, fidelity

fīdēns, ntis *adj* confident; bold

fidēs¹, ēī *f* faith, trust, confidence; belief, credence; loyalty; honesty; allegiance; promise; security; protection

fidēs², fidis *f* [usu. pl. **fidēs, ium**] lyre

fidicen, inis *m* lyre-player

fidicina, ae *f* female lyre-player

fīdō, fīsus sum ③ *v semi-dep with dat or abl* trust (in), have confidence (in)

fidūcia, ae *f* trust, confidence; boldness, courage
□ **fidūciā** on the responsibility (of); trusting in

fidūciārius, a, um *adj* holding on trust; held on trust

fīdus, a, um *adj* trusty, faithful, loyal

figlīnae, ārum *fpl* pottter's workshop, pottery

figlīnum, ī *nt* earthenware pottery

figō, īxī, īxum ③ *v* fix, fasten; transfix; establish

figulus, ī *m* potter

figūra, ae *f* shape, figure, form; image

figūrō ① *v* form, fashion, shape

fīlia, ae *f* daughter

fīliola, ae *f* little daughter

fīliolus, ī *m* little son

fīlius, (i)ī *m* son

filix, cis f fern, bracken

fīlum, ī nt thread; cord; string; texture

fimum, ī nt, **fimus, ī** m dung, excrement

findō, fidī, fissum ③ v cleave, split; divide

fingō, finxī, fictum ③ v shape, form, fashion, make; contrive; invent; make a pretence of, deceive

finiō ④ v limit; define; end, finish; mark out the boundaries of

finis, is m/f boundary, limit; end; purpose; death
■ **finēs, ium** pl country, territory

finitimus, a, um adj bordering on, adjoining, neighbouring

fīō, fierī, factus sum v ir semi-dep be made or done; happen; become; take place

firmāmen, inis nt (poet), **firmāmentum, ī** nt support, prop, mainstay

firmitās, ātis f firmness, strength

firmiter adv firmly, strongly; steadfastly

firmitūdō, inis f stability; strength

firmō ① v make firm or steady; strengthen; harden; confirm; establish; encourage

firmus, a, um adj firm; strong; steady; valid; bold

fiscella, ae f, **fiscina, ae** f small wicker-basket

fiscus, ī m money-bag, purse; imperial exchequer

fissilis, e adj easily split; split

fistula, ae f pipe, tube; shepherd's pipe

fīsus pple from ▶ **fīdō**

fixus, a, um adj fixed fast, immovable; fitted with

flābra, ōrum ntpl gusts or blasts of wind

flaccidus, a, um adj flaccid, flabby

flagellum, ī nt whip, scourge; thong; vine-shoot

flāgitātiō, ōnis f importunate request, demand

flāgitātor, oris m one who makes pestering demands, demander

flāgitiōsus, a, um adj disgraceful, scandalous; infamous

flāgitium, (i)ī nt shameful or base action; crime; scandal, disgrace

flāgitō ① v demand importunely; ask repeatedly (for)

flagrāns, ntis adj blazing, glowing; ardent, passionate

flagrantia, ae f blaze

flagrō ① v blaze, flame, burn; be inflamed; be excited

flāmen¹, inis m priest of one particular deity

flāmen², inis nt blast; gale, wind

flamma, ae f blaze, flame; ardour; fire of love; object of love

flammeus, a, um adj flaming, fiery; fiery red
■ **flammeum, ī** nt flame-coloured bridal veil

flammō ① v inflame, set on fire; excite

flātus, ūs m blowing; snorting; breath; breeze

flāveō ② v be yellow or gold-coloured

flāvēscō ③ *v* turn yellow or gold

flāvus, a, um *adj* yellow, flaxen, gold-coloured, blonde

flēbilis, e *adj* lamentable; doleful; tearful

flectō, xī, xum ③ *v* bend, bow, curve, turn; prevail on, soften

fleō, ēvī, ētum ② *v* weep, cry; weep for

flētus, ūs *m* weeping; tears

flexanimus, a, um *adj* persuasive

flexibilis, e *adj* flexible, pliant

flexilis, e *adj* pliant, pliable, supple

flexus, ūs *m* turning, winding; swerve; bend; turning point

flō ① *v* blow; sound; cast (by blowing)

floccus, ī *m* tuft of wool
  □ **nōn floccī faciō** consider of no importance

flōreō ② *v* blossom; flourish; be in one's prime

flōrēscō ③ *v* (begin to) blossom; increase in physical vigour or renown

flōreus, a, um *adj* flowery

flōridulus, a, um *adj* flowery, bright

flōridus, a, um *adj* blooming, flowery; florid

flōrifer, era, erum *adj* flowery

flōs, ōris *m* blossom, flower; youthful prime

flōsculus, ī *m* little flower, floweret; the best of anything, the 'flower'

fluctuō ① *v*, **fluctuor** ① *v dep* rise in waves, surge; float; be in a state of agitation; waver

fluctus, ūs *m* flood; wave, billow

fluentisonus, a, um *adj* resounding with the noise of the waves

fluentum, ī *nt* stream; river

fluidus, a, um *adj* liquid; soft, feeble

fluitō ① *v* float; flow; waver

flūmen, inis *nt* stream, river
  □ **adversō flūmine** against the current
  □ **secundō flūmine** with the current

fluō, ūxī, ūxum ③ *v* flow; stream; emanate; proceed (from); fall gradually; hang loosely

fluviālis, e *adj* river...

fluvius, (i)ī *m* river; running water

fluxus, a, um *adj* flowing; fluid; loose; transient; frail; dissolute

focilō ① *v* revive

focus, ī *m* fireplace, hearth; family, household

fodiō, fōdī, fossum ③ *v* dig, dig up; stab

foederātus, a, um *adj* allied (to Rome)

foeditās, ātis *f* foulness; ugliness; shame

foedō ① *v* defile; pollute; disfigure, disgrace, sully

foedus¹, eris *nt* league, treaty; agreement
  □ **~ feriō** enter into or conclude a treaty

foedus², a, um *adj* foul, filthy; ugly; base, vile; abominable

foen- ▶ **faen-**

foenebris, bre *adj* pertaining to usury; lent at interest

foenerātiō, ōnis *f* usury, money-lending

foenerātor, ōris *m* usurer, money-lender

foenīlia, ium *ntpl* place for storing hay, barn

foenum, ī *nt* hay

foenus, eris *nt* interest; profit; gain

folium, (i)ī *nt* leaf

folliculus, ī *m* bag or sack; pod; shell

follis, is *m* pair of bellows; bag; scrotum

fōmentum, ī *nt* poultice; alleviation, consolation

fōmes, itis *m* chips of wood, *etc.* for kindling a fire

fōns, ntis *m* spring, fountain; (fig) source; principal cause

fontānus, a, um *adj* of a spring

for 🔟 *v dep* speak, talk; say

forāmen, inis *nt* aperture, hole

forās *adv* out of doors, abroad, forth, out

forceps, ipis *f* pair of tongs, pincers

fore *infin* be about to be

forēnsis, e *adj* public; pertaining to the courts

forfex, icis *f* pair of shears; tongs, pincers

foris *adv* out of doors; abroad

foris, oris *f* (often pl. **forēs, um**) door, gate; opening, entrance

fōrma, ae *f* form, figure, shape; mould; pattern; sort; beauty

formīca, ae *f* ant

formīcātiō, ōnis *f* sensation of ants crawling over the skin

formīdābilis, e *adj* terrifying

formīdō¹, inis *f* fear, terror,
dread; a thing which frightens, bogey

formīdō² 🔟 *v* dread; be afraid of

formīdolōsus, formīdulōsus, a, um *adj* fearful; terrible

fōrmō 🔟 *v* shape, fashion, form; model

fōrmōsus, a, um *adj* beautiful, handsome

fōrmula, ae *f* set form of words, formula; principle, rule, legal process

fornāx, ācis *f* furnace, oven

fornicātus, a, um *adj* arched, vaulted

fornix, cis *m* arch, vault; brothel

forō 🔟 *v* bore, pierce

fors, rtis *f* fortune, chance; accident

forsan, forsit, forsitan, fortasse *adv* perhaps

forte *adv* by chance; as luck would have it

fortis, e *adj* strong, powerful; hardy; courageous; valiant; manful

fortitūdō, inis *f* strength; firmness; courage, valour; manfulness

fortuītus, a, um *adj* casual; accidental

fortūna, ae *f* fortune; chance; luck; prosperity; condition; fate, destiny

■ **fortūnae, ārum** *pl* possessions

fortūnātus, a, um *adj* lucky, happy, fortunate; rich

forulī, ōrum *mpl* bookcase

forum, ī *nt* market; court of justice; forum (at Rome)

forus, **ī** *m* gangway in a ship; row of benches erected for spectators at games

fossa, **ae** *f* ditch, trench

fossor, **ōris** *m* one who digs the ground

fovea, **ae** *f* pit; pitfall

foveō, **fōvī**, **fōtum** ② *v* keep warm; favour; cherish; maintain, foster

frāga, **ōrum** *ntpl* wild strawberries

fragilis, **e** *adj* brittle, frail; impermanent

fragilitās, **ātis** *f* brittleness, frailty

fragmen, **inis** *nt* fragment
■ **fragmina**, **um** *pl* fragments, ruins; chips

fragmentum, **ī** *nt* fragment

fragor, **ōris** *m* crash; noise

fragōsus, **a**, **um** *adj* brittle; ragged

frāgrō ① *v* smell strongly

frangō, **ēgī**, **āctum** ③ *v* break, dash to pieces, smash; crush; weaken; wear out; vanquish; break in

frāter, **tris** *m* brother; cousin; ⟨LM⟩ monk, religious brother

frāternus, **a**, **um** *adj* brotherly, fraternal; friendly

fraudō ① *v* cheat; defraud; steal

fraudulentus, **a**, **um** *adj* swindling

fraus, **dis** *f* deceit, fraud; crime; responsibility for an action

fraxinus, **ī** *f* ash-tree; spear or javelin of ash

frēgī ▶ **frangō**

fremitus, **ūs** *m* roaring; shouting; clashing; muttering; loud murmur or buzz of applause, *etc.*

fremō, **muī** ③ *v* roar; growl; rage; murmur; clamour for

fremor, **ōris** *m* low, confused noise, murmur

frendeō, **frēsum** ② *v*, **frendō** ③ *v* gnash the teeth, grind up small

frēnō ① *v* bridle; curb

frēnum, **ī** *nt* bridle, bit; check

frequēns, **ntis** *adj* frequent; usual, general; crowded; populous

frequenter *adv* often, frequently; in crowds

frequentia, **ae** *f* frequency; crowd; abundance of persons *or* things

frequentō ① *v* frequent; repeat often; haunt; throng; crowd; celebrate

fretum, **ī** *nt*, **fretus**, **ūs** *m* strait, narrow sea; sea

frētus, **a**, **um** *adj with abl* relying upon, trusting to

fricō, **fricuī**, **frictum** ① *v* rub, chafe

frīgeō ② *v* be cold; lack vigour; have a cold reception

frīgēscō, **īxī** ③ *v* become cold

frīgidārium, **(i)ī** *nt* cooling room

frīgidulus, **a**, **um** *adj* chilly, cold

frīgidus, **a**, **um** *adj* cold, cool, chilly; dull; torpid
■ **frīgida**, **ae** *f* cold water, cold bath

frīgus, **oris** *nt* cold, coldness; frost, winter

fringilla, **ae** *f* a songbird, perhaps the chaffinch

frit *nt indec* a tiny particle, perhaps the grain at the top of an ear of corn

fritillus, **ī** *m* dice-box

fritinniō 4 *v* chirp, twitter

frīvolus, **a**, **um** *adj* frivolous, trifling; silly; worthless; trashy

frondātor, **ōris** *m* pruner

frondeō 2 *v* be in leaf, become leavy

frondēscō, **duī** 3 *v* become leafy, shoot

frondeus, **a**, **um** *adj* leafy

frondōsus, **a**, **um** *adj* leafy, abounding in foliage

frōns¹, **ndis** *f* leafy branches; foliage, leaves

frōns², **ntis** *f* forehead; brow; foremost part of anything

frūctuōsus, **a**, **um** *adj* fruitful; profitable

frūctus¹ *pple from* ▶ **fruor**

frūctus², **ūs** *m* fruit, crops; profit

frūgālitās, **ātis** *f* thrift, sober habits, self-restraint

frūgī *adj indec* honest, worthy; virtuous; thrifty

☐ **∼ sum** do one's duty, do the right thing

frūgifer, **era**, **erum** *adj* fruit-bearing, fertile

frūmentārius, **a**, **um** *adj of or* concerned with corn

☐ **rēs frūmentāria** corn supply

frūmentātiō, **ōnis** *f* the collecting of corn; foraging

frūmentātor, **ōris** *m* forager

frūmentor 1 *v dep* forage

frūmentum, **ī** *nt* corn, grain

frūnīscor, **frūnītus sum** 3 *v dep* enjoy, have the pleasure of

fruor, **frūctus/fruitus sum** 3 *v* dep with abl enjoy, profit by

frūstrā *adv* in vain, to no purpose

frūstrātiō, **ōnis** *f* deceiving, disappointment

frūstror 1 *v dep* disappoint, frustrate; deceive

frustum, **ī** *nt* morsel, scrap of food

frutex, **icis** *m* shrub, bush; blockhead

fruticōsus, **a**, **um** *adj* bushy

frūx, **ūgis** *f* [*usu. pl.* **frūgēs**, **um**] fruits, crops

fūcō 1 *v* colour; paint; dye

fūcōsus, **a**, **um** *adj* sham, bogus

fūcus, **ī** *m* dye; bee-glue; drone; pretence, sham

fuga, **ae** *f* flight; fleeing; avoidance; exile

fugāx, **ācis** *adj* flying swiftly; swift; avoiding; transitory

fugiō, **fūgī** 3 *v* flee or fly, run away; go into exile; shun, avoid

fugitāns, **ntis** *adj* inclined to avoid

fugitīvus, **a**, **um** *adj* fugitive
■ **∼**, **ī** *m* runaway

fugō 1 *v* put to flight, chase away, rout; drive into exile

fuī ▶ **sum**

fulciō, **lsī**, **ltum** 4 *v* prop up, support; stop

fulcrum, **ī** *nt* head- or back-support of a couch

fulgeō, **lsī** 2 *v* gleam; glitter, shine forth, be bright

fulgor, **ōris** *m* lightning; flash; glittering, brightness; glory

fulgur, **uris** *nt* lightning

fulgurat 1 *v impers* there is lightning

fulica, ae f a water-fowl, probably the coot

fūlīgō, inis f soot; lamp-black

fulmen, inis nt lightning, thunderbolt; crushing blow

fulmineus, a, um adj of lightning; destructive

fulminō ① v lighten; cause lightning to strike; strike like lightning

fultūra, ae f prop

fulvus, a, um adj reddish yellow, tawny

fūmeus, fūmidus, a, um adj, **fūmifer, era, erum** adj full of smoke, smoky

fūmō ① v smoke, steam

fūmōsus, a, um adj full of smoke, smoky; smoked

fūmus, ī m smoke, steam, vapour

fūnāle, is nt torch of wax- or tallow-soaked rope; chandelier

fūnambulus, ī m tightrope walker

funda, ae f sling; casting-net

fundāmen, inis nt foundation

fundāmentum, ī nt foundation, groundwork, basis

fundātor, ōris m founder

funditor, ōris m slinger

funditus adv from the very bottom; utterly, totally

fundō¹, ūdī, ūsum ③ v pour out, shed; cast (metals); rout; scatter; produce; give birth to; utter freely

fundō² ① v found; establish; give a firm base to

fundus, ī m bottom; land; farm; estate

fūnebris, bre adj funereal; deadly; fatal

fūnereus, a, um adj funereal; deadly; fatal

fūnerō ① v bury; kill

fūnestō ① v pollute by murder

fūnestus, a, um adj fatal, deadly; destructive

fungor, fūnctus sum ③ v dep with acc or abl perform; discharge (a duty)

fungus, ī m fungus, mushroom

fūnis, is m rope, cable

fūnus, eris nt burial, funeral; funeral rites; corpse; death

fūr, ris m/f thief

furca, ae f (two-pronged) fork; prop

furcifer, erī m scoundrel, gallows bird

furcilla, ae f wood pitchfork; prop

furfur, ris m bran

furiae, ārum fpl frenzy; mad craving for; Furies, avenging spirits

furiālis, e adj frenzied, mad; avenging

furibundus, a, um adj raging, mad, furious; inspired

furiō ① v madden, enrage

furiōsus, a, um adj furious, mad, frantic, wild

furnus, ī m oven

furō, ruī ③ v rage, be mad or furious; be wild

furor, ōris m fury, rage, madness

fūror ① v dep steal, plunder

fūrtim adv by stealth, secretly; imperceptibly

fūrtīvus, a, um adj stolen; secret, furtive

fūrtum, ī nt theft; stolen article; trick, deception

fuscus, a, um *adj* dark, swarthy, dusky; husky; hoarse

fūsilis, e *adj* molten

fūstis, is *m* staff; club; stick

fūstuārium, (i)ī *nt* death by beating (a punishment meted out to soldiers)

fūsus, ī *m* spindle

fūtilis, futtilis, e *adj* vain; worthless

futuō, tuī, tūtum ③ *v* have sexual relations with (a woman)

futūrus, a, um *adj* future; about to be. *fut pple* from ▸ **sum**

futūtiō, ōnis *f* copulation

• • • • • • • • • • • • • • • • • • • •

Gg

gaesum, ī *nt* Gallic javelin

galea, ae *f* helmet

galērum, ī *nt*, **galērus, ī** *m* cap or hat made of skin

gallīna, ae *f* hen

gallus, ī *m* cock

gānea, ae *f*, **gāneum, ī** *nt* common eating house (the resort of undesirable characters); gluttonous eating

gāneō, ōnis *m* glutton, debauchee

ganniō ④ *v* whimper, snarl

garcifer, erī *m* LM boy

garriō ④ *v* chatter, jabber; talk nonsense

garrulus, a, um *adj* chattering, garrulous; blabbing

gaudeō, gāvīsus sum ② *v semi-dep* rejoice, be glad, be pleased with

gaudium, (i)ī *nt* joy, gladness; delight

gausapa, ae *f*, **gausape, is** *nt* cloth of woollen frieze; cloak of this material

gāvīsus *pple* from ▸ **gaudeō**

gāza, ae *f* (royal) treasure

gelidus, a, um *adj* icy, cold; frozen

gelō ① *v* freeze

gelū, ūs *nt* frost; ice, snow; cold, chilliness

gemellus, a, um *adj* twin-born ■ ∼, **ī** *m* twin

geminō ① *v* double; repeat; double the force of; pair (with)

geminus, a, um *adj* twin-born; double; both

gemitus, ūs *m* sigh, groan; roaring

gemma, ae *f* bud; jewel; cup; seal, signet

gemmātus, a, um *adj* jewelled

gemmeus, a, um *adj* set with precious stones

gemō, muī ③ *v* moan, groan; lament (over); grieve that

gena, ae *f* cheek, eyes

gener, erī *m* son-in-law

generātim *adv* by kinds, by tribes; generally

generātor, ōris *m* begetter, father, sire

generō ① *v* beget, father, produce

generōsus, a, um *adj* of noble birth; noble; of good stock

genesta ▸ **genista**

genetīvus, a, um adj acquired at birth

genetrīx, īcis f mother

geniālis, e adj connected with marriage; merry, genial; festive

genista, ae f Spanish broom, greenweed and similar shrubs

genitālis, e adj generative; fruitful

genitor, ōris m begetter; father; creator; originator

genius, (i)ī m tutelary deity or genius; talent

gēns, ntis f clan; tribe; family; race; nation

gentiles, ium mpl **LM** pagans, heathens

gentīlicius, a, um adj of or belonging to a particular Roman gēns

gentīlis, e adj of the same gēns

genū, ūs nt knee

genuīnus, ī m back-tooth, molar

genus, eris nt birth, descent, origin; offspring; race; kind; family; nation; gender

geōmetrēs, ae m geometrician, surveyor

geōmetria, ae f geometry

germānitās, ātis f brotherhood, sisterhood; affinity between things deriving from the same source

germānus, a, um adj (of brothers and sisters) full; genuine, true
- **germāna, ae** f sister
- **germānus, ī** m brother

germen, inis nt sprout, bud; shoot

gerō, gessī, gestum ③ v bear, carry; wear; have; carry on, perform, do; govern, administer; achieve; carry in the womb

□ **~ mōrem** gratify, accommodate oneself to

□ **sē gerere** behave

gestāmen, inis nt something worn or carried on the body; load, burden; means of conveyance

gestātor, ōris m bearer, traveller

gestiō ④ v exult; desire eagerly

gestō ① v carry (about); wear

gestus¹, a, um adj pple from
▶ **gerō**
■ **rēs gestae** fpl exploits

gestus², ūs m movement of the limbs; bodily action, gesture; gesticulation

gibber, era, erum adj humpbacked

gignō ③ v beget, bear, bring forth, produce

gilvus, a, um adj dun-coloured

gingīva, ae f gum (in which the teeth are set)

glaber, bra, brum adj hairless, smooth

glaciālis, e adj icy, frozen

glaciēs, iēī f ice

gladiātor, ōris m gladiator

gladiātōrius, a, um adj gladiatorial

gladius, (i)ī m sword

glaeba, ae f clod; cultivated soil; lump, mass

glāns, ndis f acorn, beach-nut; missile discharged from a sling

glārea, ae f gravel

glāreōsus, a, um adj gravelly

glaucus, a, um adj bluish grey

glēba ▶ **glaeba**

glīs, ris m dormouse

glīscō ③ v swell; increase in power

or violence

globōsus, a, um *adj* round, spherical

globus, ī *m* sphere; dense mass; closely packed throng

glomerō v form into a ball; assemble, mass together

glomus, eris *nt* ball-shaped mass

glōria, ae *f* glory, fame, renown; vainglory, boasting

glōrior v dep boast; glory in

glōriōsus, a, um *adj* glorious, famous; vainglorious, boasting

glubō v strip the bark from, peel

glūten, inis *nt* glue

gnāruris, e *adj* acquainted with, knowing

gnārus, a, um *adj* having knowledge or experience of; known

gnāv- ▶ nāv-

gnāviter *adv* (also **nāviter**) diligently; wholly

gnāvus, a, um *adj* (also **nāvus**) active, industrious

grabātus, ī *m* low couch or bed; camp-bed

gracilis, e *adj* thin, slender; meagre, lean; scanty, poor; simple, plain

grāculus, ī *m* jackdaw

gradātim *adv* step by step, by degrees

gradior, gressus sum v dep step, walk

gradus, ūs *m* step, pace; position; rank; degree; rung (of ladder); stair

□ **suspēnsō gradū** on tiptoe

□ **addō gradum** gather pace, speed up

Graeculus, a, um *adj* Grecian, Greek (mostly in a contemptuous sense)

grallae, ārum *fpl* stilts

grāmen, inis *nt* grass; herb, plant

grāmineus, a, um *adj* of grass, grassy; made of grass or turf

grammaticus, a, um *adj* grammatical

■ ~, **ī** *m* grammarian, scholar, expert on linguistic and literary questions

grandaevus, a, um *adj* of great age, old

grandēscō v grow, increase in size or quantity

grandis, e *adj* old; grown up; great; grand; tall; lofty; powerful

grandō, inis *f* hail, hail-storm

grānum, ī *nt* grain, seed

graphium, (i)ī *nt* sharp-pointed writing implement; stylus

grassor v dep march on, advance; roam in search of victims, prowl; proceed; run riot

grātēs, ium *fpl* thanks

□ **grātēs agō** thank

grātia, ae *f* grace; gracefulness; good-will; kindness; favour; obligation

□ **referō grātiam** render thanks

□ **grātiās agō/habeō** thank, be thankful to

□ **grātiam faciō dē** politely decline an invitation

□ **grātiā** with gen for the sake of, for the purpose of

grātificor v dep gratify; bestow

grātiōsus, a, um *adj* agreeable, enjoying favour; kind

grātīs *adv* without payment, for nothing

grātor ☐ *v dep with dat* congratulate; rejoice with

grātuītus, a, um *adj* free of charge; unremunerative

grātulābundus, a, um *adj* congratulating

grātulātiō, ōnis *f* congratulation; rejoicing, joy

grātulor ☐ *v dep* congratulate; rejoice

grātum, ī *nt* favour

grātus, a, um *adj* agreeable; pleasing; popular; thankful

gravātē *adv* grudgingly; reluctantly

gravēdō, inis *f* cold in the head, catarrh

gravidus, a, um *adj* pregnant; laden, weighed down with

gravis, e *adj* heavy; weighty, burdensome; burdened; important; solemn; serious; grievous; difficult; deep (of sound); strong (of smell)

gravitās, ātis *f* weight, heaviness; severity; authority

graviter *adv* heavily, severely; grievously; with reluctance

gravō ☐ *v* load, burden; oppress, aggravate
  ☐ **gravor** regard as a burden, show reluctance or annoyance

gregālis, e *adj* common; living in a flock or herd; belonging to the same flock or herd

gregārius, a, um *adj* belonging to the rank and file
  ☐ **miles ~** common soldier

gregātim *adv* in flocks

gremium, (i)ī *nt* lap, bosom; female genital parts; interior

gressus, ūs *m* going; step; *pl* the feet

grex, gis *m* flock, herd; company; crew

grūs, gruis *m/f* crane

grȳps, grȳphis *m* griffin

gubernāculum, ī *nt* helm, rudder; helm of 'ship of state'

gubernātiō, ōnis *f* steering; direction, control

gubernātor, ōris *m* helmsman, pilot; one who directs or controls

gubernō ☐ *v* steer (a ship); govern

gula, ae *f* gullet, throat; appetite

gulōsus, a, um *adj* fond of choice food

gurges, itis *m* whirlpool, eddy; 'flood', 'stream'

gustō ☐ *v* taste; sip; have some experience of

gutta, ae *f* drop; spot; speck

guttur, uris *nt* gullet, throat; appetite

gymnasium, (i)ī *nt* sports centre

gymn(ast)icus, a, um *adj* gymnastic, athletic

gynaecēum, ī *nt* women's apartments in a Greek house

gȳrus, ī *m* circle; circuit; course

Hh

habēna, ae f rein; thong; whip

habeō ② v have, hold, possess; contain; handle, use; manage; esteem; regard, treat (as); marry
□ ~ **male** bother, annoy
□ **prō certō** ~ know for certain

habilis, e adj handy, manageable; apt, fit

habitābilis, e adj habitable

habitātiō, ōnis f lodging, residence

habitātor, ōris m dweller, inhabitant

habitō ① v inhabit, dwell; live (in a place)

habitus, ūs m condition, state, dress, 'get-up'; expression, demeanour; character

hāc adv by this way; on this side

hāctenus adv hitherto; thus far; thus much

haedus, ī m kid

haereō, haesī, (haesum) ② v stick, cling, adhere, be fixed; be in difficulties; doubt; linger

haeresis, is f LM heresy

haereticus, ī m LM heretic

haesitō ① v stick hesitate, be undecided; be stuck

hālitus, ūs m breath; steam, vapour

hālō ① v emit (vapour, etc.); be fragrant

(h)ama, ae f water-bucket

Hamadryas, ados f wood-nymph, hamadryad

hāmātus, a, um adj hooked

hāmus, ī m hook; fish-hook; barb of arrow

hara, ae f coop, pigsty

harenga, ae f herring

hariola, ae f female fortune-teller

hariolor ① v dep tell fortunes

hariolus, ī m prophet, seer

harmonia, ae f harmony; coupling

harpagō, ōnis m grappling-hook

harund- ▶ arund-

harundō, inis f (also **arundō**) reed; fishing rod; arrow-shaft; arrow; pen; shepherd's pipe

haruspex, icis m soothsayer

hasta, ae f spear, lance, pike; spear stuck in the ground at public auctions

hastātus, a, um adj armed with a spear
■ **hastātī, ōrum** mpl first line of a Roman army

hastīle, is nt shaft of a spear; spear; cane

hau, haud adv not, by no means

haudquāquam adv by no means, in no way

hauriō, hausī, haustum ④ v draw (up or out); drink; drain; swallow; derive; have one's fill of; experience to the full

haustus, ūs m drinking; drink, draught; the drawing (of water)

hebdomas, ados f week, terminal point of a seven-day period

hebenus, ī m/f ebony

hebeō ② v be blunt; be sluggish

hebes, etis *adj* blunt, dull; languid; stupid

hebēscō ③ *v* grow blunt or feeble

hebetō ① *v* blunt, make dull, weaken

hedera, ae *f* ivy

hederiger, era, erum *adj* ivy-bearing

hei *int* exclamation expressing anguish or similar

heia *int* exclamation expressing deprecation, concession, astonishment or urgency

helciārius, (i)ī *m* one who tows boats

hēlluō, ōnis *m* glutton, squanderer

hēlluor ① *v dep* be a glutton; squander; spend immoderately

hem *int* what's that? ah! alas!

hendecasyllabī, ōrum *mpl* verses consisting of eleven syllables

herba, ae *f* grass; herb

herbidus, a, um *adj* grassy

herbifer, era, erum *adj* full of grass or herbs; bearing magical or medicinal plants

herbōsus, a, um *adj* grassy

herc(u)le *int* by Hercules!

hērēditās, ātis *f* heirship; inheritance

hērēs, ēdis *m/f* heir, heiress

heri *adv* yesterday

hērōicus, a, um *adj* heroic, epic

hērois, idis *f* heroine

hērōs, ōos/ōis *m* hero

hērōus, a, um *adj* heroic

Hesperia, ae *f* the western land, Italy

hesperius, a, um *adj* western

Hesperus, erī *m* evening-star

hesternus, a, um *adj* of yesterday

hetaeria, ae *f* religious brotherhood, fraternity

heu *int* oh! alas!

heus *int* ho! ho there! listen!

hiātus, ūs *m* opening, cleft; wide-opened jaw

hīberna, ōrum *ntpl,* **hībernāculum, ī** *nt* winter-quarters

hībernō ① *v* spend the winter; be in winter-quarters

hībernus, a, um *adj* of winter; wintry

hibiscum, ī *nt* marsh mallow

hīc *adv* here; in the present circumstances

hic, haec, hoc *pn* this

hicine, haecine, hocine *pn* this?

hiemālis, e *adj* of or belonging to winter, wintry

hiemō ① *v* pass the winter; be stormy

hiem(p)s, mis *f* winter; stormy weather

hilaris, e *adj* cheerful, lively, light-hearted

hilaritās, ātis *f* cheerfulness, light-heartedness

hilaritūdō, inis *f* merriment

hilarō ① *v* gladden

hilarus, a, um *adj* cheerful, lively, light-hearted

hinc *adv* from this place; henceforth; from this cause

hinniō ④ *v* neigh

hinnītus, ūs *m* neighing

hiō ① *v* be wide open, gape; be

greedy for; be open-mouthed
(with astonishment, *etc.*)

hircus, **ī** *m* he-goat

hirsūtus, **a**, **um** *adj* rough, hairy,
shaggy, bristly, prickly; rude

hirūdō, **inis** *f* leech

hirundinīnus, **a**, **um** *adj* of
swallows

hirundō, **inis** *f* swallow

hīscō ① *v* (begin to) open, gape;
open the mouth to speak

hispidus, **a**, **um** *adj* rough,
shaggy, hairy; bristly; dirty

historia, **ae** *f* history; story

historicus, **a**, **um** *adj* historical

histriō, **ōnis** *m* actor; performer
in pantomime

histriōnālis, **e** *adj* concerning an
actor; theatrical

hiulcō ① *v* cause to crack, crack
open

hiulcus, **a**, **um** *adj* gaping, cracked

hodiē *adv* today; at the present
time

hodiernus, **a**, **um** *adj* of this day;
present

holus ▶ olus

homicīda, **ae** *m/f* murderer;
killer of men

homō, **inis** *m* human being,
person; man, woman; fellow
□ **novus ~** nouveau riche,
upstart

homunculus, **ī** *m* little man;
worthless *or* puny person

honestās, **ātis** *f* honourableness,
honour; integrity

honestō ① *v* honour (with);
adorn, grace

honestus, **a**, **um** *adj* worthy;
decent; of high rank; honourable;
handsome

honor, **ōris** *m* honour; regard;
office, dignity; grace

honōrārius, **a**, **um** *adj*
complimentary, supplied
voluntarily

honōrificus, **a**, **um** *adj*
conferring honour

honōrō ① *v* honour

honōrus, **a**, **um** *adj* conferring
honour

hōra, **ae** *f* hour; season (of the
year); time
■ **Hōrae**, **ārum** *fpl* the Seasons
(personified)

hordeum, **ī** *nt* barley

hōria, **ae** *f* fishing boat

hornō *adv* this year

hornus, **a**, **um** *adj* this year's

horrendus, **a**, **um** *adj* dreadful,
terrible, horrible

horreō ② *v* stand on end, bristle;
have a rough appearance; shiver,
tremble; shudder at

horrēscō, **ruī** ③ *v* bristle up, grow
rough; begin to shake; tremble,
shudder at

horreum, **ī** *nt* storehouse; barn

horribilis, **e** *adj* rough; terrible,
horrible; monstrous

horridus, **a**, **um** *adj* rough,
bristly; horrible; unkempt; grim

horrifer, **era**, **erum** *adj*,
horrificus, **a**, **um** *adj* dreadful,
frightening; chilling

horrisonus, **a**, **um** *adj* sounding
dreadfully

horror, **ōris** *m* shivering; dread,
awe; rigidity (from cold, *etc.*)

horsum *adv* in this direction

hortāmen, **inis** *nt*

encouragement

hortātiō, ōnis *m*
encouragement; exhortation

hortātor, ōris *m* encourager;
exhorter

hortātus, ūs *m* exhortation

hortor 1 *v dep* exhort; encourage

hortulus, ī *m* small garden; *pl*
pleasure-grounds

hortus, ī *m* garden; *pl* pleasure-
grounds

hospes, itis *m* guest; visitor; host;
stranger

hospita, ae *f* female guest,
hostess; landlady

hospitālis, e *adj* of or for a guest;
hospitable

hospitāliter *adv* in a hospitable
manner

hospitium, (i)ī *nt* hospitality;
entertainment; guest
accommodation; lodgings

hostia, ae *f* sacrificial animal

hosticus, a, um *adj* of or
belonging to an enemy, hostile

hostilis, e *adj* of an enemy, hostile

hostis, is *m/f* stranger, foreigner;
enemy

hūc *adv* hither; to this place; so far

huiusmodī *adj indec* of this kind

hūm- ▸ ūm-

hūmānitās, ātis *f* human nature;
civilization, culture; humane
character

hūmāniter *adv* moderately; in a
friendly manner

hūmānus, a, um *adj* human;
humane; civilized; considerate

humī *adv* on the ground

hūmidus, a, um *adj* (also

ūmidus) moist, wet; full of sap

humilis, e *adj* low; low-lying;
mean; humble, lowly

humilitās, ātis *f* lowness;
meanness; insignificance

humō 1 *v inter*, bury

humus, ī *f* earth, soil, ground

hyacinthinus, a, um *adj*
belonging to the hyacinth

hyacinthus, ī *m* hyacinth;
sapphire

Hyadēs, um *fpl* group of five
stars in the constellation of Taurus
associated with rainy weather

hyalus, ī *m* glass

hydra, ae *f* water-serpent; snake

hydrōps, ōpis *m* dropsy

hydrus, ī *m* water-snake

Hymen, nis *m* god of marriage;
marriage; wedding-refrain

Hymenaeus, ī *m* god of
marriage; marriage; wedding-
refrain

Hyperboreus, a, um *adj*
northern

hypocauston, ī *nt* system of hot-
air channels for heating baths

hypogēum, ī *nt* underground
room or chamber

- -

Ii

- -

iaceō 2 *v* lie; be situated; be still;
lie still; lie dead; lie in ruins

iaciō, iēcī, iactum 3 *v* throw,
cast, hurl; throw away; utter; pile
up (structures)

iactanter *adv* arrogantly

iactantia, ae *f* boasting, ostentation

iactātiō, ōnis *f* shaking; boasting; showing off

iactō ▣ *v* throw, hurl; toss; utter with force; boast (of); torment □ **sē iactāre** glory (in)

iactūra, ae *f* throwing (away, overboard); loss; cost

iactus, ūs *m* throwing, throw, cast

iaculātor, ōris *m* javelin-thrower

iaculor ▣ *v dep* throw a javelin; hurl; shoot at

iaculum, ī *nt* dart, javelin

iam *adv* now, already

iambus, ī *m* iambus (a metrical foot consisting of one light syllable followed by one heavy syllable), a line of verse made up of iambī

iamdūdum *adv* just now; already for a long time; long ago

iamprīdem *adv* a long time ago; for a long time now

iānitor, ōris *m* door-keeper, porter

iānua, ae *f* door, house-door; entrance

iānuārius, (i)ī *m* January

iānus, ī *m* Janus (a Roman god of gates and doorways)

iaspis, idis *f* jasper

ibī *adv* there

ibidem *adv* in that very place; at that very instant

ībis, idis/is *f* ibis (Egyptian bird)

ictus, ūs *m* blow, stroke; musical or metrical beat

idcircō *adv* therefore, for that reason

īdem, eadem, idem *pn* the same

identidem *adv* continually; repeatedly; again and again

ideō *adv* for the reason (that); for that reason, therefore

īdōlon, ī *nt* spectre, apparition

idōneus, a, um *adj* fit, suitable; able

Īdus, ūs *fpl* Ides (the 15th day of March, May, July, October, the 13th day of the other months)

iēcī ▸ iaciō

iecur, iecinoris/iecoris *nt* liver

iēiūnus, a, um *adj* fasting; hungry; barren; insignificant; poor; uninteresting

igitur *adv* therefore

ignārus, a, um *adj* ignorant (of), having no experience of; unknown

ignāvia, ae *f* laziness; faint-heartedness

ignāvus, a, um *adj* idle, sluggish; cowardly

ignēscō ▣ *v* take fire, kindle; become inflamed (with passion)

igneus, a, um *adj* of fire; fiery; ardent

ignifer, era, erum *adj* bearing or containing fire

ignipotēns, ntis *adj* god of fire

ignis, is *m* fire; brightness; glow of passion

ignōbilis, e *adj* unknown; ignoble; obscure; of low birth

ignōbilitās, ātis *f* obscurity

ignōminia, ae *f* ignominy, dishonour

ignōminiōsus, a, um *adj* disgraced; disgraceful

ignōrantia, ae *f* ignorance

ignōrātiō, ōnis *f* ignorance

ignōrō ☐ *v* be ignorant of; fail to recognize

ignōscō, ōvī, ōtum ☐ *v* with *dat* forgive, pardon

ignōtus, a, um *adj* unknown; ignorant (of)

īlex, icis *f* holm-oak

īlia, ium *ntpl* side part of the body extending from the hips down to the groin; private parts; inwards

īlicet *adv* at once, immediately; *int* it's all up! off with you!

īlicētum, ī *nt* oak coppice

īlicō *adv* just here, just there; directly, immediately

īlignus, a, um *adj* of the holm-oak

illābor, lāpsus sum ☐ *v dep* slide or flow (into); fall or sink (onto)

illāc *adv* that way, on this side

illacessītus, a, um *adj* unattacked, free from invasion

illacrimābilis, e *adj* unlamented; inexorable

illacrimō ☐ *v*, **illacrimor** ☐ *v dep* bewail, lament

illaesus, a, um *adj* uninjured; inviolate

illaetābilis, e *adj* joyless

illaqueō ☐ *v* ensnare, entangle

ille, a, illud, īus *pn* he, she; it; that; the well-known; the former

illecebra, ae *f* allurement, enticement

illepidus, a, um *adj* lacking grace or refinement

illī *adv* there

illīberālis, e *adj* ungentlemanly, unladylike; not having the qualities of a free man

illīc *adv* there, over there

illiciō, lexī, lectum ☐ *v* allure, entice

illicita, ōrum *ntpl* forbidden things; disloyalty

illicitus, a, um *adj* forbidden, unlawful, illicit

illīdō, īsī, īsum ☐ *v* strike or dash against

illigō ☐ *v* bind or tie up; bind

illinc *adv* thence; on that side

illinō, lēvī, litum ☐ *v* smear over; anoint

illō *adv* thither; to that point

illūc *adv* thither

illūcēscō, lūxī ☐ *v* begin to dawn

illūdō, ūsī, ūsum ☐ *v* speak mockingly of; trick out; use for sexual pleasure

illūminō ☐ *v* light up; brighten

illūnis, e *adj* moonless

illūstris, tre *adj* clear, bright; famous

illūstrō ☐ *v* illuminate; make famous or illustrious; make clear

illuviēs, iēī *f* dirt, filth; filthy condition

imāginātiō, ōnis *f* fancy, thought

imāginor ☐ *v* picture, imagine

imāgō, inis *f* image, likeness; idea; appearance; echo; ghost, phantom

imbēcillitās, ātis *f* weakness, feebleness; moral or intellectual weakness

imbēcillus, a, um *adj* weak, feeble

imbellis, e *adj* unwarlike; not suited or ready for war

imber, bris *m* (shower of) rain; (any) liquid; shower of missiles

imberbis, e *adj* beardless

imbibō, bibī ③ *v* imbibe, absorb into one's mind

imbrex, icis *f* (sometimes *m*) tile

imbrifer, era, erum *adj* rain-bringing, rainy

imbuō, uī, ūtum ③ *v* wet, soak; give initial instruction (in)

imitābilis, e *adj* that may be imitated

imitāmen, inis *nt* imitation; copy

imitātiō, ōnis *f* imitation; mimicking; copy

imitātor, ōris *m* one who imitates or copies

imitātrīx, īcis *f* female imitator

imitor ① *v dep* imitate; simulate; copy; resemble

immadēscō, duī ③ *v* become wet *or* moist

immānis, e *adj* huge, vast, immense, monstrous; inhuman, savage

immānitās, ātis *f* vastness; brutality; barbarity

immānsuētus, a, um *adj* savage

immātūrus, a, um *adj* unripe, immature, untimely

immedicābilis, e *adj* incurable

immemor, oris *adj* forgetful; heedless

immēnsus, a, um *adj* endless, vast, immense
■ **(per) immēnsum** *adv* to an enormous extent or degree

immerēns, ntis *adj* undeserving (of ill-treatment), blameless

immergō, rsī, rsum ③ *v* plunge into, immerse

immeritus, a, um *adj* undeserving; undeserved
■ **immeritō** *adv* unjustly; without cause

immētātus, a, um *adj* unmeasured

immigrō ① *v* move (into)

immineō ② *v* overhang; threaten, be imminent; be a threat (to)

imminuō, uī, ūtum ③ *v* diminish; impair

immīsceō, īxtum ② *v* mix in, mingle; confuse

immītis, e *adj* harsh, sour; merciless

immittō, mīsī, missum ③ *v* send (into); admit; throw (into); put in; give the rein to

immō *adv* rather, more correctly

immōbilis, e *adj* immovable, unalterable

immoderātus, a, um *adj* unlimited; immoderate; disorderly

immodestia, ae *f* lack of self-control, licentiousness

immodicus, a, um *adj* excessive, immoderate

immolō ① *v* offer (a victim) in sacrifice

immorior, morī, mortuus sum ③ *v dep* die (in a particular place, position, *etc.*)

immortālis, e *adj* immortal, eternal

immortālitās, ātis *f* immortality

immōtus, a, um *adj* unmoved, immovable; unchanged; inflexible

immūgiō ④ *v* bellow

immundus, a, um *adj* unclean, impure, filthy

immūnis, e *adj* exempt from

tribute or taxation; free or exempt from

immūnitās, ātis f freedom, immunity

immūnitus, a, um adj unfortified

immurmurō ① v murmur, mutter (at or to)

immūtābilis, e adj unchangeable

immūtō ① v change, alter

impācātus, a, um adj not pacified

impār, aris adj uneven, unequal; inferior

imparātus, a, um adj not prepared; unready

impatiēns, ntis adj impatient (of)

impatientia, ae f impatience

impavidus, a, um adj fearless, intrepid

impedīmentum, ī nt hindrance, impediment; pl baggage of an army

impediō ④ v entangle; hamper; hinder

impedītus, a, um adj obstructed; not easily passable; difficult

impellō, pulī, pulsum ③ v push or thrust against; impel; urge on

impendeō ② v hang over; impend; threaten

impendium, (i)ī nt expense, expenditure, payment

impendō, ndī, ēnsum ③ v expend, spend; devote (to)

impēnsa, ae f outlay, cost, expense

impēnsē adv without stint; lavishly

impēnsus, a, um adj immoderate, excessive

imperātor, ōris m commander-in-chief; person in charge, ruler

imperātōrius, a, um adj of or belonging to a commanding officer; imperial

imperātum, ī nt command, order

imperfectus, a, um adj unfinished, imperfect; not complete in every respect

imperiōsus, a, um adj masterful; domineering; dictatorial

imperītia, ae f inexperience, ignorance

imperītō ① v command, govern

imperītus, a, um adj inexperienced (in), unskilled, ignorant (of)

imperium, (i)ī nt command; rule; empire; supreme power

impermissus, a, um adj not permitted, illicit

imperō ① v with dat command, rule (over)

imperterritus, a, um adj fearless

impertiō ④ v impart; give a share of

impervius, a, um adj impassable

impetrābilis, e adj easy to achieve or obtain; effective, successful

impetrō ① v get, obtain by request

impetus, ūs m assault, attack; vigour; violent mental urge

impexus, a, um adj uncombed

impietās, ātis f failure in duty or respect, *etc.*

impiger, gra, grum *adj* active, energetic

impingō, pēgī, pāctum ③ *v* thrust, strike or dash against

impiō ① *v* stain by an act of impiety

impius, a, um *adj* irreverent; wicked; impious

implācābilis, e *adj* relentless, irreconcilable

implācātus, a, um *adj* not appeased, insatiable

implacidus, a, um *adj* restless, unquiet

impleō, ēvī, ētum ② *v* fill; fulfil

implicō, cāvī/cuī, cātum/ citum ① *v* enfold; involve; encumber; entangle
□ **implicor** be intimately connected with

implōrō ① *v* invoke, entreat, appeal to; ask for (help, protection, favours, *etc.*)

implūmis, e *adj* unfledged

impluō, ūvī/uī ③ *v* rain (upon)

impluvium, (i)ī *nt* quadrangular basin in the floor of an atrium which receives the rain-water from the roof

impōnō, posuī, positum ③ *v* put upon or in; impose; assign; place in command or control (of)

importō ① *v* bring or convey in, import; bring about, cause

importūnitās, ātis f persistent lack of consideration for others; relentlessness

importūnus, a, um *adj* inconvenient; troublesome

importuōsus, a, um *adj* having no harbours

impotēns, ntis *adj* powerless, impotent, wild, headstrong; having no control (over), incapable (of)

impotentia, ae f weakness; immoderate behaviour, violence

imprānsus, a, um *adj* without having had one's morning meal

imprecor ① *v dep* call down upon, pray for; utter curses

impressiō, ōnis f push, thrust, assault

imprīmīs *adv* especially, above all; firstly

imprimō, pressī, pressum ③ *v* impress, imprint; press upon; stamp

improbitās, ātis f want of principle, shamelessness

improbō ① *v* express disapproval of, condemn

improbus, a, um *adj* morally unsound; disloyal; ill-disposed, shameless; excessive; presumptuous

imprōvidus, a, um *adj* improvident; thoughtless, unwar-

imprōvīsus, a, um *adj* unforeseen, unexpected
□ **dē/ex imprōvīsō** unexpectedly

imprūdēns, ntis *adj* ignorant; foolish; unwarned

imprūdentia, ae f imprudence; ignorance

impūbēs, beris/bis *adj* below the age of puberty; beardless

impudēns, ntis *adj* shameless, impudent

impudentia, ae f

shamelessness, effrontery

impudīcitia, ae *f* sexual impurity (often of homosexuality)

impudīcus, a, um *adj* unchaste, flouting the accepted sexual code

impugnō ① *v* fight against, attack, assail

impulsor, ōris *m* instigator

impulsus, ūs *m* shock, impact; incitement

impūne *adv* safely, with impunity; scot-free

impūnitās, ātis *f* impunity

impūnītus, a, um *adj* unpunished

impūrus, a, um *adj* unclean, filthy, foul; impure; morally foul

imputō ① *v* impute, charge; ascribe

︙mulus, a, um *adj* lowest in position, bottommost

︙mus, a, um *adj* inmost, deepest, bottommost

︙n *prep with acc* to; into; against; for; towards; until; *with abl* at; in; on; within; among

☐ ~ **diēs** day by day, every day

☐ ~ **perpetuum** for ever

☐ ~ **rem** to the point

☐ ~ **prīmīs** especially

☐ **in mediō** open to all

︙naccessus, a, um *adj* inaccessible

︙naedificō ① *v* build (in a place); wall up

︙naequālis, e *adj* uneven; unequal

︙naestimābilis, e *adj* beyond all price

︙namābilis, e *adj* disagreeable, unattractive

inambulātiō, ōnis *f* the action of walking up and down; walk, promenade

inambulō ① *v* walk up and down

inamoenus, a, um *adj* unlovely, disagreeable

inanimus, a, um *adj* lifeless, inanimate

ināniō ④ *v* empty

inānis, e *adj* empty, void; foolish
■ **ināne, is** *nt* the void

inarātus, a, um *adj* unploughed, untilled

inardēscō, arsī ③ *v* kindle, take fire; become glowing

inassuētus, a, um *adj* unaccustomed

inaudāx, ācis *adj* not daring, timid

inaudiō ④ *v* get an inkling of, hear mention of

inaudītus, a, um *adj* unheard (of), novel, new

inaugurātō *adv* with the taking of omens by augury

inaugurō ① *v* take omens by the flight of birds; consecrate by augury

inaurō ① *v* gild, make rich

inausus, a, um *adj* undared

inb- ▶ **imb-**

inbēcillitās, ātis *f* (also **imbēcillitās**) weakness, feebleness; moral *or* intellectual weakness

inbēcillus, a, um *adj* (also **imbēcillus**) weak, feeble

inbellis, e *adj* (also **imbellis**) unwarlike; not suited *or* ready for war

inberbis, e *adj* (also **imberbis**)

beardless

inbibō, bibī, itum 3 v (also
imbibō) imbibe, absorb into
one's mind

incaeduus, a, um adj not felled

incalēscō, luī 3 v grow hot;
become heated

incallidus, a, um adj not shrewd,
simple

incandēscō, duī 3 v become
red-hot

incānēscō, nuī 3 v turn grey
or hoary

incānus, a, um adj quite grey,
hoary

incarnatio, onis f LM incarnation

incassum adv without effect, to
no purpose

incautus, a, um adj incautious,
off one's guard; unprotected

incēdō, essī, essum 3 v step,
walk, march along; advance; befall

incelebrātus, a, um adj
unrecorded

incēnātus, a, um adj without
having had dinner

incendiārius, (i)ī m incendiary,
fire-raiser

incendium, (i)ī nt fire,
conflagration; passion; fiery heat

incendō, ndī, ēnsum 3 v set fire
to, kindle; inflame; aggravate

incēnsus, a, um adj not
registered at a census

inceptō 1 v begin

inceptum, ī nt beginning,
undertaking

incertus, a, um adj uncertain;
doubtful, inconstant; variable

incessō, ss(īv)ī 3 v assault,
attack; reproach, abuse

incessus, ūs m walking; advance;
gait; procession

incestō 1 v pollute, defile

incestus, a, um adj unchaste;
unholy

inchoō ▶ incohō

incidō, cidī, cāsum 3 v fall
(into); meet (with); arise, occur

incīdō, īdī, īsum 3 v cut into;
make an end to; engrave

incingō, īnxī, īnctum 3 v gird
(with); wrap (tightly) round (with)

incipiō, cēpī, ceptum 3 v begin;
undertake

incircumcisus, ī m LM one who
is uncircumcised, gentile

incitāmentum, ī nt incentive,
stimulus

incitātus, a, um adj fast-moving,
aroused, passionate

◻ **equō incitātō** at full gallop

incitō 1 v incite; stir up, spur on;
set in rapid motion

incitus, a, um adj rushing,
headlong

inclāmō 1 v cry out (to), call
upon; abuse, revile

inclārēscō, ruī 3 v become
famous

inclēmēns, ntis adj harsh

inclēmentia, ae f harshness

inclīnātiō, ōnis f the act of
leaning; tendency, inclination

inclīnō 1 v bend; lower; incline;
decay; grow worse; set (of the
sun); deject

inclitus, a, um adj renowned,
famous, celebrated

inclūdō, ūsī, ūsum 3 v shut in
up; enclose

incōgitāns, ntis adj thoughtless

incognitus, **a**, **um** *adj* not known, untried; untested

incohō ① *v* start; set going

incola, **ae** *m/f* inhabitant; resident alien

incolō, **luī** ③ *v* dwell in, inhabit

incolumis, **e** *adj* uninjured, safe; unimpaired

incolumitās, **ātis** *f* safety

incomitātus, **a**, **um** *adj* unaccompanied

incommodus, **a**, **um** *adj* inconvenient, troublesome; disadvantageous, disagreeable
■ **incommodum**, **ī** *nt* inconvenience; misfortune; set-back

incomparābilis, **e** *adj* beyond comparison, unequalled

incompertus, **a**, **um** *adj* not known

incompositus, **a**, **um** *adj* clumsy, disorganized

incōmptus, **a**, **um** *adj* dishevelled; untidy; unpolished

inconcessus, **a**, **um** *adj* forbidden

inconcinnus, **a**, **um** *adj* awkward; clumsy

inconditus, **a**, **um** *adj* rough, crude; uncivilized; disordered, not disciplined

incōnstāns, **ntis** *adj* changeable, fickle

incōnstantia, **ae** *f* changeableness; fickleness

incōnsultus, **a**, **um** *adj* rash, ill-advised

incontinēns, **ntis** *adj* intemperate

incoquō, **coxī**, **coctum** ③ *v* boil

in *or* down; boil

incorruptus, **a**, **um** *adj* unspoilt, uncorrupted

increb(r)ēscō, **b(r)uī** ③ *v* become stronger *or* more intense; spread

incrēdibilis, **e** *adj* incredible

incrēdulus, **a**, **um** *adj* disbelieving

incrēmentum, **ī** *nt* growth, increase

increpatio, **onis** *f* ᴸᴹ rebuke

increpitō ① *v* chide, utter (noisy) reproaches at

increpō, **puī**, **pitum** ① *v* make a sharp, loud noise; protest at; remark indignantly

incrēscō, **ēvī** ③ *v* grow (in *or* upon)

incruentus, **a**, **um** *adj* bloodless, without shedding of blood

incubō, **buī**, **bitum** ① *v with dat* lie in *or* on; sit upon; brood over; keep a jealous watch (over)

incūdō, **ūdī**, **ūsum** ③ *v* hammer out

inculcō ① *v* force upon, impress, drive home

incultus, **a**, **um** *adj* uncultivated; unkempt; rough, uncouth
■ **incultus**, **ūs** *m* want of cultivation *or* refinement; uncouthness, disregard

incumbō, **cubuī**, **cubitum** ③ *v* lay oneself upon, lean *or* recline upon; apply oneself earnestly (to); press forward

incūnābula, **ōrum** *ntpl* the apparatus of the cradle; one's earliest years; birth-place

incūria, **ae** *f* carelessness, neglect

incūriōsus, a, um *adj* careless, negligent; indifferent

incurrō, (cu)currī, cursum *v* run into or towards, attack, invade; meet (with); befall

incursiō, ōnis *f* attack; raid

incursō ① *v* run against, dash against, attack; make raids upon

incursus, ūs *m* attack, raid

incurvō ① *v* make crooked or bent; cause to bend down

incurvus, a, um *adj* crooked, curved

incūs, ūdis *f* anvil

incūsō ① *v* blame; criticize; condemn

incustōdītus, a, um *adj* not watched over; unsupervised

incutiō, ussī, ussum ③ *v* strike on or against; instil

indāgō, inis *f* ring of huntsmen or nets

inde *adv* thence, from that place; from that time; from that cause; thence-forwards; next

indēbitus, a, um *adj* that is not owed, not due

indecoris, e *adj* inglorious, shameful

indecorō ① *v* disgrace

indecōrus, a, um *adj* unbecoming, unseemly; ugly

indēfēnsus, a, um *adj* undefended; defenceless

indēfessus, a, um *adj* unwearied; indefatigable

indemnātus, a, um *adj* uncondemned

index, icis *m/f* informer, tale-bearer; sign, token

indicium, (i)ī *nt* information;

token; disclosure; evidence (before a court)

indicō, dīxī, dictum ③ *v* declare publicly; inflict (on) by one's pronouncement

indicō ① *v* betray; reveal; give information

indictus, a, um *adj* not said or mentioned
□ **indictā causā** without the case's being pleaded; unheard

indidem *adv* from the same place, source or origin

indigena, ae *m* native

indigēns, ntis *adj* needy, indigent

indigeō ② *v* need, require; lack

indigestus, a, um *adj* chaotic; jumbled

Indigitēs, um *mpl* deified heroes, tutelary deities (local as opposed to foreign gods)

indignātiō, ōnis *f* indignation; anger; angry outburst

indignitās, ātis *f* unworthiness, shamelessness; baseness; humiliation

indignor ① *v dep* regard with indignation, resent; be indignant

indignus, a, um *adj* unworthy, undeserving; undeserved; shameful

indigus, a, um *adj* having need (of); lacking; needy

indīligēns, ntis *adj* careless, negligent

indīligentia, ae *f* negligence, want of care; want of concern (for)

indipīscor, deptus sum ③ *v dep* overtake; acquire

indiscrētus, a, um *adj*

indistinguishable

indistīnctus, a, um *adj* not
properly arranged, applied
without distinction

indō, didī, ditum ③ *v* put in or
on; introduce

indocilis, e *adj* unteachable,
ignorant

indoctus, a, um *adj* untaught;
unlearned; ignorant; untrained

indolēs, lis *f* innate character;
inborn quality

indolēscō, luī ③ *v* feel pain of
mind; grieve

indomitus, a, um *adj* untamed;
untamable; fierce

indormiō ④ *v* sleep (in or over)

indōtātus, a, um *adj* not
provided with a dowry

indubitō ① *v* have misgivings
(about)

indūcō, dūxī, ductum ③ *v* lead
or conduct into; bring in; bring
(performers) into the arena, on to
the stage, *etc.*; introduce; put on;
persuade; spread (with)

nductiō, ōnis *f* leading or
bringing in; application

ndulgēns, ntis *adj* kind, mild

ndulgentia, ae *f* kindness;
gentleness

ndulgeō, lsī, ltum ② *v* with *dat* be
kind or lenient (to); grant; give way
to; accede (to)

nduō, uī, ūtum ③ *v* put on;
dress oneself in; assume; fall or be
impaled (upon)

ndūrō ① *v* make hard

ndusiātus, a, um *adj* wearing an
indusium (a kind of tunic)

dusium, (i)ī *nt* outer tunic

industria, ae *f* diligence,
assiduity, industry
□ **dē/ex industriā** on purpose

industrius, a, um *adj* diligent,
assiduous, industrious

indūtiae, ārum *fpl* truce,
armistice

inedia, ae *f* fasting, starvation

inēlegāns, ntis *adj* lacking in
taste; clumsy, infelicitous

inēluctābilis, e *adj* from which
there is no escape

inēmptus, a, um *adj* not bought

inēnarrābilis, e *adj*
indescribable

ineō, īre, iī/īvī, itum *v* ir go into,
enter (into or upon); commence;
form a plan

ineptiae, ārum *fpl* foolery,
absurdities

ineptus, a, um *adj* silly, foolish;
having no sense of what is fitting

inermis, e *adj* unarmed,
defenceless; (fig) unprepared

inerrō ① *v* wander in, on or among

iners, rtis *adj* unskilful; sluggish;
unadventurous; feeble

inertia, ae *f* unskilfulness;
idleness, sloth

inēvītābilis, e *adj* unavoidable

inexcūsābilis, e *adj* inexcusable

inexōrābilis, e *adj* inexorable,
relentless, stubborn

inexpertus, a, um *adj*
inexperienced (in); untried

inexpiābilis, e *adj* inexpiable;
implacable

inexplēbilis, e *adj* insatiable

inexplōrātus, a, um *adj*
unexplored; not investigated

inexpugnābilis, e *adj*

impregnable; invincible

inex(s)pectātus, a, um *adj* unforeseen

inex(s)tīnctus, a, um *adj* that is never extinguished

inex(s)uperābilis, e *adj* insurmountable; invincible; unsurpassable

inextrīcābilis, e *adj* impossible to disentangle or sort out

īnfabrē *adv* without art, crudely

īnfacētus, a, um *adj* coarse, boorish

īnfācundus, a, um *adj* unable to express oneself fluently

īnfāmia, ae *f* ill-fame, dishonour

īnfāmis, e *adj* disreputable, infamous

īnfāmō ① *v* bring into disrepute; defame

īnfandus, a, um *adj* unutterable; abominable

īnfāns, ntis *adj* speechless; inarticulate; newly born, young
■ **īnfāns, ntis** *m/f* little child

īnfantia, ae *f* infancy; inability to speak

īnfaustus, a, um *adj* unlucky, unfortunate; inauspicious

īnfectus, a, um *adj* not done, unmade; unfinished, impossible

īnfēcunditās, ātis *f* barrenness

īnfēcundus, a, um *adj* unfruitful, infertile

īnfēlīcitās, ātis *f* misfortune

īnfēlīcō ① *v* bring bad luck on

īnfēlīx, īcis *adj* unfortunate, unhappy; inauspicious

īnfēnsō ① *v* treat in a hostile manner

īnfēnsus, a, um *adj* hostile,

bitterly hostile, enraged

īnferī, ōrum *mpl* the dead

īnferiae, ārum *fpl* offerings to the dead

īnferior, ius *adj* [comp of **īnferus**] lower, later, inferior, worse
■ **īnferius** *adv* further down, at a lower level

īnfernus, a, um *adj* lower; infernal;
■ **īnfernum, i** *nt* [LM] Hell

īnferō, ferre, intulī, illātum *v ir* bring into or upon; bring forward (with hostile intention); produce, cause; inflict; bury

īnferus, era, erum *adj* below, underneath, lower
■ **īnferior, ius** *comp*
■ **īnfimus** *sup*

īnfestus, a, um *adj* hostile; dangerous; disturbed

īnficētiae, ārum *fpl* gaucheries

īnficiō, fēcī, fectum ③ *v* dye; stain; infect; imbue; corrupt

īnfidēlis, e *adj* treacherous, disloyal

īnfidēlitās, ātis *f* faithlessness; inconstancy

īnfidus, a, um *adj* faithless; treacherous

īnfigō, īxī, īxum ③ *v* fix, thrust in; fasten on

īnfimus, a, um *sup adj* lowest, worst

īnfindō, idī, issum ③ *v* cleave; plough a path into

īnfinītus, a, um *adj* boundless, endless, infinite in quantity or amount

īnfirmitās, ātis *f* weakness; sickness

īnfirmō [1] v weaken; diminish;
annul

īnfirmus, a, um adj weak, feeble;
sickly; irresolute

īnfit v ir (s)he begins (to speak)

īnfitiās adv
□ **~ eō** refuse to acknowledge as
true, deny

īnfitior [1] v dep deny, disown

īnflammō [1] v set on fire, kindle;
excite; inflame

īnflātus, a, um adj puffed up;
turgid, bombastic

īnflectō, exī, exum [3] v bend;
curve; change

īnflexibilis, e adj inflexible, rigid

īnflīgō, īxī, īctum [3] v knock or
dash (against); inflict, impose

īnflō [1] v blow into or upon;
puff out

īnfluō, ūxī, ūxum [3] v flow into

īnfodiō, ōdī, ossum [3] v bury,
inter

īnfōrmis, e adj shapeless;
deformed, ugly

īnfōrmō [1] v shape, form; fashion;
form an idea of

īnfortūnium, (i)ī nt misfortune,
punishment

īnfrā adv/prep with acc below,
underneath; under; later (than);
less (than)

īnfrāctus, a, um adj broken;
humble in tone

īnfremō, ī [3] v bellow, roar

īnfrendō [3] v gnash the teeth
(usually in anger)

īnfrēnis, e adj, **īnfrēnus, a, um**
adj not bridled; unrestrained

īnfrēnō [1] v bridle

īnfrequēns, ntis adj not

crowded; below strength; present
only in small numbers

īnfrequentia, ae f insufficient
numbers; depopulated condition
(of a place)

īnfringō, frēgī, frāctum [3] v
break, crush; weaken; diminish,
dishearten; foil, invalidate

īnfula, ae f woollen headband
knotted with ribands

īnfundō, ūdī, ūsum [3] v pour
into or on; pour out

īnfuscō [1] v darken; corrupt

ingeminō [1] v redouble; increase
in intensity

ingemō, muī [3] v groan (over)

ingenerō [1] v implant

ingeniōsus, a, um adj clever,
ingenious; naturally suited (to)

ingenium, (i)ī nt innate quality,
nature; natural disposition;
capacity; talent; gifted writer

ingēns, ntis adj vast, huge; great;
momentous

ingenuus, a, um adj indigenous,
natural; free-born; generous; frank

ingerō, essī, estum [3] v throw
upon; heap on; obtrude; force or
thrust on a person

inglōrius, a, um adj obscure,
undistinguished

ingluviēs, iēī f gullet, jaws;
gluttony

ingrātus, a, um adj unpleasant;
unthankful

ingravēscō [3] v grow heavy;
increase in force or intensity

ingravō [1] v aggravate, make
worse

ingredior, gressus sum [3] v dep
step or go into, enter; begin; walk

ingruō, uī ③ *v* advance threateningly; make an onslaught (upon)

inguen, inis *nt* groin; the sexual organs

inhabilis, e *adj* difficult to handle; not fitted; awkward

inhaereō, haesī, haesum ② *v* stick in, cling (to); be firmly attached (to)

inhibeō ② *v* restrain, curb; prevent

inhiō ① *v* gape; be open-mouthed with astonishment; covet

inhonestō ① *v* disgrace

inhonestus, a, um *adj* shameful; of ill repute

inhonōrātus, a, um *adj* not honoured

inhorrēscō, ruī ③ *v* bristle up; quiver; tremble, shudder at

inhūmānitās, ātis *f* churlishness

inhūmānus, a, um *adj* inhuman; uncivilized, churlish

inhumātus, a, um *adj* unburied

iniciō, lēcī, iectum ③ *v* throw in or into; put on; instil (a feeling, etc.) in the mind

inimīcitia, ae *f* hostility, enmity

inimīcus, a, um *adj* hostile, inimical, harmful
  ■ **inimīcus, ī** *m* enemy, foe

inīquitās, ātis *f* inequality; unfairness; unevenness of terrain

inīquus, a, um *adj* unequal, uneven; disadvantageous; unjust; unkind; hostile

initiō ① *v* initiate (into); admit (to) with introductory rites

initium, (i)ī *nt* beginning
  □ **ab initiō** from the beginning

initus, ūs *m* entry, start

iniūcundus, a, um *adj* unpleasant

iniungō, ūnxī, ūnctum ③ *v* join or fasten (to); attach to; impose (upon)

iniūrātus, a, um *adj* unsworn

iniūria, ae *f* wrong, injury; abuse, insult; offence; sexual assault

iniūriōsus, a, um *adj* wrongful, insulting

iniūrius, a, um *adj* unjust, harsh

iniussū *adv with gen* without (the) orders (of)

iniussus, a, um *adj* unbidden

iniūstus, a, um *adj* unjust, wrongful; severe; excessive; unsuitable

inl- ▸ **ill-**

inm- ▸ **imm-**

innāscor, nātus sum ③ *v dep* be born (in or on)

innatō ① *v* swim (in or on); swim (into); float upon

innātus, a, um *adj* natural, inbor

innāvigābilis, e *adj* unnavigable

innectō, exuī, exum ③ *v* tie, fasten (to); devise, weave (plots)

innītor, nīxus/nīsus sum ③ *v dep with dat* lean or rest (upon)

innō ① *v* swim or float (in or on); sail (on)

innocēns, ntis *adj* harmless; innocent; virtuous

innocentia, ae *f* harmlessness; innocence; integrity

innocuus, a, um *adj* harmless; innocent

innōtēscō, tuī ③ *v* become known

innoxius, a, um *adj* harmless, innocuous; innocent; unhurt

innūbō, **ūpsī** ③ *v with dat* marry (into a family)

innumerābilis, **e** *adj* countless

innumerus, **a**, **um** *adj* numberless

innuō, **uī**, **ūtum** ③ *v* nod or beckon (to)

innūptus, **a**, **um** *adj* unmarried

innūtrītus, **a**, **um** *adj* nourished, brought up

inobservābilis, **e** *adj* difficult to trace

inobservātus, **a**, **um** *adj* unobserved

inoffēnsus, **a**, **um** *adj* free from hindrance; uninterrupted

nolēscō, **ēvī**, **litum** ③ *v with dat* grow in or on

nopia, **ae** *f* want, scarcity; destitution; dearth

nopīnāns, **ntis** *adj* not expecting, off one's guard

nopīnātus, **a**, **um** *adj* unexpected, unforeseen

nopīnus, **a**, **um** *adj* unexpected

nops, **pis** *adj* destitute (of), needy; helpless; poor, meagre

nōrnātus, **a**, **um** *adj* unadorned; uncelebrated

np- ▶ imp-

pār, **aris** *adj* (also **impār**) uneven, unequal; inferior

parātus, **a**, **um** *adj* (also **imparātus**) not prepared; unready

patiēns, **ntis** *adj* (also **mpatiēns**) impatient (of)

patientia, **ae** *f* (also **mpatientia**) impatience

pavidus, **a**, **um** *adj* (also **mpavidus**) fearless, intrepid

inpedīmentum, **ī** *nt* (also **impedīmentum**) hindrance, impediment; baggage of an army

inpedīō ④ *v* (also **impedīō**) entangle; hamper; hinder

inpedītus, **a**, **um** *adj* (also **impedītus**) obstructed; not easily passable; difficult

inpellō, **pulī**, **ulsum** ③ *v* (also **impellō**) push or thrust against; impel; urge on

inpendeō ② *v* (also **impendeō**) hang over; impend; threaten

inpendium, **(i)ī** *nt* (also **impendium**) expense, expenditure, payment

inpendō, **ndī**, **ēnsum** ③ *v* (also **impendō**) expend, spend; devote (to)

inpēnsa, **ae** *f* (also **impēnsa**) outlay, cost, expense

inpēnsē *adv* (also **impēnsē**) without stint; lavishly

inpēnsus, **a**, **um** *adj* (also **impēnsus**) immoderate, excessive

inperātor, **ōris** *m* (also **imperātor**) commander-in-chief; person in charge, ruler

inperātōrius, **a**, **um** *adj* (also **imperātōrius**) of or belonging to a commanding officer; imperial

inperātum, **ī** *nt* (also **imperātum**) command, order

inperfectus, **a**, **um** *adj* (also **imperfectus**) unfinished, imperfect; not complete in every respect

inperiōsus, **a**, **um** *adj* (also **imperiōsus**) masterful; domineering; dictatorial

inperītia, **ae** *f* (also **imperītia**)

inexperience, ignorance

inperitō ① v (also **imperitō**) command, govern

inperitus, a, um adj (also **imperitus**) inexperienced (in), unskilled, ignorant (of)

inperium, (i)ī nt (also **imperium**) command; rule; empire; supreme power

inperō ① v (also **imperō**) with dat command, rule (over)

inperterritus, a, um adj (also **imperterritus**) fearless

inpertiō ④ v (also **impertiō**) impart; give a share of

inpervius, a, um adj (also **impervius**) impassable

inpetrābilis, e adj (also **impetrābilis**) easy to achieve or obtain

inpetrō ① v (also **impetrō**) get, obtain by request

inpetus, ūs m (also **impetus**) assault, attack; vigour; violent mental urge

inpexus, a, um adj (also **impexus**) uncombed

inpietās, ātis f (also **impietās**) failure in duty or respect, etc.

inpiger, gra, grum adj (also **impiger**) active, energetic

inpingō, ēgī, āctum ③ v (also **impingō**) thrust, strike or dash against

inpius, a, um adj (also **impius**) irreverent; wicked; impious

inplācābilis, e adj (also **implācābilis**) relentless, irreconcilable

inplācātus, a, um adj (also **implācātus**) not appeased, insatiable

inplacidus, a, um adj (also **implacidus**) restless, unquiet

inpleō, ēvī, ētum ② v (also **impleō**) fill; fulfil

inplicō, cāvī/ cuī, cātum/ citum ① v (also **implicō**) enfold; involve; encumber; entangle □ **implicor** be intimately connected with

inplōrō ① v (also **implōrō**) invoke, entreat, appeal to; ask for (help, protection, favours, etc.)

inplūmis, e adj (also **implūmis**) unfledged

inpluvium, (i)ī nt (also **impluvium**) quadrangular basin in the floor of an atrium which receives the rain-water from the roof

inpōnō, positum ③ v (also **impōnō**) put upon or in; impose; assign; place in command or control (of)

inportō ① v (also **importō**) bring or convey in, import; bring about, cause

inportūnitās, ātis f (also **importūnitās**) persistent lack of consideration for others; relentlessness

inportūnus, a, um adj (also **importūnus**) inconvenient; troublesome

inportuōsus, a, um adj (also **importuōsus**) having no harbours

inpotēns, ntis adj (also **impotēns**) powerless, impoter wild, headstrong; having no contr (over), incapable (of)

inpotentia, ae f (also **impotentia**) weakness; immoderate behaviour, violence

inprecor [1] *v dep* (also **imprecor**) call down upon, pray for; utter curses

inpressiō, ōnis *f* (also **impressiō**) push, thrust, assault

inprīmīs *adv* (also **in prīmīs/imprīmīs**) especially, above all; firstly

inprīmō, essī, essum [3] *v* (also **imprīmō**) impress, imprint; press upon; stamp

inprobitās, ātis *f* (also **improbitās**) want of principle, shamelessness

inprobō [1] *v* (also **improbō**) express disapproval of, condemn

inprobus, a, um *adj* (also **improbus**) morally unsound; disloyal; ill-disposed, shameless; excessive; presumptuous

inprōvidus, a, um *adj* (also **imprōvidus**) improvident; thoughtless, unwary

inprōvīsus, a, um *adj* (also **imprōvīsus**) unforeseen, unexpected

inprūdēns, ntis *adj* (also **imprūdēns**) ignorant; foolish; unwarned

inprūdentia, ae *f* (also **imprūdentia**) imprudence; ignorance

inpūbēs, beris/bis *adj* (also **impūbēs**) below the age of puberty; beardless

inpudēns, ntis *adj* (also **impudēns**) shameless, impudent

inpudentia, ae *f* (also **impudentia**) shamelessness, effrontery

inpudīcitia, ae *f* (also **impudīcitia**) sexual impurity

inpudīcus, a, um *adj* (also **impudīcus**) unchaste, flouting the accepted sexual code

(often of homosexuality)

inpugnō [1] *v* (also **impugnō**) fight against, attack, assail

inpulsor, ōris *m* (also **impulsor**) instigator

inpulsus, ūs *m* (also **impulsus**) shock, impact; incitement

inpūne *adv* (also **impūne**) safely, with impunity; scot-free

inpūnitās, ātis *f* (also **impūnitās**) impunity

inpūnitus, a, um *adj* (also **impūnitus**) unpunished

inpūrus, a, um *adj* (also **impūrus**) unclean, filthy, foul; impure; morally foul

inputō [1] *v* (also **imputō**) impute, charge; ascribe

inquam *v ir* say

inquiēs, ētis *adj* restless, impatient; full of tumult

inquiētus, a, um *adj* restless; sleepless

inquinō [1] *v* daub; stain, pollute; soil; 'smear'

inquīrō, īs(iv)ī, īsītum [3] *v* search out; inquire into

inquīsitiō, ōnis *f* search; inquiry

inquīsitor, ōris *m* investigator, examiner

inr- ▸ **irr-**

īnsānābilis, e *adj* incurable; irremediable

īnsānia, ae *f* madness, folly; mad extravagance

īnsāniō [4] *v* be mad, act crazily

īnsānus, a, um *adj* mad, insane; frenzied; wild

■ **īnsānum** adv outrageously, awfully

īnsatiābilis, e adj insatiable

īnscēnsiō, ōnis f going aboard, embarkation

īnsciēns, ntis adj not knowing, unaware

īnscientia, ae f ignorance

īnscītia, ae f ignorance

īnscītus, a, um adj ignorant, uninformed

īnscius, a, um adj not knowing, ignorant; unskilled

īnscrībō, psī, ptum ③ v write in or on, inscribe; brand; record as

īnscrīptiō, ōnis f inscription

īnsculpō, psī, ptum ③ v carve (in or on), engrave; engrave on the mind

īnsecō, secuī, sectum ① v cut; incise

īnsectātiō, ōnis f hostile pursuit; criticism

īnsectō ① v, **īnsector** ① v dep pursue with hostile intent; pursue with hostile speech, etc.

īnsenēscō, nuī ③ v grow old in; wane

īnsepultus, a, um adj unburied

īnsequor, īnsecūtus sum ③ v dep follow closely, pursue; persecute; come after in time

īnserō¹, ēvī, situm ③ v sow or plant in; graft on; implant

īnserō², ruī, rtum ③ v put in; insert

īnsertō ① v thrust in, introduce

īnserviō ④ v with dat serve the interests of; take care of

īnsideō, sēdī, sessum ② v sit (at or on); lie in ambush (in); be troublesome (to)

īnsidiae, ārum fpl ambush; plot, snare

īnsidiātor, ōris m one who lies in wait (to attack, rob, etc.)

īnsidior ① v dep lie in ambush

īnsidiōsus, a, um adj deceitful; insidious; hazardous

īnsīdō, sēdī, sessum ③ v sit down in or on, settle on; take possession of; be firmly implanted in

īnsigne, is nt distinctive mark, emblem; badge of honour

■ **īnsignia, um** pl dress, insignia

īnsigniō ④ v mark with a characteristic feature; distinguish

īnsignis, e adj notable; famous; remarkable; manifest

īnsiliō, luī/līvī ④ v leap into or on

īnsimulō ① v accuse, charge; allege

īnsincērus, a, um adj corrupt; not genuine

īnsinuō ① v work in; insinuate; creep into

īnsistō, stitī ③ v stand or tread on; set foot in, visit; stop; persevere (with); set about

īnsitus, a, um adj innate

īnsociābilis, e adj intractable, implacable

īnsolēns, ntis adj unaccustomed (to), arrogant; insolent; excessive

īnsolentia, ae f unfamiliarity; strangeness; haughtiness; extravagance

īnsolēscō ③ v grow proud

īnsolitus, a, um adj unaccustomed (to)

īnsomnis, e adj sleepless

īnsomnium, (i)ī nt wakefulness

vision, dream

īnsonō, nitum ③ v make a loud noise; sound; resound

īnsōns, ntis adj guiltless; harmless

īnsōpītus, a, um adj unsleeping, wakeful

īnspectō ① v look at, observe; look on, watch

īnspērāns, ntis adj not expecting

īnspērātus, a, um adj unhoped for, unexpected; unforeseen
□ **ex īnspērātō** unexpectedly

īnspiciō, spexī, spectum ③ v look into or at, inspect; examine; observe

īnspīrō ① v blow into or on; inspire; excite

īnstabilis, e adj shaky; unstable; inconstant

īnstāns, ntis adj present; urgent

īnstar nt indec counterpart, equal; moral worth; standard; to the extent, degree, etc. (of); image, likeness; manner

īnstaurātiō, ōnis f renewal, repetition

īnstaurō ① v renew, repeat; restore

īnsternō, strāvī, strātum ③ v spread or strew on; cover (with); lay over

īnstigō ① v urge on; incite, rouse

īnstillō ① v pour in drop by drop, drop in

īnstimulō ① v goad on

īnstinctor, ōris m instigator

īnstinctus¹, ūs m inspiration; instigation, impulse

īnstinctus², a, um adj roused, fired; infuriated

īnstipulor ③ v dep make

conditions, bargain

īnstita, ae f band on a dress

īnstitor, ōris m shopkeeper, pedlar

īnstituō, uī, ūtum ③ v set up; institute; found; build; make; establish; instruct, educate; start on

īnstitūtiō, ōnis f arrangement; instruction, education

īnstitūtum, ī nt plan; habit, custom; mode of life

īnstō, stitī ③ v stand in or upon; threaten; press hard (on); press on (with)

īnstrēnuus, a, um adj sluggish, inactive; spiritless

īnstrepō, puī, pitum ③ v make a loud noise

īnstrūctus, a, um adj equipped, fitted out; learned, trained, skilled

īnstrūmentum, ī nt equipment, tools; an item of such equipment; means

īnstruō, ūxī, ūctum ③ v build, construct; draw up; set in order; instruct, teach; equip, furnish (with)

īnsuēscō, ēvī, ētum ③ v become accustomed (to); accustom

īnsuētus, a, um adj unaccustomed, unused, unusual

īnsula, ae f island; tenement-house, block of flats

īnsulsitās, ātis f dullness, stupidity

īnsulsus, a, um adj boring, stupid

īnsultō ① v leap, jump, dance or trample (upon or in); behave insultingly, mock (at)

īnsum, inesse, īnfuī v ir with

dat be in or on; belong to; be involved in

īnsuō, uī, ūtum ③ *v* sew up (in); sew (on or in)

īnsuper *adv/prep with acc* above, on top; in addition (to); over

īnsuperābilis, e *adj* insurmountable; unconquerable

īnsurgō, surrēxī, surrēctum ③ *v* rise; rise up against

intābēscō, buī ③ *v* pine away; melt away

intāctus, a, um *adj* untouched; intact; untried; virgin

intāminātus, a, um *adj* undefiled; untainted

intectus, a, um *adj* uncovered; naked; open

integellus, a, um *adj* unharmed

integer, gra, grum *adj* whole; entire; safe; healthful; fresh; undecided, open-minded; heartwhole; innocent; pure; upright
□ **ab/dē/ex integrō** afresh, anew

integō, ēxī, ēctum ③ *v* cover

integritās, ātis *f* soundness; chastity; integrity

integrō ① *v* renew; refresh

integumentum, ī *nt* covering, shield, guard

intellegēns, ntis *adj* intelligent; discerning

intellegentia, ae *f* intellect, understanding

intellegō, intelligō, ēxī, ēctum ③ *v* understand

intemerātus, a, um *adj* undefiled; chaste

intemperāns, ntis *adj* unrestrained; licentious

intemperiēs, iēī *f* lack of temperateness (of weather, *etc.*); outrageous behaviour

intempestīvus, a, um *adj* unseasonable, ill-timed; untimely

intempestus, a, um *adj* unseasonable; stormy, unhealthy
□ **nox intempesta** the dead of night

intemptātus, a, um *adj* unattempted; not attacked, unassailed

intendō, ndī, ēnsum ③ *v* stretch; strain, exert; direct

intentō ① *v* point (at); point (weapons, *etc.*) in a threatening manner; threaten

intentus, a, um *adj* intent (upon); eager; strict

intepēscō, puī ③ *v* become warm

inter *prep with acc* between, among; during

interaestuō ① *v* be periodically inflamed

interbītō ③ *v* fail, come to nothing

intercalārius, a, um *adj* (of days or months) inserted in the calendar for the purposes of adjustment, intercalary

intercalō ① *v* insert (a day or month) into the calendar; postpone

intercēdō, essī, essum ③ *v* come between, intervene; put a veto on; interrupt; go bail (for); forbid; oppose; interfere

interceptor, ōris *m* usurper, embezzler

intercessiō, ōnis *f* intervention, veto (of a magistrate)

intercessor, ōris *m* mediator; one who vetoes

intercidō, **idī** ③ *v* happen; perish; fall from memory; cease to exist

intercīdō, **īdī**, **īsum** ③ *v* cut through, sever

intercipiō, **cēpī**, **ceptum** ③ *v* intercept; steal; interrupt

interclūdō, **ūsī**, **ūsum** ③ *v* cut off; hinder; blockade

intercursō ① *v* run in between

intercursus, **ūs** *m* interposition

interdīcō, **īxī**, **ictum** ③ *v* forbid; interdict; prohibit, debar (from)

interdictum, **ī** *nt* prohibition; provisional decree of a praetor

interdiū *adv* by day

interdius *adv* in the daytime

interdō, **dare**, **dedī**, **datum** ① *v* put between

interdum *adv* sometimes, now and then

intereā *adv* meanwhile

intereō, **īre**, **iī**, **itum** *v ir* perish, die; be ruined; cease

interequitō ① *v* ride among or between

interfector, **ōris** *m* murderer, assassin

interficiō, **fēcī**, **fectum** ③ *v* kill; destroy

interfluō, **ūxī** ③ *v* flow between or through

interfor ① *v dep* interrupt; break in upon a conversation

interfūsus, **a**, **um** *adj* poured or spread out between; suffused here and there

interiaceō ② *v* lie between

interibi *adv* meanwhile

intericiō, **iēcī**, **ectum** ③ *v* throw between; introduce, insert

interim *adv* meanwhile; at the same time

interimō, **ēmī**, **ēm(p)tum** ③ *v* do away with; kill; destroy

interior, **ius** *adj* inner, more inward; more remote; more intimate

interitus, **ūs** *m* violent or untimely death; extinction; dissolution

interluō, **uī** ③ *v* flow between

intermisceō, **mixtum** ② *v* intermingle, mix

intermissiō, **ōnis** *f* intermission; pause

intermittō, **mīsī**, **missum** ③ *v* leave off; leave off temporarily; leave a gap (between)

intermorior, **morī**, **mortuus sum** ③ *v dep* perish; pass out

internāscor, **nātus sum** ③ *v dep* grow between or among

interneciō, **ōnis** *f* massacre; extermination

internōdium, **(i)ī** *nt* space between two joints in the body

internōscō, **ōvī**, **ōtum** ③ *v* distinguish between; pick out

internūntius, **(i)ī** *m* intermediary, go-between

internus, **a**, **um** *adj* inward, internal; domestic

interō, **trīvī**, **trītum** ③ *v* powder or crumble (on or into); crumble up

interpellātiō, **ōnis** *f* interruption in speaking

interpellō ① *v* interrupt (in speaking); obstruct

interpolis, e *adj* having received a new appearance, refurbished; not genuine

interpolō ☐ *v* refurbish, touch up, improve

interpōnō, posuī, positum ③ *v* put, lay or set between; interpose; insert; introduce

interpres, etis *m/f* intermediary, go-between; interpreter; translator

interpretātiō, ōnis *f* interpretation; meaning

interpretor ☐ *v dep* interpret; explain; regard

interprimō, pressī, pressum ③ *v* interrupt by pressing, throttle

interrēgnum, ī *nt* space between two reigns, interregnum

interrēx, gis *m* one who holds office between the death of a supreme magistrate and the appointment of a successor

interritus, a, um *adj* fearless

interrogātiō, ōnis *f* question; inquiry; questioning

interrogō ☐ *v* ask, question; examine; indict

interrumpō, ūpī, uptum ③ *v* drive a gap in, break up; cut short, interrupt

intersaepiō, psī, ptum ④ *v* separate; block

interscindō, idī, issum ③ *v* cut through, sever

intersum, esse, fuī *v ir* be or lie between, be in the midst; be present; take part in; be different □ **interest** it makes a difference, it matters; it is of advantage or importance

intervāllum, ī *nt* space between two things, interval; distance; respite

interveniō, vēnī, ventum ④ *v* come between; intervene; occur, crop up; occur by way of a hindrance

interventus, ūs *m* intervention; occurrence of an event

intervertō, rtī, rsum ③ *v* embezzle; cheat

intestābilis, e *adj* detestable, infamous

intestīna, ōrum *ntpl* intestines, guts

intestīnus, a, um *adj* internal; domestic, civil

intexō, xuī, xtum ③ *v* weave (into), embroider (on); cover by twining; insert (into a book, *etc.*)

intimus, a, um *adj* inmost; most secret; most intimate

intolerābilis, e *adj*, **intolerandus, a, um** *adj* insupportable, insufferable

intolerāns, ntis *adj* unable to endure, impatient (of); insufferable

intolerantia, ae *f* impatience

intonō, tonuī ☐ *v* thunder; make a noise like thunder; thunder fort

intōnsus, a, um *adj* uncut; unshaven, unshorn; not stripped of foliage

intorqueō, rsī, rtum ② *v* twist or turn round, sprain; hurl or launch a missile at

intrā *prep with acc* within; within the space of; under, fewer than; *adv* within; under

intractābilis, e *adj* unmanageable, intractable

intremō, muī ③ *v* tremble

intrepidus, **a**, **um** *adj*
undaunted, fearless, untroubled

intrinsecus *adv* on the inside

intrō[1] *adv* within, inside, indoors

intrō[2] [1] *v* go into; enter; penetrate

intrōdūcō, **dūxī**, **ductum** [3] *v*
lead or bring in; introduce

introeō, **īre**, **iī/īvī**, **itum** *v ir* go
inside, enter; invade

introitus, **ūs** *m* going in, entry;
invasion

intrōmittō, **mīsī**, **missum** [3] *v*
send in; admit

intrōrsum, **intrōrsus** *adv* to
within, inwards; internally

intrōspiciō, **spexī**, **spectum** [3]
v examine; inspect; look upon

intubum, **ī** *nt*, **intubus**, **ī** *m*
endive or chicory

intueor [2] *v dep* look at or on;
consider; observe; consider; bear
in mind

intumēscō, **muī** [3] *v* swell up,
rise; become swollen

intumulātus, **a**, **um** *adj*
unburied

intus *adv* inside, within; at home

intūtus, **a**, **um** *adj* defenceless;
unsafe

inultus, **a**, **um** *adj* punished;
scot-free

inumbrō [1] *v* cast a shadow

inundō [1] *v* overflow, inundate,
flood; swarm

inurbānus, **a**, **um** *adj* rustic,
boorish, dull

inūrō, **ussī**, **ustum** [3] *v* burn
in (with a hot iron); brand (on
or with)

inūsitātus, **a**, **um** *adj* unusual

inustus, **a**, **um** *adj* branded into

inūtilis, **e** *adj* useless;
unprofitable; disadvantageous,
inexpedient

invādō, **āsī**, **āsum** [3] *v* go into;
invade; rush into; take possession
of, usurp; seize; attack; rush on (in
order to embrace)

invalidus, **a**, **um** *adj* infirm,
weak, feeble; ineffectual

invehō, **ēxī**, **ectum** [3] *v* carry or
bring in; import
   □ **invehor** ride, drive, sail, *etc.* in;
inveigh against

inveniō, **vēnī**, **ventum** [4] *v*
invent; contrive; find; discover;
manage to get

inventor, **ōris** *m* inventor;
author, contriver; discoverer

inventrīx, **īcis** *f* inventress

inventum, **ī** *nt* invention,
discovery

invenustus, **a**, **um** *adj* unlovely,
unattractive

inverēcundus, **a**, **um** *adj*
shameless; immoral

invergō [3] *v* tip (liquids) upon

invertō, **rtī**, **rsum** [3] *v* turn
upside down; pervert; change

investīgō [1] *v* search out, track
down

investitura, **ae** *f* [LM] investiture

inveterāscō, **ī** [3] *v* grow old;
become established or customary

invicem *adv* by turns, in turn;
reciprocally, mutually

invictus, **a**, **um** *adj* unconquered;
invincible

invideō, **vīdī**, **vīsum** [2] *v with dat*
envy, grudge; hate; refuse

invidia, **ae** *f* envy, jealousy; spite;
dislike

invidiōsus, a, um adj arousing hatred, odium or envy; envious

invidus, a, um adj ill-disposed; envious

invigilō ① v with dat stay awake (over); watch (over) diligently

inviolābilis, e adj sacrosanct, imperishable

inviolātus, a, um adj unhurt; unviolated; inviolable

invīsitātus, a, um adj unvisited, unseen

invīsō, īsī, īsum ③ v go to see, visit; watch over

invīsus, a, um adj hateful, hated

invītāmentum, ī nt inducement

invītātiō, ōnis f invitation

invītō ① v invite; entertain; allure, entice; incite

invītus, a, um adj against one's will, reluctant

invius, a, um adj impassable; inaccessible

invocō ① v call upon; invoke; pray for

involō ① v fly into or at, rush upon; seize on

involvō, lvī, lūtum ③ v wrap (in), cover, envelop; roll along

iō int ritual exclamation uttered under strong emotion

iocor ① v dep jest, joke

iocōsus, a, um adj fond of jokes; full of fun; funny

ioculāris, e adj laughable

ioculor ① v dep jest; joke

ioculus, ī m little joke

iocus, ī m jest, joke; sport

ipse, a, um pn he, she, it; self, very, identical

īra, ae f anger, wrath, rage

īrācundia, ae f irascibility; passion

īrācundus, a, um adj irascible, angry

īrāscor, īrātus sum ③ v dep be angry, fly into a rage

īrātus, a, um adj angry; enraged

īre infin from ▶ eō

irpex, icis m a kind of harrow

irrāsus, a, um adj unshaven

irreligātus, a, um adj unbound, unmoored

irremeābilis, e adj along or across which one cannot return

irreparābilis, e adj irreparable, irrecoverable

irrepertus, a, um adj not found, undiscovered

irrēpō, psī ③ v creep in or into; steal into; insinuate oneself (into)

irreprehēnsus, a, um adj blameless

irrētiō ④ v entangle; catch in a ne[t]

irreverēns, ntis adj disrespectfu[l]

irreverentia, ae f disrespect

irrevocābilis, e adj irrevocable, unalterable

irrīdeō, rīsī, rīsum ② v laugh at, mock, make fun of

irridiculē adv without wit

irrigō ① v water, irrigate; inundat[e] wet, moisten; diffuse

irriguus, a, um adj watering; well-watered

irrīsor, ōris m mocker, scoffer

irrīsus, ūs m mockery; laughing-stock

irrītābilis, e adj easily provoked sensitive

irrītāmen, inis nt,

irrītāmentum, **ī** *nt* incentive, stimulus

irrītātiō, **ōnis** *f* incitement, provocation

irrītō Ⅰ *v* provoke, annoy; excite; stimulate; aggravate

irritus, **a**, **um** *adj* invalid, void; of no effect; vain, useless

irrōrō Ⅰ *v* wet with dew; besprinkle; water; rain on

irrumātiō, **ōnis** *f* being sucked off

irrumō Ⅰ *v* be sucked off

irrumpō, **ūpī**, **uptum** ③ *v* break or burst or rush into; interrupt; invade

irruō, **uī** ③ *v* rush or dash in; charge (at)

irruptiō, **ōnis** *f* violent or forcible entry; assault

is, **ea**, **id** *pn* he, she, it; this, that

iste, **a**, **ud** *pn* this or that of yours; that which you refer to; the well-known

isthmus, **ī** *m* isthmus; strait

istī, **istīc** *adv* there by you; over there; here

istic, **istaec**, **istoc/istuc** *pn* that of yours; that which you refer to

istinc *adv* from over there, from here; from or on your side

istō, **istōc** *adv* to the place where you are; to the point you have reached; to this place

istōrsum *adv* in that direction

istūc *adv* to the place where you are; to the point you have reached

ita *adv* so, thus; even so; yes

itaque *conj* and so; therefore, consequently

item *adv* similarly, likewise

iter, **itineris** *nt* journey; march;

route; road, foot-way
  □ **ex itinere** out of the way, away from the road

iterato *adv* Ⓛ a second time

iterō Ⅰ *v* do a second time, repeat; renew, revise

iterum *adv* again, for the second time

itidem *adv* in the same manner, likewise

itiō, **ōnis** *f* going

itus, **ūs** *m* going, gait; departure

iuba, **ae** *f* mane of a horse; crest (of a helmet)

iubar, **aris** *nt* radiance of the heavenly bodies, brightness; first light of day; source of light

iubeō, **iussī**, **iussum** ② *v* order, command; decree
  □ **salvēre iubeō** greet, welcome

iūcunditās, **ātis** *f* pleasantness, charm

iūcundus, **a**, **um** *adj* pleasant, agreeable; delightful

iūdex, **icis** *m/f* judge; arbitrator; umpire; juror; critic

iūdicium, **(i)ī** *nt* judicial investigation; judgment; verdict; opinion; discernment

iūdicō Ⅰ *v* judge, give judgement; sentence; decide; appraise

iugālis, **e** *adj* yoked together; nuptial

iugerum, **ī** *nt* two-thirds of an acre of land

iūgis, **e** *adj* continual, constant; ever-flowing

iugō Ⅰ *v* marry; join (to)

iugulō Ⅰ *v* cut the throat, kill; butcher

iugulum, **ī** *nt*, **iugulus**, **ī** *m*

collar-bone; throat

iugum, ī nt yoke (for oxen); team; pair (of horses, etc.); ridge (of a mountain)

iūmentum, ī nt beast of burden

iūnctūra, ae f joint; association

iuncus, ī m rush

iungō, iūnxī, iūnctum ③ v yoke, harness; join; clasp (hands); unite

iūnior, ōris adj younger

iūniperus, ī f juniper

Iūnius, (i)ī m June

iūre adv justly, rightly; deservedly

iūrgium, (i)ī nt quarrel, dispute; abuse

iūrgō ① v quarrel, scold

iūriscōnsultus, ī m lawyer, jurist

iūrisdictiō, ōnis f jurisdiction, legal authority; administration of justice

iūrō ① v swear, take an oath; conspire

iūs¹, iūris nt broth, soup, sauce

iūs², iūris nt law; right; authority; court of justice; code; (war) conventions

iūs iūrandum, iūris iūrandī nt oath

iussū m abl only with possessive adj or gen by order of

iussum, ī nt order, command

iūstitia, ae f justice; equity

iūstitium, (i)ī nt cessation of judicial and all public business, due to national calamity

iūstus, a, um adj just, equitable; lawful; legitimate; well grounded; proper; right; regular; impartial
■ **iūsta, ōrum** ntpl due observances; funeral offerings

iuvenālis, e adj youthful, young

iuvenca, ae f young cow, heifer

iuvencus, ī m young bull; young man

iuvenēscō, nuī ③ v grow up; grow young again

iuvenīlis, e adj youthful

iuvenis, is adj young, youthful
■ **iuvenis, is** m/f youth, young man or woman

iuventa, ae f youth

iuventās, ātis f, **iuventūs, ūtis** f youth

iuvō, iūvī, iūtum ① v help, assist; delight; benefit
□ **iuvat** v impers it pleases

iuxtā prep with acc near by, near to; adv close; alike; equally
□ ~ **ac** as much as

. . . .

K k

. . . .

Kalendae, ārum fpl the first day of the month

Kyrie int/n indec 'Lord', (the first word of) part of the Mass

L

labāscō ③ v fall to pieces, break up; waver

labefaciō, fēcī, factum ③ v loosen; shake; cause to totter; undermine

labefactō ① v shake; cause to waver; make unsteady, loosen; undermine

labellum, ī nt lip

lābēs, bis f land-slip; subsidence; disaster, ruin; fault; stain, blemish, dishonour

labō ① v totter, be ready to fall; waver

lābor, lāpsus sum ③ v dep slide or glide down; fall down; drop; perish; go wrong

labor, ōris m labour, toil, exertion; hardship, distress

labōriōsus, a, um adj laborious, painstaking

labōrō ① v labour, take pains; strive; be sick; be oppressed or troubled; be in danger; work (at)

lābrum, ī nt basin, vat; bathing-place

labrum, ī nt lip; edge (of a vessel, ditch, river, etc.)

lābrusca, ae f wild vine

labyrinthēus, a, um adj of a labyrinth

labyrinthus, ī m labyrinth, maze

lac, lactis nt milk; milky juice

lacer, era, erum adj mangled, torn; rent

lacerātiō, ōnis f mangling; tearing

lacerna, ae f cloak

lacerō ③ v tear, mangle; shatter, torment, harass; 'lash'

lacerta, ae f lizard

lacertōsus, a, um adj muscular, brawny

lacertus, ī m lizard; muscular part of the arm; strength

lacessō, ssīvī/ssiī, ssītum ③ v excite, provoke, challenge; harass; assail

lacinia, ae f edge of garment, fringe, hem

lacrima, ae f tear

lacrimābilis, e adj mournful; tearful

lacrimō ① v **lacrimor** ① v dep shed tears, weep

lacrimōsus, a, um adj tearful, weeping; causing tears

lactēns, ntis adj unweaned, sucking; juicy

lacteolus, a, um adj milk-white

lacteus, a, um adj milky; milk-white

☐ ~ **orbis / circulus** Milky Way

lactūca, ae f lettuce

lacūna, ae f pool; hollow, pit, cavity

lacūnar, āris nt panelled ceiling

lacus, ūs m lake; pond; tank, reservoir, trough

☐ ~ **Curtiī** an area in the Roman forum

laedō, laesī, laesum ③ v hurt; injure; annoy

laena, ae f woollen double cloak

laetābilis, e adj joyful

laetitia, ae f joy; gladness

laetor ① *v dep* rejoice, be joyful

laetus, a, um *adj* joyful, cheerful, glad; fortunate; luxuriant; lush; pleasing, welcome, beautiful; rich

laevus, a, um *adj* left; unfavourable, harmful
■ **laeva, ae** *f* left hand

lagēna, ae *f* flask; bottle

lagōna, ae *f* bottle with a narrow neck

laguncula, ae *f* small flask

laicus, a, um *adj* 🔒 lay (i.e. not belonging to the clergy)

lambō, ③ *v* lick; wash

lāmenta, ōrum *ntpl* wailing, weeping, groans, laments

lāmentābilis, e *adj* doleful; lamentable

lāmentātiō, ōnis *f* lamentation, wailing

lāmentor ① *v dep* lament; bewail

lamia, ae *f* witch

lampas, adis *f* torch; lamp

lampyris, idis *f* glow-worm, fire-fly

lāna, ae *f* wool; soft hair; down

lānātus, a, um *adj* woolly

lancea, ae *f* light spear, lance

lancinō ① *v* tear in pieces, rend apart, mangle

lāneus, a, um *adj* woollen

langueō ② *v* be sluggish; be unwell; wilt; lack vigour

languēscō, uī ③ *v* become faint or languid or weak; wilt

languidulus, a, um *adj* drooping, wilting; drowsy

languidus, a, um *adj* languid, faint, weak; ill; sluggish; inert

languor, ōris *m* faintness,
feebleness; languor; apathy

laniēna, ae *f* butcher's shop

lānificus, a, um *adj* wool-working, spinning, weaving

lāniger, era, erum *adj* wool-bearing, fleecy; woolly

laniō ① *v* tear, mutilate; pull to pieces

lanista, ae *m* manager of a troop of gladiators, trainer

lānūgō, inis *f* down, youth

lānx, ancis *f* plate, dish; pan of a pair of scales

lapathum, ī *nt*, **lapathus, ī** *m/f* sorrel

lapicīda, ae *m* stone-cutter

lapideus, a, um *adj* of stone; stony

lapidō ① *v* throw stones at; stone
■ **lapidat** *v impers* it rains stones

lapidōsus, a, um *adj* full of stones, stony; gritty

lapillus, ī *m* little stone, pebble; precious stone, gem

lapis, idis *m* stone; milestone; precious stone

lappa, ae *f* bur; plant bearing bur

lāpsō ① *v* slip, lose one's footing

lāpsus¹ *pple* from ▶ **lābor**

lāpsus², ūs *m* gliding, sliding; slipping and falling

laqueāre, is *nt* panelled ceiling

laqueātus, a, um *adj* panelled

laqueus, ī *m* noose, snare; trap

lār, aris *m* tutelary household god; home

lārdum, ī *nt* bacon

largior ④ *v dep* give bountifully; give presents corruptly; bestow, grant, permit; overlook, condone

largitās, ātis f abundance; munificence

largiter adv plentifully; liberally; greatly

largitiō, ōnis f distribution of doles, land, etc., largess; bribery

largītor, ōris m liberal giver; briber

largus, a, um adj lavish; plentiful; bountiful

āridum ▶ lārdum

āsarpīcifer, era, erum adj silphium-bearing

ascīvia, ae f playfulness; wantonness, lasciviousness

ascīviō, īī v frisk; sport; run riot

ascīvus, a, um adj wanton; frolicsome; sportive; mischievous; free from restraint in sexual matters

assitūdō, inis f faintness, weariness

assō v tire, weary; wear out

assulus, a, um adj tired, weary

assus, a, um adj languid, weary, tired

atē adv widely, far and wide

atebra, ae f hiding-place, retreat; air; subterfuge

atebrōsus, a, um adj full of urking places; lurking in concealment

ateō v lie hid, lurk; escape notice

ater, eris m brick; ingot

atericius, a, um adj made of bricks

atex, icis m water; (any) liquid; spring water; juice; wine; oil

atibulum, ī nt hiding-place, den

atīnē adv in Latin

Latīnus, a, um adj Latin

latitō v remain in hiding; be hidden

lātitūdō, inis f breadth, width; extent

lātor, ōris m mover or proposer (of a law)

lātrātor, ōris m barker, one who barks

lātrātus, ūs m barking

latrō, ōnis m brigand, bandit; plunderer

lātrō v bark; bark at

latrōcinium, (i)ī nt robbery with violence; bandit raid; pillage; band of robbers

latrōcinor v dep engage in brigandage or piracy

latrunculus, ī m robber, brigand

latus, eris nt side; flank

lātus, a, um adj broad, wide; spacious; extensive

laudābilis, e adj praiseworthy

laudātiō, ōnis f praising; eulogy

laudātor, ōris m one who praises, eulogist

laudō v praise, extol; deliver a funerary eulogy of

laurea, ae f flaurel-tree; laurel wreath or branch; triumph, victory

laureātus, a, um adj adorned with a laurel
　□ **laureātae litterae** a despatch reporting a victory

laureus, a, um adj of the laurel tree, laurel

lauriger, era, erum adj crowned with laurel

laurus, ī f bay-tree; laurel; laurel crown; triumph

laus, **dis** f praise; glory; excellence; merit

■ **laudes** pl [LM] lauds (part of the daily cycle of prayer)

lautumiae, **ārum** fpl stone-quarry, especially used as a prison

lautus, **a**, **um** adj clean; well-turned-out, fine; sumptuous

lavātiō, **ōnis** f the action of washing; facilities for washing

lavō, **lāvī**, **lautum/lavātum/lōtum** ① v wash; bathe, soak

laxāmentum, **ī** nt respite; opportunity

laxitās, **ātis** f roominess, largeness

laxō ① v expand, extend; open up; slacken; relax; weaken

laxus, **a**, **um** adj wide, loose; roomy; slack; open; lax

lea, **ae** f lioness

leaena, **ae** f lioness

lebēs, **ētis** m caldron

lectīca, **ae** f litter

lectīcārius, **(i)ī** m litter-bearer

lēctiō, **ōnis** f reading (aloud); perusal; choosing

lectisternium, **(i)ī** nt special feast of supplication at which a banquet was offered to the gods, couches being spread for them to recline upon

lēctitō ① v read repeatedly; be in the habit of reading

lēctor, **ōris** m reader

lectulus, **ī** m bed or couch

lectus, **ī** m couch, (bridal-)bed

lēgātiō, **ōnis** f embassy

lēgātum, **ī** nt bequest, legacy

lēgātus, **ī** m ambassador, legate; deputy; commander

lēgerupa, **ae** m law-breaker

lēgerupiō, **ōnis** f law-breaking

lēgifer, **era**, **erum** adj law-giving

legiō, **ōnis** f Roman legion; army

legiōnārius, **a**, **um** adj of a legion, legionary

lēgitimus, **a**, **um** adj lawful, right; legitimate; real, genuine; just; proper

legō, **lēgī**, **lēctum** ③ v gather; choose; furl; traverse; read

lēgō ① v send as an envoy; choose as deputy; bequeath

legūmen, **inis** nt pulse, leguminous plant

lembus, **ī** m small fast-sailing boa...

lemurēs, **um** mpl malevolent ghosts of the dead, spectres, shades

lēna, **ae** f procuress; brothel-keeper

lēnīmen, **inis** nt alleviation, solace

lēniō ④ v mitigate; allay; ease; explain away

lēnis, **e** adj smooth, soft, mild, gentle, easy, calm

lēnitās, **ātis** f slowness; gentleness, mildness

lēnō, **ōnis** m brothel-keeper, bawd, procurer

lēnōcinium, **(i)ī** nt pandering; allurement, enticement; flattery

lēnōnius, **a**, **um** adj of a pimp

lēns, **ntis** f the lentil-plant

lentēscō ③ v become sticky; rela...

lentitūdō, **inis** f slowness in action; apathy

lentō ① v bend under strain

lentus, **a**, **um** adj pliant; tough;

145

clinging; slow; lazy; calm; procrastinating; phlegmatic

lēnunculus, ī *m* skiff

leō, ōnis *m* lion

leopardus, ī *m* leopard

lepidus, a, um *adj* agreeable, charming, delightful, amusing; witty

lepōs, ōris *m* charm, grace; wit; humour

leprae, ārum *fpl* leprosy

lepus, oris *m* hare

lētālis, e *adj* deadly, fatal, mortal

lēthaeus, a, um *adj* of Lethe; causing forgetfulness; of the underworld

Lēthē, ēs *f* Lethe, the river of forgetfulness

lētifer, era, erum *adj* deadly; fatal

lētum, ī *nt* death; death and destruction

leuuga, ae *f* 〔LM〕 league (approx. 3 miles)

levāmen, inis *nt* alleviation, solace

levāmentum, ī *nt* alleviation, mitigation, consolation

levis, e *adj* light; nimble; trivial, trifling; gentle; capricious; fickle, inconstant

lēvis, e *adj* smooth; polished; free from coarse hair; smooth

levitās, ātis *f* lightness; restlessness; mildness; fickleness; shallowness

levō 〔 〕 *v* lift; support; relieve; lessen; free from

lēvō 〔 〕 *v* smooth; polish

lēx, gis *f* law; rule; principle; condition

□ ~ **cūriāta** law passed by the assembly of the thirty divisions of the Roman people

lībāmen, inis *nt*,

lībāmentum, ī *nt* drink-offering; first-fruits

libella, ae *f* small silver coin; plumb-line, level

libellus, ī *m* little book; memorial; petition; pamphlet, defamatory publication; programme

libēns, ntis *adj* willing; cheerful

Līber, erī *m* Bacchus; wine

liber, brī *m* inner bark of a tree; book; volume

līber, era, erum *adj* free; unimpeded; void of; frank, free-spoken; licentious; outspoken

līberālis, e *adj* gentlemanly; well-bred; liberal; open-handed; generous; lavish

līberālitās, ātis *f* nobleness, kindness; frankness; liberality; gift

līberātor, ōris *m* deliverer, liberator

līberē *adv* freely; frankly; shamelessly

līberī, ōrum *mpl* children

līberō 〔 〕 *v* release, free; acquit; absolve

līberta, ae *f* freedwoman

lībertās, ātis *f* freedom; liberty; frankness of speech, outspokenness

lībertīnus, a, um *adj* of a freedman
  ■ **lībertīna, ae** *f* freedwoman
  ■ **lībertīnus, ī** *m* freedman

lībertus, ī *m* freedman

libet, uit, libitum est 〔 〕 *v impers* it pleases, is agreeable

◻ **libet mihi** I feel like, I want

libīdinōsus, a, um *adj* lustful, wanton; capricious

libīdō, inis *f* desire; lust; passion

Libitīna, ae *f* goddess of funerals

libō ① *v* nibble, sip; pour in offering; impair; graze, skim

libra, ae *f* Roman pound (about three-quarters of a modern pound); level; balance; scales; one of the twelve signs of the zodiac

librāmentum, ī *nt* weight, counterpoise

librārius, a, um *adj* of books ■ **librārius, (i)ī** *m* copyist, secretary; bookseller

librō ① *v* weigh; level; balance, poise

libum, ī *nt* cake; consecrated cake

liburna, ae *f* light, fast-sailing warship

liburnica, ae *f* a fast warship

licēns, ntis *adj* free, unrestrained

licentia, ae *f* liberty, licence; freedom; disorderliness; outspokenness

liceō ② *v* fetch (a price)

liceor ② *v dep* bid at an auction

licet, uit, licitum est ② *v impers with dat of person* permitted it is lawful or permitted; one may or can; *int* yes, all right!; *conj* with verb in subj although

licitus, a, um *adj* lawful, permitted

lícium, (i)ī *nt* thread; leash or heddle (in weaving)

līctor, ōris *m* lictor

ligāmen, inis *nt*, **līgāmentum, ī** *nt* bandage; string

lignārius, (i)ī *m* carpenter; timber-merchant

lignātiō, ōnis *f* collecting firewood

lignātor, ōris *m* one who collects firewood

ligneus, a, um *adj* of wood, wooden

lignor ① *v dep* collect firewood

lignum, ī *nt* wood; firewood; timber; 'stump'

ligō¹, ōnis *m* mattock, hoe

ligō² ① *v* bind, fasten; attach; tie up

ligustrum, ī *nt* privet, white-flowered shrub

līlium, (i)ī *nt* lily

līma, ae *f* file; polishing, revision

limbus, ī *m* ornamental border to a robe

līmen, inis *nt* lintel, threshold; entrance; house

līmes, itis *m* strip of uncultivated ground to mark the division of land; stone to mark a boundary; boundary; track; channel; route

līmō ① *v* file; polish; file down; detract gradually from

līmōsus, a, um *adj* miry, muddy

limpidus, a, um *adj* clear

līmus¹, ī *m* mud; slime

līmus², a, um *adj* oblique, sidelong

līnea, ae *f* string, cord; fishing-line; plumb-line; finishing-line

līneāmentum, ī *nt* line; *pl* outlines, features

līneus, a, um *adj* made of flax or linen

lingō, līnxī, līnctum ③ *v* lick

lingua, ae *f* tongue; speech, language; dialect

līniger, **era**, **erum** *adj* wearing linen

linō, **lēvī**, **litum** 3 *v* smear, plaster (with); erase; befoul

linquō, **līquī** 3 *v* leave, quit, forsake; abandon

linter, **tris** *f* small light boat; trough, vat

linteum, **ī** *nt* linen cloth; linen; sail; napkin; awning

linteus, **a**, **um** *adj* of linen

linum, **ī** *nt* flax; linen, thread; rope; fishing-line; net

lippitūdō, **inis** *f* inflammation or watering of the eyes

lippus, **a**, **um** *adj* having watery or inflamed eyes

liquefaciō, **fēcī**, **factum** 3 *v* melt, dissolve

liqueō, **licuī/liquī** 2 *v* be clear to a person; be evident

liquēscō 3 *v* become liquid, melt; decompose

liquidus, **a**, **um** *adj* liquid, fluid; clear; manifest; smooth; melodious; evident

liquō 1 *v* melt; strain

liquor 3 *v dep* dissolve; waste away; flow

liquor, **ōris** *m* fluid, liquid

līs, **lītis** *f* quarrel; lawsuit

litania, **ae** *f* [LM] prayer, litany

lītera, **ae** *f* letter of the alphabet
■ **literae**, **ārum** *pl* letter, literature; writings; the elements of education

literātus, **a**, **um** *adj* learned; cultured

litigiōsus, **a**, **um** *adj* quarrelsome, contentions

litigō 1 *v* quarrel; go to law

litō 1 *v* obtain or give favourable omens from a sacrifice; make an (acceptable) offering (to)

lītōrālis, **e** *adj*, **lītoreus**, **a**, **um** *adj* of the seashore

litt- ▶ **līt-**

littera, **ae** *f* (also **lītera**) letter of the alphabet
■ **litterae**, **ārum** *pl* letter, literature; writings; the elements of education

litterātus, **a**, **um** *adj* (also **līterātus**) learned; cultured

litūra, **ae** *f* smearing; erasure; blot

lītus, **oris** *nt* seashore, coast

lituus, **ī** *m* curved staff carried by augurs; a kind of war-trumpet curved at one end

līveō 2 *v* be livid or discoloured; be envious

līvidus, **a**, **um** *adj* livid, slate-coloured; discoloured by bruises; envious, spiteful

līvor, **ōris** *m* bluish discoloration (produced by bruising, *etc.*), envy, spite

lixa, **ae** *m* camp-follower

locātiō, **ōnis** *f* hiring out or letting (of property)

locō 1 *v* place, station; contract (for); farm out (taxes) on contract

locuplēs, **ētis** *adj* rich, well-to-do; rich (in)

locusta, **ae** *f* locust; lobster

locūtus *pple* from ▶ **loquor**

logi *int* fairy-tales! rubbish!

lolium, **(i)ī** *nt* a grass found as a weed in corn, darnel

longaevus, **a**, **um** *adj* of great age, ancient

longē *adv* far off; far; a great while;

very much; by a large margin
□ ~ **lātēque** far and wide

longinquitās, ātis f length;
distance; duration

longinquus, a, um adj far off,
distant; of long duration
□ **ē longinquō** from a distance

longitūdō, inis f length

longus, a, um adj long, tall;
lasting a long time, tedious

lopas, adis f limpet

loquācitās, ātis f talkativeness

loquāx, ācis adj talkative,
loquacious

loquēla, loquella, ae f speech,
utterance

loquor, locūtus sum ③ v dep
speak, talk, say; mention

lōrārius, (i)ī m strap-man, slave
constable

lōrīca, ae f cuirass; parapet,
breast-work

lōrum, ī nt thong; pl rawhide
whip; reins

lōtus, ī f lotus plant; nettle plant

lub- ▸ **lib-**

lubēns, ntis adj (also **libēns**)
willing; cheerful

lubet, uit, lubitum est ② v
impers (also **libet**) it pleases, is
agreeable
□ ~ **mihi** I feel like, I want

lubīdō, inis f (also **libīdō**)
desire; lust; passion

lūbricus, a, um adj slippery;
sinuous; inconstant; hazardous;
ticklish; deceitful

lūcar, āris nt sum of
money allocated for public
entertainments

lucellum, ī nt small or petty gain

lūceō, lūxī ② v shine; glitter; be
conspicuous

lucerna, ae f oil lamp

lucernaris, e adj LM by
candlelight

lūcēscō ③ v begin to shine, grow
light

lūcidus, a, um adj bright, shining;
clear

Lūcifer¹, erī m morning star LM
Lucifer, the Devil

lūcifer², era, erum adj light-
bringing

lūcifugus, a, um adj avoiding the
light of day

Lūcīna, ae f goddess of childbirth
childbirth

lucripeta, ae m one who is
avaricious or money-grubbing

lucror ① v dep gain, win; make a
profit (out of)

lucrōsus, a, um adj gainful,
lucrative

lucrum, ī nt gain, profit; avarice
□ **faciō lucrī** make a profit

luctāmen, inis nt struggling,
exertion

luctātor, ōris m wrestler

lūctificus, a, um adj dire,
calamitous

luctor ① v dep wrestle; struggle;
fight (against)

lūctuōsus, a, um adj mournful,
grievous

lūctus, ūs m sorrow, lamentation;
mourning; instance or cause
of grief

lūcubrō ① v work by lamp-light,
'burn the midnight oil'; make or
produce at night

lūculentus, a, um adj excellent

ne; beautiful

cus, ī m grove

dibrium, (i)ī nt mockery; aughing-stock

dibundus, a, um adj having un; carefree

dicer, lūdicrus, cra, crum dj connected with sport or the tage

lūdicrum, ī nt stage-play; how; source of fun, plaything

dificātiō, ōnis f mockery

dificātor, ōris m mocker

dificō ① v, **lūdificor** ① v dep nake sport of, trifle with

dō, ūsī, ūsum ③ v play; sport; ease; trick

dus, ī m play, game, pastime; port, entertainment, fun; school, lementary school

ēs, uis f plague, pestilence; courge, affliction

geō, lūxī, lūctum ② v mourn, ament; be in mourning

gubris, bre adj mourning; nournful; grievous

mbus, ī m the loins; the loins as he seat of sexual excitement

men, inis nt light; daylight; day; amp, torch; life; eye; (of a person) lory, cynosure

na, ae f moon; month

nāris, e adj lunar

nātus, a, um adj crescent-shaped

nō ① v make crescent-shaped,

ō¹, luī ③ v wash

ō², luī, lūtum/luitum ③ v pay; tone for

ə poenam ~ suffer punishment

pa, ae f she-wolf; prostitute

lupānar, āris nt brothel

lupātus, a, um adj furnished with jagged teeth
■ **lupātī, ōrum** mpl jagged toothed bit

Lupercālia, ium ntpl festival promoting fertility held on 15 February

Lupercus, ī m priest in the Lupercalia

lupīnus, a, um adj of or belonging to a wolf; made of wolf-skin

lupus, ī m wolf; grappling iron; sea-bass

lūridus, a, um adj sickly yellow; sallow, wan, ghastly

luscinia, ae f nightingale

luscus, a, um adj blind in one eye

lūsor, ōris m player; tease; one who treats (of a subject) lightly

lūstrālis, e adj relating to purification; serving to avert evil

lūstrō ① v purify; illuminate; move round, over or through; go about; review, survey

lūstrum, ī nt purificatory ceremony; period of five years

lustrum, ī nt haunts of wild beasts; pl den of vice

lūsus, ūs m play, game; sport, amusement; amorous sport

lūteolus, a, um adj yellow

lūteus, a, um adj yellow; saffron

luteus, a, um adj of mud or clay; good for nothing

lutulentus, a, um adj muddy; turbid; dirty; morally polluted

lutum, ī nt mud, clay; dirt

lūtum, ī nt yellow dye; any yellow colour

lūx, lūcis f light (of the sun, stars, *etc.*); daylight, day; splendour; eyesight

luxuria, ae f, **luxuriēs, iēī** f luxury, extravagance, rankness, thriving condition

luxuriō ⓘ v, **luxurior** ⓘ v dep grow rank or luxuriant; frisk; indulge oneself

luxuriōsus, a, um adj luxuriant, exuberant; immoderate; wanton; luxurious; self-indulgent

luxus, ūs m luxury, soft living; sumptuousness

lychnus, ī m lamp

lympha, ae f water; water-nymph

lymphātus, a, um adj frenzied, frantic

lynx, yncis m/f lynx

lyra, ae f lyre; lyric poetry; Lyre (constellation)

lyricus, a, um adj lyric

lyristēs, ae m lyre-player

. . . .

Mm

. . . .

macellum, ī nt provision-market

macer, cra, crum adj lean, meagre, poor

mācēria, ae f wall of brick or stone

mācerō ⓘ v make soft, soak; worry, annoy

machaera, a f single-edged sword

māchina, ae f machine; siege-engine

māchināmentum, ī nt siege-engine

māchinātiō, ōnis f mechanism, engine of war

māchinātor, ōris m engineer; (fig) projector

māchinor ⓘ v dep devise; plot

maciēs, iēī f leanness, meagreness; poverty

macrēscō, ruī ③ v become thin, waste away

macte int well done! bravo!

mactō ⓘ v honour; sacrifice; slaughter

macula, ae f spot; stain, blemish; mesh in a net

maculō ⓘ v spot; pollute; dishonour, taint

maculōsus, a, um adj spotted; disreputable

madefaciō, fēcī, factum ③ v make wet; soak
□ **madefīō, fierī** be moistened, be made wet

madeō ② v be wet or sodden; be wet with tears, perspiration, *etc.*

madēscō, duī ③ v become moist or wet

madidus, a, um adj moist, wet, drenched; drunk

maenas, adis f Bacchante, female votary of Bacchus; frenzied woman

maereō ② v be sad, grieve, lament; bewail

maeror, ōris m sadness, grief, mourning

maestitia, ae f sadness, grief

maestus, a, um adj sad, melancholy; gloomy; woeful; distressing

māgālia, ium *ntpl* huts

mage ▶ magis

magicus, a, um *adj* magical

magis *adv* more, rather

magister, trī *m* master, chief; expert, tutor, teacher; pilot of a ship
□ **magister equitum** dictator's lieutenant; master of the horse

magisterium, (i)ī *nt* office of a president; instruction

magistra, ae *f* instructress

magistrātus, ūs *m* magistracy; office; magistrate

magnanimus, a, um *adj* noble in spirit, brave, generous

magnēs, ētis *m* magnet

magnidicus, a, um *adj* boastful

magnificentia, ae *f* greatness, nobleness; grandeur; splendour

magnificus, a, um *adj* noble, eminent, stately; sumptuous, magnificent, boastful

magniloquentia, ae *f* exalted diction; braggadocio

magniloquus, a, um *adj* boastful

magnitūdō, inis *f* greatness, bulk; intensity; importance

magnopere *adv* much, greatly, especially, strongly

magnus, a, um *adj* great, large, tall; loud; much; noble, grand; mighty

magus, a, um *adj* magical
■ **magus, ī** *m* magician, sorcerer

maiestās, ātis *f* majesty; authority; grandeur; high treason

maior, ius *adj* greater
□ **nātū ~** older
□ **maiōre opere** all the more

maiōrēs, ōrum *mpl* ancestors

Maius, (i)ī *m* May

māla, ae *f* cheeks, jaws

malacia, ae *f* dead calm

male *adv* badly, ill, wickedly, unfortunately; amiss
□ **habēre male** bother, annoy

maledīcō, īxī, ictum ③ *v* speak ill of, abuse

maledictum, ī *nt* reproach, taunt

malefaciō, fēcī, factum ③ *v* do evil or wrong, injure

maleficium, (i)ī *nt* misdeed, crime; injury

maleficus, a, um *adj* wicked, criminal, harmful

malesuādus, a, um *adj* ill-advising

malevolus, a, um *adj* spiteful, malevolent

mālifer, era, erum *adj* apple-bearing

malignitās, ātis *f* ill-will, spite, malice; niggardliness

malignus, a, um *adj* spiteful; niggardly; narrow

malitia, ae *f* wickedness; vice, fault

malleolus, ī *m* fire-dart

malleus, ī *m* hammer, mallet

mālō, mālle, māluī *v ir* wish or choose rather, prefer

malum, ī *nt* evil, calamity, misfortune
■ **~** *int* the devil! the hell! for goodness' sake!

mālum, ī *nt* apple

mālus¹, ī *m* pole; mast of a ship

mālus², ī *f* apple-tree

malus, a, um *adj* bad, evil,

wicked; unfortunate; weak

malva, ae f mallow-plant

mamma, ae f breast, udder

manceps, ipis m contractor, agent

mancipium, (i)ī nt formal mode of purchase; property; right of ownership; slave

mancipō ① v transfer, sell; surrender

mancus, a, um adj maimed, crippled; powerless

mandātum, ī nt order, commission

mandō¹, ndī, mānsum ③ v chew, champ

mandō² ① v commit to one's charge, commission; command; entrust (to)

māne nt indec morning
■ ∼ adv in the morning; early next day

maneō, mānsī, mānsum ② v stay, remain; await; abide by; last; endure

mānēs, ium mpl gods of the Lower World; shades or ghosts of the dead; mortal remains; underworld; death

mangō, ōnis m slave-dealer

manica, ae f long sleeve; handcuff

manifestus, a, um adj clear, evident; plainly guilty; flagrant
■ **manifestō** adv in the act, openly

manipulāris, e adj belonging to the ranks, private
■ **manipulāris, āris** m common soldier; marine

manipulātim adv in handfuls; in companies

manipulus, ī m handful, bundle; company of soldiers

mannus, ī m pony

mānō ① v flow, pour; be shed; be wet; spring

mānsiō, ōnis f stay, visit; stopping-place on a journey

mānsitō ① v spend the night, sta[y]

mānsuēfaciō, fēcī, factum ③ tame; civilize, make mild

mānsuēscō, ēvī, ētum ③ v tame; become or grow tame

mānsuētūdō, inis f mildness, clemency

mānsuētus, a, um adj tame; mild, gentle

mantēle, is nt, **mantēlium, (i)ī** nt hand-towel; napkin

mantica, ae f travelling-bag, knapsack

mantō ① v remain, stay, wait for

manubiae, ārum fpl general's share of the booty; prize-money; profits

manūmittō, īsī, issum ③ v sometimes as two words
□ **manū mittō** set at liberty, emancipate, free

manus, ūs f hand; fist; trunk (of an elephant); handwriting; band or soldiers; company; armed force of any size; workman; legal power of a husband
□ **cōnferō manum** join battle

mapālia, ium ntpl huts in which the Nomadic Africans lived

mappa, ae f table-napkin; cloth dropped as a signal to start a race in the circus

marceō ② v be enfeebled, weak or faint

marcēscō ③ v pine away; become weak, enfeebled or languid

marchia, ae f LM march, area governed by a marquis

marchio, onis m LM marquis

marcidus, a, um adj withered, rotten; exhausted

mare, ris nt sea; sea-water

margarītum, ī nt pearl

marginō ① v provide with borders

margō, inis m/f edge; rim; border

marīnus, a, um adj of or belonging to the sea, marine; sea-born
  □ rōs marīnus rosemary

marisca, ae f fig; haemorrhoids, piles

maritimus, a, um adj sea..., maritime; (of people) used to the sea
  ■ **maritima, ōrum** ntpl sea-coast

marītō ① v marry, give in marriage

marītus, a, um adj married, united, 'wedded'
  ■ **marita, ae** f wife
  ■ **marītus, ī** m husband; mate

marmor, oris nt marble; marble statue; sea

marmoreus, a, um adj made of marble; marble-like

Mars, rtis m (also **Māvors**) god of war; war, battle; warlike spirit; the advantage in war

marsuppium, (i)ī nt pouch, bag, purse

Martiālis, e adj of or belonging to Mars

Martius, a, um adj of or belonging to Mars; March

martyrium, (i)ī nt LM martyrdom

mās, maris adj male; masculine; manly

māsculus, a, um adj male; manly; virile

massa, ae f lump, mass; bulk, size

Massicum, ī nt Massic wine

mastīgia, ae m one who deserves a whipping, rascal

matara, ae f Gallic throwing spear

māter, tris f mother; matron; origin, source; motherland, mother-city

mātercula, ae f affectionate term for mother

māterfamiliās,
mātrisfamiliās f mistress of the house; respectable married woman

māteria, ae f, **māteriēs, iēī** f material; timber; subject-matter

māternus, a, um adj motherly, maternal

matertera, ae f maternal aunt

mathēmaticus, ī m mathematician; astrologer

mātrimōnium, (i)ī nt marriage, matrimony

mātrimus, a, um adj having a mother living

mātrōna, ae f wife, matron

mātrōnālis, e adj of or befitting a married woman

matula, ae f jar; chamber-pot; blockhead, fool

mātūrēscō, ruī ③ v become ripe, ripen; mature

mātūritās, ātis f ripeness

mātūrō ① v make ripe; hasten; make haste to

mātūrus, a, um adj ripe; mellow;

m

mature; seasonable, timely; early; speedy

mātūtīnus, a, um *adj* of or belonging to the early morning ■ **matutinae, arum** *fpl*, **matutinum, ī** *nt* LM morning prayers, matins

Māvors, tis ▶ alternative name for **Mars**

maximus, a, um *adj* sup of □ **magnus** greatest, *etc.*; □ **maximō opere** most urgently

mē *pn acc/abl of* **▶ ego**

meātus, ūs *m* movement, course

medēns, ntis *m* physician, doctor

medeor ② *v dep* heal, cure; remedy

mēdica, ae *f* a kind of clover, lucerne

medicābilis, e *adj* curable

medicāmen, inis *nt* drug, remedy, medicine; dye

medicāmentum, ī *nt* drug, remedy, medicine

medicīna, ae *f* medical art; medicine; treatment, remedy

medicīnus, a, um *adj* medical

medicō ① *v* heal, cure; medicate; dye

medicor ① *v dep* heal, cure

medicus, a, um *adj* healing, medical ■ **medicus, ī** *m* physician, doctor

medimnum, ī *nt*, **medimnus, ī** *m* a dry measure, Greek 'bushel' (six **modiī**)

mediocris, cre *adj* middling, moderate, tolerable, mediocre

mediocritās, ātis *f* medium, moderateness; mediocrity

meditāmentum, ī *nt* training

exercise

meditātiō, ōnis *f* contemplation, meditation; practising

mediterrāneus, a, um *adj* remote from the coast, inland

meditor ① *v dep* think about constantly, ponder; intend; devise; reflect; practise; work over in performance

medium, (i)ī *nt* middle; public, publicity □ **in mediō** open to all □ **ē mediō abeō** die

medius, a, um *adj* mid, middle; neutral; ambiguous; middling, ordinary; moderate

medulla, ae *f* marrow, kernel; innermost part; quintessence

medullitus *adv* to the very marrow

medullula, ae *f* the marrow of one's bones; inmost part

megistānes, um *mpl* nobles of Parthia and other eastern countries, grandees

mehercle ▶ hercle

meiō, mi(n)xī, mi(n)ctum ③ *v* urinate

mel, mellis *nt* honey; sweetness; darling

melicus, a, um *adj* musical, lyrica ■ **melicus, ī** *m* a lyric poet

mēlinum, ī *nt* white pigment, Melian white

melior, ius *adj* [comp of **bonus**] better

mellifer, era, erum *adj* honey-producing

mellītus, a, um *adj* sweetened with honey; honey-sweet

melos, ī *nt* song

membrāna, ae *f* membrane; skin; parchment

membrātim *adv* limb by limb

membrum, ī *nt* limb; the genital member

meminī, isse *v ir* remember; retain in the mind; attend to; recall in writing, speech, *etc.*

memor, oris *adj* mindful (of), remembering, unforgetting; grateful; commemorative

memorābilis, e *adj* memorable, remarkable

memoria, ae *f* memory; recollection; time within remembrance; history

memoriter *adv* word for word, verbatim

memorō ① *v* remind of; mention; relate

menda, ae *f* blemish, fault; error

mendācium, (i)ī *nt* lie; counterfeit

mendāx, ācis *adj* lying, false; deceitful; counterfeit

mendīcitās, ātis *f* beggary

mendīcō ① *v* beg for; be a beggar

mendīcus, ī *m* beggar

mendōsus, a, um *adj* faulty, erroneous; prone to error

mendum, ī *nt* blemish, fault; error

mēns, mentis *f* mind, intellect; reason, judgement; frame of mind; disposition, intention

mēnsa, ae *f* table; meal; course (at a meal); banker's counter

mēnsārius, (i)ī *m* money-changer, banker; treasury official

mēnsis, is *m* month

mēnsor, ōris *m* land-surveyor; surveyor of building-works

mēnstruus, a, um *adj* monthly

mēnsula, ae *f* little table

mēnsūra, ae *f* measuring; length, area, capacity, *etc.*

mentiō, ōnis *f* mention

mentior ④ *v dep* lie, deceive; feign; speak falsely about; give a false impression; mimic

mentula, ae *f* the male sexual organ

mentum, ī *nt* chin

meō ① *v* go along, pass, travel

merācus, a, um *adj* undiluted, neat

mercātor, ōris *m* trader, merchant

mercātūra, ae *f* trade, commerce

mercātus, ūs *m* gathering for the purposes of commerce; market; fair

mercēnnārius, a, um *adj* hired, mercenary
■ ∼, **(i)ī** *m* hired worker; mercenary

mercēs, ēdis *f* hire, pay, wages, salary; reward; rent, price

mercimōnium, (i)ī *nt* merchandise, purchase

mercor ① *v dep* trade; buy

merda, ae *f* dung, excrement

merenda, ae *f* afternoon meal

mereō ② *v*, **mereor** ② *v dep* earn, get; deserve; be rewarded
□ ∼ **stipendia** serve as soldier; draw pay as a soldier

meretrīcius, a, um *adj* of, belonging to, or typical of a courtesan

meretrīcula, ae *f* courtesan

m

meretrīx, īcis f courtesan, kept woman

merges, itis f sheaf of corn

mergō, rsī, rsum ③ v immerse; plunge; bury; hide; drown; overwhelm; plunge in ruin

mergus, ī m a sea-bird, probably a gull

merīdiānus, a, um adj pertaining to noon; southern

merīdiēs, iēī f midday, noon; south

merīdiō ① v take a siesta

meritum, ī nt desert; service, kindness; due reward

meritus, a, um adj deserved, due

mersō ① v dip (in), immerse; overwhelm, drown

merula, ae f blackbird; a dark-coloured fish, the wrasse

merus, a, um adj pure, unmixed; bare, only, mere; sheer
■ **merum, ī** nt wine unmixed with water

merx, cis f a commodity; pl goods, merchandise

messis, is m/f harvest, crop; harvest time

messor, ōris m reaper, harvester

mēta, ae f cone-shaped turning post at either end of a race-track; limit; end; conical shape; cone

metallum, ī nt metal; mine; quarry

mēticulōsus, a, um adj timorous; involving fear, awful

mētior, mēnsus sum ④ v dep measure; traverse; walk or sail through; estimate, gauge

metō, messuī, messum ③ v reap, mow, cut off

mētor ① v dep measure off, mark out

metuō, uī, ūtum ③ v be afraid of; be afraid to; fear

metus, ūs m fear; anxiety; awe; object of dread

meus, a, um adj my, mine

mī dat of ▶ **ego**

mīca, ae f particle, grain, crumb

micō, micuī ① v move quickly, quiver; dart; throb; flash, glitter

migrātiō, ōnis f change of abode; move

migrō ① v change one's residence or position; pass into a new condition; move, shift

mihī pn dat of ▶ **ego**

mīles, itis m soldier; foot-soldier; soldiery

mīli ▶ **milli**

mīliārium, (i)ī nt (also **mīlliārium**) milestone

mīliēns adv a thousand times

mīliēs adv (also **mīlliēs**) a thousand times

mīlitāris, e adj military; warlike

mīlitia, ae f military service; campaign

mīlitō ① v serve as a soldier

milium, ī nt millet

mille adj indec (in pl **milia** or **millia**) thousand; thousands; innumerable
□ **mille passūs** mpl a mile

millē(n)simus, a, um adj a thousandth

mīlliārium, (i)ī nt milestone
□ ~ **aureum** golden milestone erected by Augustus at the head of the forum in Rome from which all distances were reckoned

mīlliē(n)s *adv* a thousand times

mīlvus, ī *m* kite

mīma, ae *f* actress performing in mimes

mīmus, ī *m* actor in mimes; mime; farce

mina, ae *f* silver (Greek) coin

mināciae, ārum *fpl* threats

minae, ārum *fpl* threats, menaces; warning signs

mināx, ācis *adj* threatening; boding ill

Minerva, ae *f* a person's natural capacity, intelligence, tastes, *etc.*; weaving; spinning

mingō ▶ meiō

minimus, a, um *adj* [sup of **parvus**] least, smallest

minister, trī *m* attendant; servant; agent; accomplice

ministerium, (i)ī *nt* service; employment; commission; public works

ministra, ae *f* female servant; female religious official

ministrō 1 *v with dat* attend (to), serve; furnish; supply

monitor 1 *v dep with dat* threaten

minor[1] 1 *v dep with dat* threaten

minor[2], **minus** *adj* [comp of **parvus**] smaller, lesser, younger, *etc.*;
  □ **nātū ~** younger
  □ **faciō minoris** consider of less importance
  ■ **minōrēs, um** *mpl* descendants

minuō, uī, ūtum 3 *v* lessen; impair; abate; make smaller; grow less

ninus *adv* less; not so well; not quite

minūtātim *adv* bit by bit

minūtus, a, um *adj* small, insignificant, petty

mīrābilis, e *adj* wonderful, marvellous, extraordinary

mīrābundus, a, um *adj* wondering

mīrāculum, ī *nt* wonder, marvel; amazing event

mīrandus, a, um *adj* remarkable

mīrātor, ōris *m* admirer

mīrificus, a, um *adj* wonderful; amazing

miror 1 *v dep* wonder at, be amazed (at); admire

mīrus, a, um *adj* wonderful, astonishing

misceō, mixtum/mistum 2 *v* mix, mingle; embroil; confound; stir up

misellus, a, um *adj* poor, wretched

miser, era, erum *adj* wretched, unfortunate, miserable; distressing

miserābilis, e *adj* pitiable; wretched

miserātiō, ōnis *f* pity, compassion

miserē *adv* wretchedly; desperately

misereor 2 *v dep* pity
  □ **mē miseret, miserētur** 2 *v impers with gen* it distresses me (for); I pity

miserēscō 3 *v with gen* have compassion (on)

miseria, ae *f* wretchedness, misery; distress; woe

misericordia, ae *f* pity, compassion; pathos

misericors, rdis *adj* merciful,

tender-hearted

miseror v dep feel sorry for

missa, ae f Mass, Eucharist; dismissal

missilis, e adj that may be thrown, missile

missiō, ōnis f sending (away); release; discharge (of soldiers); reprieve

missitō v send repeatedly

missus, ūs m sending (away); despatch; shooting, discharge of missiles

mītēscō v become soft and mellow; ripen; grow mild; soften

mītigō v soften; lighten, alleviate; soothe; civilize

mītis, e adj mild; sweet and juicy, mellow; placid; soothing; clement

mitra, ae f an oriental head-dress

mittō, mīsī, missum v send; cast, hurl; throw away; dismiss; disregard, say nothing of; subject (to)
□ **manū ~** set free, manumit

mnēmosynum, ī nt souvenir

mōbilis, e adj quick, active; movable; changeable; inconstant

mōbilitās, ātis f agility, quickness of mind; mobility; inconstancy

moderābilis, e adj controllable

moderāmen, inis nt rudder; management, government

moderātiō, ōnis f moderation; guidance, government

moderātor, ōris m governor, master; user; one who restrains

moderātus, a, um adj moderate; restrained; sober; temperate

moderor v dep guide; control;

regulate; govern

modestia, ae f restraint, temperateness; discipline; modesty

modestus, a, um adj restrained; mild; modest; reserved; disciplined

modicus, a, um adj moderate; temperate, restrained

modius, (i)ī m Roman dry measure, peck

modo adv only; just now; provided that; if only
□ **modo ... modo** at one time ... at another

modulor v dep sing; play; set to music

modus, ī m measure; size; rhythm; metre; mode; manner; bound, limit; end; moderation

moecha, ae f adulteress

moechor v dep commit adultery

moechus, ī m adulterer

moenia, ium ntpl town walls, fortified town

mola, ae f millstone; pl mill; cake of ground barley and salt (for sacrifices); sacrificial meal

molāris, is m rock as large as a millstone used as a missile; molar tooth

mōlēs, lis f huge, heavy mass, lump; monster; massive structure; danger; trouble; effort; vast undertaking

molestus, a, um adj troublesome, tiresome

mōlīmen, inis nt effort, vehemence; bulk; weight

mōlīmentum, ī nt exertion, labour

mōlior ④ *v dep* labour to bring about; strive; labour at, perform with effort; propel, set in motion; build

mollēscō ③ *v* become soft; become gentle *or* effeminate

molliculus, a, um *adj* soft, delicate; somewhat unmanly

molliō ④ *v* soften; mitigate; make easier; tame, enfeeble

mollis, e *adj* soft, tender, mild; mellow; pleasant; weak; effeminate; impressionable; sensitive

mollitia, ae *f*, **mollitiēs, iēī** *f* softness; tenderness; weakness; effeminacy

molō, luī ③ *v* grind

mōmen, inis *nt* movement; impulse; a trend

mōmentum, ī *nt* movement; impulse; effort; moment; importance; influence

momordī ▸ mordeō

monachus, ī *m* 〖LM〗 monk

monasterium, (i)ī *nt* 〖LM〗 monastery

monazon, ontis *m* 〖LM〗 monk

monēdula, ae *f* jackdaw

moneō ② *v* warn; advise; presage

moneta, ae *m* 〖LM〗 money

monial, lis *f* 〖LM〗 nun

monīle, is *nt* necklace; collar; collar (for horses and other animals)

nonimentum ▸ monumentum

nonitiō, ōnis *f* advice; warning

nonitor, ōris *m* counsellor, preceptor; prompter

nonitus, ūs *m* warning;

command; advice, counsel

mōns, ntis *m* mountain; towering heap; huge rock

mōnstrātor, ōris *m* guide, demonstrator

mōnstrō ① *v* show, point out; teach; reveal

mōnstrum, ī *nt* unnatural thing *or* event regarded as on omen, portent, sign; monstrous thing; monster; atrocity

mōnstruōsus, a, um *adj* strange, monstrous, ill-omened

montānus, a, um *adj* mountain...; mountainous
■ **montānus, ī** *m* mountain- *or* hill-dweller

monticola, ae *m/f* mountain-dweller

montuōsus, a, um *adj* mountainous

monumentum, ī *nt* memorial, monument; tomb; record; a literary work, book; history

mora, ae *f* delay; hindrance, obstacle

morātor, ōris *m* delayer; loiterer

mōrātus, a, um *adj* endowed with character *or* manners of a specified kind; gentle, civilized

morbidus, a, um *adj* diseased; unhealthy

morbus, ī *m* sickness, disease, illness, distress; weakness, vice

mordāx, ācis *adj* biting, snappish; tart; cutting, sharp; caustic

mordeō, momordī, morsum ② *v* bite; sting; hurt, distress; vex; criticize, carp at

mordicus *adv* by biting, with the teeth; tenaciously

moribundus, **a**, **um** *adj* dying

mōrigerus, **era**, **erum** *adj* compliant, indulgent

morior, **morī**, **mortuus sum** ③ *v dep* die; fail; decay

moror ① *v dep* delay, stay behind; devote attention to

mōrōsus, **a**, **um** *adj* hard to please, pernickety

mors, **mortis** *f* death; corpse; annihilation

morsus, **ūs** *m* bite; sting; anguish, pain

mortālis, **e** *adj* mortal; transient; human; of human origin

mortālitās, **ātis** *f* mortality; death

mortārium, **(i)ī** *nt* mortar

mortifer, **mortiferus**, **era**, **erum** *adj* death-bringing, deadly

mortuus, **a**, **um** *adj* dead, deceased

mōrum, **ī** *nt* fruit of the black mulberry

mōrus, **ī** *f* black mulberry-tree

mōs, **mōris** *m* custom, usage; manner; style; civilization; law ■ **mōrēs** *pl* character; behaviour; morals □ **gerō mōrem** gratify, accommodate oneself to; behave

mōtō ① *v* set in motion, shake, stir, *etc.*

mōtus, **ūs** *m* moving, motion; commotion; disturbance; emotion; prompting; manoeuvre

moveō, **mōvī**, **mōtum** ② *v* move, stir; brandish; agitate; affect; provoke; set in motion; shift; influence

mox *adv* soon, next in position

mucrō, **ōnis** *m* sharp point; sword

mūcus, **ī** *m* mucus, snot

mūgil, **mūgilis**, **lis** *m* grey mullet

mūgiō ④ *v* low, bellow; make a loud deep noise

mūgītus, **ūs** *m* lowing, bellowing; roaring, rumble

mūla, **ae** *f* she-mule; mule

mulceō, **lsī**, **lsum** ② *v* stroke, touch lightly; soothe, appease; charm, beguile

Mulciber, **eris/erī** *m* Vulcan; fire

mulcō ① *v* beat up; worst

mulctra, **ae** *f*, **mulctrum**, **ī** *nt* milking-pail

mulgeō, **lsī**, **lsum/lctum** ② *v* milk

muliebris, **bre** *adj* womanly, female, feminine; womanish, effeminate □ **muliebria patī** be used as a catamite

mulier, **eris** *f* woman; wife, mistress

muliercula, **ae** *f* (little, weak, foolish, *etc.*) woman

mūliō, **ōnis** *m* muleteer, mule-driver

mullus, **ī** *m* red mullet

mulsum, **ī** *nt* drink from honey and wine

multa, **ae** *f* fine; penalty

multicavus, **a**, **um** *adj* porous

multifāriam *adv* in many places

multifidus, **a**, **um** *adj* splintered

multigenus, **a**, **um** *adj* of many different sorts

multimodīs *adv* in many different ways

multiplex, **icis** adj having many windings; having many layers or thicknesses; multifarious; changeable

multiplicō ☐ v multiply; increase

multitūdō, **inis** f great number, multi-tude; crowd; mob

multivolus, **a**, **um** adj that lusts after many, amorous

multō[1] adv much, by far; long (before or after)

multō[2] ☐ v punish; fine

multum adv much, plenty

multus, **a**, **um** adj much, great; many a; large, intense; assiduous; tedious

mūlus, **ī** m mule

munditia, **ae** f, **mund: tiēs**, **iēī** f cleanness, elegance of appearance, manners or taste

mundus[1], **ī** m toilet, ornaments; world; universe

mundus[2], **a**, **um** adj clean, elegant; delicate, refined

mūnia, **ōrum** ntpl duties, functions

mūniceps, **ipis** m citizen of a municipium; native of the same municipium

mūnicipālis, **e** adj of, belonging to or typical of a **municipium**; (in contempt) provincial

mūnicipium, **(i)ī** nt town subject to Rome, but governed by its own laws; free town

mūnificentia, **ae** f bountifulness, munificence

mūnificus, **a**, **um** adj bountiful, liberal, munificent

mūnīmen, **inis** nt fortification; defence

mūnīmentum, **ī** nt fortification; bulwark; defence

mūniō[4] v fortify; build (a road); defend; safeguard

mūnītiō, **ōnis** f fortifying; fortification; repair

mūnītor, **ōris** m one who builds fortifications

mūnus, **eris** nt function, duty; gift; public show

mūnusculum, **ī** nt small present or favour

mūrālis, **e** adj of walls; of or connected with a (city) wall; turreted

mūrena, **ae** f kind of eel, the moray

mūrex, **icis** m purple dye; purple cloth

murmur, **ris** nt murmur, murmuring; humming; growling; whisper; rustling; roaring (of the sea, a lion or the thunder)

murmurō ☐ v hum, murmur, mutter; roar

murreus, **a**, **um** adj having the colour of myrrh, i.e. reddish-brown

mūrus, **ī** m wall; city wall

mūs, **ris** m mouse

Mūsa, **ae** f Muse; poetic composition

  ■ **Mūsae** pl sciences, poetry

musca, **ae** f fly

muscārium, **(i)ī** nt fly-swat

muscōsus, **a**, **um** adj mossy

mūsculus, **ī** m mouse; mussel

muscus, **ī** m moss

mūsicē adv musically; luxuriously

mūsicus, **ī** m musician

mussītō ☐ v mutter; keep quiet (about)

m

mussō ① *v* say in an undertone, mutter; keep quiet (about)

mustēla, mustella, ae *f* weasel

mustum, ī *nt* unfermented grape-juice, must

mūtābilis, e *adj* changeable; inconstant

mūtātiō, ōnis *f* changing; exchange

mutilō ① *v* maim, mutilate; lop off

mutilus, a, um *adj* mutilated; hornless, having stunted horns

mūtō ① *v* alter, change; exchange; shift; substitute (for)

muttiō ④ *v* mutter, murmur

mūtuātiō, ōnis *f* borrowing

mūtuor ① *v dep* borrow

mūtus, a, um *adj* silent, dumb, mute; speechless

mūtuus, a, um *adj* borrowed, lent; mutual, in return
  ■ **mūtuum, ī** *nt* loan

myoparōn, nis *m* light naval vessel

myrīcē, ēs *f* tamarisk (bush)

myrtētum, ī *nt* myrtle-grove

myrteus, a, um *adj* of myrtle

myrtum, ī *nt* myrtle-berry

myrtus, ī *f* myrtle, myrtle-tree

mystērium, (i)ī *nt* sacred mystery; secret

mysticus, a, um *adj* belonging to the sacred mysteries; mysterious

Nn

naevus, ī *m* mole (on the body); birth-mark

Nāias, adis *f*, **Nāis, idos** *f* water-nymph; nymph

nam *conj* for

namque *conj* certainly; for; now, well then

nancīscor, nactus/nānctus sum ③ *v dep* get, obtain, receive; meet with

nānus, ī *m* dwarf

narcissus, ī *m* the flower narcissus

nardum, ī *nt*, **nardus, ī** *f* nard; nard-oil

nāris, is *f* nose
  ■ **nārēs, ium** *pl* nostrils; nose

nārrābilis, e *adj* that can be narrated

nārrātiō, ōnis *f* narrative, story

nārrātus, ūs *m* narrative, story

nārrō ① *v* tell, narrate; describe, tell about

nāscor, nātus sum ③ *v dep* be born; proceed (from), rise; grow

nāsus, ī *m* nose; sense of smelling

nāsūtus, a, um *adj* having a long nose

nāta, ae *f* daughter

nātālēs, ium *mpl* parentage, origin

nātālis, e *adj* of or belonging to birth, natal; native
  ■ **~, is** *m* birthday
  ■ **natale, is** *nt* feastday, esp. Christmas

natātor, ōris *m* swimmer

natēs, ium *fpl* buttocks

nātiō, ōnis *f* race, nation, people; class, set

nativitas, tatis *f*⟨ʟᴍ⟩ Christmas

nātīvus, a, um *adj* innate; natural, native

natō ⟨1⟩ *v* swim; float; be inundated; sway, lack firmness, waver
  □ **rērum ~** the way things happen

nātūra, ae *f* nature; character

nātūrālis, e *adj* natural; innate

nātus, a, um *adj* born
  ■ **~** *m/f* son, daughter; *pl* children, offspring

nātū *adv* by birth
  □ **~ maior** older
  □ **~ minor** younger

nauarchus, ī *m* commander of a warship

naucum, ī *nt* a thing of trifling value

naufragium, (i)ī *nt* shipwreck; ruin; wreckage

naufragus, a, um *adj* shipwrecked; causing shipwreck; ruined

naupēgus, ī *m* shipwright

nausea, ae *f* sea-sickness; nausea

nauseō ⟨1⟩ *v* be sea-sick; feel sick

nauta, ae *m* sailor, seaman

nauticus, a, um *adj* nautical
  ■ **nauticī, ōrum** *mpl* seamen, sailors

nāvālis, e *adj* nautical, naval
  ■ **nāvāle, is** *nt* dock, slipway

nāvicula, ae *f* little ship, boat

nāviculārius, (i)ī *m* ship-owner

nāvifragus, a, um *adj* shipwrecking

nāvigābilis, e *adj* navigable, suitable for shipping

nāvigātiō, ōnis *f* sailing, sea-voyage

nāviger, era, erum *adj* ship-bearing, navigable

nāvigium, (i)ī *nt* vessel, ship

nāvigō ⟨1⟩ *v* sail, navigate

nāvis, is *f* ship
  □ **~ longa** ship of war
  □ **~ onerāria** merchant ship
  □ **nāvem solvō** set sail

nāvita ▶ **nauta**

nāviter *adv* diligently; wholly

nāvō ⟨1⟩ *v* devote oneself to; accomplish
  □ **operam ~** devote energies to

nāvus, a, um *adj* active, industrious

nē *particle* (usu. only with **ego, tu, ille, iste** or **hic**) (*affirmative*) verily; indeed

-ne *particle in direct questions* interrogative not implying anything about the answer expected e.g. **vidēsne** do you see? *in indirect questions* whether

nē *adv/conj* not; that not; in order that not; lest
  □ **~ ... quidem** not even

nebula, ae *f* mist, fog; cloud

nebulō, ōnis *m* rascal, scoundrel

nec *adv/conj* (also **neque**) neither; nor; and not
  □ **nec nōn** and also
  □ **nec ... nec** neither ... nor

necdum *conj* and (but) not yet

necessārius, a, um *adj* necessary; indispensable; connected by close ties of friendship, relationship *or* obligation
  ■ **~, (i)ī** *m* close relative; near friend

necesse *adv* essential; inevitable

necessitās | nēquam

necessitās, ātis f necessity; constraint; poverty

necessitūdō, inis f obligation, affinity; compulsion

necessum ▶ necesse

necne conj or not

necnōn conj strong affirmative (and) also, (and) furthermore

necō 1 v kill

necopīnāns, ntis adj not expecting; unawares

necopīnātus, a, um adj, **necopīnus, a, um** adj unexpected, unforeseen

nectar, aris nt nectar, the drink of the gods; anything sweet, pleasant or delicious

nectareus, a, um adj sweet as nectar

nectō, nex(u)ī, nexum 3 v bind, tie or join together; link; contrive

nēcubi adv (so) that at no place, lest at any place; (so) that on no occasion, lest on any occasion

nēcunde adv (so) that from nowhere, lest from anywhere

nēdum conj still less; not to speak of; much more

nefandus, a, um adj impious, wicked; abominable

nefārius, a, um adj offending against moral law, wicked

nefās nt indec sin, crime (against divine law); wicked action; portent, horror
■ **nefās!** int oh horror!

nefāstus, a, um adj contrary to divine law
□ **diēs nefāstī** days unfit for public business

negitō 1 v deny or refuse repeatedly

neglegēns, ntis adj heedless, neglectful

neglegentia, ae f heedlessness, neglect

neglegō, neglígō, ēxī, ēctum 3 v not to heed, neglect; overlook; do without

negō 1 v say no, deny; refuse, decline

negōtiātor, ōris m wholesale trader or dealer

negōtior 1 v dep do business, trade

negōtiōsus, a, um adj active, occupied

negōtium, (i)ī nt business; difficulty; trouble; situation

nēmō m/f no one, nobody
□ ~ **nōn** every(one)

nemorālis, e adj belonging to a wood or forest, sylvan

nemorivagus, a, um adj forest-roving

nemorōsus, a, um adj well-wooded

nempe conj without doubt; why, clearly; admittedly

nemus, oris nt wood, forest

nēnia, ae f funeral dirge sung; incantation; jingle

neō, nēvī, nētum 2 v spin; weave; produce by spinning

nepōs, ōtis m grandson; descendant; spendthrift, playboy
■ **nepōtēs** pl descendants

neptis, is f granddaughter; female descendant

Neptūnus, ī m Neptune; sea

nēquam adj indec worthless; bad

nēquāquam *adv* by no means, not at all

neque *adv/conj* neither; nor; and not

neque ... neque neither ... nor

nequedum ▸ necdum

nequeō, īre, īvī *v ir* be unable (to)

nēquicquam, nēquīquam *adv* in vain

nē ... quidem *particle* not even

nēquiter *adv* badly; wickedly

nēquitia, ae *f*, **nēquitiēs, iēī** *f* (moral) badness, vice; villainy; naughtiness

Nēreis, idos *f* sea-nymph

Nēreus, ei/eos *m* Nereus; the sea

nervōsus, a, um *adj* sinewy; vigorous

nervus, ī *m* sinew; nerve; bow-string; string (of a lute, *etc.*); fetter; strength, vigour

nesciō *v* not to know; be unfamiliar with

nescioquis, quid *pn* someone or other

nescius, a, um *adj* not knowing; ignorant

nex, cis *f* violent death, murder

nexilis, e *adj* woven together; intertwined

nexum, ī *nt*, **nexus, ūs** *m* obligation between creditor and debtor

nexus, ī *m* one reduced to quasi-slavery for debt, bondman

nī *adv/conj* if ... not; unless
□ **quid ~?** why not?

nictō 🔲 *v* blink

nīdāmenta, ōrum *ntpl* materials for a nest

nīdor, ōris *m* rich, strong smell, fumes

nīdulus, ī *m* little nest

nīdus, ī *m* nest; set of nestlings; eyrie

niger, gra, grum *adj* black, dark; discoloured, sombre; ill-omened

nigrāns, ntis *adj* black, dark-coloured; shadowy; murky

nigrēscō, ruī 🔲 *v* become black, grow dark

nigrō 🔲 *v* be black

nihil *nt indec* nothing; nothing

nihilōminus *adv* nevertheless, notwithstanding

nihilum¹ *adv* nothing as yet

nihilum², ī *nt* nothing
□ **dē nihilō** for nothing; for no reason

nīl *nt indec* [contraction of **nihil**] nothing

nimbōsus, a, um *adj* full of, *or* surrounded by, rain clouds

nimbus, ī *m* rain-cloud; cloud; cloud-burst; shower

nimiō *adv* by a very great degree, far

nīmīrum *adv* without doubt, evidently, forsooth

nimis *adv* too much; exceedingly

nimium *adv* too much, too, very much

nimius, a, um *adj* excessive, too great, too much; intemperate; over-confident

ningit, nīnxit ③ *v impers* it snows

nisi *conj* if not; unless

nīsus, ūs *m* resting one's weight on the ground; endeavour; exertion; strong muscular effort; advance

niteō ② *v* shine, glitter; be sleek and plump

nitēscō ③ *v* begin to shine

nitidus, a, um *adj* shining, glittering, bright; polished; spruce; sleek

nītor, nīsus/nīxus sum ③ *v dep* lean or rest (on); endeavour; exert oneself; rely (on)

nitor, ōris *m* brightness, splendour; beauty; elegance, smartness

nivālis, e *adj* snowy, snow-covered; snow-like

niveus, a, um *adj* snowy; snow-white

nivōsus, a, um *adj* full of snow, snowy

nix, nivis *f* snow; white hair

nixus, ūs *m* straining; *pl* the efforts of childbirth, travail

nō ③ *v* swim; float

nōbilis, e *adj* famous, celebrated; high-born; superior
  ■ ∼, is *m* nobleman

nōbilitās, ātis *f* renown, glory; high birth; excellence; nobleness

nōbilitō ① *v* make known; render famous; render notorious

noceō ② *v with dat* hurt, injure, impair

noctivagus, a, um *adj* night-wandering

noctū *adv* by night, at night

noctua, ae *f* the little owl

nocturnus, a, um *adj* nocturnal; under conditions of night

nōdō ① *v* tie in a knot or knots

nōdōsus, a, um *adj* tied into many knots, full of knots; knotty

nōdus, ī *m* knot; rope; difficulty; intricacy; bond

nōlo, nōlle, nōluī *v ir* not to wish; be unwilling; refuse

nōmen, inis *nt* name; family; celebrity

nōmenc(u)lātor, ōris *m* slave whose duty it was to attend his master and inform him of the names of those he met; announce

nōminātim *adv* by name, expressly

nōminātiō, ōnis *f* naming; nomination (to an office)

nōminitō ① *v* name, term

nōminō ① *v* name; nominate; accuse, mention, speak of, make famous

nōn *adv* not

nona, ae *f* none(s), afternoon prayers

Nōnae, ārum *fpl* the Nones; the fifth day of the month, except in March, May, July, and October, when the Nones fell on the seventh day

nōnāgintā *adj indec* ninety

nōnānus, a, um *adj* of the ninth legion

nōndum *adv* not yet

nōngentī, ae, a *adj* nine hundred

nōnne *particle* is it not the case that ...?

nōnnēmō *m/f* some persons, a few

nōnnihil *nt indec* a certain amount

adv in some measure

nōnnūllus, **a**, **um** *adj* not a little; some, several

nōnnunquam *adv* sometimes

nōnus, **a**, **um** *adj* the ninth

norma, **ae** *f* carpenter's square; standard, pattern

nōs *pn* we

nōscitō ① *v* recognize; be acquainted with

nōscō, **nōvī**, **nōtum** ③ *v* get a knowledge of, learn to know; know

noster, **tra**, **trum** *adj* our, our own, ours; one of us, our friend; favourable to us; dear, good

nota, **ae** *f* mark, sign; letter; word; writing; spot; brand, tattoo-mark

notābilis, **e** *adj* remarkable, notable

notārius, **(i)ī** *m* secretary, shorthand writer

notātiō, **ōnis** *f* marking

nōtēscō, **tuī** ③ *v* become known; become famous

nothus, **a**, **um** *adj* spurious; illegitimate; (of animals) cross-bred

nōtiō, **ōnis** *f* judicial examination or enquiry

nōtitia, **ae** *f*, **nōtitiēs**, **lēī** *f* celebrity; knowledge; conception; acquaintance; carnal knowledge

notō ① *v* mark; write down; observe; censure; brand, stain, scar

Notus, **Notos**, **ī** *m* south wind

nōtus, **a**, **um** *adj* known; notorious; familiar

novācula, **ae** *f* razor

novāle, **is** *nt*, **novālis**, **is** *f* fallow-land; enclosed land, field

novellus, **a**, **um** *adj* young, tender

novem *adj indec* nine

November, **Novembris**, **bris** *m* November

novendiālis, **e** *adj* lasting nine days; held on the ninth day after a person's death

novēnus, **a**, **um** *adj* nine each; nine at a time

noverca, **ae** *f* stepmother

novercālis, **e** *adj* of a stepmother

novīcius, **a**, **um** *adj* new, new kind of

noviē(n)s *adv* nine times

novissimus, **a**, **um** *adj* last, rear; most recent; utmost

novitās, **ātis** *f* newness, novelty; unfamiliarity, surprise

novō ① *v* make new, renew; alter

novus, **a**, **um** *adj* new; young, fresh, recent

◻ **~ homō** first in one's family to attain the consulate

nox, **noctis** *f* night; darkness; blindness

◻ **nocte/noctū** by night

noxa, **ae** *f* hurt, injury; crime; punishment; harm

noxia, **ae** *f* wrongdoing, injury

noxius, **a**, **um** *adj* harmful, noxious; guilty, criminal

nūbēs, **bis** *f* cloud; smoke; swarm; gloominess; threat (of war, calamity, *etc.*)

nūbifer, **era**, **erum** *adj* cloud-capped; that brings clouds

nūbigena, **ae** *m* cloud-born

nūbilis, **e** *adj* marriageable; nubile

nūbilus, **a**, **um** *adj* cloudy; lowering

■ **nūbilum**, **ī** *nt* cloudy sky *or* weather

nūbō, psi, ptum ③ v with dat marry (a husband)

nudius adv [from **nunc** and **diēs**]: □ ~ **tertius** (by Roman reckoning) the day before yesterday

nūdō ① v bare; strip, uncover; plunder; reveal, disclose

nūdus, a, um adj naked, bare; destitute; unarmed

nūgae, ārum fpl trifles, nonsense; trash; frivolities; bagatelle

nūgātor, ōris m one who plays the fool; teller of tall stories

nūgātōrius, a, um adj trifling, worthless, futile, paltry

nūgor ① v dep play the fool, talk nonsense; trifle

nullātenus adv LM by no means

nūllus, a, um adj not any, no

num particle is it the case that ...?; in indirect questions whether

nūmen, inis nt nod; bias; divine will; divine presence; deity, god

numerābilis, e adj possible or easy to count

numerō ① v count, number

numerōsus, a, um adj numerous; harmonious

numerus, erī m number; rhythm; poetry, metre; class

nummātus, a, um adj moneyed

nummus, ī m coin, money

numquam adv at no time, never; not in any circumstances

nūmus ▶ nummus

nunc adv now, at present □ **nunc ... nunc** one time ... another time

nunciam adv here and now; now at last

nuncupō ① v call, name; express

nūndinae, ārum fpl market-day; (fig) traffic

nūndinor ① v dep buy or sell in the market; practise trade of a discreditable kind

nūndinum, ī nt the period from one market-day to the next

nunquam ▶ numquam

nūntiō ① v announce; relate, inform

nūntius, a, um adj bringing tidings, reporting ■ ~, (i)ī m messenger; message

nūper adv recently, not long ago; in modern times

nūpta, ae f wife, married woman

nūptiae, ārum fpl marriage

nūptiālis, e adj nuptial

nurus, ūs f daughter-in-law; young woman

nusquam adv nowhere, in no place; to no place; on no occasion □ **nusquam esse** not exist

nūtō ① v nod; sway to and fro; waver; waver in allegiance

nūtrīcius, (i)ī m tutor; foster-father

nūtrīcula, ae f nurse

nūtrīmen, inis nt, **nūtrīmentum, ī** nt nourishment, sustenance

nūtriō ④ v suckle, nourish, foster, bring up; tend; deal gently with

nūtrīx, īcis f wet-nurse, nurse

nūtus, ūs m nod; will, command

nux, cis f nut; thing of no value

nympha, ae f, **nymphē, ēs** f nymph, young wife, maiden

Oo

ō *int* o! oh!

□ ~ **sī** if only

ob *prep with acc* for; by reason of; on behalf of; in payment for

obaerātus, a, um *adj* involved in debt

■ ~, **ī** *m* debtor

obambulō ① *v* walk up to, so as to meet; traverse

obarmō ① *v* arm

obarō ① *v* plough up

obc- ▸ **occ-**

obcaecō ① *v* (also **occaecō**) blind; darken; conceal

obcallēscō, ī ③ *v* (also **occallēscō**) become callous; acquire a thick skin

obcumbō, buī, itum ③ *v* (also **occumbō**) meet with (death); meet one's death

obcurrō, (cu)currī, ursum ③ *v* (also **occurrō**) *with dat* run towards or to meet; appear before; counteract; occur

obcursō ① *v* (also **occursō**) run repeatedly or in large numbers; mob; obstruct

obdō, didī, ditum ③ *v* put before or against; shut; expose to danger

obdormiō ④ *v*, **obdormīscō** ③ *v* fall asleep, sleep off

obdūcō, dūxī, uctum ③ *v* lead or draw towards; cover or lay over; overspread; wrinkle; screen

obdūrēscō, ī ③ *v* be persistent, endure

obdūrō ① *v* persist, endure

obeō, īre, lī/īvī, itum *v ir* meet with; visit; review; enclose; accept; die; set

obequitō ① *v* ride up to

obēsus, a, um *adj* fat, stout, plump

obex, icis *m/f* bolt, bar; barrier; obstacle

obf- ▸ **off-**

obferō, offerre, tulī, lātum *v ir* (also **offerō**) bring before; offer; exhibit; bring forwards; inflict; offer one's services

obfundō, ūdī, ūsum ③ *v* (also **offundō**) pour or spread over

obiaceō ② *v* lie at hand

obiciō, iēcī, iectum ③ *v* throw before or towards; expose (to); interpose; lay to one's charge

obiectō ① *v* expose (to); lay to one's charge

obiectus, ūs *m* placing something in the way of; barrier

obīrātus, a, um *adj with dat* angry with or at

obitus, ūs *m* approaching; approach, visit; setting (of the sun, *etc.*); death

obiurgō ① *v* chide; rebuke

oblectāmen, inis *nt*, **oblectāmentum, ī** *nt* delight, pleasure, source of pleasure

oblectātiō, ōnis *f* delighting

oblectō ① *v* delight, please, amuse

oblīdō, īsī, īsum ③ *v* squeeze; crush, stifle

obligō ① *v* bind or tie around; swathe; render liable; place under a moral obligation; bind (by

n
o

oath, *etc.*)

oblīmō [] *v* cover with mud; silt up

oblinō, lēvī/līvī, litum [] *v* smear, daub; sully, defame

obliquus, a, um *adj* slanting, oblique; indirect; zigzag

oblitterō [] *v* cause to be forgotten

oblīviō, ōnis *f* oblivion; forgetfulness

oblīviōsus, a, um *adj* forgetful, having a bad memory

oblīviscor, oblītus sum [] *v dep* often with gen forget

oblīvium, (i)ī *nt* forgetfulness, oblivion

oblongus, a, um *adj* of greater length than breadth, elongated

obloquor, locūtus sum [] *v dep with dat* interpose remarks, interrupt

obluctor [] *v dep with dat* struggle against

obmōlior [] *v dep* put in the way as an obstruction; block up

obmurmurō [] *v* murmur in protest (at)

obmūtēscō, tuī [] *v* lose one's speech; become silent

obnītor, nīsus/nīxus sum [] *v dep* thrust or press against; struggle against

obnoxius, a, um *adj* indebted, accountable, subservient (to); exposed to; submissive; vulnerable

obnūbō, psī, ptum [] *v* veil, cover (the head)

obnūntiō [] *v* announce adverse omens

oboediēns, ntis *adj* obedient, submissive

oboediō [] *v with dat* obey; comply with

oboleō [] *v* smell, stink

oborior, ortus sum [] *v dep* arise, appear or spring up before; well up (of tears)

obp- ▶ opp-

obpetō, īvī/iī, ītum [] *v* (also **oppetō**) meet, encounter; perish

obpōnō, posuī, positum [] *v* (also **oppōnō**) put against or before; oppose; pledge; wager; object, say in answer

obprimō, essī, essum [] *v* (also **opprimō**) press on or against; crush; overpower; beat down; surprise; suppress; conceal, cover

obprobrium, (i)ī *nt* (also **opprobrium**) scandal, disgrace; reproach, taunt

obpugnātiō, ōnis *f* (also **oppugnātiō**) assault

obpugnātor, ōris *m* (also **oppugnātor**) attacker

obpugnō [] *v* (also **oppugnō**) attack, assault; batter

obrēpō, psī, ptum [] *v* creep up to; approach unawares; sneak in

obruō, ruī, rutum [] *v* overwhelm; bury; sink; drown; suppress; smother (in)

obsaepiō, psī, ptum [] *v* enclose, seal up; block, obstruct

obscēnus, a, um *adj* inauspicious, repulsive; ill-boding; detestable; foul; obscene (applied to the sexual and excretory parts)

obscūritās, ātis *f* darkness; obscurity; unintelligibility

obscūrō [] *v* darken, obscure; conceal; make indistinct; cause to be forgotten

obscūrus, **a**, **um** *adj* dark, shady, obscure; gloomy; uncertain; incomprehensible

obsecrātiō, **ōnis** *f* supplication, entreaty; public act of prayer

obsecrō ① *v* implore; beg
■ **obsecrō (tē)** *int* please

obsequēns, **ntis** *adj* with *dat* compliant (with)

obsequenter *adv* compliantly; obediently; with deference

obsequium, **(i)ī** *nt* compliance (with), deference; servility; discipline

obsequor, **secūtus sum** ③ *v dep with dat* comply (with), gratify, submit (to)

obserō[1], **ēvī**, **itum** ③ *v* sow, plant; sow (with)

obserō[2] ① *v* bolt, fasten; obstruct

observātiō, **ōnis** *f* observation

observō ① *v* watch, observe; attend to; respect; pay court to

obses, **idis** *m/f* hostage; security, bail

obsessiō, **ōnis** *f* besieging, blockade

obsessor, **ōris** *m* besieger; frequenter

obsideō, **sēdī**, **sessum** ② *v* besiege, blockade; frequent; surround; occupy; throng

obsidiō, **ōnis** *f* siege, blockade

obsidium, **(i)ī** *nt* siege

obsīdō ③ *v* besiege; occupy

obsignō ① *v* seal up; stamp; impress

obsistō, **stitī**, **stitum** ③ *v with dat* stand in the way; resist, oppose; hinder

obsitus, **a**, **um** *adj* overgrown,

covered (with)

obsolēscō, **ēvī**, **ētum** ③ *v* fall into disuse; be forgotten about

obsolētus, **a**, **um** *adj* worn-out, dilapidated; hackneyed

obsōnium, **(i)ī** *nt* purchasing of food, getting provisions, catering; dish of food; pension

obsōnō ① *v* buy provisions, furnish an entertainment, feast

obstetrīx, **īcis** *f* midwife

obstinātiō, **ōnis** *f* firmness; stubbornness

obstinātus, **a**, **um** *adj* steady; stubborn

obstinō ① *v* be determined on

obstīpus, **a**, **um** *adj* awry, crooked, bent sideways or at an angle

obstō, **stitī** ① *v with dat* stand in the way of; block the path of; withstand; hinder

obstrepō, **puī** ③ *v* roar against; make a loud noise

obstringō, **īnxī**, **ictum** ③ *v* bind, tie or fasten up; place under an obligation; involve or implicate in

obstruō, **ūxī**, **ūctum** ③ *v* pile before or against; block up; stop, stifle

obstupefaciō, **fēcī**, **factum** ③ *v* strike dumb with any powerful emotion, daze; paralyse
□ **obstupefīō**, **fierī** *v* be astonished

obstupēscō, **puī** ③ *v* be stupefied; be struck dumb; be astounded

obsum, **esse**, **obfuī/offuī** *ir v with dat* hurt; be a nuisance to; tell against

obsuō, **uī**, **ūtum** ③ v sew up

obtegō, **ēxī**, **ēctum** ③ v cover over; conceal; protect

obtemperō ① v with dat comply with, obey

obtendō, **ndī**, **ntum** ③ v stretch or spread before; conceal; plead in excuse

obtentus, **ūs** m spreading before; cloaking, disguising, spreading out or over as a veil or covering; excuse, pretext

obterō, **trīvī**, **trītum** ③ v crush; destroy; trample on, speak of or treat with the utmost contempt

obtestātiō, **ōnis** f earnest entreaty, supplication

obtestor ① v dep call upon as a witness; invoke, entreat; aver

obtexō, **xuī** ③ v veil, cover

obticēscō, **cuī** ③ v meet a situation with silence

obtineō, **tentum** ② v hold; support; obtain; gain; prevail

obtingō, **igī** ③ v with dat fall to one's lot; occur to the benefit or disadvantage of

obtorpēscō, **puī** ③ v become numb; lose feeling

obtorqueō, **rsī**, **rtum** ② v bend back; twist or turn

obtrectātiō, **ōnis** f detraction, disparagement

obtrectātor, **ōris** m detractor, malicious critic

obtrectō ① v detract from; disparage, belittle

obtruncō ① v cut to pieces, mutilate, kill

obtueor ② v dep look or gaze at

obtundō, **udī**, **ūsum** ③ v strike, beat, batter; make blunt; deafen

obtūsus, **a**, **um** adj blunt; dull; obtuse

obtūtus, **ūs** m gaze; contemplation

obumbrō ① v overshadow; darken; conceal; defend

obuncus, **a**, **um** adj bent, hooked

obustus, **a**, **um** adj having the extremity burnt to form a point; scorched by burning

obveniō, **vēnī**, **ventum** ④ v with dat come to one by chance; happen; fall to the lot of; come up

obversor ① v dep appear before one; go to and fro publicly

obvertō, **rtī**, **rsum** ③ v turn or direct towards; direct against

obviam adv with dat in the way of; towards, against; at hand
□ ~ **eō** go to meet

obvius, **a**, **um** adj in the way, easy; hostile; exposed (to)

obvolvō, **lvī**, **lūtum** ③ v wrap round, muffle up, cover; cloak

occaecō ① v blind; darken; conceal

occallēscō, **luī** ③ v become callous; acquire a thick skin

occāsiō, **ōnis** f opportunity, right or appropriate time

occāsus, **ūs** m sun-setting, west; ruin, end, death

occidēns, **ntis** m quarter of the setting sun, the west

occīdiō, **ōnis** f massacre; wholesale slaughter

occidō, **cidī**, **cāsum** ③ v fall down; set (of the sun, etc.); die, perish; be ruined

occīdō, **īdī**, **īsum** ③ v kill, slay

occiduus, a, um *adj* going down, setting; western; declining

occinō, nuī ③ *v* break in with a song *or* call; interpose a call

occipiō, cēpī, ceptum ③ *v* begin

occlūdō, ūsī, ūsum ③ *v* shut up, close; lock

occō ① *v* harrow (ground)

occubō ① *v* lie dead

occulcō ① *v* trample down

occulō, luī, cultum ③ *v* cover up; conceal

occultātiō, ōnis *f* concealment

occultō ① *v* keep hidden, conceal; cover up

occultus, a, um *adj* hidden, concealed

occumbō, cubuī, cubitum ③ *v* meet with (death); meet one's death

occupātiō, ōnis *f* taking possession of; preoccupation with business, *etc.*; employment

occupō ① *v* occupy; seize; reach (a destination); engross

occurrō, (cu)currī, cursum ③ *v* run towards *or* to meet; appear before; counteract; occur

occursō ① *v* run repeatedly *or* in large numbers; mob; obstruct

occursus, ūs *m* meeting

Ōceanus, ī *m* ocean

ocellus, ī *m* (little) eye; darling

ōcior, ius *adj* swifter, more speedy; sooner

ocrea, ae *f* greave, leg-covering

octāvus, a, um *adj* eighth
■ **octava, ae** *f* LM period of celebration following the major Christian feasts, the eighth day following the feast; reckoned

inclusively), being the end of this period, octave

octingentī, ae, a *adj* eight hundred

octo *adj indec* eight

Octōber, bris *m* October

octōgēnī, ae, a *adj* eighty each

octōgintā *adj indec* eighty

octōnī, ae, a *adj* eight each

octuplus, a, um *adj* eightfold

octussis, is *m* eight asses

oculārius, a, um *adj* dealing with the eyes

oculus, ī *m* eye; eyesight; bud

ōdī, isse *v ir* hate; dislike

odiōsus, a, um *adj* disagreeable, offensive; tiresome, annoying

odium, (i)ī *nt* hatred, spite; unpopularity

odor, ōris *m* smell, scent, odour; perfume

odōrātus, a, um *adj* sweet-smelling, fragrant

odōrifer, era, erum *adj* fragrant

odōrō ① *v* perfume, make fragrant

odōror ① *v dep* smell out, scent; get a smattering (of)

odōrus, a, um *adj* odorous, fragrant; keen-scented

oestrus, trī *m* gad-fly; wild passion, desire, frenzy

offa, ae *f* lump of food, cake

offendō, ndī, ēnsum ③ *v* strike *or* dash against; light upon; stumble; offend, displease; upset; harm

offēnsa, ae *f* offence, displeasure; offence to a person's feelings; resentment

offēnsiō, ōnis *f* striking against,

o

stumbling-block; offence

offēnsō ① v knock or strike against, bump into

offēnsus¹, ūs m collision, knock

offēnsus², a, um adj offended; offensive, odious

offerō, ferre, obtulī, oblātum v ir bring before; offer; exhibit; bring forwards; inflict; offer one's services

officīna, ae f workshop

officiō, fēcī, fectum ③ v with dat block the path (of); check; impede

officiōsus, a, um adj dutiful, attentive; officious

officium, (i)ī nt service; duty; courtesy

offīgō, īxī, īxum ③ v fasten, nail down

offirmō ① v secure; make inflexible

offūcia, ae f paint, wash; make up

offula, ae f (small) piece of food (esp. meat)

offulgeō, lsī ② v with dat shine forth in the path of

offundō, ūdī, ūsum ③ v pour or spread over

ogganniō ④ v growl at, snarl

ōh int oh! ah!

ohē int hey! hey there!

olea, ae f olive; olive-tree

oleaster, trī m wild olive-tree

olēns, ntis adj fragrant; stinking

oleō, ī ② v smell; smell of; be fragrant; stink

oleum, ī nt olive-oil; oil

olfaciō, fēcī, factum ③ v smell

olidus, a, um adj stinking

ōlim adv formerly, in times past; at a future time, some day; sometimes

olitor, ōris m vegetable-grower

olitōrius, a, um adj pertaining to vegetables

olīva, ae f olive; olive-tree; olive-branch; staff of olive-wood

olīvētum, ī nt olive-yard

olīvifer, era, erum adj olive-bearing

olīvum, ī nt olive-oil; wrestling

ōlla, ae f pot, jar

olle, a, ud pn [archaic form of **ille**] he, she; it; that; that; the well-known; the former

olor, ōris m swan

olōrinus, a, um adj belonging to a swan or swans

olus, eris nt vegetables

ōmen, inis nt augury, sign, token (of good or bad luck)

ōmentum, ī nt the fatty membrane covering the intestines

ōminor ① v dep forebode, presage

ōminōsus, a, um adj presaging ill; ill-omened

omittō, mīsī, missum ③ v let go; lay aside; give up; neglect; disregard; cease

omnigenus, a, um adj of every kind

omnimodīs adv in every way

omninō adv altogether, utterly; in all; in general

omniparēns, ntis adj parent or creator of all things

omnipotēns, ntis adj almighty

omnis, e adj all, every

omnivolus, a, um adj that desires all

onager, **grī** *m* wild ass

onerārius, **a**, **um** *adj* that carries loads, cargo, *etc.*

  ☐ **nāvis onerāria** merchant-ship

onerō ☐ *v* load, burden, freight; overload; overwhelm; oppress; aggravate

onerōsus, **a**, **um** *adj* burdensome, heavy; tiresome

onus, **eris** *nt* load, burden; affliction, trouble, responsibility

onustus, **a**, **um** *adj* laden, burdened, freighted; weighed down

onyx, **ychis** *m* yellow marble; onyx box

opācō ☐ *v* shade, overshadow

opācus, **a**, **um** *adj* shady; darkened, overshadowed; retired

opalus, **ī** *m* opal

opella, **ae** *f* little effort; trifling duties

opera, **ae** *f* pains, work, labour; task; care, attention, endeavour

  ■ **operam dō** *with dat* apply oneself to; be at the service of, help

  ■ **operae** *pl* labourers; hired rowdies

operīmentum, **ī** *nt* cover, lid, covering

operiō, **ruī**, **rtum** ☐ *v* cover over; shut; conceal

operōsus, **a**, **um** *adj* painstaking; laborious; elaborate

opertus, **a**, **um** *adj* hidden; obscure, secret

opifer, **era**, **erum** *adj* bringing help

opifex, **icis** *m/f* craftsman, artificer; artisan; ☐☐ creator

ōpiliō, **ōnis** *m* shepherd, herdsman

opīmus, **a**, **um** *adj* fruitful; rich; sumptuous; plentiful

  ☐ **spolia opīma** spoils taken by a victorious Roman general from the enemy leader he had killed in single combat

opīniō, **ōnis** *f* opinion, belief; report, imagination; reputation

opīnor ☐ *v dep* hold as an opinion, think, believe

opitulor ☐ *v dep with dat* bring aid to; help; bring relief to

oportet ☐ *v impers* it is necessary or proper (that); it is inevitable that

opperior, **per(ī)tus sum** ☐ *v dep* wait (for); await

oppetō, **īvī/iī**, **ītum** ☐ *v* meet, encounter; perish

oppidānus, **a**, **um** *adj* of or in a town (other than Rome); provincial, local

  ■ **oppidānī**, **ōrum** *mpl* townsmen, townsfolk

oppidō *adv* exceedingly, utterly, altogether

oppidulum, **ī** *nt* small town

oppidum, **ī** *nt* town

oppīlō ☐ *v* stop up, block

oppleō, **ēvī**, **ētum** ☐ *v* fill (completely); overspread

oppōnō, **posuī**, **positum** ☐ *v* put against or before; oppose; pledge; wager; object, say in answer

opportūnitās, **ātis** *f* convenience, advantageousness; right time; opportuneness; opportunity

opportūnus, **a**, **um** *adj*

convenient; opportune; advantageous; ready to hand; liable to

opprimō, essī, essum ③ *v* press on *or* against; crush; overpower; beat down; surprise; suppress; conceal, cover

opprobrium, (i)ī *nt* scandal, disgrace; reproach, taunt

opprobrō ① *v* reproach, criticize

oppugnātiō, ōnis *f* assault

oppugnātor, ōris *m* attacker

oppugnō ① *v* attack, assault; batter

ops- ▶ **obs-**

ops, pis *f* power, might, strength, ability, help

■ **opēs, opum** *fpl* wealth; resources; assistance

opt- ▶ **obt-**

optābilis, e *adj* desirable

optimās, ātis *m* aristocrat; *pl* the best class of citizens

optimus, a, um *adj* best

optiō¹, ōnis *f* choice

optiō², ōnis *m* junior officer

optō ① *v* choose; wish for, desire

opulentia, ae *f* riches, wealth; sumptuousness

opulentus, a, um *adj* wealthy; abounding with resources; well supplied (with); sumptuous

opus¹, eris *nt* work, effort; structure *pl* siege-works

□ **maiōre opere** all the more

□ **maximō opere** most urgently

opus² *nt indec* need, necessity

□ **opus est** it is needful

□ **opus est mihi** *with abl of thing needed* I have need of

opusculum, ī *nt* little work, trifle

ōra, ae *f* border, edge; sea-coast; bank; region; climatic region

ōrāculum, ī *nt* oracle

ōrātiō, ōnis *f* speech; conversation; LM prayer

ōrātor, ōris *m* speaker, orator; ambassador; advocate

oratorium, (i)ī *nt* LM place of prayer

orbis, is *m* disc, circle; orb; ring; wheel; circuit; the world

□ **~ terrārum/terrae** the world

orbita, ae *f* wheel-track, rut; orbit

orbitās, ātis *f* bereavement; loss of a child; orphanhood; childlessness

orbō ① *v* bereave (of parents, children, *etc.*), deprive (of)

orbus, a, um *adj* bereaved; parentless, orphan; childless; deprived or destitute (of anything)

Orcus, ī *m* the god of the underworld, Dis; death; the underworld

ōrdinārius, a, um *adj* regular; usual

ōrdinātim *adv* in good order

ōrdinō ① *v* set in order, arrange, regulate

ōrdior, ōrsus sum ④ *v dep* begin, undertake; embark on

ōrdō, inis *m* row, regular series; order; class of citizens; arrangement; method; degree; rank; LM monastic order

Orēas, adis *f* mountain-nymph, Oread

orgia, ōrum *ntpl* secret rites (of Bacchus)

orichalcum, ī *nt* yellow copper ore, brass

ōricilla, ae f little ear

oriēns, ntis m east, orient; daybreak, dawn

orīgō, inis f beginning, source; birth, origin

orior, ortus sum ④ v dep rise; appear on the scene; arise; begin; be born

oriundus, a, um adj descended; originating from

ōrnāmentum, ī nt equipment; ornament, decoration, jewel; (mark of) distinction

ōrnātus, ūs m military equipment; armour; costume, garb, get-up; adornment

ōrnātus, a, um adj adorned, well-dressed; beautiful

ōrnō ① v adorn; honour; praise

ornus, ī f ash-tree

ōrō ① v plead; pray (to); beseech, supplicate

ōrsa, ōrum ntpl words, utterance

ōrsus pple from ▶ **ordior**

ortus¹ pple from ▶ **orior**

ortus², ūs m rising, sunrise; birth; beginnings, origin

ōs, ōris nt mouth; speech; face; assurance

ōs, ossis nt bone

ōscen, inis m bird which gives omens by its cry; song-bird

ōscillum, ī nt a small mask hung on trees

ōscitō ① v gape; yawn

ōsculātiō, ōnis f kissing

ōsculor ① v dep kiss

ōsculum, ī nt mouth; kiss

ōstendō, ndī, tentum/ tēnsum ③ v hold out for

inspection, show; exhibit; demonstrate; offer

ostentātiō, ōnis f exhibition, display; 'showing off'

ostentō ① v show off, display; offer

ostentum, ī nt prodigy; marvel

ostentus, ūs m display; demonstration; advertisement

ōstium, (i)ī nt mouth (of a river); entrance; exit; door

ostrea, ae f oyster; sea-snail

ostrifer, era, erum adj bearing oysters

ostrum, ī nt purple; anything dyed purple

ōtior ① v dep be at leisure, enjoy a holiday

ōtiōsus, a, um adj at leisure, unoccupied; free from public affairs; quiet; free, unemployed; undisturbed (by); superfluous; useless

ōtium, (i)ī nt leisure; rest; peace; ease; lull

ōvātus, a, um adj egg-shaped, oval

ovīle, is nt sheepfold

ovis, is f sheep

ovō ① v celebrate a minor triumph; exult, rejoice

ovum, ī nt egg; wooden balls set up in the Circus, and removed one by one at the completion of each lap

□ **ab ovō usque ad māla** from the hors d'oeuvre to the dessert, i.e. from beginning to end

Pp

pābulātiō, ōnis f foraging

pābulātor, ōris m forager

pābulor ① v dep forage

pābulum, ī nt food, nourishment; fodder; food, sustenance

pācālis, e adj associated with peace

pācātus, a, um adj peaceful, calm

pācifer, era, erum adj bringing peace, peaceful

pācificātiō, ōnis f peace-making

pācificātor, ōris m peace-maker

pācificō ① v negotiate about peace, appease

pācificus, a, um adj making or tending to make peace

pacīscō, pactum ③ v, **paciscor, pactus sum** ③ v dep make a bargain or agreement; agree, enter into a marriage contract; negotiate

pācō ① v impose a settlement on; bring under control

pactiō, ōnis f agreement, compact

pactum, ī nt agreement, compact; manner, way
 □ **quō pactō?** how?

paeān, nis m hymn, hymn usually of victory

paedagōgium, (i)ī nt training establishment for slave-boys

paedagōgus, ī m slave in charge of children

paedīcō ① v commit sodomy with

paedor, ōris m filth, dirt

paelex, icis f mistress

paene adv nearly, almost, practically

paenīnsula, ae f peninsula

paenitentia, ae f regret; chang of mind

paenitet ② v impers it gives reaso for regret
 □ **mē paenitet** with gen of thing regretted I repent (of)

paenula, ae f hooded weatherproof cloak

paenulātus, a, um adj wearing a paenula

paetus, a, um adj having a cast i the eye, squinting slightly

pāgānus, a, um adj rustic; civilia

pāgina, ae f column or page of writing; piece of writing

pāgus, ī m country district or community

pāla, ae f spade

palaestra, ae f wrestling-place; gymnastics

palaestricus, a, um adj of wrestling

palam adv/prep with abl openly, publicly; openly in the presence of

Palātīnus, a, um adj the name of one of the hills of Rome, the Palatine

Palātium, (i)ī nt the Palatine Hill

palātum, ī nt palate; sense of taste

palea, ae f chaff, husk

palear, āris nt dewlap

Palīlia, ia ntpl Feast of Pales (a tutelary deity of sheep and herds) on 21 April

palimpsestum, ī nt palimpsest

paliūrus, **ī** *m* the shrub, Christ's thorn

palla, **ae** *f* rectangular outdoor garment worn by women, mantle of a tragic actor

palleō ② *v* be or look pale; fade; become pale at

pallēscō, **luī** ③ *v* grow pale; blanch; fade

pallidulus, **a**, **um** *adj* pale, wan

pallidus, **a**, **um** *adj* pale

palliolum, **ī** *nt* small cloak

pallium, **(i)ī** *nt* rectangular outdoor garment worn by men; bed-cover

pallor, **ōris** *m* paleness, wanness

palma, **ae** *f* palm of the hand; hand; palm-tree; date; oar; victory, first place

palmātus, **a**, **um** *adj* having a palm-leaf pattern

palmes, **itis** *m* vine-branch or -shoot

palmētum, **ī** *nt* palm-grove

palmifer, **era**, **erum** *adj* palm-bearing

palmula, **ae** *f* oar

pālor ① *v dep* wander abroad, stray; scatter; wander aimlessly

palpātor, **ōris** *m* confidence trickster

palpebra, **ae** *f* eyelid

palpitō ① *v* throb, beat, pulsate

palpō ① *v* stroke, caress; act in a soothing manner

palūdāmentum, **ī** *nt* military cloak; general's cloak

palūdātus, **a**, **um** *adj* wearing a military cloak

palūdōsus, **a**, **um** *adj* fenny, boggy, marshy

palumbēs, **bis** *m/f* wood-pigeon, ring-dove

pālus, **ī** *m* stake, prop

palūs, **ūdis** *f* flood-water, fen, swamp

palūster, **tris**, **tre** *adj* marshy; of marshes

pampineus, **a**, **um** *adj* of or covered with vine-shoots or foliage

pampinus, **ī** *m/f* vine-shoot, vine foliage

pānārium, **(i)ī** *nt* bread basket

pandō, **ndī**, **pānsum/passum** ③ *v* spread out, extend; unfold; reveal

pandus, **a**, **um** *adj* spreading round in a wide curve; arched

pangō, **pepigī/pānxī**, **pāctum** ③ *v* fix; drive in; (fig) settle, stipulate for; conclude; compose

pānicum, **ī** *nt* Italian millet

pānis, **is** *m* bread, loaf; food

pannōsus, **a**, **um** *adj* dressed in rags, tattered

pannus, **ī** *m* cloth, garment; charioteer's coloured shirt; rags

panthēra, **ae** *f* leopard

panticēs, **um** *mpl* belly, paunch, guts

pantomīmus, **ī** *m* mime performer in a pantomime

papa, **ae** *m* LM Pope

papāver, **eris** *nt* poppy; poppy-seed

papāvereus, **a**, **um** *adj* of poppy, poppy-

pāpiliō, **ōnis** *m* butterfly, moth

papilla, **ae** *f* nipple, teat, dug (of mammals)

papula, **ae** *f* pimple, pustule

papȳrifer, **era**, **erum** *adj*
papyrus-bearing

papȳrum, **ī** *nt*, **papȳrus**, **ī** *f*
paper-reed; papyrus

pār, **aris** *adj* equal; fair; fit
m/f equal; mate, partner *nt* pair;
couple

parābilis, **e** *adj* procurable, easily
obtainable

parabola, **ae** *f* explanatory
illustration, comparison; parable

paramenta, **orum** *npl* ⟨LM⟩
vestments, altar hangings

parasceve, **es** *f* ⟨LM⟩ day of
preparation (for the Passover),
Good Friday

parasītus, **ī** *m* guest, parasite,
sponger, hanger-on; ⟨LM⟩ deceiver

parātus¹, **ūs** *m* preparation;
equipment, paraphernalia; attire

parātus², **a**, **um** *adj* prepared,
ready; equipped

parcō, **pepercī/parsī** ③ *v with
dat* act sparingly, be thrifty with;
spare; pardon; forbear; refrain
from

parcus, **a**, **um** *adj* sparing,
economical; niggardly,
parsimonious; moderate

parēns, **ntis** *m/f* father, mother,
parent; ancestor; originator;
producer, source

parentālis, **e** *adj* of or belonging
to parents

parentō ① *v* perform the rites
at the tombs of the dead; make
an offering of appeasement (to
the dead)

pāreō ② *v* be visible; *with dat*
obey; comply with; be subject to;
submit to

pariēs, **etis** *m* wall (of a house)

parilis, **e** *adj* like, equal

pariō, **peperī**, **par(i)tum** ③ *v*
bring forth; bear; produce, create;
procure, get

pariter *adv* equally, as well;
together; in the same manner;
simultaneously

parma, **ae** *f* small round shield

parō ① *v* get ready, prepare,
furnish, provide; intend; plan;
obtain; buy

parochus, **ī** *m* commissary

parricīda, **ae** *m/f* parricide
(murderer); murderer of a near
relative; traitor

parricīdium, **(i)ī** *nt* parricide
(murder); murder of a near
relation, treason, rebellion

pars, **rtis** *f* part, piece, portion,
share; function, office; role;
party, side

□ **pars … pars** some … others
■ **partēs**, **ium** *fpl* party; faction

parsimōnia, **ae** *f* frugality, thrift;
parsimony; temperance

parthenicē, **ēs** *f* a flower,
perhaps camomile

particeps, **ipis** *adj* sharing in *m/f*
participant, sharer

participium, **(i)ī** *nt* participle

participō ① *v* inform of; share
with others in; partake of; make
a party to

particula, **ae** *f* small part, little
bit, particle, atom

partim *adv* partly, in part

partiō ④ *v* share, divide up

partior ④ *v dep* share, distribute,
divide up

partum, **ī** *nt* a thing acquired,
acquisition

parturiō ④ v be in travail or labour; bring forth; produce; be pregnant with

partus, **ūs** m bringing forth, birth; foetus, embryo; offspring, progeny

parum nt indec used as adv too little, not enough; encore!

parumper adv for a short while

parvulus, **a**, **um** adj tiny, small, little, petty, slight

parvus, **a**, **um** adj little, small, petty, mean; young; cheap

pasceolus, **ī** m small leather purse

pascha, **ae** f, **pascha**, **atis** nt ⫽LM⫽ Easter

pāscō, **pāstum** ③ v feed, pasture; provide food for; nurture; feast

pascua, **ae** f⫽LM⫽ pasture

pāscuum, **ī** nt pasture

passer, **eris** m sparrow; blue thrush

passim adv here and there, hither and thither; at random

passio, **onis** f⫽LM⫽ suffering, passion

passum, **ī** nt raisin-wine

passus¹ pple from ▶ **patior**

passus², **ūs** m step, pace (five Roman feet); track, trace
■ **mille passūs** pl a mile

passus³, **a**, **um** adj spread out; dried (of grapes, etc.)

pāstor, **ōris** m herdsman, shepherd; ⫽LM⫽ bishop

pāstōrālis, **e** adj pastoral; ⫽LM⫽ episcopal

pāstus, **ūs** m pasture, feeding ground; pasturage

patefaciō, **fēcī**, **factum** ③ v

open, throw open; disclose, bring to light

patella, **ae** f small dish or plate; knee-cap

pateō ② v be open; be accessible; be visible; be exposed to; stretch out, extend; be evident; be available

pater, **tris** m father
□ **pater familiās** head of a family
■ **patrēs (cōnscrīptī)** pl senators
□ **patrēs** forefathers

patera, **ae** f broad, shallow offering dish

paterfamiliās, **patrisfamiliās** m mistress of the house; respectable married woman

paternus, **a**, **um** adj fatherly, paternal

patēscō, **tuī** ③ v open; extend; become clear or known

pathicus, **a**, **um** adj submitting to sexual intercourse

patibulātus, **a**, **um** adj fastened to a yoke

patibulum, **ī** nt fork-shaped yoke; gibbet

patiēns, **ntis** adj patient; capable of enduring

patientia, **ae** f patience; forbearance; submissiveness

patina, **ae** f dish, pan, stew-pan, casserole

patior, **passus sum** ③ v dep bear, undergo; suffer; allow; leave, let be

patria, **ae** f fatherland, native country; home, source

patricīd- ▶ **parricīd-**

patricīda, **ae** m/f (also **parricīda**) parricide (murderer)

murderer of a near relative; traitor

patricius, **a**, **um** adj patrician, noble

patrimōnium, **(i)ī** nt private possessions, estate, fortune

patrīmus, **a**, **um** adj having a father still living

patrissō ① v take after one's father

patrius, **a**, **um** adj belonging to a father, paternal; hereditary; of one's native land

patrō ① v accomplish, bring to completion

patrōcinium, **(i)ī** nt protection, defence, patronage, legal defence

patrōcinor ① v dep champion, defend

patrōna, **ae** f protectress, patroness

patrōnus, **ī** m protector, patron; pleader, advocate

patruēlis, **is** m/f of or belonging to a paternal uncle

patruus, **ī** m paternal uncle; type of harshness and censoriousness

patulus, **a**, **um** adj wide open, gaping; wide-spreading

paucitās, **ātis** f small number, fewness

pauculus, **a**, **um** adj very few, little

paucus, **a**, **um** adj few, little
■ **pauca** ntpl a few words

paulātim adv by degrees, gradually

paull- ▶ **paul-**

paullātim adv by degrees, gradually

paullisper adv for a little while, for a short time

paullō adv by a little; somewhat

paullum adv a little, somewhat

paullus, **a**, **um** adj little, small
■ **paullum**, **ī** nt a little, a little bit

paulō adv by a little; somewhat

paulum adv a little, somewhat

paulus, **a**, **um** adj little, small
■ **paulum**, **ī** nt a little, a little bit

pauper, **eris** adj poor; meagre, unproductive

pauperēs, **ēī** f, **paupertās**, **ātis** f poverty

pauxillātim adv little by little

pauxillum, **ī** nt a little
□ **ex pauxillō** little by little

pavefaciō, **fēcī**, **factum** ③ v terrify

paveō, **pāvī** ② v be frightened or terrified at

pavēscō ③ v become alarmed

pavidus, **a**, **um** adj fearful, terrified, panic-struck

pavīmentum, **ī** nt paved surface or floor, pavement

pavitō ① v be in a state of fear or trepidation (at)

pāvō, **ōnis** m peacock

pavor, **ōris** m fear, dread, alarm, terror, anxiety

pāx, **pācis** f peace; tranquillity of mind; favour, grace; leave
□ **pāce tuā** by your leave

paxillus, **ī** m wooden pin, peg

peccātum, **ī** nt error, sin

peccō ① v make a mistake; err; commit a fault; sin

pecten, **inis** m comb; quill with which the lyre is struck

pectō, **pexī**, **pexum/pectitum** ③ v comb, card (wool, etc.)

pectus, **oris** *nt* breast; soul; feeling; courage; understanding

pecuārius, **(i)ī** *m* cattle-breeder, grazier

pecūlātor, **ōris** *m* embezzler of public money

pecūlātus, **ūs** *m* embezzlement of public money *or* property

pecūliāris, **e** *adj* one's own

pecūlium, **(i)ī** *nt* private property of a son, daughter, *or* slave, held with the father's *or* master's consent

pecūnia, **ae** *f* property, wealth; money

pecus[1], **oris** *nt* cattle; herd, flock

pecus[2], **udis** *f* farm animal; animal; sheep

pedālis, **e** *adj* measuring a foot

pedes, **itis** *m* pedestrian, foot-soldier

  ▪ **peditēs** *pl* infantry

pedester, **tris**, **tre** *adj* on foot, pedestrian

pedetem(p)tim *adv* step by step, slowly; cautiously

pedica, **ae** *f* shackle, fetter; snare

pēdīcō ▸ **paedīcō**

pēdis, **is** *m/f* louse

pedisequa, **ae** *f* waiting-woman

pedisequus, **ī** *m* male attendant, manservant

peditātus, **ūs** *m* infantry

pēditum, **ī** *nt* fart

pedum, **ī** *nt* shepherd's crook

peior, **ius** *adj* worse

peiūrium, **(i)ī** *nt* perjury, dishonesty

pelagus, **ī** *nt* open sea

pellāx, **ācis** *adj* seductive, glib

pēllex ▸ **paelex**

pelliciō, **lexī**, **lectum** ③ *v* attract; seduce; charm; inveigle

pellicula, **ae** *f* skin, hide

pellis, **is** *f* skin, hide; leather

pellītus, **a**, **um** *adj* covered with skins

pellō, **pepulī**, **pulsum** ③ *v* push, strike; drive out, banish; impel

pelōris, **idis** *f* mussel

pelta, **ae** *f* crescent-shaped shield

peltātus, **a**, **um** *adj* armed with the pelta

pēlvis, **is** *f* shallow bowl *or* basin

Penātēs, **ium** *mpl* the household gods; the gods of the state; one's home; dwelling

pendeō, **pependī** ② *v* hang (down), be suspended; hang loose; be unstable, movable; be uncertain; depend (on)

pendō, **pependī**, **pēnsum** ③ *v* weigh; pay, pay out; consider

pendulus, **a**, **um** *adj* hanging down; suspended

penes *prep with acc* in the possession *or* power of

penetrābilis, **e** *adj* that can be pierced; penetrable; piercing

penetrālis, **e** *adj* innermost; penetrating

  ▪ **penetrāle**, **is** *nt* inner part of a place; inner shrine

penetrō ① *v* pierce, penetrate (into); gain entrance

pēnis, **is** *m* male sexual organ, penis

penitus *adv* inwardly; deep, deeply, far within; utterly, completely

penna, **ae** *f* feather; wing

pennātus, a, um *adj* winged

pēnsiō, ōnis *f* payment, instalment; rent

pēnsō ▯ *v* weigh, weigh out; pay or punish for; counterbalance, compensate; ponder, examine

pēnsum, ī *nt* quantity of wool given to be spun or woven; task, stint

pēnūria, ae *f* want, need, scarcity

penus, ī *m/f*, **penus, ūs** *m/f* provisions, food

pependī ▸ pendō

pepercī ▸ parcō

pepulī ▸ pellō

per *prep with acc* through, throughout, all over; during; by (means of); for the sake of; *in compounds* thoroughly, very; by (in oaths, *etc.*)

pēra, ae *f* satchel

perabsurdus, a, um *adj* highly ridiculous

perācer, cris, cre *adj* very sharp

peracūtus, a, um *adj* very penetrating; very sharp

peraequē *adv* equally

peragitō ▯ *v* harass with repeated attacks

peragō, ēgī, āctum ▯ *v* execute, finish, accomplish; pierce through; pass through; relate

peragrō ▯ *v* travel over every part of, scour

perambulō ▯ *v* walk about in, tour; make the round of

perangustus, a, um *adj* very narrow

perantīquus, a, um *adj* very ancient

perarō ▯ *v* furrow; inscribe

(scratch on a waxen tablet)

perbeātus, a, um *adj* very fortunate

perbene *adv* splendidly

perbibō, bibī ▯ *v* drink deeply, drink in

perbītō ▯ *v* perish

percallēscō, luī ▯ *v* become callous

percārus, a, um *adj* very dear

percelebrō ▯ *v* make thoroughly known

percellō, culī, culsum ▯ *v* strike down; strike; overpower; dismay, demoralize, upset

perciëō ▯ *v*, **perciō, ītum** ▯ *v* excite; set in motion

percipiō, cēpī, ceptum ▯ *v* take possession of; perceive, take in

percommodus, a, um *adj* very convenient

percontātiō, ōnis *f* question, interrogation

percontor ▯ *v dep* question; investigate

percoquō, coxī, coctum ▯ *v* cook thoroughly; bake, heat

percrēb(r)ēscō, b(r)uī ▯ *v* become very frequent, become very widespread

percūnctor ▯ *v* investigate

percurrō, (cu)currī, cursum ▯ *v* run or hasten through or over; traverse; pass quickly over

percussor, ōris *m* assassin

percussus, ūs *m* buffeting; beating

percutiō, ussī, ussum ▯ *v* strike forcibly; kill; shock, make a deep impression on

perdiscō, didicī ▯ *v* learn

thoroughly

erditor, **ōris** *m* destroyer

erditus, **a**, **um** *adj* ruined, lost, desperate, abandoned, morally depraved

erdiū *adv* for a long while

erdīx, **īcis** *m/f* partridge

erdō, **didī**, **ditum** ③ *v* lose; destroy; ruin; waste; spoil, impair

erdoceō, **doctum** ② *v* teach (thoroughly)

erdomō, **muī**, **mitum** ① *v* tame thoroughly, subjugate completely

erdūcō, **dūxī**, **ductum** ③ *v* lead or bring through, conduct; prolong; cover over, coat

erduelliō, **ōnis** *f* treason

erduellis, **is** *m* national enemy

eredō, **ēsse**, **ēdī**, **ēsum** *v ir* eat up, consume, waste

eregrē *adv* abroad; to, in, or from foreign parts

eregrīnātiō, **ōnis** *f* foreign travel

eregrīnor ① *v dep* travel about or abroad; reside abroad

eregrīnus, **a**, **um** *adj* outlandish, strange, foreign *m/f* foreigner, alien

erendinus, **a**, **um** *adj* after tomorrow

erennis, **e** *adj* continuing throughout the year; constant, uninterrupted; enduring

ereō, **īre**, **iī**/**īvī**, **itum** *v ir* pass from view, vanish, disappear; be destroyed, perish; be desperately in love (with)

⌐ a periī I am ruined

erequitō ① *v* ride (through or

perditor | perfungor

over), traverse; ride hither and thither, ride or drive about

pererrō ① *v* wander through, roam or ramble over

perexiguus, **a**, **um** *adj* very little or small

perfacilis, **e** *adj* very easy

perfectus, **a**, **um** *adj* finished, complete, perfect

perferō, **ferre**, **tulī**, **lātum** *v ir* bear or carry through; convey; report; tell; endure; undergo

perficiō, **fēcī**, **fectum** ③ *v* finish, complete; perform; accomplish

perfidia, **ae** *f* faithlessness, treachery

perfidiōsus, **a**, **um** *adj* treacherous

perfidus, **a**, **um** *adj* faithless, treacherous, false, deceitful; **LM** heretic(al)

perflō ① *v* blow through or over

perfluō, **ūxī** ③ *v* flow (through)

perfodiō, **ōdī**, **ossum** ③ *v* dig or pierce through

perforō ① *v* bore through; pierce

perfringō, **frēgī**, **frāctum** ③ *v* break through; break or dash in pieces; smash

perfruor, **frūctus sum** ③ *v dep with abl* have full enjoyment of, enjoy

perfuga, **ae** *m* deserter

perfugiō, **ūgī** ③ *v* take refuge, escape; go for refuge (to the enemy)

perfugium, **(i)ī** *nt* refuge; asylum; excuse

perfundō, **ūdī**, **ūsum** ③ *v* pour over, wet; overspread, imbue

perfungor, **fūnctus sum** ③

perfurō | permoveō

v dep with abl perform, discharge; have done with

perfurō 3 *v* rage, storm (throughout)

pergama, orum *npl* ⓛ citadel(s)

pergō, rrēxī, rrēctum 3 *v* advance; continue, proceed, go on

pergrandis, e *adj* very large, of very advanced age

pergrātus, a, um *adj* very agreeable *or* pleasant

perhibeō 2 *v* present, give, bestow; regard, hold; name

perhorrēscō, ruī 3 *v* tremble *or* shudder greatly; recoil in terror from

perīclitor 1 *v dep* risk; try, test; be in danger; risk

perīculōsus, a, um *adj* dangerous, hazardous, perilous

perīc(u)lum, ī *nt* trial, proof; danger, peril; risk; liability

perīdōneus, a, um *adj* very suitable, very well-fitted

perimō, ēmī, emptum 3 *v* destroy; kill; prevent

perinde *adv* just (as), equally □ ~ ac just, as if

perītia, ae *f* practical knowledge, skill, expertise

perītus, a, um *adj* experienced, practised, skilful, expert

periūcundus, a, um *adj* very welcome, agreeable

periūrium, (i)ī *nt* false oath, perjury

periūrō 1 *v* swear falsely

periūrus, a, um *adj* perjured; false, lying

perlābor, lāpsus sum 3 *v dep* glide along, over *or* through, skim

perlegō, lēgī, lēctum 3 *v* scan, survey; read through

perlīberālis, e *adj* very decent, ladylike

perlitō 1 *v* make auspicious sacrifice

perlūceō 2 *v* be transparent; shine through; shine out

perlūcidulus, a, um *adj* transparent, translucent

perlūcidus, a, um *adj* transparent, pellucid

perluō, luī, ūtum 3 *v* wash off thoroughly; bathe

perlūstrō 1 *v* go or wander all through; view all over, scan, scrutinize

permadefaciō, fēcī, factum *v* drench thoroughly

permagnus, a, um *adj* very great

permaneō, ānsī, ānsum 2 *v* continue *or* persist in staying; persist

permānō 1 *v* flow through; leak through; permeate

permeō 1 *v* go *or* pass through, cross, traverse; pervade

permētior, mēnsus sum 4 *v dep* measure exactly; travel over

permisceō, mixtum 2 *v* mix *or* mingle together; confound; embroil; disturb thoroughly

permissus, ūs *m* permission, authorization

permittō, mīsī, missum 3 *v* let go through; allow full scope to; give rein to; allow, permit; leave (to another) to do *or* decide; grar

permoveō, mōvī, mōtum 2 *v* move *or* stir up thoroughly; move deeply; excite

ermulceō, lsī, lsum/lctum ② v rub gently, stroke, touch gently; charm, please, beguile; soothe, alleviate

ermultus, a, um adj very much, very many

ermūniō ④ v fortify thoroughly

ermūtātiō, ōnis f change; exchange, barter

ermūtō ① v exchange (for); swap

erniciēs, iēī f destruction; ruin; fatal injury

erniciōsus, a, um adj destructive, ruinous, fatal

ernīcitās, ātis f nimbleness

ernix, īcis adj nimble, agile, travelling quickly

ernoctō ① v spend the night

ernōscō, ōvī, ōtum ③ v get a thorough knowledge of

ernōtēscō, tuī ③ v become known

ernox, ctis adj lasting all night

ernumerō ① v reckon up, count out (money) in full

ērō, ōnis m thick boot of raw hide

erobscūrus, a, um adj very obscure, very vague

erōdī, isse, ōsus sum v ir hate greatly, detest

eropportūnus, a, um adj very favourably situated, very convenient

erōrō ① v deliver the final part of a speech, conclude

rpācō ① v subdue completely

erparvus, a, um adj very little, very trifling

erpaucus, a, um adj very few

---

perpellō, pulī, pulsum ③ v compel, constrain, prevail upon; enforce

perpendiculum, ī nt plummet
□ **ad ~** perpendicularly

perpendō, ndī, ēnsum ③ v weigh carefully; assess carefully

perperam adv wrongly, incorrectly

perpetior, pessus sum ③ v dep endure to the full

perpetrō ① v carry through, accomplish

perpetuitās, ātis f continuity; permanence

perpetuus, a, um adj uninterrupted; continuous; lasting; invariable
□ **in perpetuum** for ever

perplaceō ② with dat please greatly

perplexus, a, um adj entangled, muddled; intricate, cryptic

perpluō ③ v let the rain through, leak; (of rain) come through

perpoliō ④ v polish thoroughly; put the finishing touches to

perpopulor ① v dep ravage, devastate completely

perpōtō ① v drink heavily; drink up

perquam adv extremely

perquīrō, īsīvī/īsiī, īsītum ③ v search everywhere for

perrārus, a, um adj very rare, exceptional

perreptō ① v creep through, crawl over

perrumpō, rūpī, ruptum ③ v break or rush through, force one's way through; cleave, sever; violate

persaepe adv very often

perscrībō, psī, ptum ③ v write in full or at length; give a full account or report of in writing

perscrūtor ① v dep search high and low; study carefully

persequor, secūtus sum ③ v dep follow perseveringly; pursue; pursue with hostile intent; strive after; go through with; catch up with

persevērantia, ae f steadfastness, persistence

persevērō ① v persist, persevere in

persicus, a, um adj
■ **concha persica** f mother of pearl

persimplex, icis adj very simple

persolvō, lvī, lūtum ③ v pay in full; pay off

persōna, ae f mask; personage, character, part

persōnātus, a, um adj masked

personō, nuī, nitum ① v resound, ring with; cause to resound; make loud music; shout out

perspectō ① v look all around; watch steadily

perspiciō, exī, ectum ③ v look or see through; look into; look at, examine, inspect; study, investigate

perspicuus, a, um adj transparent, clear; evident

perstō, stitī ① v stand firm; last, endure; persevere, persist in

perstringō, īnxī, ictum ③ v graze, graze against; make tight all over; offend; make unfavourable mention of; paralyse; travel round

the edge of

persuādeō, āsī, āsum ② v with dat persuade, convince; prevail upon, persuade to do

persultō ① v leap or skip or prance about; range (over); scour

pertaedet, pertaesum est ② impers be very wearied with

pertegō, ēxī, ēctum ③ v cover completely; thatch

pertemptō ① v test, try out; explore thoroughly; agitate thoroughly

pertendō, ndī, ēnsum ③ v persevere, persist; press on

perterreō ② v frighten or terrify, thoroughly

pertica, ae f pole, long staff, measuring rod, perch

pertimēscō, muī ③ v become very scared (of)

pertinācia, ae f obstinacy, defiance

pertināx, ācis adj firm, constant, steadfast, obstinate

pertineō ② v continue or extend through or to, reach; belong or pertain to, be relevant to

pertrahō, āxī, actum ③ v draw or drag through or to, bring or conduct forcibly to; draw on, lure

pertundō, tudī, tūsum ③ v bore through, perforate

perturbātiō, ōnis f confusion, disturbance; mental disturbance; perturbation; passion

perturbō ① v disorder, confuse; disturb; frighten

perūrō, ussī, ustum ③ v burn up; fire; scorch; make sore

pervādō, āsī, āsum ③ v go or

come through; spread through; penetrate; pervade

pervagor ① v *dep* wander or range through, rove about; pervade, spread widely; extend

pervastō ① v devastate completely

pervehō, ēxī, ectum ③ v bear, carry or convey through
□ **pervehor** sail to, ride to

perveniō, vēnī, ventum ④ v come through to, arrive at, reach

perversus, a, um *adj* askew, awry; perverse, evil, bad

pervertō, rtī, rsum ③ v overthrow; subvert; destroy, ruin, corrupt

pervestīgō ① v make a thorough search of; explore fully

pervetus, eris *adj* very old

pervicācia, ae f stubbornness, obstinacy; firmness, steadiness

pervicāx, ācis *adj* stubborn, obstinate; firm, steadfast

pervideō, vidī, vīsum ② v take in with the eyes or mind

pervigil, lis *adj* keeping watch or sleepless all night long

pervigilium, iī *nt* vigil, watch

pervigilō ① v remain awake all night; keep watch all night

pervincō, vīcī, victum ③ v conquer completely; carry (a proposal), gain an objective; persuade

pervius, a, um *adj* passable, traversable; penetrable

pervolō ① v fly or flit through; wing one's way; move rapidly through the air

pervor- ▶ **perver-**

pervulgō ① v make publicly known, spread abroad

pēs, pedis m foot; metrical foot; foot (as a linear measure); sheet (of a sail)

pessimus, a, um *adj* worst

pessum *adv* to the lowest part, to the bottom
□ **~ dō** destroy, ruin

pestifer, era, erum *adj* pestilential; destructive

pestilēns, ntis *adj* pestilential, unhealthy, unwholesome; destructive

pestilentia, ae f pestilence, unhealthy atmosphere or region; plague

pestis, is f plague, pestilence; destruction, ruin, death

petauristārius, (i)ī m acrobat

petītiō, ōnis f attack, thrust; request, petition; candidature; lawsuit

petītor, ōris m seeker, striver after; applicant, candidate; claimant, plaintiff

petō, īvī/iī, ītum ③ v make for; seek; fetch; seek after; attack; ask for; desire; be a candidate for

petulāns, ntis *adj* pert, saucy, impudent, petulant; wanton, lascivious

petulantia, ae f impudent or boisterous aggressiveness; wantonness, immodesty

petulcus, a, um *adj* butting

phalānx, angis f body of soldiers drawn up in close order

phalerae, ārum *fpl* ornaments worn by men of arms and horses

phalerātus, a, um *adj* with fine trappings

P

phantasma, atis *nt* spectre, apparition

pharetra, ae *f* quiver

pharetrātus, a, um *adj* wearing a quiver

pharmacopōla, ae *m* medicine- or drug-seller; quack

phasēlus, ī *m/f* kidney-bean; light ship

Philippus, ī *m* two-drachma coin, minted by Philip II of Macedon

philomēla, ae *f* nightingale

philosophia, ae *f* philosophy

philosophor ⓵ *v dep* philosophize

philosophus, ī *m* philosopher

philtrum, ī *nt* love-potion

philyra, ae *f* linden-tree, lime-tree

phōca, ae *f*, **phōcē**, **ēs** *f* seal

piāculāris, e *adj* atoning, expiatory

piāculum, ī *nt* expiatory offering or rite; sin

piāmen, inis *nt* atonement

pīca, ae *f* magpie; jay

picātus, a, um *adj* sealed with pitch

picea, ae *f* spruce

piceus, a, um *adj* made of pitch; pitchblack

pictor, ōris *m* painter

pictūra, ae *f* art of painting; picture; mental image

pictūrātus, a, um *adj* decorated with colour

pīcus, ī *m* woodpecker

pietās, ātis *f* piety; dutifulness; affection, love; loyalty; gratitude

piger, gra, grum *adj* slow, sluggish, inactive; inert

piget ② *v impers* it affects with revulsion or displeasure, it irks

pigmentum, ī *nt* colour, colouring, paint

pignerō ⓵ *v* pledge, pawn; appropriate

pignus, oris/eris *nt* pledge, pawn, surety; token, proof; stake; Lᴹ child

pigritia, ae *f*, **pigritiēs**, iēī *f* sloth, sluggishness, laziness, indolence

pīla, ae *f* squared pillar; pier, pile

pila, ae *f* ball

pīlānus, ī *m* a soldier of the third rank

pilentum, ī *nt* luxurious carriage used by women

pileum, ī *nt*, **pileus**, ī *m*, **pilleus**, ī *m* felt cap; freedom, liberty

pilleātus, a, um *adj* wearing the felt cap of manumission

pīlum, ī *nt* javelin

pilus, ī *m* hair; trifle

pīlus, ī *m* the first century of the first cohort of a legion
□ **prīmum pīlum dūcō** command the first century of the first cohort of a legion

pinacothēca, ae *f* picture-gallery

pīnētum, ī *nt* pine-wood

pīneus, a, um *adj* of the pine, covered in pines

pingō, pīnxī, **pictum** ③ *v* paint; embroider; embellish; tattoo

pinguēscō ③ *v* grow fat; become strong or fertile

pinguis, e *adj* fat; plump; rich;

dull, slow-witted; slothful

inifer, pīniger, era, erum *adj* pine-bearing

inna, ae *f* feather; wing; raised part of an embattled parapet

inniger, era, erum *adj* winged; finny

innipēs, edis *adj* having wings on the feet

inus, ī *f*, **pīnus, ūs** *f* pine-tree; ship; pine-wood torch

iō ① *v* appease, propitiate; cleanse, expiate

ipiō ① *v* (of birds) cheep

irāta, ae *m* corsair, pirate

irāticus, a, um *adj* piratical

irum, ī *nt* pear

irus, ī *f* pear-tree

iscārius, a, um *adj* of or connected with fish

iscātor, ōris *m* fisherman

iscātōrius, a, um *adj* of or for fishing

iscātus, ūs *m* catch of fish, seafood

iscīna, ae *f* fish-pond; swimming-pool

iscis, is *m* fish

iscor ① *v dep* fish

iscōsus, a, um *adj* teeming with fish

isculentus, a, um *adj* fishy, full of fish

istor, ōris *m* miller, baker

istrīnum, ī *nt* mill, bakery (also as a place of punishment or drudgery)

istris, is *f* sea monster; whale

ituīta, ae *f* mucus, phlegm

ius, a, um *adj* pious, religious,

faithful, devout; dutiful

pix, picis *f* pitch

plācābilis, e *adj* easily appeased, placable; appeasing, pacifying

plācātus, a, um *adj* kindly disposed; peaceful; calm

placenta, ae *f* a kind of flat cake

placeō ② *v with dat* be pleasing (to), satisfy
□ **placet** it seems good (to); it is resolved or agreed on (by)

placidus, a, um *adj* gentle, calm, mild, peaceful, placid

plācō ① *v* calm, assuage, placate, appease, reconcile (with)

plāga, ae *f* blow, stroke; wound

plaga, ae *f* open expanse (of land, sea or sky); tract; hunting-net

plāgigerulus, a, um *adj* bearing (the marks of) blows, much beaten

plāgipatidēs, ae *m* one who has suffered whipping

plāgōsus, a, um *adj* lavish with blows

plagūsia, ae *f* shellfish, scallop

plānē *adv* plainly, clearly; utterly, quite

plānēta, ae *m* wandering star, planet

planeta, ae *f* [LM] chasuble

plangō, ānxī, ānctum ③ *v* strike, beat; beat the breast in mourning, mourn for

plangor, ōris *m* beating, striking; lamentation

plānitiēs, iēī *f* flat or even surface, level ground, plain

planta, ae *f* sprout, shoot; sole of the foot

plantāria, ium *ntpl* slips, cuttings

plānus, a, um *adj* level, flat,

plane, even; obvious

platanus, **ī** f plane-tree

platea, **platēa**, **ae** f street

plaudō, **plausī**, **plausum** 🔲 v clap, strike, beat; *with dat* applaud

plausor, **ōris** m applauder

plaustrum, **ī** nt wagon, cart; Charles's Wain

plausus, **ūs** m clapping; applause

plēbēcula, **ae** f mob, common people

plēbēius, **a**, **um** adj pertaining to the common people, plebeian; common, everyday

plēbicola, **ae** m one who courts the favour of the people

plēbiscītum, **ī** nt resolution of the people

plēbs, **bis/bī** f, **plēbēs**, **ēī** f common people, plebeians; mob, common herd, masses

plectō[1], **exī**, **exum** 🔲 v plait, twine

plectō[2] 🔲 v buffet, beat; punish

plectrum, **ī** nt quill to strike the strings of a musical instrument

plēnus, **a**, **um** adj full, filled with; plump, stout; plenteous; entire; whole

plērumque adv generally, mostly, commonly, often

plērusque, **plēraque**, **plērumque** adj the greater part or number of, most of
■ **plēraque**, **plēraeque**, **plēraque** pl most (people), very many

plicō 🔲 v fold, bend; twine, coil

plōrātus, **ūs** m wailing, crying

plōrō 🔲 v wail, weep aloud, weep over

plūma, **ae** f feather, plumage; down

plumbeus, **a**, **um** adj leaden; blunt, dull; heavy; stupid

plumbum, **ī** nt lead

plūmeus, **a**, **um** adj feathery; composed of or filled with feather(

plūmiger, **era**, **erum** adj feathered

plūmipēs, **edis** adj having feathers on the feet, feather-footed

plūmōsus, **a**, **um** adj feathered

pluō, **pluī/plūvī** 🔲 v rain; fall like rain
■ **pluit** impers it rains, is raining

plūrēs, **a** adj more, a number of; very many

plūrimus, **a**, **um** adj very much or many, (the) most, very long or large or big

plūs n/adj more
□ **plūris** of more value

pluteus, **ī** m movable screen of wood or wickerwork used for protection in siege warfare; upright board forming the back of a couch

pluvia, **ae** f rain

pluviālis, **e** adj rainy; consisting (rain; rain-swollen

pluvius, **a**, **um** adj rainy, causing or bringing rain

pōculum, **ī** nt drinking-vessel, cup; drink

podagra, **ae** f gout

poēma, **atis** nt poem

poena, **ae** f punishment, penalty
□ **dō poenās** pay the penalty

poenitudo, **inis** f [LM] repentance

poēsis, **is** f poetry; poem

poēta, **ae** *m* poet

poēticus, **a**, **um** *adj* poetic

pol *int* by Pollux!

polenta, **ae** *f* barley-meal

poliō ④ *v* smooth, polish; refine, give finish to

polītus, **a**, **um** *adj* refined, polished

pollēns, **ntis** *adj* strong, potent, exerting power

pollentia, **ae** *f* power

polleō ② *v* exert power *or* influence; be strong

pollex, **icis** *m* thumb

polliceor ② *v dep* promise

pollicitātiō, **ōnis** *f* promise

pollicitor ① *v dep* promise (assiduously)

pollūcibilis, **e** *adj* sumptuous; ostentatious

polluō, **luī**, **lūtum** ③ *v* soil, defile, pollute; contaminate; violate; defile with illicit sexual conduct

polus, **ī** *m* pole; heaven, sky

polyandrium, **(i)ī** *nt* ⅬⅯ cemetery

polypus, **ī** *m* octopus, nasal tumour

polyspaston, **ī** *nt* crane

pōmārium, **(i)ī** *nt* orchard

pōmerium, **(i)ī** *nt* space left free from buildings round the walls of a Roman *or* Etruscan town

pōmifer, **era**, **erum** *adj* fruit-bearing

pōmōsus, **a**, **um** *adj* rich in fruit

pompa, **ae** *f* ceremonial procession

pōmum, **ī** *nt*, **pōmus**, **ī** *f* fruit; fruit-tree

ponderō ① *v* weigh; weigh up

pondō *adv* in *or* by weight

pondus, **eris** *nt* weight; burden; value; importance, gravity; pound's weight

pōne *adv/prep with acc* behind

pōnō, **posuī**, **positum** ③ *v* put, place; lay; station; plant; lay aside; appoint

pōns, **ntis** *m* bridge; deck (of a ship); floor of a tower

ponticulus, **ī** *m* little bridge

pontifex, **icis** *m* Roman high priest; ⅬⅯ bishop, pontiff

pontificalis, **e** *adj* pontifical, of *or* pertaining to a **pontifex**; ⅬⅯ of a bishop, episcopal; of the Pope, papal

pontificātus, **ūs** *m* pontificate, the office of **pontifex**; ⅬⅯ see, bishopric; papacy

pontificius, **a**, **um** *adj* pontifical, of *or* pertaining to a **pontifex**

pontus, **ī** *m* sea

popīna, **ae** *f* cook-shop, bistro, low-class eating house

poples, **itis** *m* knee

poposcī ▶ poscō

populābilis, **e** *adj* that may be ravaged *or* laid waste

populābundus, **a**, **um** *adj* intent on pillage *or* plunder

populāris, **e** *adj* popular; of the common people; of the same country

  □ **~ aura** the breeze of popular favour

  ■ **~ m** fellow-citizen, compatriot; member of the 'popular' party

populāritās, **ātis** *f* courting of popular favour

populāriter adv in everyday language; in a manner designed to win popular support

populātiō, ōnis f plundering, devastation

populātor, ōris m devastator, ravager, plunderer

pōpuleus, a, um adj of a poplar

populō ⚀ v, **populor** ⚀ v dep ravage, devastate; plunder; despoil

populus, ī m people, nation

pōpulus, ī f poplar-tree

porca, ae f female pig, sow

porculus, ī m piglet

porcus, ī m hog, pig

porrigō, rēxī, rēctum ⚂ v put forward, extend; stretch or spread (oneself) out; offer

porrīgō, inis f scaly condition, scurf, dandruff

porrō adv onward, further off; further; besides; again, moreover

porrum, ī nt, **porrus, ī** m leek

porta, ae f gate; entrance

portendō, ndī, ntum ⚂ v portend, presage; reveal by portents

portentum, ī nt omen, portent; something unnatural or extraordinary, monster, monstrosity; fantastic story

porticus, ūs f colonnade, portico

portiō, ōnis f part, portion, share; proportion
□ **prō portiōne** proportionally

portitor, ōris m ferryman; Charon; toll-collector, customs-officer

portō ⚀ v carry, bear, convey

portōrium, (i)ī nt duty, toll

portuōsus, a, um adj well provided with harbours

portus, ūs m harbour, haven, port; mouth of a river

poscō, poposcī ⚂ v ask for insistently, demand; demand for punishment, trial, etc.

positor, ōris m builder, founder

positus, ūs m situation, position; arrangement

possessiō, ōnis f possession; estate

possessor, ōris m owner, occupier

possibilis, e adj possible

possideō, sēdī, sessum ⚁ v possess, have

possum, posse, potuī v ir be able; have power; can

post[1] adv behind, back; backwards; after

post[2] prep with acc behind; after; inferior to

posteā adv hereafter, thereafter, afterwards

posteāquam adv after, ever sinc

posterior, ius adj later in order; later, latter; inferior

posteritās, ātis f future time; posterity

posterus, a, um adj following, next, ensuing, future
■ **posterī, ōrum** mpl posterity, descendants

postgenitus, a, um adj born at later time, yet to be born

posthabeō ⚁ v esteem less, subordinate (to); postpone

posthāc adv hereafter, henceforth, in future

postīcum, ī nt back door

postīcus, a, um adj back, rear

postibi, postid *adv* afterwards

postilla *adv* after that, afterwards

postis, is *m* post, door-post; door

postmodo, postmodum *adv* afterwards, presently, later

postmoenium, (i)ī *nt* area or part behind a wall

postpōnō, posuī, positum ③ *v* esteem less than; postpone

postquam *conj* after, since

postrēmō *adv* at last

postrēmus, a, um *adj* last; worst

postrīdiē *adv* on the day after, on the following or next day

postulātiō, ōnis *f* petition, request

postulātum, ī *nt* demand, request

postulō ① *v* ask for, demand, require, request, desire; accuse, prosecute

postumus, a, um *adj* last; last-born; born after the death of the father

potēns, ntis *adj* able, mighty, powerful, potent, efficacious
□ **suī** ~ one's own master

potentātus, ūs *m* dominion, command

potentia, ae *f* power; efficacy, virtue; ability

potestās, ātis *f* power, faculty, opportunity; authority; dominion; command

pōtiō, ōnis *f* drink, draught; potion, philtre

potior[1] ④ *v dep* take possession of, get, obtain, acquire, receive; possess

potior[2]**, ius** *adj* more powerful; preferable

potis, e *adj* able (to), capable (of); possible

potissimus, a, um *adj* principal, most powerful, chief

potius *adv* rather, preferably; more (than)

pōtō, pōt(āt)um ① *v* drink; tipple; drink to excess

prae *prep with abl* before, in front of; in comparison with; in the face of, under the pressure of

praeacūtus, a, um *adj* sharpened at the end, very sharp

praealtus, a, um *adj* very high; very deep

praebeō ② *v* offer; present; show; give; expose

praecaveō, cāvī, cautum ② *v* guard (against), beware

praecēdō, essī, essum ③ *v* go before, precede; surpass

praecellō ③ *v* excel; surpass

praecelsus, a, um *adj* exceptionally high or tall

praeceps, cipitis *adj* headlong; impetuous, sheer; involving risk of sudden disaster
□ **in** ~ headlong

praeceptor, ōris *m* teacher, instructor

praeceptum, ī *nt* rule, precept; order, instruction; teaching

praecerpō, psī, ptum ③ *v* pluck before time; pluck or cut off

praecīdō, īdī, īsum ③ *v* cut off in front; cut back, cut short

praecingō, īnxī, īnctum ③ *v* gird, surround, encircle; encompass

praecinō, inuī, centum ③ *v* sing before; predict

praecipēs ▶ praeceps

praecipiō, cēpī, ceptum ③ *v* take or obtain in advance, anticipate; teach, recommend, order

praecipitō ① *v* throw down headlong, precipitate; destroy; suffer ruin; drive headlong; fall headlong

praecipuus, a, um *adj* particular, peculiar, especial; special

praecīsus, a, um *adj* abrupt, precipitous; clipped, staccato

praeclārus, a, um *adj* very bright; beautiful; splendid, noble, excellent, brilliant; glorious

praeclūdō, ūsī, ūsum ③ *v* block up, bar; prevent; forbid access to

praecō, ōnis *m* crier; auctioneer

praecōnsūmō, mpsī, mptum ③ *v* use up prematurely

praecoquis, e *adj*, **praecox, ocis** *adj* ripened too soon; premature; unseasonable; precocious

praecordia, ōrum *ntpl* vitals, diaphragm; breast; chest as the seat of feeling

praecurrō, (cu)currī, cursum ③ *v* run before, hasten on before; precede; anticipate

praecursor, ōris *m* forerunner; member of advance-guard

praecursōrius, a, um *adj* travelling in advance, precursory

praeda, ae *f* booty, spoil, loot; prey, game

praedābundus, a, um *adj* pillaging

praedātor, ōris *m* plunderer, pillager; hunter

praedātōrius, a, um *adj*

plundering, rapacious; piratical

praedicamentum, i *nt* ⃞ category (in Aristotelian philosophy)

praedicātiō, ōnis *f* proclamation, publication; commendation

praedicator, oris *m* ⃞ preacher

praedicō ① *v* publish; proclaim; cite; describe (as), call; praise; ⃞ preach

praedīcō, īxī, ictum ③ *v* say or mention beforehand; foretell; warn; recommend

praedictum, ī *nt* prediction; forewarning; command

praediscō ③ *v* learn in advance

praeditus, a, um *adj* endowed (with)

praedium, (i)ī *nt* land, estate

praedīves, itis *adj* very rich; richly supplied

praedō, ōnis *m* brigand; pirate

praedor ① *v dep* plunder, loot, pillage, spoil; take as plunder

praedūcō, ūxī, ductum ③ *v* run (a ditch *or* a wall) in front

praedulcis, e *adj* very sweet

praedūrus, a, um *adj* very hard; very strong

praeeō, īre, iī/īvī, itum *v* ir go before, precede; dictate

praefectūra, ae *f* command; office of praefectus; district

praefectus, ī *m* director, president, chief; governor

praeferō, ferre, tulī, lātum *v* bear before; prefer; display, reveal; give precedence to

praeferōx, ōcis *adj* very high-spirited

praefestīnō ① v be in a hurry

praeficiō, fēcī, fectum ③ v put in charge (of); appoint to the command (of)

praefīgō, īxī, īxum ③ v fasten before; fix on the end or surface (of); obstruct

praefīniō ④ v fix the range of; determine

praefodiō, ōdī ③ v dig a trench in front of; bury beforehand

praefor ① v dep say or utter beforehand, mention first; recite (a preliminary formula); address with a preliminary prayer

praefrīgidus, a, um adj very cold

praefringō, āctum ③ v break off at the end, break off short

praefulgeō, lsī, ltum ② v shine with outstanding brightness; be outstanding

praegelidus, a, um adj outstandingly cold

praegestiō ④ v have an overpowering desire, be very eager (to)

praegnāns, ntis adj, **praegnās, ātis** adj with child, pregnant

praegravis, e adj very heavy; burdensome

praegravō ① v weigh down; burden

praegredior, gressus sum ③ v dep go ahead; go before, precede; surpass

praegustō ① v taste in advance

praeiūdicium, (i)ī nt precedent, example; prejudgement

praeiūdicō ① v prejudge

praelābor, lāpsus sum ③ v dep flow, glide ahead or past

praelegō, lēgī, lēctum ③ v select; sail along; read aloud

praelongus, a, um adj exceptionally long

praelūceō, ūxī ② v shine forth; outshine; light the way (for)

praemātūrē adv prematurely, very early or promptly

praemeditor ① v dep consider in advance

praemetuō ③ v fear beforehand

praemittō, mīsī, missum ③ v send in advance (of)

praemium, (i)ī nt booty, plunder, prize; reward; punishment; payment

praemoneō ② v forewarn

praemonitus, ūs m forewarning

praemorior, morī, mortuus sum ③ v dep die beforehand

praemūniō ④ v fortify, defend in advance; safeguard

praenatō ① v swim by; flow by

praenōmen, inis nt first name

praenōscō, nōvī ③ v foreknow

praenūntiō ① v announce in advance

praenūntius, a, um adj acting as harbinger; heralding

praeoccupō ① v seize upon beforehand; anticipate

praeoptō ① v choose in preference; prefer

praeparātiō, ōnis f preparation

praeparō ① v furnish beforehand; provide in readiness; plan in advance; prepare

praepediō ④ v shackle, fetter; hinder

praependeō ② v hang down in front

praepes, etis adj flying straight ahead; nimble, fleet; winged

praepinguis, e adj outstandingly rich

praepōnō, posuī, positum ③ v put before; prefer (to); put in charge (of)

praepositus, ī m LM abbot; provost (deputy to an abbot)

praeposterus, a, um adj in the wrong order; wrong-headed; topsy-turvy

praepotēns, ntis adj very powerful

praeproperus, a, um adj very hurried, precipitate; too hasty

praeripiō, ripuī, reptum ③ v snatch away (before the proper time); seize first; forestall

praerogātīva, ae f tribe which voted first

praerumpō, rūpī, ruptum ③ v break off

praeruptus, a, um adj broken off; precipitous; hasty, rash

praes, dis m surety, bondsman

praesaepe, is nt, **praesaepēs, is** f, **praesaepium, (i)ī** nt stall; brothel

praesaepiō, psī, ptum ④ v fence in front

praesāgiō ④ v have a presentiment (of); portend

praesāgium, (i)ī nt sense of foreboding; prognostication

praesāgus, a, um adj having a foreboding; ominous

praescius, a, um adj foreknowing, prescient

praescrībō, psī, ptum ③ v write before; prescribe, appoint

praescrīptum, ī nt precept, rule; route

praesecō, secuī, sec(ā)tum ① v cut in front, cut

praesēns, ntis adj present, in person, at hand, ready; prompt; favourable; effectual; immediate; present, aiding
◻ **in** ~ for the present

praesentārius, a, um adj quick, ready; paid on the spot in cash, in ready money

praesentia, ae f presence; helpful presence

praesentiō, nsī, ēnsum ④ v feel or perceive beforehand; have a presentiment of

praesep- ▶ **praesaep-**

praesēpe, is nt (also **praesaepe**) stall; brothel

praesēpiō, psī, ptum ④ v (also **praesaepiō**) fence in front

praesertim adv especially, particularly

praeses, idis m guardian, warden, custodian

praesideō, sēdī ② v with dat preside (over); guard, protect, defend; superintend

praesidium, (i)ī nt help, assistance; defence, protection; convoy, escort; garrison; stronghold

praesignis, e adj pre-eminent, outstanding

praestābilis, e adj pre-eminent, distinguished, excellent

praestāns, ntis adj excellent; distinguished (for)

praestituō, uī, ūtum ③ v

determine in advance

praestō¹ adv ready, at one's service

praestō², **stitī**, **stitum/stātum** ① v stand out; be superior (to); surpass; answer for; fulfil; maintain; show; furnish

praestōlor ① v dep expect; await

praestringō, **īnxī**, **ictum** ③ v bind or tie up; graze, weaken, blunt

praestruō, **ūxī**, **ūctum** ③ v block up, contrive beforehand

praesultō ① v dance before

praesum, **esse**, **fuī** v ir with dat be in charge (of), be in control (of); take the lead (in)

praesūmō, **m(p)sī**, **mptum** ③ v consume beforehand; perform beforehand; spend or employ beforehand; presuppose

praetendō, **ndī**, **ntum** ③ v stretch out; spread before; extend in front; allege in excuse; offer or show deceptively, make a pretence of

praeter prep with acc/adv past; except; excepting; along; beyond; unless, save; besides

praetereā adv besides; moreover

praetereō, **īre**, **iī/īvī**, **itum** v ir go by or past; pass by; escape the notice of; neglect; surpass

praeterfluō ③ v flow past

praetergredior, **gressus sum** ③ v dep march or go past

praeterhāc adv beyond this point; further

praeteritus, **a**, **um** adj past

praeterlābor, **lāpsus sum** ③ v dep glide or slip past

praetermittō, **mīsī**, **missum** ③ v let pass; omit, neglect; pass over, make no mention of

praeterquam adv beyond, besides; except, save

praetervehor, **vectus sum** ③ v dep drive, ride or sail by; pass by

praetervolō ① v fly past; slip by

praetexō, **xuī**, **xtum** ③ v weave in front, fringe; cloak (with); pretend

praetexta, **ae** f toga with a purple border worn by curule magistrates and children

praetextātus, **a**, **um** adj wearing the **toga praetexta**

praetextus, **ūs** m show; pretext

praetor, **ōris** m Roman magistrate

praetōriānus, **a**, **um** adj praetorian

praetōrium, **(i)ī** nt general's headquarters building or tent; imperial bodyguard

praetōrius¹, **(i)ī** m an ex-praetor

praetōrius², **a**, **um** adj of or belonging to a commander (of a Roman military force), praetorian

praetrepidō ① v tremble in anticipation

praetūra, **ae** f praetorship

praeūrō, **ussī**, **ustum** ③ v scorch at the extremity or on the surface

praevaleō ② v have greater power, influence or worth; prevail

praevalidus, **a**, **um** adj very or outstandingly strong; strong in growth

praevehor, **vectus sum** ③ v dep travel past or along

praeveniō, **vēnī**, **ventum** ④ v arrive first or beforehand;

anticipate, forestall

praevertō, rtī, rsum ③ *v* anticipate; preoccupy; attend to first; outstrip, outrun

praevideō, vidī, vīsum ② *v* foresee, see in advance

praevius, a, um *adj* going before, leading the way

prandeō, ndī, pransum ② *v* eat one's morning or midday meal

prandium, (i)ī *nt* meal eaten about midday, luncheon

prātum, ī *nt* meadow

prāvitās, ātis *f* bad condition; viciousness, perverseness, depravity

prāvus, a, um *adj* crooked; misshapen, deformed; perverse, vicious, corrupt; faulty; bad

precārius, a, um *adj* obtained by prayer; doubtful, precarious

precātiō, ōnis *f* prayer, supplication

precēs, um *fpl* prayer, entreaty; good wishes

precor ① *v dep* pray to, beseech, entreat; ask for; invoke

prehendō, ndī, ēnsum ③ *v* take hold of, seize hold of; catch in the act

prelatus, ī *m* 🄻 prelate, bishop

prēlum, ī *nt* wine- or oil-press

premō, essī, essum ③ *v* press, squeeze; oppress; curb; thrust; overpower; keep in subjection; afflict; pursue; have intercourse with

prēnsō ① *v* grasp at; accost; canvass

pressō ① *v* press, squeeze

pressus, a, um *adj* firmly planted,

deliberate

pretiōsus, a, um *adj* valuable, precious; costly

pretium, (i)ī *nt* price, worth, value; wages, reward; bribe
□ **(operae)** ∼ **est** it is worth while

prīdem *adv* some time ago, previously

prīdiē *adv* on the day before

prīma, ae *f* 🄻 prime (part of the daily cycle of prayer)

prīmaevus, a, um *adj* youthful

prīmānus, a, um *adj* of the first legion

prīmārius, a, um *adj* of the first rank

prīmipīlus, ī *m* senior centurion of a legion

prīmitiae, ārum *fpl* first-fruits; beginnings

prīmordium, (i)ī *nt* beginnings, origin

prīmōris, is *adj* first; foremost, extreme
■ **prīmōrēs** *mpl* nobles, men of the first rank

prīmum *adv* first, in the first place, at the beginning; for the first time
□ **quam** ∼ as soon as possible

prīmus, a, um *adj* first, foremost, most distinguished
□ **prīma lux** early dawn
□ **in prīmīs** especially
□ **ad prīma signa** in the front line

prīnceps, ipis *adj* first; *m/f* *adj* general; prime mover
□ ∼ **senatūs** senator whose name stood first on the censors' list

rīncipālis, e *adj* first, original,
principal; imperial, with the
emperor

rīncipātus, ūs *m* pre-
eminence; supremacy, post
of commander-in-chief; rule;
beginning

rīncipium, (i)ī *nt* beginning,
origin, principle

rior, ius *adj* former, previous; in
front; better

■ **priōrēs, um** *mpl* ancestors

■ **prior, is** *m* LM abbot

rīscus, a, um *adj* old, ancient;
archaic

rīstinus, a, um *adj* former,
antique, ancient

rius *adv* before, sooner

riusquam *conj* before

rīvātim *adv* in private, privately

rīvātus, a, um *adj* private

rīvigna, ae *f* stepdaughter

rīvignus, ī *m* stepson

rīvilegium, (i)ī *nt* LM privilege,
charter, bull

rīvō ① *v* deprive (of); free or
release (from)

rīvus, a, um *adj* one's own,
private; separate, single

rō¹ *prep with abl* before, in front of;
from the front of; for, in favour of;
instead of; in proportion to

■ **~ certō habeō** know for
certain

rō² *int with voc, acc or nom* Good
God! good heavens!

roavia, ae *f* great-grandmother

roavītus, a, um *adj* ancestral

roavus, ī *m* great-grandfather;
remote ancestor

robābilis, e *adj* probable;

commendable

probātor, ōris *m* one who
approves

probitās, ātis *f* honesty, probity;
virtue

probō ① *v* test; recommend;
approve of; prove

probrōsus, a, um *adj* shameful;
disreputable

probrum, ī *nt* disgrace; abuse,
insult; disgrace, shame

probus, a, um *adj* good; clever;
honest, virtuous

procāx, ācis *adj* pushing,
impudent; undisciplined; frivolous

prōcēdō, essī, essum ③ *v*
go forward or before, proceed;
advance; get on; be successful;
make progress

procella, ae *f* storm, gale;
tumult, commotion

procellōsus, a, um *adj* stormy,
boisterous

procer, eris *m* usu. in pl. great
men, noblemen

prōcēritās, ātis *f* height; great
length

prōcērus, a, um *adj* high, tall;
long

prōcessus, ūs *m* advance,
progress

prōcidō, idī ③ *v* fall prostrate,
collapse

prōcinctus, ūs *m* readiness for
battle

prōclāmō ① *v* call or cry out;
appeal noisily

prōclīnō ① *v* tilt forward; cause
to totter

prōclīvis, e *adj* sloping down;
downward; prone (to); easy

P

Procnē, ēs *f* swallow

prōcōnsul, lis *m* ex-consul; governor of a province

prōcōnsulāris, e *adj* proconsular

prōcrāstinō ① *v* put off till the next day, postpone; delay

prōcreō ① *v* bring into existence, beget, procreate; produce, create

prōcrēscō ③ *v* grow on to maturity, grow larger

prōcubō ① *v* lie outstretched

prōcūdō, ūdī, ūsum ③ *v* forge, hammer out, beat out

procul *adv* far, some way off, far away

prōculcō ① *v* trample on

prōcumbō, ubuī, ubitum ③ *v* lean *or* bend forward; sink down, prostrate oneself

prōcūrātiō, ōnis *f* charge, management; superintendence

prōcūrātor, ōris *m* manager, overseer; agent; governor; LM proctor

prōcūrō ① *v* attend to; administer; expiate (by sacrifice)

prōcurrō, (cu)currī, cursum ③ *v* run *or* rush forwards; extend, project

prōcursātiō, ōnis *f* sudden charge, sally

prōcursō ① *v* run frequently forward, dash out

prōcursus, ūs *m* forward movement; outbreak

prōcurvus, a, um *adj* curved outwards *or* forwards

procus, ī *m* wooer, suitor

prōdeō, īre, iī, itum *v ir* go *or* come forward *or* forth; project; appear in public, appear on the stage; advance, proceed

prōdīcō, īxī, ictum ③ *v* give notice of *or* fix a day

prōdigiōsus, a, um *adj* prodigious, strange, wonderful, unnatural

prōdigium, (i)ī *nt* omen, portent, monster; marvel; monstrous creature

prōdigus, a, um *adj* wasteful, lavish, prodigal

prōditiō, ōnis *f* betrayal, treachery

prōditor, ōris *m* traitor; betrayer

prōdō, didī, ditum ③ *v* give birth to; nominate; publish; betray; hand down

prōdūcō, dūxī, ductum ③ *v* lead *or* bring forward; draw out; accompany to the tomb; lengthen, prolong; bring forth

proelior ① *v dep* join battle, fight; contend

proelium, (i)ī *nt* battle, combat; conflict, dispute

profānō ① *v* desecrate, profane

profānus, a, um *adj* secular, profane; not initiated; impious

profectiō, ōnis *f* setting out; departure

profectō *adv* without question, undoubtedly, assuredly

profectus, ūs *m* progress, succes

profectus *pple* from
  ▶ **proficiscor**

prōferō, ferre, tulī, lātum *v ir* carry *or* bring out, bring forth; extend; prolong; defer; reveal; utter; produce; publish

profēstus, a, um *adj* not kept as a holiday, common, ordinary

prōficiō, fēcī, fectum ③ *v* mak

headway; advance; help; develop; be successful

proficīscor, profectus sum ③ *v dep* set out, depart; proceed, arise *or* spring from

profiteor, professus sum ② *v dep* declare publicly; promise, volunteer; profess (oneself) to be

prōflīgātus, a, um *adj* profligate, depraved

prōflīgō ① *v* defeat decisively, crush, overwhelm; ruin *or* destroy utterly

prōflō ① *v* blow out, exhale

prōfluō, ūxī, ūxum ③ *v* flow forth *or* along; emanate (from)

profor ① *v dep* speak out

profugiō, ūgī ③ *v* flee, run away (from)

profugus, a, um *adj* fugitive; runaway; refugee

prōfundō, ūdī, ūsum ③ *v* pour out; lavish, squander; break out

prōfundus, a, um *adj* deep, profound; boundless; insatiable
■ **profundum, ī** *nt* depths, abyss, chasm; boundless expanse

prōfūsus, a, um *adj* excessive; lavish; extravagant

prōgeniēs, iēī *f* race, family, progeny

prōgenitor, ōris *m* ancestor

prōgignō, genuī, genitum ③ *v* beget; produce

prōgnātus, a, um *adj* born (of), descended (from)

prōgredior, gressus sum ③ *v dep* march forwards, go on, proceed

prōgressus, ūs *m* advance, progress

prohibeō ② *v* keep off, hold at bay; prevent, restrain; stop, forbid; avert; defend

prōiciō, iēcī, iectum ③ *v* throw forth *or* before, fling down *or* away; expose; expel; renounce

prōiectus, a, um *adj* jutting out, projecting; precipitate; abject, grovelling

proinde *adv* accordingly, so then
□ ~ **ac** just as if

prōlābor, lāpsus sum ③ *v dep* glide *or* slip forwards; fall into decay, go to ruin; collapse

prōlātiō, ōnis *f* postponement; enlargement

prōlātō ① *v* lengthen, enlarge; prolong; put off, defer

prōlectō ① *v* lure, entice

prōlēs, lis *f* offspring, progeny, descendants, race

prōliciō ③ *v* lure forward, lead on

prōlogus, ī *m* prologue

prōloquor, locūtus sum ③ *v dep* speak out, declare

prōlūdō, ūsī, ūsum ③ *v* carry out preliminary exercises before a fight; rehearse for

prōluō, uī, ūtum ③ *v* wash out; wash away; wash up; purify

prōluviēs, iēī *f* overflow, flood; bodily discharge

prōmereō ② *v*, **prōmereor** ② *v dep* deserve, merit; deserve well of; earn; gain

prōmineō ② *v* jut out, stick up

prōmiscam, prōmiscē *adv* without distinction, all at the same time *or* in the same place; commonly

prōmiscuus, a, um *adj*

common, shared; general,
indiscriminate

prōmissum, **ī** nt promise

prōmissus, **a**, **um** adj hanging
down, long

prōmittō, **mīsī**, **missum** ③ v
send or put forth, let hang down;
promise, guarantee

prōmō, **prōm(p)sī**,
prōmptum ③ v take or bring out
or forth; bring into view; bring
out or display on the stage; make
known

prōmonturium, **(i)ī** nt
promontory, headland; mountain
spur

prōmoveō, **mōvī**, **mōtum** ②
v move forwards; advance, push
forward

prōmptuārium, **(i)ī** nt store-
room, cupboard

prōmptus[1], **ūs** m:
◻ **in prōmptū sum** be in full
view; be obvious; be within easy
reach for use

prōmptus[2], **a**, **um** adj plainly
visible, evident; at hand, ready,
prompt, quick; glib, insincere

prōmulgō ① v make known by
public proclamation; publish

prōmontōrium ▸
prōmontorium

prōmus, **ī** m butler; steward

pronepōs, **ōtis** m great-
grandson

prōnuba, **ae** f a married woman
who conducted the bride to the
bridal chamber

prōnūntiātiō, **ōnis** f
proclamation; delivery; verdict

prōnūntiō ① v proclaim,
announce; recite, declaim; tell;

report; promise publicly

prōnus, **a**, **um** adj stooping,
bending down; inclined
downwards; setting, sinking;
disposed, prone to; easy

propāgātiō, **ōnis** f propagation;
prolongation; the action of
extending

propāgō[1] ① v propagate; extend,
enlarge, increase

propāgō[2], **inis** f a layer or set
by which a plant is propagated;
offspring, children, race, breed

prōpalam adv openly

prope adv/prep with acc near, almost

propediem adv before long,
shortly

prōpellō, **pulī**, **pulsum** ③ v
drive or push forwards; propel;
drive away; impel

propemodo, **propemodum**
adv just about, pretty well

prōpēnsus, **a**, **um** adj ready,
eager, willing; favourably disposed

properanter adv hurriedly,
hastily

properipēs, **edis** adj swift-footed

properō ① v hasten; do with haste

properus, **a**, **um** adj quick,
speedy

prōpexus, **a**, **um** adj combed so
as to hang down

propheta, **ae** m LM prophet

prophetō ① v LM prophesy

propinquitās, **ātis** f nearness,
proximity; relationship, affinity;
intimacy

propinquō ① v bring near;
draw near

propinquus, **a**, **um** adj near,
neighbouring

■ ~, ī *m* kinsman

propior, ius *adj* nearer; more like; closer

propitiō [1] *v* win over, propitiate; soothe

propitius, a, um *adj* favourably inclined, well-disposed, propitious

prōpōnō, posuī, positum [3] *v* put out; set or post up; display; expose (to); report; propose, intend

prōpositum, ī *nt* intention, purpose; theme, point

prōpraetor, ōris *m* an ex-praetor; one sent to govern a province as *praetor*

proprietās, ātis *f* quality; special character; ownership

proprius, a, um *adj* one's own; personal; special; peculiar, proper ■ **proprior, ius** *comp* better suited

propter *adv/prep* with acc near, hard by, at hand; because of; on account of

proptereā *adv* therefore, on account of that

prōpugnāculum, ī *nt* bulwark, rampart; defence

prōpugnātor, ōris *m* defender; champion

prōpugnō [1] *v* fight; fight in defence of

prōpulsō [1] *v* drive off; ward off, repel

prōquaestor, ōris *m* deputy or treasurer; ex-quaestor

prōra, ae *f* prow; ship

prōrēpō, psī, ptum [3] *v* crawl or creep forth

prōrēta, ae *m* look-out (at the

prow of a ship)

prōripiō, ripuī, reptum [3] *v* drag or snatch away; rush or burst forth

prōrogātiō, ōnis *f* extension of a term of office; postponement

prōrogō [1] *v* prolong, keep going; put off, defer

prōrsus *adv* forward; straight ahead; absolutely

prōrumpō, rūpī, ruptum [3] *v* rush forth, break out

prōruō, ruī, rutum [3] *v* rush forward; tumble down; overthrow; hurl forward

prōsāpia, ae *f* family, lineage

proscaenium, (i)ī *nt* scaffold before the scene for the actors to play on; stage

proscindō, idī, issum [3] *v* cut, plough; castigate, lash

prōscrībō, psī, ptum [3] *v* announce publicly; post up, advertise (for sale); outlaw, proscribe

prōscrīptiō, ōnis *f* advertisement; proscription

prōscrīptus, ī *m* proscribed person, outlaw

prōsequor, secūtus sum [3] *dep* follow up, pursue; accompany

prōsiliō, luī [4] *v* leap or spring forth; start out; gush

prōspectō [1] *v* gaze out (at); look out on

prōspectus, ūs *m* view, prospect

prōspeculor [1] *v dep* look out for

prosperō [1] *v* cause to succeed, further

prosperus, a, um *adj* favourable, prosperous; successful; propitious

p

prōspiciō, exī, ectum 3 *v* see in front; foresee; take care (that); see to

prōsternō, strāvī, strātum 3 *v* throw to the ground, overthrow, prostrate; overthrow, cause the downfall of

prōstituō, tuī, tūtum 3 *v* prostitute; dishonour

prōstō, stitī 1 *v* prostitute oneself

prōsubigō, ēgī, āctum 3 *v* dig up in front of one

prōsum, prōdesse, fuī *v ir with dat* do good, benefit, profit

prōtegō, exī, ectum 3 *v* cover; furnish with a projecting roof; protect; defend

prōtēlō 1 *v* rout

prōtendō, ndī, ntum 3 *v* stretch out, extend; prolong

prōterō, trīvī, trītum 3 *v* crush, tread under foot; oppress

prōterreō 2 *v* frighten off or away

protervus, a, um *adj* violent, reckless; impudent, shameless

prōtinam *adv* at once, forthwith; straight on

prōtinus *adv* forward, straight on; immediately

prōtrahō, āxī, actum 3 *v* drag forward; bring to light, reveal; prolong

prōtrūdō, ūsī, ūsum 3 *v* thrust forwards or out; put off

prōturbō 1 *v* drive or push out of the way

prout *adv* according as, in proportion as; inasmuch as

prōvectus, a, um *adj* advanced, late; elderly

prōvehō, exī, ectum 3 *v* carry forward; convey out to sea

prōveniō, vēnī, ventum 4 *v* come forth; come into being; prosper

prōventus, ūs *m* growth; crop, produce; success; successful course

prōverbium, (i)ī *nt* proverb, saying

prōvidentia, ae *f* foresight, foreknowledge; providence

prōvideō, vīdī, vīsum 2 *v* provide (for); foresee

prōvidus, a, um *adj* prophetic; provident; characterized by forethought

prōvincia, ae *f* command, government, administration, province

prōvinciālis, e *adj* provincial

prōvīsor, ōris *m* one who foresees; one who takes care (of)

prōvocātiō, ōnis *f* challenge; appeal; right of appeal

prōvocō 1 *v* call forth, call out; challenge, excite

prōvolō 1 *v* fly forth; rush out

prōvolvō, lvī, lūtum 3 *v* roll forward or along, bowl over □ **prōvolvor** prostrate oneself

proximitās, ātis *f* near relationship; resemblance; similarity

proximus, a, um *adj* nearest; next; immediately preceding, immediately following; next of kin

prūdēns, ntis *adj* foreseeing, aware (of); intelligent, prudent, skilled (in)

prūdentia, ae f practical understanding; intelligence; prudence; practical grasp; foreknowledge

prūīna, ae f hoar-frost, rime

pruīnōsus, a, um adj frosty

prūna, ae f glowing charcoal, a live coal

prūnum, ī nt plum

prūrīgō, inis f itching, irritation; sexual excitement

prūriō 4 v itch; be sexually excited

psallō, ī 3 v play on the cithara

psalmodia, ae f [LM] psalm-singing, psalmody

psalmus, ī m psalm

psalterium, (i)ī nt psalter, book containing the Psalms

psaltria, ae f female player on the lute

psittacus, ī m parrot

pte particle own

pūbēns, ntis adj full of sap, vigorous

pūbertās, ātis f puberty; virility

pūbēs¹, bis f manpower, adult population; private parts

pūbēs², eris adj adult, grown-up; full of sap

pūbēscō, buī 3 v reach physical maturity; ripen

pūblicānus, ī m contractor for public works, farmer of the Roman taxes

pūblicitus adv at public expense

pūblicō 1 v confiscate; make public property

pūblicus, a, um adj public, common

■ **pūblicē** adv publicly, at public expense, officially

■ **pūblicum, ī** nt public purse; public property; public place, agora

■ **pūblicus, ī** m public slave

pudendus, a, um adj disgraceful, scandalous

pudēns, ntis adj modest; bashful

pudeō 2 v be ashamed; make ashamed

□ **mē pudet** I am ashamed

pudibundus, a, um adj shamefaced, blushing

pudīcitia, ae f chastity, purity

pudīcus, a, um adj chaste, virtuous

pudor, ōris m shame, shyness, modesty; decency; dishonour

puella, ae f girl, maiden; sweetheart

puellāris, e adj girlish, maidenly

puellula, ae f young girl

puer, erī m boy, son, young male slave

□ **ā puerō** from boyhood

puerīlis, e adj childish, boyish, youthful; immature

pueritia, ae f boyhood; callowness

puerpera, ae f a woman in labour

puerperium, (i)ī nt childbirth

pugil, lis m boxer, pugilist

pugilātōrius, a, um adj for punching, for boxing

pugillārēs, ium mpl writing-tablets

pugiō, ōnis m dagger, poniard

pugna, ae f fight; battle, combat; conflict, dispute

pugnātor, ōris m fighter, combatant

pugnāx, ācis adj combative, pugnacious; quarrelsome

pugneus, a, um adj of fists, 'fisty'

pugnō ① v fight; contend, clash

pugnus, ī m fist

pulc(h)er, c(h)ra, c(h)rum adj beautiful, handsome; glorious; illustrious; noble

pulc(h)ritūdō, inis f beauty; attractiveness

pullārius, (i)ī m keeper of the sacred chickens

pullātī, ōrum mpl people in mourning-dress

pullitiēs, iēī f set of young birds, brood

pullulō ① v sprout, send forth new growth; spring forth

pullus¹, ī m young animal; young chicken; darling, pet

pullus², a, um adj dingy, sombre

pulmō, ōnis m lungs; jellyfish

pulmōneus, a, um adj of the lungs

pulpitum, ī nt stage

puls, ltis f a dish made by boiling crushed spelt or other grain in water, a kind of porridge

pulsō ① v push, strike, beat, batter; assail

pulsum ▶ pellō

pulsus, ūs m stroke; beat; pulse; impulse

pultiphagus, a, um adj eating porridge

pultō ▶ pulsō

pulvereus, a, um adj, **pulverulentus, a, um** adj dusty

pulvīnar, āris nt, **pulvīnus, ī** m cushioned couch on which images

of the gods were placed

pulvis, eris m dust, powder, arena, battlefield

pūmex, icis m pumice

pūmiliō, ōnis m dwarf

pūn- ▶ poen-

pūnctim adv with the point

pūnctum, ī nt prick, small hole, puncture; spot; vote

◻ ~ **temporis** a moment

pungō, pupugī, pūnctum ③ v prick, puncture; vex, trouble

pūniceus, a, um adj scarlet, crimson

pūniō ④ v punish; avenge

pupa, ae f doll

pūpillus, ī m ward

puppis, is f stern, poop; ship

pūpula, ae f pupil of the eye

pūpulus, ī m little boy

pūrgāmen, inis nt impurity; means of purification

pūrgāmentum, ī nt means of cleansing or purifying, rubbish, filth

pūrgātiō, ōnis f cleaning

pūrgō ① v make clean, clean, cleanse, purify; justify, excuse, clear, exonerate

pūrificatio, onis f ⓛⓜ purification; Candlemas

purpura, ae f purple colour; purple; purple dye; purple-dyed cloth

purpurātus, a, um adj dressed in purple

purpureus, a, um adj purple-coloured, purple; radiant, glowing

purpurissum, ī nt dark red or purple cosmetic, rouge

pūrus, a, um adj clean, pure, undefiled; clear, chaste, naked, unadorned; without an iron point

pusillus, a, um adj very little, petty, insignificant

pustula, ae f inflamed sore, blister

putāmen, inis nt hard outer cover; nutshell

putātor, ōris m pruner

puteal, ālis nt structure surrounding the mouth of a well (in the Comitium at Rome)

puteālis, e adj derived from a well

pūteō ② v stink

puter, tris, tre adj (also **putris, e**) rotten, decaying; stinking; putrid, crumbling

pūtēscō ③ v begin to rot, go off

puteus, ī m well

pūtidus, a, um adj rotten; stinking; unpleasant; offensive; tiresomely affected; pedantic

putō ① v trim, prune; assess, estimate, regard (as); think, suppose, believe

putrefaciō, fēcī, factum ③ v cause to rot, putrefy

putrēscō ③ v rot, putrefy; crumble, moulder

pyra, ae f funeral pile, pyre

pȳramis, idis f pyramid

pyrōpus, ī m an alloy of gold and bronze; a red precious stone

pyxis, idis f small box or casket; [LM] pyx

Qq

quā adv in which direction; where; by what means, how; in so far as

quācumque adv wherever

quadra, ae f segment, slice

quadrāgēnī, ae, a adj forty each

quadragesimalis, e adj [LM] lenten

quadrāgēsimus, a, um adj fortieth

■ **quadragesima, ae** f [LM] Lent

quadrāgiē(n)s adv forty times

quadrāgintā adj indec forty

quadrāns, ntis m fourth part, quarter; coin worth a quarter of an **ās**

quadrātus, a, um adj squared, square-set

quadrīduum, ī nt period of four days

quadriennium, (i)ī nt period of four years

quadrifāriam adv in four ways, into four parts

quadrifidus, a, um adj split into four

quadrīgae, ārum fpl chariot with four horses

quadriiugus, a, um adj yoked four abreast

quadrīmus, a, um adj four years old

quadringēnārius, a, um adj of four hundred each

quadringēnī, ae, a adj four hundred each

quadringentē(n)simus, a, um *adj* the four hundredth

quadringentī, ae, a *adj* four hundred

quadrirēmis, mis *f* galley with four rowers to every 'room'

quadrivium, (i)ī *nt* ᴸᴹ the four 'higher' subjects of the medieval university curriculum, viz. mathematics, geometry, astronomy and music

quadrō 1 *v* quadruple; form a rectangular pattern

quadrupedāns, ntis *adj* galloping

quadrupēs, edis *adj* four-footed
 ∎ ∼, edis *m/f* quadruped

quadruplex, icis *adj* fourfold; quadruple

quaeritō 1 *v* seek; search for

quaerō, sīvī/siī, sītum 3 *v* look or search for; get, procure; inquire into

quaesītiō, ōnis *f* inquisition

quaesītus, a, um *adj* elaborate, contrived

quaesō 3 *v* ask (for); pray; please

quaestiō, ōnis *f* inquiry, investigation, question; examination by torture

quaestor, ōris *m* quaestor

quaestōrius, a, um *adj* of a quaestor
 ∎ ∼, (i)ī *m* ex-quaestor

quaestuōsus, a, um *adj* profitable

quaestūra, ae *f* quaestorship; public money

quaestus, ūs *m* gaining, acquiring; gain, profit, income

quālibet *adv* wherever one likes; no matter how

quālis, e *adj* of what sort, kind or nature, of what kind

quāliscumque,

quālecumque *adj* of whatever sort or quality; any kind of

quālum, ī *nt*, **quālus**, ī *m* wicker basket

quam *adv/conj* how; how much; in what way; than
 □ **tam … ∼** as … as *with sup* as … as possible
 □ ∼ **prīmum** as soon as possible *with comp*
 □ ∼ **ut/quī** [too …] to …

quamdiū *adv* as long as; how long

quamlibet *adv* however, however much

quamobrem *adv* why? for what reason? for which reason

quamprīmum *adv* as soon as possible

quamquam *conj* although; yet

quamvīs *adv/conj* to any degree you like; although; however

quandō *adv* at what time? when? at any time

quandōcumque *adv* whenever, as often as, as soon as

quandōque *adv* whenever; at some time or other

quandoquidem *conj* since, seeing that

quantillus, a, um *adj* how little?

quantō *adv* (by) how much

quantopere *adv* how greatly; in what degree

quantulus, a, um *adj* how little, how small, how trifling

quantuluscumque,

quantulacumque,

quantulumcumque adj however small or insignificant

quantus, a, um adj how great, as great as
□ **quantī** at what price?

quantuscumque, quantacumque, quantumcumque adj however great (or small); whatever

quantuslibet, quantalibet, quantumlibet adj no matter how great; however great

quantusvīs, quantavīs, quantumvīs adj however great

quāpropter adv wherefore; why

quārē adv in what way? how? whereby; wherefore, why

quārtus, a, um adj fourth

quasi adv as if, just as; as good as, practically

quassātiō, ōnis f violent shaking

quassō ① v shake repeatedly; wave, flourish; batter; weaken

quassus, a, um adj shaking, battered, bruised

quātenus adv how far; to what extent; how long, seeing that, since

quater adv four times

quaternī, ae, a adj four each, by fours; four together

quatiō, assum ③ v strike, shatter; shake; agitate, discompose; urge on

quattuor a indec four

quattuordecim a indec fourteen

quattuorvirī, ōrum mpl body of four men; board of chief magistrates

que conj and
□ **-que … et** both … and

quemadmodum adv how, in what way

queō, īre, īvī v ir dep be able (to)

quercus, ūs f oak, oak-tree; garland of oak leaves

querēla, querella, ae f complaint; plaintive sound

querimōnia, ae f complaint; 'difference of opinion'

quernus, a, um adj of oak, made of oak-wood

queror, questus sum ③ v dep complain; protest that or at

querulus, a, um adj complaining, querulous; giving forth a mournful sound

questus, ūs m complaint

quī¹ adv why? by what means? how?

quī², quae, quod pn who, which, that; which? any

quia conj because; LM that

quianam adv why ever?

quīcumque, quaecumque, quodcumque pn whoever, whatever

quid adv why? how? in what respect?

quīdam, quaedam, quoddam pn a certain

quidem adv indeed, certainly, in fact
□ **nē … ~** not even

quidnam adv what? how?

quidnī adv why not?

quiēs, ētis f rest, quiet, repose; peace; sleep; death

quiēscō, ēvī, ētum ③ v rest, keep quiet; repose in sleep

quiētus, a, um adj calm, quiet; peaceful, sleeping; undisturbed

quīlibet, quaelibet, quidlibet/quodlibet *pn* whoever or whatever you please

quīn *conj* that not; (but) that; indeed; why not? nay more

Quīnctilis, lis *m* July

quīncūnx, uncis *m* five-twelfths (of an **ās**); a pattern in which trees were planted; interest at five per cent

quīndecim *adj indec* fifteen

quīndecimvirī, ōrum *mpl* college or board of fifteen; college of priests who had charge of the Sibylline books

quīngēnī, ae, a *adj* five hundred each

quīngentē(n)simus, a, um *adj* five-hundredth

quīngentī, ae, a *adj* five hundred

quīnī, ae, a *adj* five each; five apiece; five at a time

quīnquāgēnī, ae, a *adj* fifty each; fifty at a time

quīnquāgē(n)simus, a, um *adj* fiftieth

quīnquāgintā *a indec* fifty

quīnquātria, ōrum *ntpl,* **quīnquātrūs, uum** *fpl* feast in honour of Minerva on 19–23 March

quīnque *adj indec* five

quīnquennālis, e *adj* quinquennial, occurring every five years

quīnquennis, e *adj* five years old; lasting for five years

quīnquennium, (i)ī *nt* (period of) five years

quīnquerēmis, e *adj* (of a galley) with five rowers to each 'room'

quīnquevirī, ōrum *mpl* board

of five

quīnquiē(n)s *adv* five times

quīntadecumānī, ōrum *mpl* soldiers of the fifteenth legion

quīntāna, ae *f* street or market in a Roman camp

quīntānī, ōrum *mpl* soldiers of the fifth legion

Quīntīlis ▶ Quīnctilis

quīntō, quīntum *adv* for the fifth time

quīntus, a, um *adj* fifth

quippe *adv* the reason is that, for; of course, naturally; seeing that; inasmuch as; as being; indeed, namely

Quirīnālia, ium *ntpl* a festival in honour of Romulus, celebrated on 17 February

quirītātus, ūs *m* cry of protest

Quirītēs, ītum *mpl* citizens of Rome collectively in their peacetime functions

quis, quid *pn* who? which? what? anyone; anything; someone; something

quisnam, quaenam, quidnam *pn* who tell me? what, tell me?

quispiam, quaepiam, quodpiam/quidpiam/ quippiam *pn* anyone, anybody, anything, any; someone, something, some

quisquam, quicquam *pn* any, any one, anybody, anything

quisque, quaeque, quodque/ quicque/quidque *pn* each, every, everybody, everything
□ **optimus ~** all the best people

quisquiliae, ārum *fpl* waste materials, refuse, trash

quisquis, quodquod/ quicquid/quidquid *pn* whoever, whatever, everyone who

quīvīs, quaevīs, quodvīs/ quidvīs *pn* who or what you please, anyone, anything

quō *adv* whither; whither? for what purpose? what for?; so that thereby

☐ **~ ... eō** *often with comp* as ... so

quoad *adv* how soon? how far? till, until; as far as; for as long as

quōcircā *conj* on account of which; wherefore

quōcumque, quōcunque *adv* whithersoever, to wheresoever

quod *conj* that, in that, because; as to the fact that; although; since

☐ **~ sī** but if

quoius, a, um *adj* whose?

quōlibet *adv* whithersoever or to wheresoever you please

quom ▶ old spelling of **cum**

quōminus *conj* so as to prevent (something happening); so that ... not

quōmodo *adv* in what manner, in what way, how

quōnam *adv* to whatever place

quondam *adv* formerly; some day; at times

quoniam *adv* seeing that, since, because

quōpiam *adv* somewhere

quōquam *adv* to any place, anywhere

quoque *conj* also, too

quōquō *adv* whithersoever, to wheresoever

quōr old spelling of **▶ cūr**

quōrsum, quōrsus *adv* to what

end? to what place?

quot *adj indec* how many? as many as; every

quotannīs *adv* every year

quōtīdiē, quottīdiē ▶ cottīdiē

quotiē(n)s *adv* how often? how many times? whenever

quotiē(n)scumque *adv* as often as

quotquot *adj indec* however many

quotus, a, um *adj* having what position in a numerical series? bearing what proportion to the total?

quōusque *adv* until what time? till when? how long?

- -

Rr

- -

rabidus, a, um *adj* mad, raging, frenzied, wild

rabiēs *f* savageness, ferocity; passion, frenzy

rabiōsus, a, um *adj* raving, rabid, mad

racēmifer, era, erum *adj* bearing clusters

racēmus, ī *m* bunch or cluster (of grapes or other fruit)

rādīcitus *adv* by the roots; utterly

radiō Ⅰ *v* beam, shine

radius, (i)ī *m* pointed rod used by teachers, *etc.*, for drawing diagrams, *etc.*; spoke (of a wheel); beam, ray

rādīx, īcis *f* root; radish; foot of a

hill; origin; base

rādō, rāsī, rāsum 3 v scrape, scratch, shave (off); erase; skirt, graze; strip off; hurt, offend

raeda, ae f four-wheeled carriage

raedārius, (i)ī m coachman

rāmālia, ium ntpl brushwood, twigs

rāmenta, ae f scraping, scrap

rāmeus, a, um adj of a bough

rāmōsus, a, um adj having many branches, branching

rāmulus, ī m twig, little bough

rāmus, ī m branch, twig

rāna, ae f frog

rancidus, a, um adj rotten, putrid, nauseating

rapāx, ācis adj rapacious; inordinately greedy

raphanus, ī m radish

rapiditās, ātis f swiftness, rapidity

rapidus, a, um adj swift, rapid

rapīna, ae f plunder, booty; the carrying off of a person

rapiō, puī, ptum 3 v snatch, tear or drag away; carry off; plunder; ravish

raptim adv hastily, hurriedly

raptō 1 v drag violently off; ravage

raptor, ōris m robber, ravisher

raptum, ī nt plunder; prey

raptus, ūs m violent snatching or dragging away; robbery, carrying off, abduction

rāpulum, ī nt little turnip

rāpum, ī nt turnip

rārēfaciō, fēcī, factum 3 v rarefy

rārēscō 3 v thin out, open out; become sparse

rārō adv seldom, rarely

rārus, a, um adj thin, loose in texture; scattered; rare; few; sporadic

rāsilis, e adj worn smooth, polished

rāstrum, ī nt drag-hoe

ratiō, ōnis f account; calculation, computation; sum, number; transaction, business; matter, affair; consideration of; judgement, reason; method, order; system, theory

ratis, is f raft; boat

ratiuncula, ae f small account; slight reason; petty argument

ratus, a, um adj pple from ▶ **reor** established, authoritative; fixed, certain

raucisonus, a, um adj hoarse-sounding, raucous

raucus, a, um adj hoarse; husky; raucous

rāvus, a, um adj greyish, tawny

rea, ae f defendant; guilty party; debtor

rebellātrīx, īcis f adj rebellious

rebelliō, ōnis f revolt, rebellion

rebellis, e adj insurgent, rebellious

rebellō 1 v revolt, rebel

reboō 1 v resound

recaleō 2 v, **recalēscō, luī** 3 v grow warm again

recalfaciō, fēcī 3 v make warm again

recalvus, a, um adj bald in front, balding

recandēscō, duī 3 v glow again with heat; become white

recantō ① *v* charm away; withdraw

recēdō, essī, essum ③ *v* retire, withdraw; depart; recede; vanish

recēns, ntis *adj* fresh, recent □ ~ **ā vulnere** fresh from a wound

recēnseō, nsuī, ēnsum ② *v* review, count; review the roll of

receptāculum, ī *nt* receptacle; place of refuge, shelter

receptō ① *v* recover; receive, admit (frequently)

receptus, ūs *m* withdrawal, retreat; refuge

recessus, ūs *m* retiring, retreat; recess; haunt, refuge

recidīvus, a, um *adj* recurring

recidō, cidī, cāsum ③ *v* fall back, lapse; rebound (on to its author)

recīdō, cīdī, cīsum ③ *v* cut away; curtail

recingō, īnxī, īnctum ③ *v* ungird, unfasten

recinō ③ *v* chant back, echo; call out

reciper- ▶ **recuper-**

reciperātor, ōris *m* recoverer; receiver; assessor

reciperō ① *v* (also **recuperō**) get again; regain, recover

recipiō, cēpī, ceptum ③ *v* get back; retake, regain, recover; withdraw; admit; accept; entertain; undertake □ **sē recipere** retreat

reciprocus, a, um *adj* moving backwards and forwards, marked by alternations of fortune

recitātor, ōris *m* reciter

recitō ① *v* read out, recite

reclāmō ① *v* cry out in protest at

reclīnis, e *adj* leaning back, reclining

reclīnō ① *v* bend *or* lean back

reclūdō, ūsī, ūsum ③ *v* open; open up, lay open; disclose, reveal

recognōscō, nōvī, nitum ③ *v* recognize; recollect; examine; inspect

recolligō, lēgī, lēctum ③ *v* recover

recolō, luī, cultum ③ *v* cultivate afresh; go over in one's mind

reconciliātiō, ōnis *f* reconciliation; the restoration (of good relations, *etc.*)

reconciliātor, ōris *m* restorer

reconciliō ① *v* restore; reconcile

reconditus, a, um *adj* hidden, concealed; abstruse, recondite, obscure

recondō, didī, ditum ③ *v* shut up; hide, bury, store away; replace; close again

recoquō, coxī, coctum ③ *v* renew by cooking, rehash; reheat, melt down

recordātiō, ōnis *f* recollection

recordor ① *v dep* think over; call to mind, remember

recreō ① *v* make anew, restore; refresh, revive

recrepō, puī ① *v* sound in answer, resound

recrēscō, crēvī, crētum ③ *v* grow again

recrūdēscō, duī ③ *v* become raw again; break out again

rēctā *adv* directly, straight

rēctē *adv* vertically; rightly, correctly, properly; well

r

rēctor, **ōris** *m* guide, director, helmsman; horseman; driver; leader, ruler, governor; preceptor

rēctus, **a**, **um** *adj* straight, upright; direct; honest; proper; morally right

recubō ① *v* recline, lie at ease

recumbō, **buī** ③ *v* lie down; recline at table; sink down

recuperātor, **ōris** *m* recoverer, receiver; assessor

recuperō ① *v* get again; regain, recover

recūrō ① *v* cure

recurrō, **currī**, **cursum** ③ *v* run or hasten back; return; have recourse (to)

recursō ① *v* keep rebounding or recoiling; keep recurring to the mind

recursus, **ūs** *m* running back, retreat, return

recurvō ① *v* bend back

recurvus, **a**, **um** *adj* bent back on itself, bent round

recūsātiō, **ōnis** *f* refusal; objection; counterplea

recūsō ① *v* decline, reject, refuse

recutiō, **ussī**, **ussum** ③ *v* strike so as to cause to vibrate

redardēscō ③ *v* blaze up again

redarguō, **guī** ③ *v* refute; prove untrue

reddō, **didī**, **ditum** ③ *v* give back, return, restore; give up, resign; assign; render; utter in reply

redēmptiō, **ōnis** *f* ransoming; purchasing

redēmptor, **ōris** *m* contractor; [LM] redeemer

redeō, **īre**, **iī**, **itum** *v ir* go or come back; return

redhibeō ② *v* give back, cancel the sale of

redigō, **ēgī**, **āctum** ③ *v* drive back, return; restore; bring down (to); reduce

redimīculum, **ī** *nt* female headband

redimiō ④ *v* encircle with a garland; surround

redimō, **ēmī**, **ēmptum** ③ *v* buy back; ransom, redeem; buy off; rescue; buy; contract for

redintegrō ① *v* restore, renew, refresh

reditiō, **ōnis** *f* return, returning

reditus, **ūs** *m* return, returning; revenue

redivīvus, **a**, **um** *adj* re-used, second-hand

redoleō ② *v* emit a scent, be odorous

redōnō ① *v* give back again; forgive

redūcō, **dūxī**, **ductum** ③ *v* lead *or* bring back; escort home; withdraw; draw back; bring *or* reduce (to)

reductor, **ōris** *m* restorer

reductus, **a**, **um** *adj* receding deeply, set back

redundō ① *v* flow back; overflow; abound (in)

redux, **cis** *adj* coming back, returning

refectorium, **(i)ī** *nt* [LM] refectory, dining-hall

refellō, **ī** ③ *v* refute, rebut

referciō, **rsī**, **rtum** ④ *v* stuff *or* cram full

referō, ferre, rettulī, relātum *v ir* carry, bring *or* put back; tell; propose; record; ascribe; restore; repay; render an account; answer □ **pedem** ~ return, go back □ ~ **grātiam** render thanks

rēfert, ferre, rētulit *v ir impers* it concerns, is of importance to □ **meā rēfert** it matters to me

refertus, a, um *adj* crammed full to bursting with; crowded

reficiō, fēcī, fectum ③ *v* make again, restore, rebuild, repair; reappoint

refīgō, īxī, īxum ③ *v* unfix, unfasten, detach

reflāgitō ① *v* demand repeatedly in a loud voice

reflectō, exī, exum ③ *v* bend back; turn back; turn round

reflō ① *v* blow back again

refluō ③ *v* flow back

refluus, a, um *adj* flowing back

reformīdō ① *v* dread, shun, shrink from

reformō ① *v* transform, remould; form (a new shape); restore

refoveō, fōvī, fōtum ② *v* refresh; revive; warm again

refrēnō ① *v* curb, check; restrain

refricō ① *v* gall; excite again

refrigerō ① *v* make cool

refrīgēscō, īxī ③ *v* grow cold, cool down

refringō, frēgī, frāctum ③ *v* break open

refugiō, ūgī ③ *v* run away; flee to; shrink back; recoil from

refugium, (i)ī *nt* refuge

refugus, a, um *adj* fleeing back; receding, drawing back

refulgeō, lsī ② *v* radiate light; gleam

refundō, ūdī, ūsum ③ *v* pour back

refūtō ① *v* check; refute

rēgālis, e *adj* kingly, royal, regal

regerō, essī, estum ③ *v* carry back; throw back; throw back by way of retort

rēgia, ae *f* palace

rēgificus, a, um *adj* fit for a king

regimen, inis *nt* control, steering; direction

rēgīna, ae *f* queen

regiō, ōnis *f* line; district, locality, region; boundary-line

rēgius, a, um *adj* kingly, royal; splendid, princely

reglūtinō ① *v* unglue, unstick

rēgnātor, ōris *m* king, lord

rēgnō ① *v* have royal power, reign; hold sway, lord it

rēgnum, ī *nt* kingship, monarchy, tyranny; kingdom

regō, rēxī, rēctum ③ *v* guide, conduct, direct; govern, rule

regredior, gressus sum ③ *v dep* go *or* come back, return; retire, retreat

regressus, ūs *m* going back, return

rēgula, ae *f* ruler, rod, bar; basic principle, rule

regularis, e *adj* LM under a (monastic) rule

rēgulus, ī *m* petty king

reiciō, lēcī, iectum ③ *v* reject; refuse; repulse; refer (a matter) for consideration, *etc.*; put off

relābor, lāpsus sum ③ *v dep* slide *or* glide back; recede, ebb

relanguēscō, guī ③ v become faint; abate; lose one's passion or ardour

relātiō, ōnis f motion, proposition

relaxō ① v loosen; open up

relēgātiō, ōnis f banishment

relēgō ① v banish; remove; remove from the scene

relegō, lēgī, lēctum ③ v pick up again; pick out; read over or out; recount

relevō ① v lift, raise; lighten; relieve; alleviate; refresh

relicus, relicuos ▸ reliquus

rēligiō, ōnis f supernatural feeling of constraint; scruple; sanction; religious awe; superstition; sanctity; ritual; conscientiousness

religiōsus, a, um adj pious, devout, religious; scrupulous

religō ① v tie out of the way; bind fast; moor

relinquō, līquī, lictum ③ v leave behind; leave; disregard

reliquiae, ārum fpl remains, relics, remnants

reliquum, ī nt remainder, residue; the future

reliquus, a, um adj remaining; future; remaining alive

relūceō, ūxī ② v shine out

relūcēscō, ūxī ③ v grow bright again

reluctor ① v dep struggle (against), resist

remaneō, nsī ② v stay behind; remain, continue to be; persist

remedium, (i)ī nt cure; remedy

remeō ① v go or come back, return

remētior, mēnsus sum ④ v dep go back over

rēmex, igis m rower, oarsman

rēmigium, (i)ī nt rowing; oarage; crew of rowers

rēmigō ① v row

remigrō ① v return

reminīscor ③ v dep recall to mind, recollect

remissiō, ōnis f sending back; relaxation

remissus, a, um adj mild, gentle; subdued

remittō, mīsī, missum ③ v send back; relax, slacken; grant, concede; remit

remōlior ④ v dep heave back

remollēscō ③ v become soft again; grow soft

remordeō, morsum ② v bite back; gnaw, nag

remoror ① v dep wait, linger; delay, hold up, check

remōtus, a, um adj distant, remote

removeō, mōvī, mōtum ② v move back; remove; withdraw

remūgiō ④ v bellow back, moo in reply; resound

remulceō, lsī, lsum ② v stroke back

remulcum, ī nt tow-rope

remūnerō v, **remūneror** ① v dep reward, recompense, remunerate

rēmus, ī m oar

renārrō ① v tell over again

renāscor, nātus sum ③ v dep be born again; be renewed, be revived

rēnēs, (i)um mpl kidneys

renīdeō ② v shine (back), gleam; smile back (at)

rēnō, **ōnis** m reindeer-skin

renovō ① v make new again; restore; refresh; resume

renūntiō ① v report, declare, announce; renounce; call off

renuō, **nuī** ③ v give a refusal, disapprove; refuse

reor, **ratus sum** ② v dep think, suppose, imagine, deem

repāgula, **ōrum** ntpl door-bars

repandus, **a**, **um** adj spread out, flattened back

reparābilis, **e** adj capable of being recovered or restored

reparcō, **persī** ③ v be sparing with, grudge

reparō ① v recover, restore, repair, renew; revive

repellō, **reppulī**, **repulsum** ③ v drive or push back; reject; repulse

rependō, **ndī**, **ēnsum** ③ v weigh or balance (against); weigh out in return; pay in return; purchase, compensate

repēns, **ntis** adj sudden, unexpected; completely new

repente, **repentīnō** adv suddenly, unexpectedly; all at once

repentīnus, **a**, **um** adj sudden, done to meet a sudden contingency

repercutiō, **ussī**, **ussum** ③ v cause to rebound; reflect; strike against

reperiō, **repperī**, **repertum** ④ v find, find out; discover; invent

repertor, **ōris** m discoverer, inventor, author

repertum, **ī** nt discovery

repetō, **īvī/īī**, **ītum** ③ v return to; get back; demand back; repeat; recall; attack again

repetundae, **ārum** fpl the recovery of extorted money

repleō, **ēvī**, **ētum** ② v fill again; fill up, replenish; restore to its full number

replētus, **a**, **um** adj full (of)

rēpō, **psī**, **eptum** ③ v creep, crawl

repōnō, **posuī**, **positum** ③ v put or lay back; replace; stage (a play) again; store away

reportō ① v carry or bring back; report; bring home from war

reposcō ③ v demand back; claim as one's due

repraesentō ① v exhibit, pay in ready money; revive

reprehendō, **ndī**, **ēnsum** ③ v catch hold of; censure, reprehend, rebuke

reprehēnsiō, **ōnis** f reproof, criticism

reprimō, **essī**, **essum** ③ v hold in check; check, restrain; repress

repudiō ① v divorce, repudiate; refuse

repudium, **ī** nt formal renouncement of marriage contract

repugnō ① v fight back, offer resistance (to); object (to); be inimical (to)

repulsa, **ae** f electoral defeat; rebuff

repulsō ① v drive back; reject

reputātiō, **ōnis** f consideration, reflection

reputō ① v think over, reflect on

requiēs, **ētis** f rest, relaxation,

recreation

requiēscō, ēvī, ētum v rest; take a holiday; quieten down; rest (upon)

requiētus, a, um adj rested; improved by lying fallow

requīritō v seek or demand repeatedly

requīrō, isīvī/isīī, īsītum ③ v seek; search for; need; ask about

rēs, ēī f thing; matter; affair; fact; condition; property; profit; advantage; world, universe, case (in law); suit; power; valour; exploit

  □ ~ frūmentāria corn supply

  ■ rēs pūblica, rēī pūblicae fsg republic, state

  ■ rēs novae fpl political changes, revolution

  ■ rēs gestae fpl exploits

  ■ rēs adversae fpl adverse circumstances

  ■ rēs secundae fpl prosperity

  □ rē vērā actually, really

  □ in rem to the point

resānēscō, ī ③ v be healed

rescindō, idī, issum v cut away; tear open; annul, rescind

resciscō, rescīvī/rescīī, rescītum ④ v find out

rescrībō, psī, ptum ③ v write in return or in answer; enrol in place of another

resecō, cuī, ctum ① v cut back; prune; cut at the base

resēminō ① v reproduce

resequor, secūtus sum ③ v dep reply to

reserō ① v unbar; open; disclose, uncover

reservō ① v keep back, hold in

reserve; preserve; reserve (for)

reses, idis adj motionless, inactive, idle, sluggish

resideō, sēdī ② v sit, remain in a place; be left

resīdō, sēdī ③ v sit down; settle; abate; subside, quieten down

residuus, a, um adj remaining

resignō ① v unseal; open; resign

resiliō, luī ④ v leap or spring back; recoil; rebound; shrink (back again)

resīmus, a, um adj turned up, snub; turned back on itself

resipīscō, pīvī/pīī/puī ③ v become reasonable again

resistō, stitī ③ v come to a standstill, stop; with dat resist, stand up (to)

resolvō, lvī, lūtum ③ v loosen, release, disperse, melt; relax; pay; enervate; pay back; break up; finish

resonō ① v resound, re-echo

resonus, a, um adj echoing

resorbeō ② v swallow down; pass ebb

respectō ① v keep on looking round or back; await; have regard for

respectus, ūs m looking back (at); refuge; regard, consideration (for)

respergō, ersī, ersum ③ v sprinkle, spatter

respiciō, spexī, spectum ③ v look round (for), look back (at); take notice of

respīrāmen, inis nt means or channel of breathing

respīrātiō, ōnis f taking of

breath

respīrō ① v breathe out; take breath; enjoy a respite

resplendeō ② v shine brightly (with reflected light)

respondeō, ndī, ōnsum ② v reply; say (write) in answer; say in refutation; answer a summons to appear

respōnsiō, ōnis f answer, refutation, defence

respōnsō ① v answer, reply (to); re-echo

respōnsor, ōris m answerer

respōnsum, ī nt answer, reply; answer given by an oracle; opinion of one learned in the law

rēspūblica, reīpūblicae f (also **rēs pública**) republic; state; the public good

respuō, uī ③ v spit out; refuse or reject (with abhorrence)

restāgnō ① v overflow; be covered with flood-water

restinguō, īnxī, īnctum ③ v quench, extinguish; slake; neutralize

restiō, ōnis m dealer in rope

restis, is f rope, cord

restituō, uī, ūtum ③ v replace, restore; rebuild; revive; give back, reverse; reinstate

restitūtiō, ōnis f rebuilding; reinstatement

restō, stitī ① v stay put; stand firm; resist; remain, be left

restringō, īnxī, ictum ③ v draw tight; fasten behind one; tie up

■ **resultō** ① v leap back, rebound; echo

resūmō, mpsī, mptum ③ v pick

up again; resume; recover

resupīnō ① v cause to be flat on one's back; knock flat on one's back; pull back, bend back

resupīnus, a, um adj lying flat on; leaning back

resurgō, surrēxī, surrēctum ③ v rise (again); flare up again, revive

resurrectiō, onis f [LM] resurrection

resuscitō ① v rouse again, reawaken

retardō ① v delay, hold up

rēte, is nt net

retegō, ēxī, ēctum ③ v uncover, lay bare, reveal; disclose

retentō ① v hold fast; hold back

retexō, xuī, xtum ③ v unweave, unravel; destroy gradually

rētiārius, (i)ī m net-fighter in the arena

reticeō ② v keep silent; leave unsaid

rēticulum, ī nt, **rēticulus, ī** m (little) net; mesh-work bag

retināculum, ī nt rope; hawser; rein; towing-rope; pl board

retineō, tentum ② v hold fast; hold back; detain; retain; maintain; restrain; cling to

retorqueō, rsī, rtum ② v twist back; cast back; fling back; turn aside

retractō ① v undertake anew; draw back, be reluctant; reconsider; withdraw

■ **retractātus, a, um** adj remote, distant; in a state of revision

retrahō, āxī, actum ③ v drag

or pull backwards; summon back;
win back; withdraw

retrō *adv* backwards, behind; back
again, conversely

**retrōrsum, retrōrsus,
retrōversus** *adv* back,
backwards; in reverse order

**retundō, re(t)tudī,
retū(n)sum** ③ *v* blunt; weaken;
repress, quell

reus, ī *m* defendant; guilty party;
debtor

revalēscō, luī ③ *v* grow well
again

revehō, ēxī, ectum ③ *v* carry or
bring back
□ **revehor** ride or sail back

revellō, vellī, vulsum ③ *v*
wrench off, tear down; tear out;
remove

reveniō, vēnī, ventum ④ *v*
come back, return

rēvērā *adv* (also **rē vērā**) in
reality, in fact

reverentia, ae *f* respect,
deference; awe, reverence

revereor ② *v dep* stand in awe of;
venerate

revertō, rtī ③ *v*, **revertor,
versus sum** ③ *v dep* turn back,
come back, return

revinciō, vīnxī, vīnctum ④ *v*
hold down or restrain with bonds;
hold firmly in place

revincō, vīcī, victum ③ *v*
conquer in one's turn; refute;
convict

revirēscō, ruī ③ *v* grow green
again; grow strong or young again

revīsō ③ *v* revisit, go back and see

revīvīscō, īxī, īctum ③ *v* come
to life again, revive (in spirit)

revocābilis, e *adj* capable of
being revoked or retracted

revocāmen, inis *nt* summons
to return

revocō ① *v* call back, recall,
summon back; restrain; reduce
(to); refer (to); revoke

revolō ① *v* fly back

revolūbilis, e *adj* that may be
rolled back to the beginning;
rolling backward

revolvō, lvī, lūtum ③ *v* roll back;
unroll; revolve; go back over in
thought or speech

revomō, muī ③ *v* vomit up again,
spew out

rēx, gis *m* king, tyrant, despot;
master; leader, head; patron;
great man

rhētor, oris *m* a teacher of public
speaking, rhetorician

rhētoricus, a, um *adj* rhetorical

rhīnocerōs, ōtis *m* rhinoceros

rhombus, ī *m* instrument whirled
on a string to produce a whirring
noise; turbot

rhonchus, ī *m* snore, snort of
disdain

rictus, ūs *m* the open mouth or
jaws

rīdeō, rīsī, rīsum ② *v* laugh;
smile; mock; laugh at or over

rīdiculum, ī *nt* joke, piece of
humour

rīdiculus, a, um *adj* laughable,
funny; silly
■ **~, ī** *m* buffoon, jester

rigeō ② *v* be stiff or numb; stand
on end; be solidified

rigēscō, guī ③ *v* grow stiff or
numb; stiffen, harden

rigidus, a, um *adj* stiff, hard, rigid; inflexible; stern

rigō ☐ *v* moisten, wet, water, irrigate

rigor, ōris *m* stiffness, rigidity, coldness, numbness, hardness; inflexibility; severity

riguus, a, um *adj* irrigating; well-watered

rīma, ae *f* narrow cleft, crack, chink, fissure; flash of lightning

rīmor ☐ *v dep* probe, search; rummage about for, examine, explore

rīmōsus, a, um *adj* full of cracks or fissures

ringor ☐ *v dep* bare one's teeth

rīpa, ae *f* bank; shore of the sea

rīsor, ōris *m* one who laughs

rīsus, ūs *m* laughter

rīte *adv* with the proper rites; duly, correctly

rītus, ūs *m* religious observance or ceremony, rite
  ☐ **rītū** *with gen* in the manner of

rīvālis, is *m* rival

rīvus, ī *m* brook, stream; channel

rixa, ae *f* violent or noisy quarrel, brawl, dispute

rixor ☐ *v dep* quarrel violently, brawl, dispute

rōbīgō, inis *f* rust; mildew, blight; a foul deposit in the mouth

rōboreus, a, um *adj* made of oak

rōborō ☐ *v* give physical strength to; reinforce

rōbur, oris *nt* any hard wood; oak; oak-wood; trunk (of such wood); strength, power, might; man-power; courage; resolve

rōbustus, a, um *adj* made of oak;

hard, firm, strong, hardy, robust; physically mature

rōdō, rōsī, rōsum ☐ *v* gnaw; eat away, erode; backbite, carp at

rogālis, e *adj* of a funeral pyre

rogātiō, ōnis *f* proposed measure

rogātū *adv* by request

rogitō ☐ *v* ask frequently or insistently

rogō ☐ *v* ask, question; propose (a law, a magistrate); request, solicit for favours

rogus, ī *m* funeral-pyre; remains

rōrifer, era, erum *adj* bringing dew

rōrō ☐ *v* drop or distil dew; drip or run with moisture

rōs, rōris *m* dew
  ☐ **rōs marīnus** rosemary

rosa, ae *f* rose

rosārium, (i)ī *nt* rose-garden

rōscidus, a, um *adj* dewy; wet

rosētum, ī *nt* garden of roses

roseus, a, um *adj* of roses; rose-coloured

rōsiō, ōnis *f* erosion

rōstra, ōrum *ntpl* platform for speakers in the Roman forum

rōstrātus, a, um *adj* having a beaked prow

rōstrum, ī *nt* snout or muzzle (of an animal), beak, bill; ship's beak

rota, ae *f* wheel; chariot; LM court

rotō ☐ *v* whirl round; revolve, rotate

rotundō ☐ *v* make round, round off

rotundus, a, um *adj* round, circular; smooth and finished

rubefaciō, **fēcī**, **factum** ③ v redden

rubēns, **ntis** adj coloured or tinged with red

rubeō ② v be red, become red

ruber, **bra**, **brum** adj red (including shades of orange)

rubēscō, **buī** ③ v turn red, redden, become red

rubētum, **ī** nt bramble-thicket

rubeus, **a**, **um** adj of or produced from a bramble

rubia, **ae** f madder

rubicundus, **a**, **um** adj suffused with red, ruddy

rūbīgō ▸ rōbīgō

rubor, **ōris** m redness; blush; modesty, feeling of shame; cause for shame

rubrica, **ae** f LM rubric

rubus, **ī** m bramble, blackberry

rudēns, **ntis** m rope

rudīmentum, **ī** nt first lesson; early training; beginning

rudis¹, **is** f wooden sword used in practice fights or presented to a gladiator on his discharge

rudis², **e** adj rough, unwrought; raw; untrained; unbroken; ill-made, rudely finished, coarse; ignorant (of)

rudō, **dītum** ③ v bellow, roar, bray, creak loudly

rūga, **ae** f wrinkle; crease, small fold

rūgiō ④ v roar

rūgōsus, **a**, **um** adj full of wrinkles, folds or creases

ruīna, **ae** f tumbling down, downfall, ruin; ruins; debris, disaster; landslide

ruīnōsus, **a**, **um** adj ruinous; ruined

rūminō ① v, **rūminor** ① v dep chew over again; chew the cud

rūmor, **ōris** m hearsay, rumour; reputation; ill repute

rumpō, **rūpī**, **ruptum** ③ v burst, break down; force open; violate; rupture; break off

ruō, **ruī**, **rutum** ③ v collapse, fall, go to ruin; rush (headlong) (towards), hurry (on); sweep headlong; disturb violently; overthrow

rūpēs, **pis** f steep rocky cliff, crag

ruptor, **ōris** m one who breaks or violates

rūricola, **ae** m/f one who tills the land; country-dweller

rūrigena, **ae** m born in the country

rūrsum, **rūrsus** adv backwards; on the other hand; again; in one's turn

rūs, **ris** nt country; country estate

ruscum, **ī** nt butcher's broom

russus, **a**, **um** adj red

rūsticānus, **a**, **um** adj living in the country

rūsticitās, **ātis** f lack of sophistication

rūsticus, **a**, **um** adj rural, rustic; agricultural; coarse, boorish; crude, clumsy; simple
  ■ **rūstica**, **ae** f countrywoman
  ■ **rūsticus**, **ī** m countryman

rūsum ▸ rūrsum

rūta, **ae** f rue

rutābulum, **ī** nt long implement with a flattened end

rutilō ① v glow with a bright or

golden red colour; colour bright or golden red

rutilus, **a**, **um** *adj* red, reddish; ruddy

rūtrum, **ī** *nt* shovel

Ss

sabbatum, **ī** *nt* LM the Sabbath, Saturday

saburra, **ae** *f* gravel (for ballast)

saccipērium, **(i)ī** *nt* wallet

sacculus, **ī** *m* little bag

saccus, **ī** *m* large bag; sack

sacellum, **ī** *nt* shrine

sacer, **cra**, **crum** *adj* holy, sacred; divine

sacerdōs, **ōtis** *m/f* priest; priestess; LM bishop

sacerdōtium, **(i)ī** *nt* priesthood

sacrāmentum, **ī** *nt* oath taken by newly enlisted soldiers; oath, solemn obligation; LM sacrament, sacred power

sacrārium, **(i)ī** *nt* sanctuary, shrine

sacrātus, **a**, **um** *adj* hallowed, holy, sacred

sacrifer, **era**, **erum** *adj* carrying sacred objects

sacrificium, **(i)ī** *nt* sacrifice, offering to a deity; LM Eucharist

sacrificō ① *v* sacrifice, offer up as a sacrifice

sacrificulus, **ī** *m* sacrificing priest

sacrificus, **a**, **um** *adj* sacrificial

sacrilegium, **(i)ī** *nt* sacrilege; robbery of sacred property

sacrilegus, **a**, **um** *adj* sacrilegious; profane, impious
■ **sacrilegus**, **ī** *m* temple-robber

sacrista, **ae** *m* LM sacristan

sacrō ① *v* consecrate; devote to destruction; doom; make subject to religious sanction; hallow, sanctify

sacrōsānctus, **a**, **um** *adj* sacrosanct, inviolable

sacrum, **ī** *nt* sacred object; consecrated place; temple

saeclum, **ī** *nt* generation, lifetime; race; century; indefinitely long period; the times

saeculāris, **e** *adj* of a generation; LM secular, not belonging to a religious order
□ **lūdī saeculārēs** games celebrated at fixed intervals
□ **carmen saeculāre** hymn sung at the **lūdī saeculārēs**

saeculum, **ī** *nt* generation, lifetime; race; century; indefinitely long period; the times
□ **in saecula saeculōrum** LM for ever and ever

saepe *adv* often, oftentimes, frequently
□ **saepenumerō** oftentimes, very often

saepēs, **pis** *f* hedge; fence

saepīmentum, **ī** *nt* fence; enclosure

saepiō, **psī**, **ptum** ④ *v* fence in; enclose; surround

saeptum, **ī** *nt* fold, paddock; enclosure; voting enclosure in the Campus Martius

saeta, **ae** *f* hair; bristle; fishing-line

saetiger, era, erum *adj* bristly

saetōsus, a, um *adj* bristly, shaggy

saevidicus, a, um *adj* spoken furiously

saeviō ④ *v* be fierce or furious, rage; be violent

saevitia, ae *f* rage, fierceness, ferocity; cruelty, barbarity, violence

saevus, a, um *adj* raging, furious, ferocious, barbarous, cruel; violent

sāga, ae *f* witch, sorceress, wise woman

sagāx, ācis *adj* keen-scented; acute, sharp, perceptive

sagīna, ae *f* stuffing, overstuffing; fatted animal; diet of gladiators and athletes

sagitta, ae *f* arrow

sagittārius, (i)ī *m* archer, bowman; Archer (constellation)

sagittifer, era, erum *adj* carrying arrows; archer

sagmen, inis *nt* bundle of grass torn up with its earth

sagulum, ī *nt* small military cloak

sagum, ī *nt* coarse woollen cloak; military cloak

sāl, salis *m* salt; sea-water; sea; shrewdness; a quality which gives 'life' to a person or thing ■ **salēs** *pl* jokes, witticisms

salapūtius, (i)ī *nt* short person, little squirt

salārium, (i)ī *nt* regular official payment to the holder of a civil or military post

salārius, a, um *adj* of, or relating to, salt

salāx, ācis *adj* highly sexed; aphrodisiac

salebra, ae *f* rut, irregularity; roughness (of style or speech)

salictum, ī *nt* collection of willows, osier-bed

saliēns, ntis *f* fountain, *jet d'eau*

salignus, a, um *adj* of willow

salillum, ī *nt* little salt-cellar

salīnae, ārum *fpl* salt-pans

salīnum, ī *nt* salt-cellar

saliō, saliī/saluī/saltum ④ *v* leap, jump; move suddenly; gush, spurt; (of male animals) mount, cover

salīva, ae *f* spittle; distinctive flavour

salix, icis *f* willow-tree, willow

salsus, a, um *adj* salted; salty, briny; salted with humour, witty, funny

saltātor, ōris *m* dancer

saltātrix, īcis *f* female dancer, dancing girl

saltātus, ūs *m* dancing, a dance

saltem *adv* at least, at all events □ **nōn/neque ~** not or nor even, not so much as

saltō ④ *v* dance, jump; portray or represent in a dance

saltuōsus, a, um *adj* characterized by wooded valleys

saltus¹, ūs *m* leap, spring, jump

saltus², ūs *m* narrow passage through forest, mountainous country, defile, pass; woodland interspersed with glades, passes, *etc.*

salūber, salūbris, bris, bre *adj* healthy, salutary, beneficial

salūbritās, ātis *f* good health; wholesomeness

salum, ī *nt* sea in motion, swell,

billow

salūs, ūtis f health, well-being, safety; greeting, salutation; ⟦ℒℳ⟧ eternal life, salvation

salūtāris, e adj healthful, salutary

salūtātiō, ōnis f greeting, salutation; formal morning call paid by a client on his patron

salūtifer, era, erum adj health-giving

salūtō ① v greet, salute; call to pay one's respects to

salvē int hail! welcome! farewell! good-bye!
□ **salvēre iubeō** greet; bid good day

salvus, a, um adj safe, well, sound, undamaged, intact

sambūcistria, ae f female player on a small harp

sānābilis, e adj curable

sanciō, sānxī, sānctum ④ v ratify solemnly, confirm; enact

sānctitās, ātis f sacrosanctity; moral purity, virtue

sānctus, a, um adj sacred, inviolable; venerable; holy; upright, virtuous; ⟦ℒℳ⟧ m/f saint

sandapila, ae f pauper's bier

sandyx, ycis f red dye; scarlet cloth

sānē adv certainly; truly, 'and that's a fact'; admittedly

sanguineus, a, um adj,

sanguinolentus, a, um adj bloody, blood-stained; blood-red

sanguis, inis m blood; race, family, consanguinity; life; vigour

saniēs f matter discharged from a wound, ulcer

sānitās, ātis f health; soundness

of mind, good sense

sānō ① v heal, cure, restore to health

sānus, a, um adj healthy; sound in mind, rational

sapa, ae f new wine

sapiēns, ntis adj wise, sensible, understanding; m/f wise person

sapientia, ae f wisdom

sapiō, īvī/iī ③ v taste (of); be intelligent, show good sense

sapor, ōris m taste, flavour; sense of taste

sarcina, ae f bundle, burden, load, pack

sarcinārius, a, um adj employed in carrying packs

sarcinula, ae f (little) pack, bundle

sarciō, rsī, rtum ④ v make good; redeem; restore

sarculum, ī nt hoe

sarmentum, ī nt shoot; pl twigs, cut twigs, brushwood

sat, satis adv sufficient, enough; adequately, sufficiently
□ **~ accipiō** take or exact security
■ **satius** comp better, preferable

sata, ōrum ntpl crops, cultivated plants

Satanās, ae m ⟦ℒℳ⟧ Satan, the Devil

satelles, itis m attendant, bodyguard; pl retinue; accomplice, violent supporter

satiās, ātis f sufficiency, abundance; distaste caused by excess

satietās, ātis f satiety; the state of being sated

satin int [satis + -ne] really?

satiō¹ ① v satisfy; satiate; fill to

repletion

satiō², **ōnis** f planting, sowing

satisfaciō, **fēcī**, **factum** ③ v with dat give satisfaction (to), satisfy; make amends; give sufficient attention (to)

satisfactiō, **ōnis** f satisfaction for an offence, apology, indemnification

sator, **ōris** m sower, planter; founder, originator

satum ▶ serō

satur, **ura**, **urum** adj well-fed, replete; rich; saturated

satura, **ae** f stage medley, satire

saturitās, **ātis** f satiety, fullness, exhaustion

Sāturnālia, **ium** ntpl festival in honour of Saturn, beginning on 17 December

saturō ① v fill to repletion, sate, satisfy; drench, saturate

satus, **a**, **um** adj sprung (from); native

satyrus, **ī** m satyr; satyric play

sauciō ① v wound; gash

saucius, **a**, **um** adj wounded; physically distressed, afflicted; pierced; stricken

sāv-▶ suāv-

sāviolum, **ī** nt tender kiss

sāvium, **(i)ī** nt kiss; sweetheart

saxātilis, **e** adj of rock, rocky; living among rocks

saxeus, **a**, **um** adj rocky, stony, made of stones

saxificus, **a**, **um** adj petrifying

saxōsus, **a**, **um** adj rocky, stony

saxum, **ī** nt rock, boulder; stone

scaber, **bra**, **brum** adj scurfy,

scabbed, having a rough surface

scabiēs, **iēī** f scurf; scab, mange, itching

scabō, **ī** ③ v scratch

scaccarium, **(i)ī** nt ⃞ chess; chessboard; exchequer

scaena, **ae** f stage of a theatre; background; the drama; sphere in which actions, etc., are on public display

scaenicus, **a**, **um** adj theatrical
■ **scaenicus**, **ī** m actor

scālae, **ārum** fpl ladder; flight of steps

scalprum, **ī** nt tool for scraping, paring or cutting away

scamnum, **ī** nt bench, stool

scandō ③ v climb, mount, ascend

scandula, **ae** f wooden slat used for roofing etc.; shingle

scapha, **ae** f light boat, skiff

scapulae, **ārum** fpl shoulder-blades; shoulders

scāpus, **ī** m stem, stalk; shaft of a column

scarabaeus, **ī** m beetle

scatebra, **ae** f gush of water from the ground, bubbling spring

scateō ② v gush out; swarm (with), be alive (with)

scatūrīgō, **inis** f bubbling spring

scelerātus, **a**, **um** adj accursed; heinously criminal; sinful

scelerō ① v defile

scelerōsus, **a**, **um** adj steeped in wickedness

scelestus, **a**, **um** adj wicked, villainous

scelus, **eris** nt crime

scēptrifer, **era**, **erum** adj

bearing a sceptre

scēptrum, ī *nt* sceptre; phallus; kingship

chisma, atis *nt* [LM] schism

choenobatēs, ae *m* tightrope-walker

chola, ae *f* lecture; school

cholasticus, ī *m* student, teacher

ciēns, ntis *adj* expert, knowledgeable

cientia, ae *f* knowledge; understanding, expert knowledge

cilicet *adv* one may be sure (that), it is clear (that); naturally; yes, but at the same time; evidently; to be sure, doubtless; I ask you!

cindō, idī, issum ③ *v* split, cleave, tear apart; separate

cintilla, ae *f* spark

cintillō ① *v* send out sparks

cio ④ *v* know; know of
□ **prō certō ~** know for certain

cipiō, ōnis *m* ceremonial rod, baton

cirpea, ae *f* large basket made of bulrushes

cirpus, ī *m* bulrush

ciscitor ① *v dep* inquire (of)

ciscō, īvī, ītum ③ *v* ascertain; vote for or approve (a resolution)

cissūra, ae *f* cleft, fissure

citor ① *v dep* seek to know; inquire (about); question

cītum, ī *nt* ordinance, statute

cītus, a, um *adj* having practical knowledge of, neat, ingenious; nice, excellent

cobis, is *f* sawdust

scomber, brī *m* mackerel

scōpārius, (i)ī *m* floor-sweeper

scopulus, ī *m* rock, boulder

scorpiō, ōnis *m* scorpion

scorteus, a, um *adj* of hide, leathern

scortillum, ī *nt* young prostitute

scortum, ī *nt* harlot, prostitute; male prostitute

scrība, ae *m* public clerk; secretary

scrīblīta, ae *f* cheese tart

scrībō, psī, ptum ③ *v* write; compose; draft

scrīnium, (i)ī *nt* receptacle for holding letters or papers, writing-case

scrīptor, ōris *m* writer, scribe, copyist

scrīptum, ī *nt* something written; written communication; literary work

scrīptūra, ae *f* writing; literary work, composition; [LM] (holy) scripture

scrobis, is *m/f* pit

scrūpeus, a, um *adj* composed of sharp rocks

scrūpulus, ī *m* cause for uneasiness or misgiving

scrūta, ōrum *ntpl* trash, a job lot

scrūtor ① *v dep* search, examine; inquire into

sculpō, psī, ptum ③ *v* carve, engrave, chisel

sculptilis, e *adj* engraved

scurra, ae *m* loafer, city-bred clown

scurrīlis, e *adj* impudent, rude

scurror ① *v dep* play the 'man

about town', *i.e.* dine off one's jokes

scūtātus, **a**, **um** *adj* armed with a long wooden shield

scutica, **ae** *f* strap

scutula, **ae** *f* small dish

scūtum, **ī** *nt* (oblong wooden) shield, buckler

scyphus, **ī** *m* two-handled drinking-vessel

sē, **sēsē** *acc*, **suī** (*gen*), **sibī** (*dat*), **sē** (*abl*) *pn* himself, herself, itself, themselves

sēbum, **ī** *nt* suet, tallow, hard animal fat

sēcēdō, **cessī**, **cessum** ③ *v* draw aside, withdraw; retire; secede

sēcernō, **crēvī**, **crētum** ③ *v* separate off; cut off; set aside; treat as distinct

sēcessiō, **ōnis** *f* withdrawal; secession; estrangement

sēcessus, **ūs** *m* withdrawal; secluded place; retirement

sēclūdō, **ūsī**, **ūsum** ③ *v* shut off, shut up

secō, **secuī**, **sectum** ① *v* cut, cut off; cut up; make an incision in; cleave a path through; form by cutting

sēcrētus, **a**, **um** *adj* separate, apart (from); private, secret; remote; hidden
■ **sēcrētum**, **ī** *nt* secret, mystic rite; retired haunt

sectilis, **e** *adj* capable of being cut into thin layers

sector ① *v dep* follow continually; pursue; pursue with punishment; hunt out; run after; attend

sectūrae, **ārum** *fpl* quarry

sēcubitus, **ūs** *m* sleeping apart from one's spouse or lover

sēcubō, **buī** ① *v* sleep apart from one's spouse or lover

secundānī, **ōrum** *mpl* soldiers of the second legion

secundō ① *v* (of winds) make (conditions) favourable for travel

secundum *prep with acc* after; along; next to; in favour of; in conformity with; according; *adv* after; along; next

secundus, **a**, **um** *adj* second; following; next; inferior, secondary; favourable
▢ **rēs secundae** prosperity

sēcurifer, **sēcuriger**, **era**, **erum** *adj* armed with an axe

secūris, **is** *f* axe, hatchet; authority

sēcūritās, **ātis** *f* freedom from care; carelessness; safety, security

sēcūrus, **a**, **um** *adj* unconcerned; careless; safe, secure; untroubled; nonchalant

secus *adv* otherwise; wrongly
▢ **nōn ~** just so

secūtus *pple* from ▶ **sequor**

sed *conj* but; however; yet; but also
▢ **~ enim** but in fact
▢ **~ etiam** but also

sēdātus, **a**, **um** *adj* calm, untroubled

sēdecim *adj indec* sixteen

sedeō, **sēdī**, **sessum** ② *v* be seated, sit; remain; rest; be decided on

sēdēs, **dis** *f* seat; home, residence

sedīle, **is** *nt* seat, bench, chair

sēditiō, **ōnis** *f* violent political discord, mutiny, sedition

sēditiōsus, a, um *adj* factious, seditious; turbulent

sēdō ① *v* settle, allay; restrain; calm down

sēdūcō, dūxī, ductum ③ *v* lead aside; separate off

sēductus, a, um *adj* distant; retired, secluded

sēdulitās, ātis *f* assiduity, painstaking attention (to)

sēdulus, a, um *adj* attentive, painstaking, sedulous

sēdulō *adv* with all one's heart

seges, etis *f* corn-field; crop

sēgnis, e *adj* slow, sluggish, inactive, unenergetic

sēgnitia, ae *f*, **sēgnitiēs, iēī** *f* sloth, sluggishness

sēgregō ① *v* separate (into parts); break off

sēiungō, ūnxī, ūnctum ③ *v* separate; exclude

sēlibra, ae *f* half-pound

sēligō, lēgī, lēctum ③ *v* select, choose

sella, ae *f* seat, chair, stool
□ **~ curūlis** magistrate's chair

sellisternium, (i)ī *nt* formal religious banquet

sellula, ae *f* sedan-chair

semel *adv* once, a single time; once and for all; the first time; at any time, once, ever
□ **~ atque iterum** once and again

sēmen, inis *nt* seed; shoot; slip; cutting; parentage, descent; germ, spark

sēmentis, is *f* sowing; crop

sēmermis, e *adj* badly- or poorly-armed

sēmēsus, a, um *adj* half-eaten

sēmiadapertus, a, um *adj* half-open

sēmianimis, e *adj*, **sēmianimus, a, um** *adj* half-alive

sēmiapertus, a, um *adj* half-open

sēmibōs, bovis *m* half-bull, *i.e.* the Minotaur

sēmicaper, prī *m* half-goat (Pan)

sēmicremātus, a, um *adj*, **sēmicremus, a, um** *adj* half-burned

sēmiermis, e *adj*, **sēmiermus, a, um** *adj* half-armed

sēmifactus, a, um *adj* half-made, half-finished

sēmifer, era, erum *adj* half-wild; half-monster

sēmihiāns, ntis *adj* half-open

sēmihomō, inis *m* half-man, half-human

sēmilacer, era, erum *adj* half-mangled

sēmilautus, a, um *adj* half-washed

sēmimarīnus, a, um *adj* belonging to the sea

sēmimās, aris *m* half-male

sēmimortuus, a, um *adj* half-dead

sēminex, cis *adj* half-dead

sēminō ① *v* plant, sow

sēminūdus, a, um *adj* half-naked

sēmiplēnus, a, um *adj* half-full; half-manned

sēmiputātus, a, um *adj* half-pruned

sēmireductus, a, um *adj* half

bent back

sēmirefectus, a, um *adj* half-repaired

sēmirutus, a, um *adj* half-ruined or demolished

sēmis, issis *m* half an as; half; interest at six per cent per annum

sēmisepultus, a, um *adj* half-buried

sēmisomnus, a, um *adj* half-asleep, drowsy

sēmisupīnus, a, um *adj* half-lying on one's back

sēmita, ae *f* side-path, track, lane

sēmitārius, a, um *adj* of or associated with by-ways, alleys *etc.*

sēmivir, rī *m* half man; ~ *adj* effeminate

sēmivīvus, a, um *adj* half-alive, almost dead

sēmōtus, a, um *adj* distant, remote

semper *adv* always

sempiternus, a, um *adj* everlasting

sēmuncia, ae *f* twenty-fourth part (of a pound, *etc.*); a minimal amount

sēmustus, a, um *adj* half-burnt, singed

senātor, ōris *m* member of the senate, senator

senātōrius, a, um *adj* senatorial

senātus, ūs *m* senate

senātūs cōnsultum *nt* decree or recommendation of the senate

senecta, ae *f*, **senectūs, ūtis** *f* old age; old men collectively

seneō ② *vb* be old

senēscō, nuī ③ *vb* grow old; grow weak, be in a decline; become

exhausted

senex, senis *m* old man ■ ~ *adj* old, aged

sēnī, ae, a *adj* six apiece; six

senīlis, e *adj* aged, senile

senior, ōris *adj* older

senium, (i)ī *nt* condition of old age; melancholy, gloom

sēnsim *adv* slowly, gradually, cautiously

sensualiter *adv* LM physically, corporeally

sēnsus, ūs *m* faculty of feeling, perception, sensation, sense; emotion; idea; epigrammatic notion; meaning

sententia, ae *f* opinion, sentiment; judgment; advice; vote; meaning; period; sentence □ **sententiā (meā)** to (my) liking, satisfactory

sentīna, ae *f* bilgewater; scum or dregs of society

sentiō, sēnsī, sēnsum ④ *v* discern by the senses; feel, hear, see; undergo; perceive, notice; think, deem; vote, declare; intend

sentis, is *m* any thorny bush or shrub, briar, bramble

sentus, a, um *adj* rough, rugged, uneven

seorsum, seorsus, sōrsum *adv* separately, apart from the rest

sēpar, aris *adj* separate

sēparātim *adv* separately, individually

sēparō ① *v* separate, divide; cut off, isolate

sepeliō, pultum ④ *v* bury, submerge, overcome; suppress

sēpia, ae *f* cuttle-fish; ink

sēpōnō, posuī, positum ③ *v*
put away from one; disregard;
isolate; reserve

septem *adj indec* seven

September, bris *adj* of
September; seventh (later the
ninth) month of the Roman year

septemdecim *adj indec* (also
septendecim) seventeen

septemfluus, a, um *adj* that
flows in seven streams

septemgeminus, a, um *adj*
sevenfold

septemplex, icis *adj* sevenfold;
of seven layers

septemtriōnēs, um *mpl* (also
septentriōnēs) Great Bear;
Little Bear; north, northern
regions, north wind

septendecim *adj indec* (also
septemdecim) seventeen

septēnī, ae, a *adj* seven each;
seven at a go; seven

septentriōnēs, um *mpl* (also
septemtriōnēs) Great Bear;
Little Bear; north, northern
regions, north wind

septiē(n)s *adv* seven times

septimānus, a, um *adj* of or
relating to the seventh; belonging
to the seventh legion; concerning
the nones of March, May, July or
October (the nones falling on the
seventh day of those months)

septimus, a, um *adj* seventh

septingentē(n)simus, a, um
adj seven hundredth

septingentī, ae, a *adj* seven
hundred

septuāgēnī, ae, a *adj* seventy
each

septuāgintā *adj indec* seventy

sepulcrālis, e *adj* sepulchral, of
the tomb

sepulcrētum, ī *nt* graveyard

sepulcrum, ī *nt* grave, sepulchre,
tomb; *pl* the dead

sepultūra, ae *f* burial

sequāx, ācis *adj* that follows
closely or eagerly; pliant, tractable

sequester, tra, trum *adj*
intermediary;
■ **sequestra, ae** *f* female go-
between, mediatress

sequor, secūtus sum ③ *v dep*
follow, come or go after, attend;
pursue; aim at; comply (with),
conform (to); succeed

sera, ae *f* bar (for fastening doors)

serēnitās, ātis *f* fine weather;
favourable conditions

serēnō ① *v* clear up, brighten;
lighten

serēnus, a, um *adj* clear, fine,
bright, cloudless; cheerful, glad,
joyous, tranquil
■ **serēnum, ī** *nt* fair weather

serēscō ③ *v* grow dry

sēria, ae *f* large earthenware jar

sēricus, a, um *adj* silken

seriēs *f* row, succession, series;
line of ancestors or descendants

sērius¹ *adv* later, too late
□ — **aut citius** sooner or later

sērius², a, um *adj* serious,
weighty, important; sober, grave
□ **sēriō** in earnest
■ **sēria, ōrum** *ntpl* business

sermō, ōnis *m* speech, talk;
conversation; gossip; subject of
talk; language, dialect

sērō *adv* late, at a late hour; too
late

serō¹, —, **sertum** ③ *v* string together; join, engage (in)

serō², **sēvī**, **satum** ③ *v* sow, plant; beget; broadcast; foment □ ~ **negōtium** cause trouble

sērōtinus, **a**, **um** *adj* late, belated, deferred

serpēns, **ntis** *f* snake, serpent; the constellation Draco

serpō, **psī** ③ *v* crawl; move slowly on, glide; creep on

serpyllum, **ī** *nt* wild thyme

serra, **ae** *f* saw

serta¹, **ae** *f* garland

serta², **ōrum** *ntpl* chains of flowers, garlands, festoons

serum, **ī** *nt* whey

sērus, **a**, **um** *adj* late; too late; slow, tardy

serva, **ae** *f* female slave

servābilis, **e** *adj* capable of being saved

servātor, **ōris** *m* watcher, observer; preserver, saviour

servātrīx, **īcis** *f* female preserver, protectress

servīlis, **e** *adj* slavish, servile; of or belonging to slaves

serviō ④ *v* with *dat* be a slave, serve, wait on; be of use (to); be subject (to); labour for

servitium, **(i)ī** *nt* slavery, servitude; slaves; the slave class

servitūs, **ūtis** *f* slavery, servitude, bondage

servō ① *v* save, preserve; protect; keep, observe; look after; pay attention to

servulus, **servolus**, **ī** *m* young (worthless) slave

servus¹, **ī** *m* slave

servus², **a**, **um** *adj* having the status of a slave, servile

sescentī, **ae**, **a** *adj* six hundred; an indefinitely large number

sesquipedālis, **e** *adj* of a foot and a half; (of words) a foot and a half long

sesquiplāga, **ae** *f* 'a blow and a half'

sessilis, **e** *adj* fit for sitting upon

sēstertium, **(i)ī** *nt* (originally *gen pl* after **centēna mīlia**) a hundred thousand sesterces

sēstertius¹, **(i)ī** *m* sesterce, two and a half **assēs**

sēstertius², **a**, **um** *adj* two and a half

sētius *adv* the less

seu ▶ sīve

sevēritās, **ātis** *f* gravity, sternness, strictness, severity

sevērus, **a**, **um** *adj* grave, strict, austere, stern, severe; forbidding

sēvocō ① *v* call apart, draw aside; separate, appropriate

sex *adj indec* six

sexāgēnī, **ae**, **a** *adj* sixty each; sixty at a time

sexāgintā *adj indec* sixty

sexangulus, **a**, **um** *adj* six-cornered, hexagonal

sexcentī ▶ sescentī

sexta, **ae** *f* [LM] sext (part of the daily cycle of prayer)

sextādecimānī, **ōrum** *mpl* soldiers of the sixteenth legion

sextāns, **ntis** *m* one-sixth of any unit

Sextīlis, **e** *adj* of the sixth, later the eighth month of the Roman year

■ **∼**, **is** m (month) August

sextus, **a**, **um** adj sixth

sexus, **ūs** m sex

sī conj if
□ **sī minus** if not

sibī pn dat of ▸ **sē**

sibilō ① v hiss; hiss at

sibilum, **ī** nt, **sibilus**, **ī** m hissing, whistling; hiss of contempt or disfavour

sībilus, **a**, **um** adj hissing

Sibylla, **ae** f prophetess, a sibyl

Sibyllīnus, **a**, **um** adj of or connected with a sibyl, sibylline

sīc adv in this or in such a manner, so, thus; to such an extent

sīca, **ae** f dagger

sīcārius, **(i)ī** m assassin, murderer

siccitās, **ātis** f dryness; drought; dried up condition

siccō ① v dry, staunch; dry up by evaporation; empty; suck dry

siccus, **a**, **um** adj dry; rainless, not carrying moisture; thirsty; abstemious
■ **siccum**, **ī** nt dry ground

sīcine adv so? thus?

siclus, **i** m LM shekel

sīcubi adv if anywhere, if at any place

sīcunde adv if from any place or source

sīcut, **sīcutī** adv just as, in the same way as; as it were; just as for instance; just as if; as indeed (is the case)

sīdereus, **a**, **um** adj relating to stars; starry; heavenly; star-like

sīdō, **ī** ③ v settle; sink down; sit down; run aground

sīdus, **eris** nt star, constellation; climate, weather; glory; pl star, the stars

sigillum, **ī** nt statuette; embossed figure, relief; figure woven in tapestry

signātor, **ōris** m witness (to a will, etc.)

signifer, **era**, **erum** adj holding the constellations
■ **signifer**, **erī** m standard-bearer

significātiō, **ōnis** f giving signs or signals; expression, indication, sign; suggestion, hint

significō ① v show, point out, indicate; intimate, signify; express

signō ① v mark; affix a seal to, seal up; coin, stamp; inscribe; indicate; LM make the sign of the cross

signum, **ī** nt mark, token, sign; standard, ensign; cohort; signal, password; image, picture, statue; seal, signet; constellation
□ **signa cōnferō** join battle
□ **ad prīma signa** in the front line

silēns, **ntis** adj silent
■ **silentēs**, **silentum/ silentium** mpl the dead

silentium, **(i)ī** nt stillness, silence; repose, tranquillity; omission to speak or write of; neglect

sileō ② v be silent, not to speak (about); be quiet; not to function

silēscō, **luī** ③ v grow quiet

silex, **icis** m/f pebble-stone, flint; boulder, stone

siliqua, **ae** f pod

silva, **ae** f wood, forest; brushwood; thicket-like growth; branches and foliage of trees, bushes, *etc.*; trees

silvānī, ōrum *mpl* gods associated with forest and uncultivated land

silvestris, tre *adj* covered with woods, wooded; found in woodland; living in woodlands; wild, untamed, savage

silvicola, ae *adj* inhabiting woodlands

silvicultor, ōris *m*, **silvicultrīx, īcis** *f* one inhabiting woodlands, woodland-dweller

sīmia, ae *f* monkey, ape

similis, e *adj* like, resembling, similar

similitūdō, inis *f* likeness, resemblance, similarity; comparison, simile

simītū *adv* at the same time, together

simplex, icis *adj* simple, unmixed; artless, ingenuous, naïve; harmless

simplicitās, ātis *f* simplicity; plainness, frankness, candour

simpliciter *adv* simply, just; candidly, frankly

simul *adv* together, at the same time, as well

simulac, simulatque *conj* as soon as, the moment that

simulācrum, ī *nt* likeness, image, statue; pictorial representation; ghost, phantom; shade; sham

simulāmen, inis *nt* imitation, simulation

simulātiō, ōnis *f* pretence, simulation; excuse, pretext

simulātor, ōris *m* one who copies or imitates; feigner

simulō 1 *v* imitate, copy, represent; simulate, counterfeit, pretend; act the part of; cause to resemble

simultās, ātis *f* state of animosity, quarrel, feud

sīmulus, a, um *adj* flat-nosed, snub-nosed

sīmus, a, um *adj* flat-nosed, snub nosed; flattened

sin *conj* if however, but if; but if (despite what has been said)

sināpi, is *nt* mustard

sincērus, a, um *adj* sound, whole; genuine, pure; faithful, straightforward

sindōn, nis *f* woven material of a fine texture, muslin

sine *prep with abl* without

singillātim *adv* singly, one by one

singulāris, e *adj* single, singular; unusual, remarkable

singulī, ae, a *adj* one to each recipient; every single; individual; isolated

singultim *adv* sobbingly, with sobs

singultō 1 *v* catch the breath, gasp; utter with sobs; gasp out (one's life)

singultus, ūs *m* sobbing; convulsive catching of breath

sinister, tra, trum *adj* left, on the left; unlucky, bad; auspicious, lucky, favourable; perverted
■ **sinistra, ae** *f* left hand or side
■ **sinistrā** *adv* on the left

sinō/, sīvī/siī, situm 3 *v* let, leave; allow, permit, leave alone, let be; grant

sīnum, ī *nt* bowl for serving wine, *etc.*

sinuō ① v bend into a curve; bend; billow out

sinuōsus, a, um adj characterized by the action of bending; winding, sinuous; full of folds or recesses

sīnus, ī m bowl for serving wine, etc.

sinus, ūs m curve; fold; hollow; bosom, lap; bay, gulf; pocket for money; asylum; inmost part; hiding-place; embrace

sīnus, ī m bowl

sīphō, ōnis m tube

sīquandō adv (also **sī quandō**) if ever, if at any time

sīquidem conj (also **sī quidem**) at any rate if, always assuming that; if it is really the case that; seeing that, inasmuch as

sīquis, quae/qua, quid pn (also **sī quis**) if any one, if any person

Sīrius, (i)ī m greater dog-star, Sirius

■ ~, **a, um** adj of the dog-star

sirpe nt the plant silphium

sīs int [contracted from **sī + vīs**] please

sistō, stetī/stitī, statum ③ v set up, erect, place firmly, plant, station; stand still; stand firm

sistrum, ī nt metal rattle used in the worship of Isis

sitiēns, ntis adj thirsting, producing thirst, arid, dry, parched; thirsty (for)

sitiō ④ v be thirsty; long greatly for; be in need of water

sitis, is f thirst; aridity, dryness; violent craving (for)

situs¹, ūs m situation, position, site; structure; neglect, disuse, stagnation; rottenness, mould

situs², a, um adj laid up, stored; positioned, situated; centred (on)

sīve conj (also **seu**) or if

  ☐ **sīve/seu ... sīve/seu** whether ... or

sixtus ▶ xystus

smaragdus, ī m emerald; beryl; jasper

smyrna, ae f myrrh

sobrīnus, ī m cousin on mother's side, child of mother's siblings

sōbrius, a, um adj sober; staid, sensible, temperate

soccus, ī m low-heeled, loose-fitting shoe or slipper, worn by Greeks; shoe worn by comic actors; comedy

socer, erī m father-in-law

  ☐ **socerī, ōrum** parents-in-law

socia, ae f sharer, partner, companion, associate; spouse; ally, confederate

sociālis, e adj social; of or relating to allies; conjugal

societās, ātis f association; partnership; trading company; society; fellowship; connection, affinity

sociō ① v unite in partnership or an alliance; associate (one's resources, etc.) with those of a partner; share; combine

socius, a, um adj sharing, associated; allied, confederate

■ ~, **(i)ī** m sharer, partner, companion, associate; spouse; ally, confederate

sōcordia, ae f sluggishness, torpor, inaction

sōcorditer adv negligently

sōcors, rdis adj sluggish, inactive

socrus, ūs f mother-in-law

sodālicium, (i)ī nt close association, partnership

sodālis, is m companion, comrade, crony

sodālitās, ātis f close association; religious fraternity; electioneering gang

sōdēs adv [contraction of sī audēs] if you do not mind, please

sōl, sōlis m sun; east; sunlight; heat of the sun; day

sōlāciolum, ī nt (little) comfort or solace

sōlācium, (i)ī nt solace, comfort, consolation

sōlāmen, inis nt source of comfort, solace

solea, ae f sole, sandal; sandal worn by a beast of burden

soleō, solitus sum ② v semi-dep be accustomed (to), be apt (to), be the common practise

solidō ① v make solid; strengthen, consolidate

solidus, a, um adj solid, firm, complete, entire; unwavering, strong; solid, lasting, real

sōlitūdō, inis f loneliness, solitariness; desert, waste; emptiness, solitude

solitus¹ pple from ▶ soleō

solitus², a, um adj accustomed, usual, customary, normal

solium, (i)ī nt throne; bath-tub

sollemnis, e adj solemn, ceremonial; traditional, customary

sollers, rtis adj clever, skilled, resourceful

sollertia, ae f skill, cleverness; resourcefulness

sollicitātiō, ōnis f incitement to

disloyalty or crime

sollicitō ① v harass, molest; tug at, shake up; disturb, pester; torment; rouse, stimulate; strive to influence; incite to revolt; attempt to seduce

sollicitūdō, inis f anxiety, uneasiness

sollicitus, a, um adj restless; in a state of turmoil; uneasy, apprehensive; accompanied by anxiety or uneasiness

sōlor ① v dep comfort, console; relieve, mitigate

solstitiālis, e adj of or belonging to the summer solstice

solstitium, (i)ī nt solstice; summer-time, heat of the summer-solstice

sōlum adv only, merely
  □ **nōn ~ ... sed** not only ... but

solum, ī nt base, foundation; earth, ground, soil; sole of the foot or shoe

sōlus, a, um adj alone, sole; solitary; lonely; deserted

solūtiō, ōnis f payment

solūtus, a, um adj unbound; free; unrestrained, profligate; free to act as one pleases; lax, careless

solvō, lvī, lūtum ③ v loosen, unbind; separate, disengage; dissolve; melt; open; fulfil, perform; pay, deliver, release; acquit
  □ **nāvem ~** set sail

somnifer, era, erum adj, **somnificus, a, um** adj inducing sleep

somniō ① v dream; dream of or see in a dream

somnium, (i)ī nt dream, vision; fantasy, day-dream

omnus, ī m sleep; sloth

onābilis, e adj noisy, resonant

onipēs, edis m horse, steed

onitus, ūs m noise, loud sound

onō, sonuī, sonitum [] v make a noise, sound, resound (with); utter; be heard

onor, ōris m sound, noise, din

onōrus, a, um adj noisy, loud, resounding, sonorous

ōns, ntis adj guilty, criminal ■ ~ m/f criminal

onus, ī m noise, sound

ophōs int well done! bravo!

ōpiō¹ [] v cause to sleep; render insensible by a blow or sudden shock

ōpiō², ōnis f penis

opor, ōris m sleep

opōrifer, era, erum adj bringing sleep or unconsciousness

opōrō [] v rend to sleep, render unconscious, stupefy

opōrus, a, um adj that induces sleep

orbeō [] v suck up, drink up, absorb, soak up; engulf

orbum, ī nt sorb, service-berry

ordeō [] v be dirty; seem mean, unworthy, not good enough, etc.

ordēs, dis f dirt, filth, nastiness; squalor; baseness, lowness; niggardliness

ordidātus, a, um adj shabbily dressed; wearing mourning clothes

ordidus, a, um adj dirty, foul, filthy; vulgar, low; poor; paltry, niggardly, sordid

oror, ōris f sister; [LM] religious sister, nun

■ **sorōrēs** pl the Muses; the Fates

sorōrius, a, um adj of or concerning a sister

sors, rtis f lot, drawing of lots; decision by lot; response of an oracle; fate, destiny; part; share; investment, capital, principal

sōrsu- ▶ seorsu-

sortior [] v dep cast or draw lots; obtain by lot; appoint by lot; choose

sortītus, ūs m process of lottery

sospes, itis adj safe and sound, unscathed

sospita, ae f female preserver (cult title of Juno at Lanuvium)

sospitō [] v preserve, defend

spadō, ōnis m eunuch

spargō, rsī, arsum [] v strew, scatter; sprinkle; discharge in large numbers, shower; let stream out in all directions; place in scattered positions; spread about

sparus, ī m hunting-spear, javelin

spatior [] v dep walk about, range, stalk; spread out

spatiōsus, a, um adj roomy, ample, spacious, long; protracted

spatium, (i)ī nt room, space; place for walking, interval; period; length; time available for a purpose

speciēs, iēī f visual appearance; look; sight; outward appearance; semblance; pretence; display, splendour, beauty; vision; image, likeness; species; artistic representation

specimen, inis nt sign, evidence; token, symbol; [LM] beauty

speciōsus, a, um *adj* showy, handsome, beautiful, splendid, brilliant; specious, plausible

spectābilis, e *adj* able to be seen or looked at; worth looking at

spectātor, ōris *m* witness, spectator; sightseer; critical observer

spectātrīx, īcis *f* female observer or watcher

spectō v look at; watch, observe; (geographically) lie, face; examine; test, prove; consider, pay regard to, regard (as)

specula, ae *f* raised look-out post

speculātor, ōris *m* spy; scout; look-out man

speculor v *dep* keep a close watch on, observe, spy out; look out, watch for

speculum, ī *nt* looking-glass, mirror

specus, ūs *adj* cave, abyss, chasm; hole, pit; hollow (of any kind)

spēlunca, ae *f* cave, grotto, cavern

spernō, sprēvī, sprētum v reject with scorn, disdain; scorn; disregard

spērō v look forward to, hope for; hope; anticipate

spēs, eī *f* hope; expectation; object of hope; joy

spīca, ae *f* ear of corn

spīceus, a, um *adj* consisting of ears of corn

spīculum, ī *nt* sting; javelin; arrow; sharp point of a weapon

spīna, ae *f* thorn; spine; backbone; thorn-bush

spīnētum, ī *nt* thicket (of thorn-bushes)

spīneus, a, um *adj* thorny, covered with thorns

spīnōsus, a, um *adj* thorny, prickly; crabbed, difficult

spīnus, ī *f* thorn-bush

spīra, ae *f* coil

spīrāculum, ī *nt* air-hole, vent

spīrāmentum, ī *nt* breathing-passage

spīritus, ūs *m* breath of air, breeze; breath, breathing; soul, mind; life

spīrō v breathe; blow; live; breathe out; exhale; breathe the spirit of

spissēscō v become more compact, thicken

spissō v thicken, condense

spissus, a, um *adj* thick, dense; closely packed, crowded

splēn, nis *m* spleen

splendeō v shine, be bright; be brilliant or distinguished

splendēscō, duī v become bright, begin to shine

splendidus, a, um *adj* bright, shining, glittering, brilliant; splendid, sumptuous; illustrious; showy, striking

splendor, ōris *m* brightness; brilliance, splendour; magnificence; personal distinction

spoliātiō, ōnis *f* robbing, plundering, spoliation

spoliātor, ōris *m* one who plunders or despoils

spoliō v strip or rob of clothing; plunder, rob, despoil

spolium, (i)ī *nt* skin, hide (of an animal, stripped off); booty, spoil

■ **spolia opīma** *ntpl* spoils taken by a general after a single combat with the opposing general

sponda, ae *f* bed, couch

spondeō, spopondī, spōnsum ② *v* give a pledge or undertaking; guarantee; act as surety for

spondēus, ī *m* spondee (metrical foot of two long syllables)

spōnsa, ae *f* woman promised in marriage, betrothed

spōnsālia, ōrum *ntpl* betrothal

spōnsiō, ōnis *f* solemn promise; wager at law

spōnsor, ōris *m* one who guarantees the good faith of another; surety

spōnsus, ī *m* affianced husband

sponte *adv* of one's own accord, freely, voluntarily, spontaneously; by oneself, alone

sporta, ae *f* basket, hamper

sportella, ae *f* little basket

sportula, ae *f* little basket; food or money given by patrons to clients

sprētor, ōris *m* one who despises or scorns

sprētum, sprēvī ▶ spernō

spūma, ae *f* foam, froth

spūmēscō ③ *v* become foamy

spūmeus, a, um *adj* foamy, frothy

spūmō ① *v* foam; be covered with foam

spūmōsus, a, um *adj* foaming, frothy

spuō, uī, ūtum ③ *v* spit, spit out

spurcō ① *v* soil, infect; deprave

spurcus, a, um *adj* dirty, foul; morally polluted

spurius, a, um *adj* LM illegitimate

spūtō ① *v* spit out

spūtum, ī *nt* spittle

squāleō ② *v* be covered with a rough or scaly layer; be dirty

squālidus, a, um *adj* having a rough surface; coated with dirt, filthy

squālor, ōris *m* dirtiness, filthiness, dirty or neglectful state as a sign of mourning

squāma, ae *f* scale; metal-plate used in the making of scale-armour

squāmeus, squāmiger, squāmōsus, a, um *adj* scaly

st *int* hush! sh!

stabiliō ④ *v* make firm or steady; hold still; fix or establish firmly

stabilis, e *adj* firm, steady, stable; lasting; immovable, constant

stabulō ① *v* house (domestic animals, poultry, *etc.*); be housed

stabulum, ī *nt* stall, shed, fold, stable; bee-hive; stabling

stacta, ae *f* myrrh oil

stadium, (iī) *nt* running-track

stāgnō ① *v* form or lie in pools; be under water

stāgnum, ī *nt* pool, lagoon; water

stāmen, inis *nt* warp (in the loom); thread (on the distaff, to spin); thread of life spun by the Fates

stāmineus, a, um *adj* of or consisting of threads

stannum, ī *nt* alloy of silver and lead

statārius, a, um *adj* stationary

statim *adv* at once, immediately,

instantly

statiō, ōnis f standing (still); halting-place; armed post; guard-duty; guard; station, place; anchorage

statīvus, a, um adj stationary, permanent

stator, ōris m one who establishes or upholds (cult-title of Jupiter)

statua, ae f statue

statūmen, inis nt support

statuō, uī, ūtum 3 v place, put up; set up, appoint; determine, resolve (to); decide; judge

statūra, ae f the height of the body in an upright position, stature

status¹, ūs m standing, position; posture; condition, circumstance, state; rank

status², a, um adj fixed, appointed; regular

stēlla, ae f star

stēllāns, ntis adj starry; having the appearance of stars

stēllātus, a, um adj furnished with star-like points of light

sterculīnum, ī nt dung-hill, muck-heap

stercus, oris nt dung, excrement, muck

sterilis, e adj barren, sterile; fruitless; unprofitable, futile

sternāx, ācis adj liable to throw its rider (of a horse)

sternō, strāvī, strātum 3 v spread, strew; extend; level, knock down; cause to subside; lay low, defeat utterly

sternuō, uī 3 v sneeze

stertō, tuī 3 v snore

stetī ▸ stō

stillicidium, (i)ī nt fall (of a liquid) in successive drops

stillō 1 v fall in drops; drip; cause to drip, pour in drops

stilus, ī m spike, stem; stylus, pen

stimulātrix, icis f female instigator, woman who goads on

stimulō 1 v urge forward with a goad, torment, 'sting'; incite, rouse to frenzy

stimulus, ī m goad; spur; pointed stake; incitement

stinguō 3 v extinguish, put out; annihilate

stīpātor, ōris m one of the train surrounding a king; bodyguard, close attendant

stīpendiārius, a, um adj mercenary; paying tribute in the form of cash

stīpendium, (i)ī nt tax, contribution; pay; (a year of) military service; campaign
□ **stīpendia mereor** complete (so many years of) military service

stīpes, itis m trunk (of a tree); stake

stīpō 1 v crowd, press together, compress, surround closely

stips, pis f small offering

stipula, ae f stalk; stubble; straw; reed played on as a pipe

stīria, ae f icicle

stirps, pis f stock, stem, stalk; root; plant, shrub; family, ancestral race; offspring, posterity

stīva, ae f shaft of a plough-handle

stō, stetī, statum 1 v stand;

Stōicus | studeō

stand still; be fixed; stand erect; be *or* become upright, endure, persist; remain; adhere (to); be one's fault

□ **per tē stetit quōminus vincerem** it was due to you that I did not conquer

Stōicus, a, um *adj* Stoic

stola, ae *f* long upper garment

stolidus, a, um *adj* dull, stupid, brutish

stomachor ① *v dep* be angry, boil with rage

stomachōsus, a, um *adj* irritable, short-tempered

stomachus, ī *m* gullet; stomach; annoyance; ill-temper

storea, ae *f* matting of rushes

strāgēs, gis *f* overthrow; massacre, slaughter, cutting down; havoc; confused heap; destruction, devastation

strāmen, inis *nt* straw for bedding, *etc.*, litter

strāmentum, ī *nt* straw, litter; coverings

strāmineus, a, um *adj* made of straw

strangulō ① *v* choke; suffocate, smother

strātum¹, ī *nt* coverlet; bed, couch; horse-blanket

strātum², strāvī ▶ sternō

strēnuitās, ātis *f* strenuous behaviour, activity

strēnuus, a, um *adj* active, vigorous, energetic

strepitō ① *v* make a loud *or* harsh noise

strepitus, ūs *m* noise, din;

crashing, rustling, clattering sound (of a musical instrument); noisy talk, uproar

strepō, itum ③ *v* make a loud noise; shout confusedly; resound

striātus, a, um *adj* striated, fluted

strictūra, ae *f* hardened mass of iron

strīdeō ② *v*, **strīdō, dī** ③ *v* creak, hiss, whistle, buzz, rattle; produce a high-pitched utterance; be filled with a shrill sound

strīdor, ōris *m* hissing, buzzing, rattling, whistling; high-pitched sound

strīdulus, a, um *adj* making a high-pitched *or* shrill sound

strigilis, is *f* instrument with a curved and channelled blade for scraping the skin

strigōsus, a, um *adj* lean, scraggy

stringō, īnxī, ictum ③ *v* draw or tie tight; skin, brush; graze; pluck, strip off; prune; unsheathe

strix, gis *f* owl

strophium, (i)ī *nt* twisted breast-band; head-band

strūctūra, ae *f* building, construction; structure; masonry, concrete

strūes, uis *f* heap, pile; row of sacrificial cakes

strūma, ae *f* swelling of the lymphatic glands

struō, ūxī, ūctum ③ *v* build, construct; arrange; devise, contrive

studeō ② *v with dat* devote oneself to, concern oneself (with), strive after; concentrate on; support; study

studiōsus, a, um *adj* eager, zealous, studious, scholarly; affectionate, fond; devoted

studium, (i)ī *nt* zeal, eagerness (for), study, application; devotion, goodwill, support

stultitia, ae *f* stupidity, folly, fatuity

stultus, a, um *adj* foolish, silly; inept

stupefaciō, fēcī, factum ③ *v* stun with amazement, astound ▪ **stupefiō, fierī, factus sum** *v ir semi-dep* be astonished

stupeō ② *v* be stunned or benumbed; be astonished or stupefied (at)

stupor, ōris *m* numbness, torpor; stupefaction; stupidity

stuppa, ae *f* tow, coarse flax

stuppeus, a, um *adj* of tow

stuprō ① *v* have illicit sexual intercourse with

stuprum, ī *nt* dishonour, shame; illicit sexual intercourse, rape

sturnus, ī *m* starling

stylus ▶ stilus

suādeō, suāsī, suāsum ②
v advise, recommend, urge; advocate

suāsor, ōris *m* adviser, counsellor

suāsus, ūs *m* persuasion

suāvidicus, a, um *adj* speaking pleasantly

suāviloquēns, ntis *adj* speaking agreeably

suāviolum, ī *nt* tender kiss

suāvior ① *v dep* kiss

suāvis, e *adj* sweet, pleasant, agreeable, delightful

suāvium, (i)ī *nt* kiss; sweetheart

sub *prep with acc* under, below, beneath; under the power of; *with acc* near to; about; a little before; to a position under; up to; directly after

subaquilus, a, um *adj* rather dark-skinned

subblandior ④ *v dep* fondle or caress a little

subc- ▶ succ-

subcidō, ī ③ *v* (also **succidō**) collapse through the lower parts giving way

subclāmō ① *v* (also **succlāmō**) shout in response (to)

subcrēscō ③ *v* (also **succrēscō**) grow up from below; grow up as a replacement or successor

subcumbō, buī, itum ③ *v* (also **succumbō**) sink to the ground; collapse; lie down (under); lower itself; give in (to)

subdō, didī, ditum ③ *v* place or insert below; place under; subject, expose (to); substitute fraudulently; supply

subdolus, a, um *adj* sly, deceitful, treacherous

subdūcō, dūxī, ductum ③ *v* draw from under or from below; withdraw (from); extricate; steal (away); reckon up, calculate

subductiō, ōnis *f* hauling up of a ship onto the beach

subedō, ēsse, ēdī, ēsum *v ir* eat away below

subeō, īre, iī/īvī, itum *v ir* go, move or pass underneath; come up to; approach; undergo, endure; come next; succeed to; steal in on, come over; suggest itself

sūber, eris *nt* cork-tree; its thick

spongy outer bark, cork

subf- ▶ **suff-**

subferō, ferre, sustulī, sublātum *v ir* (also **sufferō**) submit to, endure, to suffer

subfodiō, ōdī, ossum 🖩 *v* (also **suffodiō**) undermine, dig under; pierce *or* prod below

subfrāgātiō, ōnis *f* (also **suffrāgātiō**) public expression of support (for)

subfrāgium, (i)ī *nt* (also **suffrāgium**) voting; vote; right of voting; recommendation

subfundō, ūdī, ūsum 🖩 *v* (also **suffundō**) pour in *or* on; cause to well up to the surface; cover *or* fill with a liquid that wells up from below

subfuscus, a, um *adj* rather dark in appearance

subg- ▶ **sugg-**

subgerō, essī, estum *v* (also **suggerō**) heap up; supply, feed; subjoin

subiciō, iēcī, ectum 🖩 *v* throw up; place below; place under; lay before; put under the control of; expose; place next; interpose; suborn; introduce

subiectō 🖩 *v* throw up from below; apply below

subiectus, a, um *adj* with *dat* situated under; open *or* exposed (to); subject (to)

subigō, ēgī, āctum 🖩 *v* conquer, subjugate; plough; force; drive under

subinde *adv* immediately after, thereupon; constantly, repeatedly

subitārius, a, um *adj* got together to meet an emergency,

hastily enrolled

subitō *adv* suddenly, unexpectedly; at short notice; in no time at all

subitus, a, um *adj* sudden, unexpected
■ **subitum, ī** *nt* emergency, crisis

subiugalis, is *m* 🅛🅜 beast of burden

subiungō, ūnxī, ūnctum *v* yoke; subjoin; add; bring under the control (of)

sublābor, lāpsus sum 🖩 *v dep* collapse; sink *or* ebb away; creep up

sublātum ▶ **tollō**

sublātus, a, um *adj* high-pitched; bold, self-assured

sublegō, ēgī, ēctum 🖩 *v* pick up from the ground, steal away

sublevō 🗓 *v* lift, raise, support; lighten, alleviate; assist, encourage

sublica, ae *f* wooden stake *or* pile

sublǐgō 🗓 *v* fasten (to)

sublīmis, e *adj* high, lofty, exalted; imposingly tall; sublime; eminent

sublīmitās, ātis *f* height; loftiness

sublūceō 🄯 *v* shine faintly, glimmer

sublūō, ūtum 🗓 *v* wash; flow at the foot of

sublūstris, tre *adj* faintly lit, dim

submergō, rsī, ersum 🖩 *v* cause to sink, submerge

subministrō 🗓 *v* supply, furnish, afford

submissus, a, um *adj* stooping; quiet

submittō, īsī, issum 🖩 *v* raise,

rear; send up; send (reinforcements); drop; make subject (to)

submoveō, mōvī, mōtum 2 *v* remove; drive off, dislodge; expel; ward off; keep at a distance

subnectō, exuī, exum 3 *v* bind under, add, subjoin, fasten up

subnīxus, a, um *adj with abl* relying on; elated by

subnūbilus, a, um *adj* somewhat cloudy, overcast

subolēs, lis *f* shoot, sucker; race; offspring; progeny

subolēscō 3 *v* grow up

subolet 2 *v impers* there is an inkling

suborior, ortus sum 4 *v dep* come into being, be provided

subortus, ūs *m* the springing up (of a fresh supply)

subp- ▶ supp-

subpeditō 1 *v* (also **suppeditō**) be available when required, supply the needs (of); make available as required; supply (with)

subpetō, īvī/iī, ītum 3 *v* (also **suppetō**) turn up as a support, give backing (to); be available for one's needs; suggest itself

subplēmentum, ī *nt* (also **supplēmentum**) supplement; reinforcement

subpleō, ēvī, ētum 2 *v* (also **suppleō**) complete, fill up; make (a whole)

subpōnō, positum 3 *v* (also **suppōnō**) place under; substitute; introduce fraudulently into a situation

subportō 1 *v* (also **supportō**) transport (supplies, *etc.*) to a centre

subprīmō, essī, essum 3 *v* (also **supprimō**) press down or under; suppress; keep back, contain; stop, check

subr- ▶ surr-

subrēmigō 1 *v* make rowing movements underneath

subrēpō, psī, ptum 3 *v* (also **surrēpō**) creep, creep (up to); steal on, insinuate itself

subrīdeō, rīsī 2 *v* smile

subrigō, ēxī, ēctum 3 *v* (also **surrigō** and **surgō**) rise, get up; rouse oneself to action; stand high; grow tall

subripiō, eptum 3 *v* (also **surripiō**) steal, kidnap, remove by stealth

subrubeō 2 *v* be tinged with red or purple

subruō, ruī, rutum 3 *v* weaken at the base, undermine

subscrībō, psī, ptum 3 *v* write underneath; append; inscribe at the foot; give support (to)

subsecō, secuī, sectum 1 *v* cut away below; pare (the nails)

subsellium, (i)ī *nt* bench, low seat; court, courts

subsequor, secūtus sum 3 *v dep* follow close behind, follow, succeed; follow the lead of

subsidiārius, a, um *adj* acting as a support to the front line

■ **subsidiāriī, ōrum** *mpl* the reserves

subsidium, (i)ī *nt* body of troops in reserve; aid; support; safeguard means of assistance

subsīdō, sēdī, essum 3 *v* squat

down; settle down; subside; lie in
wait (for); fall to the ground

subsistō, stitī ③ *v* stop short;
stand firm; stop short, cease from;
remain, tarry, settle down

substernō, strāvī, strātum ③ *v*
spread out (as an underlay)

substringō, īnxī, ictum ③ *v*
draw in close, gather up; draw
tight
□ **aurem ~** strain to hear

substrūctiō, ōnis *f* (act of
building) a foundation,
substructure

substruō, ūxī, ūctum ③ *v* build
up from the base; support by
means of substructures

subsum, esse *v ir with dat* be
underneath; be a basis for
discussion; be close at hand as a
reserve or refuge

subsūtus, a, um *adj* stitched at
the bottom

subter *prep with abl* below,
beneath, under, underneath; *with
acc* to a position under; *adv* below,
beneath, under, underneath; to a
position underneath

subterfugiō, ūgī ③ *v* evade,
avoid by a stratagem

subterlābor ③ *v dep* glide or flow
beneath, slip away

subterrāneus, a, um *adj*
underground

subtexō, xuī, xtum ③ *v* weave
beneath; veil; subjoin, attach as a
sequel (to)

subtīlis, e *adj* fine-spun, fine;
slender, delicate, exact; minutely
thorough

subtrahō, āxī, actum ③ *v* draw
from under, undermine; withdraw

(from); detach from the main
body; rescue from the threat (of);
remove

subūcula, ae *f* under-tunic worn
by both sexes

subulcus, ī *m* swineherd

Subūra, ae *f* valley between the
Esquiline and Viminal hills of Rome
(a centre of night life)

suburbānī, ōrum *mpl* people
dwelling near the city

suburbānus, a, um *adj* situated
close to the city; growing or
cultivated near the city

suburgeō ② *v* drive up close

subvectiō, ōnis *f* transporting
(of supplies) to a centre

subvectō ① *v* convey (often or
laboriously) upwards

subvehō, ēxī, ectum ③ *v* convey
upwards; convey up
□ **subvehor** sail upstream

subveniō, vēnī, ventum ④
v with dat come to the help (of);
relieve

subvertō, rtī, rsum ③ *v*
overturn, cause to topple;
overthrow, destroy, subvert

subvexus, a, um *adj* sloping up

subvolō ① *v* fly upwards

subvolvō ③ *v* roll uphill

succēdō, cessī, cessum ③ *v*
go below or under; come to the
foot (of); come up (to); move
on upwards; move up into the
position (of); take the place (of);
succeed (to)

succendō, endī, ēnsum ③ *v* set
alight, kindle from beneath; inflame

succēnseō, sum ② *v* be angry

succenturiātus, ī *m* reservist

successiō, ōnis f succession (of a person) to a position of authority, ownership

successor, ōris m successor

successus, ūs m the action of coming up close; success, good result

succīdō, idī ③ v collapse through the lower parts giving way

succīdō, īdī, īsum ③ v cut from below, cut down

succiduus, a, um adj giving way under one

succingō, īnxī, īnctum ③ v gather up with a belt or girdle; prepare for action; surround

succlāmātiō, ōnis f answering shout

succlāmō ① v shout in response (to)

succrēscō ③ v grow up from below; grow up as a replacement or successor

succumbō, cubuī, cubitum ③ v sink to the ground; collapse; lie down (under); lower itself; give in (to)

succurrō, currī, cursum ③ v with dat run or move quickly to the rescue (of); come into one's mind

succutiō, ussī, ussum ③ v shake from below

sūcinum, ī nt amber

sūcinus, a, um adj made of amber, amber-coloured

sūcōsus, a, um adj full of sap, juicy

sūcula, ae f windlass

sūcus, ī m juice, sap; vital fluid in trees and plants

sūdārium, (i)ī nt handkerchief, napkin

sūdātor, ōris m one who sweats

sudis, dis f stake, pointed stick; spike

sūdō ① v sweat, perspire; become damp with surface moisture

sūdor, ōris m sweat, perspiration

sūdus, a, um adj clear and bright

suēscō, ēvī, ētum ③ v become accustomed (to)

suētus, a, um adj wont, accustomed; usual, familiar

sufferō, ferre, sustulī, sublātum v ir submit to, endure, to suffer

sufficiō, fēcī, fectum ③ v supply, provide; suffuse, imbue, steep; appoint in place of another; have sufficient strength (to), stand up (to); have sufficient wealth or resources for; be sufficient for; be available for

suffigō, īxī, īxum ③ v fasten beneath as a support; crucify

suffīmen, inis nt,
suffīmentum, ī nt a substance used to fumigate

suffiō ④ v fumigate

sufflō ① v puff up

suffodiō, ōdī, ossum ③ v undermine, dig under; pierce or prod below

suffrāgātiō, ōnis f public expression of support (for)

suffrāgium, (i)ī nt voting; vote; right of voting; recommendation

suffrāgor ① v dep express public support (for), canvass or vote for; lend support (to)

suffugium, (i)ī nt shelter

suffulciō, lsī, ltum ④ v

underprop, keep from falling

uffundō, ūdī, ūsum ③ *v* pour in or on; cause to well up to the surface; cover *or* fill with a liquid that wells up from below

uggerō, essī, estum ③ *v* heap up; supply, feed; subjoin

uggestus, ūs *m* raised surface; platform, dais

uggillō, sūgillō ① *v* insult, humiliate

ūgō, sūxī, sūctum ③ *v* suck; (fig) take in

uillus, a, um *adj* of pigs

ulcō ① *v* furrow, plough; cleave

ulcus, ī *m* furrow; rut; trail of a meteor; track, wake

ulfur, sulp(h)ur, ris *nt* brimstone, sulphur

ultis *int* [contraction of **sī + vultis**] please

um- ▶ subm-

umma, ae *f* total number *or* amount; sum; sum-total; a whole; the whole of a thing; the overall matter in question; an activity's general purpose

ummātim *adv* summarily, briefly

ummē *adv* in the highest degree, intensely

ummus, a, um *adj* highest, greatest, very great; chief, principal; the farthest, utmost, last, extreme; very deep □ **~ mōns** the top of the mountain

ūmō, mpsī, mptum ③ *v* take, take up; take hold of; receive; spend; have recourse to; adopt as

suitable; adopt; embrace; assume; take on

sūmptuārius, a, um *adj* concerned with the spending of money

sūmptuōsus, a, um *adj* expensive, costly, sumptuous

sūmptus, ūs *m* expense, lavish expenditure; expenses; charge

suō, suī, sūtum ③ *v* sew, stitch together

suovetaurīlia, ium *ntpl* purificatory sacrifice consisting of a boar, a ram, and a bull

supellex, lectilis *f* furniture, furnishings; outfit, paraphernalia

super *adv/prep* with *acc/abl* above, on, over; beyond; on top of; besides; about; concerning; in addition to

supera, ōrum *ntpl* heaven

superābilis, e *adj* that may be got over *or* surmounted; that may be conquered

superaddō, didī, ditum ③ *v* add *or* affix on the surface

superātor, ōris *m* conqueror

superbia, ae *f* pride, lofty self-esteem, disdain

superbiō ④ *v* with *abl* show pride or disdain on account (of), plume oneself (on)

superbus, a, um *adj* haughty, proud, arrogant; disdainful; glorying (in); that is a source of pride; grand, proud, sumptuous

supercilium, (i)ī *nt* eyebrow; gravity, haughtiness, stern looks, pride; overhanging edge, brow

superēmineō ② *v* overtop, stand out above the level of

superfluō, ūxī ③ *v* overflow;

2

superfundō | **superveniō**

superabound; be superabundantly supplied with

superfundō, **ūdī**, **ūsum** ③ *v* pour over

supergredior, **gressus sum** ③ *v dep* pass over or beyond; exceed, surpass

superī, **ōrum** *mpl* gods above

superiaciō, **iēcī**, **iactum** ③ *v* throw or scatter on top or over the surface; shoot over the top of

superimmineō ② *v* stand above in a threatening position

superimpōnō, **posuī**, **positum** ③ *v* place on top or over

superincidēns, **ntis** *adj* falling on top

superincubāns, **ntis** *adj* lying on top

superincumbō, **buī** ③ *v* lean over

superiniciō, **iēcī**, **iectum** ③ *v* throw or scatter on over the surface

superinsternō, **strāvī**, **strātum** ③ *v* lay on over the surface

superior, **ius** *adj* higher, upper, superior, better; past, previous; elder, stronger; victorious

supernē *adv* at or to a higher level, above; in the upper part; on top

supernus, **a**, **um** *adj* situated above

superō ① *v* climb over; overtop; rise to a higher level; get beyond; surpass; be superior; defeat, surmount; survive; be present in excess of one's needs; abound; remain; remain alive; be situated beyond; vanquish

superoccupō ① *v* take by

surprise from above

superpendēns, **ntis** *adj* overhanging

superpōnō, **posuī**, **positum** ③ *v* place over or on top; put in charge

superscandō ③ *v* climb over

supersedeō, **sēdī**, **sessum** ② *with abl* refrain (from), desist (from

superstagnō ① *v* spread in flood overflow

supersternō, **strāvī**, **strātum** ③ *v* spread or lay on top

superstes, **itis** *adj* outliving, surviving; standing over

superstitiō, **ōnis** *f* superstition; irrational religious awe

superstitiōsus, **a**, **um** *adj* superstitious, full of unreasoning religious awe

superstō ① *v* stand over or on top (of)

supersum, **esse**, **fuī** *v ir* have th strength (for); be superfluous (to be left over; remain alive, survive; remain to be performed

superus, **a**, **um** *adj* upper; earthly; heavenly; celestial
□ **superum mare** the Adriatic Sea
■ **superior** *comp*
■ **suprēmus** *sup*

supervacāneus, **a**, **um** *adj* redundant; unnecessary

supervacuus, **a**, **um** *adj* superfluous, redundant; unnecessary

supervādō ③ *v* surmount

supervehor, **vectus sum** ③ *v dep* ride, sail, *etc.*, over or past

superveniō, **vēnī**, **ventum** ④ *v* arrive on the scene; *with dat* come up (with a person, catching him in a given activity or situation)

supervolitō 🔲 v fly to and fro over

supervolō 🔲 v fly over

supīnō 🔲 v lay on the back; turn up; tilt back

supīnus, a, um adj lying face upwards, flat on one's back; turned palm upwards; directed or flowing backwards; flat, low-lying; languid, passive

suppeditō 🔲 v be available when required, supply the needs (of); make available as required; supply (with)

suppernātus, a, um adj having the leg cut from beneath, hamstrung

suppetiae, ārum fpl help, rescue

suppetō, īvī/iī, ītum 🔲 v turn up as a support, give backing (to); be available for one's needs; suggest itself

supplēmentum, ī nt supplement; reinforcement

suppleō, ēvī, ētum 🔲 v complete, fill up; make (a whole)

supplex, icis adj suppliant, making humble entreaty; expressing or involving supplication

supplicātiō, ōnis f offering of propitiation to a deity

suppliciter adv suppliantly, in an attitude of humble entreaty

supplicium, (i)ī nt act performed to propitiate a deity; punishment; torment; penalty, punishment

supplicō 🔲 v with dat make humble petition to; make propitiary

offerings to, do worship

suppōnō, posuī, positum 🔢 v place under; substitute; introduce fraudulently into a situation

supportō 🔲 v transport (supplies, etc.) to a centre

supprimō, pressī, pressum 🔢 v press down or under; suppress; keep back, contain; stop, check

suprā prep with acc above, over, on the upper side of; beyond; earlier than; more than

suprāscandō 🔢 v climb on top of

suprēma, ōrum ntpl funeral rites or offerings; last rites

suprēmus, a, um adj highest; topmost; last, latest, dying; greatest

□ **manus suprēma** finishing touches

sūra, ae f calf of the leg

surculus, ī m twig; cutting, graft

surditās, ātis f deafness

surdus, a, um adj deaf; unresponsive to what is said; falling on deaf ears; muffled, muted

surgō, surrēxī, surrēctum 🔢 v rise, get up; rouse oneself to action; stand high; grow tall

surrēpō, psī, ptum 🔢 v creep, creep (up to); steal on, insinuate itself

surripiō, puī, eptum 🔢 v steal, kidnap, remove by stealth

surrupiō ▶ surripiō

sūrsum adv upwards; on high, above

sūs, suis m/f pig, sow

suscipiō, cēpī, ceptum 🔢 v take (up), catch from below; support; receive; take under one's protection; adopt; undertake, perform; venture upon; accept; acknowledge (a new-born child); get or have a child

suscitō ① v dislodge, cause to rise; restore to health; venture upon; enter on the performance of; face, accept; rouse

suspectus, ūs m looking up; high regard

suspendium, (i)ī nt the act of hanging oneself

suspendō, ndī, nsum ③ v hang (up); keep poised; keep in suspense

suspēnsus, a, um adj in a state of anxious uncertainty or suspense; light

□ **suspēnsō gradū** on tiptoe

suspicāx, ācis adj mistrustful

suspiciō, spexī, spectum ③ v look upwards (at); look up at; esteem, admire; be suspicious of

suspiciō, ōnis f suspicion, mistrustful feeling; trace

suspicor ① v dep suspect; have an inkling of; infer

suspīrātus, ūs m sigh; deep breath

suspīritus, ūs m sigh

suspīrium, (i)ī nt sigh; heartthrob

suspīrō ① v sigh; utter with a sigh

sustentō ① v support, hold up; uphold, bear up against; delay

sustineō, tentum ② v hold up, support, sustain; stand up to, withstand; shoulder; have the necessary endurance (to); submit (to); endure; hold back

sustollō ③ v raise on high

sustulī ▸ tollō

susurrō ① v whisper; rustle

susurrus¹, ī m whisper, whispered report; soft rustling sound

susurrus², a, um adj whispering

sūtilis, e adj made by sewing, consisting of things stitched together

sūtor, ōris m shoemaker; cobbler

sūtrīnus, a, um adj of a shoe maker

sūtūra, ae f seam, stitch, piece of sewing

suus, a, um adj his own, her own, its own, their own; especially dear to him; belonging to him at birth; normal to him; due or allotted to him; convenient for him

syllaba, ae f syllable

symphōnia, ae f harmony, group of singers or musicians

synodus, ī m LM synod

Tt

tabānus, ī m gadfly

tabella, ae f tablet; voting-tablet board for games; placard; board; pl wax-coated wooden tablets, threaded together to form a notebook

tabellārius, (i)ī m letter-carrier, courier

tābeō ② v rot away, decay

taberna, ae f hut, booth, inn; tavern; shop or stall

tabernāculum, ī nt tent

tabernārius, (i)ī m shopkeeper

tradesman

tābēs, **bis** f wasting away; decay; putrefaction; fluid resulting from corruption or decay

tābēscō, **ī** ③ v waste or dwindle away; melt away; decompose

tābidus, **a**, **um** adj wasting away, emaciated, putrefying, rotten; accompanied by wasting

tābificus, **a**, **um** adj causing decay or wasting

tābitūdō, **inis** f wasting away

tabula, **ae** f board, plank; votive-tablet; writing-tablet; letter; will; panel; picture; game board; tablet of stone or metal set up as a permanent record; pl account-books; document; will

tabulārium, **(i)ī** nt collection of (inscribed) tablets; record-office, registry

tabulātiō, **ōnis** f structure of boards, boarding

tabulātum, **ī** nt floor, storey, tier formed by the horizontal branches of a tree

tābum, **ī** nt viscous fluid consisting of putrid matter, gore

taceō ② v be silent; say nothing about

taciturnitās, **ātis** f maintaining silence

taciturnus, **a**, **um** adj saying nothing, making no noise

tacitus, **a**, **um** adj silent; quiet; secret, hidden; unmentioned; tacit

tāctilis, **e** adj able to be touched

tāctus, **ūs** m touch, sense of touch

taeda, **ae** f pine-wood, pine-torch; wedding; pine-tree

taedet, **uit**, **taesum est** ② v impers with gen or infin and acc of person affected be tired or sick (of)

taedifer, **era**, **erum** adj torch-bearing

taedium, **(i)ī** nt weariness, ennui; an object of weariness

taenia, **ae** f ribbon

taeter, **tra**, **trum** adj foul, monstrous, vile, horrible

tālāria, **ium** ntpl skirts; winged sandals

tālāris, **e** adj reaching down to the ankles

tālea, **ae** f long, thin piece of wood, metal, etc.

talentum, **ī** nt talent of silver (currency)

tālis, **e** adj such, of such a kind; such (a)

talpa, **ae** f sometimes m mole (animal)

tālus, **ī** m ankle, ankle-bone; knuckle-bone of a sheep; pl the game played with such bones

tam adv so; so much (as)

tamen conj nevertheless, all the same; yet

   □ ~ **etsī** even though

tametsī conj even though

tamquam adv just as; just as if

tandem adv at length, at last, after some time; really, I ask you, after all

tangō, **tetigī**, **tāctum** ③ v touch; put one's hand on; reach; be next to, border on; arrive (at); affect, move; touch on, make a mention of

tantillus, **a**, **um** adj so small; so small a quantity

tantīsper adv for so long (as); for

the present

tantopere *adv* so very, to such a great degree

tantulus, a, um *adj* so small, such a little

tantum *adv* so much, to such a degree, so; only, just, merely
□ ∼ **nōn** all but, almost
□ ∼ **abest ut … ut …** it is so far from being the case that … (that the result is) that …

tantummodo *adv* only, merely

tantus, a, um *adj* so great

tantusdem, tantadem, tantundem *adj* just as great
■ **tantundem, ĭdem** *nt* the same quantity, just as much

tapēs, ētis *m*, **tapēte, is** *nt*, **tapētum, ī** *nt* woollen cloth or rug used as a covering, hanging, *etc.*

tarandrus, ī *m* reindeer

tardēscō ③ *v* become slow

tardipēs, edis *adj* slow-footed, lame

tarditās, ātis *f* slowness of movement, action, *etc.*

tardō ① *v* delay, check

tardus, a, um *adj* slow; tardy, late; dull, stupid

tarmes, itis *m* woodworm

Tartara, ōrum *ntpl*, **Tartarus, ī** *m* the infernal regions, the underworld

Tartareus, a, um *adj* of or belonging to the underworld; Tartarean

taurea, ae *f* leather whip

taureus, a, um *adj* derived from a bull

tauriḟōrmis, e *adj* having the

form of a bull

taurīnus, a, um *adj* of or derived from a bull; made of ox-hide

taurus, ī *m* bull; the constellation Taurus

taxus, ī *f* yew-tree

tē *acc/abl of* ▶ **tū**

techna, ae *f* trick, ruse

tēctum, ī *nt* roof; house, dwelling; (rough *or* improvised) shelter

tēgillum, ī *nt* piece of rush matting

tegimen, inis *nt* covering, cover

tegō, tēxī, tēctum ③ *v* cover; hide, conceal; roof over; shield, protect

tēgula, ae *f* roof-tile

tegumen, inis *nt*, **tegumentum, ī** *nt* ▶ **tegimen**

tēla, ae *f* cloth in the process of being woven on a loom; the upright threads in a loom; a loom

tellūs, ris *f* earth; ground

tēlum, ī *nt* missile, javelin; sword; (any offensive) weapon; sunbeam, thunderbolt

temerārius, a, um *adj* accidental; rash, foolhardy, thoughtless, reckless, hasty

temere *adv* blindly, heedlessly; without due thought or care; without reason; at random, casually; readily, easily

temeritās, ātis *f* recklessness, thoughtlessness, impetuosity

temerō ① *v* violate; defile, pollute; violate sexually

tēmētum, ī *nt* strong wine; intoxicating liquor

temnō ③ *v* scorn, despise

tēmō, ōnis *m* beam *or* pole of a cart, chariot, *etc.*; Charles's Wain

temperāns, ntis *adj* restrained, self-controlled

temperantia, ae *f* moderation, restraint, self-control

temperātus, a, um *adj* temperate, moderate

temperī *adv* at the right time, seasonably

temperiēs, iēī *f* mixture of substances, qualities, *etc.*, in due proportion; climate, temperateness; (moderate) temperature

temperō ① *v* exercise restraint, exercise moderation (in respect of); be moderate in one's conduct towards); restrain oneself, refrain from); temper; cause to moderate violence, *etc.*; modify; control physically; control, regulate

tempestās, ātis *f* portion of time, season; weather; storm; violent disturbance

tempestīvus, a, um *adj* seasonable; opportune, physically n one's prime, ripe (for marriage); timely

templum, ī *nt* temple, shrine; zone, space, region; plank

tempt-▸ tent-

temptō ① *v* (also **tentō**) handle, feel; attempt, try; prove; test; try out; attack; brave; make an attempt on

tempus, oris *nt* time, season; a sufficiency of time (for a particular purpose); opportunity; season (of the year); condition *pl* times; temples of the head

■ **temporī, temperī** *adv* at the right time

tēmulentus, a, um *adj* drunken

tenācitās, ātis *f* the quality of holding on to a thing

tenāx, ācis *adj* holding fast, tenacious; persistent, steadfast; stubborn, obstinate

tendō, tetendī, tentum/ tēnsum ③ *v* stretch out, extend; pitch tents; encamp; string *or* draw (a bow, *etc.*); distend; direct one's course, proceed; reach; exert oneself; aim (at); aim (to do)

tenebrae, ārum *fpl* darkness, obscurity; night; dark corner; ignorance; concealment; gloomy state of affairs; Ⓛ vespers

tenebricōsus, a, um *adj* dark

tenellulus, a, um *adj* tender, delicate

tenellus, a, um *adj* tender

teneō, tentum/tēnsum ② *v* hold, keep, possess; occupy; retain; hold a position; include; reach in journeying; maintain; detain, hold up; keep in check; bind

tener, era, erum *adj* soft, delicate, tender; immature, young; soft, effeminate

tenor, ōris *m* a sustained and even course of movement; course, tenor

tēnsa, ae *f* wagon on which the images of the gods were carried to public spectacles

tentābundus, a, um *adj* testing every stop *or* move

tentāmen, inis *nt* attempt, effort

tentāmentum, ī *nt* trial, attempt, experiment

tentō ① *v* handle, feel; attempt, try; prove; test; try out; attack;

brave; make an attempt on

tentōrium, (i)ī *nt* tent

tenuis, e *adj* thin, slender; slight, faint; fine; weak; trivial

tenuō ① *v* make thin; reduce, lessen; wear down

tenus *prep with abl* reaching to, as far as, up to

tepefaciō, fēcī, factum ③ *v* make warm

tepefactō ① *v* be in the habit of warming

tepeō ② *v* be (luke)warm; feel the warmth of love, glow; be lukewarm in one's feelings

tepēscō, puī ③ *v* become warm

tepidārium, (i)ī *nt* 'warm' room in Roman baths

tepidus, a, um *adj* lukewarm, tepid; mild, warm

tepor, ōris *m* warmth, mild heat

ter *adv* three times

terebinthus, ī *f* terebinth tree or its wood

terebrō ① *v* bore through, drill a hole in

teres, etis *adj* smooth and rounded

tergeminus, a, um *adj* threefold, triple

tergeō ② *v*, **tergō, rsī, rsum** ③ *v* rub clean, polish; press

tergiversor ① *v dep* turn one's back on a task or challenge; hang back

tergum, ī *nt*, **tergus, oris** *nt* back; hide, skin; surface
  □ **terga dō/vertō** to turn tail, flee
  □ **ā tergō** from behind

Terminālia, ium *ntpl* festival of

the god of boundaries (Terminus) on 23 February

terminātiō, ōnis *f* marking the boundaries of a territory

terminō ① *v* mark the boundaries of, form the boundaries of; restrict; conclude

terminus, ī *m* boundary, limit; end; post, stone, *etc.*, marking the boundary of a property

ternī, ae, a *adj* three each; three

terō, trīvī, trītum ③ *v* rub, bruise, grind; polish, rub smooth; wear out or away; handle constantly; use up (time)

terra, ae *f* earth; land, ground, soil; country; region

terrēnus, a, um *adj* belonging to the ground, earthy, earthly; mortal

terreō ② *v* terrorize, overawe, terrify; deter

terrestris, tre *adj* by or on land, terrestrial

terreus, a, um *adj* one born of the earth

terribilis, e *adj* frightening, terrible

terrificō ① *v* terrify

terrificus, a, um *adj* terrifying, awe-inspiring

terrigena, ae *m* one born of the earth

terriloquus, a, um *adj* uttering frightening words

territō ① *v* frighten, terrify; try to scare

terror, ōris *m* dread, terror

tersus, a, um *adj* neat, spruce

tertia, ae *f* [LM] terce (part of the daily cycle of prayer)

ertium *adv* for a third time

ertius, a, um *adj* third

essera, ae *f* square tile; die; tablet on which the password was written; fragment of earthenware, shard

esta, ae *f* object made from burnt clay; earthenware jar; fragment of earthenware, shard

estāmentum, ī *nt* will, testament

□ ~ **Vetus/Novum** LM Old/New Testament

estātiō, ōnis *f* action of testifying to a fact

estātus, a, um *adj* known on good evidence

estificor ③ *v dep* assert solemnly, testify (to a fact); demonstrate; invoke as a witness

estimōnium, (i)ī *nt* testimony; proof

estis¹, is *m/f* witness; spectator

estis², is *m* testicle

estor ③ *v dep* be a witness, testify (to); declare solemnly; invoke as a witness

estū *nt indec,* **testum, ī** *nt* earthenware pot

estūdineus, a, um *adj* made of tortoiseshell

estūdō, inis *f* tortoise; tortoise shell; roof; lyre; a covering formed of the shields of soldiers held over their heads; movable wooden screen for siege-engines or men engaged in siege operations

etendī ▸ tendō

etigī ▸ tangō

etrarchēs, ae *m* tetrarch (a minor king under Roman protection)

tetricus, a, um *adj* austere

tetulī *old pf of* ▸ **ferō**

texō, texuī, textum ③ *v* weave; plait (together); construct with elaborate care

textilis, e *adj* woven

textor, ōris *m* weaver

textum, ī *nt* woven fabric, cloth; framework; web

textūra, ae *f* weaving, texture

thalamus, ī *m* an inner chamber; bedroom; marriage

theātrālis, e *adj* theatrical, of the stage

theātrum, ī *nt* theatre

thermae, ārum *fpl* hot baths

thermopōlium, (i)ī *nt* hot-drink counter

thēsaurus, ī *m* treasure-chamber, vault; treasure

thiasus, ī *m* orgiastic Bacchic dance

tholus, ī *m* circular building with a domed roof, rotunda

thōrāx, ācis *m* breastplate, cuirass

Thrāx, ācis *m* Thracian; gladiator with sabre and short shield, gladiator

thronus, ī *m* throne

thymbra, ae *f* an aromatic plant, perhaps Cretan thyme

thymum, ī *nt* thyme

thynnus, ī *m* tunny-fish

thyrsus, ī *m* Bacchic wand tipped with a fir-cone, tuft of ivy or vine leaves

tiāra, ae *f,* **tiārās, ae** *m* ornamented felt head-dress

tibī *pn dat of* ▸ **tū**

tībia, **ae** f reed-pipe

tībīcen, **inis** m piper, prop

tībīcina, **ae** f female performer on the **tībia**

tigillum, **ī** nt small plank or beam

tīgnum, **ī** nt timber, beam, board

tigris, **is**/**idis** m/f tiger; tigress

tilia, **ae** f lime-tree

timeō 2 v fear, be afraid (of); be afraid (to)

timidus, **a**, **um** adj fearful, timid

timor, **ōris** m fear; object or source of fear

tīnctilis, **e** adj obtained by dipping

tīnctus, **ūs** m dyeing; dipping

tinea, **ae** f grub, maggot

tinnīmentum, **ī** nt ringing sound

tinnītus, **ūs** m ringing, clanging, jangling

tinnulus, **a**, **um** adj emitting a ringing or jangling sound

tintinnō, **tintinō** 1 v make a ringing or jangling sound

tīnus, **ī** m laurustinus (kind of bay-tree)

tīrō, **ōnis** m recruit; beginner, novice

tīrōcinium, **(i)ī** nt inexperience in military service; first campaign; apprenticeship, youthful inexperience

tītillō 1 v tickle, titillate; provoke; stimulate sensually

titubō 1 v stagger, totter; falter

titulus, **ī** m placard, tablet, label; inscription; title; pretext; distinction, honour

tōfus, **ī** m tufa

toga, **ae** f the formal outer

garment of a Roman citizen, toga; peace;

□ **toga candida** toga worn by candidates for office

□ **toga virīlis** toga worn by adults (without the purple border)

togātus, **a**, **um** adj dressed in or wearing a toga; having a civilian occupation

tolerābilis, **e** adj bearable, tolerable, patient; able to be withstood

tolerō 1 v bear, endure, tolerate; support; provide food for

tollō, **sustulī**, **sublātum** 3 v lift, raise; acknowledge (a new-born child); remove; eliminate; steal

tolūtim adv at a trot

tōmentum, **ī** nt stuffing

tondeō, **totondī**, **tōnsum** 2 v shear, clip; prune back; browse on

tonitrus, **ūs** m thunder

tonō, **nuī**, **nitum** 1 v thunder; speak in thunderous tones, utter thunderously; make or resound with a noise like thunder

tōnsa, **ae** f oar

tōnstrīna, **ae** f barber's shop

tōnsūra, **ae** f shearing, clipping

tormentum, **ī** nt twisted rope; machine for discharging missiles in war, catapult, ballista, etc.; torture, torment

tornus, **ī** m turner's lathe

torōsus, **a**, **um** adj muscular, brawny

torpeō 2 v be numb or lethargic; be struck motionless from fear

torpēscō, **puī** 3 v grow numb, become slothful

torpidus, **a**, **um** adj numbed,

paralysed

torpor, **ōris** *m* numbness, torpor, paralysis

torquātus, **a**, **um** *adj* wearing a collar *or* necklace

torqueō, **torsī**, **tortum** ② *v* turn, twist; hurl; torture; torment; bend, distort; spin, whirl; wind (round)

torquēs, **torquis**, **quis** *m/f* collar of twisted metal; wreath

torrēns¹, **ntis** *m* torrent, rushing stream

torrēns², **ntis** *adj* burning hot; rushing; torrential

torreō, **tostum** ② *v* parch, roast, scorch, burn; dry up

torrēscō ③ *v* be scorched

torridus, **a**, **um** *adj* parched, dried up; shrivelled, desiccated

torris, **is** *m* firebrand

tortilis, **e** *adj* twisted, coiled

tortor, **ōris** *m* torturer

tortuōsus, **a**, **um** *adj* winding; tortuous

tortus, **a**, **um** *adj* crooked, twisted

torus, **ī** *m* muscle; marriage-bed, marriage; bolster, cushion; couch

torvus, **a**, **um** *adj* pitiless, grim; savage

tot *adj indec* so many

totidem *adj indec* the same number as, as many

tōtus, **a**, **um** *adj* all, the whole of, entire

toxicum, **ī** *nt* poison

trabālis, **e** *adj* of *or* used for wooden beams

trabea, **ae** *f* short purple *or* partly purple garment

trabēs, **trabs**, **bis** *f* tree-trunk, beam, timber; ship

tractābilis, **e** *adj* manageable; tractable; easy to deal with

tractātiō, **ōnis** *f* management; treatment; discussion

tractim *adv* in a long-drawn-out manner

tractō ① *v* handle, manage; practise; manipulate; perform; examine, discuss, treat (a subject)

tractus, **ūs** *m* dragging *or* pulling along; drawing out; extent; tract, region; lengthening

trādō, **didī**, **ditum** ③ *v* hand *or* pass over; deliver; surrender; hand down, bequeath; entrust; introduce; relate, tell of

trādūcō, **dūxī**, **ductum** ③ *v* lead *or* bring across *or* over; lead along *or* parade; transfer; convert

tragicus, **a**, **um** *adj* tragic; suitable to tragedy

 ■ **tragicus**, **ī** *m* tragic poet, tragic actor

tragoedia, **ae** *f* tragedy

tragoedus, **ī** *m* tragic actor

trāgula, **ae** *f* spear fitted with a throwing strap

trahea, **ae** *f* a drag used as a threshing implement

trahō, **āxī**, **actum** ③ *v* draw, drag, haul; drag along; trail; draw *or* stretch out; extend; contract; drink; breathe in; carry off as plunder; attract; protract, delay; spend *or* get through (time)

trāiciō, **iēcī**, **iectum** ③ *v* throw, cast *or* shoot over *or* across; convey across, transport; transfix, thrust through; transfer; cross over

trāiectus, **ūs** *m* crossing over;

trāma, ae f cloth

trāmes, itis m footpath; track; bed (of a stream)

trānō ① v swim across or through; fly across

tranquillitās, ātis f tranquillity; calmness, fair weather

tranquillus, a, um adj quiet, calm, still, peaceful
■ **tranquillum, ī** nt calm weather; calm state of affairs

trāns prep with acc across, over, beyond, through

trānsabeō, īre, iī v ir go away beyond

trānsadigō, ēgī, āctum ③ v pierce through; thrust through

trānscendō, ndī, ēnsum ③ v climb or step over, transgress, overstep

trānscrībō, psī, ptum ③ v copy; transfer

trānscurrō, (cu)currī, cursum ③ v run across; run or hasten through

trānscursus, ūs m rapid movement across a space

trānsd- ▶ **trād-**

trānsdūcō, dūxī, ductum ③ v (also **trādūcō**) lead or bring across or over; lead along or parade; transfer; convert

trānsenna, ae f snare (for birds)

trānseō, īre, iī/īvī, itum v ir go over or across, pass over; pass by; go through; go over (to a side, etc.); omit, say nothing of; pass away

trānsferō, ferre, tulī, lātum v ir carry or bring over; transport; transfer; bring over (to a new

course of action)

trānsfīgō, īxī, īxum ③ v pierce through; thrust (through)

trānsfodiō, ōdī, ossum ③ v dig through to the other side of; run through

trānsfōrmis, e adj that undergoes transformation

trānsfōrmō ① v change in shape, transform

trānsfuga, ae m deserter

trānsfugiō, ī ③ v go over to the enemy, desert

trānsfugium, (i)ī nt desertion

trānsgredior, gressus sum ③ v dep step over; change one's policy; surpass; omit

trānsgressus, ūs m crossing to the other side

trānsigō, ēgī, āctum ③ v thrust or run through, pierce through; come to terms about, settle; conclude, finish

trānsiliō, siluī/silīvī ④ v leap across or over; skip; overstep, exceed

trānsitiō, ōnis f passing over, passage; desertion; infection, contagion

trānsitus, ūs m passage; passage over; transition

trānslūceō ② v shine through or across; be transparent

trānslūcidus, a, um adj transparent

trānsmarīnus, a, um adj (from over the sea

trānsmigrō ① v change one's residence from one place to another

trānsmissus, ūs m crossing

trānsmittō, īsī, issum v send or pass over; go to the other side of; travel to the other side (of)

trānsmūtō v change about

trānsnō v swim across, sail across; swim to the other side

trānsportō v carry across; convey across

trānstrum, ī nt cross-beam; rower's seat

trānsultō v spring across

trānsuō, suī, ūtum v pierce through

trānsvehō, ēxī, ectum v carry across; carry past
  □ **trānsvehor** sail, ride or travel to the other side

trānsverberō v transfix

trānsversus, a, um adj lying across, moving across

trānsvolitō v fly over or through

trānsvolō v fly across

trāvehō ▸ trānsvehō

trecēnī, ae, a adj three hundred each; three hundred; lots of three hundred (men)

trecentī, ae, a adj three hundred; (used to denote a large number)

tredecim adj indec thirteen

tremebundus, a, um adj trembling, quivering, vibrating

tremefaciō, fēcī, factum v cause to tremble

tremendus, a, um adj terrible, awe-inspiring

tremēscō v tremble, quiver, vibrate; tremble at

tremō, muī v tremble, quake; tremble (at)

tremor, ōris m trembling, shuddering; quivering, quaking

tremulus, a, um adj shaking; moving tremulously; quivering

trepidanter adv tremblingly, anxiously

trepidātiō, ōnis f trepidation, perturbation

trepidō v be in a state of alarm or trepidation; scurry, bustle; tremble, quiver, shake; be nervous

trepidus, a, um adj alarmed, anxious; marked by apprehensiveness or alarm; behaving in an excited manner; quivering, trembling

trēs, tria adj three

trēsvirī, ōrum mpl board of three

triāriī, ōrum mpl the third line of the early Roman army; the reserves

tribūlis, is m fellow tribesman

tribūnal, ālis nt dais, platform

tribūnātus, ūs m the office of tribune

tribūnicius, a, um adj belonging to a tribune
  ■ **tribūnicius, (i)ī** m ex-tribune

tribūnus, ī m tribune; military tribune

tribuō, uī, ūtum v grant, bestow, award (to); allocate

tribus, ūs f (division of the people) tribe

tribūtim adv by tribes

tribūtum, ī nt tribute, tax

tribūtus, a, um adj organized by tribes

trīcae, ārum fpl tricks, nonsense, complications

trīclīnium, (i)ī nt dining-room

tricorpor, oris adj having three bodies

tricuspis, **idis** *adj* having three prongs

tridēns, **ntis** *adj* three-pronged ■ ~, **ntis** *m* trident

tridentifer, **tridentiger**, **erī** *m* carrying a trident

trīduum, **ī** *nt* space of three days; [LM] esp. the final three days of Holy Week (i.e. Maundy Thursday, Good Friday and Holy Saturday)

triennia, **ium** *ntpl* triennial festival

triennium, **(i)ī** *nt* period of three years

triēns, **ntis** *m* third part, third; third part of an **as**

trietēricus, **a**, **um** *adj* triennial ■ **trietērica**, **ōrum** *ntpl* triennial rites

trietēris, **idis** *f* period of three years

trifāriam *adv* in three ways, into three parts

trifaucis, **e** *adj* having three throats

trifidus, **a**, **um** *adj* divided to form three prongs

trifolium, **(i)ī** *nt* clover

trifōrmis, **e** *adj* of three forms, triple, threefold

trīgeminus, **a**, **um** *adj* born as one of triplets

trīgintā *adj indec* thirty

trilībris, **bre** *adj* of three pounds weight

trilinguis, **e** *adj* that has three tongues

trilīx, **īcis** *adj* having a triple thread

trīmus, **a**, **um** *adj* three years old

trīnī, **ae**, **a** *adj* three in each case, three at a time; three, triple

trinitas, **tatis** *f* [LM] the Trinity

trinōdis, **e** *adj* having three knots or bosses

triōbolum, **ī** *nt* three-obol piece (a trivial sum)

Triōnēs, **um** *mpl* the constellations Great and Little Bea

tripēs, **edis** *adj* three-legged

triplex, **icis** *adj* threefold, triple, tripartite

tripudiō *ī* v leap, jump, dance, caper

tripudium, **(i)ī** *nt* solemn religious dance; favourable omen (when the sacred chickens ate so greedily that the food dropped to the ground)

tripūs, **podis** *m often in pl* three-legged stand, tripod; the oracle at Delphi

triquetrus, **tra**, **trum** *adj* three-cornered, triangular

trirēmis, **e** *adj* having three oars to each bench ■ **trirēmis**, **is** *f* trireme

trīste *adv* sadly, sorrowfully; harshly, severely

tristis, **e** *adj* depressed, gloomy, unhappy; bitter; ill-humoured; stern, austere; unhappy; grim, unpleasant; sour

trīstitia, **ae** *f* unhappiness, despondency, gloom; sourness

trisulcus, **a**, **um** *adj* divided into three forks or prongs

trīticeus, **a**, **um** *adj* of wheat

trīticum, **ī** *nt* wheat

trītūra, **ae** *f* rubbing, friction; threshing

trītus, **a**, **um** *adj* well-trodden,

well-worn; worn; common; familiar

riumphālis, **e** *adj* of or associated with the celebration of a triumph; having triumphal status; triumphant
■ **triumphālia**, **ium** *ntpl* the insignia of a triumph

riumphō 🔟 *v* triumph; celebrate a triumph; exult, triumph over

riumphus, **ī** *m* triumphal procession, triumph

triumvir, **rī** *m* one of the three **triumvirī**, who were the 'board of three' or triumvirate
□ **triumvirī capitālēs** superintendents of public prisons and executions

riumvirātus, **ūs** *m* triumvirate

rivium, **(i)ī** *nt* place where three roads meet; 'the gutter'; 🔠 the three 'lower' subjects of the medieval university curriculum, viz. grammar, rhetoric and logic

rivius, **a**, **um** *adj* having a temple at a spot where three roads meet

roc(h)lea, **ae** *f* a block with pulleys, block-and-tackle equipment

rochus, **ī** *m* metal hoop (used for games or exercise)

roclea ▸ trochlea

rōiugena, **ae** *adj* born of Trojan stock

ropa *adv* in a drinking game

ropaeum, **ī** *nt* trophy; monument, victory

ropice *adv* 🔠 figuratively

rucidātiō, **ōnis** *f* slaughtering, massacre

rucidō 🔟 *v* slaughter, butcher, massacre

---

triumphālis | tum

truculentus, **a**, **um** *adj* ferocious, aggressive

trudis, **dis** *f* metal-tipped pole; barge-pole

trūdō, **ūsī**, **ūsum** ③ *v* thrust, push, shove; drive, force; drive on

trulla, **ae** *f* scoop, ladel

trulleus, **ī** *m* wash-basin

truncō 🔟 *v* maim, mutilate; strip of branches, foliage; cut off

truncus¹, **ī** *m* trunk (of a tree); body of a man, trunk, torso

truncus², **a**, **um** *adj* maimed, mutilated, dismembered; trimmed of its branches; stunted in growth

trusō 🔟 *v* keep pushing or thrusting

trux, **cis** *adj* harsh, savage, pitiless, cruel

tū *pn* you (*sg*)

tuba, **ae** *f* (straight) trumpet; war-trumpet

tūber, **eris** *nt* tumour, protuberance, excrescence

tubicen, **inis** *m* trumpeter

Tubilūstrium, **(i)ī** *nt* feast of trumpets (on 23 March and 23 May)

tueor ② *v dep* look at, scan, view; keep safe, protect, watch over; preserve from danger; defend; look after; uphold
□ **torva ~** look grim

tugurium, **(i)ī** *nt* primitive dwelling, hut, shack

tulī ▸ ferō

tum *adv* then; at that time; besides; afterwards; in that case; at that moment
□ **quid tum?** what then? what further?

tumefaciō | turgeō

□ **tum ... tum** both ... and; ...
as well as ...; first ... then; at this
moment ... at that moment

□ **cum ... tum** both ... and
especially; not only ... but also

□ **tum dēmum, tum dēnique**
then and not till then

□ **tum prīmum** then for the
first time

tumefaciō, fēcī, factum ③ v
cause to swell; puff up

tumeō ② v swell, become inflated;
be puffed up; be bombastic;
be swollen with conceit,
presumption, *etc.*

tumēscō, mui ③ v (begin to)
swell; become inflamed with
pride, passion, *etc.*

tumidus, a, um adj swollen,
swelling, distended; puffed up
with pride or self-confidence;
bombastic

tumor, ōris m swollen or
distended condition; swell (of the
sea, waves); excitement, passion,
conceit

tumulō ① v cover with a burial
mound

tumulōsus, a, um adj full of
hillocks

tumultuārius, a, um adj raised
to deal with a sudden emergency;
improvised; unplanned; haphazard

tumultuātiō, ōnis f confused
uproar

tumultuō ① v, **tumultuor** ① v
dep make a confused uproar; make
an armed rising

tumultuōsus, a, um adj
turbulent, full of commotion or
uproar

tumultus, ūs m tumult, uproar,
disturbance; turbulence; alarm;

agitation (of the mind or feelings)
sudden outbreak of violence or
disorder; muddle

tumulus, ī m rounded hill, knoll;
burial-mound, grave

tunc adv then, at the very time,
at that

tundō, tutudī, tū(n)sum ③ v
beat; bruise; pulp, crush

tunica, ae f tunic

tunicātus, a, um adj wearing
a tunic

turba, ae f disorder; dense or
disorderly mass of people,
multitude, crowd; confusion,
disturbance

turbāmentum, ī nt means of
disturbing

turbātiō, ōnis f disturbance

turbātor, ōris m one who
disturbs

turbidus, a, um adj wild,
confused, disordered; muddy,
turbid; foggy; troubled, turbulent
gloomy; unruly, mutinous

turbineus, a, um adj gyrating
like a spinning-top

turbō¹ ① v disturb, confuse,
trouble, disorder; make muddy
or turbid

turbō², inis m whirlwind, tornad[]
whirlpool, eddy; spinning-top;
whirling motion; whorl or fly-
wheel of a spindle

turbulentus, a, um adj violentl[]
disturbed, stormy, turbulent;
turbid; marked by turmoil or
violent unrest; unruly, riotous

turdus, ī m thrush

tūreus, a, um adj of or connecte[]
with incense

turgeō, tursī ② v swell out,

become swollen or tumid

turgēscō ③ v begin to swell

turgidulus, a, um adj (poor little) swollen

turgidus, a, um adj swollen, inflated

tūribulum, ī nt censer, thurible

tūricremus, a, um adj burning incense

tūrifer, era, erum adj yielding or producing incense

tūrilegus, a, um adj incense-gathering

turma, ae f small troop, squadron (of cavalry); company

turmālis, e adj belonging to a squadron of cavalry

turmātim adv in troops or squadrons of cavalry

turpiculus, a, um adj somewhat ugly

turpis, e adj ugly; foul; disgraceful, dishonourable, degrading; loathsome; guilty of disgraceful behaviour; indecent, obscene

turpō ① v make ugly; pollute, disfigure

turriger, era, erum adj bearing a tower; wearing a turreted crown

turris, is f tower; howdah

turrītus, a, um adj crowned with towers; tower-shaped

turtur, uris m turtle-dove

tūs, tūris nt frankincense

tussicula, ae f slight cough

tussis, is f cough

tūtāmen, inis nt,

tūtāmentum, ī nt means of protection

tūte [= tū + te] you yourself

tūtēla, ae f protection, guardianship, tutelage, defence; charge

tūtō ① v, **tūtor** ① v dep guard, protect, defend; guard against, avert

tūtor, oris m protector; guardian

tūtus, a, um adj safe, secure; watchful; free from risk; that may safely be trusted
  ■ **tūtō** adv safely

tuus, a, um adj your (sg)

ty(m)panum, ī nt small drum; revolving cylinder

tȳphōn, nis m whirlwind, cyclone

tyrannis, idis f tyranny, position or rule of a tyrant

tyrannus, ī m despot, tyrant; monarch

Uu

ūber, eris adj plentiful, abundant, copious; rich, luxuriant, fertile
  ■ ~, **eris** nt teat, pap, udder; soil rich in nourishing quality; fertility

ūbertās, ātis f fruitfulness, fertility; abundance, plenty

ūbertim adv plentifully, copiously

ubī adv where; where? when

ubī cumque adv wherever; in any place whatever

ubinam adv where in the world?

ubiquāque adv everywhere

ubique adv everywhere, anywhere, wherever

ubivīs adv anywhere you like, no

matter where

ūdus, **a**, **um** adj wet

ulcerō [1] v cause to fester

ulcerōsus, **a**, **um** adj full of sores

ulcīscor, **ultus sum** [3] v dep take vengeance (on) or revenge (for); avenge

ulcus, **eris** nt ulcer, sore

ūlīgō, **inis** f waterlogged ground, marsh

ūllus, **a**, **um** (gen, **ūllīus**) adj any, any one

ulmeus, **a**, **um** adj of elm

ulmus, **ī** f elm-tree; elm-wood

ulna, **ae** f forearm; the span of the outstretched arms

ulterior, **ius** f farther away, more distant; additional, further

ulterius adv farther away; to a further degree; any more

ultimus, **a**, **um** adj last; utmost; farthest; greatest; lowest, meanest; least; latest; earliest □ **ultima ratiō** the last resort

ultiō, **ōnis** f revenge, vengeance, retribution

ultor, **ōris** m avenger, revenger

ultrā adv beyond, farther off, more, besides; prep with acc beyond, past; more than

ultrīx, **īcis** f adj avenging, vengeful

ultrō adv into the bargain; conversely; of one's own accord, on one's own initiative
■ ~ **tē** int away with you!
□ ~ **citrōque** to and fro

ultus pple from ▶ **ulcīscor**

ulula, **ae** f the tawny owl

ululātus, **ūs** m howling, yelling

ululō [1] v howl, yell, shriek; celebrate or proclaim with howling

ulva, **ae** f sedge

umbilīcus, **ī** m navel; centre of a country, region; ornamental end of the cylinder on which a book was rolled, middle, centre

umbō, **ōnis** m boss (of a shield)

umbra, **ae** f shade, shadow; ghost (of a dead person); sheltered conditions, privacy; darkness; empty form, phantom

umbrāculum, **ī** nt shelter, shade; parasol

umbrifer, **era**, **erum** adj providing shade, shady

umbrō [1] v cast a shadow on, shade

umbrōsus, **a**, **um** adj shady, shadowy

ūmectō [1] v moisten, make wet

ūmeō [2] v be wet; be moist

umerus, **erī** m shoulder

ūmēscō [3] v become moist or wet

ūmidulus, **a**, **um** adj somewhat moist

ūmidus, **a**, **um** adj moist, wet; full of sap

ūmor, **ōris** m moisture; liquid; bodily fluid or discharge

umquam adv at any time, ever; at some time

ūnā adv at the same time; in one company, together

ūnanimitās, **ātis** f unity of purpose, concord

ūnanimus, **a**, **um** adj acting in accord

uncia, **ae** f twelfth part, twelfth; ounce; inch

unciārius, **a**, **um** adj concerned with a twelfth part

unciatim adv ounce by ounce

ūnctitō | urgeō

ūnctitō 1 *v* smear often

ūnctus, a, um *adj* oily, greasy; anointed, oiled

ūncus¹, ī *m* hook; hook used to drag executed criminals, clamp

ūncus², a, um *adj* hooked, curved round at the extremity

ūnda, ae *f* wave, sea; sea-water; river, spring; water; advancing mass

ūnde *adv* from what place? where ... from? whence? from whom; out of which; from what source, cause, *etc.*? from what stock, family, rank, *etc.*?

ūndecim *adj indec* eleven

ūndecimus, a, um *adj* eleventh

ūndēvīgintī *adj indec* nineteen

ūndique *adv* from all sides or directions, from every side or place; in all respects

ūndō 1 *v* rise in waves; surge, seethe; well up; billow; undulate

ūndōsus, a, um *adj* abounding in waves, flowing water, *etc.*

ūnetvīcēsimānus, a, um *adj* of the 21st legion

ūngō ► **unguō**

ūnguen, inis *nt* fat, grease

ūnguentārius, (i)ī *m* dealer in ointments, maker of ointments

ūnguentātus, a, um *adj* anointed or greased with ointments

ūnguentum, ī *nt* ointment, unguent

ūnguis, is *m* nail (of a human finger or toe), claw, talon, hoof
□ **ad/in unguem** to an exact measurement or standard

ūngula, ae *f* hoof

unguō, ūnxī, ūnctum 3 *v* smear with oil, grease, *etc.*; anoint with oil, unguents, *etc.*

ūnicē *adv* to a singular degree; especially

ūnicus, a, um *adj* one and only, sole; unique, singular

ūnigena, ae *adj* one sharing a single parentage, *i.e.* brother or sister

ūnigenitus, a, um *adj* LM only-begotten

ūnimanus, a, um *adj* one-handed

ūniter *adv* so as to form a singular entity

ūniversus, a, um *adj* occurring all at once; the whole of, entire; whole; *pl* all without exception; taken all together

unquam ► **umquam**

ūnus, a, um *adj* one; a, an; only; a single, alone, sole; one and the same; the one and only; a certain
□ **in ūnum** so as to form a single mass
□ **ad ūnum** to a man; without exception

ūnusquisque, ūnaquaeque, ūnumquodque/ **ūnumquidque** *pn* everyone

urbānitās, ātis *f* sophistication, polish, suavity

urbānus, a, um *adj* of or belonging to the city; elegant, sophisticated, witty; polished, refined

urbs, bis *f* city; (city of) Rome

urgeō, ursī 2 *v* press, squeeze; push, thrust, shove; spur on; weigh down; be oppressive to; press hard in attack; follow hard on the heels

of; crowd in; 'keep on at'; pursue
with vigour

ūrīnātor, ōris m diver

urna, ae f water-jar; urn; cinerary
urn; urn used in drawing lots;
voting urn; (fig) urn of fate; a liquid
measure (about thirteen litres)

ūrō, ussī, ustum ③ v burn; burn
up; destroy by fire; scorch; make
sore, cause to smart; corrode;
inflame with desire; keep alight

ursa, ae f she-bear; Great Bear

ursus, ī m bear

urtica, ae f stinging-nettle

ūrūca, ae f caterpillar

ūrus, ī m aurochs, the long-horned
wild ox of primeval Europe

ūsitātus, a, um adj familiar,
everyday

uspiam adv anywhere,
somewhere

usquam adv at or in any place,
anywhere; to any place; at any
juncture

ūsque adv continuously,
constantly; all along, all the way;
all the while, as long or as far
as, until
■ ~ **ad** with acc right up to

ūsquequāque adv in every
conceivable situation; wholly,
altogether

ustor, ōris m someone employed
to burn dead bodies

ustulō ① v scorch, char, burn
partially

ūsūcapiō, cēpī, captum ③ v
acquire ownership of (a thing) by
virtue of uninterrupted possession

ūsūrpō ① v make use of; employ;
practise, perform; carry out; take
possession of; take to oneself;

assert one's possession of (a
right or privilege) by exercising
it; make frequent use of (a word,
expression); call habitually (by a
name); speak habitually of (as)

ūsus, ūs m use, employment;
practical experience; practice;
habitual dealings; value, utility;
requirement, need

ut adv/conj (also **utī**) in what
manner, how; in the manner that,
as; however; such as; for, as being,
inasmuch as; how much or greatly
when, as soon as
□ **ut ... ita** as well as ... no less;
while ... while; conj so that; in order
that; as if; as if it were; to wit,
namely; although; as is usual

utcumque, utcunque adv in
whatever manner or degree; no
matter how; whenever; in any
event; as best one can

utēnsilia, ium ntpl necessaries

ūter, tris m leather bag for wine,
oil, etc.; inflated bag to keep one
afloat

uter, tra, trum adj whichever or
which of the two, either one of
the two

uterque, utraque, utrumque
pn each of the two

uterus, erī m womb; belly,
abdomen

utī ▶ **ut**

ūtibilis, e adj useful, serviceable

ūtilis, e adj useful, serviceable,
advantageous, profitable, helpful

ūtilitās, ātis f the quality of
being useful, usefulness, utility,
advantage, expediency

utinam adv how I wish that! if
only!

utīque *adv* in any case; certainly; at all costs

ūtor, ūsus sum ③ *v dep with abl* use, make use of, employ, apply, enjoy; practise, exercise; experience

utpote *adv* as one might expect, as is natural

utrārius, (i)ī *m* water-carrier

utrimque *adv* from *or* on both sides; at both ends

utrō *adv* to which side (of two)

utrobīque ▸ utrubīque

utrōque *adv* to both sides, in both directions

utrubīque *adv* in both places; in both cases

utrum *adv* whether; whether?

ūtut *adv* however, in whatever manner

ūva, ae *f* grapes; bunch of grapes; cluster

ūvēscō ③ *v* become wet

ūvidulus, a, um *adj* wet, damp

ūvidus, a, um *adj* wet, soaked, dripping; moistened with drinking

uxor, ōris *f* wife
□ **uxōrem dūcō** marry (a woman), take as wife

uxōrius, a, um *adj* of *or* belonging to a wife; excessively fond of one's wife

Vv

vacātiō, ōnis *f* exemption, immunity; vacation; exemption from military service

vacca, ae *f* cow

vaccīnium, (i)ī *nt* whortleberry

vacēfīō, fierī *v ir semi-dep* become empty

vacillō ① *v* stagger, totter; be in a weak condition

vacō ① *v* be empty or unfilled; be without occupants; be devoid (of), be free (from); be available (for); have leisure; be unemployed; have time for
□ **vacat** there is room, space or opportunity (to)

vacuō ① *v* empty

vacuus, a, um *adj* empty, void; insubstantial; destitute or devoid (of); empty-handed; plain, bare; unobstructed, clear; unoccupied, deserted; ownerless; idle, having leisure; fancy-free

vadimōnium, (i)ī *nt* bail, security, surety

vādō ③ *v* go, advance, proceed

vador ① *v dep* accept sureties from (the other party) for his appearance or reappearance in court at an appointed date

vadōsus, a, um *adj* full of shallows

vadum, ī *nt* shallow, ford; bottom of the sea; shoal; *pl* waters

vae *int* ah! alas! woe!
□ ~ **victīs** alas for the

vafer | variō

conquered!

vafer, fra, frum *adj* sly, cunning, crafty

vagē *adv* so as to move in different directions over a wide area

vāgīna, ae *f* scabbard, sheath

vāgiō ④ *v* utter cries of distress, wail, squall

vāgītus, ūs *m* cry of distress, wail, howl, squalling

vagor ① *v dep* wander, roam, rove; move freely to and fro; vary, fluctuate

vagus, a, um *adj* roving, wandering; moving at random, shifting, inconstant; scattered

valdē *adv* in a high degree, intensely, strongly; exceedingly

valēns, ntis *adj* strong, stout, vigorous; healthy; powerful; potent, effective

valeō ② *v* be healthy, be well; be strong *or* vigorous; have the ability *or* power to; take effect; be powerful; have influence; be worth
□ **valēre iubeō/dīcō** to bid farewell *or* goodbye
□ **valē!** goodbye!

valēscō ③ *v* become sound in health; become powerful

valētūdō, inis *f* health, soundness; good health; bad health, indisposition, illness

validus, a, um *adj* strong, stout, sturdy, powerful; healthy, sound, well; fit, active; brisk; influential, telling

vāllāris, e *adj*
□ **corōna ~** crown *or* garland awarded to the first soldier to cross the **vāllum** surrounding an enemy camp

vāllō ① *v* surround *or* fortify (a camp, *etc.*) with a palisaded rampart; furnish with a palisade

vāllum, ī *nt* a palisade of stakes on top of an **agger**, a palisaded earthwork

vāllus, ī *m* stake; palisade, palisaded earthwork

valvae, ārum *fpl* double *or* folding-door

vānēscō ③ *v* melt into nothingness, vanish; become useless

vāniloquentia, ae *f* idle talk, chatter; boastful speech

vānitās, ātis *f* emptiness; untruthfulness; futility, foolishness; empty pride; fickleness

vannus, ī *f* winnowing basket

vānus, a, um *adj* empty, hollow, illusory; vain, useless; foolish, fatuous, trifling; silly; unreliable, ineffectual; devoid (of)

vapor, ōris *m* steam, exhalation, vapour; heat

vapōrō ① *v* cover *or* fill with vapour; heat, warm; be hot

vappa, ae *f* flat wine
■ ~, **ae** *m* a worthless person

vāpulō ① *v* be beaten *or* thrashed; be battered

variantia, ae *f* diversity, variety

variātiō, ōnis *f* divergence of behaviour

vāricus, a, um *adj* straddling

varietās, ātis *f* diversity, variety; change, vicissitude

variō ① *v* mark with contrasting colours, variegate; vary; cause (opinions) to be divided; waver; fluctuate, undergo changes

arius, a, um *adj* variegated; arious; changeable, inconstant; vavering; multifarious; many-ided

kirus, a, um *adj* bent-outwards; andy; bow-legged; contrasting

as, adis *m* surety

as, sis *nt*, **vāsa, ōrum** *ntpl* vessel, tensil; equipment, kit

asculum, ī *nt* cooking utensil

nstātiō, ōnis *f* flaying waste, avaging

astātor, ōris *m* destroyer, avager

astitās, ātis *f* desolation; evastation

astō v leave desolate; plunder, estroy, lay waste; ravage

astus, a, um *adj* desolate; vast, uge, enormous; awe-inspiring; umsy, ungainly

ātēs, ātis *m/f* prophet; poet, bard

āticinātiō, ōnis *f* prophesying, redicting

āticinātor, ōris *m* prophet

āticinor v dep prophesy; rave, alk wildly

āticinus, a, um *adj* prophetic

ve *conj* or

ēcordia, ae *f* frenzy

ēcors, rdis *adj* mad; frenzied

ectīgal, ālis *nt* revenue derived rom public property

ectīgālis, e *adj* yielding taxes, subject to taxation

ectis, is *m* crowbar, lever

ectō v carry, convey
□ **vector** ride, travel

ector, ōris *m* passenger; one hat carries or transports

vectōrius, a, um *adj* used for transporting or conveying

vectūra, ae *f* transportation, carriage; charge for transportation

vegetus, a, um *adj* vigorous, active

vēgrandis, e *adj* far from large, puny

vehemēns, ntis *adj* violent, vehement; vigorous, powerful, strong

vehiculum, ī *nt* cart, wagon

vehō, ēxī, ectum v carry, convey
□ **vehor** ride; sail; travel

vel *conj* or; even; for instance; or rather; even; *with sup* quite, altogether
□ **vel ... vel** either ... or

vēlāmen, inis *nt* covering, clothing

vēlāmentum, ī *nt* cover; olive-branch wrapped in wool carried by a suppliant

velatus, a, um *adj* **LM** veiled

vēles, itis *m* light-armed foot-soldier

vēlifer, era, erum *adj* carrying a sail

vēlitāris, e *adj* of or belonging to the **vēlitēs**

vēlivolus, a, um *adj* speeding along under sail; characterized by speeding sails

velle *infin* from ▶ **volō**

vellicō v pinch, nip; criticize carpingly

vellō, vellī/vulsī, ulsum v pluck or pull out, tear or pull up; tug at, pluck

vellus, eris *nt* fleece; hide, fur;

v

piece or lump of wool

vēlō v cover, clothe; conceal, cover up

vēlōcitās, ātis f swiftness, rapidity, speed

vēlōx, ōcis adj swift, rapid, speedy

vēlum, ī nt sail; curtain, awning; a woven cloth; □ veil
□ **vēla dō** expose the sails to the wind

velut, velutī adv just as, just like; as for example; as it were; as if, as though; as being

vēmēns ▶ vehemēns

vēna, ae f blood-vessel, vein; artery; pulse; fissure, pore, cavity, (underground) stream; vein of ore, etc.; supply or store (of talent)

vēnābulum, ī nt hunting-spear

vēnālīcius, (i)ī m slave-dealer

vēnālis, e adj for sale; on hire; open to the influence of bribes

vēnāticus, a, um adj for hunting

vēnātiō, ōnis f hunting, chase; beasts hunted, game; animal hunt in the arena

vēnātor, ōris m hunter

vēnātrīx, īcis f huntress

vēnātus, ūs m hunting, hunt

vēndibilis, e adj that can (easily) be sold, marketable

vēnditātor, ōris m one who puffs up the merits (of)

vēnditiō, ōnis f sale

vēnditō v offer for sale; cry up; pay court (to)

vēndō, didī, ditum v sell, betray for money; promote the sale of

venēficium, (i)ī nt poisoning; magic, sorcery

venēficus, a, um adj of or connected with sorcery
■ **venēfica, ae** f female poisoner, sorceress
■ **venēficus, ī** m poisoner

venēnātus, a, um adj poisonous, venomous; poisoned

venēnifer, era, erum adj venomous

venēnō v imbue or infect with poison

venēnum, ī nt poison; potent herb used for medical or magical purposes

vēneō, īre, iī/īvī, itum v ir be sold (as a slave); be disposed of for financial gain

venerābilis, e adj venerable, august

venerābundus, a, um adj expressing religious awe (towards)

venerātiō, ōnis f reverence, veneration

venerātor, ōris m one who reveres

venerō v, **veneror** v dep worship, revere, venerate; honour supplicate

venia, ae f pardon, forgiveness; leave, permission; favour, indulgence; relief, remission

veniō, vēnī, ventum v come; go; arrive; arise, come to pass; proceed

vēnor v dep hunt

venter, tris m belly; paunch, abdomen; stomach; swelling; embryo

ventilō v expose to a draught; fan; brandish

ventitō v come frequently, reso

ventōsus, a, um adj windy; swift

(as the wind); fickle, changeable; vain, puffed up

ventus, **ī** m wind; puff, breeze

dat vēnō sale:

vēnum m [only in acc **vēnum** and

□ **vēnum/vēnō dō** (**vēndō**) sell
□ **vēnum eō** (**vēneō**) be sold

vēnumdō, dare, dedī, datum
① v put up for sale

Venus, eris f goddess of love; beloved person; object of love; loveliness; beauty; charm; (planet) Venus; best throw at dice; sexual intercourse

venustās, ātis f attractiveness, charm, grace

venustus, a, um adj attractive, charming, graceful, pretty, neat

vēpallidus, a, um adj deathly pale

vepris, is m thorn-bush

vēr, ris nt spring; spring-time of life

vērāx, ācis adj speaking the truth, truthful

verbēna, ae f a leafy branch or twig from various aromatic trees or shrubs used in religious ceremonies or for medicinal purposes

verber, eris nt lash, thong of a sling; blow, stroke; pl an instrument for flogging

verberō¹ ① v lash, scourge, flog; batter, hammer; assail

verberō², ōnis m one worthy of a beating, scoundrel

verbōsus, a, um adj prolix, lengthy; long-winded

verbum, ī nt word; language; discourse, wording; talk
■ **verba dō** with dat deceive

vērē adv truly, really, indeed; correctly

verēcundia, ae f modesty; respect; uncertainty, diffidence; sense of shame

verēcundus, a, um adj modest

verendus, a, um adj that is to be regarded with awe or reverence
■ **verenda, ōrum** ntpl genitals

vereor ② v dep show reverence or respect for; be afraid of, fear; be afraid (to do something); be afraid (that)

vergō ③ v slope down (towards); look towards; sink (towards something); tilt down

vērīsimilis, e adj (also **vērī similis**) having the appearance of truth

vēritās, ātis f truth, truthfulness, frankness
□ **Veritas** LM Christ

vermiculus, ī m grub, larva

vermis, is m worm, maggot

verna, ae m/f slave born in the master's household

vernāculus, a, um adj domestic, home-grown; indigenous, native, belonging to the country; low-bred, proletarian

vernilis, e adj servile, obsequious

verniliter adv obsequiously, fawningly

vernō ① v carry on or undergo the process proper to spring

vernus, a, um adj of the spring, vernal

vērō adv in fact, certainly, to be sure, indeed; moreover; on the other hand; yet

verpa, ae f penis

verrēs, ris m boar

verrō, ersum ③ v sweep clean; sweep together; sweep (to the ground); skim, sweep; sweep along

verrūca, ae f wart

verruncō ① v turn out

versābundus, a, um adj revolving

versātilis, e adj revolving; versatile

versicolor, ōris adj having colours that change

versiculus, ī m brief line of verse

versipellis, is m werewolf

versō ① v keep turning round, spin, whirl; keep going round, keep turning over; turn over and over; stir; drive this way and that; turn this way and that; manoeuvre; sway, 'manipulate'; adapt; ponder; maintain
□ **versor** come and go frequently; be in operation; be involved (in), concern oneself (in); dwell (upon); pass one's time (in)

versus, ūs m line; row; furrow; bench of rowers; line of writing; line of verse

versūtia, ae f cunning, craft

versūtus, a, um adj full of stratagems or shifts, wily, cunning, adroit

vertex, icis m whirlpool, eddy; crown of the head; peak, top, summit (of anything); pole

verticōsus, a, um adj full of whirlpools or eddies

vertīgō, inis f whirling or spinning movement, gyration, giddiness, dizziness

vertō, rtī, rsum ③ v turn, turn around or about; turn upside down; overthrow; alter, change; transform; turn out; cause to develop (into); pass into a new frame of mind; translate
□ **tergum ~** turn tail, flee

verū, ūs nt, **verum, ī** nt spit, point of javelin

vērum[1] conj but; but at the same time

vērum[2], **ī** nt truth

vērumtamen conj nevertheless, but even so

vērus, a, um adj true, real, genuine; just; right; proper

verūtum, ī nt short throwing spear

vervēx, cis m wether

vēsānia, ae f madness, frenzy

vēsāniēns, ntis adj raging, frenzied

vēsāniō ④ v act in a frenzy, rage

vēsānus, a, um adj mad, frenzied; wild

vēscor ③ v dep take food, eat; enjoy, put to use; feed on, devour

vēscus, a, um adj thin, attenuated

vēsīca, ae f bladder; balloon

vēsīcula, ae f small bladder-like formation

vespa, ae f wasp

vesper, eris/erī m evening; evening-star; west
□ **sub vesperum** towards evening
□ **vespere/vesperī** in the evening

vespera, ae f evening; ⒧ vesper

vesperāscō, ī ③ v grow towards evening

vespertiliō, ōnis m bat

vespertīnus, a, um *adj* evening..., of the evening; situated in the west

vespillō, ōnis *m* man of disreputable trade

vester, tra, trum *adj* your *(pl)*

vestiārius, a, um *adj* concerned with clothes

vestibulum, ī *nt* fore-court, entrance

vestīgium, (i)ī *nt* footprint, track; sole of the foot; trace, mark, imprint, vestige; instant
□ **ē vestīgiō** at once, immediately

vestīgō ☐ *v* track down, search for; search out; try to find out by searching; investigate

vestīmentum, ī *nt* clothing; *pl* clothes

vestiō ④ *v* dress, clothe; cover

vestis, is *f* garments, clothing, clothes; cloth
□ **mūtō vestem** change into mourning garments

vestītus, ūs *m* clothes, dress
□ **redeō ad vestītum** resume (normal) dress (after mourning)

veterāmentārius, a, um *adj* dealing with old or worn articles

veterānus, a, um *adj* veteran, having experience of action

veternus, ī *m* morbid state of torpor

vetō, vetuī, vetitum ☐ *v* forbid; prohibit, be an obstacle to

vetulus, a, um *adj* elderly, ageing

vetus, eris *adj* aged, old; as he was in previous days
■ **veterēs, um** *mpl* 'old-timers'; old authors *or* writers

vetustās, ātis *f* old age;

antiquity; long duration

vetustus, a, um *adj* ancient, old-established; long-established

vexāmen, inis *nt*, **vexātiō, ōnis** *f* shaking; disturbance, upheaval

vexillārius, (i)ī *m* standard-bearer
■ **vexillāriī** *pl* troops serving for the time being in a special detachment

vexillum, ī *nt* standard, banner; detachment of troops

vexō ☐ *v* agitate, buffet; harry, ravage; afflict, upset; persecute; disturb

via, ae *f* way; road, passage; channel; march, journey; manner, method, means

viāticum, ī *nt* provision for a journey, travelling allowance; money saved by soldiers from day to day

viātor, ōris *m* traveller

vībēx, ēcis *f*, **vībīx, īcis** *f* weal, mark from a blow

vibrō ☐ *v* brandish, wave; crimp, corrugate; rock; propel suddenly; flash; dart; glitter

vīburnum, ī *nt* guelder rose

vicārius, (i)ī *m* substitute, deputy; successor

vīcātim *adv* by (urban) districts, street by street; in or by villages

vīcēnī, ae, a *adj* twenty each

vīcēsimānus, a, um *adj* of the 20th legion

vīcī ▶ vincō

vicia, ae *f* vetch

vīcīnālis, e *adj* of or for the use of local inhabitants

vīcīnia, ae *f* neighbourhood; nearness; neighbours

vīcīnitās, ātis *f* neighbourhood; nearness; neighbours

vīcīnus, a, um *adj* neighbouring, in the neighbourhood, near; similar

■ **vīcīnum, ī** *nt* neighbourhood, neighbouring place, vicinity (of)
■ **vīcīnus, ī** *m* neighbour

vicis *gen f no nom* change; succession; place, turn; part; exchange, retaliation, return, interchange

□ **in vicem** by turns; reciprocally; instead of

□ **vicem** after the manner of, in the place of

□ **meam vicem** in my place

□ **vice** after the manner of

vicissim *adv* in turn; conversely

vicissitūdō, inis *f* change, alternation; vicissitude

victima, ae *f* an animal offered in sacrifice; a full-grown victim

victitō ⬚ *v* live, subsist

victor, ōris *m* conqueror, victor

victōria, ae *f* victory

victrīx, īcis *f* female conqueror; *f adj* victorious

victus, ūs *m* livelihood, food; way of life

vīculus, ī *m* small village, hamlet

vīcus, ī *m* street; village; district of Rome

vidēlicet *adv* it is clear (that), evidently, plainly; namely; (expressing irony) of course, no doubt

videō, vidī, vīsum ② *v* see; look at, behold, perceive; understand; regard; take care; pay regard to *in passive* appear, seem;

be seen; be deemed

□ **vidētur** it seems good

viduitās, ātis *f* widowhood

vīdulus, ī *m* bag for carrying one' belongings

viduō ⬚ *v* widow; bereave of a husband

viduus, a, um *adj* bereft, deprived (of); widowed; divorced; not supporting a climbing plant, unsupported

viētus, a, um *adj* shrivelled, wrinkled

vigeō ② *v* be strong *or* vigorous; thrive, flourish, be active; be effective

vigēscō ③ *v* acquire strength

vigil, lis *adj* awake, on the watch, alert; wakeful

■ ~, **is** *m/f* sentry, guard; membe of fire brigade

vigilāns, ntis *adj* watchful, vigilan

vigilantia, ae *f* vigilance, alertnes

vigilia, ae *f* wakefulness, lying awake; watch, guard; patrol; watchfulness, vigilance

■ **vigiliae nocturnae** *fpl* Ⓛ Ⓜ vigils, night prayer

vigilō ⬚ *v* watch; be awake; stay awake; spend time (on a task) by remaining awake; spend (a night, *etc.*) awake; be watchful *or* alert

vīgintī *adj indec* twenty

vigor, ōris *m* vigour; physical *or* mental energy

vīlica, ae *f* wife of a farm overseer

vīlicus, ī *m* farm overseer, manager

vīlipendō ③ *v* despise, slight

vīlis, e *adj* cheap; worthless; contemptible; humble, mean, common

vīlitās, ātis f cheapness; worthlessness

villa, ae f rural dwelling with associated farm buildings

villōsus, a, um adj shaggy, hairy

villula, ae f small farmstead or country-house

villus, ī m shaggy hair, tuft of hair

vīmen, inis nt flexible branch, withy; basket

vīmineus, a, um adj of wickerwork

Vīnālia, ium ntpl wine-festivals (on 22 April and 19–20 August)

vīnārius, (i)ī m wine-merchant

vincibilis, e adj likely to win; that can be won

vinciō, vīnxī, vīnctum ④ v tie up; bind, encircle; bond; link; fetter

vincō, vīcī, victum ③ v conquer, overcome; defeat; subdue; win; surmount; exceed, excel; prevail

vinculum, ī nt band, bond, cord, rope, chain, fetter; band; prison; imprisonment; tether; mooring-rope; restraint, tie

vindēmia, ae f grape-gathering; produce of a vineyard in any given year

vindex, icis m/f champion, defender; protector; avenger, revenger; one who punishes (an offence)

vindiciae, ārum f interim possession (of disputed property)

vindicō ① v vindicate, lay legal claim to; save, preserve; free; avenge, punish; defend, protect

vindicta, ae f the ceremonial act of claiming as free one who

contends he is wrongly held in slavery; vengeance; punishment

vīnea, ae f vines; movable penthouse used to shelter siege-workers

vīnētum, ī nt vineyard

vīnitor, ōris m vineyard worker

vīnōsus, a, um adj immoderately fond of wine; intoxicated with wine

vīnum, ī nt wine

viola, ae f violet stock, gillyvor; violet colour

violābilis, e adj that may be violated or suffer outrage

violāceus, a, um adj violet-coloured

violārium, (i)ī nt bed of violets

violātiō, ōnis f profanation, violation

violātor, ōris m profaner, violator

violēns, ntis adj vehement, violent

violentia, ae f violence, aggressiveness

violentus, a, um adj violent, aggressive

violō ① v profane; defile, pollute; dishonour, outrage; transgress against; pierce, wound; violate

vīpera, ae f viper

vīpereus, a, um adj, **vīperīnus, a, um** adj of vipers

vir, rī m man; male; husband, lover; a true man; soldier

virāgō, inis f a warlike or heroic woman

virectum, ī nt area of greenery

vireō ② v be green or verdant; be lively or vigorous; be full of youthful vigour

vīrēs, ium fpl strength; control; resources, assets; value; meaning

v

virēscō ③ v turn green

virga, ae f twig, shoot, spray, rod, stick; magic wand

virgātus, a, um adj made of twigs; striped

virgeus, a, um adj consisting of twigs or shoots

virgineus, a, um adj of or belonging to or characteristic of a girl of marriageable age; virgin

virginitās, ātis f maidenhood, virginity

virgō, inis f a girl of marriageable age; virgin; Virgo (constellation); aqueduct at Rome noted for the coolness of its water

virgultum, ī nt shrub; pl low shrubby vegetation, brushwood

viridis, e adj green; fresh, blooming, sappy; marked by youthful vigour

viridō ① v make green; be green

virīlis, e adj male, masculine; of a man; manly; bold; firm; vigorous
□ **prō virīlī parte** with the utmost effort; as far as a man may
□ **toga ~** the plain white toga worn by a Roman on reaching puberty

virītim adv man by man, per man, individually

virōsus, a, um adj having an unpleasantly strong taste or smell, rank

virtūs, ūtis f manliness, manhood; goodness, virtue; excellence, worth; resolution, valour
□ **tuā virtūte** thanks to you
■ **virtutes, um** mpl LM miracles

vīrus, ī nt venom; poisonous fluid; malignant quality; secretion with medicinal or magical potency

vīs f strength, force; vigour, power, energy; violence; meaning, signification; nature; efficacy, virtue (of drugs, etc.)
■ **vīrēs** fpl strength; power; military strength

vīscātus, a, um adj smeared with bird-lime

vīscerātiō, ōnis f a communal sacrificial feast at which the flesh of the victim was shared among the guests

viscum, ī nt, **viscus, ī** m mistletoe; bird-lime

vīscus, eris nt, **vīscera, um** ntpl the soft fleshy parts of the body, internal organs; entrails, flesh; offspring; innermost part, heart (of)

vīsō, īsī, īsum ③ v go and look (at), look, view; visit

vīsum, ī nt vision

vīsus, ūs m the faculty of seeing; sight, vision; supernatural manifestation

vīta, ae f life; living, manner of life; the course of a life

vītābilis, e adj to be avoided

vītābundus, a, um adj taking evasive action

vītālis, e adj of life; vital; life-giving, alive

vītāliter adv so as to endow with life

vitellus, ī m little calf; yolk of an egg

vīteus, a, um adj belonging to a vine

vītigenus, a, um adj produced from the vine

vitiō ① v spoil, harm, impair;

279

vitiōsus | volturius

deflower; invalidate

vitiōsus, a, um *adj* faulty, defective; corrupt; wicked, vicious

vitis, is *f* vine; vine-branch; centurion's staff

vitisator, ōris *m* vine-planter

vitium, (i)ī *nt* fault, defect, blemish; error; shortcoming

vitō ① *v* avoid, shun, keep clear of

vitreārius, (i)ī *m* maker of glassware

vitreus, a, um *adj* of glass; resembling glass in its colour (greenish), translucency, or glitter

vitricus, ī *m* stepfather

vitrum, ī *nt* glass; woad

vitta, ae *f* linen headband; woollen band

vittātus, a, um *adj* wearing or carrying a ritual **vitta**

vitula, ae *f* calf, young cow

vitulīna, ae *f* veal

vitulus, ī *m* (bull-)calf

vituperō ① *v* find fault with, criticize adversely

vīvārium, (i)ī *nt* game enclosure or preserve

vīvāx, ācis *adj* long-lived, tenacious of life; vivifying; lively, vigorous

vīvēscō ③ *v* come to life

vīvidus, a, um *adj* lively, vigorous, spirited; lifelike

vīvificō ① *v* restore to life

vīvō, īxī, īctum ③ *v* live, be alive; really live; live (on); live (by); pass one's life (in); survive

vīvus, a, um *adj* alive, living; lively

vix *adv* hardly, scarcely, not easily

vixdum *adv* scarcely yet, only just

vocābulum, ī *nt* word used to designate something, term, name

vōcālis, e *adj* able to speak; having a notable voice; tuneful

vocāmen, inis *nt* designation, name

vocātiō, ōnis *f* invitation

vocātus, ūs *m* peremptory or urgent call

vōciferātiō, ōnis *f* loud outcry, shout, roar

vōciferor ① *v dep* utter a loud cry, shout, yell, cry out, announce loudly

vocitō ① *v* call

vocō ① *v* call; call upon, summon; name; invite; challenge; demand

vol- ▶ **vul-**

volaemum, ī *nt* a large kind of pear

volantēs, ium *mpl* birds

volātilis, e *adj* equipped to fly, flying, fleeing; fleeting, transient

volātus, ūs *m* flying, flight

Volcānus, ī *m* (also **Vulcānus**) Vulcan, the god of fire; fire

volēns, ntis *adj* willing, welcome

volitō ① *v* fly about; flutter, move swiftly through the air; go to and fro

volnus, eris *nt* (also **vulnus**) wound; emotional hurt; injury

volō¹ ① *v* fly; speed

volō², velle, voluī *v ir* be willing; wish, desire; want; mean, signify; maintain, claim

volōk¹, ōnis *m* volunteer

voltur, uris *m* (also **vultur**) vulture

volturius, (i)ī *m* (also **vulturius**) vulture

voltus, **ūs** *m* (also **vultus**) countenance, facial expression; face; looks, features

volūbilis, **e** *adj* spinning, rotating; rolling; coiled; flowing, fluent

volūbilitās, **ātis** *f* rotundity

volucer, **cris**, **cre** *adj* flying, winged; swift; fleeting, transitory ■ **volucris**, **is** *f* bird

volūmen, **inis** *nt* roll of papyrus, book; coil, twist

voluntārius, **a**, **um** *adj* of one's own free will, voluntarily undergone

voluntās, **ātis** *f* will, wish, choice, desire, inclination; good-will, sympathy; approval

volup *adv* agreeably, delightfully

voluptās, **ātis** *f* delight, pleasure; source of pleasure; sexual intercourse

volūtābrum, **ī** *nt* place where pigs wallow

volūtō ① *v* roll, wallow; turn over in one's mind; think *or* talk over

volvō, **lvī**, **lūtum** ③ *v* roll, roll over; cause to roll, wrap up; cause (the eyes) to travel restlessly; unroll; turn over in the mind; grovel; turn round

vōmer, **eris** *m* ploughshare

vomitus, **ūs** *m* throwing up, vomit

vomō, **muī** ③ *v* be sick, vomit; discharge, spew out; belch out

vorāgō, **inis** *f* deep hole, chasm, watery hollow

vorāx, **ācis** *adj* ravenous; insatiable; devouring

vorō ① *v* devour; engulf, eat away

vort- ▸ **vert-**

vōs *pn* you (*pl*)

voster ▸ **vester**

vōtīvus, **a**, **um** *adj* offered in fulfilment of a vow

votō ▸ **vetō**

vōtum, **ī** *nt* vow; votive offering; prayer; desire, hope

voveō, **vōvī**, **vōtum** ② *v* vow; pray *or* long for

vōx, **ōcis** *f* voice, sound, word, words; speech; language

Vulcānus, **ī** *m* Vulcan, the god of fire; fire

vulgāris, **e** *adj* usual, common, commonplace, everyday; of the common people; shared by all

vulgātor, **ōris** *m* divulger

vulgātus, **a**, **um** *adj* common, ordinary; conventional; well-known

vulgivagus, **a**, **um** *adj* widely ranging; promiscuous

vulgō[1] *adv* commonly, publicly; en masse; far and wide

vulgō[2] ① *v* make common to all; make public, publish; spread abroad; prostitute; publish the news (that)

vulgus, **ī** *nt* the common people, general public, crowd

vulnerō ① *v* wound, hurt, distress

vulnificus, **a**, **um** *adj* causing wounds

vulnus, **eris** *nt* wound; emotional hurt; injury

vulpēcula, **ae** *f* (little) fox

vulpēs, **pis** *f* fox

vultur, **uris** *m* vulture

vulturius, **(i)ī** *m* vulture

vultus, **ūs** *m* countenance, facial expression; face; looks, features

Xx

Zz

xiphiās, ae *m* swordfish

xystus, ī *m* open-air walk; cloisters

zea, ae *f* emmer wheat

zelus, i *m* zeal

Zephyrus, ī *m* a west wind

zizania, orum *npl* tares

zōna, ae *f* belt, girdle; celestial zone

zōnula, ae *f* (little) girdle

Aa

a *indefinite article* (generally unexpressed in Latin); unus, una, unum; quidam; is, ea, id

aback *adj:*
□ **taken ∼** stupefactus, attonitus, consternatus

abandon *vt* relinquo, derelinquo, desero, destituo, abicio, omitto, neglego ③

abandoned *adj* derelictus; desertus; *fig* flagitiosus, perditus

abandonment *n* derelictio, destitutio *f*

abashed *adj* pudibundus

abbreviate *vt* imminuo, contraho ③

abbreviation *n* contractio *f*

abdicate *vt&i* me abdico ① + *abl*; depono ③

abdomen *n* abdomen *nt*

abduct *vt* rapio ③

abduction *n* raptus *m*

aberration *n* error *m*

abet *vt* adiuvo, instigo ①; faveo ② + *dat*

abetter *n* instigator, impulsor *m*

abhor *vt* abhorreo ②; detestor, aversor ①

abhorrence *n* odium *nt*

abhorrent *adj* perosus; odiosus; alienus

abide *vt* (endure) patior ③; tolero ①; subeo ④; exspecto ①
■ ∼ *vi* (dwell) habito ①; maneo ②
□ ∼ **by** sto ① + *abl*

ability *n* facultas; peritia *f*; ingenium *nt*
□ **to the best of one's ∼** summa ope

abject *adj* abiectus, vilis; humilis

ablaze *adj* ardens, fervens

able *adj* potens; capax, peritus; ingeniosus
□ **be ∼ (to)** posse, quire *ir*; valere ②; sufficere ③

able-bodied *adj* validus, robustus, firmus

aboard *adv* in nave
□ **go ∼ a ship** navem conscendere ③

abode *n* domicilium *nt*; sedes *f*; (sojourn) commoratio; mansio *f*

abolish *vt* aboleo ②; extinguo, tollo, rescindo ③

abolition *n* abolitio, dissolutio *f*

abominable *adj* detestabilis, exsecrabilis, infandus; odiosus

abomination *n* detestatio *f*; odium *nt*
□ ∼**s** (vile acts) nefaria *ntpl*

abortive *adj* abortivus; *fig* irritus

abound *vi* abundo, redundo ①; supersum *ir*; supero ③
□ ∼ **in** abundo ① + *abl*

abounding *adj* abundans; copiosus, largus; creber

about *prep* circa, circum ad, apud; circiter; sub *all* + *acc*; de + *abl*
■ ∼ *adv* circiter; ferme; (more or less) quasi

a

□ be ~ to ... (e.g. write, etc.), scriptura, etc.

□ go ~ aggredior, incipio ③

□ bring ~ efficio ③

above prep (higher) super, supra; (beyond, more than) ante; praeter, ultra all + acc

■ ~ adv supra; insuper; plus, magis; (upwards) sursum

□ from ~ desuper, superne

□ be ~ emineo ②; fig dedignor ①; fastidio ④

□ over and ~ insuper

□ ~ all super omnia

above-board adv aperte, candide

above-mentioned adj quod supra dictum est

abrasion n attritus m

abreast adv ex adverso

abridge vt contraho ③

abridgement n contractio f

abroad adv (out of doors) foris; (to the outside of a house) foras; (in foreign parts) peregre; (here and there) passim, undique

□ from ~ extrinsecus; peregre

□ be or live ~ peregrinor ①; patria careo ②

abrupt adj praeruptus; praeceps; fig subitus, repentinus; improvisus

abruptly adv raptim

abscess n ulcus nt

abscond vi me clam subduco, me abdo, lateo ②; latito ①

absence n absentia; peregrinatio f; fig (of mind) oblivio f

absent adj absens

□ be ~ abesse ir, peregrinari ①

absentee n peregrinator m

absent-minded adj obliviosus

absolute adj absolutus; summus

■ ~ly adv absolute; prorsus; (entirely) penitus

absolution adj absolutio; indulgentia f

absolve vt veniam do ①; absolvo ③; libero ①; dimitto ③

absorb vt absorbeo ②; haurio ④; combibo ③; fig teneo ②

absorbent adj bibulus

abstain vi abstineo ②

abstemious adj abstemius; sobrius

abstinence n abstinentia f, (fasting) ieiunium nt

abstinent adj abstinens

■ ~ly adv abstinenter, continenter

abstracted adj (in mind) parum attentus

■ ~ly adv parum attente

abstraction n (concept) imago f

abstruse adj abstrusus; reconditus; obscurus, occultus

■ ~ly adv abdite, occulte

absurd adj absurdus, insulsus; ineptus, ridiculus

■ ~ly adv inepte, absurde

absurdity n ineptia; insulsitas; res inepta f

abundance n abundantia, copia, ubertas f

abundant adj abundans; amplus; copiosus, plenus; uber

□ be ~ abundo ①

abundantly adv abunde, abundanter, copiose; effuse; (fruitfully) feliciter

abuse[1] vt (misuse) abutor ③ + abl; fig (insult, etc.) maledico ③ + dat; convicior, lacero ①

abuse[2] n (wrong use) abusus; perversus mos m; (insult) iniuria f, convicium nt; violatio f

abusive adj contumeliosus; maledicus
■ ~ly adv contumeliose; maledice

abyss n profundum nt; (whirlpool) gurges m; fig vorago f

academic adj academicus
■ ~ally adv ut solent academici

academy n Academia f; collegium nt

accede vi accedo, annuo ③; assentior ④

accelerate vt accelero, festino, appropero ①

acceleration n festinatio f

accent[1] n accentus; tenor; fig sonus m; lingua f

accent[2] vt (in speaking) acuo ③; (in writing) fastigo ①

accept vt accipio; recipio ③; (approve of) probo ①; (agree to) assentior ④ + dat

acceptable adj acceptus, gratus; iucundus

acceptance n acceptio; approbatio f

access n aditus; accessus m
□ **gain** ~ admittor ③

accessible adj patens; fig affabilis, facilis

accession n (to the throne) regni principium nt

accessory adj adiunctus; (to crimes) conscius + gen
■ ~ n particeps m/f, conscius m

accident n casus m
□ **by** ~ casu, fortuito, temere

accidental adj fortuitus
■ ~ly adv casu; fortuito

acclamation n acclamatio f, clamor, consensus, plausus m

acclimatize vt assuefacio ③

accommodate vt accommodo, apto ①; fig (have room for) capio ③

accommodation n (lodging) deversorium nt

accompany vt comitor ①; (escort) deduco ③; (mus) concino ③

accomplice n particeps, conscius + gen; (in crimes or vices) satelles m

accomplish vt exsequor, perficio; perago ③; impleo ②

accomplished adj eruditus; doctus

accomplishment n exsecutio, effectio; (skill) ars f

accord[1] n consensus m, concordia f
□ **of one's own** ~ sponte; ultro
□ **with one** ~ uno ore

accord[2] vt (grant) concedo ③;
■ ~ vi (agree) congruo ③; concordo ①; convenio ④

accordance n ▶ accord n
□ **in** ~ **with** secundum + acc

according prep
□ ~ **to** de, ex, pro all + abl; secundum + acc

accordingly adv itaque; ita; (therefore) igitur, ergo

account[1] n (reckoning, of money) ratio f; (narrative) memoria; narratio f; (esteem) reputatio f; (advantage) commodum nt
□ **on** ~ **of** ob, propter + acc
□ **on that** ~ propterea; ideo
□ **call to** ~ rationem posco ③
□ **of little or no** ~ nullius pretii, vilis
□ **take into** ~ rationem habeo ② + gen

account[2] vt (esteem) aestimo ①; habeo ②; pendo, pono ③
■ ~ **for** vi rationem reddo ③

accountable *adj* reus, rationem reddere debens

accountant *n* tabularius *m*

accrue *vi* orior; accresco ③; provenio ④

accumulate *vt* accumulo, coacervo ①; congero ③ □ ~ *vi* cresco; congeror ③

accumulation *n* (heap, *etc.*) cumulus; acervus; fig congestus *m*

accuracy *n* cura; subtilitas *f*

accurate *adj* accuratus; subtilis ■ ~**ly** *adv* accurate, subtiliter

accusation *n* accusatio *f*; crimen *nt*

accuse *vt* accuso; criminor ①; (blame) reprehendo ③

accuser *n* accusator; (informer) delator *m*

accustom *vt* assuefacio ③ □ ~ **oneself** assuefieri *ir*, consuescere ③ □ **be** ~**ed** soleo ②

accustomed *adj* assuetus, consuetus, solitus

ache[1] *vi* doleo ② □ **my head** ~**s** caput mihi dolet

ache[2] *n* dolor *m*

achieve *vt* patro ①; consequor, conficio, perficio ③

achievement *n* res gesta *f*; facinus *nt*

aching *n* dolor *m*

acid *adj* acidus; acidulus

acidity *n* aciditas *f*

acknowledge *vt* agnosco, recognosco ③; fateor, confiteor ②

acknowledgement *n* agnitio; confessio *f*

acme *n* fastigium *nt*; (the acme of folly) summa dementia

aconite *n* aconitum *nt*

acorn *n* glans *f* ■ ~**-bearing** *adj* glandifer

acquaint *vt* certiorem facio ③ □ ~ **oneself (with)** noscere, cognoscere ③

acquaintance *n* scientia; (friendship with) familiaritas; notitia *f*; (person) familiaris *m/f*

acquainted *adj* (with) gnarus; prudens; peritus *all* + *gen* □ **become** ~ noscere, cognoscere ③

acquiesce *vi* acquiesco, inacquiesco ③; assentior ④; probo ①

acquiescence *n* assensus *m*; approbatio *f*

acquire *vt* comparo ①; nanciscor, consequor, comparatio *f*; pario, adipiscor ③; fig disco ③

acquisition *n* (acquiring) conciliatio, comparatio *f*; (thing acquired) quaesitum *nt*

acquit *vt* absolvo ③; libero, purgo ① □ ~ **oneself** se gerere ③

acquittal *n* absolutio *f*

acre *n* iugerum *nt*

acrid *adj* acerbus, acer

acrimonious *adj* acerbus; fig asper, truculentus

acrimony *n* acrimonia; amaritudo *f*

acrobat *n* funambulus *m*

across *prep* trans + *acc* ■ ~ *adv* ex transverso, in transversum

act[1] *vi* ago, facio; gero ③; (behave) me gero ③; (exert force) vim habeo ②; (on the stage) in scaenam

prodeo *ir*
■ ~ *vt* (as actor) (comoediam, primam partem) ago ③

act² *n* (deed, action) factum; gestum *nt*; (exploit) facinus *nt*; (decree) decretum *m*; (in a play) actus *m*
□ **be caught in the** ~ deprehendor ③
■ ~**s** *pl* acta *ntpl*

action *n* actio *f*; actus *m*; (battle) pugna *f*; (gesture) gestus *m*; (law) actio *f*
□ **bring an** ~ **against someone** actionem alicui intendere ③

active *adj* agilis; impiger, industrius, operosus; strenuus; vividus
■ ~**ly** *adv* impigre; strenue

activity *n* agilitas, mobilitas; industria, navitas *f*

actor *n* (in a play) comoedus, histrio; mimus; artifex scaenicus; (doer) auctor; qui agit *m*

actress *n* mima *f*

actual *adj* verus, ipse
■ ~**ly** *adv* re vera, re ipsa

acumen *n* sagacitas *f*; ingenium *nt*

acute *adj* acutus; acer; (perspicacious) sagax, subtilis
■ ~**ly** *adv* acute; acriter; (shrewdly) sagaciter

adamant *n* adamas *m*

adapt *vt* accommodo, apto ①

adaptable *adj* habilis

adaptation *n* accommodatio *f*

add *vt* addo; appono, adiungo, adicio ③; (in speaking) adicio ③; (in writing) subiungo ③
□ ~ **up** computo ①
□ **be** ~**ed** accedo ③

adder *n* coluber *m*, vipera *f*

addicted *adj* deditus, studiosus
□ **be** ~ **(to)** deditus esse

addition *n* additamentum *nt*; adiectio; accessio
■ **in** ~ *adv* insuper

addle-headed *adj* inanis, vanus, fatuus, stultus

address¹ *vt* (direct to) inscribo ③; (speak to) alloquor, aggredior ③

address² *n* (speaking to) alloquium *nt*; allocutio; (direction) inscriptio *f*; (petition) libellus supplex *m*; (speech) oratio, contio *f*

adduce *vt* (witnesses) profero *ir*; (quote) cito ①; adduco ③

adept *adj* peritus

adequate *adj* sufficiens, par

adhere *vi* adhaereo; cohaereo ②; fig sto (in) ① + *abl*

adherent *n* assectator; fautor; particeps *m/f*; socius *m*; (dependant) cliens *m*

adhesive *adj* tenax, lentus

adieu *int* ave, salve, vale
□ **bid** ~ valedico ③; valere iubeo ②

adjacent *adj* confinis, conterminus; vicinus

adjoining *adj* adiacens, confinis, vicinus

adjourn *vt* comperendino ①; differo, profero ③
■ ~ *vi* differor *ir*

adjournment *n* dilatio, prolatio *f*

adjudge *vt* adiudico ①

adjudicate *vt* addico, decerno ③

adjudication *n* addictio; (verdict) sententia *f*, arbitrium *nt*

adjust *vt* apto ①; dispono ③; (settle) compono ③; ordino ①

adjustment *n* accommodatio,

compositio *f*

adjutant *n* optio *m*

administer *vt* (manage, etc.)
administro, curo, procuro ①;
(medicine, etc.) adhibeo ②; (an
oath) adigo ③; (justice) exerceo ②;
reddo ③

administration *n* administratio;
cura; procuratio *f*; magistratus *m*;
(of public affairs) summa rerum

administrator *n* administrator;
procurator *m*

admirable *adj* admirabilis;
mirabilis, admirandus; insignis

admirably *adv* admirabiliter;
praeclare, insigniter

admiral *n* praefectus classis *m*

admiration *n* admiratio *f*

admire *vt* admiror; amo ①

admirer *n* admirator; mirator;
laudator; amans *m*

admission *n* admissio *f*; aditus,
accessus *m*; (confession) confessio *f*

admit *vt* admitto; recipio;
introduco; (adopt) ascisco ③;
(confess) fateor, confiteor ②
□ **it is ~ted** constat ①

admittance *n* admissio, aditus,
accessus *m*

admonish *vt* moneo, commoneo ②

admonition *n* monitio;
admonitio; adhortatio *f*;
monitum *nt*

admonitory *adj* monitorius

ado *n* tumultus *m*
□ **with much ~** aegre, vix
□ **without more ~** statim

adolescence *n* adolescentia *f*

adolescent *adj* adolescens

adopt *vt* (a child) adopto, (an adult)
arrogo ①; *fig* ascisco; assumo ③; (a

policy) capio ③; ineo ①

adoption *n* adoptio, adoptatio; (of
an adult) arrogatio; *fig* assumptio *f*

adoptive *adj* adoptivus

adorable *adj* adorandus,
venerandus; (lovable) amandus

adoration *n* adoratio *f*; (love)
amor *m*

adore *vt* adoro, veneror, *fig*
admiror, amo ①

adorer *n* cultor *m*; (lover) amator *m*

adorn *vt* orno, decoro, illustro ①;
excolo, como ③

adornment *n* exornatio *f*;
ornatus *m*; ornamentum *nt*

adrift *adv* in salo fluctuans
■ **be ~** *vi* fluctuor ①

adroit *adj* callidus, dexter, sollers,
peritus, ingeniosus
■ **~ly** *adv* callide, sollerter, perite,
ingeniose

adroitness *n* dexteritas *f*

adulation *n* adulatio, assentatio *f*

adult *adj* adultus; pubes
■ **~** *n* adultus homo *m*

adulterate *vt* adultero, vitio ①;
corrumpo ③

adulterer *n* adulter; moechus *m*

adulteress *n* adultera; moecha *f*

adulterous *adj* adulterinus
■ **~ly** *adv* adulterio, per
adulterium

adultery *n* adulterium;
stuprum *nt*
□ **commit ~** moechor ①

advance *vt* promoveo ②; (lift up)
tollo, attollo ③; exalto ①; (an opinion)
exhibeo ②; profero *ir* ③; (lend)
commodo ①; (accelerate) maturo ①
□ **~ someone's interests**
alicui consulo ①; rebus alicuius

studeo ②
■ ~ *vi* procedo, progredior, incedo ③; (mil) gradum *or* (pedem) infero *ir*; fig proficio ③

advance² *n* progressus; (attack) incursio *f*; (in rank) accessio dignitatis *f*; (increase, rise) incrementum *nt*

advanced *adj* provectus; (of age) grandis

advance-guard *n* antecursores *mpl*, primum agmen *nt*

advantage *n* lucrum, commodum, emolumentum *nt*; utilitas *f*; fructus; usus *m*; (blessings) bona *ntpl*
□ have the ~ over praesto ① + *dat*; superior sum *ir*
□ make *or* take ~ of utor ③ + *abl*
□ be of ~ to prosum *ir* + *dat*

advantageous *adj* fructuosus; utilis; commodus
■ ~ly *adv* utiliter; bene; commode

advent *n* adventus *m*

adventure *n* casus *m*; (as action) facinus *nt*

adventurous *adj* audax
■ ~ly *adv* audacter

adversary *n* adversarius *m*; inimicus *m*; inimica *f*

adverse *adj* adversus, infestus; fig asper
■ ~ly *adv* secus, infeliciter

adversity *n* res adversae *fpl*; calamitas *f*; res asperae *fpl*

advertise *vt* (publish) divulgo ①; (try to sell) vendito ①

advertisement *n* venditatio ①

advertiser *n* venditator *m*

advice *n* consilium *nt*; (information, intelligence) indicium *nt*
□ ask ~ consulo ③
□ give ~ moneo ②

advisable *adj* commodus, utilis
□ it is ~ expedit ④

advise *vt* moneo; (recommend) suadeo ② + *dat*; consulo ③; (counsel against) dissuadeo ②; (exhort) hortor ①; (inform) certiorem facio ③

adviser *n* consultor, monitor, suasor, auctor *m*

advocacy *n* patrocinium *nt*

advocate¹ *n* advocatus, causidicus; patronus; (one who recommends) suasor *m*; (defender) defensor *m*

advocate² *vt* suadeo ②

aedile *n* aedilis *m*

aegis *n* aegis *f*

afar *adv* procul, longe
□ from ~ e longinquo

affability *n* comitas, affabilitas, facilitas *f*

affable *adj* affabilis, comis, facilis

affably *adv* comiter

affair *n* res *f*; negotium *nt*

affect *vt* afficio ③; commoveo ②; percutio ③; (pretend) simulo ①

affection *n* (of mind *or* body) affectus *m*; affectio *f*; (love) amor *m*; gratia; benevolentia *f*; (feeling) affectus, impetus, motus; sensus *m*

affectionate *adj* amans, benevolus, pius; blandus
■ ~ly *adv* amanter; pie, blande

affinity *n* affinitas; cognatio, proximitas *f*

affirm *vt* affirmo, assevero, testificor ①

affirmation *n* affirmatio *f*; asseveratio *nt*

affix *vt* affigo ③

afflict vt torqueo ②; vexo, crucio ①

affliction n miseria f; res adversae fpl

affluence n abundantia, copia f; (wealth) divitiae fpl

affluent adj abundans, affluens; (rich) dives

afford vt praebeo ②; (yield) reddo, fero, fundo ③; (supply) sufficio ③; (buy) emo ③

affront vt irrito ①; contumelia afficio ③
  ■ ~ n contumelia, iniuria f

afloat vi:
  □ **be** ~ navigo ①, navi vehor ③

afoot adv
  □ **be** ~ parari

afraid adj timidus, pavidus
  □ **be** ~ **(of)** timeo ②; (much) pertimesco ②; expavesco ③
  □ **make** ~ terreo ②; territo ①
  □ **not** ~ impavidus, intrepidus

afresh adv de integro, ab integro, iterum, denuo

after prep post + acc; a, de, e, ex + abl; (following immediately upon) sub; (of degree or succession) iuxta; secundum; (in imitation of) ad (all + acc
  □ **one** ~ **another** alius ex alio
  ■ ~ adv (afterwards) exinde, postea, posterius; post
  □ ~ **all** tamen; saltem
  □ **a little** ~ paulo post
  □ **the day** ~ postridie
  ■ ~ conj (when) postquam, posteaquam

after-ages n posteritas f

afternoon n post meridiem nt
  ■ ~ adj postmeridianus, pomeridianus

afterthought n posterior

cogitatio f

afterwards adv post; postea; deinde, deinceps, dehinc

again adv iterum, denuo, rursum, rursus; (likewise, in turn) invicem, mutuo, vicissim; contra; (besides) praeterea
  □ **over** ~ ab integro
  □ ~ **and** ~ iterum atque iterum

against prep (opposite to), contra; adversus; (denoting attack) in; (by, at) ad, ante all + acc
  □ **be** ~ adversor, oppugno ①
  □ **fight** ~ pugno cum

age n aetas f; (century) saeculum; (time in general) tempus nt; (old ~) senectus f
  □ **under** ~ impubis
  □ **of the same** ~ aequaevus

aged adj aetate provectus; senilis; (of a certain age) natus + acc of annus
  □ ~ **five** natus annos quinque

agent n actor m; auctor; (assistant) satelles m/f; administer m

aggrandize vt amplifico ①; attollo ③; augeo ②

aggrandizement n amplificatic f; incrementum nt

aggravate vt augeo ②; exaggero ①

aggravation n exaggeratio f

aggression n incursio f

aggressive adj arma (ultro) inferens; (pugnacious) pugnax

aggrieved adj:
  □ **feel** ~ aegre fero ③

aghast adj attonitus, consternatus

agile adj agilis; pernix

agility n agilitas; pernicitas f

agitate vt agito ①; commoveo ②; perturbo ①
  ■ ~**d** adj tumultuosus;

turbulentus; (anxious) sollicitus

agitation n agitatio; commotio; iactatio f; fig tumultus m; trepidatio f

agitator n concitator; turbator (populi or vulgi) m

ago adv abhinc
□ **long ∼** iamdudum
□ **how long ∼?** quamdudum
□ **some time ∼** pridem

agog adv (astonished) attonitus

agonizing adj crucians

agony n dolor m; cruciatus m

agree vi (be in agreement) congruo ③; concordo ①; concino ③; consentio ④; (make a bargain) paciscor ③; (be agreeable) placeo ②; (assent) annuo ③; assentior ④
□ **it is ∼d** constat

agreeable adj gratus, acceptus; amabilis
□ **very ∼** pergratus

agreeably adv grate, iucunde; suaviter

agreement n consensus m; (covenant) pactum nt; stipulatio f; conventum nt; (bargain) condicio f; (harmonious arrangement) concinnitas f; (fig harmony) consensio f

agricultural adj rusticus

agriculture n agri cultura f; res rustica f

aground adv:
□ **run ∼** in terram appello ③; (be stranded) eicior ③
□ **be ∼** (touch bottom) sido ③

ah int ah! eia! vah! vae!

ahead adv ante
□ **get ∼ of** praetereo ir

aid¹ n auxilium; subsidium nt
□ **with the ∼ of** opera

aid² vt adiuto, iuvo ① + acc;

agitation | alienation

succurro ③ + dat; subvenio ④ + dat

aide-de-camp n optio m

ailment n malum nt; morbus m; aegritudo, aegrotatio f

aim¹ n propositum nt

aim² vt intendo; dirigo, tendo ③; fig (∼ at) affecto; specto ①; expeto ③; molior ④

air¹ n aer m, aura f; (sky) caelum nt; fig habitus; gestus m; (appearance) species f; (tune) numeri mpl, modus m
□ **in the open ∼** sub divo

air² vt sicco ①
□ **∼ opinions** profero ③

airy adj aerius; apertus, patens, ventosus; fig levis

aisle n ala f

ajar adj (of doors) semiapertus; semiadapertus

akin adj cognatus; propinquus; fig finitimus, cognatus

alacrity n alacritas f; studium nt

alarm¹ n (signal in war, etc.) classicum nt; (sudden fear) trepidatio f; tumultus m

alarm² vt terreo ②; consterno, territo ①
□ **be ∼ed** perturbor ①

alarming adj terribilis

alas int eheu! heu, hei mihi misero! (alas for the conquered!) vae victis!

alcove n (corner) angulus m

alder n alnus f

alert adj alacer, promptus, vigil

alertness n alacritas f

alien adj & n peregrinus; alienigena m

alienate vt alieno; abalieno ①; fig averto ③

alienation n abalienatio;

alienatio; (estrangement) disiunctio, alienatio f

alight[1] vi descendo ③; (from a horse) desilio ④; (of birds, etc.) insido ③

alight[2] adj ardens

alike adj aequus, par, similis
■ ~ adv pariter, similiter

alive adj vivus; fig vividus, alacer
□ **be** ~ vivo ③; supersum ir

all[1] adj omnis, cunctus; universus; (whole) totus; (every one individually) unusquisque
□ **by** ~ **means** quoquomodo
□ **on** ~ **sides** ubique, passim, undique
□ ~ **this while** usque adhuc
□ ~ **the better** tanto melius
□ ~ **the more** eo plus
□ **it is** ~ **over with** actum est de + abl
□ **it is** ~ **one to me** nihil mea interest

all[2] n omnia ntpl
□ **at** ~ omnino
□ **not at** ~ nihil (nullus, etc.) admodum
□ **in** ~ in summa

allay vt lenio ④; mitigo ①; (quench) restinguo ③; sedo ①

allegation n affirmatio f

allege vt arguo ③; affirmo ①; (bring forward) affero ③

allegiance n fides f

alleviate vt levo, allevo, sublevo ①

alleviation n levamen nt

alley n (narrow street) angiportus m; ambulatio f

alliance n (by blood) consanguinitas f; (by marriage) affinitas f; (of states) foedus nt; (mutual connection) societas f

allied adj cognatus; propinquus; (of states) foederatus, socius

all-mighty adj omnipotens

allot vt distribuo ③; assigno ①; tribuo ③; do ①

allotment n assignatio, portio f; pars f

allow vt concedo, permitto ③; (permit) patior, sino ③
□ ~ **of** admitto ③; (confess) fateor, confiteor ②
□ ~ **for** indulgeo ② + dat
□ **I am** ~**ed** licet + dat

allowable adj licitus, concessus

allowance n (daily ration of food) cibarium nt
□ **make** ~**s for** indulgeo ② + dat

alloy[1] n mixtura f

alloy[2] vt misceo ③; vitio ③; adultero ①

all-powerful adj omnipotens

allude vi (~ to) attingo ③; designo, denoto; specto ①

allure vt allicio ③; allecto ①

allurement n illecebra f; fig blandimentum nt; blanditiae fpl

alluring adj blandus
■ ~**ly** adv blande

allusion n significatio f

allusive adj obliquus
■ ~**ly** adv oblique

ally[1] n socius m

ally[2] vt socio ①

almighty adj omnipotens

almond n amygdala f; amygdalum nt

almost adv fere, paene, prope; tantum non
□ **it** ~ **happens that** paulum abest ut, haud multum abest ut

alms n stips f

aloft *adv* sublime

alone *adj* solus; unus; solitarius
- ■ ~ *adv* solum; tantum
- □ **leave** ~ desero ③
- □ **let** ~ omitto, mitto ③

along *prep* secundum, praeter + *acc*
- □ ~ **with** cum + *abl*

aloof *adv* procul
- □ **stand** ~ discedo ③; removeo (me) ②; non attingo ③

aloud *adv* clara voce, clare

alpine *adj* Alpinus

already *adv* iam

also *adv* etiam; item, quoque, necnon; (moreover) praeterea, porro, insuper

altar *n* ara *f*; altaria *ntpl*

alter *vt* muto, commuto, vario, novo ①; verto ③
- ■ ~ *vi* mutor, commutor ① *etc.*

alterable *adj* mutabilis, commutabilis

alteration *n* mutatio; commutatio *f*

altercation *n* altercatio *f*, iurgium *nt*

alternate¹ *adj* alternus

alternate² *vt&i* alterno, vario ①

alternately *adv* in vicem, per vices; alternis

alternation *n* vicissitudo *f*; vices *fpl*

alternative *n* (condition) condicio *f*; (refuge) refugium *nt*
- □ **I have no** ~ nihil mihi reliqui est
- ■ ~ *adj* alternus

although *conj* etsi, tametsi, quamquam, quamvis, licet

altitude *n* altitudo, sublimitas *f*

altogether *adv* omnino; prorsus; plane, penitus

always *adv* semper; in aeternum

am *vi* sum *ir* ▶ **be**

amain *adv* vi, strenue

amalgamate *vt* misceo ②
- ■ ~ *vi* coeo ④

amalgamation *n* mixtura *f*; (combination) coitus *m*

amaranth *n* amarantus *m*

amass *vt* coacervo, cumulo ①

amateur *adj* (unskilful) rudis, imperitus

amaze *vt* obstupefacio ③

amazed *adj* attonitus, stupefactus
- □ **be** ~ stupeo ②; obstupesco ③

amazement *n* stupor *m*

amazing *adj* mirus, mirabilis, mirandus
- ■ ~**ly** *adv* mirabiliter, admirabiliter

ambassador *n* legatus *m*

amber *n* sucinum, electrum *nt*
- ■ ~ *adj* sucineus

ambiguity *n* ambiguitas *f*, ambages *fpl*

ambiguous *adj* ambiguus, dubius, anceps
- ■ ~**ly** *adv* ambigue

ambition *n* ambitio *f*

ambitious *adj* laudis *or* gloriae cupidus; ambitiosus
- ■ ~**ly** *adv* ambitiose

amble *vi* tolutim incedo ③

amblingly *adv* tolutim

ambrosia *n* ambrosia *f*

ambrosial *adj* ambrosius

ambush *n* insidiae *fpl*
- □ **lie in** ~ insidior ①

ameliorate *vt* meliorem *or*

a

melius facio *ir*
■ ~ *vi* melior or melius fio ③

amenable *adj* oboediens, docilis

amend *vt* emendo ①; corrigo ③
■ ~ *vi* proficio ③

amendment *n* correctio,
emendatio *f*

amends *n*
□ **make** ~ expio ①; satisfacio, luo
③; compenso ①

amenity *n* amoenitas *f*

amiability *n* lenitas, humanitas,
suavitas *f*

amiable *adj* amabilis, suavis, lenis,
humanus

amiably *adv* amabiliter, suaviter,
leniter, humaniter

amicable *adj* pacatus; benevolus;
benignus

amicably *adv* pacate; amice,
benevole

amid *prep* (also **amidst**) inter
+ *acc*

amiss *adv* perperam, prave, male;
secus

ammunition *n* arma *ntpl*;
apparatus bellicus *m*

amnesty *n* impunitas, venia,
oblivio *f*

amok *adv*
□ **run** ~ furo ③

among *prep* (also **amongst**)
inter; apud; ad *all* + *acc*
□ **from** ~s e, ex + *abl*

amorous *adj* amatorius; amore
captus

amount[1] *n* summa *f*

amount[2] *vi*
□ **it** ~s **to the same thing**
idem est, par est

amphitheatre *n*

amphitheatrum *nt*

ample *adj* amplus; copiosus;
largus; (enough) satis

amplification *n* amplificatio *f*

amplify *vt* dilato; amplifico ①

amply *adv* ample, abunde, satis

amputate *vt* amputo; seco ①

amputation *n* amputatio;
sectio *f*

amuse *vt* oblecto, delecto ①
□ ~ **oneself** ludo ③; mihi
placeo ②

amusement *n* delectatio,
oblectatio *f*; delectamentum,
oblectamentum *nt*; (game) ludus *m*

amusing *adj* festivus; (funny)
iocosus

analyse *vt* enodo, explico ①

anarchical *adj fig* turbulentus

anarchist *n* civis seditiosus et
turbulentus *m*

anarchy *n* licentia *f*

ancestor *n* avus, proavus, atavus;
auctor *m*
■ ~**s** *pl* maiores; priores *mpl*

ancestral *adj* avitus, proavitus

ancestry *n* stirps *f*; genus *nt*;
▶ **ancestors**

anchor[1] *n* ancora *f*
□ **weigh** ~ ancoram tollo or
solvo ③
□ **cast** ~ ancoram iacio ③
□ **ride at** ~ in ancoris consisto ③

anchor[2] *vt&i* ancoras iacio ③; (of
ships) sto ①

anchorage *n* statio *f*

ancient *adj* antiquus, vetus,
vetustus; priscus; (former) pristinus
□ **from** ~ **times** antiquitus
□ **the** ~**s** (forefathers, ancestors)
veteres, priores *mpl*; (authors) antiqui

mpl; (abstractly) antiquitas f

and conj et, ac, atque; -que; necnon

anecdote n fabella; narratiuncula f

anew adv denuo; ab integro

anger[1] n ira, iracundia, bilis f; furor m

anger[2] vt irrito, exacerbo ①; commoveo ②

angle n angulus m

angler n piscator m

angrily adv iracunde, irate

angry adj iratus, iracundus
□ **be ~** irascor ③; suscenseo ②; stomachor ①
□ **make ~** irrito, exacerbo ①

anguish n angor, dolor m

anguished adj animo fractus

angular adj angularis; (full of angles) angulosus

animal n animal nt; (wild beast) fera f; (beast) pecus f

animate[1] vt (give life to) animo; fig hortor; excito ①; erigo ③

animate[2] adj (living) animans; (of nature) vividus

animated adj (lively) vividus, alacer

animation n alacritas f; ardor; spiritus m

animosity n (grudge) simultas, acerbitas, malevolentia f; odium m

ankle n (**ankle-bone**) talus m

annals n annales, fasti mpl

annex vt annecto, adiungo, suppono ③; (seize) rapio ③

annihilate vt deleo ②; extinguo, everto ③

annihilation n exstinctio; internecio f; (ruin) excidium nt

anniversary adj anniversarius;

annuus
■ ~ n festus dies anniversarius m

annotate vt annoto, commentor ①

annotation n annotatio; nota f

announce vt nuntio; (report) renuntio ①; (laws) promulgo ①

announcement n nuntiatio; renuntiatio f; (news) nuntius m

annoy vt incommodo ①; male habeo ②; (vex) irrito ①
□ **be ~ed** stomachor ①; offensus sum

annoyance n molestia f; (anger) ira f

annoying adj molestus, incommodus

annual adj anniversarius, annuus
■ ~**ly** adv quotannis

annul vt abrogo ①; rescindo, tollo ③

annulment n abolitio, abrogatio f

anoint vt ungo, inungo, perungo ③

anointer n unctor m

anointing n unctio f

anon adv statim, illico; mox

anonymous adj
■ ~**ly** adv sine nomine

another adj alius
□ ~'**s** alienus
□ **one ~** alius alium, inter nos (vos, se)

answer[1] vt respondeo ②; (in writing) rescribo ③; (correspond to) respondeo ②
□ ~ **for** rationem reddo ③; praesto ①

answer[2] n responsio f, responsum nt; (of an oracle) sors f; (solution of a problem) explicatio f

answerable *adj* (responsible) reus; obnoxius
□ **be** ~ praesto 🗆
□ **make** ~ obligo 🗆

answering *adj* congruens; (echoing) resonus

ant *n* formica *f*

antagonism *n* adversitas *f*; (dislike) inimicitia *f*

antagonist *n* adversarius *m*; adversatrix *f*; aemulus, hostis, inimicus *m*

antechamber *n* vestibulum *nt*

antelope *n* dorcas *f*

anthem *n* canticum *nt*

anticipate *vt* anticipo 🗆; praesumo 🗆; (forestall) praevenio 🗆

anticipation *n* anticipatio; praesumptio *f*

antidote *n* antidotum *nt*; antidotus *f*; remedium *nt*

antipathy *n* odium, fastidium *nt*

antiquarian *n* (also **antiquary**) antiquarius, rerum antiquarum studiosus; rerum antiquarum peritus *m*

antiquated *adj* obsoletus

antique[1] *adj* antiquus

antique[2] *n* opus antiqui artificis; monumentum antiquitatis *nt*

antiquity *n* antiquitas; vetustas *f*

antler *n* ramus *m*

anvil *n* incus *f*

anxiety *n* anxietas; sollicitudo, trepidatio *f*

anxious *adj* anxius; sollicitus; trepidus
□ **be** ~ **(to)** laboro (ut *or* ne) 🗆; anxium esse de aliqua re

anxiously *adv* anxie; sollicite; trepide

any *pn* quivis, quilibet; (*after* negative) ullus (*after* si, nisi, num, ne) quis; (interrogatively) ecquis; (all) omnis
□ ~ **longer** diutius
□ ~ **more** amplius
□ **at** ~ **time** unquam

anybody *pn* quivis, quilibet (*after* negative) quisquam; (*after* si, nisi, num, ne) quis; (interrogatively) ecquis; (all) omnis

anyhow *adv* quoquomodo

anything *pn* quicquam, quidpiam, quodvis; (*after* si, nisi, num, ne) quid

anywhere *adv* ubilibet, alicubi, ubivis
□ **if** ~ sicubi

apace *adv* celeriter; cito, propere

apart *adv* seorsum, separatim
□ ~ **from** praeter, extra + *acc*
□ **stand** ~ disto 🗆
□ **set** ~ sepono 🗆

apartment *n* conclave *nt*

apathetic *adj* lentus; socors

apathy *n* stupor *m*; ignavia, socordia, lentitudo *f*

ape *n* simius *m*; simia *f*
■ ~ *vt* imitor 🗆

aperture *n* apertura *f*; foramen *nt*

apex *n* cacumen *nt*; apex *m*

aphorism *n* sententia *f*

apiece *adv* singuli (*pl*); quisque

apologize *vi* excuso 🗆; defendo, veniam peto 🗆

apology *n* excusatio; defensio *f*; (written treatise) apologia *f*
□ **make an** ~ **for** excuso 🗆

appal *vt* exterreo 🗆; percello 🗆

appalling *adj* horrendus

apparatus *n* apparatus *m*

apparel n vestis f, vestitus m

apparent adj manifestus; (feigned) simulatus, fictus
□ be ~ appareo, videor [2]

apparently adv (plainly) aperte, manifeste; (pretendedly) per speciem
□ he is ~ dead mortuus esse videtur

apparition n spectrum, simulacrum nt

appeal[1] vi appello; provoco; obsecro [1]

appeal[2] n (law) appellatio; provocatio; (entreaty) obsecratio f

appealing adj (pleading) supplex; (charming) lepidus

appear vi appareo, compareo [2]; me ostendo [3]; (seem) videor [2]; (arise) exorior [4]; surgo [3]; (before a court) me sisto [3]
□ it ~s patet, liquet [2]

appearance n (becoming visible) aspectus m; (outward show) species f; (vision) spectrum nt; (arrival) adventus m
□ first ~ exortus m
□ to all ~s he has been killed occisus esse videtur

appease vt placo, mitigo, expio; (hunger, etc.) sedo [1]

append vt addo [3]

appendage n appendix; accessio; appendicula f

appertain vt (to) pertineo ad; attineo ad [2] + acc

appetite n appetitus m; cupiditas f
□ have an ~ esurio [4]

applaud vt applaudo [3]; laudo [1]; plaudo [3]

applause n plausus, applausus m; laus f

apple n malum, pomum nt; (of the

eye) pupula, pupilla f

apple-tree n malus f

appliance n (instrument) instrumentum nt

applicable adj commodus, conveniens
□ not be ~ alienum esse ir

applicant n petitor m

application n (use) usus m; usurpatio f; (zeal) studium nt, sedulitas, diligentia, cura f

apply vt adhibeo; admoveo [2]; appono [3]; apto, accommodo [1]
■ ~ vi pertineo [2]; (~ to someone for something) aggredior [3]

appoint vt creo [1]; facio [3]; designo, destino [1]; constituo [3]

appointment n (office) munus nt; (order) mandatum; (rendezvous) constitutum nt

apportion vt divido, distribuo [3]

apposite adj aptus, idoneus; appositus
■ ~ly adv apte; apposite

appraisal n aestimatio f

appraise vt aestimo [1]

appreciable adj quod aestimari potest

appreciate vt aestimo [1]; (value highly) magni facio [3]

appreciation n aestimatio; (praise) laus f

apprehend vt comprehendo, apprehendo; percipio [3]; (fear) timeo [2]; (suspect) suspicor [1]; (seize) capio [3]; (take unawares) intercipio [3]; (arrest) comprehendo [3]

apprehension n (fear) timor m; (suspicion) suspicio; (seizing) comprehensio f; (understanding) ingenium nt, intelligentia f

apprehensive *adj* timidus

apprentice *n* discipulus; tiro *m*

apprenticeship *n* tirocinium *nt*

approach *vt&i* appropinquo
① + *dat*; accedo ③; adeo *ir*; (be imminent) immineo ②; insto ①

approachable *adj* patens; *fig* affabilis, facilis

approbation *n* approbatio, laus *f*

appropriate¹ *vt* mihi arrogo ①; mihi assero ③; vindico ①; assumo ③

appropriate² *adj* proprius; congruens
■ ~**ly** *adv* apte, congruenter

appropriateness *n* convenientia *f*

approval *n* approbatio *f*

approve *vt* approbo, probo, laudo ①

approximate *adj* propinquus

approximately *adv* fere, prope

appurtenance *n* appendix *f*

April *n* Aprilis *m*

apron *n* subligaculum *nt*

apt *adj* aptus, idoneus; (inclined, prone) pronus, propensus, proclivis

aptitude *n* habilitas *f*; ingenium *nt*

aptly *adv* apte, apposite

aptness *n* convenientia, congruentia; (tendency, propensity) proclivitas *f*

aquatic *adj* aquatilis; aquaticus

aqueduct *n* aquae ductus, aquarum ductus *m*

Arab *n* Arabs *m*

arable *adj* arabilis
■ ~ **land** *n* arvum, novale *nt*; novalis *f*

arbiter *n* arbiter; dominus *m*

arbitrarily *adv* ad arbitrium; ad libidinem

arbitrary *adj* imperiosus; superbus

arbitrate *vt&i* discepto, diiudico ①

arbitration *n* arbitrium *nt*

arbitrator *n* arbiter; (private) disceptator *m*

arbour *n* umbraculum *nt*

arbute *n* (tree) arbutus *f*; (fruit) arbutum *nt*
■ ~-**berry** *n* arbutum *nt*

arc *n* arcus *m*

arcade *n* porticus *f*

arch¹ *n* arcus, fornix *m*

arch² *vt* arcuo ①

archaeology *n* scientia antiquitatis *f*

archaic *adj* obsoletus

arched *adj* curvus

archer *n* sagittarius *m*

archery *n* ars sagittandi *f*

archetype *n* archetypum, exemplum *nt*

architect *n* architectus *m*; artifex *m*

architectural *adj* architectonicus

architecture *n* architectura *f*

archives *n* tabulae *fpl*; tabularium *nt*

archway *n* porticus *f*

arctic *adj* arcticus; Arctous

ardent *adj* ardens, fervidus
■ ~**ly** *adv* ardenter

ardour *n* ardor, fervor *m*

arduous *adj* (difficult) arduus; difficilis
■ ~**ly** *adv* difficulter

area *n* area; superficies *f*

arena *n* arena *f*

argonaut *n* argonauta *m*

argue *vt&i* disputo, discepto ①; dissero ③; (prove) arguo, evinco ③; probo ①

argument *n* disceptatio, disputatio *f*; (subject) argumentum *nt*

argumentative *adj* (fond of dispute) litigiosus

arid *adj* aridus, siccus

aridity *n* ariditas, siccitas *f*

aright *adv* recte, bene

arise *vi* surgo ③; orior ④; (be born from) nascor ③

aristocracy *n* optimates, nobiles *mpl*

aristocrat *n* optimas, patricius *m*

aristocratic *adj* patricius
  ■ ~**ally** *adv* more patricio

arithmetic *n* arithmetica *ntpl*

arithmetical *adj* arithmeticus

arm¹ *n* bracchium *nt*; lacertus *m*; (weapon) telum *nt*; ▶ **arms**

arm² *vt* armo ①
  ■ ~ *vi* armor ①; arma capio ③; bellum paro ①

armament *n* armatura *f*; apparatus bellicus *m*

armed *adj* armatus

armistice *n* indutiae *fpl*

armour *n* armatura *f*; armatus *m*; arma *ntpl*
  ■ ~-**bearer** *n* armiger *m*

armoury *n* armamentarium *nt*

arms *n* arma; fig bellum *nt*
  □ **lay down** ~ ab armis discedere; arma dedere
  □ **take (up)** ~ sumere arma
  □ **be under** ~ in armis esse

army *n* exercitus *m*; (in battle array) acies *f*; (on the march) agmen *nt*;

(forces) copiae *fpl*

aroma *n* odor *m*

aromatic *adj* fragrans

around *adv&prep* circum, circa + *acc*
  □ **all** ~ undique

arouse *vt* suscito, excito, concito ①; (produce) cieo, moveo ②; conflo ①; (encourage) erigo ③
  □ ~ **oneself** expergisci ③

arraign *vt* accuso ①

arraignment *n* accusatio *f*

arrange *vt* instruo, struo, (battle) instituo ③; ordino ①; dispono ③; colloco ①; (make a plan) constituo ③

arrangement *n* collocatio, compositio; dispositio; (of battle) ordinatio *f*; (plan) consilium *nt*

array¹ *n* (of battle) acies *f*; (clothing) vestitus *m*; (arrangement, order) ordo *m*; dispositio, compositio *f*

array² *vt* vestio ④; adorno ①; compono, instruo ③

arrears *n* reliqua *ntpl*; residuae *fpl*
  □ **be in** ~ reliquor ①

arrest¹ *n* comprehensio *f*

arrest² *vt* comprehendo ③; (detain); detineo ②; (stop) sisto ③

arrival *n* adventus *m*

arrive *vi* advenio, pervenio ④; (as a ship) advehor, appellor ③

arrogance *n* arrogantia; superbia, insolentia *f*

arrogant *adj* arrogans; superbus; insolens
  ■ ~**ly** *adv* arroganter; insolenter

arrow *n* sagitta, arundo *f*; telum *nt*

arsenal *n* armamentarium *nt*; navalia *ntpl*

arson *n* incendium *nt*

art *n* ars *f*; (cunning) artificium *nt*;

(skill) sollertia f
□ **fine** ~**s** artes elegantes or ingenuae pl
□ **black** ~ magice f

artery n arteria; vena f

artful adj callidus, subtilis; subdolus
■ ~**ly** adv callide, subtiliter, subdole

artfulness n artificium nt; calliditas f

arthritic adj arthriticus

article n (item) res; (part of treaty) condicio; pactio; (for sale) merx f

articulate[1] adj distinctus, dilucidus

articulate[2] vt articulo, enuntio ①

artifice n artificium nt; ars f; dolus m; fraus f

artificer n artifex m; opifex m/f

artificial adj artificiosus; facticius
■ ~**ly** adv arte

artillery n tormenta ntpl

artisan n faber m; artifex m; opifex m/f

artist n artifex m

artistic adj artificiosus
■ ~**ally** adv artificiose; affabre

artless adj incomptus; incompositus; ingenuus, simplex
■ ~**ly** adv incompte; ingenue

artlessness n simplicitas f

as adv & conj (of time) dum, cum; (of manner) ut; quam; ita ut; sicut; velut
□ ~ **far** ~ quoad, quantum; usque ad + acc
□ ~ **for** de + abl
□ ~ **if** quasi, perinde ac si; ita ut si
□ ~ **it were** ceu, tanquam, velut
□ ~ **long** ~ quamdiu
□ ~ **many** ~ quotquot, quotcunque

□ ~ **much** tantum
□ ~ **often** ~ quoties
□ ~ **soon** ~ cum primum, simul atque
□ ~ **yet** adhuc
□ **not** ~ **yet** nondum

ascend vt&i ascendo, conscendo, scando ③

ascension n ascensio f; ascensus m

ascent n ascensio f; ascensus m; acclivitas f

ascertain vt comperio, pro certo scio ④; cognosco ③

ascribe vt imputo ①; ascribo, tribuo ③

ash n (tree) fraxinus f; (cinders) cinis m; ▶ **ashes**

ashamed adj pudibundus
□ **be** ~ erubesco ③
□ **I am** ~ **of** use me pudet ② + gen or inf

ashen adj (of the tree) fraxineus; (pale) pallidus

ashes n cinis m; favilla f

ashore adv in terram, ad litus
□ **be cast** ~ eicior
□ **go** ~ egredior
□ **put** ~ expono ③

Asian adj Asiaticus, Asius

aside adv seorsum, oblique
□ **call** ~ sevoco ①
□ **lay** or **set** ~ sepono ③

asinine adj asininus

ask vt (for) rogo ①, posco, peto, quaero ③; (a question) interrogo ①

askance adv
□ **look** ~ torva tueor ②

askew adv in obliquum

aslant adv oblique, in obliquum

asleep adj dormiens

□ **be** ~ dormio 4
□ **fall** ~ obdormio
□ **lull** ~ sopio, consopio 4

aspect n (what is seen) aspectus; prospectus; (face) vultus m, facies f

asperity n acerbitas f

asphalt n bitumen nt

aspiration n (desire) affectatio f; (longing) votum nt

aspire vt (~ to) affecto, aspiro ①; peto, annitor ③

aspiring adj appetens + gen

ass n asinus m, asina f; (wild ~) onager
■ ~**-driver** n asinarius m

assail vt aggredior ③; oppugno ①; invehor ③

assassin n sicarius m

assassinate vt insidiis interficio ③

assassination n caedes f

assault¹ n impetus m; oppugnatio; (violence) vis f; ▶ **attack**

assault² vt adorior 4; oppugno ①; manus infero ③

assemblage n congregatio; (multitude) multitudo f

assemble vt congrego, convoco ①; contraho ③
■ ~ vi convenio 4

assembly n coetus, conventus m; concilium nt; (in politics) comitia ntpl; contio f; (small) conventiculum nt; (of people standing round) corona f

assembly-room n curia f

assent¹ vi assentior 4; annuo ③

assent² n assensus m

assert vt affirmo, assevero ①; (vindicate) defendo ③; tueor ②

assertion n affirmatio, asseveratio; sententia f

assess vt (tax) censeo ②; (value) aestimo ①

assessment n census m; aestimatio f; (tax) vectigal; tributum nt

assessor n (judge) assessor; (of taxes) censor m

assets n bona ntpl

assiduity n assiduitas, diligentia f

assiduous adj assiduus, sedulus
■ ~**ly** adv assidue, sedulo

assign vt attribuo ③; delego, assigno ①; (determine) statuo, constituo ③

assignation n constitutum nt

assignment n assignatio; attributio f

assimilate vt assimulo; (make equal) aequo ①; (digest) concoquo ③

assimilation n assimilatio f

assist vt iuvo, adiuvo; auxilior ①; succurro ③, subvenio 4 both + dat

assistance n auxilium nt, opis gen sing f

assistant n adiutor m, adiutrix f, administer, auxiliator, advocatus m

associate¹ vt consocio ①; adscisco ③; (impute) ascribo
■ ~ vi (with) versor cum ① + abl

associate² adj socius

associate³ n socius m; consors m/f; particeps m/f

association n societas; communitas; consociatio; congregatio f; (corporation) collegium nt

assuage vt allevo, levo ①; lenio ④

assume vt induo; assumo ③; (claim) arrogo ①; (pretend) simulo ①; (take for granted) pono ③

assumption n (the taking for

assurance | attain

granted) sumptio *f*

assurance *n* fiducia; (confidence) audacia, (presumptuousness) impudentia *f*; (pledge) pignus *nt*

assure *vt* confirmo, affirmo ①; promitto ③; (encourage) adhortor ①
□ **be ~d** confido ③

assuredly *adv* profecto, certe

astern *adv* in puppi; a puppi

asthma *n* dyspnoea *f*, asthma *nt*

asthmatic *adj* asthmaticus

astonish *vt* obstupefacio ③
□ **be ~ed** miror ①; obstupesco ③

astonishing *adj* mirabilis, mirandus
■ **~ly** *adv* admirabiliter

astonishment *n* admiratio *f*; stupor *m*

astound *vt* stupefacio, obstupefacio ③

astray *adj*
□ **go ~** erro ①
□ **lead ~** via recta abducere, transversum agere ③

astringent *adj* astrictorius

astrologer *n* astrologus; mathematicus *m*

astrological *adj* Chaldaicus

astrology *n* astrologia; mathematica *f*

astronomer *n* astrologus; astronomus *m*

astronomical *adj* astronomicus

astronomy *n* astrologia; astronomia *f*

astute *adj* callidus, astutus, sagax
■ **~ly** *adv* callide, astute, sagaciter

astuteness *n* calliditas, sagacitas *f*

asunder *adv* seorsum, separatim; (in two) dis...

□ **cut ~** disseco ①
□ **pull ~** distraho ③

asylum *n* asylum *nt*

at *prep* ad, apud; (during) inter all + acc; in + abl; (of time) use abl; (of cost) use gen or abl

athirst *adv* sitiens

athlete *n* athleta *m*

athletic *adj* athleticus

atmosphere *n* aer *m*; caelum; inane *nt*

atom *n* atomus *f*; corpus individuum, corpus insecabile *nt*; fig mica, particula *f*
□ **not an ~ of** nihil omnino + *gen*

atone *vt* pio; expio ①; solvo, luo ③

atonement *n* piaculum *nt*; expiatio; compensatio, satisfactio *f*

atrocious *adj* nefarius, nefandus; (monstrous) immanis; (of crimes) dirus; atrox

atrocity *n* atrocitas *f*; nefas, facinus *nt*

attach *vt* annecto, adiungo ③; applico ①
□ **be ~ed (to)** haereo, adhaereo ②; (be fond of) amo ①

attachment *n* (affection) amor *m*, caritas *f*

attack[1] *n* (onset) impetus *m*; oppugnatio *f*; incursus *m*; fig (of a disease) tentatio *f*

attack[2] *vt* (the enemy) aggredior, irruo ③; (a town) oppugno; fig provoco ①; lacesso ③; (verbally) invehor ③; (of diseases) corripio, invado ③; tento ①

attacker *n* oppugnator; provocator *m*

attain *vt* adipiscor, consequor ③; pervenio ④ ad + acc

attainable *adj* impetrabilis

attainment *n* comparatio, impetratio *f*

attempt[1] *n* conatum; inceptum, ausum, periculum *nt*
□ **a first ~** tirocinium *nt*

attempt[2] *vt* conor ①; nitor ③; molior ④; audeo ②; tento ①

attend *vt* (accompany) comitor ①; (escort) deduco ③; (be present) intersum, (be present at) adsum *ir* + *dat*
□ **~ to** curo, procuro ①; servio ④; (comply with) obtempero ①; invigilo ①; (pay attention) animum adverto ③

attendance *n* (service) obsequium; officium, ministerium *nt*; (care) cura, diligentia *f*; (retinue) comitatus *m*; (presence) praesentia *f*

attendant *n* comes; assector, assecla, apparitor; famulus *m*; famula *f*
■ **~s** *pl* comitatus *m*

attention *n* animus attentus *m*; intentio; sedulitas *f*; cultus *m*; observantia *f*
□ **pay ~ to** observo ①; operam do ①; colo ③; studeo ②

attentive *adj* attentus; sedulus; officiosus
■ **~ly** *adv* attente, intento animo; sedulo; officiose

attest *vt* testor, testificor ①

attire[1] *n* ornatus; vestitus *m*

attire[2] *vt* adorno ①; vestio ④

attitude *n* (appearance) habitus; status *m*; (opinion) sententia *f*

attorney *n* cognitor, causidicus, advocatus *m*

attract *vt* traho, attraho; allicio ③

attraction *n* illecebra *f*;
▶ **charm**

attractive *adj* lepidus, blandus

attractiveness *n* lepos *m*

attribute[1] *vt* tribuo, attribuo, ascribo ③; (falsely) affingo ③; imputo ①

attribute[2] *n* (characteristic) proprium *nt*

attrition *n* attritus *m*

attune *vt* modulor ①

auburn *adj* flavus; aureus

auction *n* auctio *f*
□ **sell by ~** auctionor ①; sub hasta vendo ③

auctioneer *n* praeco *m*

audacious *adj* audax; confidens
■ **~ly** *adv* audacter; confidenter

audacity *n* confidentia, audacia *f*

audible *adj* quod audiri potest

audibly *adv* clara voce, ut omnes exaudire possint

audience *n* (admittance) aditus *m*; (conversation) colloquium *m*; (hearers) auditores *mpl*; (bystanders) corona *f*

audit *vt* rationes inspicio ③

auditor *n* (hearer) auditor *m*

auditorium *n* auditorium *nt*

auger *n* terebra *f*

augment *vt* augeo ②; amplio ①
■ **~ vi** (be augmented) augeor ②; cresco, accresco ③

augmentation *n* incrementum *nt*

augur[1] *n* augur *m/f*; hariolus, haruspex *m*

augur[2] *vi&t* auguror; vaticinor, hariolor ①

augury *n* augurium, auspicium *nt*; auguratio *f*

august[1] *adj* augustus; magnificus

August[2] *n* Sextilis, Augustus *m*

aunt n (on the father's side) amita; (on the mother's side) matertera f

auspices n auspicium nt
□ **under your ~** te auspice

auspicious adj faustus; secundus; prosperus; auspicatus
■ **~ly** adv auspicato; feliciter; prospere

austere adj austerus, severus

austerity n austeritas, severitas f

authentic adj certus; verus; fide dignus

authentically adv certo auctore; cum auctoritate

authenticate vt recognosco ③; firmo, confirmo ①

authentication n auctoritas; confirmatio f

authenticity n auctoritas; fides f

author n auctor; scriptor; (inventor) conditor, inventor; (beginner) princeps m; (of a crime) caput (sceleris) nt

authoritative adj auctoritate firmatus; (imperious) imperiosus

authority n auctoritas; potestas; (leave) licentia f; (power) ius; imperium nt; (office or official) magistratus m

authorization n confirmatio, licentia f

authorize vt potestatem or copiam do ①; (excuse) excuso ①; (approve) probo ①

autobiography n res gestae fpl

autocrat n dominus m

autograph n chirographum nt

autumn n autumnus m

autumnal adj autumnalis

auxiliary adj auxiliaris, auxiliarius
■ **~** n adiutor m

auxiliaries npl (mil) auxilia ntpl

avail[1] vi
□ **~ oneself of** utor ③ + abl

avail[2] n
□ **be of no ~** usui non esse

available adj utilis; efficax; (at hand) praesto (indecl)

avalanche n nivis casus m

avarice n avaritia, parsimonia, sordes f

avaricious adj avarus, sordidus
■ **~ly** adv avare, sordide

avenge vt vindico ①; ulciscor ③

avenger n ultor m, ultrix f; vindex m/f

avenging adj ultrix, vindex

avenue n aditus, introitus; (of trees) xystus m

average[1] n medium inter maximum et minimum nt; aequa distributio f
□ **on ~** peraeque; (about) circiter

average[2] adj medius inter maximum minimumque

averse adj alienus; aversus, abhorrens
□ **be ~ to** abhorreo ② + dat

aversion n odium, fastidium nt
□ **~ to** taedium + gen nt

avert vt amoveo ②; averto, depello ③; (beg off) deprecor ①

aviary n aviarium nt

avid adj avidus

avidity n aviditas f

avoid vt fugio ③; vito, devito ①; (turn aside, decline) declino, detrecto ①

avoidable adj evitabilis, qui effugi potest

avoidance n vitatio; declinatio f; (flight from) fuga f + gen

avow *vt* profiteor, confiteor ②

avowal *n* professio, confessio *f*

avowedly *adv* ex professo, aperte

await *vt* exspecto ①

awake¹ *adj* vigil, vigilans; (sleepless) exsomnis
- □ **be** ～ vigilo ①

awake² *vt* (also **awaken**) excito, suscito ①; expergefacio ③
- ■ ～ *vi* expergiscor ③

award¹ *n* sententia *f*; iudicium, arbitrium *nt*

award² *vt* adiudico ①; addico, tribuo ③; assigno ①

aware *adj* (of) gnarus, conscius + *gen* ; sciens
- □ **not** ～ **of** ignarus, nescius + *gen*
- □ **be** ～ **(of)** sentio, scio ④

awareness *n* scientia *f*

away *adv* procul
- □ ～**I** abi! apage!
- □ **be** ～ absum *ir*
- □ **go** ～ abeo *ir*
- □ **take** ～ aufero *ir*, tollo ③

awe *n* reverentia *f*; (fear) metus, terror *m*, formido *f*
- □ **stand in** ～ metuo ③; timeo ②

awestruck *adj* pavefactus

awful *adj* (awe-inspiring) verendus; (dreadful) formidolosus, terribilis, dirus
- ■ ～**ly** *adv* formidolose

awhile *adv* paulisper

awkward *adj* ineptus; rusticus, rudis, inscitus; (things) incommodus
- ■ ～**ly** *adv* inepte; rustice; inscite

awkwardness *n* imperitia, rusticitas *f*; (inconvenience) incommoditas *f*

awning *n* velarium, velum *nt*

awry *adj* obliquus

- ■ ～ *adv* oblique; perverse; prave, perperam

axe *n* securis, ascia; (battle-axe) bipennis; (pickaxe) dolabra *f*

axis *n* axis *m*

axle *n* axis *m*

azure *adj* caeruleus

Bb

baa *vi* (like a sheep) balo ①

babble *n* garrulitas *f*

babble² *vi* blatero ①; garrio ④

babbling *adj* garrulus, loquax

baby *n* infans, parvulus *m*

babyhood *n* infantia *f*

babyish *adj* puerilis

Bacchanalia *n* Bacchanalia *ntpl*

bacchanalian *adj* bacchanalis

Bacchante *n* Baccha *f*

Bacchic *adj* Bacchicus

bachelor *n* caelebs *m*

back¹ *n* tergum, dorsum *nt*
- □ **wound in the** ～ aversum vulnero ①
- □ **turn one's** ～ tergum verto ③

back² *adv* retro; retrorsum; re...

back³ *vt* (support) faveo ② + *dat*; (help) adiuvo ①
- □ ～ **water** navem remis inhibeo ②
- ■ ～ *vi* me recipio ③
- □ ～ **out of** evado ③

backbite *vt* maledico + *dat*, dente carpo ③

backbiter *n* maledicus,

obtrectator *m*
backbiting *n* obtrectatio *f*
backbone *n* spina *f*
back door *n* posticum ostium *nt*
backer *n* adiutor *m*
background *n* scaena *f*; fig recessus *m*
■ **~** *vt* (keep in the background) abscondo ③
backing *adj* (help) auxilium, (political) suffragium *nt*
backward *adj* (slow) piger, tardus, segnis; (averse to) alienus; (lying on the back) supinus
□ **be ~** (delay) cunctor ①
backwardness *n* tarditas; pigritia *f*
backwards *adv* (also **backward**) retro; retrorsum
bacon *n* lardum *nt*
bad *adj* malus, pravus, nequam; improbus; (ill) aeger; (unfortunate) malus, tristis
□ **~ weather** tempestas adversa *f*
badge *n* insigne, signum, indicium *nt*
badger *n* meles, melis *f*
badly *adv* male, prave, nequiter; improbe
badness *n* nequitia; improbitas *f*
baffle *vt* decipio, fallo, eludo ③
bag *n* saccus; crumena *f*; (of leather) uter *m*; (of netting) reticulum *nt*
baggage *n* sarcinae *fpl*; impedimenta *ntpl*
bail[1] *n* vadimonium *nt*; (surety) vas; (for debt) praes *m*
bail[2] *vt* (give **~** for) spondeo ②; fidepromitto ③; (accept **~** for) vador ①

bailiff *n* (of a farm) vilicus; (of a court of justice) apparitor *m*
bailiwick *n* iurisdictio *f*
bait[1] *n* esca *f*; fig incitamentum *nt*
bait[2] *vt* inesco ①; (tease) lacesso ③
bake *vt* torreo ②; coquo ③; igne obduro ①
baker *n* pistor *m*
■ **~'s shop** *n* pistrina *f*; pistrinum *nt*
bakery *n* pistrina *f*
balance[1] *n* (scales) libra, statera, trutina *f*; (equipoise) aequipondium *nt*; (in book-keeping) reliquum *nt*
□ **lose one's ~** labi
balance[2] *vt* libro ①, pendo ③; (weigh one thing against another) penso, compenso ①; (accounts) dispungo ③
balcony *n* maeniana *ntpl*
bald *adj* calvus, glaber; fig ieiunus, aridus
balderdash *n* farrago *f*
baldness *n* calvitium *nt*
baldric *n* cingulum *nt*, balteus *m*
bale *n* sarcina *f*, fascis *m*
baleful *adj* funestus; perniciosus; exitialis, noxius
balk *vt* (frustrate) frustror ①; eludo, decipio, fallo ③
ball *n* globus, globulus *m*; (to play with) pila *f*
ballad *n* nenia *f*; carmen triviale *nt*
ballast *n* saburra *f*
ballet *n* pantomimus *m*; embolium *nt*
ballet-dancer *n* pantomimus *m*; pantomima *f*
ballot[1] *n* (token used in voting) tabella *f*; (voting) suffragor *f*
ballot[2] *vi* tabella *or* tabellis

suffragor 🔲

ballot-box n cista f

balm n balsamum; fig solatium nt

balustrade n (rails enclosing a place) cancelli mpl

ban¹ n interdictio f

ban² vt interdico 🔲

banal adj ieiunus

band¹ n (chain) vinculum; (headband) redimiculum nt; (troop) caterva f; (chorus) grex m; fig catena, copula f; vinculum nt

band² vt socio, consocio
■ ~ vi (league together) coniuro 🔲

bandage¹ n fascia f

bandage² vt deligo 🔲

bandit n latro m

bandy-legged adj loripes, valgus

bane n venenum nt; pestis; pernicies f

baneful adj pestifer; perniciosus; funestus; exitialis

bang¹ vt&i crepo 🔲; (hit) ferio 🔲

bang² n crepitus, sonitus m; (blow) plaga f; (shock) percussus m

banish vt in exilium mitto, pello 🔲; relego 🔲; fig pono 🔲

banishment n (act) eiectio; relegatio f; (state) exilium nt; fuga f

bank n (hillock) tumulus m; (of a river) ripa f; (for money) argentaria taberna f

banker n argentarius, mensarius, trapezita m

bankrupt n decoctor m
■ **be** or **go** ~ rationes conturbare 🔲; decoquo 🔲

bankruptcy n novae tabulae fpl

banner n vexillum nt

banquet¹ n convivium nt; epulae,

dapes fpl

banquet² vi convivor; epulor 🔲
■ ~ vt convivio excipio 🔲

banqueter n epulo, conviva m

banqueting n epulatio f

banter¹ n iocus m; cavillatio f

banter² vt cavillor 🔲; derideo 🔲

banteringly adj per ludibrium

bar¹ n vectis; (of a door) obex m; repagulum nt; pessulus m; fig impedimentum nt; (ingot) later m; (in a court of justice) cancelli mpl; claustra ntpl; (barristers) advocati mpl; iudiciale nt

bar² vt (a door, etc.) obsero 🔲; (shut out) excludo 🔲; (prevent) prohibeo 🔲; veto 🔲

barb n (hook) uncus; hamus m

barbacan n turris; specula f

barbarian adj & n barbarus m

barbaric adj barbaricus

barbarity n barbaries; feritas, truculentia f

barbarous adj barbarus; ferus; immanis; saevus, truculentus; (uncultivated) rudis, barbarus
■ ~**ly** adv barbare; saeve

barbed adj hamatus

barber n tonsor m, tonstrix f
□ ~**'s shop** tonstrina f

bard n vates m/f

bare¹ adj (unclothed) nudus; (mere) merus; (of style) pressus; (plain) manifestus; (empty) nudus, vacuus

bare² vt nudo, denudo 🔲; aperio 🔲

barefaced adj impudens; audax

barefoot adj (also **barefooted**) nudo pede, nudis pedibus; discalceatus

bareheaded adj nudo capite

barely | batter

barely *adv* vix, aegre

bargain¹ *n* pactio *f*, pactum *nt*

bargain² *vi* stipulor ①; paciscor ③

barge *n* navicula, linter *f*

bargeman *n* portitor *m*

bark¹ *n* (of trees) cortex *m/f*; (inner bark) liber *m*

bark² *n* (of dogs) latratus *m*

bark³ *vi* (sound) latro ①
□ ∼ **at** (also fig) allatro ①

barking *n* latratus *m*

barley *n* hordeum *nt*

barmaid *n* ministra cauponae *f*

barn *n* granarium, horreum *nt*

barque *n* navicula, ratis, linter *f*

barracks *n* castra (stativa) *ntpl*

barrel *n* (cask) cadus *m*, dolium *nt*; orca *f*; (cylinder) cylindrus *m*

barren *adj* sterilis; infecundus

barrenness *n* sterilitas, infecunditas *f*

barricade¹ *n* agger *m*; vallum *nt*

barricade² *vt* obstruo ③

barrier *n* cancelli *mpl*; saepta *ntpl*; (in the circus) carcer *m*; claustra *ntpl*; fig impedimentum *nt*

barrister *n* advocatus, causidicus *m*

barrow *n* (vehicle) ferculum *nt*; (mound) tumulus *m*

barter¹ *n* permutatio *f*; commercium *nt*

barter² *vt&i* muto, commuto, permuto ①; paciscor ③

base¹ *adj* humilis, ignobilis, obscurus; inferior; infamis, vilis, turpis; foedus
■ ∼**ly** *adv* abiecte; turpiter

base² *n* basis *f*; fundus *m*; fundamentum *nt*

baseless *adj* vanus, inanis; falsus

baseness *n* humilitas; turpitudo; nequitia *f*

bashful *adj* pudens; pudicus, pudibundus, modestus; verecundus
■ ∼**ly** *adv* timide; modeste; verecunde; pudenter

bashfulness *n* pudor; rubor *m*; verecundia, modestia *f*

basin *n* (for washing the hands) pelvis *f*, trulleus *m*; (tub) labrum *nt*; (lake) lacus *m*; (dock) navalia *ntpl*

basis *n* fundamentum *nt*; (cause) causa *f*

bask *vi* apricor ①

basket *n* corbis *f*; canistrum; qualum *nt*; calathus *m*; (large basket) cophinus *m*

bass *n* (sound) sonus gravis *m*

bastard *n* nothus, spurius *m*; fig fictus, falsus
■ ∼ *adj* spurius

baste *vt* perfundo, conspergo ③

bastion *n* propugnaculum, castellum *nt*

bat¹ *n* (animal) vespertilio *m*

bat² *n* (club) clava *f*, fustis *m*

batch *n* (troop) turma *f*; (of things) numerus *m*
■ **in** ∼**es** *adv* turmatim

bath *n* balneum *nt*; lavatio *f*; (tub) alveus *m*, labrum *nt*

bathe *vt* lavo; (steep) macero ①; (sprinkle) perfundo ③
■ ∼ *vi* lavor ①

bathing *n* lavatio *f*

bath-keeper *n* balneator *m*

battalion *n* cohors *f*; (army in battle-array) acies *f*

batter *vt* verbero, pulso ①;

percutio, obtundo, diruo ③; ferio ④

battering-ram n aries m

battery n (mound for artillery) agger m; (artillery) tormenta ntpl; (assault) vis f

battle[1] n proelium nt, pugna f

battle[2] vi proelior, pugno ①; (with someone) contendo ③

battle-array n acies f

battle-axe n bipennis f

battlefield n acies f, campus m

battlement n pinna f

bauble n tricae, nugae fpl

bawd n lena f; leno m

bawdy adj impudicus, immodestus

bawl vi clamito, vociferor ①

bawling n vociferatio f; clamor m

bay[1] n (of the sea) sinus m

bay[2] n (tree) laurus, laurea f

bazaar n forum nt

be vi sum, esse, fui ir; (exist) existo ③
□ **how are you?** quid agis?
□ ~ **against** adversor ①; abhorreo ②
□ ~ **amongst** or **between** intersum
□ ~ **away** absum
□ ~ **for (one)** faveo ②; cum aliquo sto ①
□ ~ **in** insum
□ **so** ~ **it** ita fiat, esto!
□ **let** ~ mitto ③
□ ~ **present** adsum
□ ~ **without** careo ② + abl

beach n litus nt; (coast) ora f

beacon n specula f; (lighthouse) pharus m; (fire) ignis m

bead n globus, globulus m

beak n rostrum nt; (of ships) rostra ntpl

beaked adj rostratus

beaker n poculum, carchesium nt

beam[1] n (wooden) tignum nt, trabs f; (of ships) transtrum nt; (of a balance) scapus m; (light) radius m

beam[2] vi radio ①; refulgeo, niteo ②

beaming adj nitens, lucidus

bear[1] vt fero ir; fig patior; gero ③; subeo ④; sustineo ②; tolero ①; (of children) pario ③; (bring forth) fero, effero ir, fundo, profundo ③
□ ~ **away** or **off** aufero ir
□ ~ **out** effero ir; praesto ①
□ ~ **witness** testor ①
□ ~ **with** indulgeo ② + dat

bear[2] n ursus m, ursa f; (constellation) septentriones mpl

bearable adj tolerandus, tolerabilis

beard n barba; (of corn) arista f

bearded adj barbatus; intonsus

beardless adj imberbis

bearer n (porter) baiulus m; (of litters, etc.) lecticarius; (of corpses) vispillo m

bearing n (physical) gestus m
□ **it has a** ~ **on** pertinet ad + acc

beast n belua; bestia f; (cattle) pecus nt
□ **wild** ~ fera f
□ ~ **of burden** iumentum nt

beat vt verbero; (knock) pulso ①; caedo ③; (conquer) vinco; (bruise) tero ③; (excel) supero ①
□ ~ **back** or **off** repello ③
■ ~ vi (of the heart) palpito ①

beaten adj victus; (of a path, etc.) tritus

beating n verberatio f; (blow) ictus m; verbera ntpl; (time in music) percussio f; (of the heart) palpitatio f

beautiful adj pulcher; (of form)

formosus

beautifully adv pulchre

beautify vt decoro, orno ①; excolo ③

beauty n pulcritudo; forma; (grace, etc.) Venus f

beaver n castor, fiber m; (cheek-piece of a helmet) buccula f

becalm vt paco, sedo ①
□ **~ed** vento destitutus

because conj quia, quod; quoniam
□ **~ of** ob, propter + acc

beckon vi nuto ①; annuo, innuo ③

become vi fio ir

becoming adj decorus; decens; conveniens

bed n lectus, torus m; cubile nt; (in a garden) areola f; (of a river) alveus m

bedaub vt lino, perunguo ③; inquino, conspurco ①

bedclothes n stragulum nt; vestis f

bedding n stragulum nt; vestis f

bedeck vt decoro, orno, exorno ①; excolo ③

bedew vt irroro, umecto ①; perfundo ③

bed-fellow n socius (m) or socia (f) tori

bedpost n fulcrum nt

bedridden adj lecto affixus

bedroom n cubiculum nt

bedstead n sponda f

bedtime n hora somni f

bee n apis f
■ **~hive** n alveus m; apiarium, alvearium nt
■ **~keeper** n apiarius m

beech n fagus f

beechen adj faginus, fagineus,

fageus

beef n bubula (caro) f

beer n cervisia f

beet n beta f

beetle n scarabaeus m

befall vi contingo, accido ③; evenio ④

befit vt convenio ④
□ **it ~s** par est, convenit ④; decet ② all + dat

befitting adj decens; conveniens, idoneus

before¹ prep ante + acc; prae, pro; (in the presence of) coram + abl; apud + acc
■ **~** adv ante; antea prius
□ **~ now** antehac
□ **long ~** iamdudum
□ **a little ~** paulo ante
■ **~** conj antequam, priusquam

before² adj prior

beforehand adv ante, prius; prae ...

befriend vt sublevo, adiuvo ①, faveo ② + dat

beg vt&i peto, posco ③; oro, precor, obsecro, flagito, rogo ①; (be a beggar) mendico ①

beget vt gigno ③; procreo, creo, genero ①

beggar¹ n mendicus m, mendica f

beggar² vt ad inopiam redigo ③

beggarly adj mendicus; vilis, abiectus; (wretched) exilis

beggary n mendicitas, egestas, paupertas f

begin vt&i initium facio ③; incoho ①; ordior ④; coepi, incipio ③; (arise) exorior ④

beginner n (originator) auctor; fig (novice) tiro m

beginning n inceptio f; initium; principium, exordium nt; origo f

begrudge vt invideo + acc of thing and dat of person

beguile vt fraudo, frustror ①; fallo ③; circumvenio ④

behalf n
□ **on ~ of** pro + abl, propter + acc, causa + gen

behave vi&t
□ **~ oneself** (conduct oneself) me gero; (~ towards) utor ③ + abl

behaviour n mores mpl; (actions) facta ntpl
□ **good ~** urbanitas f
□ **bad ~** rusticitas f

behead vt decollo ①; securi percutio ③

behind adv pone, a tergo, post; (remaining) reliquus
□ **be left ~** relinquor ③
■ **~** prep post + acc

behold¹ vt conspicio ③; obtueor ②; specto ①; cerno ③; aspicio ③

behold² int ecce! en! aspice!

beholden adj obnoxius
□ **be ~ to** obligor ①; gratiam debeo ②

being n natura; (essence) essentia f; (man) homo m
□ **supreme ~** numen nt

belabour vt verbero, pulso ①

belated adj serus

belch¹ vi ructo; eructo ①

belch² n ructus m

beleaguer vt obsideo ②

belief n fides, opinio, persuasio, religio f; (teaching) doctrina f

believe vt credo ③; (trust to) confido ③; (think) existimo, opinor, arbitror, puto ①

□ **~ in the gods** deos esse credo ③

belittle vt rodo ③

bell n tintinnabulum nt

bellow vi rugio, mugio ④

bellowing n mugitus m

bellows n (a pair of ~) follis m

belly n venter m; abdomen nt; alvus f; stomachus, uterus m

belong vi (~ to) pertineo ad ② + acc

belongings n bona ntpl

beloved adj delectus, carus; amatus

below prep infra; subter + acc
■ **~** adv infra; deorsum, subter
□ **from ~** ab inferiore parte

belt n cingulum nt; zona f; (sword-belt) balteus m

bemoan vt ingemo ③; deploro ①; defleo ②

bench n scamnum, sedile, (of the senate) subsellium nt; (court of justice) subsellia ntpl

bend¹ vt flecto ③; curvo, inclino ①; fig domo ①
□ **~ down** deflecto ③
■ **~** vi flector ③; curvor ① etc

bend² n sinus, flexus m, curvamen nt; fig inclinatio f

beneath adv ▶ **below**
□ **it is ~ me to ...** me indignum est

benefaction n largitio f; beneficium nt

benefactor n patronus m

benefactress n patrona f

beneficent adj beneficus, benignus, liberalis

beneficial adj utilis, commodus; salutaris

■ ~ly adv utiliter

benefit¹ n beneficium nt, gratia f

benefit² vt iuvo ①; prosum ir + dat
■ ~ vi lucror ①

benevolence n benevolentia; largitio f

benevolent adj benevolus; benignus
■ ~ly adv benevole, benigne

benign adj benignus

bent¹ adj curvus, flexus; (backwards) recurvus; (forwards) pronus; (inwards) camur; (winding) sinuosus

bent² n fig (inclination) ingenium nt; animus m; voluntas f

bequeath vt lego ①; relinquo ①

bequest n legatum nt

bereave vt (of) orbo, spolio, privo ①

bereavement n orbitas; spoliatio; (loneliness) solitudo f

bereft adj (~ of) orbus (ab) + abl

berry n baca f; acinus m

berth n (of ship) statio f; (sleeping-place) cubiculum nt; (place, office) munus m

beseech vt obsecro, imploro, supplico, obtestor ①

beset vt circumdo ①; obsideo; circumsedeo; urgeo ②; vexo ①

beside prep (in addition to) ad, (outside) extra, (near) iuxta, (except) praeter; (along) secundum all + acc
□ be ~ oneself deliro ①

besides prep (in addition to) ad, (outside) extra, (except) praeter; all + acc
■ ~ adv porro, praeterea, praeterquam; insuper

besiege vt circumsedeo,

obsideo ②

besieger n obsessor m

best¹ adj optimus, praestantissimus
■ ~ of all adv optime, potissimum
□ to the ~ of one's ability pro viribus

best² adv optime

bestir vi
□ ~ oneself expergiscor; (make an effort) incumbo ③

bestow vt tribuo, confero ③; dono ①; largior ④

bet¹ n pignus nt; sponsio f;
▶ wager

bet² vt pignore contendo ③

betoken vt indico ①; portendo ③

betray vt trado, prodo ③, (leave in the lurch) desum ir + dat; fig (reveal one's presence) oleo ② + acc; (show) profero ir; (give proof of) arguo ③

betrayal n proditio f

betrayer n proditor m

betroth vt spondeo, despondeo ②

betrothal n sponsalia ntpl

betrothed adj & n sponsus m; sponsa f

better¹ adj melior, potior, praestantior; superior
□ get the ~ (of) supero ①; vinco ③; praevaleo ②
□ it is ~ praestat ①

better² adv melius, potius; rectius; satius
□ get ~ (in health) convalesco ③

better³ vt emendo ①; corrigo ③

between prep inter + acc, in medio + gen

beverage n potio f, potus m

bewail vt deploro [1]; ingemo, queror [3]; lamentor [1]; defleo [2]

beware vi&t caveo, praecaveo [2]
■ ~I cave, cavete

bewilder vt perturbo [1]; confundo [3]

bewilderment n perturbatio f

bewitch vt fascino [1]; (charm) demulceo [2]; capio [3]

beyond prep ultra, supra; praeter; (across) trans all + acc
■ ~ adv supra, ultra; ulterius

bias[1] n inclinatio f; momentum nt; impetus m

bias[2] vt inclino [1]

bibulous adj bibulus, vinosus

bicker vi altercor, rixor [1]

bickering n altercatio, rixa f; iurgium nt

bid[1] vt iubeo [2]; impero + dat, mando; (invite) invito, rogo, (money for wares) licitor [1]; liceor [2]
□ ~ **goodbye** valedico [3]

bid[2] n licitatio f

bidding n iussum, mandatum nt; (at the ~ of) iussu + gen; (auction) licitatio f

bide vi (one's time) expecto [1]

bier n feretrum nt, sandapila f

big adj ingens, immanis, vastus, grandis; (in bulk) crassus; fig potens; (with pride) tumidus
□ **talk** ~ ampullor [1]

bigamist n bimaritus m; bigamus m

bigoted adj superstitiosus; (obstinate) pervicax

bigotry n superstitio f; (obstinacy) pervicacia f

bile n bilis f

bilge-water n sentina f

bilious adj biliosus

bill[1] n (of a bird) rostrum nt; (in writing) libellus m; (law proposed) rogatio; lex f; plebiscitum nt; (account) syngrapha f

billet vt milites per hospitia dispono [3]

bill-hook n falx, falcula f

billow n fluctus m

billowy adj fluctuosus, undabundus

bin n (in a wine-cellar) loculus m

bind vt ligo [1]; necto, stringo [3]; vincio [4]; fig astringo [3]; (by oath, law) obligo [1]; devincio [4]
□ ~ **down** deligo [1]
□ ~ **over** obligo; vador [1]
□ ~ **together** colligo [1]
□ ~ **up** ligo; alligo; colligo [1]; substringo [3]; (be bound up in) fig contineor [2]

binding[1] adj obligatorius

binding[2] n religatio f; (wrapper) involucrum nt

biographer n vitae rerumque gestarum alicuius scriptor m

biography n vitae descriptio f

birch n betulla f

bird n avis, volucris, ales f; (bird of omen) praepes f; oscen m

birdcage n cavea f

birdcatcher n auceps m

birdcatching n aucupium nt

birdlime n viscum nt

birth n partus; ortus m; (race) stirps f, genus nt, natales mpl
□ **give** ~ pario [3]

birthday n dies natalis m

birthplace n solum natale or genitale nt

birthright n ius ex genere

ortum nt

bit n (for a horse) frenum; (little piece) frustum nt, offa, offula f

bitch n canis f

bite¹ n morsus m

bite² vt mordeo ②; (as pepper, etc.) uro ③

biting adj mordax; fig asper

bitter adj amarus; acerbus; asper; gravis; infensus
■ ~**ly** adv amare; acerbe, aspere; graviter; infense

bitterness n amaritudo; acerbitas; asperitas, gravitas f

bitumen n bitumen nt

bivouac¹ n excubiae fpl

bivouac² vi excubo ①

black¹ adj niger; ater; fig (gloomy) tristis; scelestus, improbus
□ ~ **and blue** lividus
□ ~ **eye** sugillatio f

black² n nigrum nt
□ **dressed in** ~ pullatus

blackberry n morum nt
■ ~**bush** n rubus m

blackbird n merula f

blacken vt (also fig) nigro; denigro ①

blacking n atramentum nt

blackish adj subniger

blackness n nigritia, nigrities, nigritudo f

Black Sea n Pontus m

blacksmith n ferrarius faber m

bladder n vesica f

blade n lamina f; (of grass, etc.) caulis m; herba f; culmus m; (of an oar) palma, palmula f

blame¹ vt reprehendo ③; culpo, vitupero ①

blame² n reprehensio; culpa f

blameless adj integer, innoxius; innocens, innocuus; irreprehensus
■ ~**ly** adv integre, innocenter

blamelessness n integritas; innocentia f

blanch vi expallesco ③, palleo ②; pallesco ③

bland adj blandus

blandishment n blanditiae fpl, blandimentum; (charm) lenocinium nt

blank¹ adj (empty) vacuus; (unwritten on) purus
□ **look** ~ confundor ③

blank² n inane nt; res vana f

blanket n stragulum nt; lodix m

blare¹ vi clango ③

blare² n sonus, strepitus m

blast n (of wind) flatus m; flamen nt; flabra ntpl; (blight) sideratio, rubigo f; (sound) clangor m

blaze¹ n flamma f; fulgor m; incendium nt

blaze² vi flagro ①; ardeo ②; ardesco ③

bleach vt candefacio ③
■ ~ vi albesco ③

bleak adj algidus, frigidus; immitis

bleakness n algor m; frigus nt

blear-eyed adj lippus
□ **be** ~ lippio ④

bleat vi (as a sheep) balo ①

bleating n balatus m

bleed vi (of blood) fluo ③; (emit blood) sanguinem effundo

bleeding¹ adj (of wounds) crudus

bleeding² n (flowing of blood) sanguinis profluvium nt

blemish n (flaw) vitium nt, labes,

macula f

blend vt misceo, immisceo, commisceo ②

bless vt benedico ③; (consecrate) consecro ①; (with good success) bene verto ③; prospero, aspiro, secundo ①

blessed adj beatus; pius; (fortunate) felix, fortunatus

blessing n benedictio; (good wish) fausta precatio f; (benefit) beneficium, bonum, munus nt

blight¹ n lues; (of corn, etc.) robigo, uredo; sideratio f

blight² vt uro ③; (ruin) deleo ②; (frustrate) frustror ①; fallo ③

blind¹ adj caecus

blind² n (screen of cloth) velum nt; fig praetextum nt

blind³ vt caeco, occaeco ①; (deceive) fallo ③

blindness n caecitas f; tenebrae fpl

blink vi coniveo ②; nicto ①

bliss n beatitudo f

blissful adj beatus
- ~**ly** adv beate

blister¹ n pustula f

blister² vt&i pustulo ①

bloated adj sufflatus; inflatus; tumefactus, tumidus; (immense) immanis

block¹ n (lump) massa f

block² vt impedio ④
- □ ~ **up** obstruo, intercludo ③

blockade¹ n obsidium nt; obsidio f

blockade² vt obsideo ②

blockage n impedimentum nt

blockhead n caudex m

blood n sanguis m; (gore) cruor m;

fig (slaughter) caedes; (lineage) natura f, genus nt

bloodless adj exsanguis; (without bloodshed) incruentus

blood-red adj cruentus; sanguineus, sanguinolentus

bloodshed n caedes f

bloodshot adj cruore suffusus

bloodstained adj cruentus, cruentatus, sanguinolentus

bloodthirsty adj sanguinarius; sanguinolentus; sanguineus; cruentus

blood-vessel n arteria, vena f

bloody adj sanguineus; sanguinolentus; sanguinarius; cruentus

bloom¹ n (also fig) flos m; robur nt

bloom² vi (also fig) floreo, vigeo ②

blooming adj florens; floridus; nitidus

blossom n & vi ▶ **bloom**

blot¹ n macula, litura; fig labes f, dedecus nt

blot² vt maculo ①
- □ ~ **out** deleo ②; extinguo ③; (erase) oblittero ①

blow¹ n (stroke) plaga f, ictus m; (with the fist) colaphus m; plaga f; vulnus nt
- □ **it came to ~s** res ad pugnam venit

blow² vi flo; (breathe) spiro ①; (musical instruments) cano ③; (pant) anhelo ①
- ■ ~ vt flo, afflo; (a wind instrument) inflo ①; (blow the nose) emungo ③
- □ ~ **out** extinguo ③

blue adj caeruleus, caerulus; (dark blue) cyaneus
- ■ ~ n caeruleum nt

bluff adj (unsophisticated) rusticus; (steep) declivis; (windy) ventosus; (hearty) vehemens

bluish adj lividus, livens

blunder[1] n mendum, erratum nt; error m

blunder[2] vi offendo ③; erro ①

blunt[1] adj hebes; obtusus; retusus; fig inurbanus, rusticus; (plain) planus
■ ~ly adv plane, libere

blunt[2] vt hebeto ①; obtundo, retundo ③

blur vt maculo ①; (darken) obscuro ①

blurt vt
□ ~ **out** divulgo, vulgo ①

blush[1] vi erubesco, rubesco ③; rubeo ②

blush[2] n rubor m

blushing adj
■ ~ly adv rubens, erubescens

boar n aper; verres m

board[1] n (plank) tabula; (table) mensa f; (food, etc.) victus; (playing-table) abacus, alveus lusorius m; (council) collegium, consilium nt
□ **on** ~ in nave

board[2] vt (cover with boards) contabulo ①

board[3] vt (a ship) navem conscendo ③

boarder n convictor; hospes m

boast[1] vi iacto, glorior ①

boast[2] n iactantia, iactatio, gloriatio, vanitas f

boaster n iactator m

boastful adj gloriosus, vaniloquus

boasting adj gloriosus, vaniloquus

boat n linter, scapha, navicula, cumba f

boat-hook n contus m

boatman n nauta f; (ferryman) portitor m

bode vt portendo ③; praesagio ④; praemonstro ①

bodiless adj incorporalis; sine corpore

bodily adj corporeus; corporalis
■ ~ adv corporaliter

body n corpus m; (corpse) cadaver nt; (trunk) truncus, om; (mil) numerus m, vis f; (collection of people) societas; multitudo f; collegium nt

bodyguard n stipatores, satellites mpl; cohors praetoria f

bog n palus f

boggy adj paludosus, palustris

boil[1] vi ferveo ②; effervesco ③; aestuo, exaestuo ①
■ ~ vt fervefacio; coquo ③

boil[2] n furunculus m; ulcus nt

boisterous adj procellosus; violentus; turbidus

bold adj audax; fortis; impavidus; intrepidus; (free) liber; (rash) temerarius; (impudent) insolens; procax
■ ~ly adv audacter; libere; insolenter; fortiter

boldness n audacia; fidentia; (of speech) libertas; impudentia; (rashness) temeritas f

bolster[1] n pulvinus m; (of a bed) cervical nt

bolster[2] vt (up) fulcio ④

bolt[1] n (of a door) pessulus m; claustrum nt; obex m; (dart) iaculum, pilum nt; (of thunder) fulmen nt; (rivet) clavus m

bolt[2] vt obsero ①; occludo ③

bombard vt tormentis verbero ①

bombastic | bother

bombastic adj inflatus, tumidus

bond n vinculum nt; nodus m; copula; catena; (imprisonment) custodia f; (obligation) necessitas, necessitudo f; (legal document) syngrapha f

bondage n servitus f, servitium nt; captivitas f

bondsman n servus m; addictus m; verna m/f

bone¹ n os nt; (of fish) spina f

bone² vt exosso 🗆

boneless adj exos

bonfire n ignes festi mpl

bonnet n mitra f

bony adj osseus, (thin) macer

booby n stultus m

book n liber, libellus m; volumen nt; codex m

bookcase n foruli mpl

bookish adj libris deditus

bookseller n bibliopola, librarius m
  □ ~'s shop taberna (libraria) f

bookshelf n pluteus m

bookworm n:
  □ be a ~ fig libris helluor 🗆

boom¹ n (of a ship) longurius m; (noise) stridor m

boom² vi resono 🗆

boon n bonum, donum nt; gratia f

boor n rusticus m

boorish adj agrestis, rusticus
  ■ ~ly adv rustice

boorishness n rusticitas f

boot n calceus m; caliga f

booth n taberna f, tabernaculum nt

booty n praeda f; spolia ntpl; (stripped from a foe) exuviae fpl

border¹ n (edge) margo m/f; (of dress) limbus m; (boundary) finis, terminus m; confinium nt

border² vt tango, attingo ③; circumiaceo ②
  ■ ~ vt praetexo ③

bordering adj affinis, finitimus

bore¹ vt terebro, perforo; cavo 🗆; fig fatigo 🗆

bore² n (hole) foramen nt; (tool) terebra f; fig (tedious person) importunus, molestus, odiosus m

boredom n taedium nt

boring adj molestus

born adj natus; genitus
  □ be ~ nascor, gignor ③; fig orior ④
  □ a ~ soldier aptus militiae

borough n municipium nt

borrow vt mutuor 🗆; mutuum sumo ③; fig imitor 🗆

borrowed adj mutuatus, mutuus; alienus

bosom n (breast) pectus nt, sinus m; gremium nt
  □ ~ friend amicus coniunctissimus

Bosphorus n Bosphorus m

boss n (of a shield) umbo m

botanist n herbarius m

botany n herbarum scientia f

botch vt fig male gero ③

both¹ adj (taken together) ambo (pair) geminus; duo; (taken individually) uterque
  □ ~ ways bifariam

both² conj
  □ ~ ... and et ... et, cum ... tum; que ... que

bother¹ vt vexo 🗆

bother² n vexatio, sollicitudo, cura f

bottle[1] n ampulla; (with handles) lagena f

bottle[2] vt in ampullas infundo ③

bottom[1] n fundus m; (of a ship) carina f; (dregs) faex f; (of a mountain) radix f; (depth of a thing) profundum nt
□ **at ~** ad imum (imam) ...
□ **go to the ~** subsido, resido ③; (sink) mergor ③
□ **from top to ~** funditus, penitus
□ **get to the ~ of** scrutor ①

bottom[2] adj imus, infimus

bottomless adj fundo carens, immensus; profundus

bough n ramus m, bracchium nt

bounce vi resilio ④; resulto ①

bound[1] n finis, terminus, limes m; meta f; (leap) saltus m

bound[2] vt finio, definio ④; termino ①; (delimit) circumscribo ③
■ ~ vi (leap) salio, exsilio ④

boundary n finis, terminus, limes m; confinium nt

boundless adj infinitus; immensus

boundlessness n infinitas; immensitas f

bounteous adj benignus, largus, munificus
■ ~**ly** adv benigne, large, munifice

bountiful adj benignus, largus, munificus
■ ~**ly** adv benigne, large, munifice

bounty n largitas; benignitas; munificentia f; praemium, munus nt

bouquet n fasciculus (florum) m; (of wine) flos m

bovine adj bubulus

bow[1] vt flecto ③; inclino ①; (one's head) demitto ③; fig submitto ③
■ ~ vi flector ③; (yield) cedo ③

bow[2] n arcus m; (of a ship) prora f

bowels n intestina, viscera ntpl; fig misericordia f

bowl n cratera; patera, phiala f; (shallow bowl) pelvis f

bow-legged adj valgus

bowman n sagittarius m

bowstring n nervus m

box[1] n arca; cista f; loculus m; capsa f; (for letters, etc.) scrinium nt; (for ointments, etc.) pyxis f
□ ~ **on the ear** alapa f

box[2] n (tree) buxus f

box[3] vi pugnis certo ①

boxer n pugil m

boxing-match n pugilatio f

boy n puer; (little ~) puerulus m

boyhood n pueritia; aetas puerilis f

boyish adj puerilis
■ ~**ly** adv pueriliter

brace[1] n (strap) fascia f; copula f; (couple) par nt

brace[2] vi (oneself) contendo ③

bracelet n armilla f, bracchiale nt

brag vi iacto ①

braggart[1] n iactator m

braggart[2] adj gloriosus

braid[1] n limbus m; (of hair) cincinnus m

braid[2] vt plecto, texo, praetexo ③

brain n cerebrum; (sense) cor nt; (understanding) mens f

bramble n (blackberry-bush) rubus m; (thicket) rubetum nt; (thorny bush) sentis, vepris m

bran n furfur nt

branch n (of a tree) ramus m; bracchium; (of a river) cornu nt; (of a pedigree) stemma nt; figs pars f

branching adj ramosus; (widespreading) patulus

brand n (mark) nota f; (torch) torris m; fax, taeda f

branding-iron n cauter m; cauterium nt

brandish vt vibro, libro, corusco ①

brand-new adj recentissimus

brass¹ n orichalcum, aes nt

brass² adj aenus, aereus, aeneus, aeratus

brat n infans m/f

brave¹ adj fortis; strenuus; animosus

 ∎ **~ly** adv fortiter; animose

brave² vt provoco ①; lacesso ③

bravery n fortitudo; virtus; magnanimitas f; (finery) splendor m

bravo int eu! euge!

brawl¹ vi rixor, iurgo ①

brawl² n rixa f; iurgium nt

brawler n rixator; rabula m

brawny adj lacertosus, torosus

bray¹ vi (of asses) rudo ③; (cry out) vociferor ①

bray² n (noise) strepitus m

brazen adj (of brass) aenus, aeneus, aereus, aeratus

 □ **~-faced** impudens

brazier n aerarius m; (coal-pan) foculus m

breach n ruptura; ruina; (of a treaty) violatio f; (falling out) discidium nt; discordia f

 □ **~ of law** lex violata f

 □ **commit ~ of duty** officium neglego ③

bread n panis; fig victus m

bread-basket n panarium nt

bread-making n panificium nt

breadth n latitudo f

break¹ vt frango; rumpo ③; fig violo ①

 ∎ **~** vi frangor ③; (cease) desino ③

 □ **~ apart** diffringo, dirumpo ③

 □ **~ down** demolior ④; destruo ③

 □ **~ forth** erumpo ③

 □ **~ in** (tame) domo ①; subigo ③

 □ **~ into** irrumpo; invado ③

 □ **~ loose** eluctor ①

 □ **~ off** abrumpo ③; (friendship) dirumpo; (a conference) dirimo; (a conversation) interrumpo ③; vi praefringor

 □ **~ open** effringo ③

 □ **~ out** erumpo; (a calamity, etc.) prorumpo ③; (a war) exorior ④

 □ **~ through** perrumpo ③

 □ **~ up** frango, effringo, dissolvo; (an army, assembly) dimitto; (ground) fodio ③

 □ **~ with** dissideo ②

break² n intermissio f; intervallum; (of day) diluculum nt

breakable adj fragilis

breakage n fractura f

breaker n (wave) fluctus m

breakfast¹ n prandium, ientaculum nt

breakfast² vt prandeo ②; iento ①

break-up n dissolutio f

breakwater n moles, pila f

breast n pectus nt; (of a woman) mamma, papilla f; (full of milk) uber nt; fig praecordia ntpl, pectus, cor nt

breastplate n lorica f; thorax m

breath n halitus, spiritus, flatus m; anima; (of air) aura f

 □ **take ~** respiro ①

breathe vt duco ③; (pant) anhelo; (whisper) susurro ①
□ ~ **out** exspiro ①; (the life) exhalo ①
■ ~ vi spiro, respiro ①

breathing n respiratio f

breathing-hole n spiraculum, spiramen, spiramentum nt

breathless adj exanimis, exanimus; exanimatus; (panting) anhelus

bred adj
□ **well** ~ humanus, urbanus

breeches n bracae fpl

breed¹ vt pario, gigno ③; genero, creo ①; (cause) produco ③; (engender) procreo ①; (horses, etc.) pasco ③; alo ③; nutrio ④; (bring up) educo ①; alo ③

breed² n genus nt

breeding n fetura; (education) educatio f
□ **good** ~ humanitas, urbanitas f

breeze n aura f

breezy adj ventosus

brevity n brevitas f

brew vt coquo ③; fig concito, conflo ①
■ ~ vi excitor, concitor ①
□ **be** ~**ing** immineo ②

briar n ▶ **bramble**

bribe¹ n pretium nt, merces, pecunia f

bribe² vt corrumpo ③

bribery n corruptio, corruptela, largitio f; ambitus m

brick n later m

bricklayer n caementarius m

brickmaker n laterarius m

brickwork n latericium nt

bridal adj nuptialis
□ ~ **song** n epithalamium nt

□ ~**-chamber** n thalamus m

bride n sponsa; nupta, nympha f

bridegroom n sponsus; novus maritus m

bridesmaid n pronuba f

bridge¹ n pons m; (of instrument or nose) iugum nt

bridge² vt
□ ~ **over** flumen ponte iungo ③

bridle¹ n (also fig) frenum nt; habena f

bridle² vt freno; fig infreno, refreno ①; coerceo ②

brief adj brevis, concisus

briefly adv breviter; paucis (verbis)

briefness n brevitas f

brier n ▶ **bramble**

brigade n (of infantry) legio; (of cavalry) turma f

brigadier n tribunus militum m

brigand n latro, latrunculus m

bright adj clarus; lucidus, splendidus; nitidus; candidus; (flashing) fulgidus; (smart, clever) argutus, sollers; (cloudless) serenus

brighten vt polio ④
■ ~ vi lucesco; splendesco; claresco ③; (gladden) hilaro, exhilaro ①

brightly adv lucide, clare, splendide, nitide

brightness n splendor; nitor; fulgor m; (of the sun) lumen nt; fig hilaritas f; (of intellect) sollertia f

brilliance n splendor m; fig (of style) lumen nt

brilliant adj splendidus; nitens; nitidus; fig luculentus; praeclarus; (clever) ingeniosus
□ **be** ~ splendeo, niteo ②

brim n ora f, margo m/f; labrum nt

brimstone n sulfur, sulpur nt

brine n muria f, salsamentum; (sea) salum nt

bring vt fero, affero, infero ir; gero, duco ③; porto ①; (by carriage, *etc.*) adveho ③
□ ~ **about** efficio ③
□ ~ **back** refero ir, reduco ③; reporto; fig revoco ①; (by force) redigo ③
□ ~ **before** defero ir; produco ③
□ ~ **down** defero ir; deduco; (by force) deicio ③
□ ~ **forth** prodo; depromo; pario ③; (yield) fero, effero ir
□ ~ **forward** profero, effero ir; ago ③
□ ~ **in(to)** infero ir; inveho; induco; (as income) reddo ③
□ ~ **off** praesto ①; (carry through) perficio ③
□ ~ **on** affero ir; adduco; fig obicio ③
□ ~ **out** effero ir; produco ③; excio ④
□ ~ **over** perduco, traduco; fig perduco, traho ③; concilio ①
□ ~ **to** adduco; appello ③; fig persuadeo ②
□ ~ **together** confero ir; (assemble, *etc.*) contraho ③; fig concilio ①
□ ~ **up** subduco ③; (children) educo ①; (vomit) evomo ③

brink n margo m/f

briny adj salsus; subsalsus

brisk adj alacer, agilis, vividus; laetus; impiger, acer
■ ~**ly** adv alacriter, acriter, impigre

briskness n alacritas f, vigor m

bristle¹ n saeta f

bristle² vi horreo ②; horresco ③

bristly adj saetiger, saetosus; hirsutus

Britain n Britannia f

British adj Britannicus

brittle adj fragilis, caducus

brittleness n fragilitas f

broach vt (a cask) (dolium) relino ③

broad adj latus, largus, amplus; fig manifestus, apertus

broadly adv late

broadness n amplitudo, latitudo f

broken adj fractus; intermissus; dirutus; (off) abruptus; (open) effractus; (in pieces) contusus; (up) dismissus; violatus; (of the heart) vulneratus

broken-hearted adj abiectus, spe deiectus, afflictus

broker n (money-changer) nummularius m

bronze¹ n aes nt

bronze² adj aenus, aeneus, aereus, aeratus

brooch n fibula f

brood¹ n proles; progenies; suboles; (of chickens) pullities f

brood² vi (as a hen) incubo ①; (~ upon) foveo ②; agito ①

brook¹ n amniculus, rivulus m

brook² vt fero, patior ③; tolero ①

broom n scopae fpl

broomstick n scoparum manubrium m

broth n ius nt

brothel n lupanar, lustrum nt

brother n frater, germanus m
■ ~**-in-law** n levir, sororis maritus m

brotherhood n germanitas;

fraternitas f; fig sodalicium, collegium nt

brotherly adj fraternus

brow n supercilium nt; frons f

browbeat vt terreo ②; deprimo ③

brown adj fulvus, fuscus, pullus, spadix
■ ~ n fulvus color m

brownish adj subniger, suffuscus

browse vt (graze on) carpo, depasco ③; tondeo ②

bruise[1] vt contundo ③; sugillo ①; infringo ③

bruise[2] n contusio; sugillatio f

brush[1] n scopula f; (painter's ~) penicillus m; (bushy tail) muscarium nt; (fray, skirmish) concursatio f

brush[2] vt verro ③; tergeo; detergeo
□ ~ **away** amoveo ②
□ ~ **up** orno ①; reficio ③

brushwood n sarmenta, virgulta, ramalia ntpl

brusque adj praeceps

brutal adj ferus; immanis; inhumanus; saevus; furiosus
■ ~ly adv inhumane; saeve

brutality n feritas, ferocitas, saevitia; immanitas f

brute n bestia, pecus f

brutish adj ferus; fatuus, stupidus

bubble[1] n bulla f

bubble[2] vi bullio ④; (gush up) scateo ②

buccaneer n pirata, praedo m

bucket n hama, situla f

buckle[1] n fibula f

buckle[2] vt fibula necto ③

buckler n parma f, ▶ shield

bucolic adj bucolicus, pastoralis, pastorius, rusticus, agrestis

bud[1] n gemma f, germen nt; (of a flower) calyx; (in grafting) oculus m

bud[2] vi gemmo, germino ①

budge vi me moveo ②; cedo, loco cedo ③

buff adj luteus

buffet[1] n (blow) alapa f, colaphus m

buffet[2] vt (strike) ferio ④

buffoon n scurra; sannio, balatro m
□ **play the ~** scurror ①

buffoonery n scurrilitas f; lascivia f; iocus m

bug n cimex m

bugle n bucina f; cornu nt

build vt aedifico; struo, construo, exstruo, condo ③; fabrico ①; (upon) inaedifico ①; fig (rely on) nitor ③ + abl

builder n aedificator; conditor, structor; fig auctor, fabricator m

building n (act) aedificatio, exstructio f; (structure) aedificium nt

bulb n bulbus m

bulge vi tumeo, turgeo ②; procurro ③
□ ~ **out** tumesco ③

bulk n amplitudo; moles f

bulky adj crassus; ingens; gravis; onerosus

bull n taurus, bos m; (edict) edictum nt

bulldog n canis molossus m

bullet n glans f

bullock n taurus castratus; iuvencus m

bully[1] n salaco, rixator m

bully[2] vt insulto ①; lacesso ③

bulrush n scirpus; iuncus m

bulwark *n* agger *m*; propugnaculum *nt*; moenia, munimenta *ntpl*; *fig* praesidium, propugnaculum *nt*

bump¹ *n* (swelling) tuber *nt*; (thump) plaga *f*

bump² *vt* (into) offendo ③; pulso ①

bumpkin *n* rusticus *m*

bun *n* libum, crustulum *nt*; placenta *f*

bunch *n* (bundle) fasciculus *m*
□ ~ **of grapes** racemus *m*

bundle¹ *n* fascis, fasciculus *m*; (pack) sarcina *f*; (of rods) fasces *mpl*

bundle² *vt* colligo ①

bungle *vt* rem inscite gero, inscite ago ③
■ ~ *vi* erro ①

bungler *n* homo rudis; imperitus *m*

buoy *vt* (up) attollo ③; sustineo ②; sustento ①; fulcio ④

buoyancy *n* levitas; *fig* hilaritas *f*

buoyant *adj* levis; *fig* hilaris

bur *n* lappa *f*

burden¹ *n* onus *nt*; fascis *m*; sarcina *f*

burden² *vt* onero, gravo ①; opprimo ③
□ **beast of** ~ iumentum *nt*

burdensome *adj* onerosus, gravis, molestus, iniquus

burglar *n* fur *m*

burglary *n* effractura *f*

burial *n* (act of burying) sepultura *f*; funus *nt*; exsequiae *fpl*

burial-place *n* locus sepulturae *m*; sepulcrum *nt*

burly *adj* corpulentus, robustus, lacertosus

burn *vt* uro ③; cremo ①; (set on fire) incendo ③
■ ~ *vi* flagro ①; ardeo ②; (with love, etc.) ardeo ②; flagro ①; caleo ②; calesco ③
□ ~ **down** deuro ③
□ **be** ~**t down** deflagro ①
□ ~ **out** *vt* exuro; *vi* exstinguor ③
□ ~ **up** concremo ①

burning *n* ustio, adustio; deflagratio *f*, incendium *nt*

burning *adj* ardens; *fig* fervens

burnish *vt* polio, expolio ④; levigo ①

burrow¹ *n* cuniculus *m*; cubile *nt*

burrow² *vi* (dig down) defodio ③

burst¹ *vt* rumpo, dirumpo; (with a noise) displodo ③
■ ~ **forth** *vi* erumpo, prorumpo ③
□ ~ **into tears** in lacrimas effundor
□ ~ **open** effringo ③; dirumpor ③; dissilio ④

burst² *n* (noise) fragor *m*

bury *vt* sepelio ④; humo ①; (hide, etc.) abdo, condo; (put into the ground) infodio, defodio ③

bush *n* frutex, dumus, sentis, vepres *m*

bushy *adj* dumosus; fruticosus; (of hair) hirsutus, horridus

busily *adv* industrie, sedulo

business *n* negotium *nt*; (calling, trade) ars; (matter) res; (employment) occupatio *f*; (duty) officium; (work) opus *nt*

bust *n* statua, effigies *f*

bustle¹ *n* festinatio *f*; tumulus *m*

bustle² *vi* (hurry) festino ①; (run to and fro) discurro ③

bustling *adj* operosus

b

busy *adj* occupatus; negotiosus; (industrious) strenuus, industrius, navus; (meddling) curiosus, molestus; (active, laborious) operosus

busybody *n* ardelio *m*

but *conj* sed, ast, at; autem; ceterum; vero, verum
□ ~ **for** absque + *abl*; (except) praeter, nisi; (only) modo, solum, tantum
□ ~ **if** sin, sin autem; quod si
□ ~ **if not** sin aliter, sin minus
□ ~ **yet** nihilominus, veruntamen
□ **I cannot** ~ non possum facere quin + *subj*

butcher¹ *n* lanius; *fig* carnifex *m*
■ ~**'s shop** *n* macellum *nt*

butcher² *vt* caedo ③; trucido ①

butchery *n* caedes, trucidatio *f*

butler *n* promus *m*

butt¹ *n* (mark) meta *f*; (cask) dolium *nt*; *fig* (laughing-stock) ludibrium *nt*

butt² *vi* arieto ①
■ ~**ing** *adj* petulcus

butter *n* butyrum *nt*

butterfly *n* papilio *m*

buttock *n* clunis *m/f*; natis *f*

buttress *vt* ulcio, suffulcio ④

buxom *adj* alacer, hilaris, laetus, lascivus, procax; (fat) pinguis

buy *vt* emo ③; mercor ①
□ ~ **back** *or* **off** redimo ③
□ ~ **up** emercor ①; coemo ③

buyer *n* emptor *m*

buying *n* emptio, mercatura *f*

buzz¹ *vi* murmuro, susurro ①; (in the ear) insusurro ①

buzz² *n* bombus *m*, murmur *nt*; susurrus *m*

buzzard *n* buteo *m*

by *prep* (of place) ad, apud; sub; (along) secundum, praeter; (near) propter, iuxta; (of time) sub; (denoting the instrument or cause) per; (in oaths) per *all* + *acc*; (of the agent, *e.g.* 'by a soldier') a, ab + *abl*
□ ~ **oneself** solus, solum
□ ~ **and** ~ mox, brevi, postmodo
□ **go** ~ praetereo ④

bygone *adj* praeteritus; priscus

by-law *n* praescriptum *nt*

bystander *n* arbiter *m*
■ ~**s** *pl* circumstantes *mpl*

byword *n* proverbium *nt*; *fig* fabula *f*
□ **be a** ~ ludibrio sum

Cc

cabbage *n* brassica *f*, caulis *m*; crambe *f*

cabin *n* (hut) tugurium *nt*; (small room) cellula *f*

cabinet *n* conclave; (piece of furniture) scrinium, armarium *nt*, cistula *f*; (government) summum principis consilium *nt*

cable *n* ancorale *nt*, rudens *m*

cackle¹ *vi* strepo ③; clango ③; (of hens) gracillo ①; *fig* garrio ④

cackle² *n* strepitus, clangor *m*; *fig* gerrae *fpl*

cadaverous *adj* cadaverosus; (thin) macer

cadet *n* tiro *m*

cage¹ *n* cavea *f*, avarium *nt*; (prison) carcer *m*; (for large animals) saeptum *nt*

cage² vt includo ③

cajole vt adulor ①; illicio ③; blandior ④

cajolery n blanditiae fpl; adulatio f

cake¹ n placenta f, libum nt; (doughy mass) massa f

cake² vi concresco ③

calamitous adj calamitosus; lacrimosus; funestus; gravis; infelix
■ **~ly** adv calamitose, infeliciter

calamity n calamitas f; clades f; malum nt; res adversa f

calculate vt&i computo, supputo, aestimo, existimo ①

calculated adj aptus, ad rem accommodatus; (intentional) meditatus

calculation n computatio, ratio f, calculus m; fig ratiocinatio f

calculator n abacus m

calendar n kalendarium nt, fasti mpl; (diary) ephemeris f

calf¹ n (animal) vitulus m

calf² n (of the leg) sura f

calibre n fig ingenium nt, indoles f

call¹ vt voco ①; (name) appello, nomino ①
- **~ aside** sevoco ①
- **~ away** avoco ①; fig devoco ①
- **~ back** revoco ①
- **~ down** devoco ①
- **~ for** postulo, flagito ①
- **~ forth** evoco, provoco ①; fig excieo ②; elicio ③
- **~ in** introvoco ①; (money) cogo ③
- **~ off** avoco, revoco ①
- **~ on** inclamo ①; cieo ②; appello ①; (visit) viso ③; saluto ①
- **~ out** evoco ①; vi exclamo ①
- **~ to** advoco ①
- **~ to mind** recordor ①

- **~ to witness** testor ①
- **~ together** convoco ①
- **~ up** excito; suscito ①; elicio ③

call² n (summons) vocatio; (sound of the voice) vox f; (shout) clamor m; (short visit) salutatio f

caller n salutator m

calling n (summoning) vocatio f; (profession) studium nt; ars f; (bent) impetus m (rank, position) condicio f
- **~ in** (of money) coactio f
- **~ together** convocatio f
- **~ upon** invocatio f

callous adj callosus; fig (insensible) durus
- **become ~** occallesco; obduresco ③

callousness n duritia f

calm¹ adj tranquillus, placidus, sedatus, placatus, quietus, serenus

calm² n tranquillitas, quies f; (a calm sea) tranquillum nt

calm³ vt paco, placo, sedo ①; mulceo ②; tranquillo ①

calmly adv placide, sedate, tranquille

calmness n tranquillitas; serenitas, quies f
- **bear with ~** aequo animo fero ③

calumny n maledictum nt, criminatio f, calumnia f

camel n camelus m

camp¹ n castra ntpl
- **winter ~** hiberna; stativa ntpl
- **summer ~** aestiva ntpl

camp² vi castra pono ③

campaign¹ n expeditio f; (service) militia f; stipendium; (war) bellum nt
- **one's first ~** tirocinium nt

campaign² vi expeditioni intersum ir, milito ①

camp-follower n lixa m

can¹ n hirnea, hirnula f

can² vi possum ir; queo ④
□ **I ~not** nequeo; nescio ④

canal n fossa f; canalis m

cancel vt deleo ②; rescindo ③; abrogo ①; tollo ③

cancer n (disease, and sign of the zodiac) cancer m

candelabrum n candelabrum nt

candid adj candidus; apertus; sincerus
■ **~ly** adv candide; sincere; sine fraude

candidate n candidatus m

candidateship n petitio f

candle n candela f

candlelight n lucerna f
□ **study by ~** lucubro ①

candlestick n candelabrum nt

candour n candor m, sinceritas f

cane¹ n canna, arundo f; baculus, calamus m; (rod for striking) ferula f

cane² vt ferula ferio ④

canine adj caninus

canister n pyxis f

canker n (of plants) robigo f; fig lues f; pestis f

cannibal n anthropophagus m

canoe n linter f

canopy n vela; (curtain) aulaea ntpl

cantankerous adj difficilis, morosus

canteen n caupona f

canter¹ vi curro ③; volo ①
■ **~ing** adj quadrupedans

canter² n cursus incitatus m

canvas n (for sails) linteum nt; carbasus f; (for painters) textile nt

canvass vt ambio; circumeo ④; prenso ①; (be a candidate) peto ③

canvassing n ambitio, petitio f; (unlawful) ambitus m

cap n pilleus, galerus m; mitra f

capability n facultas f

capable adj capax; idoneus, potens

capacious adj capax; amplus

capaciousness n capacitas; amplitudo f, spatium nt

capacity n (measure) mensura f; modus m; (intelligence) ingenium nt; facultas f

cape n (headland) promontorium; (garment) umerale nt; lacerna f

caper¹ n saltus m, exsultatio f

caper² vi tripudio, exsulto ①

capital¹ adj (of crimes) capitalis; fig (outstanding) insignis, eximius

capital² n (chief city) caput; (money) caput nt, sors f

Capitol n Capitolium nt

capitulate vi arma trado, me dedo ③

capitulation n deditio f

caprice n libido; inconstantia f

capricious adj levis, inconstans; mobilis; ventosus
□ **~ly** ex libidine; inconstanter ③

capsize vi everto ③

captain n (of infantry) centurio; (of cavalry) praefectus; (of a merchantship) navicularius, magister m; (general) dux, imperator m

captivate vt mulceo ②; capto ①; capio, allicio ③

captive n captivus m
■ **~** adj captivus

captivity n captivitas f;

(confinement) custodia f; (chains) vincula ntpl

captor n expugnator m

capture¹ n captura; expugnatio f

capture² vt capio, excipio ③; expugno ①

carbuncle n (tumour) carbunculus, furunculus; (precious stone) carbunculus m

carcass n cadaver nt

card vt (wool) pecto, carpo ③; carmino ①

carder n carminator m

cardinal adj (chief) praecipuus

care¹ n cura, sollicitudo; (heed) cautio; (diligence) diligentia; (anxiety) anxietas; (protection, guardianship) tutela; (management) procuratio; curatio; custodia f
□ **take ~** caveo ②
□ **take ~ of** curo ①

care² vi curo ①
□ **~ for** vt provideo ②, invigilo ① + dat
□ **I don't ~** non mihi curae est

career n curriculum nt; cursus, decursus m; (life) vita f

carefree adj hilarus, hilaris

careful adj (diligent) diligens; attentus; (cautious) cautus, providus; (of things) accuratus
■ **~ly** adv caute; diligenter; accurate, exquisite
□ **be ~l** cave, cavete

carefulness n cura; (diligence) diligentia; (caution) cautio f

careless adj securus; neglegens; imprudens
■ **~ly** adv neglegenter; secure; incuriose

carelessness n incuria; neglegentia; imprudentia;

securitas f

caress¹ n blanditiae fpl; complexus m

caress² vt blandior ④; foveo, permulceo ②; osculor ①

cargo n onus nt

carnage n caedes, strages, trucidatio f

carnival n saturnalia ntpl; festum nt

carnivorous adj carnivorus

carouse vt&i comissor, poto; perbacchor ①

carp vt (~ at) carpo, rodo ③; vellico ①; mordeo ②

carpenter n faber tignarius m

carpentry n ars fabrilis, opera fabrilis f

carpet n tapete nt; stragulum nt

carping n cavillatio f

carriage n (act of carrying) vectura f; (vehicle) vehiculum nt; raeda f; currus m; carpentum nt; fig habitus, gestus, incessus m

carrion n cadaver nt, caro morticina f

carrot n pastinaca f

carry vt porto ①; fero ①; gero ③; gesto ①; (by carriage) veho; (lead) duco, conduco ③
□ **~ away** aufero ir; aveho; fig rapio ③
□ **~ along** perduco; ago ③
□ **~ back** refero ir; reveho ③
□ **~ in** importo ①; inveho ③
□ **~ off** aufero ir; rapio; abstraho ③
□ **~ on** (continue) permaneo ② in + abl, perduco ③; fig exerceo ②; gero ③
□ **~ out** effero ir; exporto ①; eveho; fig exsequor ③
□ **~ round** circumfero ir

c

□ **~ together** comporto ①; confero ir

□ **~ through** perfero ir; fig exsequor ③

cart n carrus m, plaustrum, vehiculum nt

□ **put the ~ before the horse** fig praeposteris consiliis uti ③

cart-horse n caballus m; iumentum nt

cartilage n cartilago f

cartwright n faber carpentarius m

carve vt sculpo, exsculpo ③; caelo ①; incido ③; (meat) seco ①

carver n (artist) caelator; (of meat) carptor, scissor m

carving n caelatura f

■ **~-knife** n cultellus m

cascade n aquae lapsus or deiectus m

case n (sheath) involucrum nt, theca; vagina; (matter) res; (in law) causa; (condition, state, etc.) condicio f, status m, quaestio f; (event) eventus m

□ **it is often the ~** saepe accidit

□ **nothing to do with the ~** nihil ad rem

cash n pecunia numerata; (deposit) praesens pecunia f

cash-book n codex m

cask n cadus m; dolium nt; amphora f

casket n arca, arcula; pyxis, cista, cistula f

cast¹ vt (throw) iacio; conicio; mitto ③; iaculor, iacto ①; (metal) fundo ③

□ **~ away** or **aside** abicio, reicio ③

□ **~ down** deicio; fig affligo ③

□ **~ off** (the skin) exuo ③; fig

amoveo ②; pono ③; repudio ①

□ **~ out** eicio, expello ③

cast² n (throw and distance) iactus; missus m; (pattern) imago f

castanet n crotalum nt

castaway n (shipwrecked) naufragus m

castigate vt castigo ①

castigation n castigatio f

casting n (of metals) fusura f; (throwing) iactatus, iactus m

□ **~-net** n iaculum, rete iaculum nt

castle n castellum nt; turris, arx f

castrate vt castro, exseco ①; excido ③

castration n castratio, castratura f

casual adj fortuitus

■ **~ly** adv fortuito; temere; (by the way) obiter

casualty n casus m

cat n feles f

catacombs n puticuli mpl

catalogue n index m; tabula f

catapult n catapulta f

cataract n cataracta, catarracta f, catarractes m; (disease of the eye) glaucoma nt

catarrh n gravedo f

catastrophe n exitus, eventus m; (ruin) pernicies f; exitium nt

catastrophic adj damnosus, exitialis

catch¹ vt capio ③; capto ①; (by surprise) deprehendo; (understand) intellego ③; comprehendo ③; (in a net) illaqueo; (with bait) inesco ①; (fire) concipio; (a disease) contraho ③

□ **~ up** excipio ③

catch² n (prize) captura f; (of locks,

etc.) ansa f

catching adj contagiosus

category n categoria f; (class) genus nt

cater vi obsonor; cibos suppedito ①

caterer n obsonator m

caterpillar n eruca f

cattle n boves mpl

cattle-market n forum boarium nt

cauldron n aenum nt, lebes m; cortina f

cauliflower n brassica f

cause¹ n causa f; (source) fons m; origo f; (matter) res; (reason) ratio; (action at law) actio, lis f

cause² vt facio, efficio ③; creo ①; excito ①; moveo ②; (induce) suadeo ②; adduco ③

causeway n agger viae m

caustic adj causticus; fig mordax, acerbus

caution¹ n cautio; cura; prudentia; (warning) monitio f

caution² vt moneo, admoneo ②

cautious adj cautus, consideratus; circumspectus; providus, prudens
■ ~ly adv caute; pedetemptim, pedetemtim

cavalcade n pompa equestris f

cavalier n eques m

cavalry n equitatus m, equites mpl, copiae equestres fpl

cave n specus m/f/nt, antrum nt; caverna, spelunca f

cavern n spelunca, caverna f, antrum nt; specus m/f/nt

cavernous adj cavus

caw vi crocio ④; crocito ①

cease vt desino; omitto; intermitto ③
■ ~ vi + inf mitto, desino; desisto; omitto ③; cesso ①; (come to an end) desino, desisto ③; cesso ①

ceaseless adj perpetuus; assiduus
■ ~ly adv perpetuo; assidue; usque; continenter

cedar¹ n cedrus f

cedar² adj cedreus

cede vt cedo, dedo ③
■ ~ vi cedo, decedo ③

ceiling n lacunar, laquear nt

celebrate vt celebro, laudo ①; (solemnize) ago ③; agito, celebro ①

celebrated adj celeber; nobilis; clarus, praeclarus, illustris, notus

celebration n celebratio f

celebrity n fama, celebritas f

celery n apium nt

celestial adj caelestis; divinus
■ ~ n caeles m; caelicola m/f

cell n cella f

cellar n cella f, cellarium nt

cement¹ n ferrumen, caementum nt

cement² vt conglutino; ferrumino ①; fig (confirm) firmo, confirmo ①

cemetery n sepulcretum nt

cenotaph n tumulus inanis m; cenotaphium nt

censer n turibulum nt

censor n censor; (one who blames) reprehensor, castigator m

censorious adj austerus, severus

censorship n censura f

censure¹ n vituperatio, censura, reprehensio f

censure² vt animadverto, reprehendo ③; vitupero,

improbo [1]

census n census m

centaur n centaurus m

centenary adj centenarius
■ ~ n centenarius numerus;
centesimus annus m

centipede n centipeda f

central adj medius
■ ~ly adv in medio

centralize vt in unum contraho [3]

centre n centrum nt; medius locus
m; (the centre of the line) media acies f

centurion n centurio m

century n (political division, subdivision
of a legion) centuria f; (number of years)
saeculum m

ceremonial adj sollemnis
■ ~ly adv rite; sollemniter

ceremonious adj sollemnis
■ ~ adv sollemniter

ceremony n caerimonia f;
sollemne, officium nt; ritus; (pomp)
apparatus m

certain adj certus; compertus
■ a ~ quidam
■ for ~ certe, pro certo
■ it is ~ constat [1]
■ ~ly adv certe, certo; profecto;
vero, sane

certainty n certum nt, veritas,
fides f

certify vt confirmo, affirmo [1]

cessation n cessatio; intermissio
f; (end) finis m/f

cesspool n cloaca f

chafe vt&i (with the hand) frico [1];
(make sore) attero [3]; (vex) vexo [1]

chaff n palea f; acus nt

chaffinch n fringilla f

chagrin n vexatio f

chain¹ n catena f; vinculum nt;

(ornament) torques m/f; fig series f; (of
mountains) iugum nt

chain² vt catenis constringo;
catenas alicui inicio [3]

chair n sella; cathedra, sedes f;
sedile nt; (sedan) lectica f

chairman n (of a club, etc.)
praeses m

chalice n calix m

chalk¹ n creta f

chalk² vt creta noto [1]; creta
illino [3]
□ ~ out designo [1]

chalky adj (chalk-like) cretaceus; (full
of chalk) cretosus

challenge¹ n provocatio; (law)
reiectio f

challenge² vt provoco [1]; lacesso;
(law) reicio [3]

chamber n cubiculum, conclave
nt; (bedroom) thalamus m

chambermaid n ancilla f

champ vt&i mando [3]; mordeo [2]

champion n propugnator;
defensor m; vindex m/f

chance¹ n (accident) casus m; fors,
fortuna, fig alea; (probability) spes f;
(opportunity) occasio f
□ by ~ casu, fortuito, forte

chance² adj fortuitus;
inexpectatus

change¹ vt muto, commuto,
novo, vario; (one's place) demigro [1];
(money) permuto
■ ~ vi mutor, vario [1]

change² n mutatio; commutatio;
vicissitudo f; vices fpl; (variety)
varietas f; (small money) nummuli mpl

changeable adj mutabilis;
inconstans; levis; (of colour)
versicolor

changeableness n mutabilitas; mobilitas, inconstantia, levitas, volubilitas f

changeless adj immutabilis, immutatus

channel n canalis; (of rivers) alveus m; (arm of the sea) fretum nt; fig cursus m; via f

chant[1] n cantus m

chant[2] vt&i canto ①

chaos n chaos nt; fig confusio f

chaotic adj confusus; indigestus

chapel n sacellum, sacrarium nt

chaplet n sertum nt; corona f

chapter n caput nt

char vt amburo ③

character n mores mpl; indoles f; ingenium nt; habitus m; natura; proprietas f

characteristic[1] adj proprius + gen ■ **~ally** adv ex more (tuo, suo, etc.)

characteristic[2] n proprium nt

characterize vt describo ③

charcoal n carbo m

charge[1] vt accuso ①; arguo ③; criminor ①; (attack) adorior ④; aggredior ③; (burden) onero; (command) impero ①; (entrust) committo, credo ③; mando ①; (exact), exigo ③ ■ **~** vi irruo, invado ③

charge[2] n accusatio f; crimen nt; (attack) impetus, incursus m; (command) mandatum nt; (trust) cura, custodia f; (office) munus nt; (cost) impensa f, sumptus m

charger n (war-horse) equus bellator, sonipes, quadrupedans m

chariot n currus m, curriculum nt; (for war) essedum nt

charioteer n auriga m

charitable adj benignus, beneficus; fig mitis

charitably adv benigne; indulgenter, in meliorem partem

charity n (love) caritas; (alms) stips f; (goodwill) benevolentia f; (indulgence) indulgentia, venia f

charlatan n pharmacopola circumforaneus; fig ostentator, iactator m

charm[1] n (incantation) cantus m; carmen nt; cantio f; incantamentum nt; fig illecebra; gratia f; (physical charms) venustas f; veneres fpl; (amulet) amuletum nt

charm[2] vt incanto, fascino, canto ①; (delight) capio ③; delecto ①

charming adj venustus, amoenus, lepidus, blandus

charnel-house n ossuarium nt

chart n tabula f

charter[1] n (privilege) licentia f

charter[2] vt conduco ③

charwoman n operaria f

chase[1] vt persequor ③; venor, sector ①; (drive) pello, ago ③; agito ①

chase[2] n (hunting) venatio f; venatus m

chasm n hiatus m; specus m/f/nt

chaste adj castus, pudicus; purus

chasten vt castigo ①

chastise vt castigo ①

chastisement n castigatio; animadversio f

chastity n pudicitia, castitas f; (modesty) pudor m

chat[1] vi fabulor ①; garrio ④

chat[2] n sermo m

□ **have a** ~ fabulor [1]; garrio [4]

chattel n bona ntpl; res f

chatter¹ vi nugor [1]; garrio, effutio [4]; (of the teeth) crepito [1]

chatter² n strepitus m; (idle talk) garrulitas f; nugae fpl; (of the teeth) crepitus m

chatterbox n lingulaca f

chattering adj garrulus

chatty adj garrulus

cheap adj vilis

cheaply adv bene, vili

cheapness n vilitas f

cheat¹ vt decipio, fallo, eludo [3]; fraudo [1]

cheat² n (act) fraus, ars f, dolus m; (person) fraudator m

check¹ vt (restrain) cohibeo, inhibeo [2]; reprimo [3]; (stop) retardo, tardo [1]; (bridle) refreno [1]; (accounts) dispungo [3]; (verify) confirmo, probo [1]

check² n (hindrance) impedimentum nt; (disadvantage) detrimentum nt; (delay) mora f; (verification) probatio f

cheek n gena, bucca f
■ ~**bone** n mala, maxilla f

cheeky adj impudens

cheer¹ vt (gladden) hilaro, exhilaro [1]; (encourage) hortor, adhortor [1]; (comfort) solor [1]; (applaud) plaudo [3]

cheer² n (shout) clamor, plausus m; (cheerfulness) hilaritas f

□ **be of good** ~ bono animo esse

cheerful adj hilaris, alacer, laetus
■ ~**ly** adv hilare, laete; (willingly) libenter

cheerfulness n alacritas, hilaritas f

cheering n acclamatio f, plausus m

cheery adj ▶ **cheerful**

cheese n caseus m

chemist n pharmacopola m

chequered adj tessellatus, distinctus; varius

cherish vt (nourish) alo [3]; (treat tenderly) foveo [2]; fig colo [3]

cherry n cerasus f; cerasum nt
■ ~**tree** n cerasus f

chess n ludus latruncularius
■ ~**board** n tabula latruncularia
■ ~**man** n latrunculus, calculus m

chest n (breast) pectus nt; (box) cista, arca, capsa f; (for clothes) vestiarium nt; (cabinet) scrinium nt

chestnut n castanea f
■ ~**tree** n castanea f

chew vt mando [3]; manduco [1]; (the cud) rumino [1]; fig meditor [1]

chicken n pullus (gallinaceus) m

chick-pea n cicer nt

chicory n cichorium, intubus m

chide vt&i obiurgo, vitupero [1]; reprehendo [3]; (sharply) corripio [3]

chiding n obiurgatio, reprehensio f

chief¹ adj primus; praecipuus, summus, supremus
■ ~**ly** adv praecipue, imprimis

chief² n princeps, procer, dux, auctor m, caput nt

chieftain n dux, ductor m

chilblain n pernio m

child n infans m/f; puer, filius m; puella, filia f; (children) liberi mpl
□ **bear a** ~ parturio [4]
□ **with** ~ gravida

child-bed n puerperium nt
□ **woman in** ~**-bed** puerpera f

childbirth n partus m; Lucinae labores mpl

childhood n infantia; pueritia f
□ **from ~** a puero or pueris; a parvo

childish adj puerilis, infans
■ **~ly** adv pueriliter

childishness n pueritilas f

childless adj orbus

childlike adj puerilis

chill¹ n frigus nt; algor m; horror m; (fever) febris f

chill² vt refrigero ①

chilly adj alsiosus; frigidulus

chime¹ n (harmony) concentus m

chime² vi (of bells) cano ③
□ **~ in** succino ③

chimera n chimaera f

chimney n caminus m

chin n mentum nt

china n murrha f, murrhina ntpl

chine n tergum nt, spina f

chink n rima, fissura f; (sound) tinnitus m

chip¹ n segmen nt, assula f; (for lighting fire) fomes m; (fragment) fragmentum, fragmen nt

chip² vt dolo, dedolo ①

chirp¹ vi (also **chirrup**) (of birds) pipio ①; pipilo ①; (of crickets) strideo ②

chirp² n (also **chirrup**) pipatus m

chisel¹ n scalprum, caelum nt

chisel² vt scalpo ③

chit-chat n garrulitas f; nugae fpl

chivalrous adj magnanimus, nobilis

chivalry n virtus f, magnanimitas f

choice¹ n delectus m; electio; (power of choosing) optio; (diversity)

varietas f

choice² adj electus, exquisitus, praestans, eximius

choir n chorus m

choke vt suffoco; strangulo ①; fauces elido ③; fig praecludo ③
■ **~** vi suffocor; strangulor ①

choler n ira, bilis f

cholera n cholera f

choose vt eligo, deligo, lego ③; opto ①
■ **~** vi (prefer) malo; (be willing) volo ir

chop¹ vt abscido ③; trunco
□ **~ off** detrunco ①; abscido
□ **~ up** concido ③

chop² n (of meat) ofella f

chord n (string) chorda f, nervus m

chore n officium, munus, eris nt

chorus n chorus m; concentus m

Christ n Christus m

Christian adj Christianus

chronicle¹ n annales, fasti mpl

chronicle² vt in annales refero ③

chronicler n annalium scriptor m

chronology n aetatum ordo m; ratio temporum f

chrysalis n chrysallis f

chubby adj bucculentus

chuckle vi cachinno ①

chum n contubernalis m

chunk n (of food) frustum nt

churchyard n caemeterium, sepulcretum nt

churl n homo rusticus, homo illiberalis m

churlish adj inhumanus; agrestis
■ **~ly** adv inhumaniter

churlishness n inhumanitas, rusticitas f

cinder n cinis m; favilla f

cinnamon n cinnamum nt

circle¹ n circulus, orbis; (whirling motion) gyrus m; (of people) corona f; (social meeting) circulus m

circle² vt circumdo ①; cingo ③
■ ~ vi (move round) circumvolvor ③

circuit n circuitus; ambitus m; circumscriptio f; (of judges) conventus m
□ **make a** ~ circumire ④

circuitous adj devius

circular adj orbiculatus, rotundus

circulate vt spargo ③, differo ir
■ ~ vi circulor ①

circulation n circumactus m
□ **come into** ~ in usum venio ④

circumcise vt circumcido ③

circumcision n circumcisio f

circumference n peripheria f, circulus, orbis m

circumlocution n circumlocutio f; ambages fpl

circumnavigate vt circumvehor ③

circumstance n res f; tempus nt; condicio f; status m
□ **under these** ~s cum res ita se habeant

circus n circus m

cistern n cisterna f; puteus m

citadel n arx f

citation n vocatio, prolatio f

cite vt (law) cito, evoco ①; (quote) profero ③

citizen n civis m/f; (townsman) oppidanus m

citizenship n civitas f

city¹ n urbs f

city² adj urbanus; urbicus

civic adj civilis, civicus

civil adj civilis; (polite) comis, urbanus
■ **~ly** adv comiter, urbane

civilian n (non-military person) togatus m

civility n urbanitas f

civilization n cultus m

civilize vt excolo ③; expolio, emollio ④

clad adj vestitus, indutus, amictus

claim¹ vt postulo; flagito ①; exposco, exigo ③; (demand for oneself) vindico ①

claim² n vindicatio; postulatio f; postulatum nt
□ **legal** ~ vindiciae fpl

claimant n petitor m

clamber vi scando, conscendo ③

clammy adj lentus, viscidus

clamour n clamor, tumultus m

clamp n confibula f

clan n gens f

clandestine adj clandestinus, furtivus

clang¹ n clangor m

clang² vi clango; strepo ③

clap¹ vi (hands) plaudo ③

clap² n (blow) ictus; (noise) crepitus; (of thunder) fragor; (with the hands) plausus m

clarify vt deliquo, defaeco ①

clarity n claritas f

clash¹ n crepitus m; concursus m; (opposition) repugnantia f

clash² vi crepito ①; concurro ③; fig confligo ③; repugno ①

clasp¹ n fibula f; (embrace) amplexus m

clasp² vt fibulo ①; (embrace) amplector; (grasp) comprehendo ③

class¹ n classis f; ordo m; genus nt; (of pupils) classis f

class² vt in classes distribuo ③; (value) aestimo ①

classification n distributio f

classify vt in classes distribuo ③

clatter¹ vi crepo, crepito ①

clatter² n strepitus, crepitus m

claw¹ n unguis m; ungula f; (of a crab) bracchium nt

claw² vt (scratch) scalpo ③; lacero ①
□ ~ **away** or **off** diripio ③

clay n argilla; creta f; lutum nt

clean¹ adj mundus, purus; nitidus

clean² vt mundo, purgo ①; (sweep) verro ③; (by wiping, brushing or rubbing) tergeo, detergeo ②; (by washing) abluo ③

cleanness n munditia f; nitor m; fig innocentia f

cleanse vt purgo, depurgo, expurgo, purifico ①

cleansing n purgatio f

clear¹ adj (bright) lucidus, clarus; (of fluids) limpidus; (transparent) liquidus; (clean) purus; (fair) serenus; (of voice) candidus; (manifest) conspicuus, manifestus; (of space) apertus, patens; (of style) lucidus; fig (in the head) sagax
□ ~ **of** (free from) solutus, liber
□ **keep** ~ **of** caveo ②

clear² vt purgo ①; (acquit) absolvo ③; (a doubt) explano ①; (from) libero ①; (land, forests) extrico; (exculpate) purgo (de aliqua re) ①
□ ~ **away** detergeo; amoveo ②; (a debt) solvo ③
□ ~ **out** emundo ①
□ ~ **up** vt enodo; explano, illustro ①; vi (of the weather) sereno ①

clearly adv clare; (of sounds) liquide;

fig dilucide; plane; aperte, haud dubie, manifesto

clearness n claritas; (of sky) serenitas f; fig candor m

cleft n rima, fissura f

clemency n clementia, mansuetudo, indulgentia f

clement adj clemens, mitis

clench vt contraho, astringo ③

clerk n (scholar) doctus; (accountant) actuarius; (scribe) scriba m

clever adj sollers, dexter; ingeniosus; (knowing) scitus; (quick) versutus; (sly, cunning) callidus, astutus

cleverly adv sollerter, perite; ingeniose; scite; astute; callide

cleverness n dexteritas, sollertia, astutia, calliditas f

click vi crepito ①

client n cliens m; (one who consults another) consultor m

clientele n clientela f

cliff n (sharp rock) cautes, rupes f, scopulus; (hill) collis m

climate n regio f; aer m; caelum nt
□ **a mild** ~ temperies f

climb vt&i ascendo, conscendo, scando, enitor, evado ③

clinch vt (an argument) astringo ③

cling vi adhaereo, haereo ②; amplector ③; (remain) maneo ②

clinging adj lentus, tenax, sequax

clink¹ vi tinnio ④

clink² n tinnitus m

clip vt tondeo ②; circumcido, praecido ③; amputo ①

clipper n (ship) celox f

clipping n tonsura f

clique n factio f

cloak[1] n pallium, sagum nt; lacerna, laena, chlamys f; amictus m

cloak[2] vt pallio vestio ④; fig dissimulo ①; praetendo, tego ③

clock n horologium nt

clod n glaeba f

clog[1] n (heavy shoes) sculponeae fpl; fig impedimentum nt; mora f

clog[2] vt impedio, praepedio ④; onero ①

close[1] vt claudo ③; operio ④; (end) finio ④; termino ①
□ ~ **in** includo ③
■ ~ vi (come together) coeo ④; (end) terminor ①
□ ~ **up** praecludo, occludo ③

close[2] adj (thick) densus; (narrow) angustus; artus; (near to) contiguus; fig taciturnus, tectus
□ ~ **by** vicinus, propinquus
□ ~ **together** confertus, continuus

close[3] adv dense; (near) prope, proxime

close[4] n (end) finis m/f; (~ of a speech) peroratio f
■ **bring to a** ~ finio ④; termino ①
□ **draw to a** ~ terminor ①

closeness n (nearness) proximitas f

closet n cella f, conclave; (for clothes) vestiarium nt

clot vi concresco ③

cloth n pannus m; (linen) linteum; (for horses) stragulum nt

clothe vt vestio, amicio ④; induo ③; velo ①

clothes n vestis f; vestitus m, vestimenta ntpl

clothing n vestitus m, vestimenta ntpl

cloud n nubes, nebula f; nubila ntpl

cloudless adj serenus, sudus

cloudy adj nubilus; (of liquids) turbidus
□ **grow** ~ nubilo ①

cloven adj bisulcus, bifidus

clover n trifolium nt

clown n (buffoon) scurra m

club n (cudgel) clava f; fustis m; (of people) sodalicium nt; sodalitas f; circulus m

cluck vi singultio ④

clue n glomus nt; (trace, mark) indicium nt

clump n massa f; globus m
□ ~ **of bushes** dumentum nt

clumsily adv crasse; rustice; inscite, ineleganter, male

clumsiness n rusticitas f

clumsy adj inhabilis; inelegans; inscitus; rusticus, agrestis

cluster[1] n (of grapes, etc.) racemus; (of flowers) corymbus m

cluster[2] vi congregor, conglobor ①

clutch[1] vt arripio ③

clutch[2] n fig
□ **in one's** ~**es** in sua potestate

coach n currus m, raeda f; pilentum, petoritum nt

coachman n raedarius m, auriga m/f

coagulate vi concresco ③

coal n carbo m; (burning) pruna f

coalesce vi coalesco ③; fig coeo ④

coalition n societas f

coalmine n fodina f

coarse adj crassus; fig incultus; rudis, rusticus, infacetus, illiberalis
■ ~**ly** adv crasse; infacete

coarseness *n* crassitudo; rusticitas *f*

coast *n* ora *f*, litus *nt*

coastal *adj* maritimus

coat¹ *n* vestis; tunica *f*
□ ~ **of arms** insignia *ntpl*
□ ~ **of mail** lorica; (skin) pellis *f*; corium *nt*; tegumentum *nt*

coat² *vt* illino, induco ③

coax *vt* mulceo ②; blandior ④; (persuade) adduco ③

coaxing¹ *n* blandimenta *ntpl*; blanditiae *fpl*

coaxing² *adj* blandus

cobble *vt* resarcio ④

cobbler *n* sutor, veteramentarius *m*

cobweb *n* aranea tela, aranea *f*; aranea texta *ntpl*

cock *n* gallus *m*

cockle *n* (shellfish) chema *f*

cockroach *n* blatta *f*

cocoon *n* globulus *m*

code *n* leges *fpl*

coerce *vt* coerceo ②; refreno ①; cogo ③

coercion *n* coercitio *f*; (force) vis *f*; (necessity) necessitas *f*

coffin *n* arca *f*; loculus *m*

cog *n* (of a wheel) dens *m*

cogent *adj* gravis, efficax
■ ~ly *adv* efficaciter, graviter

cogitate *vi* meditor, reputo ①

cogitation *n* reputatio *f*

cohabitation *n* concubitus *m*

cohere *vi* cohaereo ②; fig consentio ④; concordo ①

coherence *n* contextus *m*; (order) ordo *m*

coherent *adj* contextus,

continens; (clear) clarus

cohesive *adj* tenax, lentus

cohort *n* cohors *f*

coil¹ *n* spira *f*; volumen, glomus *nt*

coil² *vt&i* glomero; glomeror ①; (wind) volvo, volvor ③

coin¹ *n* nummus *m*; (collectively) pecunia *f*; (small ~) nummulus *m*

coin² *vt* (money) cudo ③; ferio ④; fig (invent) fingo ③

coinage *n* res nummaria; (coined money) pecunia publice signata, moneta; (invention) fictio *f*

coincide *vi* congruo ③; convenio ④

coincidence *n* concursio fortuitorum *f*; (agreement) consensus *m*

colander *n* colum *nt*

cold¹ *adj* frigidus, gelidus
□ **be** ~ frigeo, algeo ②
□ **become** ~ frigesco ③

cold² *n* frigus *nt*, algor *m*; (illness) gravedo *f*
□ **catch** ~ perfrigesco, algesco ③

coldly *adv* fig frigide, gelide, lente

coldness *n* frigus *nt*; algor *m*; fig lentitudo *f*

collapse¹ *vi* collabor; concido, corruo ③

collapse² *n* lapsus, casus *m*; labes, ruina *f*

collar *n* (of a garment) collare *nt*; (ornament) torques *m/f*; monile *nt*; (for horses) helcium *nt*; (for dogs) mellum *nt*

colleague *n* collega *m*; consors *m/f*

collect *vt* lego, colligo, confero ③; (an army) comparo, convoco ①; (gather) cogo ③; comporto ①; (money) exigo ③; (heap up)

coacervo 🔟
□ **~ oneself** se or animum
colligere
■ **~ vi** convenio 🔟, coeo 🔢;
congregor 🔟

collection n collectio;
conquisitio; (of money) collatio f

college n collegium nt; academia f

collide vi confligo, concurro 🔢

colliery n fodina f

collision n conflictio f;
concursus m

colloquial adj communis
(sermo) m

collusion n collusio;
praevaricatio f

colonist n colonus m

colonize vt coloniam deduco 🔢
in + acc

colonnade n porticus f, xystus m

colony n colonia f

colossal adj (of statues) colossicus,
colosseus; (huge) ingens, immanis

colossus n colossus m

colour¹ n color m, pigmentum nt;
(ensign) vexillum, signum nt

colour² vt coloro 🔟; (dye) tingo,
inficio, imbuo 🔢
■ **~ vi** erubesco 🔢

coloured adj coloratus

colouring n color; fig ornatus m

colt n equulus m, pullus equinus m

column n columna f

comb¹ n pecten m

comb² vt pecto 🔢

combat¹ n pugna f, proelium;
certamen nt

combat² vt&i pugno, proelior
🔟; certo, dimico 🔟; contendo

🔢; (oppose) repugno, adversor 🔟
both + dat

combatant n miles, pugnator,
proeliator m

combination n coniunctio,
iunctura f; concursus m

combine vt coniungo 🔢; misceo 🔢
■ **~ vi** coeo 🔢

combustion n crematio,
deflagratio f

come¹ vi venio 🔢; (arrive) pervenio
🔢 ad + acc; (happen) fieri ir
□ **~ about** evenio 🔢, accido 🔢
□ **~ after** sequor 🔢
□ **~ again** revenio 🔢
□ **~ along** procedo 🔢
□ **~ away** abscedo 🔢; abeo ir
□ **~ back** revenio 🔢; redeo ir
□ **~ before** praevenio 🔢
□ **~ by** praetereo 🔢; (get) acquiro 🔢
□ **~ down** descendo 🔢; (fall down)
decido 🔢
□ **~ forth** exeo ir; egredior 🔢; fig
exorior 🔢
□ **~ forward** procedo 🔢
□ **~ in(to)** introeo ir, intro 🔟
□ **~ in!** intra, intrate
□ **~ near** appropinquo 🔟;
accedo 🔢
□ **~ of** originem traho (de or e,
both + abl
□ **~ off** recedo 🔢; fig discedo 🔢; (of
hair, etc.) cado 🔢
□ **~ on** procedo, pergo 🔢
□ **~ on!** agite!
□ **~ out** (be published) edor,
emittor 🔢; (become known) evulgor
🔟; ► **~ forth** and ► **~ off**
□ **~ round** circumagor, fig
adducor 🔢; (recover one's senses) me
recipio 🔢
□ **~ to** advenio ad; pervenio 🔢
ad + acc
□ **~ to pass** evenio 🔢; fio ir

□ ~ **together** convenio, coeo ir
□ ~ **up** subvenio 4; (spring up)
provenio 4; (surprise) deprehendo 3
come² int age! eia!
comedian n comoedus;
comicus m
comedy n comoedia f; soccus m
comely adj decens, pulcher,
venustus
comet n cometes m, stella crinita f
comfort¹ vt consolor, solor 1
comfort² n solacium, solamen nt,
consolatio f
comfortable adj (commodious)
commodus
comfortably adv commode
comforter n consolator m
comic adj (also **comical**)
comicus m
comically adv comice; ridicule
coming¹ n adventus m
coming² adj venturus, futurus
command¹ vt impero 1,
praecipio 3 both + dat; iubeo 2
command² n mandatum,
praeceptum, imperium nt; (order)
iussus m; iussum nt; (office, place)
praefectura f, imperium nt
commander n dux, praefectus,
imperator m
commandment n
▶ **command²**
commemorate vt celebro 1
commemoration n celebratio f
commence vt&i incipio 3; incoho
1; ordior 4; coepi 3
commencement n initium,
principium nt
commend vt (commit) commendo
1; (committo 3; (approve) approbo,

laudo, probo 1
commendable adj
commendabilis, probabilis,
laudabilis
commendably adv laudabiliter
commendation n
commendatio, laus f
comment¹ vt&i commentor,
interpretor 1; (remark)
animadverto 3
comment² n (criticism)
animadversio f
commentary n commentarius
m, commentarium nt
commentator n interpres m/f
commerce n commercium nt;
mercatus m; mercatura f
commiserate v:
■ ~ **with** vt miseror, commiseror
1; miseresco 3 + gen
commiseration n miseratio f
commission¹ n mandatum nt; (in
the army) tribunatus m
□ **a ~ of two** duumviri mpl
commission² vt delego 1
commit vt (give) do 1; (trust)
committo 3; (be guilty of) patro,
perpetro 1; (admitto 3; (imprison) in
custodiam do 1
□ ~ **oneself** se dedere 3
committee n delecti
□ ~ **of ten** decemviri mpl
commodity n res venalis, merx f
common¹ adj communis;
publicus; (ordinary, etc.) vulgaris;
(well known) pervulgatus; fig tritus;
mediocris; (social status) plebeius
common² :
□ **in ~** in medium, in commune;
communiter; promiscue
commoner n plebeius m

commonly adv vulgo, fere, plerumque

commonplace n locus communis m
■ ~ adj (hackneyed) vulgaris, pervulgatus, tritus
■ ~-**book** n commentarius m

commonwealth n respublica, civitas f

commotion n agitatio f; tumultus, motus, concursus m

communicate vt impertio ④; communico ①

communication n communicatio f; commercium; colloquium nt; (message) nuntius m
□ **cut off** ~**s** omnes aditus intercludo ③

communicative adj affabilis, apertus

community n communitas; (partnership) societas; (state) civitas, respublica f

compact¹ adj densus, spissus; solidus; (of style) pressus
■ ~**ly** adv dense, spisse; presse

compact² n pactum nt; conventio f; foedus nt

companion n socius, sodalis, comes; (as soldier) contubernalis; (in games and gambling) collusor m
□ **boon** ~ compotor m

companionship n sodalitas f; contubernium nt

company n societas, sodalitas; (of soldiers) cohors f, manipulus m; (at table) convivium nt; (troop) caterva; turba, manus f; (corporation) collegium nt

comparable adj comparabilis

comparative adj comparativus

comparatively adv use the comparative, e.g.
□ ~ **slow** tardior

compare vt comparo, aequo ①; confero ③

comparison n comparatio, collatio f
■ **in** ~ **with** prep prae + abl

compartment n loculus m, cella f

compass n (circuit) ambitus, circuitus m; (limits) fines mpl; (pair of compasses) circinus m

compassion n misericordia, miseratio f

compassionate adj misericors
■ ~**ly** adv misericorditer

compatibility n congruentia; (conformity) convenientia f

compatible adj congruus, conveniens

compatriot n civis m/f; popularis m

compel vt cogo, compello ③

compensate vt (for) penso, compenso ①

compensation n compensatio f

compete vi contendo ③; certo ①

competence n (also **competency**) facultas f

competent adj capax; (suitable) congruens, idoneus; (of authorities) locuples
■ ~**ly** adv idonee, satis

competition n contentio, aemulatio f, certamen nt

competitive adj aemulus

competitor n aemulus, rivalis m

compilation n collectio f; excerpta ntpl

compile vt colligo, conscribo, compono ③

complacency n delectatio f

complacent *adj* (contented) contentus; (smug) qui sibi placet

complacently *adv* aequo animo

complain *vt* (of) queror, conqueror ③; ploro ①
■ **~** *vi* gemo ③; lamentor ①

complaining *adj* querulus

complaint *n* querela, querimonia *f*; (charge) crimen *nt*; lamentatio *f*; (disease) morbus *m*

complaisant *adj* officiosus, comis, facilis, humanus

complement *n* complementum, supplementum *nt*

complete[1] *adj* plenus; integer; perfectus
■ **~ly** *adv* plane, prorsus

complete[2] *vt* compleo; suppleo; expleo ②; (accomplish) perficio ③

completeness *n* integritas; perfectio *f*

completion *n* (accomplishment) perfectio *f*

complex *adj* multiplex

complexion *n* (of the skin) color *m*

complexity *n* ambages *fpl*; difficultas *f*

compliance *n* obtemperatio *f*, obsequium *nt*

compliant *adj* officiosus; facilis

complicate *vt* impedio ④; confundo ③; turbo ①

complicated *adj* nodosus, difficilis, perplexus

complication *n* nodus *m*; ambages *fpl*; difficultas *f*

complicity *n* conscientia *f*

compliment[1] *n* verba honorifica *ntpl*; blanditiae *fpl*
□ **pay one's ~s (to)** saluto ①

compliment[2] *vt* laudo ①

complimentary *adj* honorificus; blandus

comply *vi* (with) concedo + *dat*; cedo ③; pareo ②; (humour) morigeror; (me) accommodo ①; (accept) accipio ③

component *n* pars *f*, elementa *ntpl*

compose *vt* compono; (arrange) digero, dispono ③; (calm) sedo ①
□ **~ oneself** tranquillor ①

composed *adj* quietus, tranquillus
■ **~ly** *adv* quiete, aequo animo

composer *n* scriptor *m*

composition *n* compositio; confectio *f*; (book) liber *m*

compost *n* stercus *nt*

composure *n* tranquillitas *f*, animus aequus *m*

compound[1] *vt* compono ③; misceo ②

compound[2] *adj* compositus; concretus

comprehend *vt* (embrace) contineo ②, complector; (understand) capio, percipio, comprehendo, intellego ③

comprehensible *adj* comprehensibilis

comprehension *n* intellectus *m*, intelligentia, comprehensio *f*

comprehensive *adj* amplus

compress *vt* comprimo, astringo ③, coarto ①

compression *n* compressio *f*

comprise *vt* contineo, cohibeo ②; comprehendo, complector ③

compromise[1] *n* compromissum *nt*; (agreement) pactum *nt*

compromise[2] *vt* compromitto

compulsion | condemn

③; (bring into disrepute) in invidiam
adduco ③
■ ~ vi pac_iscor ③

compulsion n vis, necessitas f

compulsorily adv vi, per vim

compulsory adj necessarius

computer n calculator m

comrade n sodalis, socius; (military)
contubernalis m

concave adj cavus; concavus

conceal vt celo, occulto ①; abdo,
condo, occulo ③; (dissemble)
dissimulo ①

concealment n occultatio;
dissimulatio f

concede vt concedo, permitto
③; do ①

conceit n (fancy) opinio; (pride)
arrogantia, superbia f
□ witty ~ lepos m

conceited adj arrogans, superbus,
tumidus

conceivable adj comprehensibilis

conceive vt concipio; (comprehend)
percipio, intellego ③; (imagine)
fingo ③

concentrate vt in unum locum
contraho
■ ~ vi fig animum intendo (in
aliquid) ③

concentration n in unum locum
contractio, fig animi intentio f

concept n imago, notio, opinio f

conception n (in the womb)
conceptus m; (idea) imago, species,
notio f

concern[1] n (affair) res f, negotium
nt; cura f; (importance) momentum
nt; (anxiety, trouble) sollicitudo f

concern[2] vt pertineo ②
□ it ~s interest, refert ir

□ **be ~ed** occupor ①; particeps
sum; (be anxious) sollicitus sum ir
□ **it does not ~ me** non mihi
curae est

concerning prep (about) de + abl;
(as to) quod ad + acc

concession n concessio f; (thing)
concessum nt; (allowance) venia f

conch n concha f

conciliate vt concilio ①

conciliation n conciliatio f

conciliatory adj pacificus;
pacificatorius

concise adj brevis, concisus; (style)
pressus
■ ~ly adv breviter, concise

conciseness n brevitas f

conclude vt&i concludo ③; finio ④;
(end) perficio, (settle) statuo ③; (infer)
concludo ③

conclusion n (end) conclusio f;
finis m/f; (of a speech) peroratio f;
epilogus m; (inference) conclusio f

conclusive adj (of arguments) certus

concoct vt concoquo ③; (contrive)
excogito, machinor ①

concord n concordia f; conspiratio
f; consensus m; (mus) concentus m

concourse n concursus;
conventus m; frequentia f

concrete adj concretus

concubinage n concubinatus m

concubine n concubina f

concur vi convenio; (agree)
consentio ④

concurrence n concursus,
consensus m

concurrently adv una, simul

concussion n concussio f

condemn vt damno, condemno;
(blame) vitupero ①

condemnation *n* damnatio, condemnatio *f*

condemnatory *adj* damnatorius

condensation *n* densatio, spissatio *f*

condense *vt* denso, condenso, spisso ①; fig coarto ①

condescend *vi* dignor ①; descendo, me summitto ③

condescending *adj* comis, facilis, officiosus
■ **~ly** *adv* comiter, officiose

condescension *n* obsequium *nt*; comitas *f*

condiment *n* condimentum *nt*

condition *n* condicio *f*, status *m*; (of agreement) pactum *nt*, lex *f*; (rank) ordo *m*

condolence *n* consolatio *f*

condone *vt* condono, veniam do ①; ignosco ③ *all + dat*

conduct¹ *n* vita, ratio *f*; mores *mpl*; (management) administratio, cura *f*; (deeds) facta *ntpl*

conduct² *vt* adduco; deduco; perduco ③; administro ①; (direct) dirigo ③; (preside over) praesum *ir + dat*

conduit *n* canalis *m*, aquaeductus *m*

cone *n* conus *m*

confectioner *n* crustularius, pistor dulciarius *m*

confectionery *n* cuppedia *ntpl*

confederacy *n* (alliance) foedus *nt*; societas *f*

confederation *n* foedus *nt*; societas *f*

confer *vt* (bestow) confero ③; (compare) comparo ①
□ **~ with** colloquor ③;

convenio ④

conference *n* colloquium *nt*; congressus *m*

confess *vt* fateor, confiteor ②

confession *n* confessio *f*

confidant *n* familiaris *m/f*

confide *vt* confido, committo; credo ③
□ **~ in** (trust) confido, fido ③ *both + dat*

confidence *n* fides; fiducia; confidentia; (boldness) audacia *f*; (self-confidence) sui fiducia *f*
□ **in ~** (secretly) clam

confident *adj* confidens; securus; (bold) audax
■ **~ly** *adv* confidenter

confidential *adj* (secret) arcanus

confine *vt* claudo, includo ③; coerceo, cohibeo ②; circumscribo ③; termino ①

confinement *n* inclusio; (imprisonment) custodia *f*; carcer *m*; (childbirth) puerperium *nt*

confirm *vt* confirmo; firmo; (prove) comprobo ①; (ratify) sancio ④

confirmation *n* confirmatio *f*

confirmed *adj* inveteratus

confiscate *vt* proscribo ③; publico, confisco ①

confiscation *n* publicatio, confiscatio, proscriptio *f*

conflagration *n* incendium *nt*

conflict¹ *n* contentio; controversia *f*; certamen *nt*; pugna *f*

conflict² *vi* contendo ③; (struggle) luctor ①; (be at variance) discrepo ①

conflicting *adj* contrarius, adversus

conform *vi* (comply with) obtempero ① *+ dat*

conformity n convenientia, congruentia f
□ **in ~ with** secundum + acc

confound vt confundo ③; permisceo ②; perturbo ①; (destroy) deleo ②; perimo ③

confront vt (match) committo ③
■ **~ vi** (meet) congredior cum + abl

confuse vt confundo ③; perturbo ①

confused adj confusus, perplexus; indistinctus; pudibundus

confusion n confusio; perturbatio f; tumultus; pudor m

confute vt confuto, refuto ①; refello, redarguo ③

congeal vt congelo, glacio ①
■ **~ vi** consisto, concresco ③

congenial adj (pleasant) gratus, consentaneus; (amicably shared) concors

congestion n congestus m

congratulate vt gratulor, grator ① both + dat

congratulation n gratulatio f

congratulatory adj gratulatorius

congregate vi congregor, conglobor ①; convenio ④

congregation n contio f; coetus m; auditores mpl

conifer n arbor conifera f

conjectural adj opinabilis, coniecturalis
■ **~ly** adv ex coniectura

conjecture[1] n coniectura f

conjecture[2] vt coniecto ①; conicio ③

conjugal adj coniugalis; coniugialis

conjunction n coniunctio f;

concursus m

conjure vt (entreat) obtestor ①
■ **~ vi** praestigiis utor ③

conjurer n magus; (juggler) praestigiator m

conjuring n (juggling) praestigiae fpl

connect vt connecto ③; copulo ①; (in a series) sero ③

connected adj coniunctus; continuus
□ **be ~** cohaereo ②

connection n coniunctio f; contextus m; (relation) affinitas; cognatio f
□ **have a ~ with** pertineo ② ad + acc

connive vi conniveo, indulgeo ②

connoisseur adj homo doctus, peritus, intellegens, elegans

connubial adj coniugalis

conquer vt vinco ③; supero; domo ①; (gain) capio ③; potior ④

conqueror n victor; domitor m, victrix f

conquest n victoria f; (what is gained) partum nt

conscience n conscientia f

conscientious adj religiosus; sanctus; (hard-working) diligens

conscientiousness n aequi reverentia, religio, fides f; (application) diligentia f

conscious adj conscius
■ **~ly** adv use adj sciens, prudens

consciousness n conscientia f; (feeling) sensus m
□ **lose ~** concido ③; exanimor ①

conscript n tiro m

conscription n (of soldiers) delectus m

consecrate vt sacro, consecro; dedico ①

consecration n consecratio; dedicatio f

consecutive adj continuus
■ ~ly adv per ordinem; continenter; deinceps

consent[1] vi assentior, consentio ④

consent[2] n consensus m, consensio f
□ **without my** ~ me invito

consequence n consequentia, consecutio; (logical) conclusio; (issue) exitus m; (importance) momentum nt

consequent adj consequens, consectarius
■ ~ly adv ergo, igitur, proinde

conservation n conservatio f

conservative adj (moderate) mediocris
□ **a ~ in politics** optimatium autor

conserve vt conservo, servo ①

consider vt considero, contemplor ①; intueor, contueor ②; (turn over in the mind) volvo ③; verso, voluto, reputo ①; (regard as) aestimo; (reckon) numero ①

considerable adj aliquantus; (of size) amplus

considerably adv aliquantum; multum, maxime

considerate adj consideratus, prudens; (kind) humanus
■ ~ly adv considerate; (kindly) humaniter

consideration n consideratio, contemplatio; prudentia f; (regard) respectus m; (kindness) humanitas f
□ **take into ~** rationem habeo ②] + gen

□ **without ~** inconsulte

considering prep (having regard to) pro + abl
□ **~ that** utpote, (since) quoniam, quando

consign vt confido ③; assigno ①; trado ③

consist vi
□ **~ of** consto ①; consisto ③; (be) sum ir

consistency n convenientia, constantia f; (hardness) firmitas f; (thickness) densitas f

consistent adj constans; congruens; consentaneus
■ ~ly adv constanter; congruenter

consolable adj consolabilis

consolation n consolatio f; solamen, solacium nt

console vt solor, consolor ①

consolidate vt consolido, firmo ①; stabilio ④

consort vi
□ **~ with** vivo cum + abl; familiariter utor ③ + abl

conspicuous adj conspicuus; insignis; manifestus
■ ~ly adv manifesto

conspiracy n coniuratio, conspiratio f

conspirator n coniuratus, conspiratus m

conspire vi coniuro, conspiro ①

constancy n constantia, firmitas; perseverantia f

constant adj constans, firmus; perpetuus; assiduus; fidelis; fidus
■ ~ly adv constanter, fideliter; perpetuo, assidue

constellation n sidus, astrum nt

consternation n consternatio, trepidatio f, pavor m

constitute vt constituo, facio ③, creo ①; (be) sum ir

constitution n (of the body, etc.) habitus m, constitutio f; (political) civitas f; fig condicio, natura f

constitutional adj legitimus, e republica; natura insitus

constrain vt cogo, compello ③

constraint n vis, coercitio, necessitas f

constrict vt constringo ③

construct vt construo, struo, exstruo ③; aedifico ①

construction n constructio, aedificatio; figura, forma f; (meaning, sense) sensus m
□ **put a bad ~ on** in malam partem accipio ③

consul n consul m

consular adj consularis

consulate n consulatus m

consulship n consulatus m

consult vt&i consulo ③; consulto; delibero ①
□ **a person's interests** consulo ③ + dat

consultation n consultatio; deliberatio f

consume vt (destroy, use up) consumo, absumo, conficio ③; (squander) effundo ③; dissipo ①; (eat) edo ③

consumer n consumptor m

consumption n consumptio; (disease) tabes; phthisis f

contact n contactus m

contagion n contagium nt

contagious adj pestilens, pestifer, contagiosus

contain vt contineo, habeo ②; comprehendo ③
□ **~ oneself** se tenere ②

container n arca f

contaminate vt inquino ①; polluo, inficio ③; foedo, violo ①

contamination n contagium

contemn vt temno, contemno, sperno, despicio ③; fastidio ④

contemplate vt&i contemplor intueor, contueor ②

contemplation n contemplat meditatio f

contemplative adj contemplativus

contemporary¹ adj aequalis, contemporaneus

contemporary² n aequalis, aequaevus m

contempt n contemptio f, contemptus m; fastidium nt

contemptible adj contemnendus; abiectus; sordid

contemptuous adj fastidiosus superbus
■ **~ly** adv fastidiose, contempti

contend vi contendo ③; pugno, certo ①; (struggle) luctor ①; (dispute verbis certo ①; (maintain) confirme affirmo ①
□ **~ against** repugno, adversc ① both + dat

contending adj adversus; rivali

content¹ adj contentus

content² vt satisfacio ③; placeo ② both + dat

content³ n aequus animus m

contented adj ▶ content adj

contentedly adv aequo animo placide

contention n contentio, lis f;

certamen nt

contentious adj litigiosus; pugnax

contentment n ▸ content n

contents n quod inest; (of a book) argumentum nt

contest[1] vt&i (oppose) repugno ① + dat

contest[2] n certatio, contentio; controversia; lis f; certamen nt

context n contextus m

continent[1] adj abstinens, continens; castus, pudicus
■ ~ly adv temperanter

continent[2] n continens f

continental adj continentem incolens; in continenti positus, ad continentem pertinens

contingency n casus, eventus m

contingent[1] adj (accidental) fortuitus
□ **it is ~ on** pendit ex + abl

contingent[2] n numerus m

continual adj continuus; perpetuus; assiduus, perennis
■ ~ly adv continenter; perpetuo; semper; assidue

continuation n continuatio; series f

continue vt persevero in + abl ①; (prolong) produco ③
■ ~ vi maneo, remaneo ②; duro ①; persisto ③; (go on) pergo ③

continuity n continuitas, perpetuitas f

continuous adj continens, continuus; perpetuus
■ ~ly adv continenter, perpetuo

contort vt distorqueo ②

contortion n distortio f

contour n lineamenta ntpl

contraband[1] adj illicitus, vetitus

contraband[2] n merces vetitae fpl

contract[1] vt (compress) contraho, astringo ③; (a disease, etc.) contraho ③
□ ~ **for** loco ①; (undertake by contract) redimo ③
■ ~ vi (make an arrangement by bargaining) paciscor ③; (shrink) contrahor ③

contract[2] n (bargain) locatio f; pactum nt

contraction n contractio f; compendium nt

contractor n (of work) susceptor, redemptor, conductor m

contradict vt contradico, obloquor ③; adversor ① all + dat

contradiction n contradictio; (of things) repugnantia f

contradictory adj contrarius, repugnans

contrary[1] adj (opposite) contrarius; diversus; adversus; repugnans

contrary[2] adv & prep
□ ~ **to** contra; praeter both + acc

contrary[3] n contrarium nt, contraria pars f
□ **on the ~** contra, e contrario; immo

contrast[1] n diversitas, varietas; dissimilitudo f

contrast[2] vt comparo ①; confero ③
■ ~ vi discrepo ①

contravene vt violo ①; frango ③

contribute vt confero ③; (give) do ①

contribution n collatio; (of money) collecta f; (gift) donum nt

contrivance n inventio,

machinatio *f*; (thing contrived)
inventum *nt*; machina *f*

contrive *vt* (invent) fingo ③;
excogito ①; invenio ④; (command)
□ ~ **to** efficio ③ *ut* + *subj*

control[1] *n* (power) potestas, dicio
f; (check) coercitio *f*; (command)
imperium, regimen *nt*; (management)
administratio *f*
□ **self-~** moderatio *f*

control[2] *vt* (check) reprimo ③;
(restrain) coerceo ②; (be at the
head of) praesum *ir* + *dat*; (manage)
administro, moderor ①; (rule)
rego ③

controversial *adj* controversus

controversy *n* controversia *f*;
concertatio; (debate) disceptatio;
(disagreement) dissensio *f*

contumely *n* contumelia *f*,
probrum, opprobrium *nt*

contusion *n* contusio *f*,
contusum *nt*

convalesce *vi* convalesco ③

convalescent *adj* convalescens

convene *vt* convoco ①

convenience *n* commoditas *f*;
commodum *nt*; utilitas *f*

convenient *adj* commodus,
idoneus, opportunus
■ **~ly** *adv* commode; opportune

convention *n* conventus *m*;
(agreement) pactum, conventum *nt*;
(custom) mos *m*

conventional *adj* usitatus,
translaticius

converge *vi* vergo ③

conversant *adj* peritus,
exercitatus

conversation *n* colloquium *nt*,
sermo *m*

converse *vi* colloquor ③

conversion *n* conversio *f*

convert *vt* converto ③; commuto
①; reduco, transfero ③

convex *adj* convexus

convexity *n* convexitas *f*

convey *vt* veho ③, asporto,
deporto ①; adveho ③; porto,
vecto; (transfer) abalieno; fig
significo ①

conveyance *n* (act) advectio,
vectura *f*; (vehicle) vehiculum *nt*;
(law) abalienatio *f*

convict[1] *vt* convinco ③; (detect)
comperio ④; (by sentence)
condemno ①

convict[2] *n* convictus, ad poenam
damnatus *m*

conviction *n* (condemnation)
damnatio; (belief) persuasio *f*

convince *vt* suadeo, persuadeo
② + *dat*

convincing *adj* gravis
■ **~ly** *adv* graviter

convivial *adj* hilaris, laetus

convoke *vt* convoco ①

convoy *n* (escort) praesidium *nt*

convulse *vt* concutio, convello ③

convulsed *adj* convulsus

convulsion *n* convulsio *f*,
spasmus *m*

cook[1] *n* coquus *m*, coqua *f*

cook[2] *vt&i* coquo ③

cookery *n* ars coquinaria *f*

cooking *n* coctura *f*
■ **~** *adj* coquinarius

cool *adj* frigidus; frigidulus; (shady)
opacus; fig sedatus; immotus;
impavidus; (indifferent) lentus;
(impudent) impudens

cool² n ▶ **coolness**

cool³ vt&i refrigero; refrigeror ①; fig frigesco, defervesco, languesco ③

coolly adv frigide; fig sedate; aequo animo; lente; impudenter

coolness n frigus nt; (pleasant ∼) refrigeratio f; (shadiness) opacum nt; fig lentitudo; cautela f; aequus animus m

coop¹ n (for hens) cavea f

coop² vt
  □ ∼ **up** includo ③

cooperate vi una ago ③; adiuvo, cooperor ①

cooperation n auxilium, adiumentum nt, cooperatio f

coot n fulica f

cope vi
  □ ∼ **with** certo ①, contendo ③ cum + abl

copious adj copiosus, abundans, uber
  ■ ∼ly adv abundanter, copiose

copper¹ n aes; cyprium nt

copper² adj aeneus, aenus, cypreus

copper-smith n faber aerarius m

coppice n (also **copse**) dumetum, fruticetum nt

copulate vi coeo (ir)

copulation n concubinus m

copy¹ n exemplar, exemplum nt; imitatio; imago f

copy² vt&i transcribo ③; imitor ①; (follow) sequor ③

coral n corallium nt

cord n funis m

cordial adj benignus; sincerus
  ■ ∼ly adv ex animo; benigne; sincere

cordiality n animus benignus m; comitas f

cordon n corona f

core n (of fruit) vulva f

cork¹ n (tree) suber nt; (bark) cortex m/f

cork² adj subereus

cork³ vt (seal up a container) obturo ①

corn n frumentum nt; (cereals) fruges fpl; annona f; (on the toes) callus m

corner n angulus m; (lurking-place) latebra f, recessus m; (of a street) compitum nt

cornfield n seges f, arvum nt
  ■ ∼s pl sata ntpl

corn-merchant n frumentarius m

cornucopia n cornu copiae nt

coronet n diadema nt

corporal¹ n decurio m

corporal² adj corporeus, corporalis

corporation n societas f, sodalicium nt

corporeal adj corporeus, corporalis

corps n legio f

corpse n cadaver nt

corpulent adj corpulentus, pinguis, obesus

correct¹ adj emendatus; rectus; accuratus; elegans
  ■ ∼ly adv emendate; recte; accurate; eleganter

correct² vt corrigo ③; emendo ①; fig animadverto; castigo ①

correction n correctio, emendatio; fig animadversio; castigatio f

correspond vi congruo ③; respondeo ②

correspondence n congruentia; (letters) epistulae fpl

correspondent n scriptor m

corresponding adj par + dat

corridor n andron m

corroborate vt confirmo ①

corrode vt erodo; peredo ③

corroding adj mordax

corrosion n rosio f

corrosive adj mordax

corrupt¹ vt corrumpo ③; depravo ①
■ ~ vi putresco ③

corrupt² adj corruptus, putridus; fig pravus; impurus; venalis

corruptible adj corruptibilis; venalis

corruption n corruptio; putredo f; fig depravatio, pravitas; (by money) corruptela f

corselet n lorica f; thorax m

cortège n pompa f

cosmetic n medicamen nt

cosmopolitan adj cosmicus

cost¹ n (price) pretium nt; (expense) impensa f

cost² vt&i consto, sto ①

costliness n caritas f

costly adj pretiosus, carus, sumptuosus

costume n vestitus m

cosy adj commodus

cot n (bed) lectulus m

cottage n casa f, tugurium nt

couch n cubile; pulvinar nt; lectus, torus m

cough¹ n tussis f

□ **have a bad ~** male tussio ④

cough² vi tussio ④

council n concilium, consilium nt; senatus m

councillor n consiliarius m

counsel¹ n (advice) consilium nt; (person) advocatus m

counsel² vt consulo ③; moneo ②

counsellor n consiliarius, consiliator; advocatus m

count¹ vt&i numero ①; censeo; (consider, deem) habeo ②; existimo ①; duco ③
□ ~ **on** confido ③ + dat

count² n (calculation) computatio f

countenance n (face, look) facies f, vultus, aspectus; (encouragement) favor m
□ **put out of ~** confundo ③; perturbo ①

counter¹ n (of a shop) mensa f; (for games) calculus m

counter² adv contra
□ **run ~ to** adversor, repugno ① + dat

counteract vt obsisto ③ + dat

counterbalance vt exaequo, penso, compenso ①

counterfeit¹ vt imitor; adultero; simulo ①

counterfeit² adj ficticius; simulatus; fictus; adulterinus

counterfeiter n imitator; falsarius m

countermand vt renuntio ①

countless adj innumerabilis, innumerus, infinitus

country n (as opposed to the town) rus nt; regio; terra f; loca ntpl
□ **native ~** solum natale nt; patria f

country-house n villa f
countryman n rusticus m
countryside n rus nt
couple¹ n par nt
couple² vt copulo ①; connecto, coniungo ③
courage n animus m, virtus, audacia, fortitudo f
courageous adj animosus, ferox; audax; fortis
  ■ ~ly adv ferociter; audacter; fortiter
courier n cursor; nuntius; (letter-carrier) tabellarius m
course n (running) cursus; (of water) ductus m; (means) ratio f
  ■ **of** ~ adv profecto, sane
court¹ n (palace) regia domus, aula f; (retinue) comitatus m; (in law) forum, tribunal nt; iudices mpl
court² vt (cultivate friendship of) colo ③; ambio, blandior ④; observo ①; (of a suitor) peto ③
courteous adj comis, humanus, benignus; affabilis
  ■ ~ly adv comiter, humaniter, benigne, affabiliter
courtesan n meretrix f
courtesy n comitas, affabilitas, urbanitas f
courtier n aulicus, purpuratus m
court martial n iudicium castrense nt
courtship n amor m
courtyard n area f, atrium nt
cousin n consobrinus m; consobrina f; patruelis m/f
cove n (small bay) sinus m
covenant n pactum nt; conventio f
cover¹ vt tego ③; operio ④; celo ①;

instruo ③; fig (protect) protego ③
cover² n tegmen; (lid) operculum; (wrapper) involucrum; (shelter) praesidium nt; (for game) operimentum nt; lustra ntpl; fig praetextus m
covering n (act) obductio f; (cover) tegmen, velamen; (wrapper) involucrum; (lid) operculum; (of a bed) stragulum nt
coverlet n stragulum nt
covert adj tectus; occultus; (indirect) obliquus
  ■ ~ly adv tecte, occulte; oblique
covet vt concupisco, cupio, appeto ③
covetous adj avidus, avarus, appetens, cupidus
  ■ ~ly adv avide, avare; appetenter
covetousness n avaritia, aviditas, cupiditas f
cow n vacca, bos f
coward n ignavus, timidus m
cowardice n ignavia; timiditas f
cowardly adj ignavus, timidus
cower vi subsido ③
cowherd n bubulcus, armentarius m
cowshed n bubile nt
coy adj modestus; timidus; verecundus
  ■ ~ly adv verecunde, timide
coyness n modestia; timiditas f
cozen vt fallo ③; ludificor ①
crab n cancer m
crabbed adj morosus; (sour) acerbus
crack¹ vt findo; frango ③; (a whip) flagello insono ①
  ■ ~ vi dehisco, displodor ③; dissilio ④

crack² n fissura, rima f; (noise) crepitus m

cracked adj (of walls, etc.) rimosus

crackle vi crepito ①

cradle n cunae fpl; fig cunabula, incunabula ntpl

craft n (cunning) astutia f; astus m; (calling, trade) ars f; (ship) navicula, linter f

craftily adv astute, callide

craftiness n astutia, calliditas; (skill) sollertia f

craftsman n artifex m

crafty adj astutus, callidus; (deceitful) subdolus, fallax, dolosus

crag n scopulus m

craggy adj scopulosus; (rough) asper

cram vt farcio ④
  □ ~ **together** constipo ①

cramp n (disease) spasmus m; (tool) uncus m

crane n (bird) grus m/f; (machine) tolleno f

cranny n rima, fissura f

crash¹ n fragor, strepitus m

crash² vi strepo ③; sono, fragorem do ①

crass adj crassus

crate n corbis f

crater n (of a volcano) crater m

crave vt (beg) rogo, imploro, efflagito ①, posco, expeto ③; (desire) cupio ③

craven adj ignavus, timidus

craving n desiderium nt; appetitus m; sitis, fames f

crawl vi repo, serpo ③; repto ①

craziness n imbecillitas, vesania, insania f, furor m

crazy adj imbecillus, insanus, vesanus

creak¹ vi strideo ②; crepito ①

creak² n stridor, crepitus m

creaking adj stridulus

cream n flos lactis m; fig (the pick of) flos m; robur nt

crease¹ n ruga f

crease² vt corrugo, rugo, replico ①

create vt creo ①; pario, gigno ③; fig formo ①; fingo ③; invenio ④; (appoint) creo ①

creation n (act) creatio f; (origin) origo f; (whole world) mundus m; fig (work of art) opus nt, ars f

creative adj creatrix; effectrix

creator n creator, procreator; fig fabricator; auctor m

creature n res creata f; animal nt

credence n (belief) fides f
  □ **give ~ to** credo ③ + dat

credentials n auctoritates, litterae fpl

credibility n fides, probabilitas f

credible adj credibilis

credibly adv credibiliter

credit¹ n (authority) auctoritas f; (belief, faith) fides; (reputation) fama, existimatio; (praise) laus f; (financial) fides f

credit² vt credo; (financial) acceptum refero ir + dat

creditable adj honorificus, honestus

creditor n creditor m

credulity n credulitas f

credulous adj credulus

creed n fides, doctrina, opinio f

creek n aestuarium nt

creep vi repo, serpo ③; repto ①

crescent-shaped adj lunatus; (of the moon) crescens

crest n (of animals) crista; (of a horse) iuba; (of a helmet) crista f; (heraldic) insigne nt; (of a hill) apex m

crested adj cristatus

crestfallen adj demissus, deiectus

crevice n rima, rimula f

crew n grex m, turba, multitudo f; (of a ship) remiges, nautae mpl

cricket n (insect) gryllus m, cicada f

crime n crimen, delictum, maleficium; facinus; (shameful deed) flagitium, scelus nt

criminal[1] n nocens m

criminal[2] adj scelestus, sceleratus, nefarius; (of a charge) capitalis

crimson n coccum nt
■ ~ adj coccineus, coccinus

cringe vt (to) adulor [1]

cripple[1] n claudus m

cripple[2] vt claudum facio [3]; fig debilito [1]; accido [3]

crippled adj claudus, mancus

crisis n discrimen, momentum nt

crisp adj crispus; (brittle) fragilis

criterion n signum, insigne; indicium nt

critic n existimator; iudex; criticus, censor m

critical adj criticus; (censorious) mordax

criticism n ars critica f; iudicium nt; censura, reprehensio f

criticize vt iudico, examino [1]; carpo, reprehendo [3]

croak[1] vi (as frogs) coaxo [1]; (as ravens) crocio [4]

croak[2] n crocitus m

crockery n fictilia ntpl

crocodile n crocodilus m

crocus n crocus m, crocum nt

crone n anicula, vetula f

crook n (of shepherds) pedum nt
□ **by hook or by ~** quocumque modo

crooked adj curvatus, curvus, incurvus, flexus; fig (dishonest) pravus; dolosus
■ ~**ly** adv torte; prave

crookedness n curvatura f, curvamen nt; fig (dishonesty) pravitas f

crop[1] n (of corn) messis f; (yield) reditus m

crop[2] vt abscido [3], decurto [1]; tondeo [2]; (browse) carpo, depasco [3]; tondeo [2]

cross[1] n crux; fig molestia f; cruciatus m; infortunium nt

cross[2] adj (ill-tempered) morosus
■ ~**ly** adv morose

cross[3] vt (pass over) transeo ir; (send across) transmitto, traicio [3]; fig (thwart) frustror [1]
□ ~ **one's mind** subeo ir; succurro [3]
□ ~ **over** transcendo, traicio, transgredior [3]

crossbar n repagulum nt

crossbow n arcuballista f

crossbowman n arcuballistarius m

cross-examination n interrogatio, percontatio f

cross-examine vt percontor [1]

crossing n transitus; traiectus m; (of roads) bivium; (of three or four roads) trivium, quadrivium nt

crossness n morositas f

cross-question vt percontor ①

crossroads n trames m

crouch vi me demitto, subsido ③; (hide) delitesco ③

crow¹ n (bird) cornix f; (voice of the cock) cantus m; gallicinium nt

crow² vi (of cocks) cano ③; canto; fig (boast) iacto ①

crowbar n (lever) vectis m

crowd¹ n turba; frequentia, caterva, multitudo f; concursus m

crowd² vt arto, stipo ①; premo ③ ■ ~ vi (around) circumfundor ③; (together) convolo, congregor ①; concurro, confluo ③

crowded adj condensus, confertus; frequens; celeber

crowing n (of the cock) gallicinium nt, cantus m

crown¹ n corona f, diadema nt; (top) vertex m; (completion) cumulus m; fig (royal power) regnum nt

crown² vt corono ①; (with a garland, etc.) cingo ③; (add finishing touch to) cumulo ①
□ **be ~ed with success** felicem exitum habeo ②

crucial adj maximi momenti (= of the greatest importance)

crucifixion n summum supplicium nt

crucify vt cruci suffigo ③

crude adj crudus; fig rudis; incultus ■ ~ly adv imperfecte, inculte

cruel adj crudelis, atrox, saevus; immanis; barbarus, durus, ferus ■ ~ly adv crudeliter, saeve; dure; atrociter

cruelty n crudelitas; atrocitas, saevitia f

cruise¹ vi pervagor,

circumvector ①

cruise² n navigatio f

crumb n (of bread) mica f; frustum nt

crumble vt frio ①; comminuo, contero ③ ■ ~ vi frior ①; collabor, corruo ③

crumple vt rugo, corrugo ①

crunch vi dentibus frango, morsu divello ③

crush vt contundo, contero ③; (press) premo, comprimo ③; elido fig opprimo; affligo ③; (weaken) debilito ①

crust n crusta f

crusty adj crustosus; fig morosus

crutch n baculum nt; (support) fulcrum nt

cry¹ vt&i clamo, exclamo, conclamo; (weep) lacrimo ①; fleo ② □ ~ **against** obiurgo ① □ ~ **out** exclamo, vociferor ①

cry² n clamor m, vox, exclamatio f; (of infants) vagitus; (weeping) ploratus m

crying n fletus, ploratus m

crypt n crypta f

cryptic adj ambiguus

crystal¹ n crystallum nt

crystal² adj crystallinus, vitreus; pellucidus

cub n catulus m

cube n cubus m

cubic adj cubicus

cubit n cubitum nt, ulna f

cuckoo n coccyx, cuculus m

cucumber n cucumis m

cud vi
□ **chew the ~** rumino ①

cuddle vt amplector ③

cudgel¹ n fustis m, baculum nt

cudgel² vt fustibus verbero ⬛

cue n (hint) nutus m; (watchword) signum nt; tessera f

cuff n (blow) colaphus m; alapa f

cuirass n lorica f; thorax; cataphracta m

culinary adj culinarius; coquinarius

cull vt carpo, lego, decerpo ③

culminate vi ad summum fastigium pervenio ④

culmination n fastigium nt

culpable adj culpandus; nocens

culprit n (person accused) reus m, rea f; (guilty person) nocens, noxius m

cult n cultus m

cultivate vt colo ③; (develop) formo ⬛; fingo, excolo ③; (train) exerceo; (show attentions to) foveo ②; observo ⬛

cultivation n cultura f, cultus m

culture n cultura f, cultus m; (of the mind) humanitas f

cumbersome adj iniquus, gravis, incommodus, onerosus

cunning¹ n peritia; astutia, calliditas, ars f

cunning² adj doctus, peritus, sollers; (in a pejorative sense) astutus, vafer

cunningly adv docte, perite, sollerter; astute, vafre, dolose

cup n poculum nt, calix m; (beaker) patera f

cup-bearer n pocillator m

cupboard n armarium nt

Cupid n Cupido, Amor m

cupidity n cupiditas f

cur n canis m/f

curable adj medicabilis, sanabilis

curative adj medicabilis

curator n curator; custos m

curb¹ n frenum nt; fig coercitio f

curb² vt freno, refreno ⬛; compesco, comprimo ③; coerceo ②

curdle vt cogo ③; coagulo ⬛
■ ~ vi coeo ④; concresco ③

cure¹ n (of wounds) sanatio f; (remedy) remedium nt, medicina f

cure² vt (heal) sano ⬛, medeor ②; (preserve) salio ④

curiosity n curiositas; audiendi or spectandi studium nt; (object) res rara, raritas f

curious adj (inquisitive) curiosus; (wondrously made) elaboratus; rarus; mirus
■ ~ly adv curiose; mirabiliter; arte

curl¹ vt (hair) crispo ⬛; torqueo ②
■ ~ vi crispor ⬛

curl² n (natural) cirrus; (artificial) cincinnus m; (curve) flexus m

curling-iron n calamister m, ferrum nt

curly adj crispus

currency n (money) moneta f; nummi mpl; (use) usus m

current¹ adj vulgaris, usitatus
☐ **be ~** valeo ②
■ ~ly adv vulgo

current² n (of a river) flumen nt; (of the sea) aestus; (of air) afflatus m; aura f

curry vt:
☐ ~ **favour with** morem gero ③ + dat

curse¹ n exsecratio f, maledictum nt

curse² vt exsecror, detestor ⬛;

devoveo ②

cursed adj exsecrabilis

cursory adj brevis, properatus

curt adj brevis, abruptus
■ ~**ly** adv breviter

curtail vt decurto, mutilo ①; praecido ③; fig coarto ①; minuo ③

curtain n velum; (in a theatre) aulaeum nt; (for beds, etc.) plagula f; (mosquito net) conopium nt

curtness n brevitas f

curve¹ n curvamen nt, flexus; sinus m; (thing curved) curvatura f

curve² vt curvo, incurvo, sinuo ①; flecto ③

curved adj curvus, incurvus, recurvus; curvatus; sinuosus; (as sickle) falcatus

cushion n pulvinar nt, pulvinus m, culcita f

custody n custodia, tutela f; (imprisonment) carcer m

custom n (use) usus, mos m, consuetudo f; (fashion) institutum, praescriptum nt; (rite) ritus m
□ ~**s duty** portorium, vectigal nt

customary adj usitatus, consuetus, translaticius

customer n emptor m

custom-house n telonium nt
■ ~**s-officer** n portitor m

cut¹ vt seco ①; (fell) caedo; (mow) succido, meto ③
□ ~ **apart** intercido ③; disseco ①
□ ~ **away** recido, abscindo ③; amputo ①
□ ~ **down** caedo; (kill) occido ③
□ ~ **to pieces** concido ③
□ ~ **off** praecido; abscindo ③; (amputate) amputo ①; (the head) detrunco ①; (intercept) intercludo ③; prohibeo ②; fig (destroy, etc.)

exstinguo, perimo, adimo ③
□ ~ **open** incido ③
□ ~ **out** exseco ①; (out of a rock, etc.) excido ③
□ ~ **short** intercido; (abridge) praecido ③; fig (interrupt) intermitto ③
□ ~ **through** disseco ①; (e.g. the enemy) perrumpo ③
□ ~ **up** minutatim concido ③

cut² n incisura f; (slice) segmentum; (wound) vulnus nt, plaga f; (a short cut) via compendiaria f

cutlery n ferramenta ntpl

cutpurse n saccularius, sector zonarius m

cut-throat n sector collorum, sicarius m

cutting¹ adj (sharp) acutus; fig mordax

cutting² n (act) sectio f; (of a plant) propago, talea f

cuttle-fish n loligo, sepia f

cycle n orbis m

cylinder n cylindrus m

cylindrical adj cylindratus

cymbal n cymbalum nt

cynic adj & n cynicus m

cynical adj mordax, difficilis, severus
■ ~**ly** adv cynice, mordaciter, severe

cypress n cupressus, cyparissus f

Dd

dab vt illino ③

dabble vt (in) strictim attingo ③

daffodil n narcissus m

dagger n pugio m, sica f

daily adj diurnus; quotidianus
■ ~ adv cotidie, in dies

daintiness n fastidium nt

dainty adj (of people) fastidiosus; elegans; (of things) delicatus; exquisitus, mollis

daisy n bellis f

dale n vallis, convallis f

dalliance n blanditiae fpl

dam¹ n (mole) moles, pila f, agger m; (barrier) obex m

dam² vt coerceo ②; obstruo ③; oppilo ①

damage¹ n damnum, incommodum; (loss) detrimentum nt; (injury) iniuria, noxa f

damage² vt (hurt) laedo ③; (impair) obsum

damn vt (condemn) damno, condemno ①

damnation n damnatio f

damp¹ adj umidus, udus

damp² n umor m

damp³ vt (also **dampen**) umecto ①; fig infringo; restinguo ③

dampness n uligo f; umor m

damsel n puella, virgo f

dance¹ n saltatus m, saltatio f; chorus m; chorea f

dance² vi salto ①

dancer n saltator m

dancing n saltatio f, saltatus m

dancing-girl n saltatrix f

dandruff n furfur m; porrigo f

danger n periculum, discrimen nt

dangerous adj periculosus, gravis
■ ~ly adv periculose; graviter

dangle vi pendeo, dependeo ②; fluctuo ①

dangling adj pendulus

dank adj umidus, uvidus, udus

dappled adj variatus, varius

dare vi audeo ②
■ ~ vt provoco ①

daring adj audens; ferox; audax; animosus
■ ~ly adv audenter, audacter, animose

dark¹ adj obscurus; fuscus; opacus; niger; caecus; tenebrosus; caliginosus; (of mourning-dress) pullus; fig obscurus, ambiguus, dubius, anceps; (gloomy) atrox
■ ~ly adv obscure; fig per ambages

dark² n tenebrae fpl; obscurum nt; nox f

darken vt obscuro; (of colours) infusco; fig occaeco ①

darkness n obscuritas, caligo f; (shadiness) opacitas f; tenebrae fpl; color fuscus m

darling n deliciae fpl; amores mpl; corculum nt
■ ~ adj suavis, mellitus; amatus

darn vt resarcio ④

darnel n lolium nt

dart¹ n iaculum, spiculum, missile nt; hasta, lancea f

dart² vi provolo ①; me inicio ③

dash¹ vt (against) allido, illido;

d

offendo ③; (frustrate) frustror ①; (confound) confundo ③
□ ~ **to pieces** discutio ③
□ ~ **out** elido ③; vi ruo ③
■ ~ vi (rush) ruo ③
dash² n (onset) impetus m
dashing adj acer, alacer; splendidus
date¹ n (of time) dies m/f; tempus nt; (fruit) balanus f; palma f
□ **out of** ~ obsoletus, desuetus
date² vt (establish age) diem ascribo ③
■ ~ vi (from) incipio, originem traho ③
daub¹ vt oblino, illino ③
daub² n litura f
daughter n filia f
daughter-in-law n nurus f
daunt vt pavefacio ③; terreo, perterreo ②
dauntless adj impavidus, intrepidus
dawdle vi (loiter) moror, cesso ①
dawn¹ vi illucesco, dilucesco ③; fig eluceo ②
□ ~ **upon** fig subeo ④; succurro ③ both + dat
dawn² n aurora, prima lux f, diluculum nt
day¹ n dies m/f; lux f, sol m; tempus nt
□ **the** ~ **before** pridie
□ **the** ~ **after** postridie
day² adj diurnus
daybreak n lux prima f
daylight n lux f, dies m
daytime n tempus diurnum nt
daze vt obstupefacio ③
dazzle vt praestringo ③; fig capio ③
dazzling adj fulgidus, splendidus

dead¹ adj mortuus; vita defunctus; (lifeless, senseless) exanimis; fig torpidus; (dull) segnis
dead² n manes mpl; (of night) intempesta (nox) f
deaden vt hebeto ①; obtundo ③; (weaken) debilito, enervo ①; (lessen) imminuo ③
deadly adj mortifer, letalis; fig capitalis, implacabilis
deadness n torpor, stupor m, inertia; (dullness) insulsitas f
deaf adj surdus
deafen vt exsurdo ①; obtundo ③
deafness n surditas f
deal¹ n (quantity) numerus m; vis, copia f; (business) negotium nt
□ **a great** ~ multum
deal² vt distribuo ③; (handle) tracto ①
□ ~ **in** (sell) vendo
□ ~ **with** utor ③ + abl
■ ~ vi mercor, negotior ①
dealer n mercator, negotiator m
dealing n (trade) negotiatio, mercatura f, commercium nt; usus m; (doing) factum nt; (treatment) tractatio f
dear adj (costly) carus, pretiosus; (beloved) dilectus, carus
■ ~**ly** adv care; valde
dearness n caritas f
dearth n inopia, penuria; fames f
death n mors f; letum nt; interitus, obitus m
□ **violent** ~ nex f; funus nt
deathbed n
□ **on one's** ~ moriens
debar vt excludo ③; prohibeo, arceo ②
debase vt depravo; adultero; vitio

359

debatable | decorate

[]; corrumpo ③; fig dedecoro []

debatable adj disputabilis, controversiosus, dubius

debate¹ vt disputo, discepto []; dissero ③

■ ~ vi cogito, meditor []

debate² n controversia, disceptatio f; (friendly) colloquium nt

debauch vt stupro; vitio []; corrumpo ③

debauchery n libido, luxuria f, stuprum nt

debit¹ n expensum nt

debit² vt expensam pecuniam alicui ferre

debris n ruina f

debt n (of money) debitum, aes alienum; fig debitum nt

debtor n (also fig) debitor m

decade n decennium nt

decay¹ vi (of buildings) dilabor, labor; (of flowers) defloresco; (rot) putresco; (waste away) tabesco ③; fig deficio ③; declino []

decay² n tabes, caries; fig defectio, deminutio f

deceased adj mortuus, defunctus

deceit n fraus, fallacia f, dolus m

deceitful adj fallax; dolosus; fraudulentus; falsus

■ ~**ly** adv fallaciter; fraudulenter; dolose; per fallacias

deceive vt decipio, fallo ③; (cheat) fraudo []; circumduco ③; circumvenio ④

■ ~ vi fig mentior ④

deceiver n fraudator m

December n December m

decency n decorum nt; pudor m

decent adj decens; decorus; pudicus; honestus

■ ~**ly** adv decore, decenter, honeste

deception n fraudatio, fraus, fallacia f

deceptive adj fallax, vanus

decide vt&i discepto, diiudico []; decerno; constituo ③

decided adj firmus, constans; (of things) certus

■ ~**ly** adv certe

decimate vt decimo; fig depopulor []

decipher vt explico []

decision n sententia f, arbitrium, iudicium nt

decisive adj decretorius, haud dubius, certus

■ ~**ly** adv haud dubie

deck n pons m; transtra ntpl

declaim vt&i declamo, declamito []; invehor (in) ③ + acc

declamation n declamatio f

declaration n professio; (of war) denuntiatio f; (speech) oratio f; (opinion) sententia f

declare vt declaro []; aperio ④; profiteor ②; (war) denuntio; (as a judge) iudico []

■ ~ vi affirmo []

decline¹ vt (recoil from) detrecto; (refuse) recuso []

■ ~ vi (slope) vergo ③; inclino []; (decay) deficio, minuor ③; (abate) laxo []

decline² n defectio; (wasting away) tabes f

decompose vt dissolvo ③

■ ~ vi dissolvor, putresco ③

decomposition n dissolutio; (decay) tabes f

decorate vt orno, exorno,

d

decoro 🔟

decoration n (act) ornatio, exornatio f; ornatus m; (ornament) ornamentum

decorator n exornator m

decorous adj decorus
■ ~ly adv decore

decorum n decorum, quod decet nt

decoy[1] vt inesco 🔟; fig allicio, illicio, pellicio ③

decoy[2] n illecebra f, illicium nt; (bird) allector m

decrease[1] vt minuo, imminuo, deminuo ③
■ ~ vi decresco, minuor ③; minor fio ir

decrease[2] n deminutio, imminutio f

decree[1] n decretum, edictum nt; (judgment) sententia f

decree[2] vt statuo; decerno, edico ③

decrepit adj decrepitus, debilis, enervatus

decry vt detrecto, obtrecto 🔟

dedicate vt dedico; consecro 🔟; voveo ②

dedication n dedicatio; consecratio; (of a book) nuncupatio f

deduce vt (infer) concludo ③

deduct vt detraho, subtraho, deduco ③

deduction n deductio f; (in logic) conclusio f

deed n factum; facinus nt; res gestae fpl; (law) syngrapha f, instrumentum nt

deem vt iudico, puto, existimo 🔟; duco ③

deep[1] adj altus, profundus; (of sounds) gravis; (of colours) satur

deep[2] n profundum, (sea) mare nt

deepen vt excavo 🔟; defodio, deprimo ③
■ ~ vi altior fio ir; (night, etc.) densor ③

deeply adv alte, profunde; (inwardly) penitus; fig graviter, valde

deepness n ▶ depth

deer n cervus m; cerva f

deface vt deformo, turpo 🔟

defamation n obtrectatio f

defamatory adj probrosus

defame vt diffamo, calumnior, obtrecto 🔟

default vi (fail) deficio ③
□ **let a legal case go by** ~ ad vadimonium non venio ④

defeat[1] n clades, calamitas; (frustration) frustratio f

defeat[2] vt (baffle) frustror 🔟; (conquer) vinco ③; supero 🔟

defect[1] n vitium, mendum nt; menda f; (want) defectus m

defect[2] vi deficio ③

defection n defectio f

defective adj mancus, vitiosus; imperfectus

defence n (act) defensio; (excuse) excusatio; (means of) tutela f; tutamen nt
□ ~s munimentum nt

defenceless adj inermis; defensoribus nudatus

defend vt defendo ③; (at law) patrocinor 🔟 + dat

defendant n reus m, rea f
□ **the** ~ iste

defender n defensor; patronus m

defensible adj quod defendi potest; excusabilis

defer vt differo, profero ir, produco ③
□ ~ **to** obsequor ③ + dat

deference n observantia; reverentia f

defiance n provocatio f
□ **in ~ of** contra + acc

defiant adj ferox

deficiency n defectio f, defectus m; pars relicta; (want) lacuna f

deficient adj mancus; (deficient in) inops + gen
□ **be ~ in** deficio ③; careo ② + abl

deficit n lacuna f

defile[1] vt contamino, inquino, maculo, commaculo; fig foedo; incesto, violo ①

defile[2] n fauces, angustiae fpl; saltus m

define vt circumscribo ③; termino ①; definio ④

definite adj certus, status, definitus
■ ~**ly** adv definite, certe

definition n definitio f

definitive adj definitivus, decretorius

deflect vt&i deflecto ③; declino ①

deform vt deformo ①

deformed adj deformis; deformatus; distortus

deformity n deformitas; pravitas f

defraud vt fraudo, defraudo ①

deft adj habilis

defunct adj vita defunctus, defunctus, mortuus

defy vt (challenge) provoco ①; (spurn) contemno ③

degenerate[1] vi degenero ①

degenerate[2] adj degener

degradation n ignominia; deiectio f

degrade vt deicio ③; loco moveo ②; fig ignominia afficio ③

degree n gradus, ordo m
□ **in the highest ~** summe
□ **by ~s** paulatim, sensim, pedetentim, gradatim

deification n apotheosis, consecratio f

deify vt divum habeo ②; in numero deorum colloco ①

deign vi dignor; non aspernor, non gravor ①; sustineo ②

deity n numen nt; deus m; dea f

dejected adj demissus, tristis

dejection n animi demissio f; animus afflictus m

delay[1] n mora, cunctatio; dilatio, retardatio f

delay[2] vt detineo ②; tardo; retardo; (keep back) remoror ①
■ ~ vi cunctor; moror, cesso ①

delectable adj amoenus

delegate[1] n legatus m

delegate[2] vt (depute) delego; (commit) commendo ①

delegation n delegatio f

deliberate[1] adj deliberatus, consideratus, cautus, prudens; lentus
■ ~**ly** adv deliberate, cogitate; lente; consulto

deliberate[2] vi consulto, delibero, considero, reputo, verso, voluto ①; volvo ③

deliberation n deliberatio f

delicacy n subilitas, tenuitas; elegantia f; cuppediae fpl; (weakness) infirmitas f

delicate adj delicatus; mollis, tener; exquisitus; elegans; fastidiosus; (of texture) subtilis; (in taste) suavis; (weak) infirmus
■ **~ly** adv delicate; exquisite; subtiliter; molliter

delicious adj suavis, suavis, exquisitus

delight¹ n delectatio f; deliciae fpl; gaudium nt; voluptas f

delight² vt delecto ①
■ **~** vi gaudeo ②; laetor ①

delightful adj suavis, iucundus, amoenus
■ **~ly** adv iucunde, suaviter

delinquency n delictum nt

delinquent n nocens m

delirious adj non sui compos, mente alienatus

delirium n mentis alienatio f; delirium nt

deliver vt do ①; (hand over) trado ③; (free) libero ①; (surrender) prodo ③; (a speech) habeo ②; (sentence) dico (ius) ③; (an opinion) promo ③; (a message) perfero ③; (of childbirth) parienti adsum ir; (~ up) cedo ③

deliverance n liberatio f

deliverer n liberator, conservator m; vindex m/f

delivery n liberatio; (of goods) traditio; (utterance) pronuntiatio f; (childbirth) partus m

delude vt decipio, deludo ③; derideo ②

deluge¹ n diluvies, inundatio f, diluvium nt

deluge² vt inundo ①

delusion n error m; fraus f

delve vi ▶ **dig**

demand¹ vt postulo, flagito ①;

posco, deposco, peto ③

demand² n postulatio, petitio f
□ **be in ~** a multis expetor ③

demarcation n designatio f; (boundary) confinium nt

demean vi:
□ **~ oneself** (condescend to) descendo ③ ad + acc

demeanour n mores mpl; (deportment) gestus m

democracy n civitas popularis f; liber populus m

democrat n plebicola, homo popularis m

democratic adj popularis
■ **~ally** adv populi voluntate, per populum

demolish vt demolior ④; everto, disicio ③

demolition n demolitio, eversio ∎

demon n daemon m

demonstrable adj demonstrabilis, manifestus

demonstrate vt demonstro, firmo ①; convinco ③

demonstration n demonstratio f

demur¹ vi haesito, dubito ①
□ **~ to** nego, repudio ①

demur² n mora; (objection) exceptio f

demure adj modestus, gravis, severus
■ **~ly** adv modeste

demurral n mora; (objection) exceptio f

den n (cave) specus m/f/nt; (of beasts) latibulum nt; spelunca, latebra f; lustra ntpl

denial n negatio; infitiatio; (refusal) repudiatio; repulsa f

denote vt significo ①

denounce vt (accuse) accuso; (blame) culpo ①

dense adj densus, spissus, confertus

■ **~ly** adv dense; crebro

density n densitas f

dent[1] n (mark) nota f

dent[2] vt (mark) noto ①

dentist n dentium medicus m

denude vt denudo, nudo ①; detego ③; (rob) spolio ①

denunciation n denuntiatio; accusatio f

deny vt nego, infitior ①; (refuse) nego, recuso, denego ①; renuo, abnuo ③

depart vi abeo; exeo ④; (leave) discedo ③; (move) demigro ①; (set out) proficiscor ③

department n (area of responsibility) provincia f; cura f; munus nt; (branch) genus nt

departure n abitus, discessus m, profectio; (deviation) digressio f

depend vi (on) pendeo ② + ab or ex + abl; (trust) confido, fido + dat

dependable adj fidus

dependant n cliens m/f; assecla m

dependence n servitus; (reliance) fiducia; fides f; (poverty) inopia f

dependent adj subiectus; (poor) inops

depict vt pingo, depingo; effingo; describo; exprimo ③

deplorable adj miserabilis, flebilis, lugendus, plorabilis, calamitosus

deploy vt explico ①

depopulate vt desolo, vasto ①

deportment n gestus, habitus m

depose vt abrogo ①; amoveo ②

deposit[1] vt depono ③; (commit) commendo ①

deposit[2] n depositum; (pledge) pignus nt; (first instalment) arrabo m

deposition n (evidence) testimonium nt

depraved adj corruptus

depravity n pravitas f

deprecate vt deprecor ①

deprecation n deprecatio f

depredation n praedatio, spoliatio f; latrocinium nt

depress vt deprimo; fig infringo; affligo ③

depressed adj (downcast) afflictus; (flat) planus; (hollow) cavus

depressing adj tristis

depression n fig animi demissio f; animus afflictus m

deprivation n (act) privatio; spoliatio; (state) orbitas; inopia f

deprive vt privo; spolio; orbo ①; (take away) adimo, eripio ③

deprived adj expers, exsors

depth n altitudo f; profundum nt; (sea) pontus m; (bottom) fundus m

deputation n legati; (spokesmen) oratores mpl

depute vt lego, mando ①

deputy n legatus; vicarius m

deranged adj (mentally) mente captus, delirus

derangement n (of mind) mens alienata, mentis alienatio f

derelict adj derelictus

deride vt rideo, derideo, irrideo ②

derision n risus, derisus m; irrisio f

derisive adj acerbus

derivation *n* derivatio; etymologia *f*

derive *vt* duco, deduco ③
■ ~ *vi* proficiscor ③; orior ④

derogatory *adj* inhonestus, turpis

descend *vt&i* descendo; (fall suddenly) delabor ③
□ **be ~ed from** orior ④ ab + *abl*; originem traho ③ ab + *abl*

descendant *n* progenies, proles, stirps *f*

descent *n* descensus *m*; descensio; (slope) declivitas *f*; fig lapsus *m*; (origin) origo *f*; genus *nt*

describe *vt* describo; depingo ③; narro ①

description *n* descriptio; narratio *f*

desecrate *vt* profano, violo ①; polluo ③

desecration *n* violatio *f*

desert¹ *n* (wilderness) desertum *nt*, vastitas, solitudo *f*

desert² *n* meritum *nt*

desert³ *vt* desero, relinquo, destituo ③
■ ~ *vi* transfugio, signa relinquo ③

deserter *n* desertor; transfuga *m*

desertion *n* derelictio; (betrayal) proditio *f*

deserve *vt&i* mereo, mereor ②; dignus sum *ir*

deservedly *adv* merito, iure

deserving *adj* dignus; bonus, optimus, probus

design¹ *vt* describo ③; fig machinor, excogito ①; molior ④; (destine) destino ①

design² *n* (drawing) descriptio *f*; fig (purpose) consilium, propositum *n*

designate *vt* designo; nomino ①

designation *n* designatio *f*; (name) nomen *nt*

designer *n* inventor; fabricator; machinator *m*

designing *adj* callidus, subdolus

desirable *adj* optabilis, expetendus

desire¹ *vt* desidero, opto ①; expeto, cupio ③

desire² *n* desiderium *nt*; cupido *f*; appetitus *m*; appetitio *f*

desirous *adj* cupidus, appetens

desist *vi* desisto; absisto; (cease) desino ③

desk *n* scrinium; pulpitum *nt*

desolate *adj* solus, desertus, vastus, desolatus; fig (of persons) afflictus

desolation *n* vastitas; solitudo *f*; (bereavement) orbitas *f*

despair¹ *n* desperatio *f*

despair² *vi* despero (de aliqua re) ①

despairingly *adv* desperanter

despatch *vt* mitto; dimitto ③; (finish) absolvo; exsequor; (settle) transigo; conficio; (kill) interficio ③

desperate *adj* (without hope) exspes, desperatus; (dangerous) periculosus
■ ~ly *adv* ita ut spes amittatur
□ **be ~ly in love** perdite amo ①

desperation *n* desperatio *f*

despicable *adj* aspernandus, vilis

despicably *adv* turpiter

despise *vt* despicio, sperno, temno, contemno ③; aspernor ①

despite *conj* (even if) etiamsi

despoil *vt* ▶ spoil *vt*

despondency *n* animi demissio *f*

despondent *adj* demissus

despot *n* dominus; tyrannus *m*

despotic *adj* imperiosus, superbus, tyrannicus
■ ~**ally** *adv* tyrannice

despotism *n* dominatio, regia potestas *f*

dessert *n* secunda mensa *f*; bellaria *ntpl*

destination *n* (purpose) destinatio *f*; propositum *nt*; (goal) meta *f*

destine *vt* destino; (mark out) designo ①

destiny *n* fatum *nt*; sors *f*

destitute *adj* egens, egenus, inops; destitutus, expers; viduus

destitution *n* inopia; egestas *f*; mendicitas *f*

destroy *vt* destruo, perdo, everto, tollo, consumo ③; aboleo, deleo ②; vasto ①
□ **be** ~**ed** intereo, pereo *ir*

destruction *n* eversio *f*; exitium *nt*; clades *f*

destructive *adj* exitialis, perniciosus; calamitosus

detach *vt* seiungo; solvo, secerno ③

detached *adj* seiunctus

detachment *n* separatio *f*; (of troops) manus *f*; (fairness) aequitas *f*

detail¹ *vt* enumero ①; singillatim dico ③

detail² *n* singulae res *fpl*; singula *ntpl*

detain *vt* retineo ②; retardo ①

detect *vt* comperio ④; deprendo ③

detection *n* deprehensio *f*; indicium *nt*

detective *n* inquisitor *m*

detention *n* mora *f*

deter *vt* deterreo, absterreo ②; averto ③

deteriorate *vi* deterior fio *ir*, in peius mutor ①

deterioration *n* depravatio, corruptio *f*

determination *n* definitio *f*; arbitrium, iudicium *nt*; mens, voluntas *f*; (purpose) consilium *nt*; (resoluteness) constantia *f*

determine *vt* determino ①; definio ④; statuo, constituo, decerno ③; diiudico ①
□ **I am** ~**d** certum est mihi

detest *vt* abominor, detestor ①; odi, perodi ③

detestable *adj* detestabilis, foedus, odiosus

detestation *n* odium *nt*; detestatio *f*

dethrone *vt* regno expello ③

detract *vt* detraho, imminuo ③; (slander) detrecto, obtrecto ①

detraction *n* obtrectatio *f*

detriment *n* detrimentum, damnum *nt*

detrimental *adj* damnosus, iniuriosus, iniquus

devastate *vt* vasto, populor, depopulor ①; fig percello ③

devastation *n* (act) vastatio, populatio; (state) vastitas *f*

develop *vt* evolvo ③; explico ①; fig excolo ③
■ ~ *vi* cresco ③

development *n* explicatio *f*; (issue) exitus *m*

deviate *vi* aberro ①; digredior ③

deviation *n* aberratio; declinatio;

d

digressio f; fig error m
device n (emblem) insigne nt; (motto) inscriptio f; (contrivance) artificium nt; machina f
devious adj devius; vagus; erraticus
□ ~ **course** ambages fpl
devise vt fingo ③; excogito ①; concoquo ③; molior ④; machinor ①
□ ~ **a plan** consilium capio ③
devoid adj inanis, vacuus; liber; expers
devote vt devoveo ②; consecro, dico ①; (set apart) sepono ③
□ ~ **oneself to** studeo ②; incumbo ③ both + dat
devoted adj studiosus; (loving) pius
devotedly adv studiose, summo studio
devotion n devotio f; (affection) pietas f; (zeal) studium nt; diligentia f
devour vt voro, devoro ①; haurio ④; consumo ③
devout adj pius, devotus
■ **~ly** adv pie, religiose, sancte
dew n ros m
dewy adj roscidus, roridus, rorulentus
dexterity n calliditas, sollertia f
dexterous adj (also **dextrous**) callidus, sollers, sciens, habilis
■ **~ly** adv callide, scienter, sollerter
diabolical adj diabolicus
diagnosis n (examination) exploratio f; (judgment) sententia f
diagonal adj diagonalis
■ **~** n diagonalis linea f
■ **~ly** adv in quincuncem, in transversum

diagram n forma; forma geometrica f
dial n solarium nt
dialect n dialectos f; sermo m
dialogue n sermo m; colloquium nt; (written discussion) dialogus m
diameter n diametros, dimetiens f
diamond n adamas m
diaphragm n praecordia ntpl
diarrhoea n profluvium nt
diary n diarium nt; ephemeris f
dice npl tali mpl; tesserae fpl; (the game) alea f
dictate vt dicto ①; praescribo ③; (command) impero ① + dat
dictation n dictatum nt; (command) imperium, praescriptum nt
dictator n dictator m
dictatorial adj dictatorius; arrogans; imperiosus
dictatorship n dictatura f
diction n dictio f
dictionary n lexicon nt; thesaurus m
die¹ n (for gaming) talus m
□ **the ~ is cast** alea iacta est
die² vi morior; fig exstinguor; (decay) labor ③; pereo, intereo ④; (fade) cado ③
diet n (food) victus m; (med) diaeta f
differ vi differo ③; discrepo, disto ①; (in opinion, etc.) dissentio ④; dissideo ②
difference n differentia; diversitas; varietas f; discrimen nt; (of opinion) discrepantia; dissensio f
different adj diversus; alius; dispar; (unlike) dissimilis; (various) diversus, varius

■ **~ly** adv aliter; diverse; secus

difficult adj difficilis; arduus

difficulty n difficultas f; (dilemma, need) angustiae fpl
□ **with ~** aegre

diffident adj diffidens; verecundus, timidus; modestus

dig vt&i fodio ③
□ **~ up** eruo, effodio ③

digest vt (food) concoquo ③; (also fig)

digestion n (of food) concoctio f; (stomach) stomachus m

digit n digitus, numerus m

dignified adj gravis

dignify vt honesto, honoro, orno ①

dignity n dignitas, gravitas f, honor m

digress vi digredior ③; aberro ①

digression n digressio f

dike n ▶ **dyke**

dilapidated adj ruinosus, prolapsus

dilapidation n ruina f

dilate vt&i dilato; dilator ①

dilatory adj cunctabundus, lentus, tardus

dilemma n dilemma nt; fig (difficulty) angustiae fpl

diligence n diligentia, sedulitas f

diligent adj diligens, sedulus
■ **~ly** adv diligenter, sedulo

dilute vt diluo ③; misceo ②; tempero ①

dilution n temperatio, mixtura f

dim adj hebes; obscurus
□ **be ~** hebeo ②
□ **become ~** hebesco ③

dimension n dimensio, mensura f

diminish vt minuo, imminuo, deminuo ③; (reduce) extenuo ①
■ **~** vi minuor ③; extenuor ①

diminution n imminutio, deminutio f

dimly adv obscure

dimness n hebetatio; obscuritas; caligo f

din n strepitus, sonitus, fragor m
□ **make a ~** strepo ③

dine vi ceno ①; prandeo ②

dingy adj fuscus, squalidus, sordidus, subniger

dining-room n cenatio f

dinner n cena f

dinner-party n convivium nt

dint n
□ **by ~ of** per + acc

dip[1] vt immergo; tingo ③
■ **~** vi mergor; tingor; (sink) premor, vergo ③; declino ①

dip[2] n declivitas f

diploma n diploma nt

diplomacy n ars, astutia f

diplomat n (ambassador) legatus m

dire adj dirus, terribilis

direct[1] adj rectus, directus
■ **~ly** adv directe, recta (via); (immediately) statim, confestim

direct[2] vt (arrange); (turn) flecto, verto; (address) inscribo ③; (order) iubeo ②; (rule) guberno; (manage) curo, procuro ①

direction n (act) directio f; (way) iter nt, via; (quarter) regio; (ruling) gubernatio; (management) administratio f; (order) praeceptum nt
□ **in both ~s** utroque

director n rector; magister; praeses, praefectus; gubernator;

(manager) curator m

dirge n nenia f, carmen funebre nt

dirt n sordes f; caenum, lutum nt; limus m

dirtiness n spurcitia; fig obscenitas f

dirty[1] adj spurcus, sordidus, immundus, lutulentus, caenosus; (unwashed) illotus; fig obscenus

dirty[2] vt foedo, spurco, maculo, commaculo [1]

disability n impotentia f

disable vt debilito; enervo [1]

disabled adj debilis; mancus

disadvantage n incommodum, detrimentum, damnum nt; (inequality) iniquitas f

disadvantageous adj incommodus; iniquus

disaffected adj alienatus; aversus; seditiosus

disaffection n alienatus animus m; seditio f

disagree vi discrepo [1]; dissideo [2]; dissentio [4]

disagreeable adj iniucundus; ingratus; molestus; insuavis; gravis; (of people) difficilis, morosus

disagreement n dissensio, discordia f

disappear vi vanesco; evanesco; dilabor [3]

disappearance n exitus m

disappoint vt fallo [3]; frustror, fraudo [1]

disappointment n frustratio f; (inconvenience) incommodum nt

disapprobation n improbatio, reprehensio f

disapproval n improbatio, reprehensio f

disapprove vt reprehendo [3]; improbo [1]

disarm vt exarmo [1]; armis exuo [3]; fig mitigo [1]

disaster n calamitas, clades f; incommodum nt

disastrous adj calamitosus, funestus; pestifer
  ■ ~**ly** adv calamitose; pestifere

disband vt dimitto [3]; missum facio [3]

disbelief n diffidentia; incredulitas f

disbelieve vt fidem non habeo [2]; non credo [3]

disc n discus m; orbis (solis, lunae) m

discard vt repudio [1]; reicio, excutio [3]

discern vt discerno, distinguo [3]

discerning adj perspicax, acutus

discernment n perspicientia f; (faculty) prudentia f; acumen nt

discharge[1] vt&i (unload) exonero [1]; (dismiss) dimitto [3]; (of rivers) effundo [3]; (perform) fungor, perfungor [3]; (pay) solvo [3]; (shoot, let fly) mitto, immitto [3]; (acquit) absolvo [3]

discharge[2] n (unloading) exoneratio; (dismissal) missio; (acquittal) absolutio; (payment) solutio f; (efflux) profluvium, effluvium nt

disciple n discipulus m; discipula f; fig sectator m

discipline[1] n disciplina f

discipline[2] vt instituo; assuefacio [3]

disclaim vt infitior [1]; diffiteor [2]; nego [1]; (let go) remitto, dimitto [3]

disclaimer n negatio, infitiatio f

disclose vt patefacio, pando,

detego ③; aperio ④; enuntio, vulgo ①

disclosure n indicium nt

discolour vt decoloro ①

discomfort n incommoda ntpl; molestiae fpl; vexatio f

disconcert vt conturbo, perturbo ①; (frustrate) frustror ①

disconnect vt disiungo, seiungo ③

disconsolate adj afflictus, tristis
■ ~ly adv insolabiliter; triste

discontent n animus parum contentus m; (anger) ira f; (hatred) odium nt

discontented adj parum contentus; (disagreeable) morosus

discontinue vt&i intermitto; desino, desisto ③

discord n discordia f

discordant adj discors; discrepans; dissonus; absonus

discount vt deduco; (disregard) neglego ③

discourage vt deterreo ②; examino ①; (dissuade) dissuadeo ②
□ **be ~d** animum demitto ③

discouragement n animi demissio f; (dissuasion) dissuasio f

discouraging adj adversus, incommodus

discourse n sermo m; colloquium nt; (written) libellus m

discourteous adj inurbanus; inhumanus
■ ~ly adv inurbane; inhumaniter

discourtesy n inhumanitas f

discover vt comperio ④; (search out) exploro, investigo ①

discoverer n inventor; repertor m; inventrix, repertrix f; (searcher)

investigator m

discovery n inventio; (searching out) investigatio f; (thing found out) inventum nt; (making known) patefactio f

discreet adj cautus, prudens
■ ~ly adv caute, prudenter

discrepancy n discrepantia f

discretion n prudentia, circumspectio f
□ **at the ~ of** arbitrio + gen, ad arbitrium + gen

discriminate vt diiudico ①; distinguo ③

discriminating adj proprius; (intelligent) acutus, perspicax, sagax

discrimination n (distinguishing) distinctio f; (discernment) iudicium; (distinction) discrimen nt

discuss vt disputo ①; dissero, ago ③

discussion n disputatio, disceptatio, controversia f

disdain¹ vt dedignor, aspernor ①; despicio, sperno, contemno ③; fastidio ④

disdain² n contemptus m; fastidium nt; superbia f

disdainful adj fastidiosus, superbus
■ ~ly adv fastidiose, contemptim, superbe

disease n morbus m, malum nt; (plague) pestilentia, pestis, lues f

diseased adj aegrotus, aeger

disembark vt&i e navi (navibus) expono; e navi egredior (in terram) ③

disembowel vt eviscero ①

disengage vt solvo, exsolvo ③; avoco ①

disentangle vt extrico, explico ①; expedio ④

disfavour n invidia f

disfigure vt deformo, turpo, mutilo ①

disfigurement n deformatio; deformitas, foeditas f; (blemish) vitium nt; labes f

disgorge vt revomo, evomo ③

disgrace¹ n (shame) infamia; ignominia f; dedecus nt; (disfavour) offensa, invidia f

disgrace² vt dedecoro, dehonesto ①

disgraceful adj turpis, inhonestus, ignominiosus
■ ~ly adv turpiter, inhoneste, ignominiose

disguise¹ n (mask) persona f; fig dissimulatio f; (false appearance) species f; (pretence) praetextum nt

disguise² vt vestem muto; fig celo; dissimulo ①

disgust¹ n (loathing) fastidium, taedium, odium nt

disgust² vt fastidium moveo ②
□ **be ~ed** piget (me rei) ②; aegre fero ③

disgusting adj foedus; fig odiosus

dish¹ n catinus m; (flat ~) patina; (a large dish) lanx f; (course) mensa f, ferculum nt

dish² vt
□ ~ **up** appono ③

dishearten vt animum frango ③; exanimo ①
□ **be ~ed** animum demitto ③

dishevelled adj passus, effusus, irreligatus

dishonest adj improbus, malus, perfidus, fradulentus
■ ~ly adv improbe, dolo malo, fraude ac dolo

dishonesty n improbitas, fraus f; dolus malus m

dishonour¹ n infamia f; dedecus nt; ignominia f

dishonour² vt dehonesto; dedecoro ①

dishonourable adj inhonestus, turpis

disinherit vt exheredo ①

disinterested adj aequus, integer

disjointed adj intermissus

dislike¹ vt aversor, non amo ①
■ **I ~ it** res mihi non placet ②; res mihi displicet ②

dislike² n aversatio f; odium, fastidium nt

dislocate vt luxo ①

dislocation n luxatura f

dislodge vt deturbo ①; depello ③

disloyal adj infidelis, perfidus, perfidiosus

disloyalty n infidelitas, perfidia f

dismal adj tristis, miser; maestus; (dreadful) dirus
■ ~ly adv misere, maeste

dismantle vt diruo ③

dismay¹ n consternatio, perturbatio f; pavor m

dismay² vt perterrefacio ③; territo, consterno, perturbo ①

dismiss vt dimitto ③; demoveo ②

dismissal n missio, demissio f

dismount vi ex equo desilio ④

disobedience n contumacia f

disobedient adj non oboediens; contumax
■ ~ly adv contra (alicuius) iussum

disobey vi non pareo ② or non oboedio ④ + dat; neglego ③; detrecto ①

disorder n confusio f; (disturbance of the peace) tumultus m; (illness) aegrotatio; (of mind) perturbatio (animi) f

disorderly adj inordinatus, turbatus; turbidus; incompositus; tumultuosus

disorganization n dissolutio f

disorganized adj dissolutus

disown vt diffiteor ②; infitior ①

disparage vt obtrecto, detrecto ①

disparagement n obtrectratio f

disparity n inaequalitas, diversitas f

dispatch vt ▶ despatch

dispel vt dispello, depello, solvo ③

dispense vt distribuo ③
□ ~ with careo + abl ②

dispenser n dispensator m

disperse vt spargo, dispergo ③; dissipo ①; (put to flight) fundo ③; fugo ①
■ ~ vi dilabor; diffugio ③

dispersion n dissipatio f

dispirited adj abiectus, animo fractus

displace vt summoveo ②; (a person) loco moveo ②

display[1] n (show) ostentus m; fig iactatio, ostentatio f

display[2] vt (expose) expono; (spread) expando ③; fig iacto, ostento ①; (exercise) praesto ①; exhibeo ②

displease vt displiceo ② + dat

displeasure n offensa; offensio; (grudge) ira f

disposable adj in promptu

disposal n arbitrium m
■ **at the ~ of** prep penes + acc

dispose vt dispono ③; ordino ①; (induce) adduco ③
□ ~ **of** (sell) vendo ③; (get rid of) tollo ③

disposed adj inclinatus + ad + acc; propensus (ad); pronus (ad)
□ **well-~** aequus
□ **ill-~** malevolus, iniquus

disposition n (arrangement) dispositio; (nature) natura, indoles f; ingenium nt; mens f; animus m

disproof n refutatio f

disproportionate adj inaequalis, impar
■ **~ly** adv inaequaliter, impariter

disprove vt confuto, refuto ①; refello, redarguo ③

disputable adj disputabilis; (doubtful) dubius, ambiguus

dispute[1] n disputatio, disceptatio, contentio; controversia f; (quarrel) rixa f; iurgium nt

dispute[2] vt&i disputo ①; contendo ③
□ **it is ~d** ambigitur; non constat

disqualification n impedimentum nt

disqualify vt impedimento esse + dat

disquiet n sollicitudo, inquies f

disregard[1] n incuria, neglegentia f; contemptus m

disregard[2] vt neglego; parvi facio ③

disreputable adj infamis

disrepute n infamia f

disrespect n neglegentia, irreverentia f

disrespectful adj irreverens

■ ~**ly** adv irreverenter

disrupt vt disturbo ①

disruption n diruptio f; fig discidium nt

dissatisfaction n taedium, fastidium nt; indignatio f

dissatisfied adj male (parum) contentus

dissect vt disseco ①; incido ③

dissection n sectio, incisio, anatomia f

dissemble vt&i dissimulo ①

dissembler n dissimulator m

dissension n dissensio f; dissidium nt

dissent¹ vi dissentio ④; dissideo ②

dissent² n dissensio f

dissident adj & n rebellis

dissimilar adj dissimilis, dispar

dissimilarity n dissimilitudo f

dissimulation n dissimulatio f

dissipate vt&i dissipo, dissipor ①

dissipated adj perditus, dissolutus

dissipation n dissipatio f

dissolute adj dissolutus, corruptus, immoderatus

dissoluteness n mores dissoluti mpl

dissolution n dissolutio; mors f

dissolve vt dissolvo; (melt) liquefacio ③; liquo ①; (break up) dirimo ③
■ ~ vi liquesco ③; (break up) dissolvor ③

dissonant adj dissonus, absonus

dissuade vt dissuadeo ② + dat; abduco ③

distaff n colus f

distance n distantia f;

intervallum, (space) spatium nt; (remoteness) longinquitas f
□ **at a** ~ procul, longe

distant adj distans, disiunctus, longinquus, remotus, amotus
■ **be** ~ absum ir

distaste n fastidium nt

distasteful adj odiosus, molestus, gravis

distend vt distendo ③

distended adj tumidus, tumefactus

distil vt&i stillo, destillo; exsudo ①

distinct adj (different) diversus, alius; (clear) clarus; distinctus
■ ~**ly** adv clare, distincte

distinction n distinctio f; (difference) differentia f; discrimen nt

distinctive adj proprius

distinguish vt&i distinguo, discerno ③
□ ~ **oneself** eniteo ②; praecello ③

distinguishable adj qui secerni or internosci potest

distinguished adj insignis, clarus, praeclarus, celeber, notus, eximius

distort vt distorqueo; detorqueo ②; depravo ①

distortion n distortio, depravatio f

distract vt distraho ③; (divert) avoco ①

distracted adj amens, demens, mente alienatus, vesanus, vecors

distress¹ n dolor m; miseria, tristitia f; angustiae fpl; (poverty) inopia f

distress² vt affligo, ango ③

distressing adj molestus, gravis

distribute vt distribuo, divido ③; dispertio ④

distribution n distributio f

district n regio f

distrust¹ n diffidentia f

distrust² vt diffido ③ + dat

distrustful adj diffidens, suspicax, suspiciosus
■ ~ly adv diffidenter

disturb vt perturbo; sollicito, inquieto ①; (break up) dirimo ③

disturbance n perturbatio; confusio f; tumultus m; seditio f

disuse n desuetudo f

ditch n fossa f

dive¹ vi mergor ③

dive² n (den of vice) lustrum nt

diverge vi deflecto ③; declino ①

divergence n declinatio f; fig discrepantia f

divergent adj diversus; (contrary) contrarius

diverse adj alius, varius, diversus

diversification n variatio f; vices fpl

diversify vt vario ①; distinguo ③

diversion n (turning aside) derivatio; fig oblectatio f; oblectamentum nt

diversity n diversitas, varietas f

divert vt diverto ③; fig oblecto ①; (distract) avoco ①

divide vt divido ③; partior ④; distribuo ③
■ ~ vi discedo; (gape open) dehisco ③

divination n divinatio, vaticinatio f

divine adj divinus; caelestis

divinity n divinitas f; numen nt; (god) deus m

divisible adj dividuus, divisibilis

division n divisio f; (army) distributio, partitio; (part) pars; fig (dissent) seditio, discordia f; dissidium nt

divorce¹ n divortium, discidium nt

divorce² vt repudio ①; dimitto ③

divulge vt vulgo, divulgo ①; palam facio ③, in medium profero ir

dizziness n vertigo f

dizzy adj vertiginosus; (precipitous) praeceps

do vt ago, facio, efficio ③
□ ~ away with tollo, perdo ③
□ ~ for conficio ③
□ ~ up (bind) constringo ③
□ ~ without egeo, careo ② both + abl
■ ~ vi (be suitable) convenio ④

docile adj docilis; tractabilis

dock¹ n navale nt

dock² vt (ships) subduco ③; (curtail) curto ①

dockyard n navalia ntpl

doctor n (physician) medicus m

doctrine n doctrina f

document n litterae fpl

dodge vt eludo ③

doe n cerva f

dog¹ n canis m/f

dog² vt indago ①

dogged adj pervicax
■ ~ly adv pervicaciter

doggedness n pervicacia f

doggerel n versus inculti mpl

dogma n dogma, placitum, praeceptum nt

dogmatic adj imperiosus

doing n factum, facinus nt

dole¹ vt
□ ~ out metior ④

dole | downfall

dole² n donatio f; congiarium nt; diurnus victus m

doll n pupa f

dolphin n delphinus, delphin m

dolt n caudex, stipes m

domestic adj domesticus, familiaris; intestinus; (private) privatus

domesticate vt (tame) mansuefacio ③

domicile n domicilium nt; domus f

dominant adj praevalens

dominate vt&i dominor ① in + acc, praevaleo ②, supero ①

domination n dominatio f

domineer vi dominor ①; imperito ①

domineering adj arrogans, imperiosus

dominion n imperium nt; potestas f; dicio f; regnum nt

donate vt dono ①

donation n donum, munus nt; stips f

donkey n asinus, asellus m

donor n donator, dator m; donatrix f

doom¹ n fatum, exitium nt

doom² vt damno, condemno ①
□ **to** ~ destino ① + dat

door n ianua, foris f; ostium nt
□ **folding** ~ valvae fpl

doorkeeper n ianitor m; ianitrix f; custos m/f

door-post n postis m

doorway n ianua f; ostium nt

dormant adj (lying idle) reses; (hidden) latens

dormitory n cubiculum,

dormitorium nt

dormouse n glis m

dot n punctum nt

dotage n deliratio f; (old age) senium nt; senectus f

dotard n senex delirus m

dote vt (on) depereo ir; deamo ①

double¹ adj duplex; (of pairs) geminus; (as much again) duplus

double² n duplum nt

double³ vt duplico ①

double-dealer n homo duplex m

double-dealing n fraus, fallacia f; dolus m

doubly adv dupliciter; bis

doubt¹ n dubitatio f; scrupulus m
□ **there is no** ~ **that** non est dubium quin

doubt² vt dubito, suspicor ①; (distrust) diffido ③ + dat
■ ~ vi haesito, dubito ①

doubtful adj (of people) dubius; (of things) incertus; ambiguus; anceps
■ ~**ly** adv (of people) dubie; (of things) ambigue

doubtless adv sine dubio, haud dubie

dove n columbus m; columba f

dove-coloured adj columbinus

dovecot n columbarium nt

down¹ adv deorsum; (on the ground) humi

down² prep
□ ~ **from** de + abl
□ ~ **to** usque ad + acc
□ **up and** ~ sursum deorsum

down³ adj declivis; (sad) tristis

downcast adj (of the eyes or head) deiectus, demissus; fig afflictus

downfall n occasus m; ruina f;

exitium nt

downhill adj declivis

downstream adv secundo flumine

downward adj declivis; pronus

downwards adv deorsum

dowry n dos f

doze vi dormito ①

dozen n duodecim; adj duodeni

drab adj cinereus; pullus

draft¹ vt (levy) conscribo, scribo ③

draft² n (first copy) exemplar nt

drag vt traho
■ ~ vi (on the ground) trahor ③

dragon n draco; anguis, serpens m

drain¹ n cloaca; fossa f

drain² vt sicco ①; (drink) exhaurio ④; ebibo ③; epoto, exsicco ①

drake n anas m

drama n drama nt; fabula f

dramatic adj dramaticus, scaenicus
■ ~ally adv scaenice

dramatist n poeta scaenicus m

dramatize vt fabulam ad scaenam compono ③

drape vt induo ③; amicio ④; velo ①

drapery n (cloth) vestis f

draught n (of drink) haustus m; (of air) aura f

draughty adj ventosus

draw vt (pull) traho; duco ③; (a picture, etc.) delineo ①; describo ③; (the sword) stringo, destringo; (teeth) extraho ③; (water) haurio ④; (attract) illicio ③
□ ~ **aside** abduco, seduco ③
□ ~ **away** averto, distraho ③
□ ~ **back** vt retraho ③; vi pedem refero, cedo; fig recedo ③
■ ~ **near** vi appropinquo; insto ①
■ ~ **off** vt detraho; abduco; (wine) promo; vi cedo ③
□ ~ **out** extraho; (prolong) educo; extendo ③; fig elicio ③
□ ~ **together** contraho ③
□ ~ **up** subduco; scribo; (troops) instruo, constituo ③

drawback n impedimentum; detrimentum; incommodum nt; mora f; retardatio f

drawing n (art) pictura linearis; (picture) tabula, imago f

drawing-room n exedra f

dread¹ n terror, pavor m; formido f

dread² vt timeo ②; metuo, expavesco ③; formido ①

dreadful adj terribilis, horribilis; dirus; (violent) atrox
■ ~ly adv foede, atrociter

dream¹ n somnium nt; quies f

dream² vt&i somnio; fig dormito ①

dreamer n somniator m

dreamy adj somniculosus

dreary adj vastus, solus, incultus; horridus; tristis

dregs n faex; sentina f

drench vt madefacio ③; irrigo ①

dress¹ n (clothing) habitus, vestitus m; vestis f; ornatus m

dress² vt vestio ④; induo ③; orno, exorno, (wounds) curo ①
■ ~ vi (I get dressed) me vestio ④

dressing n ornatus m; (of food) coctura; (wounds, etc.) curatio f; (poultice) fomentum f

dribble vi stillo ①

drift¹ n (meaning) propositum nt; (purpose) consilium; (of sand) cumulus m; (of snow) vis f

drift² vi feror ③; fluito ①

drill¹ vt terebro, perforo ①; (troops) exerceo ②; (discipline) instituo ③

drill² n terebra; (of troops) exercitatio f

drink¹ vt&i bibo ③; poto ①
□ ~ **in** absorbeo ②; bibo ③
□ ~ **up** ebibo ③; haurio ④; epoto ①
□ ~ **to** propino ① + dat

drink² n potus m; potio f

drinkable adj potabilis

drinker n potor, potator m

drinking n (act) potatio; (drunkenness) ebrietas f
■ ~**-bout** n compotatio f

drip¹ vi stillo; roro, mano ①

drip² n stillicidium nt

drive vt ago; impello; (force) compello, cogo ③; (horses, carriages) ago ③
■ ~ vi (in a carriage) vehor; (be carried along) deferor ③
□ ~ **along** ▸ ~ **on**
□ ~ **away** abigo; depello ③; fugo ①
□ ~ **back** repello ③
□ ~ **in(to)** (a nail, etc.) infigo; (sheep, etc.) cogo; fig compello ③
□ ~ **off** abigo; vi avehor ③
□ ~ **on** impello ③
□ ~ **out** expello ③
□ ~ **past** praetervehor ③

drivel n fig ineptiae fpl

driver n agitator; agaso m; (of carriages) auriga m/f

drizzle¹ vi roro, irroro ①

drizzle² n pluvia f

droll adj facetus, iocosus; ridiculus

drone¹ n fucus; (person) deses; (noise) bombus m

drone² vi murmuro, susurro ①

droop vi langueo ②; marcesco; tabesco ③
■ ~ vt demitto ③

drop¹ n gutta, stilla f; (a little bit) paululum nt
□ ~ **by** ~ guttatim, stillatim

drop² vt (pour) stillo ①; (let slip) omitto ③; (pour out) effundo; (dismiss) dimitto ③
■ ~ vi stillo ①; (fall or glide down) delabor ③; (decrease) deminuor ③

dross n scoria; spurcitia f; (dropsy) aqua intercus f; fig quisquiliae fpl; faex f

drought n siccitas, ariditas f

drover n pecuarius, armentarius m

drown vt immergo, demergo; fig opprimo ③
□ **his voice was ~ed by shouts** vox prae clamoribus audiri non potuit

drowsily adv somniculose

drowsiness n somni cupiditas f

drowsy adj somniculosus

drudge¹ vi me exerceo ②; laboro ①

drudge² n (a slave) mediastinus; fig homo clitellarius m

drudgery n opera servilis f

drug¹ n medicamentum, medicamen nt; medicina f

drug² vt medico ①

Druids npl Druidae mpl

drum n tympanum nt

drummer n tympanista m

drunk adj ebrius, potus

drunkard n use adj temulentus, ebriosus, vinolentus m

drunken adj ▸ **drunk**

drunkenness n ebrietas, temulentia f

dry¹ adj aridus, siccus; (thirsty) siticulosus; fig ieiunus; insulsus

dry² vt sicco, desicco ①; arefacio ③; (in the sun) insolo ①
■ ~ vi aresco ③

dryness n ariditas, siccitas f

dual adj duplex

dub vt (name) nomino ①

dubious adj dubius
■ ~**ly** adv dubie

duck¹ n anas f

duck² vt mergo, submergo, demergo ③
■ ~ vi (head) caput demitto ③

duckling n anaticula f

dudgeon n ira, indignatio f

due¹ adj debitus; iustus; meritus; idoneus, aptus

due² n debitum; ius; (tax) vectigal nt

duel n singulare certamen nt

duet n bicinium nt

dull¹ adj hebes; obtunsus; surdus; (cloudy) caliginosus; nebulosus; fig tardus; languidus; tristis; segnis; insulsus; stupidus

dull² vt hebeto ①; obtundo, stupefacio ③

duly adv rite; recte

dumb adj mutus
□ **be ~** obmutesco ③

dumbfound vt obstupefacio ③

dunce n homo stupidus, stipes m

dung n stercus nt; fimus m

dungeon n carcer m; ergastulum nt

dunghill n sterculinium, fimetum nt

dupe¹ n homo credulus m;

victima f

dupe² vt decipio ③; ludifico ①; fallo ③

duplicate¹ adj duplex

duplicate² n exemplum, exemplar, apographum nt

duplicity n fraus; fallacia f

durable adj stabilis; durabilis; solidus; constans

duration n spatium (temporis) nt; diuturnitas f

during prep per; inter both + acc

dusk n crepusculum nt

dusky adj obscurus, tenebrosus; fuscus

dust¹ n pulvis m; (of filing or sawing) scobis f

dust² vt detergeo ②

duster n peniculus m

dustman n scoparius m

dusty adj pulverulentus, pulvereus

dutiful adj pius; officiosus, oboediens; obsequens
■ ~**ly** adv pie; officiose; oboedienter

duty n officium; munus; (tax) vectigal nt; (mil) statio f

dwarf¹ n nanus, pumilio m

dwarf² vt (diminish) imminuo ③; (overtop) superemineo ②

dwell vi habito ①; incolo ③; fig (upon) commoror ①

dwelling-place n domicilium nt; sedes, domus, habitatio f

dwindle vi decresco, imminuor ③

dye¹ vt tingo, inficio, imbuo ③; coloro ①

dye² n tinctura f; color m

dying adj moriens, moribundus; (last) extremus, ultimus

dyke n (ditch) fossa f; (dam, mound) agger m

dynasty n imperium nt; domus regnatrix f

dysentery n dysenteria f

Ee

each adj (every) quisque; (every one) unusquisque
- □ ~ **other** alter alterum
- □ ~ **of two** uterque
- □ **one** ~ singuli

eager adj acer, studiosus, cupidus, avidus; (fierce) ferox; (earnest) vehemens
- ■ ~**ly** adv acriter; avide, cupide

eagerness n aviditas, cupiditas; fig alacritas f; impetus m; studium nt

eagle n (bird, also legionary standard) aquila f

ear n auris; (of corn) spica f; (hearing) aures fpl

ear-ache n aurium dolor m

earliness n maturitas f

early[1] adj (in the morning) matutinus; (of early date) antiquus; (beginning) novus; (forward) maturus; praematurus, praecox

early[2] adv (in the morning) mane; (untimely) mature; (too ~) praemature; (quickly, soon) cito

earn vt lucror ①; mereo ②; consequor, quaero ③

earnest[1] adj intentus; impensus; vehemens; ardens; (important) gravis; (serious) serius
- ■ ~**ly** adv acriter; impense,

intente

earnest[2] adv
- □ **in** ~ serio; bona fide

earnings n stipendium nt

earring n inaures fpl

earshot n unde quis exaudiri potest

earth n (land) terra, tellus f; (world) orbis m; (of a fox) specus m/f/nt; (ground) solum nt; humus f

earthenware n fictilia ntpl

earthly adj terrenus; terrestris; humanus

earthquake n terrae motus m

earth-work n agger m

earthy adj terrosus; fig terrenus

ease[1] n otium nt; quies, requies f; fig (grace) lepor m; facilitas; (pleasure) voluptas f
- □ **with** ~ facile

ease[2] vt levo, exonero, laxo ①

easily adv facile

east[1] adj orientalis

east[2] n oriens; ortus m

easterly adj (also **eastern**) orientalis; ad orientem vergens

eastwards adv ad orientem versus

east wind n Eurus m

easy adj facilis; solutus; expeditus; (at leisure) otiosus; quietus; (graceful) lepidus; (of temper) facilis

eat vt&i edo, comedo ir, vescor; fig rodo ③
- □ ~ **away** peredo ir; fig corrodo ③
- □ ~ **up** comedo ③; voro, devoro ①

eatable adj esculentus, edulis

eating n esus m
- ■ ~-**house** n popina f

eaves n suggrunda ntpl
eavesdrop vi subausculto ①
eavesdropper n auceps m
ebb[1] n recessus m
ebb[2] vi recedo; fig decresco ③
echo[1] n imago, echo; resonantia f
echo[2] vt repercutio ③; resono ①
■ ~ vi resulto ①; (resound, be loud) sono, resono, persono ①
eclipse[1] n defectus m; defectio f
eclipse[2] vt obscuro, obumbro ①
□ **be ~d** deficio ③
economical adj oeconomicus; (sparing) parcus
■ ~**ly** adv parce
economize vt&i (with) parco ③ + dat
economy n oeconomia; (stinginess) parsimonia f
ecstasy n ecstasis, insania f; furor m
ecstatic adj furibundus, lymphatus
eddy[1] n vortex m
eddy[2] vi circumferor ir
edge n (brink) margo m/f; (of a knife, etc.) acies; (of a forest, etc.) ora f; (lip) labrum nt
edible adj esculentus, edulis
edict n edictum, decretum nt
edit vt edo ③
edition n editio f
educate vt educo ①; erudio ④
education n educatio; eruditio; disciplina f
educational adj scholasticus
eel n anguilla f
eerie[1] n nidus m
eerie[2] adj lugubris
effect n vis f; effectus m
□ **in ~** re vera; etenim

□ **take ~** bene succedere ③; efficax sum ir
effective adj efficax; potens
■ ~**ly** adv efficaciter
effects npl bona ntpl
effectual adj efficax, valens, potens
effeminacy n mollitia f
effeminate adj effeminatus, mollis, muliebris
efficacious adj efficax
■ ~**ly** adv efficaciter
efficacy n efficacitas, vis f
efficiency n efficacitas, vis f
efficient adj efficiens; efficax
■ ~**ly** adv efficaciter
effigy n imago, effigies f
effort n conatus, nisus, impetus, labor m
□ **make an ~** nitor ③, molior ④
effrontery n audacia, impudentia f
egg[1] n ovum nt
□ **lay ~s** ova pario ③
egg[2] vt (on) impello, incendo ③; excito ①
eggshell n ovi putamen nt; ovi testa f
egotism n sui iactantia f
eight adj octo
□ ~ **times** octies
eighteen adj duodeviginti
eighteenth adj duodevicesimus
eighth adj octavus
■ ~ n octava pars f
eight hundred adj octingenti
eightieth adj octogesimus
eighty adj octoginta
either[1] pn alteruter; uter; alter; (whichever of two) utervis, uterlibet

□ **not ~** neuter

either² conj:
  □ **~ ... or** aut ... aut; vel ... vel; -ve ... -ve

eject vt eicio; expello ③

ejection n eiectio f

eke vt
  □ **~ out** suppleo ②; (livelihood) colligo ③

elaborate¹ vt elaboro, evigilo ①

elaborate² adj elaboratus; accuratus
  ■ **~ly** adv accurate

elapse vi praetereo ④; labor ③

elastic adj (pliant) lentus

elasticity n lentitia f

elate vt inflo ①; effero ③
  □ **be ~d** intumesco ③

elation n superbia f; animus elatus m

elbow n cubitum nt; ulna f

elbow-room n fig spatium nt

elder adj maior natu; (in date) prior

elderly adj aetate provectior

eldest adj maximus natu; antiquissimus

elect vt eligo ③; creo ①

election n electio f, delectus m; (political) comitia ntpl

electioneering n petitio, ambitio, prensatio f
  ■ **~ adj** candidatorius

elegance n elegantia f; nitor m

elegant adj elegans; nitidus; lautus; concinnus
  ■ **~ly** adv eleganter, nitide, laute

elegy n elegia f; elegi mpl

element n elementum nt
  ■ **~s** pl principia rerum; fig rudimenta ntpl

elementary adj simplex, puerilis, primus

elephant n elephantus, elephas m

elevate vt levo ①; effero ir, attollo ③; fig inflo ①

elevation n elatio f; (loftiness) altitudo f; (rising ground) locus superior m

eleven adj undecim
  □ **~ times** undecies

eleventh adj undecimus

elicit vt elicio ③; evoco ①

eligible adj dignus

eliminate vt amoveo ②

elm n ulmus f

elocution n elocutio f

elongate vt produco ③

elope vi (domo) clam fugio, aufugio ③

elopement n fuga clandestina f

eloquence n eloquentia, facundia f; eloquium nt

eloquent adj eloquens, disertus, facundus
  ■ **~ly** adv diserte, eloquenter

else¹ adj alius
  □ **no one ~** nemo alius; nemo alter

else² adv praeterea; (otherwise) aliter; (if not) si non

elsewhere adv (at another place) alibi; (to another place) aliquo

elucidate vt illustro, explico ①

elucidation n explicatio f

elude vt eludo, effugio ③; frustror ①; evito ①

elusive adj fallax, fugax

emaciated adj macer, macilentus

emaciation n macies; tabes f

emanate vi emano ①; orior ④

emancipate vt emancipo ①;
manumitto ③; fig libero ①

emancipation n (of a slave)
manumissio; (of a son) emancipatio;
fig liberatio f

embalm vt condio ④, pollingo ③

embankment n agger m; moles f

embark vt (goods, troops) in navem
impono ③
  ■ ~ vi in navem conscendo ③

embarkation n (in navem)
conscensio f

embarrass vt (hinder) impedio ④;
(entangle) implico; fig perturbo ①

embarrassment n implicatio
f; angustiae fpl; scrupulus
m; perturbatio f; (hindrance)
impedimentum nt; mora f

embassy n legatio f; legati mpl

embellish vt orno, exorno ①

embellishment n ornamentum,
decus, insigne nt

embers n cinis m/f; (live coals)
favilla f

embezzle vt averto ③

embezzlement n peculatus m

embezzler n interceptor,
peculator m

embitter vt exacerbo ①

emblem n signum nt; imago f;
(example) exemplum nt

embolden vt animo, confirmo ①

emboss vt caelo ①

embrace[1] vt complector ③;
(contain) contineo ②; amplector ③

embrace[2] n amplexus,
complexus m

embroider vt acu pingo ③

embroidery n (art) ars plumaria f

embroil vt confundo ③

permisceo ②; fig implico ①;
impedio ④; (match, set to fight)
committo ③

embryo n semen nt

emerald n smaragdus m

emerge vi emergo; (arise) exsisto ③

emergency n (accident) casus m;
(crisis) discrimen nt; necessitas f

emigrant n colonus m

emigrate vi migro ①

emigration n migratio (in alias
terras) f

eminence n praestantia f

eminent adj eminens; egregius,
eximius, insignis, praestans
  ■ ~ly adv eximie, insigniter

emit vt emitto ③; (breathe out)
exhalo ①

emolument n lucrum,
emolumentum nt; quaestus m

emotion n animi motus, affectus
m; commotio; perturbatio f

emperor n imperator, princeps m

emphasis n vis f; pondus nt

emphasize vt vehementer dico ③

emphatic adj gravis
  ■ ~ally adv graviter

empire n imperium, regnum nt

employ vt adhibeo; exerceo
②; occupo ①; (use) utor ③ + abl;
usurpo ①

employer n conductor;
dominus m

employment n occupatio f;
(business) negotium, studium nt

empower vt potestatem (alicui)
facio ③; copiam (alicui) do ①

empress n imperatrix f

emptiness n inanitas f; fig vanitas f

empty[1] adj vacuus, inanis; fig vanus

empty[2] *vt* vacuo 1; vacuefacio 3; exinanio 4; (drink up) haurio, exhaurio 4

emulate *vt* aemulor; imitor 1

emulation *n* aemulatio *f*

enable *vt* facultatem (alicui) facio 3

enact *vt* decerno 3; sancio 4

enactment *n* sanctio; (law) lex *f*; decretum *nt*

enamoured *adj*
□ **be ~** amo, deamo 1

encampment *n* castra *ntpl*

enchant *vt* fascino 1; fig capio 3; delecto 1

enchanted *adj* cantatus, incantatus

enchanting *adj* venustus, suavissimus, pulcherrimus

enchantment *n* incantamentum *nt*; fig illecebrae *fpl*; (magic) carmen *nt*

enchantress *n* maga; cantatrix *f*; (beloved one) amata *f*

encircle *vt* circumplector; cingo 3; circumdo 1

enclose *vt* saepio 4; includo; (encircle) cingo 3; circumdo 1

enclosure *n* saeptum *nt*

encounter[1] *n* (meeting) congressus *m*; (fight) certamen *nt*; pugna *f*

encounter[2] *vt&i* congredior 3 + cum + *abl*; obviam eo 4, incurro 3 *both* + *dat*

encourage *vt* hortor, cohortor, animo, confirmo 1

encouragement *n* hortatus *m*; cohortatio, confirmatio *f*

encroach *vi* usurpo 1; praesumo 1

encroachment *n* usurpatio *f*

encumber *vt* onero 1; impedio 4; (weigh down) praegravo 1

encumbrance *n* impedimentum; onus *nt*; (trouble) molestia *f*

end[1] *n* finis *m/f*; terminus; exitus *m*; (aim, design) propositum *nt*; (death) mors *f*; obitus *m*

end[2] *vt* finio 4; termino 1; concludo 3
■ ~ *vi* (cease) desino 3; finior 4

endanger *vt* periclitor 1; in periculum deduco 3

endearing *adj* carus

endearment *n* blanditiae *fpl*; blandimenta *ntpl*

endeavour[1] *vi* tempto, conor 1; nitor, enitor 3; contendo 3

endeavour[2] *n* conatus, nisus *m*; conamen *nt*

ending *n* exitus *m*

endless *adj* infinitus; perpetuus; aeternus; sempiternus
■ ~**ly** *adv* sine fine, perpetuo; in aeternum

endorse *vt* confirmo 1

endorsement *n* confirmatio *f*

endow *vt* doto 1; instruo 3; orno 1
□ ~**ed with** praeditus + *abl*

endowment *n* dos *f*

endurable *adj* tolerabilis

endurance *n* patientia; (stability) stabilitas *f*

endure *vt* tolero 1; patior, perpetior, fero 3; sustineo 2
■ ~ *vi* duro 1; permaneo 2

enemy *n* hostis, inimicus *m*

energetic *adj* strenuus; alacer, acer
■ ~**ally** *adv* strenue; acriter

energy *n* vis; alacritas;

vehementia f; impetus m

enervate vt enervo; debilito 1

enfeeble vt debilito, infirmo, labefacto 1

enforce vt (compel) cogo 3; (put in execution) exerceo 2

enfranchise vt libero 1; manumitto 3; civitatem do 1

engage vt (hire) conduco 3; (involve, entangle) implico 1; (occupy) occupo 1
■ ~ vi (in battle) confligo 3; (promise) spondeo 2; (undertake) suscipio 3

engaged adj (to marry) sponsus

engagement n (agreement) stipulatio f; pactum nt; (occupation) occupatio f; (battle) proelium nt; (betrothal) pactio nuptialis f; (promise) fides f

engine n machina; machinatio f

engineer n machinator; architectus m

England n Anglia f

English adj Anglicus, Britannicus

Englishman n Anglus m

engrave vt scalpo, sculpo; incido 3; caelo 1

engraver n scalptor, sculptor m

engraving n (art) sculptura, sculptura f

engrossed adj (~ in) deditus + dat

engulf vt devoro, ingurgito 1

enhance vt augeo 2; amplifico, orno 1; (raise) accendo 3

enigma n aenigma nt; ambages f

enigmatic adj aenigmaticus, ambiguus
■ ~ally adv ambigue

enjoin vt iubeo 2; iniungo, praecipio 3 both + dat

enjoy vt fruor 3 + abl; percipio 3;

enervate | enslavement

(rejoice in) gaudeo in + abl; (possess) possideo 2
□ ~ **oneself** me oblecto 1

enjoyable adj gratus

enjoyment n fructus m; gaudium nt; possessio f; oblectatio; voluptates f pl

enlarge vt amplifico; dilato 1
■ ~ vi amplificor; dilator 1
□ ~ **upon** (a subject), uberius dico de + abl 3

enlargement n amplificatio f; (increase) auctus m

enlighten vt erudio 4; doceo 2

enlightened adj (cultivated) cultus

enlightenment n eruditio f; (culture) humanitas f

enlist vt conscribo 3; (win over) concilio 1
■ ~ vi sacramentum dico 3

enliven vt animo; incito; exhilaro 1

enmity n inimicitia f; odium nt

enormity n immanitas; fig atrocitas f

enormous adj ingens, enormis, immensus; vastus, immanis
■ ~ly adv admodum, multum, mire

enough adv satis, sat, affatim
□ ~ **of this** sed haec hactenus

enquire vt&i ▶ **inquire**

enrage vt irrito; exaspero 1

enraged adj iratus, furens

enrich vt locupleto, dito 1

enrol vt inscribo 3
■ ~ vi (enlist) sacramentum dico 3

ensign n (flag) vexillum, signum, insigne nt; (officer) signifer m

enslave vt subigo, in servitutem redigo 3

enslavement n servitus f;

servitium nt

ensnare vt illaqueo ①; irretio ④; (fig) illicio, capio ③

ensue vi sequor, insequor ③

ensuing adj sequens, insequens, posterus, proximus

ensure vt (guarantee) praesto ①; (see to it that) curo ① ut + subj

entail vt affero ③

entangle vt implico, illaqueo ①; irretio; impedio ④

enter vt&i intro ①; ineo ④; ingredior ③
 □ ~ **in a book** refero ③
 □ ~ **on** or **upon** (undertake) incipio, suscipio ③

enterprise n (undertaking) inceptum; ausum nt; (boldness) audacia f

enterprising adj audax, strenuus, acer

entertain vt (a guest) accipio, excipio ③; (an opinion) habeo ②; (amuse) oblecto ①

entertainment n (by a host) hospitium; (feast) convivium nt; (amusement) oblectatio, delectatio f

enthral vt mancipo ①; servum facio ③; fig capio ③

enthusiasm n fervor m; alacritas f

enthusiast n fanaticus m

enthusiastic adj fervidus, fanaticus
 ■ ~**ally** adv fanatice

entice vt allicio ③; allecto ①

enticement n allectatio; illecebra f

enticing adj blandus

entire adj integer, totus
 ■ ~**ly** adv omnino; penitus, prorsus

entitle vt (name) appello, nomino ①; inscribo (titulum) ③; (give a right) potestatem ① do + dat

entrails n viscera ntpl

entrance[1] n (act) aditus; introitus m; (beginning) principium nt

entrance[2] vt rapio, capio ③

entrance-hall n vestibulum nt

entreat vt obsecro; oro; deprecor, obtestor ①; (beg) peto ③

entreaty n obsecratio f; preces fpl

entrust vt committo, credo ③; mando, commendo ①

entry n (act of entering) introitus m; (in a book) nomen nt

entwine vt implico; circumplico ①; necto ③

enumerate vt enumero ①; recenseo ②

envelop vt involvo ③; amicio ④

envelope n involucrum nt

enviable adj dignus cui invideatur, fortunatus

envious adj invidus, invidiosus

envoy n nuntius, legatus m

envy[1] n invidia; malignitas f; livor m

envy[2] vt invideo ② + dat

ephemeral adj brevis; caducus

epic adj epicus
 □ ~ **poem** epos nt

epidemic[1] n lues, pestilentia f

epidemic[2] adj epidemus

epigram n epigramma nt

epilepsy n morbus comitialis, morbus caducus m; epilepsia f

epileptic adj epilepticus

epilogue n epilogus m

episode n embolium nt; (affair) res f

epistle n epistula f; litterae fpl

epitaph n epitaphium; carmen nt

epitome n epitome f; breviarium nt

epoch n saeculum nt; aetas f; tempus nt

equal¹ adj aequalis, aequus, par
■ **~ly** adv aeque; aequaliter; pariter

equal² n par m/f

equal³ vt aequo, adaequo, aequiparo ①; assequor ③

equality n aequalitas f; aequum nt

equalize vt aequo, adaequo, exaequo ①

equanimity n aequus animus m

equestrian adj equestris
■ **~** n eques m

equilibrium n aequilibrium nt

equinoctial adj aequinoctialis

equinox n aequinoctium nt

equip vt armo; exorno ①; instruo ③

equipment n armamenta ntpl; armatura f

equitable adj aequus, iustus

equivalent adj tantusdem; par

era n tempus nt; aetas f; saeculum nt

eradicate vt eradico, exstirpo ①; tollo ③

eradication n exstirpatio f; excidium nt

erase vt erado ③; deleo ②

erect¹ adj erectus, arrectus

erect² vt (raise) erigo, educo; (build up) exstruo; fig statuo, (found) condo ③

erection n exstructio; aedificatio f

erode vt erodo ③

erotic adj amatorius

err vi erro, aberro; fig pecco ①; delinquo ③

errand n mandatum nt

erratic adj erraticus; fig inconstans

erroneous adj falsus, vanus
■ **~ly** adv falso

error n (fault) delictum, peccatum, erratum nt; (mistake) fraus f, error m

erudite adj eruditus, doctus

erudition n eruditio f

eruption n (of a volcano) eruptio; (of the skin) scabies f

escapade n ausum nt

escape¹ vt&i evado, effugio, elabor ③; (secretly) subterfugio ③; (with difficulty) eluctor ①

escape² n fuga f; effugium nt

escort¹ n comitatus m; (protection) praesidium nt; custodia f

escort² vt comitor ①; deduco ③; prosequor ③

especial adj ▸ **special**

especially adv ▸ **specially**

espy vt conspicor ①; aspicio ③; video ②
■ **~** vi speculor ①

essay n (treatise) libellus, tractatus m

essence n essentia; natura, vis f

essential adj proprius, necessarius
■ **~ly** adv natura, necessario

establish vt statuo; constituo ③; firmo, confirmo ①; stabilio ④

estate n fundus, ager m; (means, wealth) bona ntpl; divitiae fpl; (class, in politics) ordo m; dignitas f

esteem¹ vt aestimo, puto ①; habeo ②; (judge) existimo ①; (respect) magni facio ③

esteem² n aestimatio f; honor m; reverentia f

e

estimate¹ vt aestimo ①; (assess) censeo ②

estimate² n (valuation) aestimatio f; pretium; iudicium nt

estimation n aestimatio; opinio f

estrangement n alienatio f; discidium nt

estuary n aestuarium nt

eternal adj aeternus, sempiternus, immortalis
■ **~ly** adv in aeternum, semper

eternity n aeternitas; immortalitas f

ethereal adj aethereus

eulogistic adj panegyricus, laudativus

eulogize vt collaudo ①

eulogy n laus, laudatio f; panegyricus m

eunuch n eunuchus m

evacuate vt vacuo ①; vacuefacio ③; (leave) relinquo ③

evacuation n (departure) excessus m

evade vt subterfugio, eludo ③

evaporate vi evaporor ①; evanesco ③
■ **~ vt** evaporo, exhalo ①

evaporation n evaporatio, exhalatio f

evasion n effugium nt; fuga; tergiversatio f

evasive adj vafer; subdolus; ambiguus
■ **~ly** adv vafre; subdole; ambigue

eve n vesper m; (of a feast) vigiliae fpl

even¹ adj aequalis, aequus; (level) planus; (of numbers) par

even² adv etiam, quoque; (with superlatives) vel
□ **not ~** ne ... quidem

□ **~ as** perinde ac si, quemadmodum
□ **~ if** etiamsi

evening¹ n vesper m

evening² adj vespertinus

Evening-star n Vesper, Hesperus m

evenly adv aequaliter, aequabiliter

event n eventus, exitus, casus m

eventful adj (remarkable) memorabilis

eventually adv denique, aliquando, tandem

ever adv unquam; aliquando; semper
□ **for ~** in aeternum
□ **who~** quicumque

evergreen adj semper viridis

everlasting adj sempiternus

every adj quisque; omnis
□ **~ day** cotidie, in dies

everybody pn quisque; unusquisque; nemo non; omnes; quivis; quilibet

everyday adj cotidianus; usitatus

everything n omnia (ntpl); quidvis; quidlibet

everywhere adv ubique, ubivis, undique

evict vt expello ③, deturbo ①

eviction n (law) expulsio ④

evidence n (proof) argumentum; (in law) testimonium nt; (witness) testis m/f; (information) indicium nt

evident adj apertus, manifestus, clarus, liquidus
□ **it is ~** apparet, liquet
■ **~ly** adv aperte, manifesto, liquide

evil adj malus, pravus, improbus
■ **~ n** malum, incommodum nt

evince vt praesto [1]

evoke vt evoco [1]; elicio [3]

evolve vt evolvo [3]

ewe n ovis femina f

exact[1] adj (attentive to detail) diligens, subtilis; (of things) exactus
■ **~ly** adv exacte, ad unguem

exact[2] vt exigo [3]

exaggerate vt exaggero, aggravo [1]; augeo [2]

exaggeration n amplificatio f; immoderatio f

exalted adj celsus, altus, sublimis

examination n investigatio; inspectio; (of witnesses) interrogatio f

examine vt investigo; exploro [1]; inspicio [3]; (witnesses) interrogo [1]

example n exemplum, exemplar, documentum nt
□ **for ~** verbi gratia

exasperate vt exaspero, exacerbo, irrito [1]

exasperation n ira f; animus iratus m

excavate vt excavo [1]; effodio [3]

excavation n excavatio f

exceed vt excedo [3]; supero [1]

exceedingly adv valde, egregie, magnopere; vehementer

excel vt praesto [1] + dat; supero [1]
■ **~** vi excello [3]

excellence n excellentia, praestantia f

excellent adj excellens, praestans, egregius, eximius

except[1] vt excipio, eximo [3]

except[2] prep extra, praeter + acc; (unless) nisi
□ **~ that** nisi quod, nisi si

evince | excruciating

exception n exceptio f
□ **take ~ to** reprehendo [3]; culpo [1]
□ **with the ~ of Cicero** Cicerone excepto

exceptional adj rarus
■ **~ly** adv raro; (outstandingly) eximie; (contrary to custom) praeter solitum

excess n exsuperantia, immoderatio; (licence) intemperantia, licentia f
□ **to ~** nimis

excessive adj nimius; immodicus; immoderatus
■ **~ly** adv nimis; immodice; immoderate

exchange[1] n (barter) mutatio, permutatio f; (of money) collybus m

exchange[2] vt muto, permuto [1]

excitable adj irritabilis; fervidus

excite vt excito, incito, stimulo [1]; (inflame) incendo [3]; (thrill) agito [1]; commoveo [2]; (produce) cieo, moveo [2]; conflo [3]

excited adj agitatus

excitement n commotio; perturbatio f

exclaim vt exclamo; (several voices) conclamo [1]

exclamation n vox; exclamatio; (of several people) conclamatio f

exclude vt excludo [3]; arceo; prohibeo; removeo [2]

exclusion n exclusio f

exclusive adj (one's own) proprius; (especial) praecipuus
■ **~ly** adv (only) solum

excrement n excrementum, stercus nt; proluvies f

excruciating adj acerbissimus

excursion n excursio, incursio; fig digressio f

excusable adj excusabilis

excuse[1] vt excuso; (exculpate) purgo 🔲; (pardon) ignosco ③ + dat; condono 🔲

excuse[2] n excusatio f; causa f; (pretence) praetextum nt

execute vt (fulfil, perform) exsequor, persequor, perficio, perago ③; (as punishment) securi ferio ④

execution f; (performance) exsecutio f; (punishment) supplicium nt; (death) mors f
□ **place of** ~ furca f

executioner n carnifex m

exemplary adj egregius, eximius, excellens

exemplify vt (give example of) exemplum do 🔲 + gen

exempt[1] vt eximo ③; immunitatem do 🔲

exempt[2] adj immunis

exemption n vacatio, immunitas f

exercise[1] n exercitatio f; (of soldiers) exercitium nt; (task) pensum nt

exercise[2] vt exerceo ②; (an office) fungor ③ + abl; (trouble) vexo 🔲
■ ~ vi exerceor ②

exert vt exhibeo, exerceo ②
□ ~ **oneself** contendo, nitor ③

exertion n contentio f; nisus m

exhalation n exhalatio f; vapor m

exhale vt exhalo, exspiro 🔲; spargo, emitto ③

exhaust vt exhaurio ④; conficio ③; debilito, infirmo 🔲

exhausted adj fessus, defessus, confectus, languidus

exhaustion n languor m; lassitudo, defectio (virium) f

exhibit vt exhibeo ②; expono, propono, profero ir, ostendo ③; (qualities) praesto nt

exhibition n prolatio f; (show) spectaculum nt

exhilarate vt exhilaro 🔲

exhilaration n hilaritas f

exhort vt hortor 🔲

exhortation n hortatio f

exile[1] n (banishment) exsilium, exilium nt; fuga f; (person banished) exsul, exul, extorris m/f

exile[2] vt relego 🔲; in exilium pello ③

exist vi sum ir, exsisto; vivo ③

existence n vita f

existing adj qui nunc est

exit n exitus m; effugium nt

exonerate vt culpa libero, excuso 🔲

exorbitant adj nimius, immodicus

exotic adj externus, peregrinus

expand vt expando; extendo ③; dilato 🔲; augeo ②
■ ~ vi expandor, extendor, cresco ③; dilator 🔲

expanse n spatium nt

expect vt&i exspecto; spero 🔲

expectant adj suspensus

expectation n exspectatio; spes f

expediency n utilitas f

expedient[1] adj utilis, commodus, salutaris
□ **it is** ~ expedit

expedient[2] n modus m; ratio f

expedite vt maturo ③

expedition n (mil) expeditio f

expel | exquisite

expel vt expello, eicio ③

expend vt expendo, impendo; consumo ③

expenditure n sumptus m; impensa f

expense n impensa f; sumptus m

expensive adj sumptuosus, pretiosus, carus
■ ~**ly** adv sumptuose, pretiose, care

expensiveness n caritas f; magnum pretium nt

experience[1] n experientia; peritia f; usus m

experience[2] vt experior ④; utor + abl, cognosco ③

experienced adj peritus, experiens; callidus

experiment[1] n experimentum, periculum nt

experiment[2] vt experimentum facio ③

experimental adj usu comparatus
■ ~**ly** adv usu, experimentis

expert[1] n artifex m

expert[2] adj callidus, sciens
■ ~**ly** adv callide, scienter

expertise n ars, calliditas, sollertia f

expiate vt expio ①; luo ③

expiration n exspiratio f; finis m/f; exitus m

expire vi (die) exspiro ①; (terminate) exeo ④

explain vt explano, explico ①; expono ③

explanation n explanatio, explicatio f

explicit adj explicatus; apertus
■ ~**ly** adv aperte, plane,

nominatim

explode vt (blow up) displodo; fig explodo, reicio ③
■ ~ vi displodor ③

exploit[1] vt utor ③ + abl

exploit[2] n res gesta f; facinus nt

exploration n indagatio, investigatio f

explore vt exploro; perscrutor; vestigio, indago ①

explorer n explorator m

explosion n crepitus, fragor m

export[1] vt eveho ③; exporto ①

export[2] n exportatio f

expose vt expono, retego ③; nudo ①
□ ~ **to** obicio ③; obiecto ①

exposition n explicatio, expositio; interpretatio f

exposure n expositio f; (disclosure) indicium nt; (cold) frigus nt

expound vt expono ③; interpretor ①

express[1] vt exprimo, loquor, dico ③; significo ①

express[2] adj clarus; certus; expressus
■ ~**ly** adv expresse, nominatim

expression n (word) vox; (maxim, epigram) sententia f; fig (of the face) vultus m

expressive adj significans; fig (of) index; (speaking) loquax; (clear) argutus
■ ~**ly** adv significanter

expulsion n exactio f

expurgate vt expurgo ①

exquisite adj conquisitus; exquisitus; elegans, subtilis, eximius
■ ~**ly** adv exquisite, eximie,

eleganter

exquisiteness n elegantia; subtilitas f

extant adj superstes
■ **be** ~ vi exsto ①

extemporary adj extemporalis

extempore adv subito; ex tempore

extemporize vt ex tempore dico ③

extend vt extendo; produco ③; propago ①
■ ~ vi extendo; porrigor ③

extension n extensio; propagatio; (of boundaries, etc.) prolatio f; (space) spatium nt

extensive adj late patens, amplus, diffusus
■ ~**ly** adv late

extent n spatium nt; (of a country) tractus m; fines mpl; (range) circuitus m; (amount) vis f

exterior¹ adj externus, exterior

exterior² n species, facies, forma f

exterminate vt exstirpo, extermino ①; deleo ②; tollo, exstinguo ③

extermination n exstirpatio f

external adj externus; extraneus
■ ~**ly** adv extrinsecus

extinct adj exstinctus; obsoletus
□ **become** ~ exstinguor, obsolesco ③

extinction n exstinctio f; interitus m

extinguish vt exstinguo ③

extol vt laudibus effero ③; laudo ①

extort vt extorqueo ②; exprimo ③

extortion n (pecuniae) repetundae fpl

extra¹ adj praecipuus

extra² adv insuper, praeterea
■ ~ n supplementum nt

extract¹ vt extraho ③

extract² n (juice) sucus m; (literary) excerptum; (epitome) compendium nt

extraction n (birth) stirps; origo f; genus nt

extraordinarily adj extra modum; praeter solitum

extraordinary adj extraordinarius, insolitus, mirabilis

extravagance n intemperantia, effusio; luxuria f

extravagant adj immodicus, nimius; profusus; effusus; luxuriosus; (dissolute) perditus
■ ~**ly** adv immodice; effuse; prodige; nimis

extreme¹ adj extremus; ultimus; summus; fig ingens
■ ~**ly** adv summe

extreme² n extremum, summum nt

extremity n extremitas f; extremum nt; (distress) miseria f; (danger) discrimen, periculum nt; (difficulty) angustiae fpl

extricate vt expedio ④; extraho ③; libero ①

exuberance n luxuria, redundantia; ubertas f

exuberant adj luxuriosus; redundans; fig

exude vt&i exsudo ①

exult vi exsulto, ovo ①; gestio ④

exultant adj laetus, ovans

exultation n laetitia f; gaudium nt

eye¹ n oculus, ocellus m; lumen nt; (of a needle) foramen nt; (sight) acies f

eye² vt aspicio ③; intueor ②;

contemplor ①

eyeball n pupula f

eyebrow n supercilium nt

eyelid n palpebra f

eyesight n acies oculi f

eyesore n res odiosa f

eyewitness n arbiter m; testis m/f; spectator m

Ff

fable n fabula f

fabric n (woven material), textile, textum nt

fabricate vt fabrico ①; struo ③

fabrication n (construction) fabricatio f; fig mendacium nt

face¹ n facies f; os nt; vultus; fig conspectus m; (boldness) audacia, impudentia f; (appearance) species f
□ ~ **to** ~ coram

face² vt aspicio ③; intueor ②; (of position) specto ad + acc ①; (meet) obeo ④ + dat; (cover in part) praetexo ③

facetious adj facetus, lepidus
■ ~**ly** adv facete, lepide

facetiousness n facetiae fpl; lepos m

facilitate vt facilius reddo ③

facility n (easiness) facilitas f; (opportunity) copia, facultas f

facing¹ prep adversus, ante both + acc

facing² adj contrarius, adversus

facsimile n imago scripturae f

fact n factum nt; res f
□ **in** ~ re ipsa; re vera, enim

faction n (party) factio f

factor n (agent) procurator m; (element) pars f

factory n officina f

faculty n facultas; vis f; ingenium nt

fade vt marcesco, defloresco ③; langueo ②; (decay) deficio ③; (become pale) albesco ③

faggot n fascis m; sarmenta ntpl

fail¹ vt (disappoint) deficio, desero ③
■ ~ vi (break down) succumbo ③; (of duty) delinquo ③; (become bankrupt) decoquo ③; (be unsuccessful) cado ③; male cedo ③

fail² n
□ **without** ~ certo

failing n (deficiency) defectus m; (fault) culpa f; delictum nt

failure n defectio f; defectus m; (fault) culpa f; delictum nt

faint¹ n exanimatio f

faint² adj (weary) defessus; (dropping) languidus; (of sight, smell, etc.) hebes; (of sound) surdus; (unenthusiastic) frigidus; (timid) demissus
■ ~**ly** adv languide; timide

faint³ vi (swoon) collabor ③

faintness n defectio f; languor m

fair adj (of complexion) candidus; (beautiful) formosus, pulcher; (of weather) serenus, sudus; (of winds) secundus, idoneus; (of hair) flavus; fig aequus; mediocris; modicus
■ ~ **play** n aequitas f

fairly adv iuste; (moderately) mediocriter

fairness n (beauty) forma, pulchritudo f; (justice) aequitas f;

candor animi *m*

faith *n* (trust) fides, (confidence) fiducia, (religion) religio *f*

faithful *adj* fidelis; fidus
- ∼**ly** *adv* fideliter, fide

faithfulness *adj* fides, fidelitas, integritas *f*

faithless *adj* infidus, infidelis, perfidus; perfidiosus

fake *adj* falsus

falcon *n* falco *m*

fall[1] *vi* cado; concido; (die) occido; (decrease) decresco; (violently and completely) corruo ③
- ∼ **apart** dilabor ③
- ∼ **away** deficio ③
- ∼ **back** recido; relabor; (retreat) pedem refero; fig recurro ③
- ∼ **down** decido; (completely) concido ③
- ∼ **forwards** procido; procumbo; prolabor ③
- ∼ **in(to)** incido ③
- ∼ **in with** (meet) incido ③; (find) invenio ④; (agree) assentior ④
- ∼ **in love with** adamo ①
- ∼ **off** decido
- ∼ **on ▶ ∼ upon**
- ∼ **out** excido; (happen) contingo, accido ③; evenio ④; (with someone) dissideo ②
- ∼ **short of** non contingo ③
- ∼ **sick** in morbum incido ③
- ∼ **under** succumbo ③; (be classed) pertineo + ad + acc ②; (be subjected to) patior ③
- ∼ **upon** accido; incido; (assail) invado, ingruo, incurro ③; occupo ①
- **let** ∼ demitto; (out of the hand) emitto ③

fall[2] *n* casus; lapsus *m*; (ruin) ruina *f*; labes *f*; (of ground, *etc.*) libramentum

nt; (waterfall) cataracta; (diminution) deminutio *f*; (autumn) autumnus *m*; (death) mors *f*

fallacious *adj* fallax, fictus, falsus
- ∼**ly** *adv* fallaciter, ficte, falso

fallible *adj* errori obnoxius

fallow *adj* (of land) inaratus; (never having been ploughed) novalis
- ∼ **land** novalis *m*; novale *nt*

false *adj* falsus; fictus; (counterfeit) adulterinus
- ∼**ly** *adv* falso, perperam, ficte

falsehood *n* (untrue story) commentum; (lie) mendacium *nt*

falseness *n* perfidia *f*; dolus *m*

falsification *n* adulteratio, corruptio *f*

falsify *vt* suppono, corrumpo ③; depravo, (documents) vitio ①; interlino ③

falter *vi* haereo ②; haesito, labo; (reel, totter) titubo ①

fame *n* fama; laus, gloria *f*; nomen, decus *nt*; (famousness) claritas; celebritas *f*

familiar *adj* familiaris; solitus; notus; intimus
- ∼**ly** *adv* familiariter

familiarity *n* familiaritas; necessitudo, notitia; (in bad sense) licentia *f*

familiarize *vt* assuefacio ③

family *n* familia; domus *f*; genus *nt*; cognatio *f*; (clan) gens *f*

famine *n* fames *f*; fig inopia *f*

famished *adj* famelicus; fame enectus

famous *adj* clarus, praeclarus, notus, celeber, inclutus
- ∼**ly** *adv* praeclare; insigniter

fan[1] *n* flabellum *nt*; (for winnowing)

vannus f

fan² vt ventilo []; (fire) accendo ③; fig excito, conflo []

fanatical adj & n fanaticus
■ ~ly adv fanatice

fanciful adj vanis imaginibus deditus; (capricious) inconstans, levis; libidinosus

fancy¹ n opinio, imaginatio; f (mind) animus m; (caprice) libido f; (dream) somnium nt; (liking, inclination) voluntas f

fancy² vt&i imaginor; somnio; (like) amo []

fang n dens; (claw) unguis m

fantastic adj (unreal) vanus; (absurd) absurdus

fantasy n phantasia f

far¹ adj longinquus, remotus

far² adv procul, longe
  □ ~ off procul
  □ by ~ multo
  □ from ~ procul + abl
  □ how ~ quousque?
  □ as ~ as quantum; quatenus
  □ so ~ hactenus
  □ ~ be it from me longe absit
  □ ~ and near longe lateque

farce n mimus m

farcical adj mimicus
■ ~ly adv mimice

fare¹ n (food) cibus, victus m; (money) vectura f; naulum nt

fare² vi ago ③; habeo (me) ②; cedo []

farewell int & n vale; salve!
  □ bid ~ valere or salvere iubeo ②; valedico + dat ③

far-fetched adj quaesitus; longe petitus

farm¹ n fundus, agellus m; praedium nt

farm² vt (till) aro []; colo ③

farmer n agricola; colonus m

farmhouse n villa f

farming n agricultura f; res rusticae fpl

farther adj ulterior
■ ~ adv longius, ulterius

farthest adj ultimus, extremus

fascinate vt fascino []; fig capio ③

fascination n fascinatio f; illecebrae fpl; gratia f

fashion¹ n (form) figura, forma f; (manner) mos, modus; ritus m; (custom) consuetudo f; usus m; (sophistication) urbanitas f

fashion² vt (shape) formo, informo, fabrico []; effingo ③

fashionable adj elegans; concinnus
  □ be ~ in usu sum ir; valeo ②

fashionably adv ad morem; eleganter

fast¹ adj (firm) firmus, stabilis; (tight) astrictus; (swift) celer; (shut) occlusus

fast² adv (unflinchingly) firmiter; (quickly) celeriter

fast³ vi cibo abstineo ②; ieiuno []

fast⁴ n ieiunium nt

fasten vt astringo, affigo ③; fig infero ir ③; (down) defigo ③; (to) annecto; impingo ir ③; (together) colligo []; configo ③

fastening n vinculum nt

fastidious adj fastidiosus; delicatus; elegans; morosus

fat¹ adj pinguis, obesus; opimus

fat² n adeps m/f; pingue nt; arvina f; (suet) sebum nt; (of a pig) lardum nt; (in general) pinguitudo f

fatal adj mortifer, letifer; exitialis; funebris; funestus

■ ~**ly** adv fataliter; fato

fate n Fatum nt; sors f
■ **the Fates** pl Parcae fpl; (fortune) fortuna f; (chance) casus m

fated adj fatalis
□ **ill-~** infaustus

father n pater, genitor, parens m
□ ~ **of a family** paterfamilias m

fatherhood n paternitas f

father-in-law n socer m

fatherless adj orbus

fatherly adj paternus, patrius

fathom n ulna f

fatigue n fatigatio, defatigatio, lassitudo f

fatness n pinguitudo, sagina f

fatten vt sagino [1]; farcio [4]

fattening n saginatio; (cramming of fowls) fartura f

fatty adj pinguis

fatuous adj stultus, fatuus

fault n delictum, mendum, vitium nt; (responsibility) culpa f; (mistake) error m; (blemish) menda, labes, macula f
□ **at ~** in culpa
□ **find ~ with** vitupero [1]; carpo [3]

faultless adj perfectus; integer

faulty adj vitiosus; mendosus

favour¹ n favor m; gratia; (goodwill) benevolentia f; beneficium nt; (present) munus nt
□ **do a ~** gratificor [1] + dat

favour² vt faveo [2] + dat; secundo [1]

favourable adj prosperus, felix, faustus; commodus, idoneus, benignus; (of the gods) propitius, aequus, secundus

favourably adv prospere, feliciter, fauste, benigne,

opportune

favourite adj dilectus, gratus; (popular) gratiosus
■ ~ n (darling, etc.) deliciae fpl

favouritism n gratia f; studium nt

fawn¹ n hinnuleus m

fawn² vi (on, upon) adulor [1]

fawning adj adulatorius, blandus

fax n imago scripturae f

fear¹ n timor, metus m; formido f

fear² vt&i timeo, metuo [2]; paveo [2]; metuo [3]; formido [1]; (reverentially) vereor [2]

fearful adj timidus, pavidus; (terrible) dirus; formidolosus
■ ~**ly** adv timide, formidolose

fearfulness n timiditas f

fearless adj impavidus, intrepidus
■ ~**ly** adv impavide

fearlessness n audacia, audentia f

feasible adj quod fieri potest

feast¹ n (holiday) dies festus m; sollemne nt; (banquet) convivium nt; epulae, dapes fpl

feast² vi epulor, convivor [1]
□ ~ **one's eyes on** oculos pasco [3]

feat n facinus; factum nt; res gesta f

feather n (big or wing ~) penna; (small, downy) pluma f

feathered adj pennatus; plumosus, penniger

feature n lineamentum nt; vultus m; os nt; fig (part) pars f

February n Februarius m

federal adj foederatus

federation n societas f

fee n (pay) merces f; praemium, pretium nt

feeble adj infirmus, debilis,

languidus

□ **grow ~** languesco ③

feebleness n infirmitas, debilitas f; languor m

feebly adv infirme; languide

feed vt (animals) pasco; (nourish) alo ③; (support) sustento ③; ■ **~** vi pascor; vescor ③

feel¹ vt&i (touch) tango ③; (handle) tracto ①; (perceive) sentio ④; concipio, percipio ③; (be moved, affected) moveor, commoveor ③
□ **how do you ~?** quid agis? ③
□ **~ for** doleo cum + abl, misereor ② + gen

feel² n tactus m

feeler n (of an insect) crinis m; fig tentamen nt

feeling n (touch) tactus m; (sensibility in general) sensus; (emotion) affectus m; (judgement) iudicium nt

feign vt&i fingo, comminiscor ③; (pretend) dissimulo ①; (lie) mentior ④

feint n simulatio; (in fencing) captatio f

fell¹ vt (trees) caedo ③; (knock down) sterno, prosterno, everto ③

fellow n (companion) socius; (in office) collega; (any individual) homo; (equal) par m

fellow-citizen n civis m/f

fellow-countryman n civis m/f

fellow-creature n homo m

fellow-feeling n (pity) misericordia f

fellow-servant n conservus m; conserva f

fellowship n societas, communitas f; sodalicium nt

fellow-traveller n convector;

socius itineris m

felt n coactilia ntpl

female¹ n femina, mulier f

female² adj femineus, muliebris

feminine adj femineus, muliebris; femininus

fence¹ n (barrier) saepes f; saeptum nt

fence² vt (barricade) saepio ④; defendo ③
■ **~** vi (spar with swords) battuo ③

fencer n gladii peritus, gladiator, lanista m

fencing n ars gladii f

fend vi
□ **~ for oneself** suis opibus nitor ③

fennel n faeniculum nt

ferment¹ n fermentum nt; fig aestus m

ferment² vt&i fermento; fermentor ①

fern n filix f

ferocious adj ferus, truculentus, saevus, atrox
■ **~ly** adv truculente, saeve, atrociter

ferociousness n saevitia, feritas, atrocitas f

ferocity n saevitia, feritas, atrocitas f

ferret¹ n viverra f

ferret² vt
□ **~ out** rimor, exspiscor ①

ferry vt traicio, transveho ③

ferry-boat n scapha, cumba f

ferryman n portitor m

fertile adj fertilis, fecundus, ferax, uber

fertility n fertilitas, ubertas f

fertilize vt fecundo ①

fervent adj ardens, fervidus; vehemens
■ **~ly** adv ardenter; vehementer

fervour n ardor, fervor, impetus m

fester vi suppuro, ulceror ①

festival n dies festus m; sollemne nt

festive adj festus, festivus

festivity adj sollemnia ntpl; (gaiety) festivitas f

festoon n sertum nt
■ **~** vt corono, adorno ①

fetch vt adduco ③, affero ir; accesso, peto ③
□ **~ back** reduco ③
□ **~ down** deveho ③
□ **~ in** importo ①
□ **~ out** depromo ③; (cause to appear) elicio ③

fetter[1] vt (alicui) compedes impingo ③; colligo ①; vincio ④; fig impedio ④; illaqueo ①

fetter[2] n compes, pedica f

feud n lis, simultas; inimicitia f; odium nt

fever n febris f

feverish adj febriculosus; fig ardens

few adj pauci, perpauci; aliquot, (indecl)
□ in a **~ words** paucis, breviter

fib n mendaciolum, mendaciunculum nt

fibre n fibra f; filum nt

fickle adj inconstans, mobilis; instabilis; levis

fickleness n inconstantia; mutabilitas; mobilitas, levitas f

fiction n fictio f; commentum nt; fabula f

fictitious adj fictus, commenticius; (simulated), simulatus
■ **~ly** adv ficte

fiddle n fides f

fidelity n fidelitas; constantia, fides f

fidget vi cursito ①

fidgety adj inquietus

field n campus, ager m; arvum, rus nt; (~ of grass) pratum; (battle) proelium nt; fig (scope) area f

field-mouse n mus agrestis m

fiend n Erinys f

fierce adj atrox; saevus; vehemens
■ **~ly** adv atrociter; saeve; ferociter; vehementer

fierceness n atrocitas; saevitia; ferocitas; ferocia; vehementia f

fiery adj igneus; fig ardens, fervidus; fig iracundus

fifteen adj quindecim

fifteenth adj quintus decimus

fifth[1] adj quintus

fifth[2] n quinta pars f

fifthly adj quintum, quinto

fiftieth adj quinquagesimus

fifty adj quinquaginta

fig n (fruit and tree) ficus f

fight[1] n pugna f; proelium nt; (struggle) contentio f

fight[2] vt&i pugno; dimico ①; contendo ③; (in battle) proelior (with sword) digladior; (hand to hand) comminus pugno ①
□ **~ against** repugno ①

fighter n pugnator, proeliator m

figurative adj translatus
■ **~ly** adv per translationem, tropice

figure n figura; forma; (shape) imago f; (appearance) species f; (of speech) tropus m; (number) numerus m

figured adj sigillatus; (chased) caelatus

filament n fibrae fpl; filum nt

filch vt surripio ③; suffuror ①

file¹ n (tool) lima f; (for or of papers) scapus m; (line, string, row) ordo m; series f

    □ **the rank and ~** milites gregarii mpl

file² vt (rub smooth) limo ①

filial adj pius

filings n scobis f

fill¹ vt compleo; impleo, expleo; (supply) suppleo ②

    □ **~ out** impleo ②

    □ **~ up** expleo; (completely) compleo ②; (heap) cumulo ①

fill² n satietas f

    □ **have one's ~ of** satior ① + abl

filter¹ n colum nt

filter² vt&i percolo; percolor ①

filth n sordes, colluvies, illuvies f; ▶ **dirt**

filthiness n foeditas f; squalor m; fig obscenitas f

filthy adj sordidus, foedus, spurcus; fig obscenus

fin n pinna f

final adj ultimus, extremus, postremus

    ■ **~ly** adv postremo; denique

finance n res familiaris f, fiscus, aerarii reditus m

financial adj aerarius

finch n fringilla f

find vt invenio, reperio ④; (hit upon) offendo ③; (catch in the act)

deprehendo ③

    □ **~ out** comperio ④; (discover) rescisco ③; nosco, cognosco ③; (guess) coniecto ①

fine¹ adj (of texture) subtilis; (thin) tenuis; (of gold) purus; (handsome) bellus; elegans; (excellent) optimus, (ironically) bonus, egregius, praeclarus

    ■ **~ly** adv subtiliter; tenuiter; fig pulchre; egregie

fine² n mul(c)ta f

fine³ vt mul(c)to ①

fineness n subtilitas; tenuitas; fig pulchritudo; elegantia, praestantia f

finery n ornatus, cultus m; lautitia f

finger¹ n digitus m

finger² vt tango ③; tracto ①

finish¹ vt conficio, perficio ③; (put an end to) termino ①; finio ④

    □ **~ off** consummo ①; ultimam manum operi impono ③

    ■ ~ vi finio ④

finish² n (end) finis m/f

finishing-touch n ultima manus f

finite adj caducus, moriturus

fir¹ n (**fir-tree**) abies, pinus f

fir² adj (of fir) abies, pinus f

fire¹ n ignis m; (conflagration) incendium nt; fig fervor, ardor, impetus m

    □ **catch ~** ignem concipio ③

    □ **set ~ to** incendo ③

    □ **on ~** incensus, inflammatus

fire² vt (weapons) mitto, dirigo ③

firebrand n torris m

fire-engine n sipho m

firemen n excubiae vigilesque adversus incendia mpl

fireplace n caminus; focus m

fireproof adj ignibus impervius

fireside n focus m

firewood n lignum nt

firm[1] adj firmus; solidus; (of purpose) tenax
□ **be ~** (endure) persevero, persto [1]

firm[2] n (company) societas f

firmly adv firme, firmiter; solide; (of purpose) tenaciter

firmness n firmitas; constantia f

first[1] adj primus; princeps

first[2] adv primum
□ **at ~** primo
□ **~ of all** imprimis

fiscal adj fiscalis

fish[1] n piscis m

fish[2] vt&i piscor; fig expiscor [1]

fish-bone n spina piscis f

fisherman n piscator m

fish-hook n hamus m

fishing n piscatus m; piscatio f

fishing-boat n piscatoria navis f

fishing-line n linum nt

fishing-net n funda f; iaculum, everriculum nt

fishing-rod n arundo f; calamus m

fishmonger n cetarius, piscarius m

fish-pond n piscina f; vivarium nt

fishy adj piscosus, pisculentus; fig suspectus

fissure n rima, fissura f

fist n pugnus m

fit[1] n (of a disease) accessio f; (whim) libido f
□ **epileptic ~** morbus caducus m
■ **by ~s and starts** adv carptim

fit[2] adj aptus, idoneus; conveniens; opportunus; habilis; (becoming) decens; (ready) paratus; (healthy) sanus

fit[3] vt accommodo, apto; (apply) applico [1]; (furnish) instruo [3]; orno [1]
□ **~ out** instruo [3]; orno, adorno [1]; suppedito [1]
■ **~** vi (of dress) sedeo [2]; fig convenio [4]

fitful adj mobilis, mutabilis, inconstans

fitness n convenientia; (healthiness) valetudo f

fitting adj decens, ▶ **fit** adj

five adj quinque
□ **~ times** adv quinquies

fix vt (attach) figo [3]; (the eyes, etc.) intendo [3]; (establish) stabilio [4]; (on, upon) eligo [3]; (appoint) statuo, constituo [3]; (repair) reficio [3]
■ **~** vi (be fixed, stick) inhaereo [2]

fixed adj fixus, firmus; certus; (intent upon) intentus
■ **~ly** adv firmiter, constanter

flabby adj flaccidus, flaccus; fluidus; (drooping) marcidus

flaccid adj flaccidus

flag[1] n (banner) vexillum; insigne nt

flag[2] vi languesco; refrigesco, remittor [3]; laxor [1]

flagon n lagena f

flagrant adj immanis, insignis; atrox, nefarius; (open) apertus

flagship n navis praetoria f

flake n floccus m; frustum nt; squama f
□ **snow~s** nives fpl

flaky adj squameus

flame[1] n flamma f; ardor m

flame[2] vi flammo, flagro [1]

□ ~ **up** fig exardesco ③

flamingo n (bird) phoenicopterus m

flank n (of an animal) ilia ntpl; (of an army) latus nt

flap¹ n lacinia f

flap² vt&i (wings) alis plaudo ③; (hang loosely) fluito ①; dependeo ②

flare vi flagro ①; fulgeo ②

flash¹ n fulgor m; (of lightning) fulmen nt

flash² vi fulgeo, splendeo ②; corusco ①

flask n ampulla, laguncula f

flat adj (even, level) planus; (not mountainous) campester; (lying on the face) pronus; (sheer) merus; (insipid; of drinks) vapidus; fig frigidus; insulsus; ieiunus

flatness n planities f; (evenness) aequalitas; (of a discourse, etc.) ieiunitas; (of drinks) vappa f

flatten vt complano, aequo ①

flatter vt adulor, assentor ①; blandior ④

flatterer n adulator, assentator m

flattering adj adulans, blandus, adulatorius

flattery n adulatio, assentatio f; blanditiae fpl

flaunt vt obicio ③; ostento ①

flautist n tibicen m

flavour¹ n sapor m

flavour² vt condio ④

flavouring n condimentum nt

flaw n (defect) vitium nt; menda, macula, labes f; (chink) rima f

flawless adj sine mendo, perfectus, integer

flax n linum nt

flaxen adj lineus; (of colour) flavus

flay vt pellem detraho ③

flea n pulex m

fleck¹ n macula f

fleck² vt maculo ①

flee vt&i fugio ③
□ ~ **away** aufugio ③
□ ~ **to** confugio ③
□ ~**from** effugio ③

fleece¹ n vellus nt

fleece² vt (shear) tondeo ②; fig spolio; privo; expilo ①

fleecy adj laniger

fleet n classis f

fleeting adj fugax; fluxus; lubricus; caducus

flesh n caro f; viscera ntpl; fig (body) corpus nt; (sensuality) libido f

fleshy adj (abounding in flesh) carnosus

flexibility n mollitia, facilitas f

flexible adj flexibilis, flexilis, mollis, lentus; fig exorabilis

flicker vi (flutter) volito; (flash) corusco ①

flight n fuga f; (escape) effugium nt; (of birds) volatus m; (of stairs) scala f
□ **put to** ~ in fugam impello ③; fugo ①; fundo ③
□ **take (to)** ~ aufugio ③

flimsiness n tenuitas, exilitas f

flimsy adj tenuis, praetenuis; fig frivolus

flinch vi abhorreo ②

fling vt iacio, mitto ③
□ ~ **away** abicio ③
□ ~ **down** deicio ③
□ ~ **off** reicio ③

flint n silex m/f

flippancy n levitas, protervitas f

flippant adj levis, protervus, petulans
■ ~**ly** adv proterve, petulanter

flirt vi ludo ②

flirtation n lusus m

flit vi volito, circumvolito ①

float vi fluito, nato, innato; fluctuor ①; pendeo ②; (hang loosely) volito ①
■ ~ vt (launch) deduco ③

flock¹ n (of sheep, birds, etc.) grex m

flock² vi (together) coeo ir, convenio ④, congregor; convolo ①

flog vt verbero ①; caedo ③

flogging n verberatio f; verbera ntpl

flood n (inundation) diluvies f; (stream) flumen nt; (tide) aestus m; fig flumen ①

floor¹ n solum nt; (paved ~) pavimentum nt; (of a barn) area; (storey) contignatio f; tabulatum nt

floor² vt pavimentum struo ③; (with planks) contabulo ①; (throw down) sterno ③; (silence) confuto ①

flooring n contabulatio f,
▶ **floor** ①

floral adj florens

florid adj (of complexion) rubicundus; fig (of style) floridus

flounder vi voluto, titubo ①

flour n farina f

flourish¹ vi floreo; vireo ②

flourish² n ornamentum nt; (of style) calamistri, flosculi mpl; (of a trumpet) cantus m

flourishing adj florens

floury adj farinulentus

flout vt derideo ②; repudio ①

flow¹ vi fluo, feror ③; mano ①; (of the tide) affluo, accedo ③

flow² n fluxus m; (gliding motion) lapsus; (of the tide) accessus m; (stream) flumen ①; (course) cursus m

flower¹ n flos, flosculus m; fig (the best) flos m

flower² vi floreo ②; floresco ③

flower-bed n area f

flowery adj floreus; floridus; florifer

fluctuate vt fluctuo; fluito, iactor ①

fluctuation n fluctuatio; fig mutatio f

flue n cuniculus fornacis m

fluency n volubilitas linguae; copia verborum f

fluent adj volubilis; profluens; (eloquent) disertus
■ ~**ly** adv volubiliter

fluid¹ adj fluidus, liquidus

fluid² n liquor, umor, latex m

flurry n perturbatio f; tumultus m

flush¹ n (sudden attack) impetus m; (abundance) copia f; (blush) rubor m

flush² vi erubesco ③

fluster vt perturbo; inquieto ①; sollicito ①

flute n tibia f

flutter vt agito, perturbo, sollicito ①
■ ~ vi (of birds) volito; (with alarm) trepido ①

fly¹ n musca f

fly² vi volo, volito ①; (flee) fugio ③
□ ~ **off** avolo ①
□ ~ **open** dissilio ④
□ ~ **out** provolo ①
□ ~ **up** subvolo ①

flying adj volatilis; volucer; ales

foal n (of the horse) equuleus m

foam[1] *n* spuma *f*

foam[2] *vi* spumo ①

foamy *adj* spumans; spumeus, spumosus, spumifer

fodder *n* pabulum *nt*

foe *n* hostis, inimicus *m*

fog *n* caligo, nebula *f*

foggy *adj* caliginosus, nebulosus

foible *n* vitium *nt*; error *m*

foil[1] *n* (for fencing) rudis *f*; (leaf of metal) lamina; (very thin) brattea *f*; (contrast) exemplum contrarii *nt*

foil[2] *vt* frustror ①; repello ③
□ be ~ed spe deicior ③

fold[1] *n* sinus *m*; (wrinkling) ruga *f*; (for cattle) stabulum; (for sheep) ovile *nt*

fold[2] *vt* plico, complico ①

folding-doors *n* valvae *fpl*

foliage *n* frons, coma *f*; folia *ntpl*

folk *n* homines *mpl*

follow *vi* sequor, insequor, consequor, insequor ③; (close) insto, sector, assector ①; (on) persequor; (out) exsequor, prosequor; (up) subsequor ③

follower *n* sectator, assectator, fig discipulus *m*

following *adj* sequens, insequens, posterus, proximus; (uninterruptedly) continuus
□ on the ~ day postridie

folly *n* stultitia; insipientia; (madness) dementia *f*

foment *vt* foveo ②; (disorder, etc.) stimulo ①; cieo ②

fond *adj* amans; deditus; cupidus; (indulgent) indulgens; (foolishly infatuated) demens
■ be ~ of amo ①
■ ~ly *adv* amanter, peramanter

fondle *vt* permulceo, foveo ②

fondness *n* amor *m*; indulgentia; caritas *f*

food *n* (for cattle, etc.) pabulum *nt*; (any nourishing substance) alimentum *nt*; (of people) cibus *m*; esca *f*

fool[1] *n* stultus, insipiens; (idiot) fatuus; (in a play) sannio *m*
□ make a ~ of ludificor (aliquem) ①
□ play the ~ ineptio ④; nugor ①

fool[2] *vt* ludificor ①; ludo, illudo ③
□ ~ around ineptio ④; nugor ①

foolery *n* ineptiae, nugae *fpl*

foolhardiness *n* temeritas *f*

foolhardy *adj* temerarius

foolish *adj* stultus, fatuus, ineptus, stolidus
■ ~ly *adv* stulte, inepte

foot *n* pes *m*; (of a mountain) radix *f*; (of a figure, etc.) basis *f*
□ on ~ pedester
□ to the ~ of sub + *acc*

football *n* pila *f*

footing *adj* (condition) status *m*; condicio *f*

footpath *n* semita *f*; callis, trames *m*

footprint *n* vestigium *nt*

foot-soldier *n* pedes *m*

footstep *n* vestigium *nt*

footstool *n* scabellum *nt*

for[1] *prep* (on behalf of) pro + *abl*; (for the sake of) causa + *gen*; (because of) ob, propter + *acc*; (after negatives) prae + *abl*
□ ~ some time aliquandiu
□ ~ food ~ a day cibus unius diei

for[2] *conj* nam, enim

forage *vt&i* pabulor; frumentor ①; fig rimor ①

forager *n* pabulator;

frumentator m

foraging n pabulatio; frumentatio f

foray n incursio, populatio f

forbear vi abstineo ②; (leave off) desisto ③

forbearance n patientia; indulgentia f

forbid vt veto ①; prohibeo ②; interdico ③

forbidding adj insuavis, odiosus; (ugly) deformis; (frightful) immanis

force¹ n vis; (law) maiestas f; (mil) copiae fpl; (weight) momentum, pondus nt; (strength) vires fpl; robur nt
□ **in ~** valens, validus

force² vt cogo; (a door, a wall, etc.) perrumpo; (drive away) expello ③
□ **~ down** detrudo ③
□ **~ in** (a nail, etc.) infigo ③
□ **~ out** extorqueo ②; depello ③
□ **~ open** rumpo ③

forced adj (unnatural) accersitus, quaesitus
□ **~ march** magnum or maximum iter nt

forceful adj validus

forcible adj per vim factus; (violent) vehemens; (compulsory) coactus

forcibly adv per vim, vi; violenter

ford¹ n vadum nt

ford² vt vado transeo ④

forearm¹ n bracchium n

forearm² vt praemunio ④

forebode vt portendo ③; praesagio ④; (forewarn) moneo ②

foreboding n portentum, praesagium nt; (prophetic feeling) praesensio f

forecast¹ vt praevideo ②;

prospicio ③; auguror ①

forecast² n providentia f; augurium nt

forefather n atavus m
■ **~s** pl maiores mpl

forefinger n digitus index m

foregoing adj prior, proximus

forehead n frons f

foreign adj externus, alienus, peregrinus

foreigner n peregrinus, externus; (stranger) advena m

foreknowledge n providentia f

foreland n promontorium nt; lingua f

forelock n cirrus m

foremost adj primus; princeps, praecipuus

forensic adj forensis

forerunner n praenuntius, antecursor m

foresee vt praevideo ②; prospicio ③

foresight n providentia, prospicientia, prudentia; (precaution) provisio f

forest n silva f; nemus nt; saltus m
■ **~** adj silvestris, nemorensis

forestall vt anticipo ①; praecipio ③

foretaste n gustus m

foretell vt praedico ③; vaticinor ①

forethought n providentia, prospicientia f

forever adv in aeternum, in perpetuum

forewarn vt praemoneo; moneo ②

forfeit¹ n mul(c)ta, poena f

forfeit² vt mul(c)tor ①; (lose)

amitto ③

forfeiture n (loss) amissio; (of goods) publicatio f

forge¹ vt (metal, etc.) cudo, procudo ③; fabricor ①; (devise) fingo; (counterfeit) corrumpo ③; (a document) interlino ③; vi

□ **~ ahead** progredior ③

forge² n fornax f

forger n fabricator; (of writings) falsarius m

forgery n (of documents) subiectio; (forged document) litterae falsae fpl

forget vt obliviscor + gen; (unlearn) dedisco ③

forgetful adj obliviosus, immemor

forgetfulness n oblivio f; oblivium nt

forgive vt condono ①; ignosco ③ + dat

forgiveness n venia f

forgiving adj ignoscens; clemens

forgo vt renuntio ①; dimitto ③; (abstain from) abstineo ② ab + abl; (lose) amitto ③

fork¹ n furca f; (of roads) bivium, trivium, quadrivium nt

fork² vi scindor ③

forked adj bifurcus, bicornis

forlorn adj solus, desertus, miser

form¹ n forma, figura f; (bench) scamnum nt; (rite) ritus m; (class in a school) classis f

form² vt formo ①; fingo; (produce) efficio ③; (constitute) sum ir

formal adj formalis; fig frigidus; (stiff) rigidus, durus

formality n ritus m

formation n conformatio; forma, figura f

former adj prior, priscus, pristinus; (immediately preceding) superior
  ■ **~ly** adv antea, prius, antehac; olim; quondam

formidable adj formidabilis, formidolosus, metuendus

formless adj informis; fig rudis

formula n formula f; exemplar nt

forsake vt desero, derelinquo, relinquo, destituo ③

fort n castellum nt; arx f

forth adv foras; (of time) inde
  □ **and so ~** et cetera

forthcoming adj promptus; in promptu

forthwith adv extemplo, protinus, statim, continuo

fortieth adj quadragesimus

fortification n munitio f; munimen, munimentum nt

fortify vt munio, circummunio ④

fortitude n fortitudo, virtus f

fortnight n semestrius nt; dies quatuordecim mpl

fortress n arx f; castellum nt

fortuitous adj fortuitus
  ■ **~ly** adv fortuito

fortunate adj fortunatus, felix, prosperus
  ■ **~ly** adv fortunate, prospere, feliciter

fortune n fortuna, fors, sors f; casus m
  □ **good ~** fortuna f; (wealth) divitiae, opes fpl
  □ **tell ~s** hariolor ①

fortune-teller n hariolus m; hariola f

forty adj quadraginta

forum n forum nt

forward¹ adv (also **forwards**)

porro, prorsus, prorsum

forward[2] *adj* (early, soon ripe) praecox; (bold) audax; (saucy) protervus

forward[3] *vt* (despatch) mitto ③; (promote) promoveo ②; consulo ③ + *dat*

foster *vt* foveo ②; nutrio ④; alo ③

foster-child *n* alumnus *m*; alumna *f*

foster-father *n* nutricius, nutritor *m*

foster-mother *n* nutrix, altrix, educatrix *f*

foul[1] *adj* (dirty) foedus, lutulentus, squalidus; (of language) obscenus; (of weather, stormy) turbidus; *fig* turpis

foul[2] *vt* foedo, inquino ①

foul-mouthed *adj* maledicus

foulness *n* foeditas *f*; (dirt) squalor *m*; (of a crime) atrocitas; *fig* turpitudo; obscenitas *f*

found *vt* fundo ③; condo, constituo, construo ③

foundation *n* fundamentum, fundamen *nt*; substructio, sedes *f*

founder[1] *n* fundator, conditor; auctor *m*

founder[2] *vi* (of ships) submergor, deprimor ③

foundling *n* expositicius *m*

fountain *n* fons *m*

four *adj* quattuor
□ ~ **times** quater
□ **on all** ~**s** repens

fourfold *adj* quadruplex, quadruplus

four-footed *adj* quadrupes

fourteen *adj* quattuordecim

fourteenth *adj* quartus decimus

fourth *adj* quartus

■ ~**ly** *adv* quarto

fowl *n* avis, volucris *f*
□ **domestic** ~ gallina *f*

fox *n* vulpes, vulpecula *f*; *fig* homo astutus *m*

fraction *n* pars exigua *f*; fragmentum, fragmen *nt*

fractious *adj* difficilis, morosus

fractiousness *n* morositas *f*

fracture[1] *n* fractura *f*

fracture[2] *vt* frango ③

fragile *adj* fragilis; *fig* caducus

fragility *n* fragilitas *f*

fragment *n* fragmentum, fragmen *nt*

fragrance *n* odor *m*

fragrant *adj* suaveolens, odorus; odorifer

frail *adj* fragilis; caducus; infirmus

frailty *n* fragilitas; infirmitas *f*

frame[1] *n* compages *f*; (of body) figura; (of a window, *etc*.) forma; (of a bed) sponda *f*; (edge) margo *m*/*f*; *fig* habitus animi *m*

frame[2] *vt* (shape) formo; (build) fabrico ①; (join together) compingo ③; (contrive) molior ④

framework *n* compages *f*

franchise *n* ius suffragii *nt*

frank *adj* candidus, liber, ingenuus, sincerus, simplex
■ ~**ly** *adv* candide, libere, ingenue, sincere, simpliciter

frankness *n* libertas *f*; candor *m*; ingenuitas; simplicitas; sinceritas *f*

frantic *adj* fanaticus, furens, insanus, amens
■ ~**ly** *adv* insane

fraternal *adj* fraternus
■ ~**ly** *adv* fraterne

fraternity n (association) sodalitas f

fraternize vi amice convenio ④

fratricide n (murderer) fratricida m; (murder) fraternum parricidium nt

fraud n fraus, fallacia f; dolus m

fraudulent adj fraudulentus, dolosus
■ ~**ly** adv fraudulenter, dolo malo

fray¹ n rixa, pugna f; certamen nt

fray² vi (wear away) atteror ③

freak n (monster) monstrum, portentum nt

freckled adj lentiginosus

freckles n lentigo f

free¹ adj liber; (from business) otiosus; (not bound by ...) solutus; (of space) vacuus; (immune) immunis; (gratuitous) gratuitus; (impudent) procax; fig candidus, sincerus
□ ~ **from** expers + gen, vacuus + abl

free² vt libero ①; (a slave) manumitto ③

freebooter n praedo, latro; (at sea) pirata m

freeborn adj ingenuus

freedman n libertus, libertinus m

freedom n libertas, immunitas; (from) vacuitas f; (franchise) civitas f

freedwoman n liberta, libertina f

freely adv libere; (of one's own accord) sponte; (liberally) large; copiose; liberaliter, munifice; (far and wide) late; (for nothing) gratis

freeman n liber m

free-will n voluntas f; liberum arbitrium nt

freeze vt congelo, gelo, glacio ①
■ ~ vi consisto, rigesco ③
□ **it is freezing** gelat

freight n onus nt

frenzied adj furens, lymphatus

frenzy n furor m; insania f

frequency n crebritas; frequentia f

frequent¹ adj creber; frequens
■ ~**ly** adv crebro; frequenter, saepe

frequent² vt frequento, celebro ① f

fresco¹ n tectorium nt

fresco²:
□ **al** ~ sub divo, foris

fresh adj (new) recens, novus; (cool) frigidulus; (lusty) vigens; (not tired) integer; (green) viridis; (not salt) dulcis

freshen vt recreo ①
■ ~ vi increbresco ③

freshly adv recenter

freshness n (newness) novitas f; (vigour) vigor m

fret vi (grieve) doleo ②; crucior ①; aegre fero ③

fretful adj morosus; difficilis

fretfulness n morositas f

fretwork n caelatum opus nt

friction n frictio f; tritus, attritus m

friend n amicus m; amica f; familiaris m/f; necessarius m; sodalis m

friendless adj amicorum inops, desertus

friendliness n benevolentia; comitas, affabilitas f

friendly adj benevolus; comis; amicus

friendship n amicitia, sodalitas, necessitudo, familiaritas f

frieze n (in architecture) zoophorus m

frigate n navis longa f

fright | fuel

fright n pavor, terror, metus m; formido f

frighten vt terreo, perterreo ②
☐ **~ away** absterreo ②

frightful adj terribilis, terrificus; dirus
■ **~ly** adv terribilem in modum

frigid adj frigidus
■ **~ly** adv frigide

frigidity n frigiditas f

frill n segmentum nt

frilly adj segmentatus

fringe n fimbriae fpl; limbus m

frisk vi lascivio; salio, exsilio ④; luxurio ①

frisky adj lascivus, procax, protervus

fritter vt
☐ **~ away** contero; comminuo ③; fig dissipo ①

frivolity n levitas, inconstantia f

frivolous adj levis; frivolus, futilis
■ **~ly** adv nugatorie, tenuiter

fro adv
☐ **to and ~** huc illuc; ultro citroque ...

frock n palla, stola f

frog n rana f

frolic¹ n lascivia f; (play, prank) ludus m

frolic² vi exsulto ①; lascivio ④

from prep a, ab, de, ex all + abl; (owing to) propter + acc
☐ **~ above** desuper
☐ **~ day to day** de die in diem
☐ **~ time to time** continuo

front¹ n frons, prior pars f; (mil) primum agmen nt

front² adj prior, primus; (mil) primoris
☐ **in ~** ex adverso

frontage n frons f

frontier n finis, terminus m

frost n gelu nt; (hoar-frost) pruina f

frostbitten adj frigore adustus

frosty adj gelidus, glacialis; fig (of manner) frigidus

froth¹ n spuma f; fig (empty words) vaniloquentia f

froth² vi spumo ①

frothy adj spumeus, spumosus; fig tumidus

frown¹ n contractio frontis f; vultus severus m

frown² vi frontem contraho ③; fig (~ upon) aversor ①

frozen adj conglaciatus, gelatus, gelu rigens, concretus

frugal adj abstinens, parcus, frugalis
■ **~ly** adv frugaliter, parce

frugality n parsimonia; frugalitas f

fruit n fructus m; frux f; fig (gain) lucrum nt; (result) fructus m

fruitful adj fecundus, fertilis; ferax, uber
■ **~ly** adv fecunde, feraciter

fruitfulness n fecunditas, fertilitas, ubertas f

fruition n fructus m

fruitless adj irritus
■ **~ly** adv frustra; re infecta

fruit-tree n pomum nt

frustrate vt frustror ①; (baffle) decipio, fallo ③; (break up) dirimo ③

frustration n frustratio f

fry vt frigo ③

frying-pan n sartago f

fuck vt futuo ③

fuel n fomes m; ligna ntpl;

nutrimen *nt*

fugitive[1] *adj* fugitivus; fugax

fugitive[2] *n* profugus *m*; profuga *f*

fulfil *vt* expleo 2; exsequor 3

fulfilment *n* exsecutio, perfectio *f*; (result) exitus *m*

full *adj* plenus; (filled up) expletus; (entire) integer; solidus; (satiated) satur; (of dress) fusus
■ ~ *adv* ▶ **fully**

full-grown *adj* adultus

full moon *n* plenilunium *nt*

fully *adv* plene; copiose; omnino, prorsus

fume[1] *n* vapor, halitus *m*

fume[2] *vt&i* exhalo 1; (fig) irascor 3

fumigate *vt* fumigo 1; suffio 4

fumigation *n* suffitus *m*; suffitio *f*

fun *n* iocus, ludus *m*; ludibrium *nt*

function *n* munus, officium *nt*

functional *adj* utilis

fund *n* pecunia *f*; opes *fpl*; fig copia *f*

fundamental *adj* primus, simplex, necessarius, stabilis
■ ~**ly** *adv* (by nature) natura; (essentially) necessario; (altogether) penitus, omnino

funeral[1] *n* funus *nt*; exsequiae *fpl*

funeral[2] *adj* funebris, funereus
□ ~ **rites** iusta funebria *ntpl*
■ ~ **pile** *n* rogus *m*; pyra *f*

fungus *n* fungus *m*

funnel *n* infundibulum *nt*

funny *adj* ridiculus, festivus

fur *n* villi *mpl*; pellis *f*

furious *adj* (frenzied) furialis, furiosus, furens; (angry) iratus

furl *vt* contraho, lego 3

furnace *n* fornax *f*

furnish *vt* ministro, suppedito;

orno, exorno 1; instruo 3

furniture *n* supellex *f*; apparatus *m*

furrow[1] *n* sulcus *m*; (groove) stria *f*

furrow[2] *vt* sulco; aro 1

furry *adj* pellicius

further[1] *adv* ultra, longius, ulterius
■ ~ *adj* ulterior

further[2] *vt* promoveo 2; proveho, consulo + *dat* 3; (aid) adiuvo 1

furthermore *adv* porro, insuper

furthest *adj* extremus, ultimus

furtive *adj* furtivus
■ ~**ly** *adv* clam, furtim, furtive

fury *n* furor *m*; ira, rabies *f*

fuse *vt* fundo, liquefacio 3; conflo 1

fusion *n* fusura *f*

fuss *n* tumultus *m*; turba *f*

fussy *adj* curiosus

futile *adj* futilis, frivolus, vanus

futility *n* futilitas *f*

future[1] *adj* futurus

future[2] *n* futura *ntpl*; posterum tempus *nt*
□ **in, for the** ~ in posterum

Gg

gabble *vi* blatero 1; garrio 4

gable *n* fastigium *nt*

gadfly *n* tabanus, oestrus, asilus *m*

gag[1] *n* oris obturamentum *nt*

gag[2] *vt* os obturo, praeligo 1; obstruo 3

gaiety n festivitas, hilaritas f; nitor, splendor m

gain¹ vt lucror ①; consequor, acquiro ③; (get possession of) potior ④

gain² n lucrum, emolumentum nt; quaestus m

gainful adj lucrosus

gait n incessus, ingressus m

galaxy n via lactea f

gale n ventus m; aura, tempestas, procella f

gall n bilis f; fel nt

gallant adj nitidus, elegans; urbanus; (brave) fortis

gallantry n virtus f; (politeness) urbanitas, elegantia f

galleon n navis oneraria f

gallery n porticus f; (open) peristylium nt; (top seats) summa cavea f

galley n navis longa, biremis, triremis f

gallop¹ n cursus citatus m

gallop² vi citato equo contendo ③; (of the horse) quadrupedo ①

gallows n patibulum nt

gamble vi alea ludo ③
  □ **~ away** ludo amitto ③

gambler n aleator; lusor m

gambling n alea f

gambling-house n aleatorium nt

gambling-table n alveus m

gambol vi lascivio ④; ludo ③; exsulto ①

game n ludus; (act of playing) lusus m; (in hunting) ferae fpl
  □ **~ of chance** alea f
  □ **make ~ of** ludificor ①

gamekeeper n saltuarius m

gaming n ▶ **gambling**

gander n anser m

gang n grex m; (troop) caterva f; sodalicium nt

gangrene n gangraena f

gangway n (in a ship) forus m

gaol n etc. ▶ **jail**, etc.

gap n rima, fissura; lacuna f; hiatus m

gape vi hio ①; dehisco ③; (with mouth open) oscito ①; fig stupeo ②
  □ **~ at** inhio ①

gaping adj hians, hiulcus; fig stupidus

garb n vestitus m

garbage n quisquiliae fpl

garden n hortus m

gardener n hortulanus
  □ **market-~** holitor m

gardening n hortorum cultus m

gargle vi gargarizo ①

garland n sertum nt; corona f

garlic n allium nt

garment n vestimentum nt; vestius m

garnish vt decoro, orno ①; (season) condio ④
  ■ **~** n ornamentum nt

garotte vt laqueo strangulo ①

garret n cenaculum nt

garrison¹ n praesidium nt

garrison² vt praesidium colloco ①

garrulous adj garrulus, loquax

gash n vulnus nt; plaga f
  ■ **~** vt seco, vulnero ①

gasp¹ n anhelitus m

gasp² vi anhelo ①

gate n ianua f; ostium nt; fores fpl;

(of a town) porta *f*

gateway *n* porta *f*

gather *vt* (assemble) congrego ①; (bring together) colligo; (of fruits) decerpo, lego; (pluck) carpo; (in logic) concludo ③; (suspect) suspicor ①
■ ~ *vi* (assemble) convenio ④
■ ~ **round** *vi* convolvo ①; confluo ③
□ ~ **up** colligo; (pick up) sublego ③

gathering *n* collectio *f*; (assembling) congregatio *f*; (assembly) coetus *m*

gaudiness *n* ornatus, nitor *m*; lautitia *f*

gaudy *adj* lautus, splendidus, speciosus

gauge¹ *vt* metior ④

gauge² *n* modulus *m*

gaunt *adj* macer

gay *adj* laetus, hilaris, floridus; splendidus

gaze¹ *n* conspectus *m*; (fixed look) obtutus *m*

gaze² *vi* intueor ②; specto, contemplor ①

gear *n* instrumenta *ntpl*; arma *ntpl*; supellex *f*

gem *n* gemma; baca *f*

gender *n* genus *nt*

general¹ *adj* generalis; vulgaris, publicus, universus
□ **in ~** in universum; (for the most part) plerumque

general² *n* dux, imperator *m*

generally *adv* generatim; universe; (commonly) plerumque, vulgo

generalship *n* ductus *m*; (skill of a commander) ars imperatoria *nt*

generate *vt* genero, procreo ①;

gigno ③

generation *n* generatio *f*; (lineage) genus *nt*; (period of time) saeculum *nt*

generosity *n* liberalitas, generositas *f*; munificentia *f*

generous *adj* generosus; liberalis; munificus; magnanimus

generously *adv* liberaliter, munifice

genial *adj* genialis, hilaris

geniality *n* geniale ingenium *nt*

genitals *n* genitalia *ntpl*

genius *n* ingenium *nt*; (nature) indoles *f*; (person) vir ingeniosus *m*

genteel *adj* elegans, urbanus

gentle *adj* (mild) lenis, mitis, clemens; (gradual) mollis

gentleman *n* homo nobilis; fig vir honestus; (well-bred man) homo liberalis *m*

gentleness *n* lenitas, clementia *f*

gently *adv* leniter; clementer; placide; (gradually) sensim; paulatim, pedetemptim

genuine *adj* sincerus; purus; verus; germanus
■ ~**ly** *adv* sincere, vere

genus *n* genus *nt*

geography *n* geographia *f*

geometrical *adj* geometricus

geometry *n* geometria *f*

germ *n* germen *nt*

germinate *vi* germino, pullulo ①

germination *n* germinatio *f*; germinatus *m*

gesticulate *vi* gestum ago ③

gesticulation *n* gestus *m*

gesture *n* gestus, motus *m*

get *vt* adipiscor, consequor, acquiro ③; (by entreaty) impetro ①

ghastly | glance

g

■ ~ vi (become) fio ir
□ ~ **away** aufugio ③
□ ~ **back** vt (receive) recupero ①; vi (return) reverto ③
□ ~ **the better of** fig supero ①; praevaleo ②
□ ~ **down** vi descendo ③
□ ~ **hold of** prehendo ③; occupo ①
□ ~ **off** vi aufugio; dimittor; absolvor ③
□ ~ **on** (succeed) bene cedo, succedo ③
□ ~ **out** vi exeo ir; (e curru) descendo ③
□ ~ **over** vt traicio, transgredior ③; supero ①
□ ~ **rid of** amoveo ②; tollo ③
□ ~ **something done** curo ① aliquid faciendum
□ ~ **through** pervenio ④; fig perago, perficio ③
□ ~ **together** vt colligo, cogo ③; vi congrego ①
□ ~ **up** surgo ③

ghastly adj (sallow) luridus; (pale) pallidus, pallens; (horrid, shocking) foedus
ghost n (phantom) larva f; (of a dead person) umbra f; manes mpl
ghostly adj (unsubstantial) inanis
giant¹ n gigas m
giant² adj praegrandis
gibberish n inanis strepitus m
gibbet n furca f; patibulum nt
gibe¹ n (sneer) sanna f; (mockery) ludibrium nt
gibe² vt illudo ③
giddiness n vertigo f; fig levitas, inconstantia f
giddy adj vertiginosus; fig levis, inconstans
gift n donum; beneficium, munus

nt; (talent) dos f
gifted adj (endowed) praeditus; fig ingeniosus
gigantic adj praegrandis, ingens
giggle vi cachinno ①
gild vt inauro ①
ginger n zingiberi nt
giraffe n camelopardalis f
girdle n cingulum nt; balteus m; (of women) zona f
girl n puella, virgo f
girlhood n puellaris aetas f
girlish adj puellaris; virginalis; virgineus
girth n fascia f; (of a horse) cingula f; (circuit) ambitus m
gist n (main point) summa f
give vt do, dono ①; confero ir; praebeo ②; (deliver) trado ③
□ ~ **away** dono ①
□ ~ **back** reddo ③
□ ~ **in** vi (yield) cedo ③
□ ~ **out** edo; emitto ③; nuntio ①; distribuo ③; vi (fail) deficio
□ ~ **up** vt trado; (betray) prodo; (abandon) dimitto ③; vi (surrender) me dedo ③
□ ~ **way** pedem refero ir; (yield) cedo; (comply with) obsequor ③ + dat
glad adj laetus, contentus; hilaris, libens
□ **be** ~ gaudeo ②; laetor ①
gladden vt laetifico, hilaro, exhilaro ①
glade n nemus nt; saltus m
gladiator n gladiator m
gladly adv laete; libenter
gladness n gaudium nt; laetitia f
glamour n pulchritudo f
glance¹ n aspectus, obtutus m
glance² vi aspicio

□ ~ **at** stringo, perstringo ③

gland n glandula f

glare¹ n fulgor, ardor m; (fierce look) oculi torvi mpl

glare² vi (of light) fulgeo, ardeo ②; (of expression) torvis oculis aspicio ③

glaring adj fulgens; fig manifestus

glass¹ n vitrum; (mirror) speculum nt; (for drinking) calix m; (glassware) vitrea ntpl

glass² adj vitreus

gleam¹ n fulgor, splendor m; iubar nt; fig aura f

gleam² vi corusco, mico ①; fulgeo ②

gleaming adj coruscus, renidens

glee n laetitia f; gaudium nt

gleeful adj laetus

glib adj volubilis

■ ~**ly** adv volubiliter

glide vi labor, prolabor ③

glimmer¹ n lux dubia f; crepusculum nt, ▶ **gleam**

glimmer² vi subluceo ②

glimpse n aspectus m

□ **have a** ~ **of** dispicio ③

glisten vi luceo, fulgeo ②; radio ①

glitter¹ n fulgor m

glitter² vi fulgeo ②; radio, mico, corusco ①

gloat vi (over) oculos pasco ③

globe n globus; fig orbis terrae or terrarum m

globule n globulus m; pilula f

gloom n tenebrae fpl; caligo; fig tristitia f

gloominess n ▶ **gloom**

gloomy adj tenebrosus, nubilus; fig maestus, tristis

glorify vt celebro, glorifico ①

glorious adj gloriosus, illustris; splendidus; eximius

glory¹ n gloria; laus, fama f

glory² vi glorior ①; superbio ④

gloss n (lustre) nitor m

glossy adj nitidus; expolitus; levis

glove n digitabulum nt

glow¹ n ardor, fervor, calor m

glow² vi candeo, caleo ②; excandesco ③

glowing adj candens, fervens; fig fervidus

glow-worm n cicindela, lampyris f

glue¹ n gluten, glutinum nt

glue² vt glutino, conglutino ①

glum adj tristis, deiectus

glut¹ n satietas f

glut² vt satio, saturo ①; (feast) pasco ③

glutton n helluo, homo gulosus m

gluttonous adj gulosus, edax

gluttony n gula f

gnarled adj nodosus

gnash vt frendeo, infrendeo ②; dentibus strido ③

gnat n culex m

gnaw vt&i rodo ③

go vi eo ir; proficiscor, incedo ③; cedo ir; fig (become) fio ir
□ ~ **around** circumeo ir; fig aggredior ③
□ ~ **abroad** peregre abeo ir
□ ~ **after** sequor ③
□ ~ **astray** aberro, vagor ①
□ ~ **away** abeo ir
□ ~ **back** revertor ③
□ ~ **before** praeeo ir; antecedo ③
□ ~ **beyond** egredior; fig excedo ③

g

□ ~ **by** praetereo *ir*; fig (adhere to) sto ① + *abl*
□ ~ **down** descendo; (of the sun) occido ③
□ ~ **for** peto ③
□ ~ **forth** exeo *ir*
□ ~ **in(to)** ineo *ir*, ingredior ③, intro ①
□ ~ **off** abeo *ir*
□ ~ **on** pergo ③; (happen) fio *ir*; (succeed, thrive) succedo ③
□ ~ **out** exeo *ir*, fig (of fire) extinguor ③
□ ~ **over** transgredior; fig (a subject) percurro ③
□ ~ **round** circumeo (locum) *ir*
□ ~ **through** transeo; obeo *ir*, pertendo ③; (endure) patior ④
□ ~ **to** adeo ③; accedo ③
□ ~ **towards** peto ③
□ ~ **under** subeo *ir*
□ ~ **up** ascendo ③
□ **let** ~ dimitto; (let fall) omitto ③
□ ~ **without** careo, egeo ②
both + *abl*

goad[1] *n* pertica *f*; stimulus *m*
goad[2] *vt* instigo; fig stimulo ①
goal *n* (in the Roman circus) meta, calx *f*; fig finis *m/f*
goat *n* caper *m*
□ **she-**~ capra *f*
gobble *vi* voro, devoro ①; exsorbeo ②
go-between *n* internuntius *m*; internuntia *f*; conciliator *m*; conciliatrix *f*
goblet *n* poculum *nt*; scyphus *m*; ▶ **cup**
god *n* deus *m*; divus *m*; numen *nt*
goddess *n* dea, diva *f*
godly *adj* pius, sanctus
gold *n* aurum *nt*
■ ~ *adj* aureus

golden *adj* aureus; (yellow) flavus
goldfinch *n* carduelis *f*
goldfish *n* hippurus *m*
gold-mine *n* aurifodina *f*
goldsmith *n* aurifex *m*
good[1] *adj* bonus; (effective) efficax; salutaris; utilis; (kind-hearted) benevolus
□ ~ **for nothing** nequam
□ **do** ~ **to** prosum *ir* + *dat*
□ **make** ~ compenso ①; restituo ③; sano ①
good[2] *n* (profit) commodum, lucrum *nt*; salus; utilitas *f*; (in abstract sense) bonum *nt*
good[3] *int* bene! euge!
goodbye *int* vale, valete
good-humoured *adj* facilis
good-natured *adj* comis, benignus, facilis
goodness *n* bonitas; probitas; benignitas *f*
goods *n* bona *ntpl*; res *f*
goodwill *n* benevolentia; gratia *f*
goose *n* anser *m*
gore[1] *n* cruor *m*; sanies *f*
gore[2] *vt* cornu ferio ④
gorge[1] *n* fauces; angustiae *fpl*
gorge[2] *vi* devoro, ingurgito ①
gorgeous *adj* nitidus, lautus, splendidus; magnificus
gorse *n* ulex *m*
gory *adj* cruentus, cruentatus, sanguineus, sanguinolentus
gossip[1] *n* (idle talk) nugae, gerrae *fpl*; (person) homo garrulus *m*; mulier loquax *f*
gossip[2] *vi* garrio ④
gouge *vt* evello, eruo ③
gout *n* morbus articularis *m*; (in the

feet) podagra f

govern vt impero, imperito ① both + dat; rego ③; (check) coerceo ②; moderor ①

governess n magistra f

government n gubernatio (civitatis); administratio f; imperium, regnum nt; provincia f

governor n gubernator; praefectus; dominus m

gown n (woman's garment) stola f; (of a Roman citizen) toga f

grab vt corripio ③

grace n gratia; (elegance, etc.) venustas f; veneres fpl; decor, lepos m; (pardon) venia f
■ **Graces** pl Gratiae fpl

graceful adj elegans; lepidus, venustus
■ **~ly** adv venuste; eleganter, lepide

gracious adj benignus; clemens; humanus; (propitious) aequus, propitius
■ **~ly** adv benigne; humane

graciousness n benignitas, humanitas, clementia f

grade n gradus, ordo m

gradient n clivus m

gradual adj per gradus
■ **~ly** adv gradatim, pedetemptim, paulatim

graft¹ n (of plants) insitum nt; surculus m

graft² vt insero ③

grain n granum nt; fig particula f

grammar n grammatica f

grammatical adj grammaticus

granary n horreum, granarium nt

grand adj grandis, magnificus; praeclarus, splendidus

grandchild n nepos m; neptis f

granddaughter n neptis f

grandeur n magnificentia; granditas; sublimitas; maiestas f; splendor m

grandfather n avus m

grandmother n avia f

grandson n nepos m

grant¹ vt concedo, permitto ③; (acknowledge) fateor ②; do ①; praebeo ②

grant² n concessio f

grape n acinus m; uva f
□ **bunch of ~s** racemus m

graphic adj expressus
■ **~ally** adv expresse

grapple vi luctor ①

grasp¹ vt prehendo, corripio ③; affecto ①; (understand) teneo ②
□ **~ at** capto ①; fig appeto ③

grasp² n complexus m; (power) potestas; (hand) manus f

grasping adj avidus, cupidus; avarus

grass n gramen nt; herba f

grasshopper n grillus m

grassy adj graminosus, gramineus, herbosus, herbidus

grate¹ n clathri, cancelli mpl

grate² vt (grind) tero, contero ③
■ **~** vi strideo ②

grateful adj gratus, iucundus
■ **~ly** adv grate; (thankfully) grato animo

gratification n expletio; gratificatio; (pleasure, delight) voluptas; oblectatio f

gratify vt (indulge) indulgeo ②; gratificor ① both + dat

gratifying adj gratus

grating n clathri, cancelli mpl; (sound) stridor m

gratitude n gratia f; gratus animus m

gratuitous adj gratuitus

gratuity n stips f; munus, praemium nt

grave[1] adj gravis, serius; (stern) severus
■ **~ly** adv graviter, serio; severe

grave[2] n sepulcrum, bustum nt; tumulus m

gravel n glarea f; sabulo m

gravestone n monumentum nt

gravity n gravitas f; pondus nt; (personal) severitas; dignitas; tristitia f

graze[1] vt (pasture) pascor; (touch lightly) stringo, perstringo ③; (scrape) rado ③

graze[2] n vulnus nt

grease[1] vt ungo, perungo, illino ③

grease[2] n unguen, pingue nt; arvina f; (for wheels) axungia f

greasy adj pinguis; unctus; (dirty) squalidus

great adj magnus; ingens; amplus, grandis; (powerful) potens
□ **so ~** tantus
□ **as ~ as** tantus, quantus

great-grandfather n proavus m

great-hearted adj magnanimus

greatly adv magnopere, valde

greatness n magnitudo f

greaves n ocreae fpl

Greece n Graecia f

greed n aviditas; voracitas f

greedily adv avide, cupide

greediness n aviditas; voracitas f

greedy adj avidus, avarus, cupidus; vorax

Greek adj & n Graecus m

green[1] adj viridis; virens; prasinus; (unripe) crudus, immaturus
□ **become ~** viresco ③

green[2] n color viridis; (lawn) locus or campus herbidus m
□ **~s** holera ntpl

greengrocer n holerum venditor m

greenish adj subviridis

greenness n color viridis m; (in abstract sense) viriditas f; fig immaturitas f

greet vt saluto ①; salutem dico ③ + dat

greeting n salutatio, salus f

gregarious adj gregalis

grey adj cinereus; (blue-grey) glaucus; (with age) canus
□ **become ~** canesco ③

grey-headed adj canus

greyish adj canescens

greyness n canities f

grief n dolor, maeror; luctus m; aegritudo; molestia, tristitia f

grievance n querimonia, querela, iniuria f; malum nt

grieve vt dolore afficio (aliquem) ③; excrucio, sollicito ①
■ **~ vi** doleo, lugeo ②

grievous adj gravis, durus, atrox, acerbus

griffin n gryps m

grill vt torreo ②

grim adj torvus; trux, truculentus, horridus
■ **~ly** adv horride

grimace n vultus distortus m; oris depravatio f

grime n squalor m, ▶ **dirt**

grimy adj squalidus

grin¹ vi ringor ③; (laugh) rideo ②

grin² n rictus m

grind vt (corn) molo ③; (in a mortar) contundo ③; (on a whetstone) exacuo ③; (the teeth) dentibus frendeo ③

grindstone n cos f

grip¹ n manus f

grip² vt comprehendo ③

grisly adj horrendus, horridus

gristle n cartilago f

gristly adj cartilagineus, cartilaginosus

grit n glarea f; arena f, sabulo m

gritty adj arenosus, sabulosus

groan¹ vi gemo, ingemo ③

groan² n gemitus m

grocer n condimentarius m

groin n inguen nt

groom¹ n agaso, equiso m

groom² vt (equum) curo ①
■ ~ n (bridegroom) sponsus m

groove n canalis m; stria f

grope vi praetento ①

gross adj (fat) crassus, densus; pinguis; (coarse) rusticus, incultus; (dreadful) atrox; (whole) totus
■ **~ly** adv graviter; crasse; turpiter

grotesque adj absurdus, ridiculus

ground n solum nt; terra; humus f; (place) locus m; fig causa f
□ **on the ~** humi
□ **gain ~** proficio ③
□ **lose ~** recedo ③
□ **~s** (sediment) faex f

groundless adj vanus, falsus; fictus

groundwork n subtructio f; fig fundamentum nt

group¹ n corona, turba f; globus, circulus m

group² vt dispono ③
■ ~ vi circulor ①

grouse n lagopus, tetrao m

grove n lucus, saltus m; nemus nt

grovel vi provolvor ③; fig servio ④

grovelling adj humilis, supplex, servilis

grow vi cresco ③; (increase) augeor ②; adolesco ③; (become) fio ir
■ ~ vt (cultivate) sero ③; (a beard, etc.) promitto ③
□ **~ out of** fig orior ④; nascor ③; (grow up) adolesco ③

grower n cultor m

growl¹ n fremitus m

growl² vi fremo ③; mussito, murmuro ①

grown-up adj adultus; puber

growth n incrementum nt; auctus m
□ **full ~** maturitas f

grub n vermiculus m

grudge¹ n odium nt; simultas f
□ **hold a ~ against** succenseo ② + dat

grudge² vt invideo ②

grudgingly adv invite, gravate

gruff adj asper, taetricus, torvus
■ **~ly** adv aspere

grumble vi murmuro, mussito ①; queror ③

grunt¹ vi grunnio ④

grunt² n grunnitus m

guarantee¹ n fides, satisdatio f

guarantee² vt satisdo, praesto ①; (promise) spondeo ②

guard¹ n custodia; tutela f; (military) praesidium nt; (person) custos m/f
□ **be on one's ~** caveo ②

guard | hair

guard[2] *vt* custodio [4]; defendo, protego [3]; munio [4]; (against) caveo [2]

guarded *adj* cautus, circumspectus

guardian *n* custos; praeses *m/f*; defensor; (of orphans) tutor; curator *m*

guess[1] *vt&i* conicio [3]; divino, suspicor [1]; (solve) solvo [3]

guess[2] *n* coniectura f

guest *n* hospes; (stranger) advena; (at a feast) conviva *m/f*

guidance *n* ductus *m*; cura, curatio, administratio f

guide[1] *n* dux *m/f*; ductor *m*

guide[2] *vt* duco [3]; (rule) guberno [1]; rego [3]

guidebook *n* itinerarium nt

guild *n* collegium nt

guile *n* dolus, astus *m*; astutia f

guilt *n* culpa, noxa f; crimen, peccatum nt

guiltless *adj* innocens, insons, innocuus

guilty *adj* sons, nocens, noxius + *abl* or *gen*; sceleratus

guise *n* (manner) modus; mos; (appearance) species f

guitar *n* cithara f

gulf *n* sinus *m*; (abyss) vorago f

gullet *n* gula f; fauces fpl

gullibility *n* credulitas f

gullible *adj* credulus

gum[1] *n* (of the mouth) gingiva f; (adhesive) cummi nt, cummis f

gum[2] *vt* glutino [1]

gush *vi* (out) effluo, profluo [3]; prosilio [4]; scateo [2]

gust *n* flatus *m*; flamen nt

gusty *adj* procellosus

gut[1] *n* intestinum nt
□ ~s viscera ntpl

gut[2] *vt* exentero [1]; fig exinanio [4]

gutter *n* canalis *m*; (of streets) colliciae fpl

gymnasium *n* gymnasium nt; palaestra f

gymnastic *adj* gymnicus, gymnasticus

gymnastics *n* palaestrica f

gyrate *vi* volvor [3]

gyration *n* gyrus *m*

Hh

habit *n* (custom) consuetudo f; mos *m*; (dress) vestitus *m*; (state) habitus *m*

habitable *adj* habitabilis
□ **not** ~ inhabitabilis

habitation *n* habitatio, domus f

habitual *adj* inveteratus, assuetus, consuetus, solitus
■ **~ly** *adv* de (ex) more

hack *vt* concido [3]; mutilo [1]

hackneyed *adj* tritus; pervulgatus

haemorrhage *n* haemorrhagia f

hag *n* anus f

haggard *adj* macer, exsanguis

haggle *vt* cavillor; (bargain) licitor [1]

hail[1] *n* grando f

hail[2] *vt* (salute) saluto [1]
■ ~ *vi* grandino [1]

hail[3] *int* salve!

hailstone *n* grando f

hair *n* capillus, crinis *m*, caesaries, coma f; (single) pilus; (of animals)

hairdresser | harbour

...illus m

☐ **grey** ~ canities f

hairdresser n capitis et capilli
:concinnator m; ornatrix f

airy adj pilosus; crinitus; comatus;
shaggy) hirsutus

alcyon n alcedo, alcyon f

alf adj dimidius

■ ~ n dimidia pars f; dimidium nt

alf-dead adj semianimis

alf-eaten adj semiesus

alf-hearted adj piger

alf-yearly adj semestris

all n atrium; (entrance-~)
vestibulum; (for business)
conciliabulum nt; (of the senate)
curia f

allucination n alucinatio f;
error m; somnium nt

alt[1] vi consisto ③; fig haesito ①

alt[2] n pausa, mora f

alve vt ex aequo divido ③

ammer[1] n malleus m

ammer[2] vt cudo ③

amper[1] n qualus m; fiscina f

amper[2] vt impedio ④; implico,
retardo ①

and[1] n manus, palma f;
(handwriting) chirographum nt; (of a
dial) gnomon m

☐ **at** ~ ad manum; prae manibus;
praesto

☐ **by** ~ manu

☐ ~ **in** ~ iunctis manibus

☐ ~ **to** ~ comminus

☐ **in** ~ (of money) prae manu

☐ **on the other** ~ altera parte

☐ **on the right** ~ ad dextram

and[2] vt trado ③

☐ ~ **out** distribuo ③

☐ ~ **over** trado ③

☐ ~ **round** circumfero ③

handcuffs npl manicae fpl

handful n manipulus, pugillus m

handicap n impedimentum nt

handicraft n ars f; artificium nt

handiwork n opus nt; opera f

handkerchief n sudarium nt

handle[1] vt tracto ①

handle[2] n manubrium nt; ansa f;
(of a sword) capulus m

handsome adj pulcher, formosus;
honestus; elegans, bellus

handwriting n manus f;
(manuscript) chirographum nt

handy adj (useful) utilis

hang vt suspendo

■ ~ vi pendeo, dependeo ②

☐ **let** ~ demitto ③

☐ ~ **back** haesito ①

☐ ~ **over** immineo ③ + dat

hanger-on n assecla, fig
parasitus m

hangman n carnifex m

hanker vi desidero ①; expeto ③

haphazard adj fortuitus

happen vi accido ③; evenio ④;
contingo ③; fio ir

happiness n vita beata; (good
fortune) felicitas f

happy adj felix, fortunatus,
faustus; beatus

harangue[1] n contio f

harangue[2] vt&i contionor ③

harass vt fatigo; vexo; inquieto ①;
lacesso ③

harbinger n praenuntius,
antecursor m

harbour[1] n portus m; fig refugium,
perfugium nt

harbour[2] vt excipio ③; (feelings,

etc.) habeo ②; afficior ③ + *abl*

hard *adj* durus; fig (difficult) arduus; (severe) acer, rigidus; (hard-hearted) crudelis

harden *vt* duro; induro ①
■ ~ *vi* duresco; obduresco ③

hard-hearted *adj* durus, ferreus, inhumanus, crudelis

hard-heartedness *n* crudelitas *f*; ingenium durum *nt*

hardihood *n* audacia *f*

hardiness *n* robur *m*

hardly *adv* (with difficulty, scarcely) vix; aegre

hardness *n* duritia *f*

hardship *n* aerumna; difficultas *f*; labor *m*; dura *ntpl*

hardware *n* ferramenta *ntpl*

hardy *adj* durus; robustus

hare *n* lepus *m*

harem *n* gynaeceum *nt*

harm[1] *n* damnum *nt*; iniuria; fraus, noxa; calamitas *f*

harm[2] *vt* laedo ③; noceo ② + *dat*

harmful *adj* noxius, perniciosus

harmless *adj* (things) innocuus, innoxius; (person) innocens

harmonious *adj* concors, consonus; canorus; fig concors, consentiens

harmonize *vt* compono ③
■ ~ *vi* concino ③; fig consentio ④

harmony *n* harmonia *f*; concentus *m*; fig concordia *f*

harness[1] *n* ornatus *m*

harness[2] *vt* adiungo, iungo, subiungo ③; (saddle) insterno ③

harp *n* lyra *f*

harpist *n* psaltes *m*; psaltria *f*

harpoon[1] *n* iaculum *nt*

harpoon[2] *vt* iaculor ①, transfigo ③

harridan *n* anus, vetula *f*

harrow *n* rastrum *nt*
■ ~ *vt* occo ①; fig crucio, excrucio ①

harsh *adj* asper; (in sound) discors, stridulus; (hoarse) raucus; (in taste) acer; fig gravis; severus, durus
■ ~**ly** *adv* aspere; graviter, acerbe, duriter

harshness *n* asperitas; acerbitas; saevitia; severitas *f*

harvest[1] *n* messis *f*

harvest[2] *vt* meto ③

harvester *n* messor *m*

hash *n* fig
□ **make a ~ of** male gero + *acc*

haste *n* celeritas; festinatio, properatio *f*
□ **in ~** propere; properanter
□ **make ~** propero, festino ①

hasten *vt* accelero, propero; (hurry on) praecipito ①
■ ~ *vi* propero, festino ①

hastily *adv* propere; raptim

hastiness *n* celeritas *f*

hasty *adj* properus; praeceps; fig iracundus

hat *n* pilleus, galerus, petasus *m*

hatchet *n* ascia, securis, bipennis *f*

hate[1] *vt* odi, perodi ③; destestor ①

hate[2] *n* ▶ **hatred**

hateful *adj* odiosus, invisus; inamabilis

hatred *n* odium *nt*; invidia; simultas, inimicitia *f*

haughtiness *n* superbia; arrogantia *f*; fastidium *nt*

haughty *adj* superbus; arrogans; fastidiosus

haul vt traho, subduco ③

haunt¹ vt frequento ①; fig (of spirits) adsum ir

haunt² n latebra f; lustra ntpl

have vt habeo; possideo, teneo ②
□ ~ **on** gero ③
□ **I would ~ you know** velim scias

haven n portus m; (fig) salus f

havoc n strages, caedes f

hawk n accipiter m

hay n faenum nt

hazard n periculum, discrimen nt; (chance) alea f

hazardous adj periculosus; anceps

haze n nebula f; vapor m

hazel¹ n (tree) corylus f

hazel² adj colurnus; (of colour) spadix, flavus

hazy adj nebulosus, caliginosus; fig (doubtful) dubius, ambiguus

he pn hic, is, ille

head¹ n caput nt; vertex m; (also fig) (mental faculty) ingenium nt; (chief) princeps m/f; (top) culmen, cacumen nt

head² adj princeps, summus

head³ vt dux sum ir + gen; praesum ir + dat
□ ~ **for** peto ③

headache n capitis dolor m

headband n vitta f

heading n titulus m

headland n promontorium nt

headlong adj praeceps; temerarius

headquarters n praetorium nt

headstrong adj pervicax, contumax; ▶ **stubborn**

heal vt sano ①; medeor ②
■ ~ vi sanesco; (wounds) coalesco ③; coeo ④

healing adj salutaris, saluber
■ ~ n sanatio f

health n sanitas, valetudo, salus f

healthful adj salutaris, saluber

healthiness n firma valetudo; (of place or things) salubritas f

healthy n sanus; integer; (places or things) saluber

heap¹ n acervus, cumulus m; congeries f

heap² vt acervo, coacervo, accumulo ①

hear vt&i audio; exaudio ④; ausculto ①; (find out) certior fio ir

hearing n (act) auditio f; (sense) auditus m

hearsay n fama f; rumor m

hearse n feretrum nt

heart n cor nt; fig (feeling) pectus nt; (courage) animus m
□ **have the ~ to** sustineo, audeo ②

heartbreaking adj miserabilis

heartbroken adj angoribus confectus, afflictus

hearten vt confirmo ①

hearth n focus m

heartily adv sincere; effuse; valde; vere; ex animo

heartless adj ferreus, crudelis, inhumanus
■ ~**ly** adv inhumane, crudeliter

heartlessness n inhumanitas, saevitia f

heat¹ n calor, ardor; fervor, aestus m

heat² vt calefacio, incendo ③
■ ~ vi calesco ③

heating n calefactio f

heave vt attollo ③; levo ①; (sighs, etc.) traho, duco ③
■ ~ vi tumeo ②; fluctuo ①

heaven n caelum nt; fig di, superi mpl

heavenly adj caelestis, divinus

heaviness n gravitas; (slowness) tarditas; (dullness) stultitia f; (drowsiness) sopor m

heavy adj gravis; onerosus, ponderosus

hedge n saepes f; saeptum nt

hedgehog n erinaceus, ericius m

heed n:
□ **pay** ~ **to** curo ①
□ **take** ~ caveo, praecaveo ②

heedless adj incautus; temerarius

heel n calx f

heifer n iuvenca f

height n altitudo; (tallness) proceritas f; (top) culmen nt; (hill) clivus, collis, tumulus m

heighten vt altius effero ③; fig amplifico; exaggero ①

heinous adj atrox; nefarius; foedus

heir n (also **heiress**) heres m/f

heirloom n res hereditaria f

hell n Tartarus m

hellish adj infernus, nefarius

hello int salve, salvete; ave, avete

helm n gubernaculum nt; calvus m

helmet n cassis, galea f

helmsman n gubernator, rector navis m

help¹ n auxilium nt; opem f (acc sing)

help² vt iuvo, adiuvo ①; succurro ③; subvenio ④ both + dat; auxilior,

helper n adiutor, auxiliator m

helpful adj utilis

helpless adj inops

helplessness n inopia f

hem¹ n ora f; limbus m

hem² vt praetexo; fig cingo ③
□ ~ **in** circumsideo ②

hemisphere n hemisphaerium nt

hemlock n cicuta f

hen n gallina f

hence adv hinc

henceforth adv posthac; dehinc, in posterum

henhouse n gallinarium nt

henpecked adj fig uxorius

her¹ pn eam

her² adj suus; eius

herald¹ n caduceator; (crier) praeco m

herald² vt nuntio ①

herb n herba f

herd¹ n grex m; fig (in contempt) vulgus m

herd² vi congregor ①

herdsman n pastor; armentarius; bubulcus m

here adv hic; (hither) huc
□ ~ **and there** raro

hereditary adj hereditarius

heritage n hereditas f

hero n heros, vir fortis; (in a play) qui primas partes agit m

heroic adj heroicus
■ ~ly adv fortiter

heroine n heroina; virago; (of a play) quae primas partes agit f

heroism n virtus, fortitudo f

heron n ardea f

herring n harenga f

hers pn eius, illius

herself n ipsa; (reflexive) se

hesitant adj haesitans
■ ~**ly** adv cunctanter

hesitate vi dubito, haesito, cunctor, cesso 🔟

hesitation n dubitatio; haesitatio f

hew vt dolo 🔟; caedo ③; seco 🔟

hey int ohe!

hiccough¹ n (also **hiccup**) singultus m

hiccough² vi (also **hiccup**) singulto 🔟

hide¹ n pellis f; corium nt

hide² vt abdo, condo, occulo, abscondo ③; celo 🔟; (dissemble) dissimulo 🔟
■ ~ vi lateo ②

hideous adj foedus, turpis, deformis

hiding n (beating) verberatio f

hiding-place n latebra f; latibulum nt

hierarchy n sacerdotium, collegium nt; (ranking) ordo m

high adj altus, excelsus, sublimis; (tall) procerus; (of price) pretiosus; carus; fig magnus; amplus
■ ~ adv alte; sublime; valde; vehementer
□ ~ **aim** magnas res appeto ③

highland n regio aspera or montuosa f

highly adv (much) valde, multum; (value) magni, permagni

high priest n summus sacerdos, pontifex maximus m

high-spirited adj generosus, animosus

highway n via f

highwayman n latro, grassator m

hike vi ambulo 🔟

hilarious adj hilaris, festivus

hill n collis; tumulus; (slope) clivus m

hilly adj montuosus, clivosus

hilt n (of a sword) capulus m

him pn eum, hunc, illum
□ **of** ~ eius, huius; illius; de illo

himself pn ipse; (reflexive) se

hind adj posterior, aversus

hinder vt impedio ④; obsto 🔟 + dat; retardo 🔟; (prevent) prohibeo ②

hindrance n impedimentum nt

hinge n cardo m

hint¹ n indicium nt; nutus m; significatio f

hint² vt&i innuo, suggero ③; summoneo ②
□ ~ **at** perstringo ③

hip n coxa, coxendix f

hippopotamus n hippopotamus m

hire¹ n merces f; stipendium nt

hire² vt conduco ③; loco 🔟

hired adj conductus, conducticius, mercenarius

his pn eius, huius; illius, ipsius
□ ~ **own** suus, proprius

hiss¹ vt&i sibilo 🔟; strideo ②

hiss² n sibilus; stridor m

historian n historicus m

historic adj historicus
■ ~**ally** adv historice

history n historia, memoria rerum gestarum f; res f; (narrative) narratio f

hit vt ferio ④; percutio ③
□ ~ **upon** (discover) invenio,

reperio ④

hitch n impedimentum nt; mora f

hither adv huc
  □ **~ and thither** huc illuc

hitherto adv adhuc

hive n alvus f; alvearium nt

hoard n acervus m
  ■ **~** vt coacervo ①

hoarder n accumulator m

hoar-frost n pruina f

hoarse adj raucus
  □ **~ly** adv rauca voce

hoarseness n raucitas f

hoax¹ n ludificatio f; fraus f; dolus m

hoax² vt ludificor ①

hobble vi claudico ①

hobby n studium nt; cura f

hoe n sarculum, pastinum nt
  ■ **~** vt sarculo ①; pastino ①; (weeds) pecto ③

hog n sus, porcus m

hoist vt sublevo ①; tollo ③

hold¹ vt teneo; possideo, habeo ②; (contain) capio ③
  ■ **~** vi permaneo ②; (think) existimo ①; censeo ②
  □ **~ back** retineo ②; vi cunctor ①
  □ **~ forth** vi contionem habeo ②
  □ **~ in** inhibeo, cohibeo ②
  □ **~ off** abstineo ②
  □ **~ out** porrigo, extendo ③; (offer) praebeo ②; fig ostendo ③; (endure) duro ①; (persevere) obduro, persevero ①
  □ **~ together** contineo ②
  □ **~ up** (lift up) attollo ③; sustineo ②; (delay) moror ①
  □ **~ with** consentio ④

hold² n manus; custodia f;

(influence) momentum nt; potestas f; (of a ship) alveus m

holder n possessor m; colonus m; (handle) manubrium nt

hole n foramen nt; rima f; fig latebra f; (of mice, etc.) cavum nt

holiday n dies festus m
  ■ **~s** pl feriae fpl

holiness n sanctitas, religio, pietas f

hollow¹ adj cavus; concavus; fig vanus

hollow² n caverna f; cavum nt; (depression) lacuna f

hollow³ vt cavo, excavo ①

hollowness n fig vanitas f

holm-oak n ilex f

holy adj sanctus; sacer, religiosus; (dutiful) pius

homage n obsequium nt; cultus m; observantia f
  □ **pay ~ to** colo ③; observo ①

home¹ n domicilium nt; domus f
  □ **at ~** domi

home² adj domesticus
  ■ **~** adv (homewards) domum

home-bred adj domesticus, vernaculus

homeless adj tecto carens, profugus

homely adj (unsophisticated) simplex; rudis; incompositus; rusticus

home-made adj domesticus, vernaculus

homesick n suorum desiderium nt

homeward adv domum

homicide n (person) homicida m; (deed) homicidium nt

honest adj probus; sincerus; integer, verus
■ ~**ly** adv probe, sincere, integre, vere

honesty n probitas, sinceritas, integritas f

honey n mel nt

honeycomb n favus m

honorary adj honorarius

honour¹ n honos m; fama, laus, gloria; honestas, fides f; (high position) dignitas f

honour² vt honoro; celebro ①; (hold in ~) in honore habeo ②; (pay homage to) colo ③; observo ①

honourable adj honestus; honorificus; bonus

hood n cucullus m; palliolum nt

hoodwink vt ludificor ①

hoof n ungula f

hook¹ n hamus; uncus m

hook² vt inunco ①; fig capio ③

hooked adj hamatus; (crooked) curvatus, aduncus, curvus, recurvus

hoop n circulus m

hoot vt&i gemo, queror ③; acclamo ①; explodo ③

hop vi salio ④; subsulto ①

hope¹ n spes f

hope² vt spero ①
□ ~ **for** expecto ①

hopeful adj bonae spei
■ ~**ly** adv cum magna spe

hopeless adj exspes; desperatus
■ ~**ly** adv sine spe, desperanter

horde n turba f; ▶ **crowd**

horizon n orbis finiens m

horizontal adj libratus
■ ~**ly** adv ad libram

horn n cornu nt; (to blow on) bucina f; cornu nt

hornet n crabro m

horoscope n horoscopus m; genesis f

horrible adj horribilis, foedus, nefarius

horrid adj horridus, horrens, immanis

horrific adj horrificus, terribilis

horrify vt horrifico ①; terreo, exterreo ②

horror n horror, pavor m; (hatred) odium nt

horse n equus m; equitatus m

horseback n
□ **on** ~ equo, ex equo
□ **ride on** ~ equito ①

horseman n eques m

horse-race n curriculum equorum nt; certatio equestris f

horseshoe n solea f

horticulture n hortorum cultus m

hose n (pipe) tubulus m

hospitable adj hospitalis, liberalis, munificus

hospital n valetudinarium nt

hospitality n hospitium nt; hospitalitas; liberalitas f

host n (of guests) hospes m; (at an inn) caupo m; (crowd) multitudo f; (army) exercitus m

hostage n obses m/f

hostess n hospita; (at an inn) caupona f

hostile adj hostilis, hosticus, inimicus, infestus

hostility n inimicitia f
□ **hostilities** (war) bellum nt

hot adj calidus; fervens, candens; fervidus; (of spices) acer; (furious) furens, iratus; (keen) vehemens, acer
- □ **grow** ~ excandesco ③

hotchpotch n farrago f; miscellanea ntpl

hotel n hospitium nt; caupona f; deversorium nt

hotly adv acriter, ardenter, vehementer

hound n catulus m; canis m/f

hour n hora f
- □ **half an** ~ semihora f
- □ **three-quarters of an** ~ dodrans horae m

hourglass n horarium nt

hourly adj & adv in singulas horas; in horas, singulis horis

house¹ n domus, sedes f; tectum; domicilium nt; fig familia; domus, gens f; (in politics) (senatorum, etc.) ordo m; (meeting place of senate) curia f

house² vt domo excipio; (store) condo ③

household n domus, familia f
- ■ ~ adj domesticus, familiaris

householder n paterfamilias m

household-god n Lar m
- □ ~**s** Penates mpl

housekeeper n promus; dispensator m; (female) dispensatrix f

housekeeping n cura rei familiaris f

housewife n materfamilias f

hovel n tugurium nt; casa f

hover vi pendeo ②; volito ①; libror ①; (over) immineo ②

how¹ adv quomodo; ut; (to what degree) quam
- □ ~ **many** quot, quam multi
- □ ~ **often** quoties
- □ ~ **much** quantum

how² adv ut! quam!

however adv -cumque, quamvis, utcumque; quantumvis
- ■ ~ conj nihilominus, tamen

howl vi ululo ①
- ■ ~ n ululatus m

hubbub n tumultus m; turba f

hue n color m
- □ ~ **and cry** conclamatio f

huff n ira f

hug¹ n complexus, amplexus m

hug² vt complector, amplector ③

huge adj ingens; vastus; immanis
- ■ ~**ly** adv immaniter, egregie

hull n (of a ship) alveus m

hum¹ vi susurro; murmuro ①

hum² n bombus m; fremitus m; murmur nt; susurrus m

human¹ adj humanus; mortalis

human² n
- □ ~ **being** homo m

humane adj humanus, misericors
- ■ ~**ly** adv humaniter; misericorditer

humanity n (humaneness) humanitas; misericordia f; (mankind) homines, mortales mpl

humble¹ adj humilis; summissus, supplex; (mean) obscurus

humble² vt infringo, deprimo ③
- □ ~ **myself** me demitto ③

humbly adv humiliter, summisse

humid adj umidus

humidity n umor m

humiliate vt humilio ①; deprimo ③

humiliation n humiliatio f;
  dedecus nt; ignominia, turpitudo f

humility n animus summissus m;
  modestia f

humorous adj facetus; lepidus;
  ridiculus

humour¹ n (frame of mind)
  ingenium nt; (whim) libido f;
  (liveliness) festivitas f; lepos m;
  facetiae fpl

humour² vt obsequor, morem
  gero ③; indulgeo ② all + dat

hump n gibber, gibbus m

humpbacked adj gibber

hundred adj centum
  □ ~ **times** centiens
  ■ ~ n centuria f

hundredth adj centesimus

hunger¹ n fames f; ieiunium nt

hunger² n esurio ④; fig cupio ③

hungrily adv voraciter

hungry adj esuriens; ieiunus; fig
  avidus, vorax

hunt¹ vi venor ①
  ■ ~ **for** vt peto, quaero ③

hunt² n venatio f; venatus m

hunter n venator; (hunting horse)
  equus venaticus m

hunting n venatio f; venatus m

hunting-spear n venabulum nt

huntress n venatrix f

huntsman n venator m

hurdle n crates f

hurl vt iacio, proicio ③; iacto ①;
  iaculor ①

hurly-burly n tumultus m

hurrah int (also **hurray**) euge!

hurricane n procella, tempestas
  f; turbo m

hurriedly adv raptim; festinanter

hurry¹ vi festino, propero,
  praecipito ①; curro ③
  ■ ~ vt urgeo ②; festino, propero,
  praecipito ①
  ■ ~ **along** vi curro ③
  ■ ~ **away** vi propero ①;
  aufugio ③

hurry² n festinatio, properatio f
  □ **in a** ~ festinanter

hurt¹ vt noceo ② + dat; laedo ③; fig
  offendo ③
  ■ ~ vi doleo ②

hurt² n vulnus; damnum nt;
  iniuria f

hurtful adj noxius, perniciosus;
  (cruel) crudelis

husband n maritus, vir, coniunx m

hush¹ int st! tace, tacete

hush² vt paco ①; comprimo ③
  ■ ~ vi taceo ②
  □ ~ **up** fig celo ①

husk n folliculus m; siliqua f; (of
  corn) gluma f

husky adj (of voice) surraucus

hustle vt proturbo ①

hut n tugurium nt; casa f

hutch n cavea f; mapalia ntpl

hyacinth n hyacinthus m

hydraulic adj hydraulicus

hyena n hyaena f

hygiene n munditia f

hygienic adj mundus

hymn n hymnus m

hypochondria n atra bilis f

hypocrisy n simulatio,
  dissimulatio; pietas ficta f

hypocrite n simulator,
  dissimulator; hypocrita m

hypocritical adj simulatus, fictus

hypothesis n (guess) coniectura;

(opinion) sententia f

hysteria n animi concitatio f

. . . .

Ii

I pn ego
□ ~ **myself** egomet, ipse ego

ice n glacies f; gelu nt

icicle n stiria f

icy adj glacialis; gelidus

idea n species, forma; imago; notitia; notio; (opinion) opinio, sententia; (suspicion) suspicio; (guess) coniectura f

ideal¹ adj perfectus; mente conceptus

ideal² n exemplar (perfectum) nt

identical adj idem; unus atque idem

identify vt agnosco ③
□ ~ **with** sto ① cum + abl

idiocy n fatuitas, stultitia f

idiomatic adj proprius linguae; vernaculus

idiosyncrasy n proprium nt

idiot n fatuus; stupidus, stultus; excors m

idiotic adj fatuus

idle adj (at leisure) otiosus, vacuus; (of people) ignavus, piger, segnis, desidiosus, iners

idleness n otium nt; ignavia, segnitia, desidia f

idly adv otiose; segniter; fig frustra, incassum

idol n idolum, simulacrum nt; fig

deliciae fpl

idolize vt (be desperately in love with) depereo ④ + acc

if conj si
□ **as ~** quasi, tamquam
□ **but ~** sin, quod si
□ **even ~** etiamsi
□ **~ only** dummodo; (would that) utinam
□ **~ not** ni, nisi, si non; si mimus

ignite vt accendo
■ ~ vi exardesco, excandesco ③

ignominious adj contumeliosus, ignominiosus, turpis

ignorance n ignoratio, ignorantia, inscitia f

ignorant adj (unaware) inscius, ignarus, nescius; (unlearned) indoctus, inscitus
□ **be ~ of** ignoro ①; nescio ④

ignore vt praetereo ④

ill¹ adj malus; (in health) aegrotus
□ **be ~** aegroto ①
□ **fall ~** in morbum incido ③

ill² n malum nt
□ **take it ~** aegre fero ③

ill-advised adj inconsideratus, inconsultus, temerarius

ill-bred adj agrestis, inurbanus

ill-disposed adj malevolus, malignus

illegal adj quod contra leges fit; illicitus
■ **~ly** adv contra leges; illicite

illegible adj quod legi non potest

illegitimacy n (of birth) ortus infamia f

illegitimate adj (of birth) haud legitimus; spurius; nothus; (wrong) vitiosus

ill health n (infirma) valetudo f

illicit *adj* illicitus
■ **~ly** *adv* illicite

illiterate *adj* illitteratus

ill-natured *adj* malevolus, malignus

illness *n* morbus *m*; aegrotatio *f*

illogical *adj* vitiosus

ill-omened *adj* dirus, infaustus

ill-temper *n* iracundia, morositas *f*

ill-tempered *adj* iracundus, acerbus, stomachosus; difficilis

ill-treat *vt* lacesso ③

illuminate *vt* illustro; illumino ①

illumination *n* lux *f*; lumen *nt*; festi ignes *mpl*

illusion *n* error *m*

illusory *adj* fallax

illustrate *vt* illustro; *fig* explano ①; patefacio ③

illustration *n* illustratio *f*; *fig* exemplum *nt*

illustrious *adj* clarus, illustris, praeclarus, inclutus, insignis

ill will *n* malevolentia, malitia, malignitas *f*

image *n* simulacrum *nt*; (likeness, portrait) effigies, imago *f*; (form) species, forma *f*

imaginary *adj* (unreal) imaginarius, fictus, falsus

imagination *n* cogitatio; imaginatio *f*; (dream) somnium *nt*

imaginative *adj* ingeniosus

imagine *vt* imaginor ①; fingo ③; (think) existimo, arbitror ①; (guess) conicio ③; (dream) somnio ①

imbecile *n* fatuus *m*

imbecility *n* imbecillitas animi *f*

imitate *vt* imitor, assimulo ①

imitation *n* imitatio *f*; imitamentum *nt*

immaculate *adj* castus, integer, inviolatus

immaterial *adj* simplex, incorporalis; (unimportant) levis

immature *adj* immaturus

immaturity *n* immaturitas *f*

immeasurable *adj* immensus, infinitus

immediate *adj* praesens
■ **~ly** *adv* confestim, extemplo, protinus; continuo

immemorial *adj*
□ **from time ~** ex omni memoria aetatum

immense *adj* ingens, immensus, enormis
■ **~ly** *adv* immensum, multum

immensity *n* immensitas; vastitas *f*

immerse *vt* mergo, demergo, immergo ③

immersion *n* immersio *f*

immigrant *n* advena *m/f*

imminent *adj* instans, praesens

immobile *adj* immobilis

immobility *n* immobilitas *f*

immoderate *adj* immodicus, nimius, immoderatus

immoral *adj* corruptus, pravus, improbus

immorality *n* improbitas morum *f*

immortal *adj* immortalis; aeternus

immortality *n* immortalitas *f*

immortalize *vt* aeterno ①; immortalem reddo ③

immovable *adj* immobilis;

immotus

immune adj immunis

immunity n immunitas f

impact n impetus m

impair vt laedo; imminuo; attero ③; debilito ①

impart vt impertio ④; communico ①

impartial adj aequus
■ ~**ly** adv sine ira et studio

impartiality n aequitas, aequabilitas f

impassable adj insuperabilis, invius, impervius

impassioned adj vehemens, ardens

impatience n impatientia f

impatient adj impatiens; iracundus
■ ~**ly** adv impatienter

impeach vt accuso ①

impede vt impedio ④; retardo ①

impediment n impedimentum nt; mora f; (in speech) haesitatio f

impel vt impello ③; excito, stimulo ①; cieo ②

impending adj praesens

impenetrable adj impenetrabilis, impervius; fig occultus

imperceptible adj quod sensu percipi non potest

imperceptibly adv (little by little) sensim; (step by step) pedetentim; obscure

imperfect adj imperfectus, mancus; (faulty) mendosus; vitiosus

imperfection n defectus m; vitium nt

imperial adj imperatorius; imperialis

imperious adj imperiosus; superbus; arrogans

imperishable adj perennis; fig immortalis

impersonate vt partes (alicuius) sustineo ②

impersonation n partes (actoris) fpl

impertinence n insolentia f

impertinent adj insolens; (things) ineptus, absurdus
■ ~**ly** adv insolenter

impervious adj impervius; (inexorable) inexorabilis

impetuous adj vehemens, fervidus
■ ~**ly** adv vehementer

impetus n vis f; impetus, impulsus m

impious adj impius; scelestus, sceleratus; nefandus, nefarius
■ ~**ly** adv impie; sceleste, scelerate; nefarie

implacable adj implacabilis, inexorabilis

implant vt ingigno; insero ③

implement n instrumentum nt; arma ntpl

implicate vt implico ①
□ **be ~d** particeps sum ir

implicit adj tacitus
■ ~**ly** adv tacite

implore vt imploro, obsecro, supplico, obtestor ①

imply vt significo ①
□ **be implied** subsum ir

impolite adj inurbanus
■ ~**ly** adv inurbane

impoliteness n rusticitas, importunitas f

import[1] vt importo ①; inveho ③;

(mean) significo 🗆

import[2] *n* (meaning) significatio; (of goods) invectio *f*

importance *n* momentum, pondus *nt*; gravitas *f*

important *adj* magni momenti, gravis

importer *n* qui merces peregrinas invehit

impose *vt* (a task) iniungo, impono ③

□ ~ **upon** (deceive) fraudo 🗆

impossibility *n* impossibilitas *f*

impossible *adj* impossibilis

impostor *n* fraudator, praestigiator *m*; planus *m*

impotent *adj* infirmus, impotens

impound *vt* confisco 🗆; (animals) includo ③

impoverish *vt* pauperem reddo ③; fig vitio 🗆

impracticable *adj* quod fieri non potest

impregnable *adj* inexpugnabilis

impress *vt* (stamp, imprint) imprimo ③; (mark) signo 🗆; fig inculco 🗆; (move) moveo ②

impression *n* (stamping) impressio *f*; (track, footstep) vestigium *nt*; (of a book) editio *f*; fig animi motus *m*; (effect) momentum *nt*

impressive *adj* gravis

imprint[1] *n* (mark) vestigium *nt*

imprint[2] *vt* imprimo ③

imprison *vt* includo, in vincula conicio ③

imprisonment *n* captivitas, custodia *f*

improbable *adj* haud verisimilis

impromptu *adj* ex tempore dictus

improper *adj* indecorus; indignus

impropriety *n* improprietas *f*; indecorum *nt*

improve *vt* emendo 🗆; excolo, corrigo ③

■ ~ *vi* melior fio *ir*, proficio ③

improvement *n* cultura *f*; (progress) profectus *m*

improvise *vt* ex tempore dico or compono ③

impudence *n* impudentia, procacitas, protervitas *f*

impudent *adj* impudens; procax, protervus

■ ~**ly** *adv* impudenter; procaciter, proterve

impulse *n* impulsus, impetus *m*

impulsive *adj* vehemens, ardens, temerarius

impunity *n*

□ **with** ~ impune

impure *adj* (of morals) impurus; incestus; impudicus

impurity *n* impuritas *f*

impute *vt* (ascribe) attribuo ③; do 🗆; verto ③; (as a fault) imputo 🗆

in *prep* in + *abl*; (in the works of) apud + *acc*

inability *n* infirmitas; (lack of means) inopia *f*

inaccessible *adj* inaccessus, difficilis aditu

inaccuracy *n* neglegentia *f*; error *m*

inaccurate *adj* parum accuratus, minime exactus; falsus

inactive *adj* iners, ignavus, otiosus

inactivity *n* inertia, socordia; cessatio *f*

inadequate *adj* impar; mancus

■ ~**ly** *adv* haud satis

inadvertent *adj* imprudens
■ **~ly** *adv* imprudenter

inane *adj* ineptus

inanimate *adj* inanimus

inanity *n* ineptiae *fpl*

inapplicable *adj*
□ **be ~** non pertineo ad + *acc*

inappropriate *adj* haud idoneus, parum aptus

inarticulate *adj* indistinctus, confusus

inattention *n* animus parum attentus *m*; neglegentia, incuria *f*

inattentive *adj* haud or parum attentus; neglegens
■ **~ly** *adv* animo parum attento; neglegenter

inaudible *adj* quod audiri nequit

inaugurate *vt* inauguro ①

inauguration *n* inauguratio, consecratio *f*

inauspicious *adj* infaustus; infelix, funestus

inborn *adj* ingenitus, innatus, insitus

inbred *adj* ingenitus, innatus, insitus

incalculable *adj* quod aestimari nequit; fig immensus; incredibilis

incapable *adj* inhabilis, imperitus

incapacitate *vt* noceo ② + *dat*; laedo ③

incense[1] *n* tus *nt*

incense[2] *vt* exaspero ①; incendo ③

incentive *n* incitamentum *nt*; stimulus *m*

incessant *adj* continuus, assiduus, perpetuus
■ **~ly** *adv* assidue; perpetuo

incest *n* incestum *nt*; incestus *m*

incestuous *adj* incestus

inch *n* uncia *f*
□ **~ by ~** unciatim; fig paulatim, sensim

incident *n* (event) eventus *m*; res *f*; casus *m*

incidental *adj* fortuitus
■ **~ly** *adv* fortuito

incision *n* incisura *f*; incisus *m*

incisive *adj* acer, acerbus

incite *vt* incito, stimulo ①; impello ③

incitement *n* incitamentum *nt*; incitatio *f*; stimulus *m*

inclination *n* (tilt) inclinatio; (slope) acclivitas; fig voluntas, inclinatio *f*

incline[1] *vt* inclino ①; fig adduco ③; inclino ①
■ **~** *vi* propendeo ②; inclino ①

incline[2] *n* acclivitas *f*

inclined *adj* proclivis; propensus

include *vt* includo, comprehendo ③

incognito *adv* dissimulato nomine

incoherent *adj* confusus

income *n* reditus; fructus *m*

incomparable *adj* incomparabilis, unicus

incompatibility *n* repugnantia *f*

incompatible *adj* discors, repugnans, contrarius

incompetence *n* inscitia, imperitia *f*

incompetent *adj* inhabilis; inscitus, imperitus

incomplete *adj* imperfectus, incohatus; mancus

incomprehensible *adj* quod comprehendi non potest

inconceivable *adj* quod cogitari or mente percipi non potest

inconclusive *adj* levis; infirmus

incongruous *adj* inconveniens, male congruens
■ **~ly** *adv* parum apte

inconsiderate *adj* inconsideratus

inconsistency *n* inconstantia, mutabilitas; repugnantia *f*

inconsistent *adj* inconstans; contrarius, absonus
■ **~ly** *adv* inconstanter

inconsolable *adj* inconsolabilis

inconspicuous *adj* obscurus

inconstant *adj* inconstans, levis, mutabilis, mobilis

incontrovertible *adj* certus

inconvenience¹ *n* incommodum *nt*

inconvenience² *vt* incommodo ①

inconvenient *adj* incommodus; molestus
■ **~ly** *adv* incommode

incorporate *vt* adiungo ③; admisceo ②

incorrect *adj* mendosus, falsus

incorrigible *adj* insanabilis

increase¹ *vt* augeo ②; amplifico ①
■ **~ vi** augeor ②; cresco; ingravesco ③

increase² *n* incrementum *nt*; auctus *m*

incredible *adj* incredibilis

incredibly *adv* incredibiliter; incredibile quantum; ultra fidem

incredulity *n* incredulitas *f*

incredulous *adj* incredulus

incriminate *vt* accuso ①

incubate *vi* incubo ①

incubation *n* incubatio *f*; incubitus *m*

inculcate *vt* inculco ①

incur *vt* incurro ③ in + *acc*; mereor ②

incurable *adj* insanabilis, immedicabilis

indebted *adj* obaeratus
□ **I am ~ to you for this** hoc tibi debeo ②

indecency *n* indecorum *nt*; indignitas *f*

indecent *adj* indecens, indecorus
■ **~ly** *adv* indecenter, indecore

indecision *n* haesitatio, dubitatio *f*

indecisive *adj* dubius, incertus, anceps, ambiguus

indeed *adv* (it is true) re vera, profecto
□ **~?** itane?
□ **very good ~** vel optimum

indefinite *adj* incertus; anceps, obscurus

indelible *adj* indelebilis

indemnity *n* indemnitas *f*
□ **act of ~** impunitas *f*

indentation *n* incisura *f*

independence *n* libertas *f*

independent *adj* sui potens; liber; *fig* sui iuris
■ **~ly** *adv* libere; suis legibus; (each by itself) singillatim

indescribable *adj* inenarrabilis, infandus

index *n* (of a book) index *m*; *fig* indicium *nt*

indicate *vt* indico; significo ①

indication *n* signum, indicium *nt*

indict *vt* accuso ①; defero ③

indictment *n* (accusation) accusatio *f*

indifference n (neutrality) aequus animus m; (carelessness) neglegentia f; (contempt) contemptus m

indifferent adj aequus, medius; remissus, neglegens, frigidus

indigent adj egens, inops

indigestion n cruditas f

indignant adj indignans, indignabundus, iratus
■ ~ly adv indignanter

indignation n indignatio; ira f

indirect adj obliquus
■ ~ly adv oblique
□ touch on ~ly perstringo ③

indiscreet adj inconsultus

indiscretion n imprudentia f

indiscriminate adj promiscuus
■ ~ly adv promiscue

indispensable adj necessarius

indisposed adj (in health) minus valens

indisposition adj (illness) aegrotatio, commotiuncula f

indisputable adj certus; haud dubius

indisputably adv haud dubie

indistinct adj indistinctus, obscurus

individual[1] adj individuus, proprius
■ ~ly adv singillatim

individual[2] n homo m

indolence n inertia, desidia, ignavia, socordia f

indolent adj iners, ignavus, deses, socors, segnis

indomitable adj indomitus, invictus

indoor adj domesticus, umbratilis

indoors adv domi

indubitable adj indubitabilis, haud dubius, certus

indubitably adv haud dubie

induce vt adduco, impello ③; persuadeo ② + dat; incito ①

inducement n incitamentum nt; causa f; stimulus m

indulge vt (in) indulgeo ② + dat

indulgence n indulgentia; (pardon) venia; (kindness) clementia f

indulgent adj indulgens, facilis, clemens
■ ~ly adv indulgenter, clementer

industrious adj industrius; diligens; sedulus; strenuus
■ ~ly adv industrie, diligenter, sedulo, strenue

industry n industria; sedulitas; diligentia f; studium nt; (manufacturing) officina f

inebriated adj ebrius

ineffective adj inefficax, inutilis

ineffectual adj inefficax, inutilis

inefficiency n inutilitas f

inefficient adj inefficax; inhabilis; inutilis

inelegant adj inelegans; inconcinnus

inept adj ineptus

inequality n inaequalitas f

inert adj iners, segnis

inertia n inertia f

inevitable adj ▶ unavoidable

inexcusable adj inexcusabilis

inexhaustible adj inexhaustus

inexorable adj inexorabilis, durus, implacabilis

inexpensive adj vilis

inexperience n imperitia, inscitia f

inexperienced adj imperitus; inexpertus inscitus; rudis

inexplicable adj inexplicabilis, inenodabilis

inexpressible adj inenarrabilis, infandus

infallible adj qui errare non potest; certus, haud dubius

infallibly adv haud dubie

infamous adj infamis; turpis, inhonestus, foedus, ignominiosus

infamy n infamia, ignominia f; opprobrium, probrum nt

infancy n infantia, aetas iniens f

infant n infans m/f

infantile adj infantilis, puerilis

infantry n peditatus m; pedestres copiae fpl

infatuated adj:
□ be ~ with depereo ④

infect vt inficio ③; contamino ①

infection n contagium nt; contagio f; contactus m

infectious adj contagiosus

infer vt conicio, infero, colligo ③

inference n coniectura, conclusio f

inferior[1] adj inferior, deterior, minor

inferior[2] n impar m/f

infernal adj infernus

infertile adj sterilis

infertility n sterilitas f

infidelity n infidelitas f

infinite adj infinitus; immensus
■ ~ly adv infinite; infinito

infinity n infinitas, infinitio f

infirm adj infirmus, debilis, imbecillus

infirmity n infirmitas,

imbecillitas, debilitas f

inflame vt inflammo ①; incendo ③

inflammation n inflammatio f

inflammatory adj turbulentus, seditiosus

inflate vt (also fig) inflo ①
□ be ~d tumeo ②

inflexibility n rigor m

inflexible adj rigidus; fig obstinatus

inflict vt infligo; impono ③; irrogo ①

influence[1] n momentum, pondus nt; auctoritas, gratia f; (prompting) impulsus m

influence[2] vt moveo ②; impello ③; valeo ②

influential adj (auctoritate) gravis, potens

inform vt (teach) doceo ②; instruo; (give information) certiorem facio; (against) defero ③

informal adj privatus

informant n (messenger) nuntius m

information n (news) nuntius m; (knowledge) scientia f

informer n delator m

infringe vt violo ①

infringement n violatio f

infuriate vt effero, exaspero ①

ingenious adj sollers; subtilis; ingeniosus

ingenuity n ingenium nt

ingot n later m

ingrained adj insitus, inveteratus

ingratiate vi (oneself) gratiam ineo ir apud (aliquem) ④; gratiam (mihi) concilio ①

ingratitude n animus ingratus m; beneficii oblivio f

ingredient n pars f

inhabit vt colo, incolo ③; habito ①

inhabitant n incola m/f; habitator, colonus m

inhale vt duco ③; haurio ④

inherent adj inhaerens, proprius

inherit vt hereditate accipio ③

inheritance n hereditas f; patrimonium nt

inhibit vt coerceo ②

inhospitable adj inhospitalis, inhospitus

inhuman adj inhumanus; crudelis
  ■ ~ly adv inhumane; crudeliter

inhumanity n inhumanitas; crudelitas f

inimitable adj inimitabilis

initial adj primus
  ■ ~ n prima verbi littera f

initiate vt initio ①

initiation n initiatio f; initiamenta ntpl

initiative n
  □ **take the ~** initium capio ③

inject vt infundo, immitto ③

injection n (act) infusio f; infusus m

injure vt noceo ② + dat; laedo; offendo ③

injury n iniuria f; damnum, detrimentum nt

injustice n iniustitia; iniquitas; iniuria f

ink n atramentum nt

inkling n (hint) rumusculus m; (suspicion) suspicio f

inlet n (of the sea) aestuarium nt

inmate n incola, inquilinus m

inmost adj intimus, imus
  □ **~ recesses** penetralia ntpl

inn n caupona, taberna f; deversorium, hospitium nt

innate adj innatus; insitus; ingenitus

inner adj interior

innermost adj intimus; imus

innkeeper n caupo m

innocence n innocentia; integritas; castitas f

innocent adj innocuus; innocens; insons; (chaste) castus
  ■ ~ly adv innocue; innocenter; caste

innocuous adj innocuus

innovation n res novae fpl

innumerable adj innumerabilis, innumerus

inoffensive adj innocens, innoxius

inopportune adj intempestivus

inordinate adj immoderatus
  ■ ~ly adv immoderate

inquest n inquisitio f

inquire vt&i quaero, inquiro ③; investigo ①

inquiry n inquisitio f

inquisitive adj curiosus
  ■ ~ly adv curiose

inroad n incursio, irruptio f
  □ **make ~s into** incurro ③ in + acc

insane adj insanus; vecors; amens; demens

insanity n insania, dementia; amentia, vecordia f

insatiable adj insatiabilis, inexplebilis, inexpletus

inscribe vt inscribo; insculpo; incido ③

inscription n inscriptio f; titulus m; carmen nt

insect n insectum nt

insecure adj intutus, periculosus; infestus, lubricus

insecurity n periculum nt

inseparable adj inseparabilis

insert vt insero; ascribo, interpono ③

inside[1] n interior pars f; interiora ntpl

inside[2] adj interior
■ ~ adv intrinsecus; intra, intro, intus
■ ~ prep intra + acc

insidious adj insidiosus; subdolus
■ ~**ly** adv insidiose; subdole

insight n prudentia, cognitio f

insignificant adj exiguus; nullius momenti; levis

insincere adj insincerus, simulatus; fallax; dolosus

insincerity n fallacia; simulatio f

insinuate vt
□ ~ **oneself into** irrepo ③; (hint) significo ①

insinuation n insinuatio f; (suspicion) suspicio f
□ **make ~s against** oblique perstringo ③

insipid adj insulsus; fig hebes; frigidus

insist vi insto ①; urgeo ②; exigo ③
□ ~ **on** flagito ①

insolence n insolentia, arrogantia, superbia f

insolent adj insolens, arrogans, superbus
■ ~**ly** adv insolenter; impudenter; superbe

inspect vt inspicio, introspicio ③

inspection n inspectio; cura f

inspector n curator; praefectus m

inspiration n (divine) afflatus m; numen nt; instinctus m

inspire vt inspiro ①; inicio ③; (kindle) incendo ③; excito ①

instability n instabilitas, inconstantia f

install vt inauguro ①; constituo ③

instalment n (payment in part) pensio, portio f

instance n exemplum nt
□ **for ~** exempli gratia

instant[1] adj (immediate) praesens
□ ~**ly** adv (at once) statim

instant[2] n momentum, punctum temporis nt
□ **this ~** statim, actutum

instantaneous adj quod momento temporis fit
■ ~**ly** adv continuo; statim

instead adv
□ ~ **of** loco, vice both + gen; pro + abl

instigate vt instigo, stimulo, incito ①; cieo ②

instigation n incitatio f; stimulus m

instil vt instillo ①

instinct n natura f

instinctive adj naturalis
■ ~**ly** adv naturaliter

institution n (thing instituted) institutum nt

instruct vt (teach) doceo ②; instruo, instituo ③; erudio ④; (order, command) mando ①

instruction n institutio, disciplina f; (order, commission) mandatum nt

instructor n praeceptor, magister m; magistra f

instrument n instrumentum nt

instrumental adj aptus, utilis

insubordinate adj seditiosus

insubordination n seditio f; tumultus m

insufferable adj intolerandus, intolerabilis

insufficiency n inopia, egestas f

insufficient adj non or parum sufficiens, impar
■ ~ly adv haud satis

insulate vt insulo ①

insult¹ n opprobrium, probrum, convicium nt; contumelia f

insult² vt maledico ③ + dat

insulting adj contumeliosus

insurmountable adj inexsuperabilis, insuperabilis

insurrection n rebellio, seditio f; tumultus m

intact adj integer; incolumis

integral adj necessarius

integrity n integritas, probitas; sinceritas, innocentia f

intellect n intellectus m; intellegentia, mens f

intelligence n ingenium nt; (cleverness) sollertia f; (news) nuntius m

intelligent adj intellegens; sollers
■ ~ly adv intellegenter

intelligible adj intellegibilis

intend vt destino ①; (resolve) constituo, decerno ③

intense adj acer, vehemens; (excessive) nimius
■ ~ly adv acriter; vehementer; (extremely) valde, magnopere

intensity n vehementia, vis f; (of winter, etc.) asperitas f

intent¹ adj intentus, attentus

■ ~ly adv intente

intent² n consilium, propositum nt; (meaning) significatio f

intention n consilium, propositum nt

intentionally adv de industria, consilio, consulto

intercede vi intercedo ③; deprecor ①

intercept vt intercipio, intercludo; deprehendo ③

interchange¹ vt permuto, commuto ①

interchange² n permutatio; vicissitudo f

intercourse n (sexual) coitus, concubitus m

interest¹ vt teneo ②; capio ③; delecto ①

interest² n (advantage) emolumentum nt; utilitas f; (for money) faenus nt, usura f; (concern) studium nt

interesting adj (appealing) iucundus

interfere vi intercedo ③; intervenio ④; (hinder) obsto ① + dat

interference n intercessio f; interventus m

interim n intervallum nt
□ in the ~ interim

interior¹ adj interior, internus

interior² n pars interior f

interjection n interiectio f

interlude n (entr'acte) embolium nt

intermarriage n conubium nt

intermediate adj medius

interminable adj infinitus

intermingle vt intermisceo, immisceo ②

ntermission n intermissio; cessatio, remissio f

ntermittent adj rarus

nternal adj intestinus, domesticus
■ ~**ly** adv intus

nternational adj
■ ~ **law** n ius gentium nt

nterpret vt interpretor ①; (figure out) conicio ③

nterpretation n interpretatio, coniectio f

nterpreter n interpres m/f

nterrogate vt interrogo, percontor ①

nterrogation n interrogatio, percontatio f

nterrupt vt interrumpo, intermitto ③; interpello ①

nterruption n interruptio; interpellatio f

ntersect vt interseco ①

ntersection n decussatio f

ntersperse vt intermisceo, immisceo ②

nterval n intervallum, spatium nt

ntervene vi (be between) interiaceo ②; (come between) intercedo ③; (hinder) intervenio ④ + dat

ntervening adj medius

ntervention n interventus, interiectus m

nterview¹ n colloquium nt; congressus m

nterview² vt convenio ④

nterweave vt intertexo; intexo ③

ntestines npl intestina; viscera ntpl

ntimacy n familiaritas, consuetudo f

intimate adj familiaris, intimus
■ ~**ly** adv familiariter, intime

intimidate vt metum inicio ③; minor ① + dat; terreo ②

intimidation n minae fpl

into prep in + acc

intolerable adj intolerabilis, intolerandus

intolerance n intolerantia, impatientia f

intolerant adj intolerans, impatiens

intoxicate vt ebrium reddo ③

intoxication n ebrietas f

intrepid adj intrepidus, impavidus

intricacy n ambages fpl

intricate adj contortus, perplexus
■ ~**ly** adv contorte; perplexe

intrigue n consilium clandestinum nt; fraus, ars f; (amour) amores mpl

intrinsic adj internus; innatus
■ ~**ally** adv intrinsecus

introduce vt introduco; (institute) instituo ③

introduction n inductio; (to a person) introductio; (preface) praefatio f; exordium, prooemium nt

introductory adj introductorius

intrude vt&i immitto, me immitto ③; molestus sum ir

intrusion n importunitas; usurpatio f

intrusive adj molestus

inundate vt inundo ①

inundation n inundatio f; diluvium nt

inure vt assuefacio ③

invade vt invado, irrumpo, bellum infero ③

invader n invasor m

invalid[1] adj infirmus, vitiosus, nugatorius, irritus

invalid[2] n aeger, aegrotus, valetudinarius m

invalidate vt irritum reddo; rescindo ③

invaluable adj inaestimabilis

invariable adj constans, immutabilis, immobilis

invariably adv immutabiliter; semper

invasion n incursio, irruptio f

invective n convicium nt

inveigle vt illicio, pellicio ③

invent vt invenio, reperio ④; (contrive) excogito ①; fingo ③

invention n (act) inventio f; (thing invented) inventum nt; (lie, etc.) commentum nt

inventive adj habilis, ingeniosus

inventor n inventor, repertor m

inventress n inventrix f

inverse adj inversus, conversus

inversion n inversio, conversio f

invert vt inverto ③

invest vt do, mando; (money) colloco ①; pono ③; (besiege) obsideo ②

investigate vt investigo, indago, scrutor ①; inquiro, cognosco ③

investigation n investigatio, inquisitio f

investment n (of money) pecunia in faenore posita

inveterate adj inveteratus

invidious adj invidus, malignus, invidiosus

■ ~**ly** adv invidiose; maligne

invigorate vt corroboro, confirmo ①

invincible adj invictus; insuperabilis

invisible adj invisibilis

invitation n invitatio f

invite vt invito, voco ①

inviting adj gratus, blandus, suavis

invocation n obtestatio f

invoke vt invoco, imploro, obtestor ①

involuntary adj invitus, coactus

involve vt (contain) contineo ②; (entangle) implico ①; (imply) habeo ②

involved adj (intricate) perplexus

invulnerable adj invulnerabilis

inward adj interior

inwardly adv intus, intrinsecus, introrsus

inwards adv intus, intrinsecus, introrsus

irascible adj iracundus

irate adj iratus

iris n (plant) iris f

irksome adj molestus, odiosus

iron[1] n ferrum nt

■ ~**s** pl vincula ntpl

iron[2] adj ferreus; fig durus

ironic adj (also **ironical**) deridens

■ ~**ally** adv ironice

ironmonger n negotiator ferrarius m

irony n ironia, dissimulatio f

irrational adj rationis expers, irrationalis

irreconcilable adj implacabilis; (incompatible) repugnans

irrefutable *adj* quod confutari non potest

irregular *adj* (disorderly) tumultuarius; (spasmodic) rarus, infrequens; (uneven) iniquus

irrelevant *adj* non pertinens, alienus

irreligious *adj* impius, irreligiosus, religionis neglegens

irreparable *adj* irreparabilis; irrevocabilis

irresistible *adj* invictus; cui nullo modo resisti potest

irresolute *adj* incertus animi; dubius; parum firmus
■ **∼ly** *adv* dubitanter

irresolution *n* dubitatio *f*; animus parum firmus *m*

irresponsible *adj* levis

irreverent *adj* irreverens, parum reverens

irrevocable *adj* irrevocabilis

irrigate *vt* rigo, irrigo ①

irrigation *n* irrigatio, inductio aquae *f*

irritability *n* iracundia *f*

irritable *adj* irritabilis, stomachosus, iracundus

irritate *vt* irrito; inflammo ①

irritation *n* irritatio *f*; stomachus *m*; ira *f*

island *n* insula *f*

isolate *vt* seiungo, secerno ③

isolation *n* solitudo *f*

issue¹ *n* (outlet) egressus *m*; (result) eventus, exitus *m*; (end) finis *m/f*; (matter) res *f*; (offspring) liberi *mpl*; (of money) erogatio *f*; (profit) reditus *m*

issue² *vt* (publish) edo; (post up) propono ③; (money) erogo ①
■ **∼** *vi* emano ①; egredior ③; (end)

evenio ④

isthmus *n* isthmus *m*

it *pn* id, hoc

Italy *n* Italia *f*

itch¹ *n* scabies, prurigo *f*

itch² *vi* prurio ④

itchy *adj* scabrosus

item *n* res *f*

itinerary *n* itinerarium *n*

itself *pn* ipsum

ivory¹ *n* ebur *nt*

ivory² *adj* eburneus; eburnus

ivy *n* hedera *f*

Jj

jackal *n* canis aureus *m*

jackdaw *n* monedula *f*

jade *n* (horse) caballus *m*; fig (woman) importuna mulier *f*

jaded *adj* defessus

jagged *adj* dentatus, serratus

jail¹ *n* carcer *m*

jail² *vt* in carcerem conicio ③

jailer *n* custos *m*

jam¹ *n* conditae baccae *fpl*

jam² *vt* comprimo ③

jangle *vi* (make a jangling sound) tinnio ④; tintinno ①

January *n* Ianuarius *m*

jar¹ *n* (pitcher, bottle, cask) olla; amphora *f*; urceus *m*

jar² *vi* discrepo, discordo ①

jargon *n* confusae voces *fpl*; barbarus sermo *m*

jarring adj dissonus, discors
jasper n iaspis f
jaundice n morbus regius, icterus m
jaundiced adj ictericus; fig morosus; invidiosus
jaunt n excursio f
javelin n pilum, iaculum; telum, veru nt
jaw n mala; maxilla f; fig fauces fpl
jawbone n maxilla f
jay n corvus glandarius m
jealous adj invidus; aemulus; invidiosus
jealousy n invidia; aemulatio f; livor m
jeer¹ vi derideo, irrideo ②
jeer² n risus; irrisus m
jelly n cylon, quilon nt
jellyfish n pulmo, halipleumon m
jeopardize vt in periculum adduco ③
jeopardy n periculum, discrimen nt
jerk¹ n impetus, subitus motus m
jerk² vt subito moveo ②
jest¹ n iocus, lusus m; facetiae fpl
□ **in ~** ioco, iocose
jest² vi iocor ①; ludo ③
jester n ioculator; (buffoon) scurra m
jet n (spout of water) scatebra f; (mineral) gagates m
jet-black adj nigerrimus
jetty n moles, pila f
Jew n Iudaeus m
jewel n gemma f
jewelled adj gemmeus, gemmifer
jeweller n gemmarius m
jewellery n gemmae fpl

jig n saltatio f
jilt vt fallo ③
jingle vi tinnio ④
jingling n tinnitus m
job n negotiolum nt; res lucrosa f
jockey n agaso m
jocular adj iocularis, iocosus, facetus
■ **~ly** adv ioculariter, facete, iocose
jocularity n facetiae fpl, animus iocosus m
jog vt concutio, quatio ③
join vt iungo, coniungo ③; (border on) contingo ③
■ **~** vi adiungor ③; cohaereo ②
□ **~ battle** vi confligo, manum consero ③; congredior ③ cum + abl
□ **~ in** (take part in) particeps or socius sum ir + gen
joiner n lignarius m
joint n commissura f; articulus m; vertebra; iunctura f
jointly adv coniuncte, coniunctim, una, communiter
joist n tignum transversarium nt
joke¹ n iocus m; sales mpl; facetiae fpl
joke² vt&i (at) iocor ①; ludo ③; irrideo ②
joker n ioculator m
jollity n festivitas, hilaritas f
jolly adj festivus, hilaris
jolt¹ vt concutio ③; iacto, quasso ①
■ **~** vi concutior ③; iactor, quassor ①
jolt² n iactatio f
jostle vt pulso, deturbo ①
journal n ephemeris f; diarium nt; (newspaper) acta diurna ntpl

journey n iter nt; profectio f; via f

Jove n Iupiter m

jovial adj hilaris, festivus

joviality n hilaritas, festivitas f

joy n gaudium nt; laetitia f

joyful adj laetus, hilaris
■ ~ly adv laete, hilare; libenter

joyous adj laetus, hilaris
■ ~ly adv laete, hilare; libenter

jubilant adj laetitia exsultans; ovans

jubilation n triumphus m; gaudium nt

Judaism n Iudaismus m

judge¹ n iudex; quaesitor, arbiter; (critic) existimator, censor m; (umpire) arbiter m

judge² vt&i iudico; existimo ①; censeo ②; (value) aestimo ①

judgment n sententia f; arbitrium; fig (opinion, faculty of judging) iudicium nt

judicial adj iudicialis

judicious adj sapiens, prudens
■ ~ly adv sapienter, prudenter

jug n urceus m

juggle vi praestigias ago ③

juggler n praestigiator; pilarius m

juggling n praestigiae fpl

juice n sucus m

juicy adj sucosus

July n Quintilis m

jumble¹ vt confundo ③; permisceo ②

jumble² n confusio, congeries, strages f

jump¹ vi salio, exsilio ④; exsulto ①

jump² n saltus m

junction n coniunctio, iunctura f

June n Iunius m

jungle n locus virgultis obsitus m

junior adj & n iunior, minor

jurisdiction n iurisdictio f

juror n iudex m

jury n iudices mpl

just¹ adj iustus; meritus; aequus

just² adv (a moment ago) modo; (only) modo; (only just) vix
□ ~ **so** haud secus

justice n iustitia, aequitas f

justifiable adj excusandus

justifiably adv iure; cum causa, excusate

justification n excusatio, purgatio f

justify vt purgo; excuso ①

justly adv iuste; iure; merito

jut vi (out) promineo ②; procurro ③

juvenile adj iuvenilis, puerilis

· ·

Kk

· ·

Kalends n Kalendae fpl

keel n carina f

keen adj acer; alacer; sagax; (sharp) acutus
■ ~ly adv acute, acriter; sagaciter

keenness n sagacitas, subtilitas f

keen-sighted adj perspicax

keep¹ vt teneo; habeo ②; (preserve) servo, conservo ①; (guard) custodio ④; (store) recondo ③; (support, sustain) alo ③; sustineo ②; (animals) pasco ③; (a holiday) celebro ①; ago ③; (reserve) reservo ①; (one's word, law,

etc.) servo 1
■ *vi* maneo 2; duro 1
□ ~ **away** *vt* arceo, prohibeo; *vi* abstineo 2
□ ~ **back** retineo, cohibeo 2; (conceal) celo 1
□ ~ **company** comitor 1
□ ~ **down** comprimo 3
□ ~ **from** *vt* prohibeo 2; *vi* abstineo 2
□ ~ **in** includo 3
□ ~ **off** ▶ ~ **away**
□ ~ **on** *vi* persevero 1
□ ~ **out** *vt* excludo 3
□ ~ **up** (maintain) *vt* tueor 2; sustineo 2; *vi* subsequor 3

keep² *n* (citadel) arx *f*; (food) cibus *m*
keeper *n* custos *m/f*
keeping *n* tutela; custodia; cura *f*
keepsake *n* pignus *nt*
keg *n* cadus *m*; testa *f*
kennel *n* cubile *nt*; stabulum *nt*
kernel *n* (of a fruit) nucleus *m*
kettle *n* lebes *m*; aenum *nt*
key *n* clavis *f*; (key position controlling access) claustra *ntpl*; fig cardo *m*
kick¹ *vi* calcitro 1; calce ferio 4
kick² *n* calcitratus *m*
kid *n* (young goat) haedus *m*
kidnap *vt* surripio 3
kidnapper *n* plagiarius *m*
kidneys *n* renes *mpl*
kill *vt* interficio, caedo, occido, interimo, perimo 3; neco 1
killer *n* interfector *m*
kiln *n* fornax *f*
kin *n* consanguinitas *f*; genus *nt*; ▶ **relation**
kind¹ *n* genus *nt*; modus *m*; species *f*
□ **of what** ~ qualis, cuiusmodi

□ **of such a** ~ talis, eiusmodi
kind² *adj* amicus; benignus; benevolus; comis; humanus; suavis
kind-hearted *adj* benignus
kindle *vt* accendo 3; fig inflammo 1
■ *vi* exardesco 3
kindly *adj* ▶ **kind**
■ ~ *adv* amice; benigne; humane; comiter
kindness *n* benignitas; humanitas *f*; (kind act) beneficium *nt*
king *n* rex *m*
kingdom *n* regnum *nt*
kingfisher *n* alcedo *f*
kinsman *n* necessarius, cognatus, consanguineus *m*
kiss¹ *n* suavium, osculum, basium *nt*
kiss² *vt* suavior, osculor, basio 1
kit *n* impedimenta *ntpl*
kitchen *n* culina *f*
kite *n* (bird) milvus *m*
kitten *n* catulus felinus *m*
knack *n* ars, sollertia *f*
knapsack *n* sarcina *f*
knavish *adj* scelestus, nefarius
knead *vt* depso, subigo 3
knee *n* genu *nt*
kneecap *n* patella *f*
kneel *vi* in genua procumbo, genibus nitor 3
knife *n* culter, cultellus *m*
knight *n* eques *m*
knighthood *n* equestris dignitas *f*
knit *vt*
□ ~ **the brow** supercilium (frontem) contraho 3
knob *n* tuber *nt*; nodus *m*; (of a

door) bulla f

knock¹ vt&i pulso ①; ferio ④; tundo ③
- □ ~ **against** (one's head, etc.) offendo ③
- □ ~ **at** (a door), pulso ①; ferio ④
- □ ~ **down** deicio, sterno ③; fig (at an auction) addico (bona alicui) ③
- □ ~ **over** deturbo ①
- □ ~ **up** (awake) suscito ①

knock² n pulsatio f

knock-kneed adj varus

knoll n tumulus m

knot¹ n nodus m; geniculum nt; fig (of people) circulus m; fig difficultas f

knot² vt nodo ①

knotty adj nodosus; fig spinosus, difficilis

know vt scio ④; (learn, become acquainted with) cognosco ③; (be acquainted with) nosco ③
- □ ~ **how to** scio ④ + inf
- □ **not** ~ ignoro ①
- □ ~ **again** recognosco ③

knowing adj sciens, prudens; (cunning) astutus
- ■ **~ly** adv scienter; prudenter; (cunningly) astute

knowledge n scientia, cognitio; (skill) peritia; (learning) eruditio f; (understanding) intellectus m

knowledgeable adj sciens

known adj notus
- □ **be** ~ enotesco ③
- □ **it is** ~ constat
- □ **become** ~ emano ①
- □ **make** ~ palam facio ③; divulgo ①
- □ **well** ~ (famous) celeber

knuckle n condylus, articulus m
- ■ **~-bones** pl (game) tali mpl

L l

label¹ n titulus m

label² vt titulum affigo ③

laborious adj laboriosus; (difficult) operosus
- ■ **~ly** adv laboriose; operose; multo labore

labour¹ n labor m; (manual) opera f; (work) opus nt; (of childbirth) partus m

labour² vt&i laboro, operor ①; (struggle, etc.) contendo ③

labourer n operarius m; opifex m/f

labyrinth n labyrinthus m

lace vt (edge) praetexo ③; (tie) necto, astringo ③

lacerate vt lacero, lanio ①

laceration n laceratio f

lack¹ vt egeo, careo ② + abl

lack² n inopia, egestas f

laconic adj Laconicus, brevis

lad n puer, adulescens m

ladder n scala f

laden adj onustus, oneratus

ladle n ligula, spatha, trulla f; coclear nt

lady n domina; matrona, era f

lag vi cesso, cunctor, moror ①

lagoon n lacuna f

lair n cubile; latibulum, lustrum nt

lake n lacus m; stagnum nt

lamb n agnus m; agna f

lame¹ adj claudus, debilis; fig inconcinnus, ineptus

lame² vt mutilo; debilito ①

lament¹ vt&i lamentor; deploro

①; fleo ②

lament ② *n* ▶ **lamentation**

lamentable *adj* miserandus; lamentabilis; luctuosus, flebilis, miser

lamentation *n* lamentatio *f*; lamenta *ntpl*; (act) ploratus, fletus *m*

lamp *n* lucerna, lampas *f*; lychnus *m*

lance *n* lancea, hasta *f*

land¹ *n* (soil) terra, tellus; (country) regio *f*; (estate) fundus *m*; praedium *nt*; (field) ager *m*

land² *vt* in terram expono ③
■ ~ *vi* egredior ③

land-forces *npl* copiae terrestres *fpl*

landing *n* egressus *m*

landlord *n* (innkeeper) caupo; (owner of land) dominus *m*

landmark *n* limes *m*

landscape *n* forma et situs agri; (picture) topia *f*

landslide *n* lapsus terrae *m*

lane *n* angiportus *m*

language *n* lingua, oratio *f*; sermo *m*; verba *ntpl*

languid *adj* languidus

languish *vi* langueo ②; languesco ③

lank *adj* (also **lanky**) macer

lantern *n* lanterna *f*

lap¹ *n* sinus *m*; gremium *nt*; (of a racecourse) spatium *nt*

lap² *vt* (lick) lambo ③

lap-dog *n* catellus *m*

lapse¹ *n* lapsus *m*; fig (error) erratum, peccatum *nt*

lapse² *vi* labor ③; (come to an end) exeo ④; (err) pecco ①

lard *n* laridum, lardum *nt*

larder *n* carnarium *nt*; cella *f*

large *adj* magnus, amplus, grandis, largus

largess *n* largitio *f*; donativum *nt*

lark *n* alauda *f*

lascivious *adj* salax; lascivus, petulans
■ ~**ly** *adv* lascive; petulanter

lasciviousness *n* salacitas, lascivia; petulantia *f*

lash¹ *n* (stroke) verber *nt*; (whip) scutica *f*; flagellum *nt*

lash² *vt* (whip) verbero, flagello; (fasten) alligo; fig castigo ①

last¹ *adj* postremus, ultimus; summus, extremus, (most recent) novissimus
□ ~ **but one** paenultimus
□ **at** ~ demum, tandem; denique, postremo

last² *adv* postremum; novissime

last³ *vi* duro, perduro ①; maneo ②

lasting *adj* mansurus; perennis; stabilis

lastly *adv* postremo, denique

latch *n* obex *m/f*; pessulus *m*

late *adj* serus; tardus; (new) recens; (dead) mortuus
■ ~ *adv* sero
□ **it grows** ~ vesperascit

lately *adv* nuper, modo

latent *adj* latens, latitans, occultus

later *adj* posterus

lateral *adj* lateralis

lathe *n* tornus *m*

lather *n* spuma *f*

Latin *adj & n* Latinus; (language) lingua Latina *f*

latitude *n* latitudo; (liberty) licenta *f*

445

latter | leak

latter *adj* posterior
□ **the ~** hic
■ **~ly** *adv* nuperrime

lattice *n* cancelli, clathri *mpl*

laudable *adj* laudabilis, laude dignus

laudatory *adj* laudativus

laugh[1] *vi* rideo ②
□ **~ at** derideo, irrideo ②

laugh[2] *n* risus *m*

laughable *adj* ridiculus

laughing-stock *n* ludibrium *nt*

laughter *n* risus *m*

launch *vt* deduco ③; (hurl) iaculor ①; contorqueo ②

laurel[1] *n* (tree) laurus *f*; laurea *f*

laurel[2] *adj* laureus

laurelled *adj* laureatus, laurifer, lauriger

lava *n* torrens igneus *m*, liquefacta massa *f*

lavatory *n* latrina *f*

lavish[1] *adj* prodigus; profusus
■ **~ly** *adv* profuse, prodige

lavish[2] *vt* prodigo, profundo, effundo ③

law *n* lex *f*; (right) ius *nt*; (rule) norma *f*; (court of justice) iurisdictio *f*
□ **~suit** lis *f*
□ **international ~** ius gentium *nt*

lawful *adj* legitimus; iustus; licitus
■ **~ly** *adv* legitime; lege

lawless *adj* exlex; illicitus; inconcessus
■ **~ly** *adv* contra leges

lawlessness *n* licentia *f*

lawn *n* (of grass) pratum *nt*; (fine linen) carbasus, sindon *f*

lawsuit *n* lis, causa *f*

lawyer *n* iurisconsultus; causidicus, advocatus *m*

lax *adj* remissus; *fig* neglegens

laxity *n* (also **laxness**) remissio, neglegentia *f*

lay *vt* pono; (eggs) pario; (spread) spargo, expando ③
□ **~ aside** amoveo ②; repono
□ **~ by** repono, recondo, sepono ③
□ **~ claim to** vindico ①
□ **~ down** depono; (state) statuo, expendo ③
□ **~ on** impono ③; *fig* imputo ①
□ **~ out** expono; (money) expendo ③
□ **~ waste** vasto ①

laziness *n* segnities, pigritia; desidia *f*

lazy *adj* iners, ignavus, piger, segnis, desidiosus

lead[1] *n* plumbum *nt*

lead[2] *vt* duco ③; praeeo ④; (pass, spend) ago, dego ③; (manage) moderor ①
□ **~ away** abduco ③
□ **~ off** diverto; adduco ③
□ **~ on** (induce) conduco ③

leaden *adj* plumbeus

leader *n* dux *m/f*; ductor; *fig* auctor *m*

leadership *n* ductus *m*

leading *adj* princeps; primarius

leaf *n* folium *nt*; (of paper) pagina; (of metal) brattea *f*

leafless *adj* fronde nudatus

leafy *adj* frondosus, frondeus, frondifer

league *n* (confederacy) foedus *nt*; societas *f*
□ **be in ~ with** consocio ① cum + *abl*

leak[1] *n* rima *f*; hiatus *m*

leak² vi perfluo; humorem transmitto ③

leaky adj rimosus

lean¹ adj macer; exilis, gracilis

lean² vt inclino, acclino ①
■ ~ vi inclino ①
□ ~ **on** vi innitor ③ + dat
□ ~ **(over)** vi incumbo ③ ad + acc

leap vi salio ④; fig exsulto ①
□ ~ **across** transilio ④

leap year n bisextilis annus m

learn vt&i disco; cognosco ③; (hear) audio ④
□ ~ **by heart** edisco, perdisco ③

learned adj eruditus, doctus

learner n discipulus m

learning n doctrina, humanitas f; litterae fpl; (knowledge) eruditio f

lease¹ n conductio, locatio f

lease² vt conduco ③; loco; (out) eloco ①

leash n (thong) lorum nt; (rein) habena, (leash) copula f

least adj minimus
■ ~ adv minime
□ **at** ~ saltem
□ **not in the** ~ ne minimum quidem

leather¹ n corium nt; (tanned) aluta f

leather² adj scorteus

leave¹ vt linquo, relinquo, desero ③; (entrust) mando ①; trado ③; (bequeath) relinquo ③; lego ①; (depart from) exeo ir ex + abl, discedo ③ ex + abl, relinquo ③
□ ~ **behind** relinquo ③
□ ~ **off** vi desino; vt fig depono; (through interruption) intermitto ③
□ ~ **out** omitto ③; praetereo ir

leave² n permissio, licentia, copia, potestas f; (of absence) commeatus m

lecherous adj libidinosus, salax

lecture¹ n schola, acroasis f; praelectio f

lecture² vt praelego ③; (reprove) obiurgo ①; corripio ③

lecturer n praelector m

ledge n dorsum nt; ora f

ledger n codex m

leech n sanguisuga, hirudo f

leek n porrum, allium nt

leer vi limis oculis intueor ③

left adj sinister, laevus
■ ~ n manus sinistra f
□ **on the** ~ a sinistra
□ **to the** ~ ad sinistram, sinistrorsum

leg n tibia f; crus nt; (of a table, etc.) pes m

legacy n legatum nt

legal adj legalis, legitimus; iudicialis
■ **~ly** adv legitime; legibus

legalize vt legibus confirmo ①

legate n legatus m

legation n legatio f

legend n fabula f

legendary adj fabulosus

legible adj quod legi potest

legion n legio f

legionary n (soldier) legionarius m

legislate vt legem fero ③

legislation n legum datio f

legislator n legum lator m

legitimate adj legitimus; licitus, fig sincerus, verus

leisure n otium nt
□ **at** ~ otiosus; vacuus

lemon | licentious

lemon n citrum nt

lend vt pecuniam mutuam do; commodo; (at interest) faeneror ①; fig praebeo ②

lender n qui pecuniam mutuam dat m

length n longitudo; (of time) longinquitas; (tallness) proceritas f
□ **at ~** tandem, demum

lengthen vt extendo, protraho; fig produco ③

lengthy adj longus; prolixus

leniency n lenitas, clementia, mansuetudo, indulgentia f; (pardon) venia f

lenient adj mitis, lenis, clemens; mansuetus

lentil n lens f

leopard n leopardus m

leprosy n leprae fpl

less adj minor
■ **~** adv minus

lessen vt minuo, imminuo
■ **~** vi decresco, minuor ③

lesson n schola f

lest conj ne …

let vt permitto ③ + dat; sino; patior ③; (lease) loco ①
□ **~ alone** omitto ③
□ **~ down** demitto ③
□ **~ in** admitto ③
□ **~ out** emitto ③; (hire) eloco ①
□ **~ pass** omitto ③; praetereo ④

lethal adj letalis

lethargic adj languidus

lethargy n languor; veternus m

letter n (of alphabet) littera f; (communication) epistula f; litterae fpl
■ **~ s** pl (learning) litterae fpl

lettering n titulus m

lettuce n lactuca f

levee n salutantium comitatus m

level¹ adj planus, aequus

level² n planities f

level³ vt aequo, coaequo, complano ①

lever n vectis m

levity n levitas; iocatio f

levy¹ n delectus m

levy² vt (troops) conscribo ③; (money) exigo ③

lewd adj incestus, impudicus; libidinosus

liability n (obstacle) impedimentum nt

liable adj obnoxius
□ **~ to** obnoxius + dat

liaison n amicitia f

liar n mendax m/f

libel¹ n libellus famosus m

libel² vt diffamo ①

libellous adj probrosus; famosus

liberal adj liberalis, munificus; fig ingenuus
■ **~ly** adv liberaliter, munifice; ingenue

liberality n liberalitas, munificentia f

liberate vt libero ①; (in law) manumitto ③

liberation n liberatio f

liberator n liberator m

liberty n libertas; licentia f
□ **at ~** liber

librarian n bibliothecae praefectus m

library n bibliotheca f

licence n licentia; (lack of restraint) licentia, intemperantia f; venia f

licentious adj dissolutus, impudicus, lascivus; incestus

■ **~ly** adv inceste, lascive

licentiousness n mores dissoluti mpl; licentia, lascivia, intemperantia f

lick vt lambo ③; (daintily) ligurrio ④

lictor n lictor m

lid n operculum; operimentum nt

lie¹ n mendacium nt
□ **tell a ~** mentior ④

lie² vi (tell falsehoods) mentior ④

lie³ vi iaceo ②; (in bed, etc.) cubo ①; (be situated) situs sum ir
□ **~ down** decumbo ③
□ **~ in wait** insidior ①
□ **~ on** incubo ①; incumbo ③ both + dat

lieu n
□ **in ~ of** loco + gen

life n vita; anima f; spiritus m; fig vigor m; alacritas f

lifeless adj inanimus; exanimis; fig exsanguis, frigidus

lifetime n aetas f; aevum nt

lift vt tollo, attollo, erigo ③; levo, sublevo ①

ligament n ligamentum, ligamen nt

light¹ n lux f; lumen nt; (lamp) lucerna f
□ **bring to ~** in lucem profero ③

light² adj (bright, etc.) lucidus, fulgens; (in weight) levis; (in of colours) candidus, dilutus; (easy) facilis; (nimble) agilis; pernix; (inconstant) instabilis

light³ vt accendo ③
■ **~** vi exardesco ③
□ **~ up** illumino ①

lighten vt (illumine) illumino, illustro ①; (a weight) allevo; exonero ①

light-hearted adj hilaris, laetus, alacer

lighthouse n pharus f

lightly adv leviter; perniciter; fig neglegenter; temere

lightness n levitas; (quickness) agilitas, pernicitas f

lightning n fulmen nt

like¹ adj similis; assimilis, consimilis all + gen; (equal) par, aequus all + dat
■ **~** adv tamquam, velut; (in ~ manner) pariter, similiter

like² vt&i (approve) comprobo ①; (be fond of) amo ①
□ **would you ~?** velis?

likelihood n verisimilitudo f

likely adj probabilis, verisimilis
■ **~** adv probabiliter

liken vt assimulo, comparo ①; confero ③

likeness n similitudo; (portrait) imago, effigies f

likewise adv pariter, similiter

liking n approbatio f; favor m; (fancy) libido f

lily n lilium nt

limb n membrum nt; artus m

lime¹ n calx f
□ **bird-~** viscum nt; (tree) tilla f

lime² vt visco illino ③

limestone n calx f; lapis calcarius m

limit¹ n limes, terminus m; finis m/f; modus m

limit² vt termino ①; finio ④; circumscribo ③

limitation n exceptio f

limited adj circumscriptus

limitless adj infinitus

limp¹ vi claudico ①

limp² n claudicatio f

limp | loathsome

limp³ *adj* flaccidus, lentus

line¹ *n* (drawn) linea *f*; (row) series *f*; ordo *m*; (lineage) stirps, progenies *f*; genus *nt*; (cord) funiculus *m*; (in poetry) versus *m*; (entrenchment) vallum *nt*; (fishing–∼) linea *f*

line² *vt* (up) in ordinem instruo ③

lineage *n* stirps *f*; genus *nt*

linear *adj* linearis

linen¹ *n* linteum *nt*; carbasus *f*; (fine) sindon *f*

linen² *adj* linteus, lineus, carbaseus

linger *vi* cunctor, cesso, moror ①

lingering *adj* cunctabundus; tardus

linguist *n* linguarum peritus *m*

link¹ *n* (of a chain) anulus *m*; (bond) vinculum *m*

link² *vt* connecto ③

lintel *n* limen superum *nt*

lion *n* leo *m*

lioness *n* leaena, lea *f*

lip *n* labrum, labellum *nt*; fig os *nt*; (edge) ora *f*

liquefy *vt* liquefacio ③
  ■ ∼ *vi* liquefio ③

liquid¹ *adj* liquidus; (transparent) pellucidus

liquid² *n* liquidum *nt*; liquor *m*

liquor *n* umor, liquor *m*

lisp¹ *n* os blaesum *nt*

lisp² *vi* balbutio ④

list *n* index *m*

listen *vi* ausculto ①; audio ④

listener *n* auscultator, auditor *m*

listless *adj* remissus, neglegens, languidus

listlessness *n* inertia, socordia *f*; languor *m*

literal *adj* accuratus
  ■ ∼ly *adv* ad litteram, ad verbum

literary *adj* ad litteras pertinens

literature *n* litterae *fpl*

litigant *n* litigator *m*

litigation *n* lis *f*

litter *n* (of straw, *etc.*) substramen, substramentum, stramentum *nt*; (vehicle) lectica *f*; (brood) partus *m*

little¹ *adj* parvus, exiguus
  □ **a** ∼ paulum
  ■ ∼ *adv* parum

little² *n* paulum, exiguum; (somewhat) aliquantulum; nonnihil *n*
  □ ∼ **by** ∼ paulatim

live¹ *vi* vivo, dego ③; spiro ①; vitam ago ③; (reside) habito ①; (on) vescor ③

live² *adj* vivus; vivens

livelihood *n* (trade) ars *f*; (means of maintenance) victus *m*

liveliness *n* vigor *nt*

lively *adj* vivus, vividus, alacer; vegetus

liver *n* iecur *nt*

livid *adj* (of colour) lividus, livens; fig (angry) iratus

living¹ *adj* vivus, vivens, spirans

living² *n* (way of life, food) victus *m*

lizard *n* lacertus *m*; lacerta *f*

load¹ *n* onus *nt*; sarcina *f*; (quantity) vehis *f*

load² *vt* onero ①

loaf *n* panis *m*

loan *n* mutua pecunia *f*

loathe *vt* fastidio ④; aspernor ①; odi, perodi ③

loathing *n* fastidium, taedium *nt*; satietas *f*

loathsome *adj* foedus; odiosus

lobby n vestibulum nt

lobster n locusta f; cammarus m

local adj loci, locorum (both gen); (neighbouring) vicinus

locality n locus m

locate vt (place) loco ①; (find) invenio ④

location n locus m

lock¹ n sera f; claustrum nt; (of hair, wool, etc.) cirrus; floccus m

lock² vt&i (a door) obsero ①
□ ~ **in** includo ③
□ ~ **out** excludo ③
□ ~ **up** occludo ③

locker n loculamentum nt; capsa f

locksmith n claustrarius artifex m

locust n locusta f

lodge¹ vi habito ①; (stick fast in) haereo ② + in + abl

lodge² n casa; cella f

lodger n inquilinus m

lodging n (stay) commoratio f; (room) cubiculum; (inn) deversorium nt

loft n cella f; tabulatum, cenaculum nt

lofty adj altus; celsus, excelsus, sublimis; fig superbus, elatus, arrogans

log n lignum nt; stipes; (trunk) truncus m

loggerhead n
□ **be at** ~**s** rixor ① + cum + abl

logic n logica, dialectica f

logical adj logicus, dialecticus
■ ~**ly** adv dialectice

loiter vi cesso, cunctor; moror ①

loll vi dependo ③; langueo ②
□ ~ **on** innitor ③ + dat

lone adj solus; solitarius

loneliness n solitudo f

lonely adj solus; solitarius; (of places) desolatus; avius

long¹ adj longus; (of time) diuturnus; diutinus; (lengthened) productus

long² adv diu
□ ~ **after** multo post
□ ~ **ago** iamdudum
□ ~ **before** multo ante

long³ vi aveo ②; (for) desidero ①; cupio ③

longevity n longaevitas f

longing n desiderium nt; appetitus m; cupido f

longitude n longitudo f

long-suffering adj patiens

look vi video ②; aspicio, conspicio ③; specto ①; (seem) videor ②
▶ **seem**
□ ~ **around** circumspicio ③
□ ~ **after** fig curo ①
□ ~ **at** intueor ②
□ ~ **back** respicio ③
□ ~ **down on** despicio ③
□ ~ **for** (seek) quaero ③
□ ~ **forward** prospicio ③; expecto ①
□ ~ **in** inspicio, introspicio ③; (examine) perscrutor ①
□ ~ **on** intueor ②
□ ~ **out** prospicio ③; (for) quaero ③
□ ~ **out!** cave! cavete!
□ ~ **round** circumspicio; respicio ③
□ ~ **through** per ... aspicio; fig perspicio ③
□ ~ **to** fig curo ①
□ ~ **up** suspicio ③
□ ~ **upon** fig (value) habeo ②; aestimo ①
□ ~ **up to** fig veneror ①

look² n aspectus, vultus; os nt; facies f; (glance) obtutus m

look³ int ecce! en! aspice!

looking-glass n speculum nt

lookout n (**lookout post**) specula f

loom¹ n tela f

loom² vi appareo, obscure videor ②

loop n laqueus m

loophole n fig effugium nt

loose¹ adj laxus; solutus; neglegens; dissolutus

loose² vt solvo, resolvo ③; laxo, relaxo ①

loosen vt solvo, resolvo ③; laxo, relaxo ①; vi solvor ③

loot n praeda f

looter n raptor m

loquacious adj loquax, garrulus

lord n dominus m

lordly adj superbus, imperiosus

lordship n imperium nt

lore n doctrina; eruditio f; (rites) ritus mpl

lose vt amitto, perdo ③; (be deprived of) privor ① + abl; (be defeated) vincor ③
  □ ~ **one's way** aberro ①
  □ **be lost** pereo ④

loss n (act) amissio, iactura f; damnum, detrimentum nt; (mil) clades f

lot n pars, portio; (chance) sors f; casus m
  □ **by** ~ sorte
  □ ~ **of** multus

lotion n medicamen nt

lottery n sortitio f

loud adj clarus, sonorus

■ ~**ly** adv clare, magna voce

loudness n claritas f

lounge¹ vi cesso, otior ①

lounge² n lectulus m

louse n pedis, pediculus m

lout n homo agrestis, rusticus m

loutish adj agrestis, rusticus

love¹ n amor, ardor m; flamma f; (desire) desiderium nt; (dearness) caritas f
  ■ **in** ~ adj amans

love² vt amo ①; diligo ③

love-letter n nota blanda f

loveliness n venustas; forma, pulchritudo f

lovely adj formosus pulcher; venustus

love-potion n philtrum nt

lover n amator, amans; (devotee) studiosus m

lovingly adv amanter, blande

low¹ adj humilis; (of price) vilis; (of birth) obscurus; (of the voice) summissus m; fig turpis; (downcast) abiectus

low² adv humiliter; summissa voce

low³ vi mugio ④

lower¹ vt (let down) demitto; (humiliate) abicio; (the price) imminuo ③; (the voice) submitto ③

lower² adj inferior

lowermost adj infimus, imus

lowing n mugitus m

lowliness n humilitas f; fig animus demissus m

lowly adj humilis, obscurus

loyal adj fidelis
  ■ ~**ly** adv fideliter

loyalty n fides, fidelitas f

lucid adj lucidus; (transparent)

pellucidus

luck n fortuna f; successus m
  □ **bad** ~ res adversae fpl
  □ **good** ~ res secundae fpl

luckily adj feliciter; fauste, prospere, fortunate

lucky adj felix, faustus, prosperus, fortunatus

lucrative adj quaestuosus, lucrosus

ludicrous adj ridiculus, iocularis

lug vt traho ③

luggage n sarcinae fpl; impedimenta ntpl; onus nt

lukewarm adj egelidus, tepidus; fig frigidus

lull¹ vt sopio ④; fig demulceo ②

lull² n quies f

luminous adj illustris, lucidus

lump n glaeba; massa; (heap) congeries f

lumpy adj glaebosus

lunacy n alienatio mentis f; amentia, dementia f

lunar adj lunaris

lunatic adj insanus, demens
  ■ ~ n homo insanus m

lunch¹ n (also **luncheon**) merenda f; prandium nt

lunch² vi prandeo ②

lung n pulmo m

lunge n ictus m; plaga f

lurch¹ n
  □ **leave in the** ~ desero, destituo ③

lurch² vi titubo ①

lure¹ n illecebra, (bait) esca f

lure² vt allicio, pellicio ③

lurk vi lateo ②; latito ①

luscious adj suavis, praedulcis

lust¹ n libido, cupido, cupiditas f; appetitus m

lust² vt (for) concupisco ③

lustful adj libidinosus, salax, lascivus

lustre n (also fig) splendor m

lusty adj robustus, vegetus

luxuriant adj luxuriosus; sumptuosus; fig luxurians

luxurious adj luxuriosus; sumptuosus; fig luxurians

luxury n luxus m; luxuria f

lying adj mendax; fallax; vanus

lynx n lynx m/f
  ■ ~-eyed adj lynceus

lyre n cithara; lyra f

lyric adj (also **lyrical**) lyricus

Mm

mace n sceptrum nt

machination n dolus m; (trick) machina; ars f

machine n machina f; machinamentum nt

machinery n machinamentum nt; machinatio f

mackerel n scomber m

mad adj insanus, vesanus, demens, amens

madam n domina, era f

madden vt mentem alieno; fig furio ①; ad insaniam adigo ③

maddening adj fig furiosus; (troublesome) molestus

madly adv insane, dementer;

furiose

madman *n* homo furiosus; fig demens *m*

madness *n* insania; rabies; amentia, dementia *f*; furor *m*

maggot *n* vermiculus, termes *m*

magic *adj* magicus
■ ~ *n* magica ars *f*; veneficium *nt*

magician *n* magus, veneficus *m*; (conjurer) praestigiator *m*

magistracy *n* magistratus *m*

magistrate *n* magistratus *m*

magnanimity *n* magnanimitas, magnitudo animi *f*

magnanimous *adj* magnanimus
■ ~**ly** *adv* pro magnitudine animi

magnet *n* magnes *m*

magnetic *adj* magnes

magnificence *n* magnificentia *f*; splendor *m*

magnificent *adj* magnificus, splendidus
■ ~**ly** *adv* magnifice; splendide

magnify *vt* amplifico ①

magnitude *n* magnitudo *f*

magpie *n* corvus pica *f*

maid *n* (female servant) ancilla, famula *f*

maiden *adj* virginalis
■ ~ **speech** *n* prima oratio *f*

maidenhood *n* virginitas *f*

mail *n* (letter-carrier) tabellarius *m*; (coat) lorica *f*; thorax *m*

maim *vt* mutilo; trunco ①

main[1] *adj* praecipuus, primus, maximus
■ ~**ly** *adv* praecipue, maxime; praesertim

main[2] *n* (sea) mare *nt*

mainland *n* terra continens *f*

maintain *vt&i* affirmo ①; (defend) tueor, sustineo ②; (keep) nutrio ④; (sustain) ① alo ③; (keep in good condition) conservo ①

maintenance *n* (support) defensio *f*; (means of living) alimentum *nt*; victus *m*

maize *n* zea *f*

majestic *adj* augustus, sublimis; imperatorius

majesty *n* maiestas; dignitas, sublimitas *f*

majority *n* pars maior *f*; plures *m/fpl*

make *vt* facio ③; (elect) creo ①; (form, fabricate) conficio; fingo ③; (render) reddo ③
□ ~ **for** peto ③
□ ~ **good** resarcio ④
□ ~ **much of** magni facio ③
□ ~ **up** (compensate) resarcio ④; (resolve) decerno ③; (numerically) expleo ②; (invent) fingo ③

maker *n* fabricator *m*; auctor *m/f*

makeshift *adj* subitarius

maladministration *n* administratio mala *f*

male[1] *adj* mas; masculinus, masculus, virilis

male[2] *n* mas, masculus *m*

malefactor *n* maleficus *m*

malevolence *n* malevolentia, malignitas, invidia *f*

malevolent *adj* malevolus, malignus

malice *n* malevolentia, malitia *f*

malicious *adj* malevolus, malitiosus
■ ~**ly** *adv* malevolo animo, malitiose

malign[1] *adj* malevolus

malign² vt obtrecto ①

malignant adj malevolus

malleable adj ductilis, mollis

mallet n malleus m

malpractice n male facta, delicta ntpl; maleficium nt

maltreat vt vexo ①; laedo ③

maltreatment n iniuria f

mammal n animal nt

man¹ n (human being) homo; (as opposed to woman) vir; mas m
- □ **a ~** (someone) aliquis
- □ **~ of war** navis longa f

man² vt (a ship) compleo ②

manacle¹ n manicae fpl; compes f

manacle² vt manicas (alicui) inicio ③

manage vt administro; curo, tracto ①; gero ③
- □ **~ vi** (cope) rem prospere gero ③

manageable adj tractabilis

management n administratio; cura, procuratio f

manager n curator; (steward) procurator, vilicus m

mandate n mandatum nt

mandatory adj necessarius

mane n iuba f

mange n scabies f

mangle¹ vt lacero, lanio, dilanio ①

mangle² n prelum nt

mangy adj scaber

manhood n pubertas; virilitas; fortitudo f

mania n fig insania, amentia f

maniac n homo furiosus m

manifest¹ adj manifestus, clarus, apertus, evidens
- ■ **~ly** adv manifeste, aperte; evidenter

manifest² vt declaro ①; ostendo ③; praebeo ②

manifestation n patefactio f

manifesto n edictum nt

manifold adj multiplex; varius

maniple n manipulus m

manipulate vt (manibus) tracto ①

manipulation n tractatio f

mankind n genus humanum nt; homines mpl

manliness n virtus, fortitudo f

manly adj virilis; strenuus; fortis

manner n modus m; ratio, consuetudo f
- □ **~s** mores mpl
- □ **good ~s** urbanitas f
- □ **bad ~s** rusticitas f

mannerism n mala affectatio f

manoeuvre¹ n (mil) decursus m; fig artificium nt

manoeuvre² vi (mil) decurro ③; (plot) machinor ①

mansion n domus, sedes f

manslaughter n homicidium nt

manual adj manualis
- ■ **~ labour** n opera f

manufacture¹ n fabrica f; opificium nt

manufacture² vt fabricor ①; fabrefacio ③

manufacturer n fabricator m, opifex m/f

manumission n manumissio f

manumit vt manumitto ③

manure¹ n stercus nt; fimus m

manure² vi stercoro ①

manuscript n codex m

many adj multi; plerique; complures
- □ **as ~ as** quot ... tot

□ **how** ~ quot
□ **so** ~ tot
□ ~ **ways** multifarie

map¹ *n* tabula geographica *f*

map² *vt* (out) designo ①

maple¹ *n* acer *nt*

maple² *adj* acernus

mar *vt* foedo, vitio ①; corrumpo ③

marauder *n* praedator *m*

marauding *n* praedatio *f*

marble *n* marmor *nt*
■ ~ *adj* marmoreus

March¹ *n* (month) Martius *m*

march² *n* iter *nt*; (step) gradus *m*

march³ *vi* iter facio, incedo, gradior, proficiscor ③
■ ~ *vt* exercitum duco ③
□ ~ **in** ingredior ③
□ ~ **off** recedo ③

mare *n* equa *f*

margin *n* margo *m*/*f*

marginal *adj* in margine positus, margini ascriptus

marine *adj* marinus, maritimus

mariner *n* nauta *m*

marital *adj* conubialis

maritime *adj* maritimus

marjoram *n* amaracum, origanum *nt*

mark¹ *n* nota *f*; signum; (brand) stigma; (impression) vestigium *nt*; (to shoot at) scopus *m*; (of a stripe) vibex; (of a wound) cicatrix *f*; fig indicium *nt*

mark² *vt* noto, signo ①; (observe) animadverto ③; (with a pencil, *etc.*) designo ①
□ ~ **out** metor ①; metior ④

market *n* (place) forum *nt*; mercatus *m*

market-day *n* nundinae *fpl*

marketing *n* emptio, mercatura *f*

market-place *n* forum *nt*

marksman *n* iaculator *m*

marriage¹ *n* conubium, coniugium, matrimonium *nt*; nuptiae *fpl*

marriage² *adj* nuptialis, coniugalis, conubialis

marriageable *adj* nubilis, adultus

married *adj* (of a woman) nupta; (of a man) maritus

marrow *n* (of bones) medulla *f*

marry *vt* (of a priest) conubio iungo; (as the man) uxorem duco; (as the woman) viro nubo ③

marsh *n* palus *f*

marshal *vt* dispono ③

marshy *adj* paluster, paludosus

martial *adj* bellicosus, ferox; militaris, bellicus
■ **court** ~ *n* castrense iudicium *nt*

martyr *n* martyr *m*/*f*

marvel *n* res mira *f*; mirum *nt*; miraculum *nt*

marvellous *adj* mirus, mirabilis
■ ~**ly** *adv* mire; mirabiliter

masculine *adj* masculus; mas; virilis

mask¹ *n* persona, larva *f*; fig praetextum *nt*

mask² *vt* personam induo ③; fig dissimulo ①

mason *n* lapicida, structor *m*

masonry *n* saxa *ntpl*

mass *n* moles, massa; immensa copia *f*; ingens pondus *nt*; (of people) multitudo, turba *f*

massacre *n* caedes, trucidatio *f*
■ ~ *vt* trucido ①

massive *adj* solidus

mast *n* (of a ship) malus *m*

master[1] *n* dominus, erus; (teacher) magister, praeceptor *m*; fig potens, compos *m/f* + *gen*; (expert) peritus *m* + *gen*

master[2] *vt* supero ①; vinco ③; dominor ①; (learn) perdisco ③

masterly *adj* (of an artist) artificiosus

masterpiece *n* opus palmare *nt*

master-stroke *n* artificium singulare *nt*

mastery *n* dominatus *m*; imperium *nt*; (skill) peritia *f*

mat *n* matta, teges *f*; stragulum *nt*

match[1] *n* (marriage) nuptiae *fpl*; (contest) certamen *nt*; (an equal) par, compar *m/f*

match[2] *vt* compono ③; adaequo, exaequo
■ ~ *vi* (be suitable) quadro ①

matchless *adj* incomparabilis, eximius, singularis

matchmaker *n* conciliator nuptiarum *m*; conciliatrix nuptiarum *f*

mate[1] *n* socius, collega *m*; coniunx *m/f*

mate[2] *vi* (of animals) coniungor ③

material[1] *adj* corporeus; fig (important) magni momenti

material[2] *n* materia *f*; (cloth) textile *nt*
■ ~s *pl* res necessariae *fpl*

maternal *adj* maternus

maternity *n* condicio matris *f*

mathematical *adj* mathematicus

mathematician *n* mathematicus *m*

mathematics *n* mathematica *f*

matricide *n* (murder) matricidium *nt*; (murderer) matricida *m/f*

matrimonial *adj* coniugalis, conubialis, nuptialis

matted *adj* concretus

matter[1] *n* (substance) materia; (affair, business, *etc.*) res *f*; negotium; (purulent) pus *nt*; sanies *f*
□ no ~ nihil interest

matter[2] *vi impers*
□ it does not ~ nihil interest, nihil refert

matting *n* tegetes *fpl*

mattress *n* culcita *f*

mature *adj* maturus; tempestivus
■ ~ *vt&i* maturo ①

maturity *n* maturitas; aetas matura *f*

maul *vt* mulco ①

mausoleum *n* mausoleum *nt*

mawkish *adj* (of taste) putidus; fastidiosus
■ ~ly *adv* putide, fastidiose

maxim *n* praeceptum *nt*; sententia *f*

May[1] *n* (month) Maius *m*

may[2] *vi* possum; licet

maybe *adv* forsitan, forsan; forte, fortasse

mayor *n* praefectus urbanus *m*

maze *n* labyrinthus *m*; ambages *fpl*

me *prep* me
□ to ~ mihi

meadow *n* pratum *nt*

meagre *adj* macer; fig aridus; ieiunus; exilis

meal *n* (flour) farina *f*; (food) cibus *m*; (dinner, *etc.*) epulae *fpl*

mealtime *n* cibi hora *f*

mean¹ adj (middle) medius; (moderate) mediocris; (low) humilis; (miserly) avarus; (unkind) malignus; fig sordidus; vilis
　□ **in the ~time** interea

mean² n medium nt; (manner) modus m; ratio f
　□ **by all ~s** quam maxime
　□ **by no ~s** nullo modo

mean³ vt & i volo; mihi volo ir; cogito; significo ①

meander¹ n cursus; flexus m

meander² vi labor ③; sinuor ①

meaning n significatio f; animus, sensus m

meanness n humilitas; fig avaritia; ignobilitas f

means n (method) modus m, ratio f

meanwhile adv interea, interim

measurable adj quod metiri potes, mensurabilis

measure¹ n mensura f; (of land, liquids) modus m
　■ **~s** pl consilium nt
　□ **in some ~** aliquatenus

measure² vt metior ④; metor ①
　□ **~out** admetior ④

measurement n mensura f

meat n caro f

mechanic n opifex m/f, faber m

mechanical adj mechanicus
　■ **~ly** adv mechanica quadam arte

mechanics n mechanica ars; machinalis scientia f

mechanism n machinatio; mechanica ratio f

medal n nomisma nt

meddle vi (with) me immisceo ②; intervenio ④

mediate vi intercedo ③

mediation n intercessio f

mediator n intercessor, conciliator m

medical adj medicus, medicinalis

medicinal adj medicus; salutaris

medicine n (science) medicina f; (remedy) medicamentum, medicamen nt

mediocre adj mediocris, modicus

mediocrity n mediocritas f

meditate vi meditor, cogito ①

meditation n meditatio, cogitatio f

meditative adj cogitabundus

Mediterranean n mare mediterraneum or internum or medium m

medium¹ n (middle) medium nt; (mode, method) modus m, ratio f; (agent) conciliator m

medium² adj mediocris

medley n farrago f

meek adj mitis; fig summissus, humilis
　■ **~ly** adv summisse

meekness n animus summissus m

meet vt obvenio ④; occurro ③; obviam eo ④ all + dat; congredior ③ + cum + abl
　□ **~ with** offendo ③; (bad) subeo ④; patior ③; (good) nanciscor ③

meeting n congressio f; congressus m; (assembly) conventus m

melancholy¹ n tristitia, maestitia f

melancholy² adj melancholicus, maestus, tristis

mellow¹ adj maturus, mitis

mellow² vi maturesco ③

melodious adj canorus, numerosus

melody n melos nt; modulatio f; numerus m

melt vt liquefacio, solvo, dissolvo ③; ■ ~ vi liquefio ir, liquesco ③

membrane n membrana f

memento n monumentum nt

memoir n commentarius m

memorable adj memorabilis, notabilis, memoria dignus

memorial n monumentum nt

memory n memoria f

menace n & vt ▶ **threat, threaten**

menagerie n vivarium f

mend vt emendo ①; corrigo ③; reparo ①; (clothes) sarcio ④ ■ ~ vi melior fio ir

menial adj servilis; sordidus

mental adj mentis, animi (gen sing); mente conceptus, internus ■ ~ly adv mente, animo

mention[1] n commemoratio, mentio f

mention[2] vt commemoro ①; mentionem facio + gen ③ ▫ **not to ~** silentio praetereo ④

mercenary[1] adj mercenarius, venalis

mercenary[2] n miles conductus m

merchandise n merx; (trade) mercatura f

merchant n mercator, negotiator m

merciful adj misericors, clemens

merciless adj immisericors, inclemens; immitis, durus

mercury n (metal) argentum vivum nt

mercy n misericordia, clementia, indulgentia f ▫ **at the ~ of** in manu + gen

mere adj merus ■ ~ly adv tantummodo, solummodo, nihil nisi

merge vt confundo ③; misceo ② ■ ~ vi commisceor cum + abl

merit[1] n meritum nt; virtus f

merit[2] vt mereo, demereor, promereo ②

merry adj hilaris, festivus

merrymaking n festivitas f

mesh n (of a net) macula f

mesmerize vt consopio ④

mess[1] n (mil) (place for eating) contubernium nt; (dirt) squalor m; fig (confusion) turba f

mess[2] vi (about) ludo ③

message n nuntius m

messenger n nuntius; (letter-carrier) tabellarius m

metal n metallum nt

metallic adj metallicus

metamorphose vt transformo, transfiguro ①

metamorphosis n transfiguratio f

metaphor n translatio f

metaphorical adj translaticius ■ ~ly adv per translationem

meteor n fax caelestis f

method n ratio, via f

methodical adj dispositus, ratione et via factus ■ ~ly adv ratione et via; disposite

meticulous adj curiosus, diligens

metre n metrum nt; numerus m; versus m

metrical adj metricus

mettle n vigor, animus m; (courage) virtus, fortitudo; magnanimitas f

mid adj medius

midday n meridies m; meridianum tempus nt
■ ~ adj meridianus

middle¹ adj medius

middle² n medium nt; (waist) medium corpus nt

middling adj mediocris; modicus

midnight n media nox f

midst n medium nt
□ in the ~ of inter + acc

midsummer n media aestas, summa aestas f

midway n media via f

midwife n obstetrix f

midwinter n media hiems f

mien n vultus m; os nt; species f

might¹ n vis, potestas, potentia f
□ with all one's ~ summa ope

might² vi in subordinate clauses often expressed by subj verb and/or subj of possum (expressing or possibility) or licet (permission)

mighty adj potens, pollens, validus; magnus

migrate vi migro, transmigro ①; abeo ir

migration n migratio, peregrinatio f

mild adj mitis, lenis; placidus; clemens; mansuetus
■ ~ly adv leniter, clementer, placide, mansuete

mildew n (mould) mucor, situs m

mildness n clementia, lenitas, mansuetudo f

mile n mille passus mpl

milestone n miliarium nt

militant adj pugnax

military adj militaris
■ ~ n milites mpl

milk¹ n lac nt

milk² vt mulgeo ②

milky adj lacteus, lactans
■ ~ way n orbis lacteus m; via lactea f

mill n mola f; pistrinum nt

miller n molitor m

millet n milium nt

million n decies centena milia f

millionaire n homo praedives m

millstone n mola f; molaris m

mime n (play and player) mimus m

mimic¹ n mimus m

mimic² vt imitor ①

mimicry n imitatio f

mince vt concido ③

mind¹ n animus m; mens f; ingenium nt; sensus m; (desire) desiderium nt; voluntas, cupido f; (recollection) memoria f

mind² vt (look after) curo ①; (regard) respicio ③; (consider) animadverto ③; considero ①
□ I don't ~ nihil moror ①

mindful adj attentus, diligens; memor

mine¹ n fodina f; metallum nt; (mil) cuniculus m

mine² vt&i effodio ③; (mil) cuniculos ago ③

mine³ adj meus

miner n (of metals) metallicus m

mineral n metallum nt
■ ~ adj metallicus

mingle vt misceo, commisceo ②; confundo ③
■ ~ vi commisceor ②

minimum n minimum nt

minion n satelles m

minister n minister; (of state) rerum publicarum administer m

minor n pupillus m; pupilla f

minority n minor pars f; (under age) pupillaris aetas f

minstrel n fidicen m

mint[1] n moneta f

mint[2] n (plant) menta f

mint[3] vt cudo ③; signo ①

minute[1] n punctum temporis nt

minute[2] adj minutus, exiguus

miracle n miraculum nt

miraculous adj prodigiosus, mirabilis

■ **~ly** adv divinitus

mirror n speculum nt

mirth n hilaritas; laetitia; festivitas f

misadventure n infortunium nt

misapprehension n falsa conceptio f; error m

misbehave vi indecore se gerere ③

misbehaviour n morum pravitas f

miscalculate vt erro ①; fallor ③

miscalculation n error m

miscarriage n (in childbirth) abortus; fig malus successus m

miscarry vi parum succedo ③

miscellaneous adj promiscuus, miscellaneus

miscellany n coniectanea, miscellanea ntpl

mischief n (harm, loss) incommodum, damnum; (injury, wrong) maleficium, malum nt; (nuisance) pestis f

mischievous adj maleficus; noxius, funestus

misconception n falsa opinio f

misconduct n delictum, peccatum nt

misconstrue vt male or perverse interpretor ①

misdeed n delictum, peccatum nt; scelus nt

misdemeanour n vitium nt

miser n avarus m

miserable adj miser, miserabilis, miserandus, aerumnosus

miserly adj avarus

misery n miseria f; aerumnae fpl; angor m

misfortune n adversa fortuna, calamitas f; infortunium, incommodum nt

misgivings n

□ **have ~** parum confido, diffido ③

misguided adj demens

mishap n incommodum nt

misinterpret vt male interpretor ①

misinterpretation n falsa interpretatio f

misjudge vt male iudico ①

mislay vt amitto ③

mislead vt decipio, fallo ③

mismanage vt male gero ③

misnomer n falsum nomen nt

misplace vt alieno loco pono ③

misrepresent vt perverse interpretor; calumnior ①; detorqueo ②

miss[1] n error m; (loss) damnum nt; (failure) malus successus m

miss[2] vt&i (pass over) omitto ③; (one's

aim) non attingo ③; (be disappointed) de spe decido ③; (not find) reperire non possum *ir*; (feel the loss of) desidero ①; careo ② + *abl*

misshapen *adj* deformis, pravus

missile *n* telum, missile *nt*

mission *n* legatio; missio *f*; (instructions) mandatum *nt*

mist *n* nebula; caligo *f*

mistake[1] *n* erratum, mendum, vitium *nt*; error *m*

mistake[2] *vt* male interpretor ①

mistaken *adj* falsus
    □ **be** ~ erro ①

mistletoe *n* viscum *nt*

mistress *n* domina, era; (sweetheart) amica; (teacher) magistra *f*

mistrust[1] *n* diffidentia, suspicio *f*

mistrust[2] *vi* diffido ③; suspicor ①

mistrustful *adj* diffidens

misty *adj* nebulosus, caliginosus; *fig* obscurus

misunderstand *vt* perperam intellego ③

misunderstanding *n* error *m*; (disagreement) offensa, offensio *f*

misuse[1] *vt* abutor ③ + *abl*

misuse[2] *n* abusus *m*; (ill-treatment) iniuria *f*

mitigate *vt* mitigo, levo ①; lenio ④; remitto ③; extenuo ①

mitre *n* mitra *f*

mix *vt* misceo, commisceo, permisceo ②
    □ ~ **up** admisceo ②
    □ ~ **with** (socially) me immisceo ②

mixed *adj* mixtus, promiscuus, confusus

mixture *n* (act and result) mixtura *f*; (hotchpotch) farrago *f*

moan[1] *vi* gemo, ingemisco ③

moan[2] *n* gemitus *m*

moat *n* fossa *f*

mob *n* turba *f*; vulgus *nt*

mobile *adj* mobilis, expeditus

mobility *n* mobilitas *f*

mock[1] *vt&i* ludo ③; ludificor ①; irrideo ②

mock[2] *adj* fictus, fucatus, simulatus

mockery *n* irrisio *f*; irrisus *m*

mode *n* modus *m*; ratio *f*; (fashion) usus *m*

model[1] *n* exemplar, exemplum *nt*

model[2] *vt* formo; delineo ①

moderate[1] *adj* moderatus, mediocris; modicus
    ■ ~**ly** *adv* moderate; modice; mediocriter

moderate[2] *vt* moderor, tempero ①; (restrain) coerceo ②

moderation *n* moderatio; temperantia, modestia *f*

modern *adj* recens; hodiernus

modest *adj* (moderate) mediocris, modicus; (not proud) verecundus; modestus
    ■ ~**ly** *adv* modeste, verecunde, mediocriter

modesty *n* pudor *m*; modestia, pudicitia, verecundia *f*

modification *n* immutatio *f*

modify *vt* immuto ①

moist *adj* umidus, uvidus, udus, madidus

moisten *vt* umecto, irroro, rigo ①

moisture *n* umor *m*; uligo *f*

molar *n* molaris *m*

mole *n* (massive structure, pile) moles, pila *f*; (earthwork) agger *m*; (on the body) naevus m; (animal) talpa m/f

molest vt vexo, sollicito ①

molten adj fusus, fusilis; liquidus

moment n (of time) punctum temporis; (importance) momentum, pondus nt; (opportunity) occasio f
□ **in a ~** statim
□ **of great ~** magni ponderis
□ **this ~** ad tempus

momentarily adv subito

momentary adj brevis, brevissimus, subitus

momentous adj magni momenti

momentum n impetus m

monarch n rex m, princeps m/f

monarchy n regnum nt

Monday n dies lunae m

money n pecunia f; argentum nt; nummus m

moneylender n faenerator m

monitor n admonitor m

monkey n simius m; simia f

monologue n soliloquium nt

monopolize vi monopolium exerceo ②; fig solus habeo ②

monopoly n monopolium nt

monotonous adj fig continuus; nulla varietate delectans

monster n monstrum; portentum, prodigium nt

monstrous adj monstruosus, portentosus, prodigiosus

month n mensis m

monthly adj menstruus

monument n monumentum; (tomb) mausoleum nt

monumental adj monumentalis

mood n animi affectus, habitus m, voluntas f

moody adj morosus; tristis

moon n luna f

moonlight n lunae lumen nt
□ **by ~** per lunam

moor[1] n loca patentia et ericis obsita ntpl

moor[2] vt (a ship) navem religo ①

mop n peniculus m
■ **~** vt detergeo ②

mope vi tristis sum ir

moral adj moralis; qui ad mores pertinet; (virtuous) integer, honestus

morality n mores mpl; (virtue) virtus f; (duty) officium nt

morals n mores mpl; instituta ntpl

morbid adj morbidus, morbosus

more adj plus, maior
■ **~** adv plus, magis; amplius; ultra
□ **~ and ~** magis et magis
□ **~ than enough** plus satis
□ **nothing ~** nihil amplius

moreover adv praeterea, ultra

morning[1] n mane nt indecl; matutinum tempus nt
□ **early ~** prima lux f
■ **good ~** int salve! (when parting) ave!

morning[2] adj matutinus

morose adj morosus, difficilis, serverus

morsel n offa f; frustum nt

mortal[1] adj mortalis; (deadly) mortifer, letifer, letalis; fig (of an enemy) infensissimus

mortal[2] n homo m
■ **~s** pl mortales mpl

mortality n mortalitas; mors; pestis f

mortar n mortarium nt

mortgage[1] n hypotheca f; pignus m

mortgage[2] vt pignori oppono ③

mosaic n tessellatum (opus) nt
■ ~ adj tessellatus

mosquito n culex m

moss n muscus m

mossy adj muscosus

most¹ adj plurimus, maximus, plerique

most² adv maxime, plurimum
■ ~ly adv (usually) plerumque; vulgo

moth n blatta, tinea f

mother n mater; genetrix f

motherhood n condicio matris f

mother-in-law n socrus f

motherless adj matre orbus

motherly adj maternus

mother-of-pearl n concha Persica f

motion n motio f; motus m; (proposal) rogatio f

motionless adj immotus, immobilis, fixus

motivate vt incito ①

motive n causa, ratio f; incitamentum nt

motto n sententia f; praeceptum nt

mould¹ n (for casting) forma f; (mustiness) mucor, situs m

mould² vt formo ①; fingo; (knead) subigo ③

moulder vi putresco, dilabor ③

mouldy adj mucidus; situ corruptus
□ **go ~** putresco ③

moult vi plumas exuo ③

mound n tumulus, agger m; moles f

mount vt&i scando, ascendo ③; supero ①; (rise) sublime feror ③; subvolo ①; (get on a horse) equum conscendo ③

mountain n mons m

mountaineer n homo montanus m

mountainous adj montuosus, montanus

mounted adj (on horseback) eques

mourn vt&i lugeo; maereo, doleo ②; lamentor ①

mourner n plorator; pullatus m

mournful adj luctuosus, lugubris; maestus; tristis, lamentabilis, flebilis
■ ~ly adv maeste; flebiliter

mourning n luctus, maeror m; (clothes) vestis lugubris f
□ **be in ~** lugeo ②
□ **go into ~** vestitum muto ①

mouse n mus m

mouse-hole n cavum (muris) nt

mousetrap n muscipulum nt

mouth n os nt; rictus m; (of a bird) rostrum nt; (of a bottle) lura f; (of a river) ostium nt

mouthful n buccella f

mouthpiece n fig (speaker) interpres m/f; orator m

movable adj mobilis

move¹ vt moveo ②
■ ~ vi moveor ②; feror ir; (change dwelling, etc.) migro ①
□ ~ **on** progredior ③

move² n motus m; fig artificium nt

movement n motus m

moving adj flebilis, miserabilis
■ ~ly adv flebiliter

mow vt meto ③

mower n faenisex m; messor m

much adj multus
■ ~ adv multum; (with comparative) multo

m

□ **as ~ as** tantus ... quantus;
tantum ... quantum
□ **how ~** quantus; quantum
□ **so ~** tantus; tantum
□ **too ~** nimius; (adv) nimis
□ **very ~** plurimus; plurimum
muck n stercus nt
mud n caenum, lutum nt; limus m
muddle¹ vt turbo; perturbo ①
muddle² n confusio, turba f
muddy adj lutosus, lutulentus;
limosus, caenosus; (troubled)
turbidus
muffle vt obvolvo ③
mug n poculum nt; ▶ **cup**
muggy adj umidus
mulberry n morum nt
■ **~ tree** n morus f
mule n mulus m; mula f
muleteer n mulio m
multiple adj multiplex
multiplication n multiplicatio f
multiply vt multiplico ①
■ **~** vi cresco ③; augeor ②
multitude n multitudo, turba,
plebs f; vulgus nt
mumble vi murmuro, musso ①
munch vt manduco ①; mando ③
mundane adj mundanus
municipal adj municipalis
municipality adj municipium f
munificence n munificentia,
largitas f
murder¹ n caedes f;
homicidium nt
murder² vt neco, trucido,
obtrunco ①
murderer n homicida m/f;
sicarius m
murderous adj sanguinarius,

cruentus
murky adj caliginosus,
tenebrosus, obscurus
murmur¹ n murmur nt; susurrus
m; fremitus m; (complaint) questus
m; querela f
murmur² vt&i murmuro, musso,
mussito, susurro ①; fremo ③;
(complain) queror ③
muscle n musculus; lacertus;
torus; m
muscular adj musculosus;
lacertosus; robustus, torosus
Muse¹ n Musa f
muse² vi cogito, meditor ①
museum n museum nt
mushroom n fungus; boletus m;
agaricum nt
music n (art) musica f; (of instruments
and voices) cantus; concentus m
musical adj musicus; (tuneful)
canorus
musician n musicus m
muslin n sindon f
mussel n (shellfish) mytilus m;
conchylium nt
must vi necesse est
□ **I ~** debeo ②; oportet ② me
+ infin
mustard n sinapi nt; sinapis f
muster¹ vt colligo ①; fig (up)
colligo ③
■ **~** vi convenio ④
muster² n
□ **pass ~** approbor ①
musty adj mucidus
mute adj mutus, tacitus
■ **~ly** adv tacite, silenter
mutilate vt mutilo, trunco ①
mutilation n mutilatio,
detruncatio f

Nn

mutineer n seditiosus; homo turbulentus m

mutinous adj seditiosus, turbulentus

mutiny[1] n seditio f; tumultus m

mutiny[2] vi tumultuor 🔲

mutter[1] vt&i murmuro, musso, mussito 🔲

mutter[2] n murmur nt; murmuratio f

mutton n ovilla (caro) f

mutual adj mutuus
  ■ ~ly adv mutuo, invicem

muzzle[1] n capistrum nt

muzzle[2] vt capistro 🔲, constringo ③

my pn meus
  □ ~ **own** proprius

myriad n decem milia ntpl; (countless number) sescenti adj

myrtle[1] n myrtus f

myrtle[2] adj myrteus

myself pn ipse, ego
  □ **I** ~ egomet

mysterious adj arcanus; occultus; mysticus
  ■ ~ly adv occulte

mystery n mysterium, arcanum nt; fig res occultissima f

mystical adj mysticus

mystify vt ludificor 🔲; fallo ③

myth n fabula f

mythical adj fabulosus

mythological adj mythologicus

mythology n mythologia f

nab vt prehendo ③

nag[1] vt sollicito 🔲

nag[2] n (horse) caballus m

Naiad n Naias f

nail[1] n unguis; (of metal) clavus m

nail[2] vt clavum pango or defigo ③

naive adj ingenuus, simplex

naivety n ingenuitas, simplicitas f

naked adj nudus, apertus; (of a sword) strictus

nakedness n nuditas f

name[1] n nomen, vocabulum nt; appellatio; fig (reputation) fama; celebritas f
  □ **by** ~ nominatim

name[2] vt nomino, appello, nuncupo 🔲; (mention) mentionem facio ③

nameless adj sine nomine, nominis expers

namely adv scilicet, videlicet

namesake n cognominis, eodem nomine dictus m

nap n somnus brevis m; (of cloth) villus m
  □ **take a** ~ obdormisco ③; (at noon) meridior 🔲

nape n
  □ ~ **of the neck** cervix f

napkin n (serviette) mappa f; (little towel) mantele nt

narcotic adj somnificus, somnifer
  ■ ~ n medicamentum somnificum nt

narrate vt narro, enarro 🔲

narration n narratio; expositio f

narrative n narratio; expositio f

narrator n narrator m

narrow[1] adj angustus; artus
■ ~**ly** adv (with difficulty) aegre

narrow[2] vt coarto ①; contraho ③

narrow-minded adj animi
angusti or parvi

narrowness n angustiae fpl

nastiness n foeditas; obscenitas f

nasty adj (foul) foedus; obscenus;
(ill-natured) malignus

nation n gens, natio f; (as political
body) populus m

national adj popularis

nationality n totum populi
corpus nt

native[1] adj nativus, vernaculus

native[2] n indigena m

native land n patria f

natural adj naturalis; nativus,
innatus; proprius; fig sincerus;
simplex
■ ~**ly** adv naturaliter; (unaffectedly)
simpliciter; (of its own accord) sponte;
(of course) plane

naturalist n rerum naturalium
investigator m

naturalization n civitatis
donatio f

naturalize vt aliquem civitate
dono ①

nature n natura f; (natural disposition)
indoles f, ingenium nt; (peculiarity)
proprietas f; (universe) mundus m

naughtiness n malitia,
petulantia f

naughty adj improbus, malus

nausea n (seasickness, feeling
sick) nausea f; (squeamishness)
fastidium nt

nauseate vt fastidium pario ③;
satio ①

nautical adj nauticus

naval adj navalis, maritimus

navel n umbilicus m

navigable adj navigabilis

navigate vt guberno ①
■ ~ vi navigo ①

navigation n navigatio f

navigator n nauta, navigator m

navy n classis f; copiae navales fpl

near[1] adj propinquus, vicinus; (of
relationship) proximus

near[2] adv prope; iuxta; proxime
■ ~ prep ad, apud, prope, iuxta
all + acc
□ ~ **at hand** propinquus, in
promptu
□ **far and** ~ longe lateque

near[3] vt appropinquo ① + dat

nearby adj propinquus, vicinus

nearly adv prope; fere; ferme;
(almost) paene

nearness adj propinquitas; vicinia;
(of relationship) propinquitas f

neat adj mundus; lautus; lepidus;
nitidus; concinnus; elegans

neatness n munditia;
concinnitas f

necessaries npl (of life)
necessitates fpl; necessaria ntpl

necessarily adv necessario

necessary adj necessarius
□ **it is** ~ necesse est

necessitate vt cogo ③

necessity n necessitas; (want)
egestas, necessitudo; (indispensable
thing) res omnino necessaria f

neck n collum nt; cervix f; (of a

bottle) collum *nt*

necklace *n* monile *nt*; (as ornament) torques *m/f*

nectar *n* nectar *nt*

need[1] *n* (necessity) opus *nt*, necessitas; (want) egestas, penuria *f*

need[2] *vt* (require) requiro ③; egeo ② + *abl*
■ ~ *vi* (must) debeo ②

needle *n* acus *f*

needless *adj* minime necessarius, supervacaneus
■ ~**ly** *adv* sine causa

needlework *n* opus acu factum *nt*

needy *adj* egens, indigens, egenus, inops

negative[1] *adj* negativus

negative[2] *n* negatio; repulsa *f*
□ **answer in the** ~ nego ①

neglect[1] *vt* neglego; desero, praetermitto ③

neglect[2] *n* neglegentia, incuria *f*; neglectus *m*

neglectful *adj* neglegens

negligence *n* neglegentia; incuria *f*

negligent *adj* neglegens, indiligens, remissus; incuriosus
■ ~**ly** *adv* neglegenter, incuriose

negligible *adj* minimi momenti

negotiable *adj* mercabilis

negotiate *vt* agere, gero ③
■ ~ *vi* negotior ①

negotiation *n* actio *f*

negotiator *n* conciliator; (spokesman) orator *m*

neigh[1] *vi* hinnio ④

neigh[2] *n* hinnitus *m*

neighbour *n* vicinus, finitimus,

propinquus *m*

neighbourhood *n* vicinitas; vicinia; proximitas; propinquitas *f*

neighbouring *adj* vicinus; finitimus; propinquus

neither *adj & pn* neuter
■ ~ *conj* nec, neque
□ ~ ... **nor** nec ... nec

nephew *n* fratris or sororis filius *m*; nepos *m*

nerve *n* nervus *m*; *fig* fortitudo *f*

nervous *adj* nervosus; (fearful) timidus, trepidus, anxius
■ ~**ly** *adv* nervose; (fearfully) trepide, timide, anxie

nervousness *n* anxietas *f*; timor *m*

nest *n* nidus *m*

nestle *vi* recubo ①

net *n* (for hunting) rete *nt*; iaculum *nt*; plaga *f*; (for fishing) funda *f*

netting *n* opus reticulatum *nt*

nettle *n* urtica *f*

network *n* reticulum *nt*

neuter *adj* neuter

neutral *adj* medius; neuter, aequus

neutrality *n* aequitas *f*

neutralize *vt* aequo; compenso ①

never *adv* nunquam
□ ~**more** nunquam posthac

nevertheless *adv* nihilominus, tamen, attamen

new *adj* novus, novellus, recens; integer

newcomer *n* advena *m/f*; hospes *m*

newfangled *adj* novicius

newly *adv* nuper, modo; recenter

newness *n* novitas *f*

n

news n res novae fpl; (report) fama f; rumor, nuntius m

newspaper n acta diurna ntpl

next[1] adj proximus; (of time) insequens

next[2] adv proxime; iuxta; (of time) deinde

nib n (of a pen) acumen nt

nibble vt rodo, arrodo ③

nice adj (dainty) delicatus; (choice) exquisitus; (exact) accuratus; subtilis; (fine) bellus; (pleasant) iucundus; (amiable) suavis
■ ~ly adv delicate; exquisite; subtiliter; accurate; belle

niche n loculamentum nt

nick n (cut, notch) incisura f
□ **in the very ~ of time** in ipso articulo temporis

nickname n nomen probrosum nt

niece n fratris or sororis filia f

niggardly adj parcus, tenax; avarus

night n nox f
□ **by ~** nocte, noctu

nightfall n
□ **at ~** sub noctem, primis tenebris

nightingale n luscinia, Philomela f

nightly adj nocturnus
■ ~ adv noctu, de nocte

nightmare n incubo m; suppressio f

night-watch n vigilia f; (person) vigil m

nimble adj pernix; agilis, mobilis

nimbleness n pernicitas, agilitas, mobilitas f

nimbly adv perniciter

nine adj novem (indecl)

□ **~ times** novies

nineteen adj undeviginti (indecl)

nineteenth adj undevicesimus

ninetieth adj nonagesimus

ninety adj nonaginta (indecl)

ninth adj nonus

nip vt vellico ①; (of cold) uro ③
□ **~ off** deseco ①

nipple n papilla f

no[1] adj nullus; nemo; nihil (indecl)
□ **~ one** nemo m/f; minime

no[2] adv haud, non; minime

nobility n nobilitas f; nobiles mpl; fig magnanimitas f

noble[1] adj nobilis, fig generosus; magnanimus

noble[2] n (**nobleman**) vir nobilis m

nobly adv praeclare; generose

nobody n nemo m/f

nocturnal adj nocturnus

nod n nutus m
■ ~ vi nuto ①; annuo, innuo ③; (be drowsy) dormito ①

noise n strepitus, stridor; fragor; sonus, sonitus; (of voices) clamor m
□ **make a ~** strepito, sono ①; fremo, strepo ③

noiseless adj tacitus; silens
■ ~ly adv tacite

noisily adv cum strepitu

noisy adj tumultuosus

nomad n vagus m

nominal adj nominalis
□ ~ly adv nomine, verbo

nominate vt nomino, designo ①

nomination n nominatio, designatio; (of an heir) nuncupatio f

nonchalantly adv aequo animo

nondescript adj nulli certo

generi ascriptus

none *adj & pn* nemo, nullus

nones *n* Nonae *fpl*

nonplus *vt* (checkmate) ad incitas redigo 3

nonsense *n* ineptiae, nugae *fpl*
□ **talk ~** absurde loquor 3; garrio 4
■ **~!** *int* gerrae! fabulae! somnia!

nonsensical *adj* ineptus, absurdus

nook *n* angulus *m*; latebra *f*

noon *n* meridies *m*

noose *n* laqueus *m*

nor *conj* nec, neque; neve, neu

normal *adj* secundum normam

normally *adv* ut solet

north *n* septentrio *m*

northerly *adj* septentrionem spectans

northern *adj* septentrionalis, aquilonius, boreus

north pole *n* Arctos *f*

northward *adv* septentrionem versus

north wind *n* aquilo *m*; boreas *m*

nose *n* nasus *m*; nares *fpl*

nostril *n* naris *f*

not *adv* non; haud; minime; (in prohibitions) ne
□ **~ at all** nullo modo
□ **~ yet** nondum

notable *adj* notabilis, insignis

notably *adv* insignite, insigniter, notabiliter; (especially) praecipue, praesertim

notch[1] *n* incisura *f*

notch[2] *vt* incido 3

note[1] *n* (mark) nota *f*; signum, indicium *nt*; (writing) chirographum *nt*

note[2] *vt* (mark) noto; (in a book) annoto 1; ▸ **notice**

notebook *n* commentarius *m*; tabulae *fpl*

noted *adj* nobilis; insignis, notus; clarus, praeclarus, celeber

noteworthy *adj* notandus, notabilis

nothing *n* nihil *nt*
□ **for ~** gratis

notice[1] *n* (noticing) animadversio, observatio *f*; (proclamation) edictum *nt*
□ **public ~** proscriptio *f*; (placard) titulus *m*
□ **escape ~** lateo 2
□ **give ~** edico 3
□ **take no ~ of** ignoro 1

notice[2] *vt* observo 1; animadverto 3

notification *n* denuntiatio, proscriptio *f*

notify *vt* significo, denuntio 1

notion *n* notio, notitia; opinio *f*

notoriety *n* notitia *f*

notorious *adj* (in a bad sense) famosus

noun *n* nomen *nt*

nourish *vt* nutrio 4; alo 3

nourishment *n* alimentum *nt*; cibus *m*

novel[1] *adj* novus

novel[2] *n* fabula *f*

novelist *n* fabulator *m*

novelty *n* novitas *f*

November *n* Novembris *m*

novice *n* tiro *m*; novicius *m*; novicia *f*

now *adv* nunc
□ **~ and then** nonnunquam

n

nowadays adv hodie, his temporibus

nowhere adv nusquam, nullo in loco

noxious adj nocens, noxius, perniciosus

nude adj nudus

nudge[1] n cubiti ictus m

nudge[2] vt fodico ①

nudity n nudatio f

nugget n massa f

nuisance n incommodum nt; molestia f

null adj (and void) irritus; nullus

numb[1] adj torpens, torpidus, hebes

numb[2] vt hebeto ①; obstupefacio ③

number[1] n numerus m; (of things) copia; vis; (of people) frequentia, multitudo f

number[2] vt numero, computo ①

numberless adj innumerus, innumerabilis

numbness n torpor; fig stupor m

numerous adj frequens, creber, multus

nuptial adj nuptialis, coniugalis, conubialis, coniugialis

nurse[1] n nutrix, altrix f

nurse[2] vt nutrio ④; fig foveo ②; (to the sick) ancillor ① + dat

nursery n (for children) cubiculum infantium nt; (of plants) seminarium nt

nurture vt educo ①; nutrio ④

nut n nux f

nutcracker n nucifrangibulum nt

nutrition n nutrimentum nt

nutritious adj (also **nutritive**) alibilis

nutshell n putamen nt; fig
□ **in a ~** paucis verbis

nymph n nympha; (girl) puella f

Oo

oaf n stultus, hebes m

oak n quercus, aesculus, ilex f; robur nt

oar n remus m

oarsman n remex m

oat(s) n avena f

oath n iusiurandum nt; (of soldiers) sacramentum m
□ **take an ~** iuro ① (in verba)

obedience n oboedientia f; obsequium m

obedient adj oboediens, obsequens
■ **~ly** adv oboedienter

obese adj obesus; ▸ **fat**

obesity n obesitas f

obey vt pareo ②, oboedio ④, obtempero ① all + dat

object[1] n obiectum nt; res f; (aim, design) consilium nt

object[2] vt (to) repugno + dat, improbo ①

objection n impedimentum nt; mora f
□ **if you have no ~** si per te licet

objectionable adj improbabilis

objective adj medius

obligation n officium;

beneficium *nt*

oblige *vt* cogo ③; obligo ①; devincio ④; (by kindness) bene de aliquo mereor ②
□ **be ~d to** debeo ② + *infin*

obliging *adj* officiosus, comis, blandus; benignus, beneficus
■ **~ly** *adv* comiter; benigne; officiose

oblique *adj* obliquus
■ **~ly** *adv* oblique

obliterate *vt* deleo ②; oblittero ①

oblivion *n* oblivio *f*; oblivium *nt*

oblivious *adj* obliviosus, immemor

oblong *adj* oblongus

obnoxious *adj* (hateful) invisus; (hurtful) noxius

obscene *adj* obscenus, spurcus, turpis

obscenity *n* obscenitas; turpitudo *f*

obscure¹ *adj* obscurus; fig perplexus; (intricate, puzzling) difficilis; (of style) intortus; (of people) ignobilis, ignotus

obscure² *vt* obscuro, obumbro ①

obscurity *n* obscuritas *f*; tenebrae *fpl*; fig ignobilitas, humilitas *f*

obsequious *adj* officiosus, morigerus
■ **~ly** *adv* cum nimia obsequentia; assentatorie

observance *n* observantia, obtemperatio *f*

observant *adj* attentus; oboediens

observation *n* observatio; animadversio *f*; (remark) dictum *nt*

observe *vt* observo ①;

animadverto ③; (utter) dico ③; (spy out) speculor ①; (obey) pareo ②, obtempero ① *both* + *dat*

observer *n* spectator *m*

obsolete *adj* obsoletus

obstacle *n* impedimentum *nt*; mora *f*

obstinacy *n* obstinatio, pertinacia, pervicacia, contumacia *f*

obstinate *adj* obstinatus, pertinax; pervicax, contumax
■ **~ly** *adv* obstinate; pervicaciter, contumaciter, pertinaciter

obstruct *vt* obstruo ③; (hinder) impedio ④

obstruction *n* obstructio *f*; impedimentum *nt*

obtain *vt* paro ①; consequor, quaero, nanciscor; adipiscor ③; (by entreaty) impetro ①

obtainable *adj* impetrabilis

obtrusive *adj* molestus; importunus

obtuse *adj* obtusus; hebes

obvious *adj* apertus, perspicuus, manifestus
■ **~ly** *adv* aperte, manifesto

occasion *n* occasio, causa *f*

occasional *adj* rarus, infrequens
■ **~ly** *adv* per occasionem, occasione oblata

occult *adj* occultus, arcanus

occupant *n* possessor *m*

occupation *n* (including military) possessio *f*; (employment) quaestus *m*; (business) studium, negotium *nt*

occupier *n* possessor *m*

occupy *vt* occupo ①; (possess) teneo ②; (inhabit) habito ①; (detain) detineo ②

occur vi occido, contingo ③; evenio; obvenio; fig in mentem venio ④

occurrence n casus, eventus m; res f

ocean n oceanus m

octagon n octagonon nt

octagonal adj octagonos

October n October m

odd adj (of number) impar; (strange) insolitus, inusitatus
■ ~**ly** adv inusitate

oddity n res inusitata f; monstrum nt

odds n discordia, dissensio, contentio f; (difference) discrimen nt
□ **be at** ~ **with someone** ab aliquo dissideo ②

odious adj odiosus, invisus; (disgusting) foedus
■ ~**ly** adv odiose

odorous adj odoratus

odour n odor m

of prep use genitive case

off¹ prep (out of) extra + acc; (from, of) de, ex + abl

off² adv procul, longe
□ **be well** ~ bene me habeo ②

offal n quisquiliae fpl

offence n (fault) offensa, culpa f; (insult) iniuria, contumelia f; (displeasure) offensio f

offend vt (insult, etc.) offendo; laedo ③; (against) violo ①
■ ~ vi (transgress) pecco ①

offender n reus m

offensive adj iniuriosus; (things) odiosus; foedus

offer¹ vt offero ③; do ①; praebeo ②; (at an auction) licitor ①

offer² n oblatio; (proposal) condicio f

offering n oblatio f; donum nt; (of a sacrifice) immolatio f

office n (duty) officium, munus; (room) tabularium m

officer n magistratus m; (in the army) praefectus, tribunus militaris m

official¹ adj publicus; (holding an official position) magistratui praepositus

official² n minister; accensus, lictor m

officiate vi officium praesto ①; (in religious ceremonies) rem divinam facio ③; (for another) alterius vice fungor ③

officious adj molestus

offspring n proles, progenies, stirps, suboles f

often adv saepe
□ **very** ~ persaepe, saepenumero

ogle vt limis oculis intueor ②

ogre n larva f

oh int oh! ah! ohe!

oil n oleum nt; olivum nt

oily adj (like oil) oleaceus; oleosus

ointment n unguentum, unguen; (as medicament) collyrium nt

old adj (in age) aetate provectus, senex; (ancient) vetus, vetustus; (out of use) obsoletus; (worn) exesus, tritus; (of former days) antiquus, priscus, pristinus
□ ~ **man** n senex m
□ ~ **woman** n anus f
□ ~ **age** n senectus f
□ ~ **of** ~ olim, quondam
□ ~**er** senior; vetustior
□ ~**est** natu maximus
□ **grow** ~ senesco ③

old-fashioned adj priscus, antiquus

oldness n antiquitas, vetustas f

oligarchy n paucorum potestas f

olive n olea, oliva f

Olympic adj Olympicus
□ **the ~ games** Olympia ntpl

omen n omen, auspicium, augurium, ostentum nt

ominous adj infaustus, infelix
■ **~ly** adv malis ominibus

omission n praetermissio f

omit vt praetermitto, omitto; (temporarily) intermitto ③

on¹ prep in, super both + abl; (near) ad + acc; (depending, hanging on) de; (immediately, after) e, ex abl + abl
□ **~ his side** cum illo

on² adv porro; (continually) usque
□ **and so ~** et cetera
□ **go ~** procedo, pergo ③

once adv (one time) semel; (formerly) olim, quondam; aliquando
□ **at ~** illico, statim; (at the same time) simul, uno tempore
□ **~ (and) for all** semel

one adj unus; (a certain person or thing) quidam
□ **~ another** alius alium
□ **~ after another** alternus; (adv) invicem
□ **~ by ~** singillatim
□ **it is all ~** perinde est
□ **~ or the other** alteruter

onerous adj gravis, praegravis, onerosus

oneself pn ipse; (with reflexive verbs) se

one-sided adj inaequalis, iniquus

onion n caepa f

only¹ adj unicus; unus, solus

only² adv solum, tantum, dumtaxat; (except) non nisi

onset n impetus, incursus m; incursio f

onslaught n impetus, incursus m; incursio f

onwards adv porro; protinus

ooze vi mano, emano; stillo, destillo ①

opal n opalus m

opaque adj densus, opacus

open vt aperio ④; patefacio, pando ③; (uncover) retego ③; (a letter) resigno ①; (begin) ordior ④
■ **~** vi patesco ③; (gape open) dehisco ③

open adj (not shut) apertus, patens; (visible) in conspectu positus; (evident) manifestus; (sincere) candidus, ingenuus; (public) communis, publicus
□ **in the ~ air** sub divo

opening n (act of making accessible) apertio f; (aperture) foramen nt; (air-hole) spiramentum nt

openly adv aperte; manifesto; (publicly) palam; fig libere, simpliciter

operate vt&i operor ①; ago ③; (cut open) seco ①; (have force) vim habeo ②

operation n effectus m; (surgical) sectio f; (business) negotium nt

operative adj efficax; potens

opinion n opinio, sententia; censura; mens f; iudicium nt; animus m; (esteem) existimatio f
□ **in my ~** mea sententia

opponent n adversarius m

opportune adj opportunus, idoneus, commodus

opportunity n occasio f; opportunitas, facultas, copia f

oppose vt oppono, obicio ③

■ ~ *vi* (resist) repugno, adversor, obsto [1]; resisto [3] *all + dat*

opposed *adj* adversus; adversarius; contrarius

opposite[1] *adj* adversus, contrarius, diversus

opposite[2] *n* contrarium *nt*

opposite[3] *adv&prep*
□ ~ **to** contra + *acc*, ex adverso

opposition *n* oppositio; repugnantia; discrepantia *f*; (obstacle) impedimentum *nt*

oppress *vt* affligo [3]; vexo; gravo, onero [1]

oppression *n* gravatio; iniuria; vexatio *f*

oppressive *adj* gravis; acerbus, molestus, iniquus

oppressor *n* tyrannus *m*

opt *vt* (for) opto [1]

optical *adj* oculorum *gen pl*

option *n* optio *f*

optional *adj* cuius rei optio est

opulence *n* opulentia *f*

opulent *adj* opulens, opulentus, dives
■ ~**ly** *adv* opulenter

or *conj* vel; aut; (interrogatively) an
□ **either ... ~** vel ... vel, aut ... aut, -ve ... -ve
□ **whether ... ~** sive ... sive, seu ... seu

oracle *n* oraculum, responsum *nt*; sors *f*

oral *adj* verbo traditus; praesens
■ ~**ly** *adv*

orange *adj* luteus

oration *n* oratio; (before the people or to the army) contio *f*

orator *n* orator *m*

oratory *n* oratoria ars, rhetorica; (eloquence) eloquentia *f*

orbit *n* orbis *m*; orbita *f*; (in astronomy) ambitus *m*

orchard *n* pomarium *nt*

orchestra *n* (body of musical performers) symphoniaci *mpl*

orchid *n* orchis *f*

ordain *vt* ordino [1]; iubeo [2]; instituo [3]

ordeal *n* fig discrimen *nt*

order[1] *n* ordo *m*; (rank) ordo *m*; (row) series *f*; (command) praeceptum, mandatum, decretum *nt*; (custom) mos *m*; consuetudo *f*; (instruction) rescriptum; (decree) edictum *nt* (association) societas *f*
□ **in ~** ordine, ex ordine
□ **out of ~** (out of turn) extra ordinem

order[2] *vt* (put in order) dispono [3]; ordino [1]; (give orders to) impero [1] + *dat*; iubeo [2]

orderly[1] *adj* compositus, ordinatus; (of people) oboediens; (quiet, sober) modestus, temperatus

orderly[2] *n* (mil) tesserarius *m*

ordinarily *adv* usitate, fere, plerumque, vulgo

ordinary *adj* usitatus, solitus, vulgaris

ordination *n* ordinatio *f*

ore *n* metallum *nt*

organ *n* (musical instrument) organum *nt*; (of the body) membrum *nt*

organism *n* compages, natura *f*

organist *n* organicus *m*

organization *n* ordinatio; temperatio *f*

organize *vt* ordino [1]; constituo,

dispono ③; formo ①
orgies n orgia ntpl
orgy n (revelry) comissatio f
oriental adj orientalis
origin n origo f; principium nt; ortus m
original¹ adj primitivus; pristinus; principalis
■ **~ly** adv ab origine; primum
original² n archetypum, exemplar; (writing) autographum nt
originality n proprietas quaedam ingenii f
originate vi orior ④; proficiscor ③
ornament¹ n ornamentum nt; ornatus m; decus nt
ornament² vt orno, decoro ①
ornamental adj quod ornamento, decori est
ornate adj ornatus; pictus
orphan adj & n orbus
orthodox adj orthodoxus
oscillate vi fluctuo ①
oscillation n fluctuatio f
osier n vimen nt; salix f
ostensible adj simulatus, fictus
ostensibly adv specie, per speciem
ostentation n ostentatio; iactatio f
ostentatious adj ambitiosus; gloriosus; vanus
■ **~ly** adv ambitiose, gloriose, iactanter
ostracism n testarum suffragia ntpl
ostrich n struthiocamelus m
other adj (another) alius; alter
□ **the ~s** ceteri, reliqui
otherwise adv alio modo, aliter;

(if not) si non; (besides) insuper
otter n lutra f
ought vi debeo, oportet ②
our prep (and **ours**) noster; (of ~ country) nostras nostri
ourselves prep nosmet, nosmet ipsi
oust vt eicio ③
out¹ adv (out of doors) foris; (to outside) foras
□ **get ~!** apage!
out² prep
□ **~ of** e, ex + abl; (on account of) propter; (~side, beyond) extra both + acc
□ **~ of the way** devius
outbreak n eruptio; fig (revolt) seditio f
outcast n exsul, extorris, profugus m
outcome n eventus m
outcry n clamor m; acclamatio f
outdo vt supero ①
outer adj exterior
outfit n apparatus m
outflank vt circumeo ④
outgrow vt fig dedisco ③
outlandish adj externus; barbarus
outlast vt durando supero ①
outlaw¹ n proscriptus m
outlaw² vt aqua et igni interdico + dat, proscribo ③
outlay n sumptus m; impensa f
outlet n exitus, egressus m
outline n forma rudis f
outlive vt supervivo ③; supersum ir; supero ①; superstes sum ir
outlook n prospectus m
outlying adj (distant) remotus

o

outnumber vt numero supero [1]

outpost n statio f

outrage[1] n iniuria f; (outrageous deed) flagitium nt

outrage[2] vt iniuria afficio [3]; laedo [3]

outrageous adj iniuriosus; atrox; (exaggerated) immodicus; immanis; immoderatus

outright adv (completely) prorsus

outrun vt praecurro [3]; cursu supero [1]

outset n principium, initium nt

outside[1] n pars exterior; superficies; (appearance) species f

outside[2] adj exterus

outside[3] adv foris, extrinsecus

outside[4] prep extra + acc

outskirts n (of towns) suburbium nt

outspoken adj candidus

outstanding adj prominens; (excellent) egregius; (of debts) solvendus

outstretch vt expando, extendo [3]

outstrip vt cursu supero [1]; praeverto [3]

outvote vt suffragiis supero [1]

outward adj externus, exterus
■ ~ adv foras

outwardly adv extrinsecus, extra

outwards adv in exteriorem partem; extra

outweigh vt praepondero [1]

outwit vt deludo [3]; circumvenio [4]

oval adj ovatus

ovation n ovatio f

oven n furnus m

over prep super; supra, trans
all + acc
■ ~ adv super; supra

□ ~ **and** ~ **again** iterum ac saepius

□ **all** ~ per totum

□ ~ **and above** insuper

overawe vt metu coerceo [2]

overbalance vt praepondero [1]

overbearing adj insolens, superbus

overcast adj nubilus, tristis

overcharge vi (in price) plus aequo exigo [3]

overcoat n lacerna, paenula f; pallium nt

overcome vt supero [1]; vinco [3]

overdo vt nimis studeo [2] + dat; nimis incumbo [3] + in + acc

overdue adj iamdudum solvendus

overflow vi exundo, redundo, restagno [1]; superfluo [3]
■ ~ vt inundo [1]

overgrown adj obductus, obsitus

overhang vi impendeo, immineo [2] both + dat

overhead adv desuper; supra, superne

overhear vt subausculto [1]

overjoyed adj ovans, exsultans

overlap vt excedo [3]

overload vt nimio pondere onero [1]

overlook vt (not notice) praetermitto; (have view of) prospecto [1]

overpower vt opprimo [3]; supero, exsupero [1]

overrate vt nimis aestimo [1]

override vt (cancel) rescindo [3]

overripe adj praematurus

overrule vt (check) coerceo [2]; (cancel) rescindo [3]

overrun[1] vt (devastate) vasto 1

overrun[2] adj obsitus

oversee vt curo 1; inspicio 3

overshadow vt obumbro, opaco; fig obscuro 1

oversight n (carelessness) incuria; neglegentia f; error m; (guardianship) cura, custodia f

overt adj manifestus, apertus
■ ~ly adv manifesto, aperte

overtake vt assequor, excipio 3; supervenio 4

overthrow vt subverto, everto, proruo; (the enemy) devinco, prosterno; (fig oppress) fig opprimo 3

overture n (proposal) condicio f; (beginning) exordium 1

overturn vt everto, subverto 3

overvalue vt nimis aestimo 1

overwhelm vt obruo; opprimo 3

owe vt debeo 2

owing prep (to) propter, ob + acc
□ **be ~ing (to)** per (aliquem) stat 1 ut + subj

owl n bubo m; strix, noctua, ulula f

own[1] adj proprius, peculiaris
□ **one's ~** suus, proprius

own[2] vt possideo, teneo, habeo; (acknowledge) confiteor 2; (claim) vindico 1

owner n dominus, possessor, erus m

ownership n dominium nt

ox n bos, iuvencus m

oyster n ostrea f

Pp

pace[1] n gressus; incessus; passus m

pace[2] vi incedo 3; spatior 1
■ ~ vt passibus emetior 4

pacific adj pacificus; tranquillus; placidus, pacifer

pacify vt placo, sedo, paco, pacifico 1; lenio 4

pack[1] n (bundle) sarcina f; fasciculus m; (crowd) grex m; turba f

pack[2] vt (cram) stipo, suffarcino 1; (bring together) colligo 3

package n sarcina f; fasciculus m

packet n fasciculus m

pact n foedus nt

pad n (cushion) pulvinus m

paddle n remus m

paddock n saeptum nt

padlock n sera f

page n (of a book) pagina f

pageant n spectaculum nt; pompa; fig species f

pageantry n species atque pompa f

pail n hama, situla f

pain n dolor; angor, cruciatus m

painful adj gravis, aeger; (laborious) operosus

painless adj sine dolore, doloris expers

pains n cura f; studium nt
□ **take ~** operam do 1

painstaking adj operosus

paint[1] vt (colour) (colore) induco; pingo, depingo 3; (the face) fuco 1

■ ~ *vi* (as artist) pingo ③

paint² *n* pigmentum *nt*

paintbrush *n* peniculus *m*

painter *n* (artist) pictor *m*

painting *n* (art) pictura; (picture) tabula, pictura *f*

pair¹ *n* (couple) par *nt*

pair² *vt* iungo, coniungo ③; copulo ①

palace *n* regia (domus) *f*; palatium *nt*

palatable *adj* sapidus; iucundus

palate *n* palatum *nt*

pale *adj* pallidus; exsanguis
  □ **be ~** palleo ②
  □ **grow ~** pallesco ③

paleness *n* pallor *m*

pall¹ *n* pallium *nt*

pall² *vi* nil sapio ③

palm¹ *n* (of the hand) palma *f*; (tree) palma *f*

palm² *vt*
  □ **~ off** vendito ①

palpitate *vi* palpito ①

palpitation *n* palpitatio *f*

paltry *adj* vilis; (trifling) minutus, exiguus

pamper *vt* indulgeo ② + *dat*

pamphlet *n* libellus *m*

pan *n* (vessel) patina *f*

panacea *n* panacea *f*; panchrestum medicamentum *nt*

pander *n* leno *m*
  ■ **~ to** *vi* lenocinor ①; indulgeo ② + *dat*

panegyric *n* laudatio *f*; panegyricus *m*

panel *n* (of a door) tympanum *nt*; (list of names) index *m*; album *nt*

pang *n* dolor, angor *m*

panic *n* terror, pavor, metus *m*; formido *f*

panic-stricken *adj* (also **panic-struck**) pavidus, exterritus

panorama *n* prospectus *m*

pant *vi* palpito; trepido; anhelo ①

panther *n* panthera *f*

panting¹ *adj* anhelus

panting² *n* anhelitus *m*

pantry *n* cella penaria *f*; promptuarium *nt*

paper *n* (for writing on) charta *f*; (newspaper) acta diurna *ntpl*
  ■ **~s** *pl* scripta *ntpl*; litterae *fpl*

parable *n* parabola *f*

parade¹ *n* (mil) decursus; locus exercendi; (display) apparatus *m*; pompa, ostentatio *f*

parade² *vt* (mil) instruo ③; *fig* ostento ①
  ■ **~** *vi* (march ceremonially) decurro ③

paradise *n* Elysii campi *mpl*

paradox *n* quod contra opinionem omnium est

paradoxical *adj* praeter opinionem accidens

paragon *n* specimen, exemplum *nt*

paragraph *n* caput *nt*

parallel¹ *adj* parallelos; *fig* consimilis

parallel² *n* parallelos *m*; (comparison) collatio, comparatio *f*

parallel³ *vt* exaequo; (compare) comparo ①; (be equal) par sum *ir*

paralyse *vt* debilito, enervo ①

paralysis *n* paralysis *f*; *fig* torpedo *f*; torpor *m*

paralytic *n* paralyticus *m*

paramount *adj* supremus;

summus

parapet n pluteus m

paraphernalia n apparatus m

paraphrase¹ n paraphrasis f

paraphrase² vt liberius interpretor ①

parasite n parasitus, assecla m

parasitic adj parasiticus

parasol n umbella f; umbraculum nt

parcel n pars f; (bundle) fasciculus m

parch vt arefacio ③; torreo ②

parched adj torridus

parchment n membrana f

pardon¹ n venia f

pardon² vt ignosco ③; condono ①
both + dat

pardonable adj condonandus

parent n parens m/f

parentage n genus nt; prosapia, origo f

parental adj paternus; maternus

parenthesis n interpositio, interclusio f

park n (for game) vivarium; (for pleasure) viridarium nt; horti mpl

parley¹ n colloquium nt

parley² vi colloquor ③

parrot n psittacus m

parry vt averto, defendo ③; propulso ①

parsimonious adj parcus, sordidus

parsimony n parsimonia f

part¹ n pars, portio; (in a play) persona f, partes fpl; (duty) officium nt; (of a town) regio f
□ **in ∼** partim

part² vt separo ①; divido ③;
■ ∼ vi (go away) discedo ③;

digredior ③, abeo ir; (gape open) dehisco, fatisco ③
□ ∼ **with** dimitto ③

partial adj per partes; (biased) iniquus
□ ∼ **to** cupidus + gen
■ ∼ly adv partim

partiality n gratia; iniquitas f

participant n particeps m/f

participate vi particeps sum or fio ④

participation n participium nt; societas f

particle n particula f

particoloured adj versicolor; varius

particular¹ adj proprius; peculiaris; singularis; (fastidious) fastidiosus; (especial) praecipuus
■ ∼ly adv particulatim; singillatim; (especially) praesertim, praecipue

particular² n singula ntpl

parting n divisio f; (from) discessus m

partisan n fautor, homo factiosus m

partition n partitio f; (enclosure) saeptum nt; (of rooms) paries m

partly adv partim; nonnulla ex parte, in parte

partner n socius m; socia f; particeps, consors m/f

partnership n societas, consociatio, consortio f

partridge n perdix m/f

party n factio; secta f; partes fpl; (detachment) manus f

pass¹ vt (go) eo ir; vado, cedo ③; (go by) praetereo; (cross) transeo ir; (a law, etc.) fero ir; (approve) approbo ①

■ ~ *vi* praetereo *ir*; praetervehor ③; (of time) praetereo *ir*; (from one to another) migro ①; (for) habeor ②; (hand over) trado ③

□ ~ **away** transeo *ir*; (die) pereo *ir*; labor, effluo ③; (cease) cesso ①

□ ~ **by** praetereo *ir*

□ ~ **over** traicio, transgredior ③; fig praetereo ③

□ ~ **round** circumfero, trado ③

□ **let** ~ praetermitto, dimitto ③

pass² *n* fauces, angustiae *fpl*; saltus *m*; (ticket) tessera *f*

passable *adj* (of a way) pervius; fig mediocris, tolerabilis

passage *n* (action) transitus *m*; transitio *f*; transmissio, traiectio; (thoroughfare) transitio pervia *f*; (of a book) locus *m*

passenger *n* viator; (by water) vector *m*

passing *adj* transiens; praeteriens; fig brevis, caducus

passion *n* cupiditas *f*; fervor *m*; impetus, animi motus *m*; (anger) ira *f*; (for) studium *nt*; (love) amor *m*

passionate *adj* fervidus, ardens, vehemens; iracundus

■ ~**ly** *adv* ardenter; iracunde, vehementer

passive *adj* patibilis; passivus

■ ~**ly** *adv* passive

passport *n* syngraphus *m*

password *n* tessera *f*

past¹ *adj* praeteritus; (immediately preceding) proximus, superior

■ ~ *n* praeteritum tempus *nt*; actum tempus *nt*

past² *prep* praeter; (beyond) ultra both + acc

paste¹ *n* gluten *nt*

paste² *vt* glutino ①

pastime *n* oblectamentum *nt*; ludus *m*

pastoral *adj* pastoralis; pastorius

pastry *n* crustum *nt*, bellaria *ntpl*; crustula *ntpl*

pasture *n* pabulum *nt*

pat *n* plaga levis *f*

patch¹ *n* pannus *m*

patch² *vt* sarcio, resarcio ④; assuo ③

patent¹ *adj* apertus, manifestus

□ ~**ly** plane

patent² *n* diploma *nt*

paternal *adj* paternus, patrius

paternity *n* paternitas *f*

path *n* semita *f*; trames, callis *m*; fig (course) via *f*

pathetic *adj* patheticus

■ ~**ally** *adv* pathetice

pathway *n* semita *f*; callis *m*

patience *n* patientia *f*; tolerantia

patient¹ *adj* patiens; tolerans

■ ~**ly** *adv* patienter; aequo animo

patient² *n* aegrotus *m*; aegrota *f*

patrician *adj* & *n* patricius

patrimony *n* patrimonium *nt*; hereditas *f*

patriot *n* amans patriae *m*; bonus civis *m*

patriotic *adj* amans patriae; bonus, pius

patriotism *n* amor patriae *m*; pietas *f*

patrol *n* vigil *m*; excubiae *fpl*

■ ~ *vi* excubias agere ③

patron *n* patronus *m*

patronage *n* patrocinium, praesidium *nt*

patronize *vt* faveo, studeo ② + dat; (be present at) adsum *ir* + dat

patter[1] n crepitus m

patter[2] vi crepo, crepito ①

pattern n (sample) exemplar, exemplum; (model) specimen nt

paunch n venter m

pauper n pauper, egens, inops m/f

pause[1] n pausa, mora; intermissio f; intervallum nt

pause[2] vi intermitto, quiesco ③

pave vt (viam saxo) sterno ③

pavement n pavimentum nt; stratura f

pavilion n tentorium nt

paw[1] n ungula f; pes m

paw[2] vt pedibus pulso (terram) ①

pawn[1] n pignus nt; (in chess) latrunculus m

pawn[2] vt pignero; oppignero, obligo ①

pawnbroker n pignerator m

pay[1] n (mil) stipendium nt; (wages, hire) merces f; (profit) quaestus, fructus m

pay[2] vt (pecuniam debitam) solvo ③; (stipendium) numero ①; fig persolvo ③
■ ~ vi pendo ③; (be profitable) prosum ir, proficio ③
□ ~ **for** (hire) conduco ③; (buy) emo ③; fig (suffer) poenas do ①
□ ~ **off** dissolvo ③

payable adj solvendus

pay-day n dies stipendii solvendi m

payment n (act) solutio f; (sum of money) pensio f

pea n pisum, cicer nt

peace n pax; quies f; otium nt; (of mind) tranquillitas animi f

peaceable adj pacis amans; placabilis; (of things) pacatus;

placidus, quietus

peaceably adv pacate; cum (bona) pace

peaceful adj pacis amans; placabilis; (of things) pacatus; placidus, quietus
■ ~**ly** adv pacate; cum (bona) pace

peacefulness n tranquillitas f

peacemaker n pacificator m

peach n malum Persicum nt

peacock n pavo m

peak n (of a mountain) cacumen, culmen nt; apex, vertex m

peal[1] n (of thunder) fragor m; (of bells) concentus m

peal[2] vi sono, resono ①

pear n pirum f
■ ~**-tree** n pirus f

pearl n margarita, baca, gemma f

pearly adj gemmeus, gemmans

peasant n rusticus, agrestis, agricola m

pebble n lapillus, calculus m

peck vt rostro impeto ③; mordeo ②

peculiar adj (one's own) proprius; peculiaris; (unusual) praecipuus, singularis
■ ~**ly** adv praesertim, imprimis; praecipue

pedantic adj litterarum ostentator, putidus; professorius
■ ~**ally** adv putide

pedantry n scholasticorum ineptiae fpl; eruditio insulsa f

pedestal n stylobates m; spira f

pedestrian adj pedester; pedibus (abl)
■ ~ n pedes m

pedigree n stemma f

pedlar n institor m

peel[1] *n* cutis, tunica *f*; cortex *m*

peel[2] *vt* decortico, desquamo ①

peep[1] *n* (look) contuitus *m*

peep[2] *vi* per rimam speculor ①

peer *n* (equal) par *m*

peer at *vt* (scrutinize) rimor ①

peevish *adj* stomachosus, morosus, difficilis
 ■ **~ly** *adv* stomachose, morose

peg *n* paxillus *m*

pelican *n* pelicanus, onocrotalus *m*

pellet *n* globulus *m*; pilula *f*

pell-mell *adv* effuse, sine ordine, promiscue

pelt[1] *n* pellis *f*

pelt[2] *vt* peto ③; lapido; (beat) verbero ①

pen[1] *n* (to write with) calamus, stylus *m*; (for sheep) ovile *nt*

pen[2] *vt* scribo, compono ③; (shut in) includo ③

penal *adj* poenalis

penalty *n* poena; mul(c)ta *f*; supplicium *nt*

penance *n* satisfactio *f*; (atonement) piaculum *nt*; (punishment) poena *f*

pencil *n* graphis *f*; peniculus, penicillus *m*

pending *adj* instans; (law) sub iudice

pendulum *n* libramentum *nt*

penetrate *vt* penetro ①

penetration *n* acies mentis; sagacitas *f*

peninsula *n* paeninsula *f*

penitence *n* paenitentia *f*

penitent *adj* paenitens

penknife *n* scalprum *nt*

pennant *n* vexillum *nt*

penniless *adj* omnium rerum egens, inops

pennon *n* vexillum *nt*

penny *n* as, nummus, denarius *m*

pension *n* merces annua *f*; annuum beneficium *nt*

pensive *adj* cogitabundus

penultimate *adj* paenultimus

people *n* populus *m*; homines *mpl*; (nation) natio *f*
 □ **~ say** dicunt
 □ **common ~** vulgus *nt*; plebs *f*

pepper *n* piper *nt*

perceive *vt* sentio ④; percipio ③; video ②; intellego ③

percentage *n* rata portio *f*

perception *n* perceptio, animadversio *f*

perch[1] *n* (for birds) sedile (avium) *nt*; (fish) perca *f*

perch[2] *vi* insido, + *dat*; assido ③ + in + *abl*

perennial *adj* perennis

perfect[1] *adj* perfectus; absolutus; (intact) plenus, integer
 ■ **~ly** *adv* perfecte; absolute; (entirely) plane

perfect[2] *vt* perficio, absolvo ③

perfection *n* perfectio; absolutio, summa *f*

perforate *vt* perforo, terebro ①

perforation *n* (hole) foramen *nt*

perform *vt* perficio; exsequor; fungor + *abl*; (bring to pass) efficio; (accomplish) perago ③

performance *n* exsecutio; actio *f*; (work) opus *nt*

performer *n* effector; (player) actor, histrio *m*

perfume[1] *n* odor *m*

perfume² vt suffio 4

perhaps adv fortasse, forte, forsitan

peril n periculum, discrimen nt

perilous adj periculosus
■ **~ly** adv periculose

period n tempus nt; aetas f

periodical adj periodicus
■ **~ally** adv temporibus certis

perish vi pereo, intereo ir; extinguor, cado 3

perishable adj fragilis, caducus, infirmus

perjure vi (oneself) peiero, periuro 1

perjury n periurium nt
□ **commit ~** peiero, periuro 1

permanent adj diuturnus, mansurus, perpetuus
■ **~ly** adv perpetuo

permeate vt penetro, pervagor, pererro 1

permission n permissio, venia f
□ **with your ~** pace tua, tua bona venia

permit vt sino, permitto, concedo 3
□ **it is ~ted** licet 2

pernicious adj perniciosus; noxius
■ **~ly** adv perniciose

perpendicular adj directus

perpetrate vt perficio; facio, committo, admitto 3; perpetro 1

perpetual adj sempiternus; perpetuus; perennis; continuus
■ **~ly** adv perpetuo, semper, usque, continenter

perplex vt (confound) turbo 1; confundo 3

perplexity n perturbatio;

anxietas f

persecute vt insector; vexo 1

persecution n insectatio; vexatio f

perseverance n perseverantia, constantia, assiduitas f

persevere vi persevero, persto 1

persevering adj constans; tenax (propositi); assiduus

persist vi persto, persevero 1

persistence n permansio (in aliqua re) f

persistent adj pertinax

person n homo m
□ **any ~** quilibet, quivis
□ **in ~** ipse (ego, ille, etc.)

personage n homo notus m

personal adj privatus
■ **~ly** adv per se; ipse

perspiration n sudor m

perspire vi sudo 1; sudorem emitto 3

persuade vt suadeo, persuadeo 2 + dat

persuasion n persuasio; fides; opinio f

persuasive adj suasorius
■ **~ly** adv apte ad persuadendum

pert adj procax

pertinent adj appositus (ad rem), aptus, idoneus

perturb vt turbo, perturbo 1

peruse vt lego, perlego 3

pervade vt perfundo 3; permano 1; pervagor 1

perverse adj perversus, pravus

perversion n depravatio f

perversity n perversitas, pravitas f

pervert vt depravo 1; perverto,

484

corrumpo ③
pest n pestis, pernicies f
pester vt infesto, sollicito, vexo ①
pet¹ n (little favourite) corculum nt;
deliciae fpl
pet² adj dilectus, carus
pet³ vt ▶ **caress, fondle**
petal n floris folium nt
petition n preces fpl; libellus m;
petitio f
petrify vt in lapidem converto ③;
fig obstupefacio ③
petty adj minutus, angustus;
(trifling) parvus
phantom n phantasma nt; vana
species f; spectrum n
phase n vices fpl
pheasant n phasiana; avis
phasiana f
phenomenal adj singularis
phenomenon n res nova f;
ostentum nt
philanthropic adj benignus,
humanus
philanthropist n generi
humano amicus m
philanthropy n benignitas,
humanitas f
philosopher n philosophus,
sapiens m
philosophical adj philosophicus
■ **~ly** adv philosophice; fig aequo
animo
philosophize vi philosophor ①
philosophy n philosophia;
sapientia; (theory) ratio f
phoenix n phoenix m
phrase¹ n locutio f
phrase² vt loquor ③
physical adj corporis gen; physicus

■ **~ly** adv natura (abl); physice
physician n medicus m
physics n physica ntpl
physique n corpus nt
pick¹ vt (pluck) carpo, decerpo ③;
lego; (choose) eligo
□ **~ off** avello ③
□ **~ out** eligo ③
□ **~ up** tollo; colligo ③
□ **~ holes in** carpo, rodo ③
pick² n (tool) dolabra f; (choicest part)
flos m, robur nt
pickaxe n dolabra f
picket n (mil) statio f
pickpocket vt&i manticulor ①
picture¹ n tabula, tabella; effigies;
fig descriptio f
picture² vt depingo ③; (imagine)
fingo ③
picture-gallery n pinacotheca f
picturesque adj venustus,
pulcher, amoenus
pie n (pastry) crustum nt
piece n (part) frustum nt; pars,
portio f; (fragment) fragmentum nt;
(coin) nummus m
□ **tear to ~s** dilanio, lacero ①
pier n pila; (massive structure) moles
f; agger m
pierce vt perforo, terebro ①; (with
a sword, etc.) transfigo, perfodio,
transadigo; fig (with grief) (aliquem)
dolore afficio ③
piercing adj penetrabilis; (of
sounds) acutissimus; fig sagax
■ **~ly** adv acute
piety n pietas f
pig n porcus, sus m
pigeon n columba f; columbus m
pigeon-hole n loculamentum nt
pigheaded adj obstinatus

485

pigment n pigmentum nt

pigsty n hara f

pike n (spear) hasta, lancea f; (fish) lucius, lupus m

pile¹ n (heap) acervus, cumulus m; congeries f; (of firewood) rogus m; (nap of cloth) villus m

pile² vt (up) coacervo, cumulo, aggero, accumulo ①; exstruo, congero ③

pilfer vt surripio ③; suffuror ①

pilfering n direptio f

pilgrim n peregrinator m

pilgrimage n peregrinatio f

pill n pilula f

pillage¹ n (act) vastatio, direptio; (booty) praeda f; spolium nt

pillage² vt populor, praedor, vasto, spolio ①; diripio ③

pillar n (support, prop) columna; pila f

pillow n pulvinus m; cervical nt

pilot¹ n gubernator, rector m

pilot² vt guberno ①; rego ③

pimp n leno m

pimple n pustula, pusula f

pin¹ n acus; acicula f; (nail, peg) clavus m

pin² vt acu figo; affigo ③

pincers n forceps f

pinch¹ vt vellico ①; (as cold) uro, aduro ③; (hurt) laedo ③

pinch² n vellicatio f
□ feel the ~ urgeor ②, premor ③

pine¹ n pinus f

pine² vi (away) tabesco ③; marcesco, conficior ③

pink adj (of colour) roseus

pinnacle n fastigium nt

pint n (measure) sextarius m

pioneer n (mil) cunicularius; explorator viae; fig praecursor m

pious adj pius; (pure) sanctus
■ ~ly adv pie, sancte

pip n (of fruit) semen nt; nucleus m; (of grapes) acinus m

pipe n (tube) tubus m; (mus) fistula f; tibia, arundo f; calamus m

piper n fistulator, tibicen m

piquant adj fig salsus, facetus; acutus

pique n offensio f; offensa f; odium nt

piracy n piratica f

pirate n praedo maritimus, pirata m

pit n fossa, fovea, scrobis f; puteus m; (abyss, gulf) barathrum nt; (in theatre) cavea f; (quarry) fodina f

pitch¹ n pix f

pitch² n summum fastigium nt

pitch³ n mus sonus m

pitch⁴ vt (a tent, the camp) pono ③; (fling) conicio ③
■ ~ vi fluctuo ①

pitch-black adj (also **pitch-dark**) fuscus, niger; obscurus, caliginosus

pitcher n urceus m

pitchfork n furca f

pith n medulla f

pithy adj medulla abundans; nervosus; fig sententiosus

pitiable adj miserabilis; flebilis; lamentabilis; afflictus

pitiful adj misericors; (pitiable) miserabilis; (contemptible, mean) abiectus
■ ~ly adv misericorditer; miserabiliter; abiecte

pitiless adj immisericors; durus,

▶ **cruel**

pity¹ n misericordia, miseratio f

pity² vt&i miseret (me alicuius), misereor ②; miseror ①; misereresco ③ all + gen

pivot n cardo m

placard n edictum nt

place¹ n locus m; (office) munus nt
□ **in the first ∼** fig primum, primo

place² vt pono ③; loco, colloco ①

placid adj placidus, tranquillus; quietus
■ ∼**ly** adv placide, tranquille, quiete

plague¹ n pestilentia; fig pestis f

plague² vt vexo, crucio ①

plain¹ n campus m; planities f; aequor nt

plain² adj (smooth) planus; (not ornamented) inornatus; (distinct) clarus; (simple) simplex; (evident) apertus, manifestus; sincerus

plainly adv distincte, clare, plane; simpliciter; (evidently) manifeste, aperte, perspicue

plaintiff n petitor m; accusator m

plaintive adj flebilis; querulus
■ ∼**ly** adv flebiliter

plait vt implico ①; intexo ③

plan¹ n (project) consilium, propositum nt; (of ground) forma, designatio f

plan² vt (scheme) excogito ①; (draw) designo ①

plane¹ n (tool) runcina f; (level surface) superficies f

plane² vt runcino ①

planet n planeta m; stella erratica f

plane-tree n platanus f

plank n axis m; tabula f

plant¹ n herba, planta f

plant² vt planto ①; sero ③

plantation n plantarium nt

plaque n tabula f

plaster¹ n tectorium; gypsum; (med) emplastrum nt

plaster² vt trullisso, gypso ①; induco; illino ③

plasterer n tector m

plate n (thin sheet of metal) lamina, brattea f; (silver for table) vasa argentea ntpl; (dish) patella f

plated adj bratteatus

platform n suggestus m; suggestum nt

plaudit n plausus, clamor m

plausible adj probabilis; speciosus

play¹ n (act of playing) ludus; lusus m; (movement) motus m; (scope) area f; locus m; (at a theatre) fabula, comoedia, tragoedia f
□ **fair ∼** aequitas f

play² vt&i ludo ③; (frolic, etc.) lascivio ④; luxurio ①; (on musical instruments) cano ③; (gamble) aleam exerceo ②; (as actor) partes ago ③

player n (on the stage) histrio, actor; (on an instrument) fidicen, tibicen, citharista m; (of a game) lusor m

playful adj lascivus, iocosus, ludibundus
■ ∼**ly** adv iocose

plaything n (rattle) crepundia ntpl; (doll) pupa f

plea n (excuse) excusatio, causa f

plead vt&i causas ago; (for one) (aliquem) defendo; (against) contra aliquem causam dico ③; (in excuse) excuso ①

pleasant adj amoenus, iucundus, gratus; urbanus, lepidus

please vt&i (give pleasure) placeo ②
+ dat; delecto ①
□ **as you** ~ ut vobis libet

pleased adj laetus, felix

pleasing adj gratus; lepidus;
iucundus

pleasure n voluptas; iucunditas
f; deliciae fpl; (caprice) libido f; (will)
arbitrium nt

plebeian adj & n plebeius; vulgaris

pledge[1] n pignus nt; (surety) vas,
praes m; (proof) testimonium nt

pledge[2] vt pignero ①; spondeo ②;
promitto ③

plentiful adj largus, affluens,
uber, copiosus, abundans
■ **~ly** adv large, abunde, copiose,
ubertim

plenty n copia, abundantia,
ubertas f

pliable adj flexibilis; lentus, mollis;
flexilis; tractabilis; mansuetus

pliant adj flexibilis; lentus, mollis;
flexilis; tractabilis; mansuetus

plight n condicio f; status m

plot[1] n (conspiracy) coniuratio f; (of
land) agellus m; (surveying) designatio
f; fig (of a play, etc.) argumentum nt

plot[2] vi coniuro ①
■ ~ vt molior ④; excogito ①

plotter n ▶ conspirator

plough[1] n aratrum nt

plough[2] vt aro ①

ploughman n arator m

pluck[1] n (courage) animus nt

pluck[2] vt (pull) vello ③; vellico ①;
(gather) carpo, decerpo; (off) avello;
deripio; (out) evello; eripio; fig
□ ~ **up** (courage) colligo ③

plug[1] n obturamentum nt

plug[2] vt obturo ①

plum n prunum nt
■ ~ **tree** n prunus f

plumage n plumae, pennae fpl

plumber n (worker in lead)
plumbarius m

plumb-line n perpendiculum nt;
linea f

plume n penna, pluma; (crest)
crista f

plummet n perpendiculum nt;
linea f

plump adj nitidus, obesus;
corpulentus

plumpness n obesitas f; nitor m

plunder[1] n (booty) praeda f;
spolium nt; (act of plundering) rapina,
direptio f; (stolen goods) furta ntpl

plunder[2] vt praedor ①; diripio ③;
spolio, vasto, populor ①

plunge vt mergo, summergo; (a
sword) condo, subdo ③ in + abl
■ ~ vi immergor; fig me mergo
③ in ...

plural adj pluralis

ply vt exerceo ②

pocket n (pouch) marsupium nt;
crumena f

pocket-money n peculium nt

pod n siliqua f

poem n poema, carmen nt

poet n poeta, vates m

poetess n poetria f

poetic adj (also **poetical**)
poeticus
■ ~**ally** adv poetice

poetry n (art) poetice; (poems)
poesis f; carmen nt

point[1] n punctum; (pointed end)
acumen nt; (of swords, etc.) mucro
m; (of a spear) cuspis f; fig quaestio f;
casus m; res f; argumentum nt

□ ~ **of view** iudicium nt

□ **main** or **chief** ~ caput nt

point² vt (aim) intendo ③

□ ~ **at** monstro ①

□ ~ **out** monstro ①

pointed adj praeacutus; acutus; fig salsus; (stinging) aculeatus

■ ~**ly** adv acriter, acute; plane, aperte

pointer n index m/f

pointless adj fig insulsus, frigidus

poise n (equilibrium) aequipondium nt; fig (sophistication) urbanitas f

poised adj libratus

poison¹ n venenum, virus nt

poison² vt (a thing) veneno; (a person) veneno neco; fig vitio ①

poisoner n veneficus m; venefica f

poisoning n veneficium nt

poisonous adj venenatus; veneficus; venenifer

poke vt (alicui) latus fodico ①; (touch) tango ③; (move) moveo ②

poker n rutabulum nt

polar adj arctous

pole n (staff) asser m; pertica f; contus m; (of the earth) polus, axis m

police n securitatis urbanae cura or custodia f

policeman n vigil, lictor m

policy n reipublicae administratio; (craft) astutia, calliditas f; (stratagem) ars f; dolus m; (in good sense) consilium nt

polish¹ vt polio; expolio ④; limo, levo ①

polish² n nitor, levor m; fig lima f

polite adj comis, urbanus; affabilis, humanus

politely adv comiter, humane

politeness n urbanitas, comitas, humanitas f

politic adj prudens

political adj publicus, civilis

■ ~**ly** adv quod ad rempublicam attinet

politician n vir rerum publicarum peritus m

politics n res publica f

poll n (voting) suffragium nt

pollen n pollen nt

polling-booth n saeptum, ovile nt

poll tax n exactio capitum f

pollute vt inquino, contamino, maculo, commaculo, foedo ①; polluo ③

pollution n colluvio; impuritas, macula, labes f

polygon n polygonum nt

polygonal adj polygonius, multangulus

pomp n pompa f; splendor, apparatus m

pompous adj magniloquus; fig inflatus

pond n stagnum nt; lacus m

ponder vt&i considero, pensito, meditor ①; perpendo ③

pony n mannulus m

pool n lacuna f; stagnum nt

poop n puppis f

poor adj pauper; egenus, inops; (of soil) macer; fig tenuis; mediocris; miser

poorly adj aeger

poplar n populus f

poppy n papaver nt

populace n vulgus nt; plebs f

popular adj popularis; gratiosus;

(common) vulgaris
■ **~ly** adv populariter, vulgo

popularity n favor populi m; studium populi nt; gratia f

population n incolae urbis, civitatis, etc. m/fpl

populous adj populo frequens, celeber

porcelain n murra f; murrina ntpl

porch n vestibulum nt; porticus f

porcupine n hystrix f

pore vi (over) incumbo ③ + dat

pork n porcina, suilla f

porous adj rarus

porpoise n porculus marinus m

porridge n puls f

port n portus m

portable adj quod (facile) portari potest

portcullis n cataracta m

portend vt praesagio ④; auguror ①; portendo ③; praemonstro, significo ①

portent n ostentum, portentum, prodigium nt

porter n ianitor, ostiarius, custos; (carrier) baiulus m

portfolio n scrinium nt

portico n porticus f

portion n pars; portio f

portly adj obesus

portrait n imago, effigies f

portray vt pingo ③; delineo ①; fig depingo, describo ③

pose n status m; (pretence) simulatio f

position n situs, positus; fig status m; condicio f

positive adj certus; fig confidens; pervicax

■ **~ly** adv praecise; confidenter; pervicaciter

possess vt possideo, teneo, habeo ②; (of feelings) occupo ①; invado ③; (induce) animum induco ③

possession n (occupancy) possessio f; (goods) bona ntpl
□ **in the ~ of** penes + acc

possessor n possessor, dominus m

possibility n possibilitas f; (opportunity) facultas, copia, potestas f

possible adj possibilis
□ **as (quickly) as ~** quam celerrime

possibly adv (perhaps) fortasse

post¹ n (stake) sudis f; stipes, palus m; (doorpost) postis m; (letter-carriers) tabellarii mpl; (station) statio, sedes f, locus m; (office) munus nt

post² vt (put up) colloco ①; pono; constituo ③; (a letter) tabellario litteras do ①

poster n tabula f

posterior adj posterior

posterity n posteri; minores mpl

posthumous adj postumus

postman n tabellarius m

postpone vt differo, profero ③; prorogo ①

posture n status, habitus, gestus m

posy n ▶ bouquet

pot n olla f; aenum, vas nt

potent adj potens

potion n potio f

potter n figulus m

pottery n (trade) figlina f; (ware) figlinum nt; fictilia ntpl; (workshop) figlina f

p

pouch n pera f; sacculus m

poultice n malagma, fomentum, cataplasma nt

poultry n aves cohortales fpl

pounce[1] n (swoop) impetus m

pounce[2] vi involo ①; insilio ④

pound[1] n (weight and money) libra f; (for cattle) saeptum nt

pound[2] vt (crush) contundo, contero; (cattle) includo ③

pour vt&i fundo; fundor ③
□ ~ **down** (of rain vi) ruo; fig ingruo ③
□ ~ **out** effundo, profundo ③; vi effundor ③

poverty n paupertas, pauperies, inopia, penuria, egestas f

powder[1] n pulvis m

powder[2] vt pulvere conspergo ③; (reduce to powder) in pulverem redigo ③

power n vis; potestas f; (authority) ius; imperium nt; (mil) copiae fpl; fig (of mind) dos animi f
□ **in** (one's) ~ penes + acc

powerful adj validus, praevalidus, potens; (effectual) efficax
■ ~**ly** adv potenter; efficaciter

powerless adj invalidus; infirmus, imbecillus; impotens; (vain) irritus; inefficax
□ **be** ~ **to** non possum ir, nequeo ④

practicable adj quod fieri potest

practical adj (opposite to theoretical) activus; (taught by experience) usu doctus
■ ~**ly** adv ex usu; (almost) paene

practice n usus m; exercitatio; experientia; (custom) consuetudo f

practise vt&i exerceo ②; tracto ①;

(do habitually) factito ①

praetor n praetor m

praetorian adj praetorius

praetorship n praetura f

praise[1] n laus, laudatio; f; praeconium nt

praise[2] vt laudo, collaudo, praedico ①; effero ③

praiseworthy adj laudabilis, laudandus

prance vi exsulto ①

prank n ludus m; fraus f

prattle[1] n garrulitas f

prattle[2] vi garrio ④; blatero ①

prawn n squilla f

pray vt precor, exoro, supplico, flagito ①; oro ①
□ ~ **for** intercedo ③ pro + abl; (for a thing) peto, posco ③
□ ~ **to** adoro; supplico ①

prayer n preces fpl; precatio f

preach vt&i praedico ①

preamble n exordium, prooemium nt

precarious adj incertus, precarius
■ ~**ly** adv precario

precaution n cautio, provisio f

precede vt antecedo, praegredior, praecurro ③; anteeo, praeeo ir

precedence n ius praecedendi nt; principatus m

precedent n exemplum nt

preceding adj praecedens, antecedens

precept n praeceptum nt

precinct n termini, limites mpl

precious adj pretiosus, carus; dilectus

precipice n locus praeceps m; praeruptum nt

precipitate[1] *vt&i* praecipito 🔟; (hurry) accelero, festino, maturo 🔟

precipitate[2] *adj* praeceps; fig inconsultus

precipitous *adj* praeceps, praeruptus, declivis

precise *adj* certus, definitus; (very) ipse; fig (exact) accuratus, exactus; (of manner) rigidus
■ ~**ly** *adv* accurate

precision *n* accuratio f

preclude *vt* praecludo 🔟; arceo, prohibeo 🔟

precocious *adj* praecox; festinatus, praematurus

preconception *n* praeiudicata opinio f

precursor *n* praenuntius, praecursor m

predatory *adj* praedatorius; rapax

predecessor *n* decessor, antecessor m

predestination *n* praedestinatio f

predestine *vt* praedestino 🔟

predicament *n* praedicamentum nt; (difficulty) angustiae fpl

predict *vt* praedico 🔟; auguror, vaticinor 🔟

prediction *n* praedictio f; praedictum; vaticinium nt; vaticinatio f

predominant *adj* praepollens
□ **be** ~ praevaleo 🔟

predominate *vi* praevaleo 🔟

pre-eminence *n* excellentia, praestantia f; (supreme rule) principatus m

pre-eminent *adj* insignis, praestans, praecipuus
■ ~**ly** *adv* praestanter, praecipue

preface *n* praefatio f; exordium, prooemium nt

prefer *vt* praefero ir, praepono 🔟, antefero ir, antepono 🔟; (like better) malo ir

preferable *adj* potior, praestantior
□ **it is** ~ praestat

preferably *adv* potius

preference *n*
□ **give** ~ (to), antepono 🔟

pregnancy *n* graviditas; praegnatio f

pregnant *adj* gravida, praegnans, gravis

prejudge *vt* praeiudico 🔟

prejudice[1] *n* opinio praeiudicata f; detrimentum nt

prejudice[2] *vt* in suspicionem adduco 🔟; (injure) laedo 🔟
□ **be ~d against** suspicor 🔟

prejudicial *adj* noxius

preliminary[1] *n* prooemium nt; prolusio f

preliminary[2] *adj* primus

prelude *n* prooemium nt; fig prolusio f

premature *adj* praematurus; fig praeproperus

premeditation *n* praemeditatio f

premises *n* (house) domus f; (estate) fundus m; villa f; praedium nt

premiss *n* praemissa f; praemissa ntpl

premium *n* praemium nt

premonition *n* praesagium nt

preoccupation *n* praeoccupatio f

preoccupy vt praeoccupo ①

preparation n praeparatio f;
paratus, apparatus m

prepare vt paro, comparo,
praeparo ①; (furnish) orno, adorno;
(study) meditor ①
■ ~ myself comparo ①; se accingere ③

prepared adj paratus

preposterous adj praeposterus;
perversus; absurdus
■ ~ly adv perverse, absurde

prerogative n praerogativa f;
privilegium nt

presage[1] n praesagium;
augurium, omen, portentum nt

presage[2] vt&i portendo ③;
significo ①; praesagio ④; praedico
③; vaticinor ①

prescribe vt praecipio;
praescribo; propono ③

prescription n praescriptum nt;
(custom) usus m

presence n praesentia f
□ **in my ~** me praesente
□ **in the ~ of** coram + abl

present[1] adj praesens; hic
□ **for the ~** in praesens
□ **be ~** adsum ir

present[2] n donum, munus nt

present[3] vt offero ③; dono, do ①;
largior ④; introduco; (law) sisto ③; fig
(~ itself) obvenio ④

presentation n donatio f

presentiment n praesagium nt
□ **have a ~ of** praesentio ④

presently adv (soon) mox;
(immediately) ilico, statim

preservation n conservatio f

preserve vt servo, conservo ①;
tueor ②; (fruits) condio ④

preside vi (over) praesideo ②;

praesum ir both + dat

presidency n praefectura f

president n praeses,
praefectus m

press[1] n (for wine, oil, clothes, etc.)
prelum nt; (of people) turba f

press[2] vt premo; comprimo ③; fig
urgeo ②; insto, flagito ①; (force to
serve) vi comparo ①
□ ~ **on** or **upon** insto ①, insisto
③ both + dat

pressing adj instans

pressure n pressura f; fig angor m;
aerumna f

prestige n gloria f

presume vt&i (be conceited) arrogo,
(hope) spero ①; (suppose) conicio ③;
(dare) audeo ②

presumption n arrogantia f;
(conjecture) suspicio f; (opinion)
sententia f

presumptuous adj arrogans;
audax, temerarius
■ ~ly adv arroganter, audacter

pretence n simulatio f;
▶ pretext

pretend vt&i simulo, dissimulo ①

pretension n (claim) postulatio;
(display) ostentatio f

pretext n species f; praetextum nt
□ **under the ~ of** specie + gen

prettiness n elegantia, venustas f

pretty adj bellus; lepidus; venustus
□ ~ **well** mediocriter

prevail vi praevaleo, polleo;
persuadeo ②; (become current)
increbresco ③
□ ~ **upon** impetro ① with ab + abl

prevalent adj vulgatus
□ **be ~** increbresco ③

prevaricate vi tergiversor, praevaricor []

prevarication n praevaricatio, tergiversatio f

prevent vt praevenio []; praeverto []; (stop) impedio []; prohibeo []

prevention n prohibitio f

previous adj antecedens, prior
■ **~ly** adv antea, antehac, prius

prey[1] n praeda f
□ **beast of ~** animal rapax nt, fera f

prey[2] vi (on, upon) praedor []; rapio []; fig vexo []

price n pretium nt
□ **at what ~?** quanti?

priceless adj inaestimabilis

prick[1] n punctus m; (goad) stimulus m

prick[2] vt pungo []; fig stimulo []
□ **~ up** (aures) arrigo []

prickle n aculeus m; spina f

prickly adj spinosus

pride[1] n superbia f; fastidium f; fastus m

pride[2] vt (oneself on) iacto []; superbio [] + abl

priest n sacerdos, antistes, vates m

priestess n sacerdos, antistita, vates f

priesthood n (office) sacerdotium nt; (collectively) sacerdotes mpl

prim adj rigidus

primarily adv praecipue

primary adj principalis; praecipuus

prime[1] n (of life) florens aetas f; fig flos m; robur nt

prime[2] adj egregius, optimus

primeval adj primigenius,

primaevus; priscus

primitive adj principalis, primitivus; (simple) simplex

prince n rex, princeps, regulus; (king's son) regis filius m

princess n regina; regia puella; regis filia f

principal[1] adj principalis, praecipuus; maximus, potissimus
■ **~ly** adv maxime, praecipue; potissimum, praesertim

principal[2] n caput nt; praeses, praefectus m

principle n principium nt; origo f; (in philosophy) ratio f; (precept) praeceptum nt; (maxim) institutum nt

print[1] vt imprimo []

print[2] n (mark) nota f; vestigium nt

prior adj prior

prise vt
□ **~ open** vecti refringo []

prison n carcer m; custodia f

prisoner n (of war) captivus; (law) reus m; rea f

privacy n solitudo f; secretum nt

private adj privatus; (domestic) domesticus
■ **~ly** adv privatim, secreto; clam

privation n privatio; (need) inopia f

privilege n privilegium, beneficium nt; immunitas f

prize[1] n (reward) praemium nt; (victory) palma f

prize[2] vt (value) aestimo []; (highly) magni facio []

probability n similitudo veri, probabilitas f

probable adj verisimilis, probabilis

probably adv probabiliter

probation n probatio f

probe[1] n specillum nt

probe[2] vt specillo tento ①

problem n (problems) problemata ntpl; quaestio f

problematical adj incertus, dubius

procedure n ratio agendi f, ordo m; forma f; (proceedings) acta, facta ntpl

proceed vi progredior; procedo, incedo; (continue) pergo ③; (advance) proficio ③; (arise, spring from) orior ④; proficiscor ③

proceeding n facinus, factum nt
□ ~s acta, facta ntpl
□ **legal** ~s actio f; controversia iudiciaria f

proceeds n reditus, proventus m

process n processus m; (method) ratio f; (law) lis, actio f

procession n pompa f

proclaim vt promulgo, pronuntio ①; edico, propono ③

proclamation n pronuntiatio, promulgatio f; edictum nt

proconsul n proconsul m; pro consule

proconsular adj proconsularis

proconsulship n proconsulatus m

procrastinate vt differo ir
■ ~ vi cunctor; moror ①

procrastination n tarditas, procrastinatio, cunctatio f

procure vt (get) acquiro, adipiscor, consequor ③; comparo ①

prod vt pungo ③

prodigal adj prodigus; profusus, effusus

prodigious adj (monstrous)

prodigiosus; (great) immanis; ingens
■ ~ly adv prodigiose; valde

prodigy n prodigium, monstrum, portentum; fig miraculum nt

produce[1] vt (bring forward) produco ③, profero ir; (bring forth) pario ③; (yield) fero, effero, profero ir; (cause) facio ③; creo ①; (incite) cieo, moveo ②

produce[2] n fructus m

product n (of earth) fructus m; fruges fpl; (of work) opus nt

production n prolatio; (manufacture) fabricatio f

productive adj ferax, fertilis, fecundus; fig efficiens

profane[1] adj profanus; fig impius

profane[2] vt violo, profano ①

profanity n impietas f; nefas nt

profess vt profiteor ②

profession n (avowal; calling, trade) professio f; (business, trade) ars f

professional adj ad professionem pertinens

professor n (literary) professor m

proffer vt offero, propono ③

proficiency n ars, peritia f

proficient adj peritus

profile n facies obliqua f; (as portrait) catagrapha ntpl

profit[1] n emolumentum; lucrum nt; reditus, fructus, quaestus m

profit[2] vi prosum ir + dat
■ ~ vi proficio ③; (get advantage) lucror ①; (fructum percipio ③)

profitable adj fructuosus, quaestuosus; lucrosus; utilis
□ **be** ~ prosum ir

profligate adj perditus, flagitiosus, nequam indecl

profound adj (deep) altus; fig

subtilis; abstrusus
■ ~**ly** *adv* penitus; subtiliter, abscondite

profundity *n* altitudo, subtilitas *f*

profuse *adj* effusus, profusus
■ ~**ly** *adv* effuse, profuse

profusion *n* effusio, profusio, ubertas; abundantia *f*

programme *n* libellus *m*

progress¹ *n* iter *nt*; progressus, processus *m*

progress² *vi* progredior, fig proficio ③

progression *n* progressus *m*

progressively *adv* (gradually) paulatim, sensim, gradatim

prohibit *vt* veto ①; interdico ③; prohibeo ②

prohibition *n* interdictum *nt*

project¹ *n* propositum, consilium *nt*

project² *vt* molior ④
■ ~ *vi* consilium capio ③; (jut out) promineo, emineo ②

projectile *n* missile *nt*

projecting *adj* prominens; proiectus

projection *n* proiectum *nt*; proiectura *f*

proletariat *n* plebs *f*; vulgus *nt*

prolific *adj* fecundus, ferax, fertilis

prologue *n* prologus *m*

prolong *vt* produco ③; prorogo ①; extendo, traho ③

prominence *n* eminentia *f*

prominent *adj* eminens; conspicuus

promiscuous *adj* promiscuus; mixtus
■ ~**ly** *adv* promiscue, sine ullo discrimine

promise¹ *n* promissum *nt*; (act) promissio, fides *f*

promise² *vt&i* promitto ③; polliceor, spondeo ②

promising *adj* bona or summa spe

promote *vt* augeo ②; tollo, effero, proveho ③; (serve) consulo + *dat* ③

promotion *n* amplior gradus *m*; dignitas *f*

prompt¹ *adj* promptus, paratus; (speedy) maturus
■ ~**ly** *adv* prompte; (speedily) mature

prompt² *vt* subicio ③; (incite, *etc.*) impello ③

prone *adj* pronus; propensus; proclivis

prong *n* dens *m*

pronounce *vt* pronuntio; (articulate syllables) enuntio ①; loquor ③

pronouncement *n* iudicium *nt*; sententia *f*

pronunciation *n* pronuntiatio *f*

proof *n* documentum, argumentum; indicium; signum; specimen *nt*; ratio demonstrandi or probandi *f*; (trial) experimentum *nt*

prop¹ *n* fulcrum; fig columen *nt*

prop² *vt* (up) fulcio ④; adminiculor ①

propagate *vt* propago; (spread) dissemino ①

propagation *n* propagatio *f*

propel *vt* impello; propello ③

propensity *n* proclivitas *f*

proper *adj* proprius; (suitable) aptus; (becoming) decorus
■ ~**ly** *adv* proprie; apte; decore

property *n* fortuna *f*; bona *ntpl*;

(characteristic) proprium nt

prophecy n praedictum nt; vaticinatio; (power) praedictio, divinatio f

prophesy vt&i vaticinor, divino, auguror ①; praedico ③

prophet n vates m/f; fatidicus, propheta m

prophetess n vates f

prophetic adj fatidicus; (of inward feeling) praesagus

propitious adj propitius; faustus, felix, secundus
■ ~ly adv fauste, feliciter

proportion n ratio, proportio; symmetria f
□ **in ~** pro portione

proposal n condicio f; (plan) consilium nt

propose vt condicionem offero ③; (intend) cogito ①; (marriage) condicionem quaero ③; (a toast) propino ①; (a law) fero ③; promulgo ①

proposition n condicio; (bill) rogatio f; (advice) consilium nt; (logic) propositio f

propound vt propono, profero ③

proprietor n dominus, erus m

propriety n decorum n, convenientia f

propulsion n impulsus m

prosaic adj pedester, solutae orationi proprior; fig aridus, ieiunus

proscribe vt proscribo ③

proscription n proscriptio f

prose n oratio soluta, prosa f; pedester sermo m

prosecute vt exsequor, persequor ③; insto ① + dat; persevero ① in + abl; (accuse) reum facio ③

prosecution n exsecutio; (law) accusatio f

prospect n prospectus, despicius m; (hope, expectation) spes, exspectatio f

prospective adj futurus

prospectus n titulus m, index m/f

prosper vi prospera fortuna utor ③; successus prosperos habeo ②; bene cedo, cedo ③

prosperity n res secundae fpl; prospera fortuna, prosperitas f

prosperous adj secundus, prosperus; florens
■ ~ly adv prospere; bene

prostitute n scortum nt; meretrix f

prostitution n meretricium nt

prostrate adj prostratus, proiectus; fig afflictus, fractus
□ **fall ~ me** (ad pedes alicuius) proicio; procumbo ③

prostration n animus fractus m

protect vt tueor ②; protego, defendo ③; servo ①; custodio ④

protection n tutela, custodia f; praesidium, tutamen nt

protector n patronus, defensor, propugnator m

protest¹ n acclamatio; intercessio; interpellatio f

protest² vi&t obtestor, acclamo, interpello ①; (against) aegre fero ir, intercedo vi; (profess) profiteor ③

prototype n exemplar m

protract vt traho, protraho ③, differo ir, produco ③

protrude vi promineo, emineo ②

protuberance n tuber nt; tumor, gibbus m

proud adj superbus, arrogans; magnificus

☐ **be** ~ superbio, fastidio [4]

■ ~**ly** adv superbe; arroganter; (of things) magnifice

prove vt probo [1]; evinco, arguo [3]; (try) experior [4]; (as false) refello [3]; (show) monstro, demonstro; (make good) praesto [1]

■ ~ vi (become) fio ir; (turn out to be) evado [3]

proverb n proverbium nt

proverbial adj proverbialis

provide vt paro, comparo [1]; (supply) praebeo [2]; suppedito [1]

■ ~ vi (against) provideo ne + subj, praecaveo [2]; (for) provideo (alicui) [2]; (with) instruo [3] + acc and dat

provided conj

☐ ~ **that** dummodo, dum, modo

providence n providentia, diligentia, cura; (divine) providentia f

provident adj providus; cautus

province n provincia; regio f; fig provincia f; munus nt

provincial adj provincialis; fig rusticus

provision n praeparatio f; apparatus m; copia f

☐ ~**s** (food) alimentum nt; victus m; penus m/f; (for an army) commeatus m; cibaria ntpl; (for a journey) viaticum nt

provisional adj temporarius

■ ~**ly** adv ad tempus

proviso n exceptio, cautio, condicio f

provocation n provocatio f; (wrong) iniuria f

provoke vt lacesso [3], provoco, irrito, stimulo [1]

prow n prora f

prowess n virtus f

prowl vi praedor; (roam about) vagor [1]

☐ ~ **round** obambulo, oberro [1]

prowler n praedator m

proximity n propinquitas, proximitas f

proxy n vicarius m

☐ **by** ~ vice, vicem both + gen

prudence n prudentia; circumspectio f

prudent adj cautus, prudens, consideratus

■ ~**ly** adv caute; considerate

prune[1] n prunum nt

prune[2] vt (trees) decacumino, amputo, puto [1]; fig reseco [1]; recido [3]

pruning-knife n falx f

pry vi scrutor, perscrutor, exploro [1]

prying adj curiosus

pseudo adj fictus, simulatus

puberty n pubertas, pubes f

public[1] adj publicus; communis; (known) pervulgatus

■ ~**ly** adv in publico; palam, aperte

public[2] n homines mpl; fig vulgus nt; multitudo f

publican n (farmer of taxes) publicanus; (innkeeper) caupo m

publication n promulgatio f; (of a book) editio f; (published book) liber m

publicity n celebritas f; fig lux f

publish vt (make known) vulgo; divulgo [1]; patefacio [1]; (a book) edo [3]

publisher n bibliopola, librarius m

publishing n (of a work) editio f

puddle n lacuna f

puerile adj puerilis

puff[1] n (of wind) flatus m

puff[2] vt inflo, sufflo
■ ~ vi (pant) anhelo 🔟
□ ~ **up** inflo 🔟
□ be ~d **up** intumesco 🔟

puffy adj sufflatus; tumens; turgidus; inflatus

pugnacious adj pugnax

pull[1] vt vello 🔟; vellico 🔟; (drag) traho 🔟
■ ~ vi vires adhibeo 🔟; annitor 🔟
□ ~ **away** avello 🔟
□ ~ **apart** diripio
□ ~ **back** revello, retraho 🔟
□ ~ **down** (houses, etc.) demolior 🔟; destruo; (violently) everto 🔟
□ ~ **off** avello; detraho 🔟
□ ~ **out** extraho, evello, eximo 🔟
□ ~ **up** extraho; eripio, eruo 🔟

pull[2] n (act) tractus; (effort) nisus m

pulley n trochlea f

pulp n (flesh) caro, pulpa f

pulpit n rostra ntpl; suggestus m; tribunal nt

pulsate vi vibro 🔟

pulsation n pulsus m

pulse n (venarum) pulsus m

pulverize vt pulvero 🔟

pumice n pumex m

pump[1] n antlia f

pump[2] vt haurio 🔟; fig (question) exploro 🔟

pumpkin n pepo, melopepo m; cucurbita f

pun n lusus verborum, iocus m

punch[1] n (blow) pugnus, ictus m; (tool) terebra f

punch[2] vt (perforate) terebro 🔟; (strike) pugno percutio 🔟

punctilious adj scrupulosus, religiosus

punctual adj promptus, accuratus, ad tempus veniens or rediens
■ ~**ly** adv ad tempus, accurate

punctuate vt interpungo 🔟

punctuation n (act) interpunctio f; (break between sentences) interpunctum nt

puncture n (act) punctio f; (hole) punctum nt

pungent adj (to the senses) acutus; fig mordax; aculeatus

Punic adj Punicus

punish vt punio 🔟; castigo 🔟; animadverto 🔟; vindico 🔟
□ be ~ed poenas do 🔟

punishment n (act) castigatio; poena f; supplicium nt

punt n ratis f

puny adj pusillus, exiguus

pup n catulus m

pupil n discipulus m; discipula f; (of the eye) pupilla, pupula f

puppet n pupa f

puppy n catulus m

purchase[1] n (act) emptio; (merchandise) merx f

purchase[2] vt emo 🔟; (procure) comparo 🔟

purchaser n emptor; mercator m

pure adj mundus; purus; (unmixed) merus; fig purus; (chaste) castus; (of character) integer

purge[1] vt purgo, mundo 🔟

purge[2] n purgatio f

purification n purgatio; purificatio; expiatio; lustratio f; lustrum nt

purify vt purifico, purgo, lustro, expio 🔟

purity *n* munditia; *fig* castitas; integritas *f*

purple[1] *n* purpura *f*; ostrum, conchylium *nt*; mureux *m*
  □ **dressed in ~** purpuratus

purple[2] *adj* purpureus

purpose[1] *n* propositum, consilium *nt*; animus *m*; (end, aim) finis *m/f*; (wish) mens, voluntas *f*
  □ **on ~** de industria; consulto; consilio
  □ **to the ~** ad rem ...
  □ **to no ~** frustra

purpose[2] *vi* propono, statuo, constituo, decerno ③

purposely *adv* consulto, consilio, de industria

purr[1] *vi* murmuro, susurro ①

purr[2] *n* murmur *nt*; susurrus *m*

purse[1] *n* crumena *f*; (money-belt) zona *f*

purse[2] *vt* (up) corrugo ①; contraho ③

pursue *vt* sequor, persequor, insequor; *fig* insisto + *dat*; utor ③ + *abl*

pursuit *n* insectatio *f*; (occupation) studium *nt*

pus *n* pus *nt*; sanies *f*

push[1] *vt* trudo, pello ③; urgeo ②
  □ **~ forward** protrudo, propello ③
  ■ **~ in** *vt* intrudo ③
  □ **~ on** impello ③; urgeo ②; *vi* contendo ③; (hasten) festino ①

push[2] *n* pulsus, impetus, impulsus, *fig* conatus *m*; (energy) strenuitas *f*

put *vt* pono ③; loco, colloco ①; (a question) quaero; (again) repono; (aside) sepono ③
  □ **~ away** sepono ③; amoveo ②; (in safety) recondo ③; (send away)

dimitto ③
  □ **~ back** repono ③
  □ **~ by** (place in safety) condo ③
  □ **~ down** depono; (lower, let down) demitto; (suppress, abolish) supprimo; tollo; (in writing) scribo ③; (in an account) fero ir
  □ **~ forward** (promote) promoveo ②; (excuses, *etc.*) profero ir; (as a candidate) produco ③
  □ **~ in** impono; (forcibly) immitto; interpono ③
  □ **~ off** (deter) repello ③; (disconcert) perturbo ①; (distract) distraho ③; (postpone) differo ③; profero ir
  □ **~ on** impono; (dress, clothes) induo; (add) addo ③
  □ **~ out** expello, eicio; (fire, light) exstinguo; (stretch out) extendo; *fig* (disconcert, *etc.*) confundo ③; perturbo ①; (dislocate) extorqueo ②
  □ **~ together** compono ③, confero ir
  □ **~ up** erigo; arrigo ③; (for sale) propono; (as a candidate) peto ③; (at auctions) auctionor ③; (with others) fero ③; (impose upon) impono (alicui) do ①
  □ **~ upon** superimpono, superpono; addo ③ *all + acc and dat*; (impose upon) impono ③

putrefy *vi* putresco ③, putrefio ir

putrid *adj* puter, putridus

puzzle[1] *n* quaestio abstrusa or obscura; *fig* difficultas *f*; nodus *m*

puzzle[2] *vt* confundo ③; perturbo ①
  ■ **~ vi** haereo ②

puzzling *adj* perplexus, obscurus

pygmy *n* nanus, pumilio *m*

pyramid *n* pyramis *f*

pyre *n* rogus *m*; bustum *nt*; pyra *f*

Qq

quadrangular adj quadriangulus

quadruped n quadrupes m/f

quadruple¹ adj quadruplex; quadruplus

quadruple² n quadruplum nt

quadruple³ vt quadruplico ①

quaestor n quaestor m

quaestorship n quaestura f

quagmire n palus, lacuna f

quail¹ n coturnix f

quail² vi despondeo ②; paveo ②

quaint adj mirus, insolitus; (strange, odd) rarus

■ **~ly** adv mire

quake vi tremo ③

qualification n (endowment) indoles; (condition) condicio f; status m

qualified adj aptus, idoneus; capax, dignus; (moderate) mediocris

qualify vt aptum reddo, instruo ③; (limit, restrict, etc.) tempero, extenuo ①

quality n qualitas; natura f; fig dos, (degree) ordo, gradus m

qualm n (of conscience) religio f

quandary n angustiae f

quantity n quantitas; magnitudo f; nervus m; vis, copia f

quarrel¹ n iurgium nt; altercatio, rixa, simultas f

quarrel² vi iurgo; altercor; rixor ①

quarrelsome adj iurgiosus, rixosus, pugnax

quarry n (stone-quarry) lapicidinae, lautumiae fpl; (prey) praeda f

quarter¹ n quarta pars f; quadrans m; (side, direction, district) regio f

■ **~s** pl (dwelling) tectum nt; habitatio f; (temporary abode) hospitium, deverticulum nt; (mil) castra

□ **winter ~s** hiberna ntpl

□ **at close ~s** comminus

quarter² vt in quattor partes divido ③; (soldiers, etc.) colloco ①; dispono ③; (receive in one's house) hospitium praebeo ②

quarterly adj (for three months) trimestris; (by the quarter) tertio quoque mense

■ **~** adv tertio quoque mense

quash vt (law) rescindo ③; aboleo ②; abrogo ①

queen n regina f

queer adj (strange) ineptus, insulsus, ridiculus

quell vt opprimo, restinguo ③; sedo; domo ①

quench vt extinguo, restinguo ③; (thirst) (sitim) sedo ①, restinguo ③

querulous adj querulus; queribundus

query n quaestio; interrogatio; dubitatio f

quest n investigatio f

question¹ n interrogatio; (doubt) dubitatio f; (disputed point) quaestio f; controversia; fig (matter) res, causa f

□ **call in ~** dubito ①

□ **without ~** non dubium est, haud dubie

question² vt&i interrogo; dubito; (examine) in ius voco; (investigate)

scrutor 🗆

questionable adj dubius, incertus

quibble[1] n captio; cavillatio f

quibble[2] vi captiose dico 🗆; cavillor 🗆

quick adj (nimble, swift) agilis, celer; pernix; (keen, sharp) acer, acutus; fig (of mind: clever) sollers
🗆 **be ~** (go fast) propero; maturo 🗆

quicken vt (enliven) animo; (hasten) celero, propero; maturo; (rouse) excito, instigo 🗆

quickly adv (also **quick**) cito; velociter; propere; (hastily) festinanter

quickness n (nimbleness) agilitas; (liveliness) vivacitas f; fig sagacitas f; acumen (ingenii) nt

quicksand n syrtis f

quick-witted adj sollers

quiet[1] adj quietus, tranquillus; placidus; (silent) tacitus; silens, mutus
🗆 **be or keep ~** quiesco 🗆; (be silent) sileo; taceo 🗆; conticesco 🗆

quiet[2] n quies, tranquillitas f; (silence) silentium nt; (peace) pax f

quiet[3] vt (also **quieten**) tranquillo; paco, sedo 🗆

quietly adv quiete, tranquille; sedate; tacite

quietness n quies, requies f; pax f; silentium nt

quill n penna f; calamus m; (of porcupines) spina f

quilt n stragulum nt

quit vt (leave) relinquo, desero 🗆
■ ~ vi discedo 🗆; migro 🗆

quite adv (completely) omnino, penitus, prorsus; valde; (fairly) satis

questionable | radiate

🗆 **~ so** ita est

quiver[1] vi tremo, contremisco 🗆; trepido 🗆

quiver[2] n pharetra f; corytus m

quota n rata pars, portio f

quotation n (passage quoted) locus allatus m

quote vt affero, profero 🗆; cito 🗆

Rr

rabbit n cuniculus m

rabble n plebecula, faex populi f; vulgus nt; (crowd) turba f; grex m

rabid adj rabidus, rabiosus

rabies n rabies f

race[1] n genus nt; stirps: prosapia; proles; (nation) gens f; (running) cursus m; (contest) certamen nt

race[2] vi cursu contendo 🗆

racecourse n stadium, spatium nt; hippodromus m

racehorse n celes m

racing n cursus m; certamen nt

rack[1] n (for punishment) eculeus m; tormentum nt; (for holding fodder) falisca f

rack[2] vt (torture) torqueo 🗆; (one's brain) cum animo reputo 🗆

racket n (noise, stir) strepitus, tumultus m

racy adj salsus

radiance n fulgor, splendor m

radiant adj radians, nitidus, clarus, fulgidus, splendidus

radiate vi radio 🗆; fulgeo, niteo 🗆

■ ~ vt spargo ③
radiation n radiatio f
radically adv radicitus; penitus
radish n raphanus f
radius n radius m
raft n ratis f
rafter n canterius m; trabs f;
tignum nt
rag n pannus; m; (ragged clothes)
pannuli mpl; dilabidae vestes fpl
rage¹ n furor m; rabies f; ira f
rage² vi furo ③; saevio ④; (as the sea)
aestuo ①
ragged adj (in tatters) lacer; (wearing
such clothes) pannosus
raging adj furens, furiosus;
furibundus, rabidus
raid¹ n incursio, irruptio f
raid² vt invado ③
rail n (fence) saepimentum nt;
(baluster) cancelli mpl
railing n (fence) saepimentum nt
rain¹ n pluvia f; imber m
rain² vi
□ **it is ~ing** pluit
rainbow n arcus pluvius, arcus m
rainwater n aqua caelestis f;
aquae pluviae fpl
rainy adj pluvius, pluvialis;
pluviosus
raise vt attollo ③; elevo ①; (erect)
erigo ③; (build) exstruo, extruo ③;
(money) cogo ③; (an army) exercitum
contraho ③; (a siege) solvo ③;
(increase) augeo ②; (up) sublevo ①
raisins n uva passa f
rake¹ n rastrum nt, irpex m
rake² vt rado; (together) corrado
③; fig
□ ~ **up** colligo ③

rally vt (troops) reduco; (recover)
recolligo ③
■ ~ vi ex fuga convenio ④
ram¹ n aries m
□ **battering** ~ n aries m
ram² vi (ram down) festuco ①; pavio
④; (stuff) inferio ④
ramble¹ n vagatio, ambulatio f
ramble² vi vagor, erro, ambulo ①
rambler n ambulator m
rambling adj vagus
rampage vi saevio ④
rampart n vallum,
propugnaculum nt; agger m
rancid adj rancidus
rancorous adj infensus, infestus;
invidus; malignus
rancour n simultas f; odium nt
random adj fortuitus
□ **at** ~ temere
range¹ n series f; ordo m; (class)
genus nt; (of mountains) iugum nt;
(tract) tractus m; (reach) teli iactus m;
(great size) magnitudo f
range² vt (wander through) pervagor,
lustro ①
rank¹ n series f; ordo; gradus m;
dignitas f
rank² vt colloco; ordino ①
■ ~ vi collocor, numeror ①
rank³ adj luxurians; immodicus; (of
smell) fetidus; rancidus
ransack vt diripio ③; (search)
exquiro ③
ransom n redemptio f; pretium nt
rant vi superbe loquor ③;
bacchor ①
rap¹ n (slap) alapa f; (blow) ictus m;
(with the knuckles) talitrum nt; (at the
door) pulsatio f

rap vt&i pulso 1; ferio 4

rapacious adj rapax; avidus

rapacity n rapacitas; aviditas f

rape[1] n raptus m; vitium virginis, stuprum nt

rape[2] vt constupro, violo 1

rapid adj rapidus, celer; velox, citus ∎ ~ly adv rapide; cito; velociter, celeriter

rapidity n rapiditas; velocitas f

rapist n stuprator, violator m

rapture n animus exsultans (laetitia); furor m

rapturous adj (of things) mirificus; iucundus; (of persons) laetitia elatus

rare adj rarus; inusitatus; (infrequent) infrequens; mirus; fig eximius, singularis ∎ ~ly adv raro

rarity n raritas; paucitas; (thing) res rara or singularis f

rascal n homo nequam, scelestus m

rash[1] adj praeceps, temerarius, inconsultus ∎ ~ly adv temere; inconsulte

rash[2] n formicatio f

rashness n temeritas, imprudentia f

rat n mus m

rate[1] n (price) pretium; (of interest) faenus nt; (speed) celeritas f (tax) census m; (manner) modus m

rate[2] vt aestimo 1; (tax) censeo 2

rather adv potius; libentius; (slightly, somewhat) aliquantum, paulo, sub ...; expressed also by the comparative of adjectives □ **I had ~** malo ir

ratification n confirmatio f

ratify vt ratum facio 3; confirmo

1; sancio 4

ratio n proportio f

ration n (portion) demensum nt; (mil) cibaria ntpl

rational adj rationis particeps; intellegens; sapiens ∎ ~ly adv sapienter

rattle[1] n crepitus, strepitus; fragor m; (children's ~) crepitaculum nt; crepundia ntpl

rattle[2] vt&i crepito; crepo 1

ravage vt vasto, spolio, populor 1; diripio 3

rave vi furo 3; saevio 4; fig (be in a frenzy) bacchor 1

raven n corvus m

ravenous adj rapax, vorax; edax

ravine n angustiae, fauces fpl; saltus m

raving adj furiosus, furens, insanus, rabiosus, rabidus

ravish vt rapio 3; (a woman) constupro 1; (delight) delecto 1

ravisher n raptor; stuprator m

ravishing adj iucundus, suavis, mirificus

raw adj crudus, incoctus; (of wounds) crudus; (unripe) immaturus; (unwrought) rudis; (of weather) frigidus; fig rudis; imperitus

ray n (of the sun) radius m

raze vt (a town, etc.) solo aequo 1; everto 3

razor n novacula f

reach[1] vt&i attingo 3; (come up to) assequor 3; (approach) appropinquo 1; (hand) trado 3; (arrive at) pervenio 4 ad + acc; consequor 3; (stretch) extendor 3

reach[2] n tractus m; spatium nt; (of a missile) iactus m; (capacity) captus m

read | recent

read vt&i lego ③; verso; (aloud) recito ①

readable adj legibilis, lectu facilis

reader n lector; recitator m

readily adv (willingly) libenter; (easily) facile

readiness n facultas, facilitas f
□ in ~ in promptu

reading n lectio; recitatio; (interpretation) lectio f

ready adj paratus; promptus; expeditus; (willing) libens; (easy) facilis
□ ~ **money** n praesens pecunia f
□ **be** ~ praesto sum ir

real adj verus; certus; germanus
■ ~**ly** adv re vera; (surely) sane, certe

reality n res; veritas f; verum nt

realization n effectio f; effectus m; (of ideas) cognitio rerum f

realize vt (fulfil) efficio, ad exitum perduco; (convert into money) redigo; (understand) comprehendo ③

realm n regnum nt

reap vt meto ③; deseco ①; fig capio, percipio ③

reaper n messor m

reaping-hook n falx f

reappear vi rursus appareo ②; redeo ④; resurgo ③

rear¹ vt educo ①; alo ③
■ ~ vi (of horses) arrectum se tollere ③

rear² n tergum nt; (mil) novissimum agmen; extremum agmen nt

reason¹ n mens, intelligentia; (faculty) ratio; (motive) causa f; (understanding) consilium nt; (right) ius, aequum nt

reason² vi ratiocinor, disputo ①

reasonable adj (rational) rationalis, rationis particeps; (sane) sanus; (judicious) prudens; (just) iustus, aequus; (moderate) mediocris, modicus

reasonably adv merito; iure; iuste

reasoning n ratio; ratiocinatio; disceptatio f

reassemble vt recolligo ③

reassure vt confirmo ①

rebel¹ adj & n rebellis, seditiosus m

rebel² vi deficio, descisco ③; rebello ①; rebellionem facio ③

rebellion n rebellio, seditio, defectio f

rebellious adj rebellis, seditiosus; (disobedient) contumax

rebound vi resilio ④; resulto ①

rebuff¹ n repulsa f

rebuff² vt repello, reicio; sperno ③

rebuild vt reficio, restituo ③

rebuke¹ vt vitupero ①; reprehendo ③

rebuke² n vituperatio, reprehensio f

recall vt revoco ①; (to the mind) in memoriam redigo ③

recapitulate vt breviter repeto, summatim colligo ③

recapture vt recipio ③; recupero ①

recede vi recedo; refugio, discedo ③

receipt n (act) acceptio; (verbal release from an obligation) acceptilatio f; (money received) acceptum nt

receive vt accipio, recipio, excipio; (get) percipio ③

recent adj recens
■ ~**ly** adv nuper, modo

receptacle n receptaculum nt; cisterna f

reception n aditus m; admissio f; (of a guest) hospitium nt

recess n (place) recessus, secessus m; latebra f; (vacation) feriae fpl; iustitium nt

recipe n praescriptum nt; compositio f

recipient n acceptor m

reciprocal adj mutuus
■ ~**ly** adv mutuo; vicissim

reciprocate vt alterno 🔟

recital n narratio; enumeratio; recitatio f

recitation n recitatio; lectio f

recite vt narro, recito 🔟

reciter n recitator m

reckless adj neglegens; (rash) temerarius; imprudens
■ ~**ly** adv temere

recklessness n neglegentia, incuria; temeritas f

reckon vt numero; computo, aestimo 🔟; (consider, estimate) duco, pendo ③; (on) confido ③ + dat/abl
□ ~ **up** enumero 🔟

reckoning n numeratio; (account) ratio f

reclaim vt reposco; repeto ③

recline vi recubo 🔟; recumbo ③; iaceo ②; (at table) accubo 🔟; accumbo ③

recognition n recognitio f
□ **in** ~ **of** pro + abl

recognize vt agnosco; recognosco, cognosco ③

recoil vi resilio ④, recido ③; (from) recedo, refugio, discedo ③

recollect vt (remember) recordor 🔟; reminiscor ③; memini ③

recollection n memoria; recordatio f

recommence vt itero, renovo 🔟; repeto ③

recommend vt commendo 🔟

recommendation n commendatio f

recompense[1] n praemium nt; merces, remuneratio f

recompense[2] vt remuneror 🔟; (indemnify) compenso 🔟

reconcile vt reconcilio 🔟; in gratiam restituo ③
□ **be** ~**d to** aequo animo fero ③
□ **be** ~**d** (in harmony) convenio ④

reconciliation n reconciliatio f; reditus in gratiam m

reconnoitre vt exploro, speculor 🔟

reconsider vt recognosco ③; retracto 🔟

record[1] vt memoro, commemoro, narro ③

record[2] n mentio, narratio f; monumentum nt; historia f
■ ~**s** pl annales mpl

recount vt refero ③; memoro, narro, enarro 🔟

recoup vt (regain) recipero 🔟

recourse n
□ **have** ~ **to** confugio, perfugio 🔟, adeo ir ad + acc

recover vt (get back) recipero 🔟; recipio ③
■ ~ vi convalesco ③

recovery n reciperatio; (from illness) recreatio, refectio f

recreation n animi remissio, oblectatio f; (for children) lusus m

recrimination n mutua accusatio f

r

recruit¹ vt (troops) suppleo ②

recruit² n tiro m

recruitment n delectus m; supplementum nt

rectangular adj orthogonius

rectify vt corrigo ③; emendo ①

recur vi recurro ③

recurrence n reditus m

recurrent adj recurrens

red adj ruber; (ruddy) rubicundus; (of hair) rufus
  □ **be** ~ rubeo ②
  □ **grow** ~ rubesco, erubesco ③

redden vt rubefacio ③
  ■ ~ vi rubesco; erubesco ③

reddish adj surrufus, surrubicundus, rubicundulus

redeem vt redimo ③; libero; (a pledge) repignero ①

red-hot adj candens

redness n rubor m

redouble vt gemino, ingemino ①

redress¹ vt emendo ①; corrigo ③; medeor ②

redress² n (remedy) remedium nt

reduce vt reduco; redigo ad or in + acc; (lessen) minuo ③

reduction n deminutio f

redundancy n redundantia f

redundant adj redundans, supervacaneus, superfluus

reed n arundo f; calamus m; canna f

reef n scopulus m; dorsum nt; cautes f

reel vi (stagger) vacillo, titubo ①

re-enter vt iterum intro ①

re-establish vt restituo, reficio ③

refectory n cenatio f

refer vt refero ir; remitto ③ ad + acc

  ■ ~ vi (allude to) perstringo, attingo ③; (regard) specto ①

referee n arbiter, disceptator m

reference n (respect) ratio f

refill vt repleo ②

refine vt purgo ①; excolo ③; expolio ④; (metals) excoquo ③

refined adj cultus, politus; elegans; urbanus; humanus

refinement n urbanitas, humanitas; elegantia f

reflect vt repercutio ③
  ■ ~ vi considero, meditor, reputo ①; revolvo ③

reflection n repercussus m; (thing reflected) imago; fig consideratio f

reform¹ vt reficio; (amend) corrigo ③; emendo ①
  ■ ~ vi me corrigo ③

reform² n correctio f

reformer n corrector, emendator m

refrain¹ n versus intercalaris m

refrain² vi abstineo ② ab + abl; parco ③ + dat

refresh vt (restore) recreo ①; reficio ③; (the memory) redintegro ①; (cool) refrigero ①

refreshing adj (cool) frigidus; (pleasant) iucundus

refreshment n refectio f; (food) cibus m

refuge n refugium, perfugium, asylum nt
  □ **take** ~ (in), confugio ③ in + acc

refugee n profugus m; exsul, exul m/f

refund vt reddo ③

refusal n recusatio; repudiatio; detrectatio; repulsa f

refuse¹ vt recuso, nego; repudio

①]; renuo ③; denego, detrecto ①

refuse² n recrementum, purgamentum nt; faex f; quisquiliae fpl

refute vt refuto, confuto ①; refello, redarguo ③

regain vt recipio ③; recupero ①

regal adj regalis, regius, regificus
■ ~**ly** adv regie, regaliter, regifice

regard¹ n respectus m; ratio; (care, etc.) cura f

regard² vt respicio ③; intueor ②; (observe) observo; (concern) specto; (mind, care) curo; (esteem) aestimo ①; pendo ③; (respect) rationem habeo ②

regarding prep ▶ concerning

regardless adj neglegens, incuriosus; ▶ heedless
■ ~ adv nihilominus

regenerate vt regenero, fig redintegro, renovo, restauro ①

regime n (government) rerum administratio f

regiment n legio, caterva f

regimental adj legionarius

region n regio, plaga f; tractus m; (neighbourhood) vicinitas f

register¹ n tabulae fpl; index m/f

register² vt in tabulas refero ③

registrar n tabularius; ab actis; actuarius m

registration n perscriptio f

registry n tabularia f; tabularium nt

regret¹ vt (be sorry for) aegre fero ③; (bemoan) doleo; piget ②; (repent) paenitet ②; (miss) desidero ①

regret² n paenitentia f; dolor m; (feeling of loss) desiderium nt

regular adj (fixed) certus; (according to law) legitimus, iustus; (usual) usitatus
■ ~**ly** adv ordine; iuste, legitime; (at fixed times) certis temporibus

regularity n symmetria; constantia; (uniformity) aequabilitas f

regulate vt ordino; dispono; praescribo ③; administro ①

regulation n ordinatio; moderatio, temperatio f; (law) lex f; (rule) praescriptum nt

rehabilitate vt restituo ③

rehearsal n (recital) narratio, recitatio; (of a play, etc.) prolusio, exercitatio, meditatio f

rehearse vt recito ①; repeto ③; (practise) meditor ①; praeludo ③

reign¹ n regnum nt

reign² vi regno; dominor ①

reimburse vt rependo ③

rein¹ n habena f; frenum, lorum nt

rein² vt freno ①; fig cohibeo ②

reindeer n tarandus m

reinforce vt suppleo ②; auxiliis confirmo ①

reinforcement n (mil) novae copiae fpl; subsidium nt

reinstate vt restituo ③

reiterate vt itero ①

reject vt reicio ③; repudio ①; repello; (scorn) sperno ③

rejection n reiectio, repudiatio, repulsa f

rejoice vi gaudeo ②; exsulto, laetor ①

rejoin vt (meet) convenio ④ cum + abl
■ ~ vi (answer) respondeo ②; resequor ③

rejoinder n responsum nt

rekindle vt refoveo ②; excito ①

relapse vi recido, relabor ③

relapse² n morbus recidivus m

relate vt refero ③; memoro, narro ①

related adj (by blood) consanguineus; (by marriage) affinis; fig propinquus, cognatus; coniunctus

relation n narratio; (reference) ratio; (relationship) cognatio f; (person) cognatus m; cognata f

relationship n propinquitas; necessitudo; cognatio; (by blood) consanguinitas; (by marriage) affinitas; fig coniunctio f

relative¹ adj cognatus

∼ly adv pro ratione

relative² n cognatus m; cognata f; ▶ related

relax vt remitto ③; laxo, relaxo ①; resolvo ③

∎ ∼ vi relanguesco; (abate) remittor ③

relaxation n remissio; relaxatio f

relay n cursus publici mpl

release¹ vt libero ①; resolvo ③; laxo ①; (relieve) exonero, levo, relevo ①

release² n liberatio; absolutio; (discharge) missio f

relegate vt relego ①

relent vi mitesco ③; mitigor ①; lenior ④

relentless adj immisericors, inexorabilis, atrox, durus

relevant adj aptus, appositus

reliable adj fidus, certus

reliance n fiducia f; fides f

relic n reliquiae fpl; monumentum nt

relief n (comfort) solacium; (alleviation) levamentum; (help) auxilium nt; (remedy) medicina f; remedium nt; (in sculpture) caelatura f

relieve vt levo, allevo; mitigo ①; (aid) succurro ③; (succeed) subeo ④ both + dat; (take over a duty) excipio ③

religion n religio, pietas f

religious adj religiosus; pius

relinquish vt relinquo ③; derelinquo, demitto, omitto, depono ③

relish¹ n (flavour) sapor m; (seasoning) condimentum; (fondness) studium nt

relish² vt (like) gusto ①; (enjoy) fruor ③ + abl

reluctance n aversatio f

reluctant adj invitus

∼ly adv invitus (adj); aegre

rely vi (trust) confido ③ + dat/abl

remain vi (stay) maneo, permaneo ②; resto ①; (last) sto, duro ①, (be left over) supersum ir

remainder n reliquum nt

remaining adj reliquus

remains npl reliquiae fpl

remark¹ vt observo ①; animadverto ③

remark² n observatio, animadversio f; (something said) dictum nt

remarkable adj insignis, memorabilis, notabilis, mirus; egregius

remarkably adv insigniter; mire; egregie

remedial adj medicus, medicabilis

remedy¹ n remedium nt;

medicina f

remedy² vt sano ①; medeor ②; corrigo ③

remember vt memini ③; recordor ①; reminiscor ③

remind vt commoneo ②; commonefacio ③

reminiscence n recordatio f

remiss adj neglegens; incuriosus

remission n remissio; venia f

remit vt (abate) remitto ③; (forgive) condono ①; (money) transmitto ③
~ vi relaxor ①

remittance n remissio f

remnant n reliquum nt; reliquiae fpl

remonstrate vt obtestor, acclamo, interpello ①; aegre fero ③

remorse n angor conscientiae m; stimuli mpl

remorseless adj immisericors; durus; crudelis

remote adj remotus; amotus; ultimus; longinquus; disiunctus

removal n remotio; exportatio; (banishment) amandatio; relegatio; (changing one's dwelling) migratio f

remove vt amoveo ②; depello, tollo, detraho ③; amando ①

remunerate vt remuneror ①

remuneration n remuneratio f

render vt reddo; facio; (hand over) trado; (a town, etc.) dedo; (translate) verto ③

rendezvous n locus praescriptus (ad conveniendum); (meeting itself) conventus m

renegade n transfuga m

renew vt renovo; novo; redintegro ①

renewal n renovatio; integratio f

renounce vt missum facio; pono, depono ③; (deny) nego ①

renovate vt renovo, redintegro ①; (repair) reparo, instauro ①

renovation n renovatio f

renown n fama, gloria f; nomen nt

renowned adj insignis, celeber, clarus; praeclarus

rent¹ n reditus m; vectigal nt; merces, pensio f; (fissure) scissura, rima f

rent² vt (let out) loco ①; (hire) conduco ③

renunciation n abdicatio, repudiatio f

reopen vt iterum aperio ④; fig (a case) retracto ①

reorganize vt restituo ③

repair¹ vt (buildings) reparo, instauro ①; (make good) reficio; restituo ③; (clothes) resarcio ④; (cure) sano ①; (make amends for) sarcio ④

repair² n refectio f

repairer n refector m

reparation n restitutio f; (amends) satisfactio f

repartee n salsum dictum nt

repay vt repono, retribuo ③; remuneror ①; (compensate) penso, compenso, repenso ①

repayment n solutio; remuneratio f

repeal¹ vt abrogo ①; rescindo, tollo ③

repeal² n abrogatio f

repeat vt itero ①; repeto ③

repeatedly adv iterum atque iterum, saepius

repel vt repello ③; fig aspernor ①

repent vi paenitet (me) ②

repentance n paenitentia f

repentant adj paenitens

repercussion n repercussio f

repetition n iteratio; repetitio f

replace vt repono; (restore) restituo; (substitute) substituo, suppono ③

replenish vt repleo, suppleo ②

reply[1] n responsum nt; responsio f

reply[2] vt&i respondeo ②; refero ir

report[1] vt fero ③; narro, nuntio ①; (state) propono ③

report[2] n (rumour) fama f; rumor m; (hearsay) auditio f; (noise) fragor, crepitus m; relatio; narratio f

repose[1] vi (rest) quiesco, requiesco ③

repose[2] n quies, requies f

represent vt repraesento ①; exprimo; propono ③; (act on behalf of) vicem impleo + gen ②; loco sum ir + gen

representation n (act) repraesentatio; (statement) editio; (likeness) imago f

representative n vicarius; procurator m

repress vt reprimo, comprimo ③; coerceo ②; (tame) domo ①

repression n refrenatio, coercitio f

reprieve[1] n dilatio (supplicii) f

reprieve[2] vt diem prorogare damnato

reprimand[1] vt reprehendo ③

reprimand[2] n reprehensio f

reprisal n talio; vindicta f

reproach vt obicio ③; exprobro; vitupero; accuso ①

reproachful adj obiurgatorius

reproduce vt refero ③

reproof n reprehensio, vituperatio, obiurgatio f

reprove vt obiurgo, vitupero ①; reprehendo ③

reptile n repens animal nt

republic n respublica, civitas popularis, libera civitas f

republican adj popularis

repudiate vt repudio ①; respuo, renuo, abnuo, sperno ③

repugnance n aversatio f; fastidium nt; fuga f

repugnant adj odiosus; alienus

repulse vt repello ③; propulso, fugo ①

repulsion n repulsus m; (dislike) odium nt

repulsive adj odiosus; foedus

reputable adj honestus, bonae famae

reputation n (also **repute**) fama, existimatio f; nomen nt

request[1] n preces fpl

  □ at the ~ of rogatu + gen

request[2] vt rogo ①; peto ③; supplico, precor ①

require vt (demand) postulo ①, posco ③; (need) egeo ② + abl; desidero ①

requirements n necessaria ntpl

requisite adj necessarius

rescue[1] vt libero, recupero; (save) servo ①

rescue[2] n liberatio, recuperatio f

research n investigatio f

resemblance n similitudo f; instar nt (indecl)

resemble vi similis sum ir

resent vt aegre or graviter fero ③;

indignor ①

resentful *adj* iracundus; indignans

resentment *n* indignatio *f*

reservation *n* retentio *f*

reserve[1] *vt* reservo ①; repono, condo, recondo ③; retineo ②

reserve[2] *n* (silence) taciturnitas *f*; (mil) subsidium *nt*

reserved *adj* (silent) taciturnus, tectus

reservoir *n* cisterna *f*; receptaculum *nt*; lacus *m*

reside *vi* habito, commoror ①

residence *n* habitatio; sedes *f*; domicilium *nt*; (sojourn) commoratio *f*

resident *n* habitator *m*

residue *n* residuum, reliquum *nt*

resign *vt* cedo, depono ③; abdico ①

□ **~ oneself to** aequo animo fero ③

resignation *n* (act) abdicatio; (surrendering (in law)) cessio *f*; fig aequus animus *m*

resin *n* resina *f*

resist *vi* resisto ③; obsto, adversor ① + *dat*

resistance *n* repugnantia; (mil) defensio *f*

resolute *adj* audax; constans; fortis; firmus

■ **~ly** *adv* constanter; fortiter; audaciter; firme

resoluteness *n* constantia *f*; consilium *nt*

resolution *n* (plan) consilium *nt*; (of mind) constantia *f*; (courage) animus *m*; (of an assembly) decretum *nt*

resolve[1] *n* constantia *f*; consilium *nt*

resentful | responsible

resolve[2] *vt* decerno, statuo, constituo ③; (solve) solvo ③; resolvo, reduco, redigo ③

resonant *adj* resonus

resort[1] *vi* (have recourse to) confugio ③; convenio ④ *both* + ad + *acc*

resort[2] *n* (refuge) refugium, perfugium *nt*

resound *vi* resono, persono ①

resource *n* refugium, auxilium *nt*

□ **~s** opes *fpl*

resourceful *adj* callidus

respect[1] *vt* revereor ②; veneror; observo ①

respect[2] *n* (regard) respectus *m*; (reverence) reverentia, observantia *f*; (relation, reference) ratio *f*

□ **with ~ to** ad + *acc*, de + *abl*; (as regards) quod attinet ad + *acc*

respectability *n* honestas *f*

respectable *adj* honestus; (fairly good) tolerabilis

respectful *adj* observans; reverens

■ **~ly** *adv* cum summa observantia; reverenter

respecting *prep* ad + *acc*, de + *abl*, quod attinet ad + *acc*

respiration *n* respiratio *f*

respite *n* (delay) mora; cessatio; intermissio *f*

resplendent *adj* resplendens, clarus, nitidus

■ **~ly** *adv* clare, nitide

respond *vi* respondeo ②

response *n* responsum *nt*

responsible *adj* obnoxius; (trustworthy) fidus; (able to pay) locuples

□ **be ~ for** praesto ① + *dat*

rest¹ n quies; requies; pax f; (prop) fulcrum nt, statumen nt; (remainder) residuum, reliquum nt; (of people) reliqui, ceteri mpl

rest² vi quiesco, requiesco ③; (pause) cesso ①; (lean) nitor; (on) innitor ③ + dat
■ ~ vt (lean) reclino ①

restaurant n caupona f

restive adj sternax, petulans

restless adj inquietus; turbidus, tumultuosus; (agitated) sollicitus
~**ly** adv turbulente

restoration n refectio; (recall) reductio f

restore vt restituo, reddo ③; restauro, reparo ①; (health, etc.) sano ①; (recall) reduco ③

restrain vt refreno ①; coerceo ②; (limit) circumscribo ③; contineo ②; (prevent) impedio ④; prohibeo ②

restraint n coercitio; moderatio f

restrict vt cohibeo ②; restringo, circumscribo ③

restriction n restrictio, limitatio f

result¹ vi orior, exorior ④; proficiscor ③; fio ir; (follow) consequor ③

result² n (effect) exitus, eventus m; (conclusion) summa f

resume vt resumo; repeto ③; redintegro ①

resuscitate vt resuscito, revoco ①

retain vt retineo ②; servo ①

retaliate vi ulciscor ③; par pro pari refero ③

retaliation n lex talionis; ultio f

retch vi nauseo ①

reticent adj taciturnus

retinue n comitatus m; pompa; turba clientium f

retire vi (go away) recedo, regredior, decedo ③; abeo ir

retirement n solitudo f; recessus m; (from office) abdicatio f

retort¹ vt regero, refero ③
■ ~ vi respondeo ②

retort² n responsum nt

retrace vt repeto ③
□ ~ one's steps revertor ③

retract vt retracto, recanto ①

retreat¹ vi recedo, refugio ③; pedem refero ir

retreat² n recessus m; refugium nt; latebrae fpl; lustrum nt; (mil) receptus m

retribution n poena, vindicta f; supplicium nt

retrieve vt (recover) recupero ①; (make good) sarcio ④; (save) sano ①

return¹ vt (give back) restituo, reddo ③; (send back) remitto ③
■ ~ vi (go back) redeo ④; revertor ③; (come back) revenio ④

return² n (coming back) reditus; regressus m; (giving back) restitutio; (repayment) remuneratio f; (income, profit, etc.) fructus, quaestus; reditus m

reunion n reconciliatio f

reunite vt&i reconcilio ①

reveal vt retego; recludo, patefacio, prodo ③; nudo; (unveil) revelo ①; (make known) evulgo, divulgo ①

revelation n patefactio f

revelry n comissatio f; orgia ntpl

revenge¹ vt ulciscor ③

revenge² n ultio, vindicta f
□ take ~ (on) vindico in + acc ③; poenas repeto ab + abl ③

revenger n ultor m; ultrix f; vindex m/f

revenue n reditus, fructus m; vectigal nt

reverberate vt repercutio ③; vi resono, persono ①

reverberation n repercussus m

revere vt revereor ②; veneror, observo ①; colo ③

reverence n reverentia, veneratio, observantia f

reverent adj reverens; pius ■ ~ly adv venerabiliter, reverenter

reversal n rescissio, infirmatio f

reverse[1] n (change) conversio, commutatio (fortunae); (defeat) clades f; (contrary) contrarium nt; (of a medal) aversa pars f

reverse[2] vt inverto; (alter) converto; (annul) rescindo ③

revert vi revertor, recurro ③; redeo ④

review[1] n recensio f; recensus m; (critique) censura f

review[2] vt recenseo ②; lustro ①

reviewer n censor m

revise vt recenseo ②; retracto ①; relego, corrigo ③; fig limo ①

revision n correctio f; (of a literary work) fig lima f

revisit vt reviso ③

revival n renovatio f

revive vt resuscito ①; (renew) renovo; (encourage) animo; (refresh) recreo; (recall) revoco ① ■ ~ vi revivisco ③

revoke vt revoco ①; (a law) rescindo, tollo ③

revolt[1] vt offendo ③ ■ ~ vi rebello ①; descisco, secedo, deficio ③

revolt[2] n rebellio; defectio f

revolution n circuitus m; circumversio f; circumactus m; (change) commutatio f; (of planets) cursus, meatus m; (political) res novae fpl

revolutionary[1] adj seditiosus, novarum rerum cupidus

revolutionary[2] n rerum novarum molitor m

revolve vt volvo ③; voluto ① ■ ~ vi circumvolvor, circumvertor, circumagor ③

revolving adj versatilis, versabundus

revulsion n taedium nt

reward[1] vt remuneror ①

reward[2] n praemium nt; merces f; fructus m

rewrite vt rescribo ③

rhetoric n rhetorice, oratoria f; rhetorica ntpl

rhetorical adj rhetoricus; oratorius

rheumatism n dolor artuum m

Rhine n Rhenus m

rhinoceros n rhinoceros m

rhododendron n rhododendron nt

Rhone n Rhodanus m

rhyme n versus m

rhythm n numerus, rhythmus m

rhythmic adj (also **rhythmical**) numerosus, rhythmicus

rib n costa f

ribald adj obscenus, spurcus, turpis

ribbon n taenia, vitta, fascia f; lemniscus m

rice n oryza f

rich adj dives, locuples, pecuniosus, opimus; abundans, copiosus; (of the soil, etc.) fertilis, uber

riches n divitiae, opes fpl

richness n opulentia, abundantia, copia; ubertas, fertilitas f

rickety adj instabilis

rid vt libero ①
□ **get ~ of** (also fig) amolior ④; amoveo, removeo ②; dimitto, depono ③;

riddle¹ n aenigma nt; ambages fpl

riddle² vt (with wounds, etc.) confodio ③

ride¹ vt (a horse) equo vehor ③
■ ~ vi equito ①
□ ~ **away or off** avehor ③
□ ~ **past** praetervehor ③

ride² n equitatio; vectatio, vectio f

rider n eques; vector m; (addition) adiectio f

ridge n iugum, dorsum; culmen nt

ridicule¹ n ludibrium nt; risus m

ridicule² vt rideo, irrideo ②

ridiculous adj ridiculus
■ ~ly adv ridicule

riding n equitatio f

riding-school n hippodromos m

rife adj frequens, vulgatus
□ **become ~** increbresco ③

riffraff n plebecula f; vulgus nt; faex populi f

rig vt adorno, armo ①; instruo ③

rigging n armamenta ntpl

right¹ adj rectus; (hand, side) dexter; fig verus; iustus; aequus; idoneus, aptus
■ ~ly adv recte; iuste; iure; vere; rite
□ **you are ~** vera dicis

right² n (hand) dextra f; (law) ius, aequum, fas nt; (permission, licence) licentia, venia f
□ **on the ~** dextrorsus
□ **I have a ~ to** mihi licet + inf

righteous adj aequus, iustus; pius, sanctus

rightful adj legitimus, iustus
■ ~ly adv legitime, iure, iuste

rigid adj rigidus

rigidity n rigor m

rigorous adj asper, severus, rigidus

rigour n asperitas, severitas f

rim n labrum nt; ora f; margo m/f

rind n crusta, cutis f; cortex, liber m

ring¹ n anulus; (hoop) circulus, orbis m; (of people) corona f; (ground for fighting) arena f; (sound) sonitus m; (of bells) tinnitus m

ring² vt tinnio ④; resono ①

ringleader n caput nt; dux, auctor m/f

ringlet n (of hair) cincinnus, cirrus m

rinse vt alluo, eluo ③

riot¹ n tumultus m

riot² vt tumultuor ①

rioter n seditiosus, turbulentus m

riotous adj seditiosus, tumultuosus, turbulentus

rip vt (unsew) dissuo; (tear) diffindo, divello ③

ripe adj maturus; tempestivus

ripen vt maturo ①
■ ~ vi maturesco ③

ripeness n maturitas f

ripple n fluctus m; unda f
■ ~ vi murmuro, lene sono ①

rise¹ vi orior, coorior ④; surgo, consurgo ③; (out of, from) exorior ④;

(mount) ascendo ③; (as a bird) evolo ①; (up) assurgo ③; (increase) cresco ③; (of rebels) consurgo ③; rebello ①
□ ~ **again** resurgo ③

rise² n (ascent) ascensus; (increase) augmentum nt; (of the sun) ortus m; (rising ground) tumulus m; (origin) origo f; fons m
□ **give ~ to** pario ③

rising¹ adj (sloping) acclivis; (about to be) futurus

rising² n (of the sun, etc.) ortus m; (insurrection) tumultus m; seditio f

risk¹ vt periclitor ①

risk² n periculum, discrimen nt

risky adj periculosus

rite n ritus m; solemne nt

ritual adj sollemnis
□ ~ n sollemne nt

rival¹ n rivalis, aemulus, competitor m

rival² vt aemulor ①

rivalry n aemulatio f; certamen nt; (in love) rivalitas f

river n flumen nt; amnis, rivus m
■ ~-**bed** n alveus m

rivet¹ n clavus m

rivet² vt fig clavo figo ③; fig teneo ②

road n via f; iter nt
□ **on the ~** in itinere

roam vi ▶ ramble

roar¹ vi fremo, rudo ③, mugio ④; (of voices) vociferor ①

roar² n fremitus m; strepitus, mugitus, clamor m

roast vt&i torreo ②; (in a pan) frigo ③; asso ①; coquo ③

rob vt latrocinor; furor; praedor; spolio, despolio ①; diriplo ③; (deprive) privo, orbo ①

robber n latro, praedo, raptor, fur m

robbery n latrocinium nt; spoliatio, direptio, rapina f

robe n vestis, palla f

robust adj robustus, validus, lacertosus, firmus

rock¹ n rupes, cautes f; saxum nt; scopulus m

rock² vt moveo ②; agito ①
■ ~ vi vibro ①; moveor ②; agitor, fluctuo ①

rocky adj saxosus, saxeus, scopulosus

rod n virga; ferula f

roe n (of fishes) ova ntpl

rogue n nequam (homo), furcifer, mastigia m

role n persona f; partes fpl

roll¹ vt volvo ③; verso ①
■ ~ vi volvor ③

roll² n volumen nt; (coil) spira f; orbis m; (of names) index m/f; album nt

roller n (tool) cylindrus m

Roman adj & n Romanus; Quiris m

romance n (story) fabula, narratio ficta f; (love) amor m

romantic adj fabulosus, commenticius; (chivalrous) sublimis; (pleasing) gratus

romp¹ n lusus m

romp² vi exsulto ①; ludo ③; lascivio ④

roof¹ n tectum; fastigium; (of the mouth) palatum nt

roof² vt contego, intego ③

roofing n tegulae fpl

rook n corvus m

room n (space) spatium nt; locus

r

m; (apartment) conclave, cubiculum, cenaculum *nt*

roomy *adj* laxus; spatiosus; amplus

roost *vi* insisto ③; insideo ②

root[1] *n* radix, stirps *f*; fig fons *m*; origo *f*
□ **by the ~s** radicitus
□ **take ~** coalesco ③; inveterasco ③

root[2] *vi* radices ago ③
□ **~ out** or **up** exstirpo, eradico ①

rope *n* funis *m*; rudens *m*

rose *n* rosa *f*

rosebud *n* calyx rosae *m*

rose-bush *n* rosa *f*

rostrum *n* rostra *ntpl*

rosy *adj* roseus

rot[1] *vi* putresco, putesco ③
■ **~** *vt* corrumpo, putrefacio ③

rot[2] *n* putor *m*; caries *f*

rotate *vi* volvor ③

rotation *n* ordo *m*

rote *n*
□ **by ~** memoriter
□ **learn by ~** edisco, perdisco ③

rotten *adj* puter, putidus, putridus; cariosus

rough *adj* asper; (with hair, thorns) hirsutus; horridus; scabrous; scaber; (of weather) procellosus; fig agrestis, durus, incultus

roughen *vt* aspero ①

roughly *adv* aspere; duriter; horride; inculte; (approximately) fere, ferme

roughness *n* asperitas *f*; (of surface) scabies; fig (coarseness) rusticitas; (brutality) feritas *f*

roughshod *adj*
□ **ride ~ over** calco, proculco ①; obtero ③

round[1] *adj* rotundus; globosus; (as a circle) circularis; (rounded) teres

round[2] *n* orbis, circulus *m*
□ **go the ~s** circumeo *ir*

round[3] *vt* (make round) rotundo; torno ①; (go round) circumeo *ir*
□ **~ off** (end) concludo ③

round[4] *adv* & *prep* circum, circa + *acc*
□ **~ about** undique

roundabout *adj* devius

rouse *vt* excito; stimulo; animo ①; cieo, moveo ②; (awaken) expergefacio ③

rout[1] *n* tumultus *m*; turba; (defeat) clades *f*; (flight) fuga *f*

rout[2] *vt* fugo, profligo ①; fundo ③

route *n* via *f*; iter *nt*

routine *n* mos, usus *m*; consuetudo *f*

row[1] *n* series *f*; ordo *m*; (quarrel) rixa *f*; (riot) turba *f*
□ **in a ~** deinceps

row[2] *vt* & *i* remigo ①; remis propello ③; (quarrel) rixor ①

rower *n* remex *m*

rowing *n* remigatio *f*; remigium *nt*

royal *adj* regalis, regius, regificus

royalty *n* maiestas regia; dignitas regia; regia potestas *f*

rub *vt* & *i* frico ①; tero ③
□ **~ against** attero ③
□ **~ off** detergeo ②
□ **~ out** deleo ②

rubbish *n* rudus *nt*; fig quisquiliae *fpl*; (nonsense) fabulae, gerrae *fpl*

ruby *n* carbunculus *m*

rudder *n* gubernaculum *nt*; clavus *m*

rude *adj* rudis, incultus; rusticus, inurbanus; (artless) incomptus, incompositus; inconditus; (insolent) insolens; (rude) asper; (unskilful) inexpertus, imperitus

rudeness n rusticitas; inhumanitas; insolentia f

rudiment n elementum, initium, rudimentum, principium nt

rudimentary adj rudis

rueful adj maestus, tristis

ruffian n homo perditus, sicarius, latro m

ruffle vt agito, turbo 🔟

rug n stragulum nt

rugged adj asper, inaequalis, confragosus; (precipitous) praeruptus

ruin¹ n pernicies f; exitium, excidium nt; ruina f
■ ~s pl ruinae fpl
□ **in** ~ ruinosus

ruin² vt perdo, corrumpo 🛐; depravo, vitio 🔟

ruinous adj damnosus; exitiosus; exitialis, perniciosus, funestus

rule¹ n (for measuring) regula f; fig praeceptum nt; lex, norma, regula, formula f; (government) regimen nt

rule² vt (a line) duco 🛐; (govern) rego 🛐; praesum ir + dat
□ ~ vi dominor; impero 🔟 + dat; (of a custom) obtineo 2️⃣

ruler n rector; regnator, gubernator, dominus, moderator m; (for drawing lines) regula f

ruling adj potens; regius; (chief, most powerful) potentissimus

rumble¹ vi murmuro, crepo 🔟

rumble² n murmur nt; crepitus, sonitus m

ruminate vi ruminor 🔟; fig meditor 🔟

rummage vt rimor, perscrutor 🔟

rumour n rumor m; fama f

rumple vt corrugo 🔟

run¹ vi curro; (flow) fluo; (of rivers) labor 🛐
□ ~ **about** curso 🔟
□ ~ **after** sequor 🛐; sector 🔟
□ ~ **away** fugio, aufugio 🛐
□ ~ **down** decurro; (as water) defluo 🛐; fig vitupero 🔟
□ ~ **off** aufugio; (as water) defluo 🛐
□ ~ **out** excurro 🛐; (of time) exeo ir
□ ~ **over** (a person) obtero; fig percurro; (touch lightly) perstringo; vi (of fluids) superfluo 🛐
□ ~ **through** (also fig) percurro; (with a sword) transfigo, traicio, transigo 🛐; (squander) dissipo 🔟
□ ~ **together** concurro 🛐
□ ~ **up** vt erigo, exstruo; vi accurro 🛐

run² n cursus m

runaway n fugitivus m; transfuga m

rung n gradus f

runner n cursor m

running adj (of water) perennis, iugis; (consecutive) continuus

rupture¹ n violatio, seditio; dissensio; (med) hernia f

rupture² vt violo 🔟; rumpo, abrumpo 🛐

rural adj rusticus; agrestis

rush¹ n iuncus, scirpus m; (hurry) festinatio f

rush² vi ruo, feror 🛐; praecipito 🔟; (on, forward) irruo, irrumpo, prorumpo, (out) erumpo 🛐; evolo 🔟

rust¹ n robigo; (of copper) aerugo; (of iron) ferrugo f

rust² vi robiginem contraho 🛐; fig torpeo 2️⃣

rustic adj rusticus; agrestis

rustle¹ vi crepito; murmuro; susurro ①

rustle² n stridor; susurrus m; murmur nt; crepitus m

rusty adj robiginosus, aeruginosus; (rust-coloured) ferrugineus

rut n (made by a wheel) orbita f

ruthless adj immisericors; immitis; immansuetus, crudelis, ferus, saevus

rye n secale nt

. . . .

Ss

. . . .

sack¹ n saccus m

sack² vt (pillage) vasto ①; diripio ③

sacking n spoliatio, vastatio f; (coarse cloth) cilicium nt

sacred adj sacer; sanctus; sacrosanctus; religiosus

sacrifice¹ n (act) sacrificium nt; (victim) victima f; fig detrimentum, damnum nt

sacrifice² vt immolo, sacrifico, macto ①; fig posthabeo ②; (give up) devoveo ②; profundo ③

sacrilege n sacrilegium nt; impietas f

sacrilegious adj sacrilegus; impius

sad adj tristis, maestus, miser, miserabilis

sadden vt contristo ①

saddle¹ n ephippium, stratum nt

saddle² vt (equum) sterno; fig impono ③; onero ①

sadness n tristitia, maestitia, miseria f

safe adj tutus; (without hurt) incolumis; (sure) certus
  □ **~ and sound** salvus

safeguard n praesidium nt; tutela f

safety n salus, incolumitas f

saffron¹ n crocus m

saffron² adj croceus

sail¹ n velum nt; carbasa, lintea ntpl; (excursion) navigatio f

sail² vi vela facio ③; navigo ①; (set out to sea) vela do ①; solvo ③
  ■ ~ vt navigo ①

sailing n navigatio f; (of a ship) cursus m

sailor n nauta m

saint n vir sanctus m; femina sancta f

saintly adv sanctus, pius

sake n
  □ **for the ~ of** gratia, causa + gen; pro + abl; (on account of) propter, ob + acc

salad n acetaria ntpl

salary n merces f; stipendium; salarium nt

sale n venditio f; (auction) auctio f
  □ **for ~** venalis
  □ **be on ~** veneo ir
  □ **put up for ~** venalem propono ③

salesman n venditor m

salient adj prominens; (chief) praecipuus

saliva n saliva f; sputum nt

sallow adj pallidus, luridus

sally¹ n eruptio f

sally² vi (mil) erumpo, excurro ③

salmon n salmo m

salt¹ n sal m

salt² adj salsus

salt³ vt salio, sale condio ④

salt-cellar n salinum m

salty adj salsus

salubrious adj salubris, salutaris

salutary adj salutaris, salubris; utilis

salute¹ n salus, salutatio f

salute² vt saluto ①

salvation n salus, salvatio f

same adj idem
  □ **it is all the ~ thing** nihil interest
  □ **at the ~ time** eodem tempore
  □ **in the ~ place** ibidem

sample n exemplum; exemplar; specimen nt

sanctify vt sanctifico; (consecrate) consecro ①

sanctimonious adj sanctitatem affectans

sanction¹ n auctoritas, confirmatio f

sanction² vt ratum facio ③; sancio ④; confirmo, firmo ①

sanctity n sanctitas; sanctimonia, religio f

sanctuary n asylum, adytum, sacrarium nt

sand n sabulo m; arena f

sandal n solea, crepida f

sandstone n tofus, tophus m

sandy n (full of sand) arenosus, sabulosus; arenaceus; (of colour) rufus

sane adj sanus, mentis compos

sanity n sanitas, mens sana f

sap n sucus m; lac nt

sapling n surculus m

sapphire n sapphirus f

sarcasm n dictum acerbum nt

sarcastic adj acerbus, mordax

sarcophagus n sarcophagus m

sardine n sarda f

sardonic adj acerbus

sash n cingulum m

satchel n saccus, sacculus m; pera f; loculi mpl

sate vt satio, saturo ①

satellite n satelles m/f; (planet) stella minor or obnoxia f

satiate vt satio, saturo ①

satiety n satietas f; fastidium nt

satire n satura f

satirical adj satyricus, acerbus

satirist n scriptor (or poeta) satyricus

satirize vt derideo ②; perstringo ③

satisfaction n satisfactio f; fig oblectatio animi; voluptas f

satisfactory adj (suitable) commodus; (pleasant) gratus, iucundus

satisfy vt (please) satisfacio ③ + dat; (fill) satio, saturo ①; fig persuadeo; (one's expectations) respondeo ② both + dat; (be satisfied) contentus sum ir

saturate vt saturo ①; imbuo, madefacio ③

satyr n satyrus m

sauce n condimentum; ius nt

saucepan n cacabus m

saucer n patella f

saucy adj petulans, procax, protervus

saunter vi ambulo ①; incedo ③

s

sausage n farcimen, tomaculum nt

savage adj ferus; ferox, immansuetus; immanis; saevus; atrox; (furious) efferus; (uncivilized) ferus, incultus
■ **~ly** adv crudeliter; immaniter; atrociter; saeve

savagery n feritas; immanitas; saevitia f

save vt servo, conservo; (from danger) libero ①; pericolo eripio; (spare) parco ③ + dat; (gain) lucror ①

savings n peculium nt

saviour n servator m

savour[1] n sapor, odor, nidor m

savour[2] vi sapio ③
■ **~ vt** fruor ③ + abl

savoury adj sapidus

saw[1] n (tool) serra f

saw[2] vt&i serra seco ①; serram duco ③

sawdust n scobis f

say vt&i dico, loquor, aio ③; fari (inf) ①
□ **he ~s** inquit
□ **they ~** dicunt, ferunt
□ **that is to ~** scilicet

saying n dictum nt

scab n (of a wound) crusta f

scabbard n vagina f

scaffold n tabulatum nt; catasta f

scaffolding n tabulatum nt

scald vt fervente aqua macero ①

scale[1] n (of a fish) squama; (of a balance) lanx f
■ **~s** pl libra; trutina f; (degree) gradus m

scale[2] vt (walls) ascendo ③; scalas admoveo ② with ad + acc

scaling-ladder n scalae fpl

scallop n (shellfish) pecten m

scalp n calva f

scalpel n scalpellum, scalprum nt

scaly adj squamosus; squameus

scamper vi ruo ③; provolo ①
□ **~ away** aufugio, effugio ③

scan vt examino, exploro, lustro ③

scandal n ignominia, turpitudo f; opprobrium nt

scandalize vt offendo ③

scandalous adj ignominiosus, probrosus, turpis

scant adj (and **scanty**) angustus, exiguus, tenuis

scapegoat n caper emissarius m

scar[1] n cicatrix f

scar[2] vt noto ①

scarce adj rarus
■ **~ly** adv vix, aegre

scarcity n paucitas; penuria, inopia f

scare vt terreo ②; territo, formido ①

scarecrow n terricula ntpl

scared adj territus

scarf n fascia f

scarlet[1] n (colour) color coccineus m

scarlet[2] adj coccineus

scatter vt spargo, dispergo ③; dissipo ①; (put to flight) fundo ③; fugo ①
■ **~ vi** dilabor ③

scene n scaena f; (spectacle) spectaculum nt; (place) locus; (landscape) prospectus m

scenery n (of nature) species regionis f
□ **beautiful ~** amoena loca ntpl; (of a theatre) scaena f

scenic adj scaenicus

scent¹ n (sense) odoratus; (fragrance) odor m; (of dogs) sagacitas f

scent² vt (perfume) odoro; (get wind of, scent out) odoror ①

scent-bottle n olfactorium nt

scented adj odoratus, odorifer, odorus, fragrans

sceptical adj (suspicious) suspicax

sceptre n sceptrum nt

schedule n libellus m

scheme¹ n consilium nt

scheme² vt&i molior ④; (plot) coniuro ①

scholar n discipulus m; discipula f; (learned man) homo doctus m

scholarship n litterae fpl; eruditio, humanitas f

school n (also fig) schola; secta f; ludus m

schoolboy n discipulus m

school-fellow n condiscipulus m; condiscipula f

schoolmaster n ludi magister, magister, praeceptor m

schoolmistress n magistra, praeceptrix f

sciatica n ischias f

science n scientia; doctrina; disciplina, ars; (theory) ratio f

scientific adj ad scientiam conformatus
■ **~ally** adv ex disciplinae praeceptis

scissors n forfipes fpl

scoff vi (mock) irrideo, derideo ②; cavillor ①; (eat) comedo ir

scold vt&i obiurgo, increpo, increpito ①

scolding n obiurgatio f; iurgium nt

scoop¹ n trulla f

scoop² vt cavo, excavo ①

scope n finis m; propositum nt; fig campus m; area f; spatium nt

scorch vt uro, aduro ③; torreo ②

score¹ n nota; (bill) ratio f; (twenty) viginti

score² vt (mark) noto ①
□ **~ a point** superior sum ir

scorn¹ vt temno, contemno, sperno ③; aspernor ①; fastidio ④

scorn² n contemptio f; contemptus m; supercilium, fastidium nt

scornful adj fastidiosus
■ **~ly** adv contemptim; fastidiose

scorpion n scorpio, scorpius m

scotch vt incido ③; vulnero ①

scot-free adj impunitus
□ **~** adv impune

scoundrel n nebulo, furcifer m

scour vt tergeo, detergeo ②; fig pervagor ①; percurro ③

scourge¹ n flagellum nt; fig pestis f

scourge² vt caedo ③; verbero ①

scout¹ n explorator, speculator, emissarius m

scout² vt speculor, exploro ①

scowl¹ vi frontem contraho ③

scowl² n frontis contractio f

scramble vi nitor, enitor ③

scrap n fragmentum, fragmen, frustum nt

scrape vt&i rado; (together) corrado ③

scraper n (tool) radula f; rallum nt

scratch¹ vt rado; scalpo ③; scabo ①; (inscribe) inscribo ③
□ **~ out** erado ③

scratch² n vulnus nt

scream¹ vi strideo ②; vociferor ①;

(of a child) vagio [4]

scream² n stridor m; vociferatio f; (of an infant) vagitus m

screech¹ vi strideo [2]; vociferor [1]; (of a child) vagio [4]

screech² n stridor m; vociferatio f; (of an infant) vagitus m

screen¹ n umbraculum nt; (protection) praesidium nt; defensio f

screen² vt occulo, protego, defendo [3]

scribe n scriba, amanuensis, librarius m

scroll n volumen nt

scrub¹ vt frico [1]; tergeo [2]

scrub² n (brushwood) virgulta ntpl

scruple¹ n scrupulus m; religio, dubitatio f

scruple² vi dubito [1]

scrupulous adj religiosus, scrupulosus

■ **~ly** adv religiose; scrupulose

scrutinize vt scrutor, perscrutor [1]

scrutiny n scrutatio, perscrutatio f

scuffle¹ n rixa; turba f

scuffle² vi rixor [1]

sculptor n sculptor, scalptor; artifex m; caelator m

sculpture¹ n (art) sculptura; scalptura f; (work) opus (marmoreum, etc.)

sculpture² vt sculpo, scalpo [3]; caelo [1]

scum n spuma; (of metals) scoria; fig sentina f

scurrilous adj scurrilis, probrosus

scurvy n scrofula f

scuttle n navis fundum perforo [1]

scythe n falx f

sea n mare, aequor, marmor nt;

pontus m

seacoast n ora f; litus nt

seafaring adj maritimus

seagull n larus m; gavia f

seahorse n hippocampus m

seal¹ n signum nt; (animal) phoca f

seal² vt signo, consigno, obsigno [1]; fig sancio [4]

sealing-wax n cera f

seam n sutura; commissura f

seaman n nauta m

seamanship n navigandi peritia f

search¹ vt&i scrutor, perscrutor [1]; (into) inquiro [3]; investigo [1]

search² n scrutatio; investigatio; inquisitio f

seasick adj nauseabundus

□ **be ~** nauseo [1]

seasickness n nausea f

seaside n ora f

season¹ n tempus (anni) nt; (right moment) opportunitas f

season² vt&i condio [4]; fig assuefacio [3]; duro, exercito [1]

seasonable adj tempestivus, opportunus

seasoned adj exercitatus

seasoning n (act) conditio f; (the seasoning itself) condimentum nt

seat¹ n sedes; sella f; sedile, subsellium nt; (dwelling-place) domicilium nt; (place) locus m; (dwelling) sedes f

seat² vt sede loco [1]; (oneself) consido [3]

sea-urchin n echinus m

seaweed n alga f; fucus m

seaworthy adj navigandi capax

secluded adj solitarius; remotus

seclusion n solitudo f; secessus

m; locus remotus m

second[1] adj secundus; alter
□ **for the ~ time** iterum

second[2] n (person) adiutor m; (of time) punctum temporis nt

secondary adj secundarius; inferior

secondly adv deinde, tum

secrecy n secretum nt; taciturnitas f; (keeping secret) silentium nt

secret[1] adj arcanus; secretus; occultus; furtivus; clandestinus
□ **in ~** clam
□ **keep ~** celo [1]
■ **~ly** adv clam; occulte, furtim

secret[2] n secretum, arcanum nt; res arcana f

secretary n scriba; amanuensis m

secrete vt celo, occulto [1]; abdo [3]
□ **~ oneself** lateo [2]; delitesco [3]

sect n secta, schola f

section n pars; (geometry) sectio f

sector n sector m

secular adj saecularis; (worldly) profanus

secure[1] adj securus; tutus
■ **~ly** adv tuto, secure

secure[2] vt confirmo [1]; munio [4]; a periculo defendo [3]; in custodiam trado [3]; (bring about, get) pario [3]; paro [1]

security n salus; incolumitas f; (pledge) satisdatio f; pignus nt; (person) vas, sponsor, praes m

sedan-chair n lectica f

sedate adj gravis, sedatus

sedentary adj sedentarius, sellularius

sediment n faex f

sedition n seditio, rebellio f;

tumultus m

seditious adj seditiosus, turbulentus

seduce vt corrumpo [3]; depravo [1]; decipio [3]

seducer n corruptor m

seduction n illecebra; corruptela f

seductive adj blandus

see vt&i video [2]; specto [1]; cerno, conspicio, aspicio [3]; (take precautions) caveo, video [2]; (understand) intellego [3]
□ **go to ~** viso [3]
□ **~ to** curo [1]

seed n semen nt

seedling n planta f

seeing conj
□ **~ that** quandoquidem, quoniam

seek vt&i quaero, peto, expeto, sequor [3]; (endeavour) conor; (strive to attain) affecto, consector [1]

seem vi videor [2]

seeming adj speciosus
■ **~ly** adv in speciem, ut videtur

seemly adj decorus, decens

seer n vates, fatidicus, augur, propheta m

seethe vi ferveo [2]; aestuo [1]; (with rage) furo [3]

segment n segmentum nt

segregate vt segrego [1]

seize vt prehendo, comprehendo; arripio [3]; (take possession) occupo [1]; (attack) invado; incesso; fig afficio [3]

seizure n comprehensio; occupatio f

seldom adv raro

select[1] vt seligo, eligo, deligo [3]

select[2] adj exquisitus

s

selection n selectio, electio f;
delectus m

self pn ipse, se, sese
□ **by one's ~** solus

self-confidence n sui fiducia f

self-conscious adj verecundus

self-control n temperantia f

selfish adj nimis se amans

selfishness n amor sui m

self-possessed adj placidus,
tranquillus, imperturbatus

self-willed adj obstinatus,
contumax

sell vt vendo ③
■ ~ vi veneo ④

seller n venditor m

semblance n similitudo, species f

semicircle n semicirculus m

semicircular adj semicirculus,
semicircularius

senate n senatus m; curia f

senate-house n curia f

senator n senator m

senatorial adj senatorius

send vt mitto ③; (on public business)
lego ①; (away) dimitto ③
□ ~ **for** accerso ③

senile adj senilis

senior adj natu maior

seniority n aetatis privilegium nt

sensation n sensus m;
(astonishment) stupor m; (subject of
talk) fabula f

sense n (faculty) sensus m; (intellect)
mens; (opinion) opinio, sententia f;
(meaning) significatio f

senseless adj nihil sentiens;
(lifeless) exanimis; fig mentis expers;
absurdus

sensible adj sensilis; sensu

praeditus, sensibilis; fig sapiens

sensitive adj mollis
□ ~ **to** impatiens + gen

sensual adj voluptarius;
libidinosus

sentence[1] n iudicium nt; (set of
words) sententia f

sentence[2] vt damno, condemno ①

sentiment n sententia, opinio
f; sensus m

sentimental adj animi mollioris
(gen); (in contempt) flebilis

sentinel n excubitor, vigil m;
excubiae fpl

sentry n excubitor, vigil m;
excubiae fpl
■ ~**-box** n specula f

separate[1] vt separo ①; disiungo,
seiungo, secerno ③
■ ~ vi separor ①; disiungor ③; (go
different ways) digredior ③

separate[2] adj separatus;
disiunctus

separation n separatio;
disiunctio f; (going different ways)
digressus m

September n September m

sequel n exitus, eventus m

sequence n ordo m; series f

serene adj serenus; tranquillus

serenity n serenitas; tranquillitas f

series n series f

serious adj gravis, serius, severus
■ ~**ly** adv graviter; serio; severe

seriousness n gravitas f; serium
nt; severitas f

sermon n oratio, contio f

serpent n serpens, anguis m/f;
coluber, draco m

servant n minister; famulus m;
ministra, ancilla f; famula f

serve *vt&i* servio ④ + *dat*; (for wages) stipendia mereo *or* mereor ②; (be useful) prosum *ir*; (be sufficient) sufficio ③ *both* + *dat*
□ ~ **up** offero *ir*

service *n* servitium; (kindness) officium *nt*; (advantage) utilitas *f*; (mil) militia *f*

serviceable *adj* utilis; commodus
□ **be** ~ prosum *ir* + *dat*

servile *adj* servilis, humilis

servility *n* humilitas *f*; animus abiectus *m*

session *n* sessio *f*; consessus, conventus *m*

set¹ *vt* pono, sisto ③; loco, colloco ①; (prescribe) praescribo ③; (an example) do ①; (enclose) includo ③; (on fire) accendo ③
□ ~ *vi* (of sun) occido ③
□ ~ **about** incipio ③
□ ~ **apart** *or* **aside** sepono; fig rescindo ③
□ ~ **down** (in writing) noto ①; perscribo
□ ~ **forth** expono; propono ③, profero *ir*; *vi* proficiscor ③
□ ~ **in** insero ③
□ ~ **off** *vt* (adorn) adorno; illustro ①; *vi* abeo ④; proficiscor ③
□ ~ **on** (incite) instigo ①; (attack) invado ③
□ ~ **out** *vi* discedo, proficiscor ③
□ ~ **up** erigo; extruo; statuo; (institute) instituo, constituo ③

set² *adj* (well-ordered) compositus

settee *n* lectulus *m*

setting *n* collocatio *f*; (of the sun) occasus *m*

settle *vt* statuo, constituo ③; (a quarrel) dirimo ③; (adjust) compono; (an account) solvo ③
■ ~ *vi* (reside) consido; (sink) subsido ③

settlement *n* constitutio; (dowry) dos *f*; (agreement) pactum *nt*; (colony) colonia *f*

settler *n* colonus *m*

seven *adj* septem
□ ~ **times** septies

seven hundred *adj* septingenti

seventeen *adj* septendecim, decem et septem

seventeenth *adj* septimus decimus

seventh *adj* septimus

seventieth *adj* septuagesimus

seventy *adj* septuaginta

sever *vt* separo ①; dissolvo ③; dissocio ①; disiungo ③

several *adj* plures, complures; diversus, varius

severe *adj* severus; gravis; durus
■ ~ **ly** *adv* severe, graviter

severity *n* severitas; gravitas; inclementia *f*

sew *vt&i* suo, consuo ③

sewer *n* cloaca *f*

sewing *n* sutura *f*

sex *n* sexus *m*

sexual *adj* sexualis; naturalis

shabby *adj* pannosus; sordidus

shackles *n* vincula *ntpl*; pedica, compes *f*

shade¹ *n* umbra *f*; (parasol) umbraculum *nt*; fig (difference) discrimen *nt*

shade² *vt* opaco; obscuro; obumbro; adumbro ①

shadow *n* umbra *f*

shadowy *adj* umbrosus, opacus; fig tenuis, inanis, vanus

shady *adj* opacus, umbrosus

shaft n sagitta f; (of a spear) hastile nt; (in a mine) puteus m; (of a column) scapus m

shaggy adj hirsutus, hirtus, villosus

shake vt quatio, concutio ③; quasso ①; (the head) nuto ①; (undermine) labefacio ③; labefacto ①
■ ~ vi concutior; (with fear) tremo ③; (totter) vacillo, nuto ①

shallow adj vadosus; fig levis

shallows n vada ntpl

sham[1] adj fictus, simulatus; fallax

sham[2] n fallacia f; dolus m; simulatio, species f

sham[3] vt simulo ①; fingo ③

shame[1] n pudor m; (disgrace) dedecus; opprobrium nt; ignominia f

shame[2] vt ruborem incutio ③ + dat

shamefaced adj pudens, pudibundus, verecundus

shameful adj turpis, probrosus
■ ~ly adv turpiter; probrose

shameless adj impudens
■ ~ly adv impudenter

shape[1] n forma, figura; species; facies f

shape[2] vt formo, figuro ①; fingo ③

shapeless adj informis; deformis, indigestus, rudis

shapely adj formosus

share[1] n pars, portio f

share[2] vt partior ④; (with another) communico ①; cum + abl
■ ~ vi particeps sum ir; in partem venio ④

sharer n particeps m/f; socius m; socia f; consors m/f

shark n (fish) pristis f; (person) fraudator m

sharp adj acutus; acer; (bitter) acerbus; (tart) acidus; fig mordax; argutus; subtilis
■ ~ly adv acute; (keenly) acriter; (bitterly) acerbe; (cleverly) subtiliter

sharpen vt acuo, exacuo ③

sharpness n (of edge) acies; (sourness) acerbitas; fig subtilitas, perspicacitas f; acumen nt

sharp-sighted adj perspicax

shatter vt quasso ①; frango, confringo; elido ③

shave vt rado ③; tondeo ②
□ ~ **off** abrado ③

shaving n ramentum nt; scobis f

shawl n amiculum nt

she pn haec, illa, ea

sheaf n manipulus, fascis m; merges f

shear vt tondeo ②; fig spolio, nudo ①

shears n forfex f

sheath n vagina f; (wrapper) involucrum nt

sheathe vt (in vaginam) recondo ③

shed[1] vt fundo, effundo, profundo, spargo ③; (blood) (one's own) do ①; (another's) haurio ④; (tears) effundo, profundo ③

shed[2] n tugurium nt

sheep n ovis, pecus, bidens f

sheepish adj timidus, modestus

sheepskin n pellis ovilla, mastruca f

sheer adj merus; purus; (precipitous) praeceps

sheet n linteum nt; (of metal) lamina f

shelf n pluteus m; tabula f

shell n concha; crusta, testa f;

(husk) folliculus *m*; (of nuts, *etc.*) putamen *nt*

shellfish *n* concha *f*

shelter¹ *n* tegmen *nt*; fig refugium, perfugium; (asylum) receptaculum *nt*

shelter² *vt* tego; protego; defendo ③

shepherd *n* pastor, upilio, pecorum custos *m*

shield¹ *n* scutum *nt*; clipeus *m*

shield² *vt* tego; protego, defendo ③

shift¹ *vt* muto ①; amoveo ②
■ ~ *vi* (as the wind) verto ③; (shuffle) tergiversor ①

shift² *n* (expedient) ratio *f*; modus *m*; (remedy) remedium *nt*; (trick) dolus *m*; ars *f*

shin *n* (**shin-bone**) tibia *f*

shine *vi* luceo, fulgeo, niteo, splendeo ②; corusco, mico ①
□ ~ **forth** eluceo; eniteo ②; exsplendesco ③
□ ~ **on** affulgeo ② + *dat*

shingle *n* glarea *f*; scandula *f*

shining *adj* lucidus, fulgidus, nitidus

shiny *adj* nitidus

ship¹ *n* navis *f*; navigium *nt*

ship² *vt* in navem (*or* naves) impono; accipio ③

shipbuilder *n* naupegus *m*

ship owner *n* navicularius *m*

shipping *n* navigia *ntpl*

shipwreck *n* naufragium *nt*; fig ruina *f*; interitus *m*

shipwrecked *adj* naufragus
□ **be** ~ naufragium facio ③

shipyard *n* navale *nt*, navalia *ntpl*

shirk *vt* detrecto ①

shirt *n* indusium *nt*; tunica *f*

shiver¹ *vi* contremisco, horresco ③; horreo ②

shiver² *n* (shudder) horror *m*
□ **cold** ~ frigus *nt*

shoal *n* (of fishes, *etc.*) caterva *f*; grex *m*; (shallow) brevia, vada *ntpl*

shock¹ *n* concussio *f*; impetus, concursus *m*; fig (of feeling) offensio; (blow) plaga *f*

shock² *vt* percutio, percello; fig offendo ③

shocking *adj* foedus; atrox

shoe¹ *n* calceus *m*; caliga; (slipper) solea *f*; soccus *m*; (for horses) solea *f*

shoe² *vt* calceos induo ③; (a horse) soleas apto ① + *dat*

shoemaker *n* sutor *m*

shoot¹ *vt* (telum) mitto; conicio ③; iaculor ①; (a person) figo, transfigo ③
■ ~ *vi* (of plants) germino ①; (of pains) vermino ①

shoot² *n* (of plants) surculus *m*; propago *f*; germen *nt*

shooting star *n* fax (caelestis), stella *f*

shop *n* taberna, officina *f*

shopkeeper *n* tabernarius *m*

shore *n* litus *nt*; ora *f*

short *adj* brevis; (little) exiguus
□ **in** ~ breviter, denique
□ **be** ~ **of** egeo ② + *abl*

shortcoming *n* defectus *m*; (fault) delictum, vitium *nt*; (failure) inopia *f*

shorten *vt* coarto ①; contraho ③
■ ~ *vi* contrahor; minuor ③

shorthand *n* notae breviores *fpl*

short-lived *adj* brevis

shortly *adv* (of time) brevi; mox
□ ~ **after** haud multum post

shortness n brevitas; exiguitas f;
(of breath) anhelitus m

short-sighted adj myops; fig
improvidus

short-sightedness n myopia;
fig minima imprudentia f

shot n ictus m; (reach, range) iactus;
(marksman) iaculator m; (bullet) glans
f; tormentum nt

shoulder n umerus m

shoulder-blade n scapulae fpl

shout¹ n clamor m; acclamatio,
vox f

shout² n clamo; acclamo;
vociferor ①

shove vt trudo ③; pulso ①

shovel n pala f; batillum; (for the
fire) rutabulum nt

show¹ vt monstro, declaro; indico
①; ostendo ③; (display) exhibeo;
(teach) doceo ②; (prove) confirmo ①;
(qualities) praebeo ②
  □ ∼ **off** ostento, vendito ①

show² n (appearance) species;
(display) ostentatio; (pretence)
simulatio; (parade) pompa f;
(spectacle) spectaculum nt

shower¹ n imber, nimbus m; fig
vis, multitudo f

shower² vt superfundo, effundo;
fig ingero ③

showery adj pluviosus, nimbosus,
pluvius, pluvialis

showy adj speciosus

shred n segmentum nt

shrewd adj acutus, astutus,
callidus; sagax; prudens
  ∼**ly** adv acute, callide; sagaciter;
astute, prudenter

shrewdness n calliditas; astutia;
sagacitas f; acumen nt; prudentia f

shriek¹ vi ululo, eiulo ①

shriek² n eiulatio f; ululatus m

shrill adj acutus, peracutus;
stridulus

shrimp n squilla f

shrine n (for holy things) sacrarium,
sacellum, adytum nt; cella f

shrink vt contraho ③
  ■ ∼ vi contrahor; (withdraw) refugio
③; (from) abhorreo ②; detrecto ①

shrivel vt corrugo ①; torreo ②
  ■ ∼ vi corrugor ①; torreor ②

shroud¹ n (of ships) rudentes mpl; (of
corpse) linteum (mortuorum) nt

shroud² vt involvo; obduco ③

shrub n frutex m; arbuscula f

shrubbery n fruticetum nt

shrug¹ n umerorum allevatio f

shrug² vt umeros allevo ①

shudder¹ n horror, tremor m

shudder² vi horreo ②; horresco ③

shuffle vt misceo ②
  ■ ∼ vi tergiversor ①

shun vt vito, devito, evito, declino,
detrecto ①; fugio ③

shut vt claudo, occludo ③; (out)
excludo ③; (up) concludo ③

shutter n claustrum nt

shuttle n radius m

shy adj timidus; pudibundus;
verecundus

shyness n timiditas; verecundia f

Sibyl n Sibylla f

sick adj aeger, aegrotus
  □ be ∼ aegroto ①; (of, with) taedet
(me rei) ②, fastidio ①

sicken vt fastidium moveo ② + gen;
satio ①
  ■ ∼ vi in morbum incido ③

sickle n falx f

■ **~-shaped** adj falcatus

sickly adj infirmus; (pale) pallidus

sickness n aegrotatio, aegritudo f; morbus m

side[1] n latus nt; (part, quarter) pars; regio; (edge) ora f; (of a hill) clivus m; (party in a contest) partes fpl

side[2] adj lateralis

side[3] vi (with) partes sequor ③ + gen; ab aliquo sto ①

sideboard n abacus m

sideways adv in obliquum, oblique

sidle vi obliquo incessu progredior ③

siege n oppugnatio, obsessio, obsidio f

siesta n meridiatio f
□ **take a ~** meridior ①

sieve n cribrum nt

sift vt cribro ①; cerno ③; fig exploro, scrutor ①

sigh[1] n suspirium nt

sigh[2] vi suspiro ①; (for) desidero, suspiro ①

sight n (sense) visus; (act of seeing) aspectus, conspectus m; (of the eye) acies (oculi or oculorum) f; (show) spectaculum nt; (appearance) species f; visum nt
□ **in ~** in conspectu
□ **out of ~** e conspectu

sign[1] n signum, indicium nt; (mark) nota f; (of a shop, etc.) insigne; fig portentum, omen; augurium nt

sign[2] vt&i subscribo; annuo ③; signum do ①

signal[1] n signum nt; (mil) classicum nt

signal[2] vt signum do ①

signature n nomen nt; subscriptio f

signet-ring n anulus m; signum nt

significance n (meaning) significatio f; sensus m; fig vis f; momentum nt

significant adj significans; fig magni momenti gen

signify vt&i significo ①; valeo ②; portendo ③

silence[1] n silentium nt; taciturnitas f
■ **~!** int tace! tacete!

silence[2] vt silentium facio ③; (confute) refuto ①; (allay) sedo ①; compesco ③

silent adj tacitus, silens
■ **~ly** adv (cum) silentio, tacite

silk[1] n sericum nt; bombyx m/f

silk[2] adj (also **silken**) sericus, bombycinus

sill n limen inferum nt

silliness n stultitia, fatuitas, insulsitas, insipientia f

silly adj stultus, fatuus, ineptus, insipiens, insulsus

silver[1] n argentum nt

silver[2] adj (also **silvery**) argenteus; (of hair) canus

silversmith n faber argentarius m

similar adj similis
■ **~ly** adv similiter

similarity n similitudo; vicinitas, proximitas f

simile n similitudo f

simmer vt fervefacio ③
■ **~** vi aestuo ①; ferveo ②

simple adj simplex; rudis; fig (silly) ineptus; ingenuus

simpleton n stultus, fatuus, ineptus m

simplicity n simplicitas f

simplify vt simpliciorem reddo ③

simply adv simpliciter; (merely) solum, modo, tantummodo

simulate vt simulo ①

simulation n simulatio f

simultaneous adj eodem tempore
■ ~ly adv simul, una

sin¹ n peccatum; delictum, flagitium, nefas, vitium nt

sin² vt pecco ①; delinquo ③

since¹ prep post + acc

since² conj cum, ex quo; (seeing that) cum; (when) quando; quoniam

since³ adv abhinc
□ **long ~** iamdudum

sincere adj sincerus, candidus; simplex, verus
■ ~ly adv sincere, vere

sincerity n sinceritas, simplicitas f; candor m

sinew n nervus; lacertus m

sinful adj impius, pravus; flagitiosus, sceleratus

sing vt&i cano ③; canto ①

singe vt aduro, amburo ③

singer n cantor m

singing n cantus m; carmen nt

single¹ adj solus, unicus, unus

single² vt (out) eligo ③

singly adv singillatim

singular adj unicus, singularis; (exceptional) peculiaris; egregius, eximius

sinister adj mali ominis gen; malevolus, iniquus

sink vi (fall to the ground) consido, subsido; (into ruins) collabor; (of a ship) deprimor, summergor ③
■ ~ vt deprimo; demergo,

summergo; (a well) demitto ③

sinner n peccans m/f

sinuous adj sinuosus

sip¹ vt sorbillo, degusto, libo, delibo ①

sip² n sorbitio f

siphon n sipho m

sir n (knight) eques m
■ ~! int (title of respect in address) bone vir! vir clarissime!

Siren n Siren f

sister n soror f

sisterhood n societas f; collegium nt

sister-in-law n glos f

sisterly adj sororius

sit vi sedeo; (at) assideo ②; (down) consido ③; (on) insideo ② + dat

site n situs; positus m; (space) area f

sitting n (act and session) sessio f

situated adj situs, positus

situation n situs, positus m; fig condicio f; status m

six adj sex
□ ~ **times** sexies

six hundred adj sescenti

sixteen adj sedecim

sixteenth adj sextus decimus

sixth adj sextus

sixtieth adj sexagesimus

sixty adj sexaginta

size n magnitudo; moles; mensura; forma f

skeleton n sceletus m; (bones) ossa ntpl
□ ~ **key** clavis adulterina f

sketch¹ n adumbratio f

sketch² vt adumbro; delineo ①; fig describo ③

skewer n veru nt

skilful adj dexter, expertus, peritus; sollers, ingeniosus
■ ~**ly** adv perite, sollerter, ingeniose

skilfulness n ars, sollertia, calliditas, peritia f

skill n ars, sollertia, calliditas, peritia f

skilled adj dexter, expertus, peritus; sollers, ingeniosus

skim vt despumo ①; fig percurro, stringo; perstringo, attingo ③; (fly over) volo per + acc ①; perlabor, verro ③

skin¹ n (of people) cutis; (of animals) pellis f; (prepared) corium nt; (membrane) membrana; (of vegetables) cutis, membrana, tunica f

skin² vt pellem detraho ③ + gen

skinny adj rugosus; macilentus; macer

skip¹ vi salio, exsilio ④; exsulto ①; lascivio
□ ~ **over** transilio ④; (leave out) omitto ③

skip² n saltus m

skirmish¹ n leve proelium nt

skirmish² vi velitor ①

skirt¹ n (dress) vestis f

skirt² vt lego ③

skull n calvaria, calva f

sky n caelum nt; aether m

skylark n alauda f

slab n quadra f

slack adj remissus, laxus; fig piger, neglegens

slacken vt remitto ③; laxo, relaxo ①; minuo ③
■ ~ vi minuor, remittor ③; laxor, relaxor ①

slag n scoria f

slake vt exstinguo ③; sedo ①; depello ③

slander¹ vt calumnior, detrecto ①

slander² n calumnia; obtrectatio f

slanderous adj maledicus

slanting adj obliquus

slap¹ n alapa f

slap² vt alapam do ①

slash¹ n (cut) incisura f; (blow) ictus m; (wound) vulnus nt

slash² vt concido, incido ③

slaughter n caedes, trucidatio f
■ ~ vt macto, trucido, neco, iugulo ①

slaughterhouse n macellum nt

slave¹ n servus m; serva f; verna m/f; mancipium nt; famulus m; famula f

slave² vi fig sudo ①

slavery n servitus f; servitium nt

slave-trade n venalicium nt

slave-trader n venalicius m

slavish adj servilis; humilis

slay vt interficio, caedo, perimo, interimo, occido ③; trucido, obtrunco ①

sledge n traha, trahea f

sleek adj levis, politus; nitidus

sleep¹ n somnus; sopor m; quies f

sleep² vi dormio ④; quiesco ③
□ ~ **off** edormio ④

sleepiness n somnolentia f; sopor m

sleepless adj insomnis; exsomnis, vigil, vigilax; pervigil

sleeplessness n insomnia; vigilantia f

sleepy adj somniculosus; fig iners

s

sleet n nivosa grando f

sleeve n manica f
□ **laugh up one's ~** furtim rideo ②

sleight n (of hand) praestigiae fpl

slender adj gracilis; tenuis; (sparing) parcus

slenderness n gracilitas; tenuitas f

slice¹ n segmentum, frustum nt; offula; (tool) spatha f

slice² vt seco ①

slide vi labor ③

slide² n lapsus m

slight¹ adj levis; exiguus, tenuis, parvus
■ **~ly** adv leviter; paulum, paulo

slight² n neglegentia; repulsa, iniuria f; contemptus m

slight³ vt neglego; contemno, despicio ③

slim adj gracilis; ▶ **slender**

slime n pituita f; (mud) limus m

slimy adj limosus, mucosus

sling¹ n funda; (for the arm) fascia, mitella f

sling² vt e funda iaculor ①; (hang) suspendo ③

slink vi (away) furtim me subduco ③; (in) irrepo ③

slip¹ vi labor ③
□ **~ away** elabor, clanculum me subtraho
□ **~ out** excido ③

slip² n lapsus m; fig peccatum nt; culpa f; error m

slipper n solea, crepida f

slippery adj lubricus; fig (deceitful) subdolus; (dangerous) periculosus

slipshod adj neglegens

slit¹ n incisura, rima f

slit² vt incido ③

slope¹ n acclivitas, declivitas f; clivus m

slope² vi proclinor ①; demittor ③
■ **~ vt** demitto ③

sloping adj acclivis; declivis; pronus

sloppy adj lutulentus, sordidus

sloth n ignavia, pigritia, inertia; socordia f

slothful adj iners, piger, segnis; ignavus, socors
■ **~ly** adv pigre, ignave, segniter

slough n (marsh) palus f

slow adj tardus, lentus; piger; (gentle) lenis
■ **~ly** adv tarde; lente; pigre; sensim

slug n limax m/f

sluggish adj piger, ignavus

sluice n obiaculum nt; cataracta f

slumber¹ n somnus, sopor m

slumber² vi obdormisco ③; dormito ①; dormio ④

slur¹ vt (smear) inquino ①

slur² n macula, labes f

slut n mulier neglegens f

sly adj astutus, vafer, callidus
□ **on the ~** clam, clanculum
■ **~ly** adv callide, vafre

smack¹ n (relish) sapor m; (slap) alapa f; (ship) lenunculus m

smack² vt (taste) gusto ①; (strike) ferio ④
■ **~ of** sapio ③ + acc

small adj parvus, exiguus, tenuis; brevis; pusillus; (insignificant) levis

smallness n exiguitas, tenuitas; parvitas; gracilitas; brevitas f

smart adj (clever) acutus, sollers, callidus; (energetic) alacer; (elegant) lautus, nitidus; (elegantly) nitide, laute

smartness n sollertia f; acumen nt; alacritas; (elegance) lautitia f, nitor m

smash¹ n ruina f

smash² vt confringo ③

smattering n (a small quantity) aliquantum nt

smear vt lino, illino, oblino, ungo ③

smell¹ vt olfacio ③; odoror ①
■ ~ vi oleo; redoleo ②; fragro ①

smell² n (sense) odoratus m; (odour) odor m

smelly adj olidus, graveolens

smile¹ vi subrideo, renideo ②; (at) arrideo ②

smile² n risus m

smiling adj renidens, subridens

smith n faber m

smithy n fabrica; officina f

smoke¹ vt fumigo, suffumigo; (dry by smoke) infumo ①
■ ~ vi fumo; vaporo ①

smoke² n fumus, vapor m

smoky adj fumeus, fumidus, fumosus, fumificus; (blackened by smoke) decolor fuligine

smooth¹ adj levis; glaber; (slippery) lubricus; (polished) teres; (calm) placidus; lenis; fig blandus
■ ~ly adv leniter, placide; fig blande

smooth² vt levigo ①; polio ④; (with the plane) runcino; fig complano ①

smother vt suffoco ①; opprimo ③; (conceal) celo ①

smoulder vi fumo ①

smudge¹ n sordes f

smudge² vt inquino ①

smug adj sibi placens

smuggle vt furtim importo, sine portorio importo ①

smut n (soot) fuligo f

snack n pars, portio; gustatio f

snail n coclea f; limax m/f

snake n anguis m/f; serpens f; vipera f; ▶ **serpent**

snap¹ vt/i (one's fingers or a whip) concrepo ①; (break) frango ③
■ ~ vi dissilio ④
□ ~ at mordicus arripio ③; fig hianti ore capto ①

snap² n crepitus m

snare¹ n laqueus m; pedica f; insidiae fpl

snare² vt illaqueo, implico ①; irretio ④

snarl¹ vi (as a dog) ringor ③; hirrio ④

snarl² n hirritus m

snatch vt rapio, corripio ③; (away) eripio; surripio; avello ③

sneak vi repo, serpo ③; latito ①
□ ~ off me subtraho ③

sneer¹ vi irrideo, derideo ②

sneer² n irrisio f; irrisus m

sneeze¹ vi sternuo ③

sneeze² n sternumentum, sternutamentum nt

sniff vi naribus capto ①; haurio ④

snip vt amputo ①; (off) decerpo, praecido ③

snob n homo novus et arrogans, divitum cultor m

snobbish adj fastidiosus

snore¹ vi sterto ③

snore² n rhonchus m

snort¹ vi fremo ③

snort² n fremitus (equorum) m

snout n rostrum nt

snow[1] n nix f

snow[2] vi impers
  □ **it is ~ing** ningit ③

snowy adj niveus, nivalis; (full of snow) nivosus

snub[1] vt repello ③

snub[2] n repulsa f

snub-nosed adj simus, resimus

so adv sic, ita; tam; adeo
  □ **and ~** itaque
  □ **~ far** eatenus
  □ **~ much** tantum; tam
  □ **~ great** tantus
  □ **~ many** tot
  □ **so-so** mediocriter
  □ **~ that** ita ut

soak vt macero ①; madefacio, imbuo, tingo ③
  ■ **~** vi (be soaked) madeo ②; madesco, madefio ③
  □ **~ through** percolor ①

soap n sapo m

soar vi in sublime feror ③; (of birds) subvolo ①

sob[1] n singultus m

sob[2] vi singulto ①

sober adj sobrius; fig moderatus

sobriety n sobrietas f

sociable adj sociabilis, socialis; facilis, affabilis, comis

social adj socialis; communis; civilis

society n societas f; (fraternity) sodalicium, collegium nt

sock n pedale nt; udo m

socket n cavum nt

sod n (clod) caespes m

sofa n lectulus, grabatus m

soft adj mollis, tener; (gentle) lenis;

clemens; mitis; (not loud) mollis; fig delicatus; effeminatus
  ■ **~ly** adv molliter; leniter; clementer

soften vt mollio ④; mitigo ①; fig lenio ④; placo, levo ①
  ■ **~** vi mollesco; (fruits) mitesco fig mansuesco, mitesco ③

softness n mollitia; teneritas; lenitas; (effeminacy) mollitia f

soil[1] n solum nt; terra f

soil[2] vt inquino, contamino, maculo ①

solace n solacium, lenimen, levamen, levamentum nt

solar adj solaris; solis (genitive)

solder[1] vt ferrumino ①

solder[2] n ferrumen nt

soldier n miles m

sole[1] n mollitia; teneritas; tenacitas; solus
  ■ **~ly** adv solum, modo, tantum

sole[2] n (of the foot) planta; (of a shoe) solea f

solecism n soloecismus m

solemn adj sollemnis; severus; gravis; serius
  ■ **~ly** adv sollemniter, graviter, severe, serio

solemnity n sollemne, festum nt; sollemnitas f

solicit vt rogo; flagito; (tempt) sollicito ①

solicitor n iuris consultus, causidicus; advocatus m

solid[1] adj solidus; densus; fig verus; firmus

solid[2] n corpus solidum nt

solitary adj solitarius; (of places) desertus, solus

solitude n solitudo f; locus solus m

soluble adj solubilis

solution n dilutum nt; fig solutio, explicatio f

solve vt solvo ③; explico ①

sombre adj (severe) tristis

some adj aliqui, nescio qui; nonnullus; quidam
□ ~ ... **other** alius ... alius

somebody n nescio quis, aliquis

somehow adv nescio quo modo

something n aliquid nt

sometime adv aliquando; quandoque
□ ~ **or other** aliquo tempore

sometimes adv quandoque, interdum; nonnunquam; (when repeated) modo ... modo

somewhat adv paullulum

somewhere adv alicubi

son n filius, natus m
■ ~-**in-law** n gener m

song n cantus m; carmen nt; (tune) melos nt

soon adv brevi, postmodo, mox
□ ~ **after** paulo post
□ **as** ~ **as** simulatque, simulac
□ **as** ~ **as possible** quam primum

sooner adv (earlier) citius, temperius, prius ... quam; (rather) libentius; potius
□ **no** ~ **said than done** dicto citius

soot n fuligo f

soothe vt mulceo, permulceo ②; mitigo, levo ①; delenio ④

soothsayer n hariolus, sortilegus m; fatidicus, haruspex m; augur, vates m/f

sooty adj fuliginosus

sop n offa, offula f

sophisticated adj lepidus

soporific adj soporus, soporifer, somnifer

sorcerer n magus, veneficus m

sorceress n maga, saga, venefica f

sorcery n fascinatio f; veneficium nt; magice f

sordid adj sordidus, turpis, foedus

sore¹ adj tener
■ ~**ly** adv graviter, vehementer

sore² n ulcus nt

sorrow n dolor, maeror, luctus, angor m; anxietas f

sorrowful adj luctuosus, tristis, miser, maestus

sorry adj
□ **I am** ~ aegre fero ③; paenitet me (alicuius rei)
□ **feel** ~ **for** misereor ② + gen

sort¹ n (kind) genus nt; species f; (manner) modus, mos m; (quality, of things) nota f

sort² vt ordino ①; dispono, digero ③

sortie n eruptio, excursio f; excursus m

soul n anima f; (person) homo m

sound¹ adj (healthy) validus, sanus; (strong) robustus; (entire) integer; (in mind) mentis compos; (true, genuine) verus; (valid) ratus; (of sleep) profundus; altus

sound² n sonus, sonitus m; vox f; (of a trumpet) clangor; (noise) strepitus m

sound³ vt (a trumpet) cano ③; (try) tento, sollicito ①
■ ~ **vi** sono, persono ①; strepo ③

soup n ius nt

sour adj acidus, acerbus; amarus;

fig morosus

source n fons m; fig origo f; principium nt

sourness n acor m; acerbitas; fig morositas f

south n meridies, auster m

southern adj australis, meridianus

southwards adv in meridiem, meridiem versus

south wind n Auster, Notus m

sovereign[1] n princeps m/f, rex, regnator m

sovereign[2] adj supremus

sovereignty n imperium nt; dominatio f; principatus m

sow[1] n sus; porca f

sow[2] vt sero ③; semino ①

space n spatium nt; area f; (of time) intervallum nt

spacious adj spatiosus, amplus

spade n (implement) ligo m; pala f

Spain n Hispania f

span n (width of the palm) palmus m

Spanish adj Hispanicus, Hispaniensis

spar[1] n (beam) trabs f

spar[2] vi dimico; fig digladior ①

spare[1] vt&i parco ③ + dat; parce utor ③ + abl

spare[2] adj parcus; exilis

sparing adj parcus

spark n scintilla f; igniculus m

sparkle vi scintillo, corusco, radio, mico ①

sparkling adj nitidus, coruscus

sparrow n passer m

Sparta n Sparta, Lacedaemon f

Spartan adj Laconicus, Spartanus, Lacedaemonius

spasm n spasmos m

spasmodic adj spasticus; fig rarus
■ ~ally adv raro

spatter vt inquino ①; aspergo ③; fig calumnior ①

spatula n spatha f

spawn[1] n ova (piscium) ntpl

spawn[2] vi ova gigno ③

speak vi&t loquor ③; for ①; dico ③
□ ~ of dico (de + abl; (mention) memoro ①
□ ~ out eloquor, proloquor ③
□ ~ to alloquor ③

speaker n orator m

spear[1] n hasta, lancea f; telum, pilum, iaculum nt

spear[2] vt transfigo ③

special adj peculiaris, specialis; praecipuus
■ ~ly adv specialiter, praecipue, peculiariter, praesertim

speciality n proprietas f; quod peculiare est

species n species f; genus nt

specific adj specialis; (definite) certus
■ ~ally adv specialiter

specify vt enumero ①; describo ③

specimen n exemplum, documentum, specimen nt

speck n macula f

speckled adj maculosus

spectacle n spectaculum nt; species f; aspectus m

spectator n spectator m; spectatrix f

spectre n simulacrum, umbra, visum nt

speculate vt&i meditor ①; coniecturam facio ③

speculation n contemplatio f

speech n lingua, loquela f; sermo m; contio, oratio f

speechless adj mutus, elinguis; fig obstupefactus

speed¹ n celeritas; festinatio f; impetus m

speed² vt propero, festino, adiuvo, prospero 🔲
■ ~ vi (hasten) propero, festino 🔲

speedy adj citus, properus

spell¹ n (charm) incantamentum, cantamen, carmen nt; cantus m

spell² vt&i ordino 🔲 syllabas litterarum

spelling n orthographia f

spend vt impendo; consumo; (time) ago, dego, consumo, contero; (exhaust) effundo ③; (squander) dissipo 🔲

spendthrift n nepos, prodigus m

spew vt&i vomo ③

sphere n sphaera f; globus m; fig provincia, area f

spherical adj sphaericus, sphaeralis, globosus

sphinx n sphinx f

spice¹ n aroma nt; odores mpl

spice² vt condio ④

spicy adj aromaticus, conditus, fragrans, odorus, odorifer

spider n aranea f
□ ~'s web araneum nt; casses fpl

spike n clavus m; (point) cuspis; (of corn) spica f

spiky adj acutus, spinosus

spill vt effundo ③

spin vt neo ②; (draw out) duco, protraho ③; (as a top) verso 🔲
■ ~ vi (be turned round) versor 🔲;

circumferor ③

spinal adj dorsualis

spindle n fusus; (of a wheel) axis m

spine n (vertebrae, thorn) spina f

spinster n innupta f

spiral¹ adj spirae formam habens

spiral² n spira f

spire n spira; (tower) turris f

spirit n spiritus m; anima f; fig ingenium nt; vigor m; (ghost) simulacrum nt; umbra, imago f; (god) deus m

spirited adj animosus; alacer

spiritual adj animi, mentis both gen; incorporalis; ecclesiasticus

spit¹ n veru nt; (of land) lingua f;
▶ **spittle**

spit² vt&i (from the mouth) spuo ③; exscreo 🔲

spite¹ n livor m; invidia, malevolentia f; odium nt
■ **in ~ of** use ablative absolute with perfect participle passive of contemno

spite² vt vexo 🔲

spiteful adj lividus, malevolus, invidus

spittle n sputum nt; saliva f

splash vt aspergo, respergo ③

splendid adj splendidus; nitidus; lautus, sumptuosus; magnificus
■ ~**ly** adv splendide; magnifice; laute, nitide, sumptuose

splendour n splendor, nitor m; fig magnificentia; lautitia f

splint n (in medicine) ferula f

splinter¹ n assula f

splinter² vt confringo ③
■ ~ vi dissilio ④

split¹ vt&i findo; findor ③

split² n fissura, rima f

split[3] *adj* fissilis

spoil[1] *n* spolium *nt*; praeda *f*; exuviae *fpl*

spoil[2] *vt* spolio; praedor; vasto [1]; diripio [3]; (mar, etc.) corrumpo; (ruin) perdo [3]; depravo, vitio [1]

spoke *n* radius *m*

spokesman *n* orator *m*

sponge[1] *n* spongia *f*

sponge[2] *vt* spongia detergeo [2]

spongy *adj* spongiosus

sponsor *n* sponsor, vas, praes *m*

spontaneously *adv* sua sponte, ultro

spool *n* fusus *m*

spoon *n* coclear *nt*

spoonful *n* coclear *nt*

sport[1] *n* ludus, lusus *m*; (hunting) venatio; (mockery) irrisio *f*
□ **in ~** *per* iocum

sport[2] *vi* ludo [3]; lascivio [4]

sportive *adj* iocosus, ludicer

sportsman *n* athleta *m*

spot[1] *n* macula; (mark) nota; (stain) labes *f*; (place) locus *m*

spot[2] *vt* (stain) inquino, maculo, commaculo; (speckle) maculis noto [1]

spotless *adj* expers maculis; *fig* purus; integer
■ **~ly** *adv* sine labe

spotted *adj* maculosus, maculis distinctus

spouse *n* coniunx *m/f*; maritus *m*; uxor *f*

spout[1] *n* canalis; (of water) torrens *m*

spout[2] *vt* eiaculor (in altum); (speeches) declamo [1]
■ **~** *vi* prosilio [4]; emico [1]

sprain[1] *vt* intorqueo [2]; convello [3]; luxo [1]

sprain[2] *n* luxatura *f*

sprawl *vi* humi prostratus iaceo [2]

spray[1] *n* aspergo, spuma *f*; (branch) ramus *m*; virga *f*

spray[2] *vt* spargo [3]

spread *vt* pando, tendo, expando, distendo, extendo; diffundo [3]; (make known) divulgo [1]
■ **~** *vi* pandor, tendor, distendor, extendor, expandor, diffundor [3]; (become known) divulgor; (of a disease, etc.) evagor [1]; glisco [3]

sprig *n* ramulus *m*; virga *f*

sprightly *adj* alacer; hilaris

spring[1] *n* (season) ver *nt*; (leap) saltus *m*; (of water) fons *m*

spring[2] *adj* vernus

spring[3] *vi* (grow from) orior [4]; enascor [3]; (as rivers, etc.) scateo [2]; effluo [3]; (leap) salio, exsilio [4]
□ **~ a leak** rimas ago [3]

springtime *n* vernum tempus *nt*

sprinkle *vt* spargo, aspergo, respergo [3]; roro, irroro [1]

sprout[1] *n* surculus *m*; germen *nt*
■ **~s** *pl* cauliculi *mpl*

sprout[2] *vi* pullulo, germino [1]

spruce *adj* lautus, nitidus, comptus

spur[1] *n* calcar; *fig* incitamentum, irritamen, irritamentum *nt*

spur[2] *vt* equum calcaribus concito [1]; equo calcaria subdo [3]; *fig* incito, excito [1]

spurious *adj* subditus, suppositus, falsus

spurn *vt* aspernor, repudio [1]; sperno [3]; proculco [1]

spurt *vi* (as liquids) exsilio [4]

spy[1] *n* explorator; speculator; emissarius *m*

spy² vt&i exploro; speculor ☐

squabble¹ vi rixor ☐

squabble² n iurgium nt; rixa f

squad n manipulus m

squadron n (of cavalry) turma, ala; (of ships) classis f

squalid adj squalidus, spurcus, sordidus, turpis

squall n vociferatio f; (sudden storm) procella f

squalor n squalor, situs m; sordes fpl; illuvies f

squander vi dissipo ☐; profundo ☐

square¹ adj quadratus; fig honestus, probus

square² n quadratum nt; quadra; (tool) norma f; (mil) agmen quadratum nt

squash vt contero, confringo ☐

squat vi succumbo, recumbo, subsido ☐

squeak vi strideo ☐

squeamish adj fastidiosus

squeeze vt comprimo, premo ☐; (out) exprimo ☐

squint vi limis oculis intueor ☐

squinting adj strabus, limis oculis

squirrel n sciurus m

squirt vt proicio ☐
■ ~ vi emico ☐; exsilio ☐

stab¹ n vulnus nt; ictus m; plaga f

stab² vt fodio ☐; perforo ☐; perfodio, transfigo ☐

stability n stabilitas f

stable¹ adj stabilis, solidus

stable² n stabulum nt
■ ~-boy n stabularius m

stack¹ n acervus m; strues f

stack² vt coacervo ☐

stadium n (running-track) stadium nt

staff n baculum nt; fustis; (baton) scipio m; (officers) legati mpl; fig (support) subsidium, fulcimentum nt

stag n cervus m

stage n proscaenium; pulpitum; suggestum; theatrum nt; fig (field of action) campus m; area f; (on a journey) iter nt

stagger vi vacillo, titubo ☐
■ ~ vt obstupefacio ☐

stagnant adj stagnans; torpens; piger, iners

stagnate vi stagno ☐; fig refrigesco ☐

stagnation n torpor m

staid adj gravis, severus

stain¹ n macula, labes; fig infamia, nota f

stain² vt maculo, commaculo, contamino ☐; (dye) tingo, inficio, imbuo ☐

stainless adj immaculatus, purus; fig integer

stair n gradus m; scala f

staircase n scalae fpl

stake¹ n palus, stipes, vallus m; sudis f; (wager) depositum nt
□ be at ~ in discrimine esse

stake² vt depono ☐; pignero, oppignero ☐

stale adj vetus; obsoletus; tritus

stalk¹ n caulis m; (of corn) culmus m

stalk² vi incedo, ingredior ☐; spatior ☐; (in hunting) venor ☐

stall n stabulum nt; (seat) subsellium nt

stallion n (equus) admissarius m

stammer¹ n haesitatio linguae f

stammer² vt&i balbutio ☐; lingua

haesito 🗌

stamp¹ n (mark) nota f; signum nt; (with the foot) vestigium nt; (kind) genus nt

stamp² vt imprimo ③; noto 🗌; (money) cudo ③; (with the feet) supplodo ③; pulso 🗌

□ ~ **out** deleo ②

stand¹ n locus m; statio; mora f; (platform) suggestus m; (counter) mensa f

□ **make a** ~ subsisto ③

stand² vi sto 🗌; consisto ③; (remain) maneo ②; (endure) tolero 🗌; sustineo ②; (against) resisto ③ + dat; (aloof) absto 🗌; (by) asto 🗌; assisto ③ both + dat; fig persto 🗌; (out) exsto 🗌; promineo ②; (still) consisto, subsisto ③

standard n signum, vexillum nt; (pattern of practice or behaviour) norma, (yardstick) mensura f

■ ~-**bearer** n vexillarius, signifer m

standing n status, ordo m; condicio f

standstill n

□ **be at a** ~ consisto ③; haereo ②

star n stella f; sidus, astrum; fig lumen nt

stare n obtutus m

■ ~ vt&i inhio 🗌; stupeo ②

□ ~ **(at)** intueor ②; haereo ②; defixus in aliquo

stark adj rigidus

starling n sturnus m

starry adj sidereus, stellans, stellatus, stellifer

start¹ vi (in agitation) trepido 🗌; subsilio ④; contremisco ③; (begin) ordior ④; incipio ③; (set out) proficiscor ③

■ ~ vt (game) excito 🗌; (set on foot) instituo ③; (put in motion) commoveo ②; (begin) incipio ③

start² n subita trepidatio f; tremor m; (departing) profectio f; (leap) saltus m; (beginning) initium, principium nt

starting-place n (at the races) carceres mpl; claustra ntpl

startle vt territo 🗌; terreo ②

starvation n fames, inedia f

starve vt fame interficio ③

■ ~ vi fame enecor 🗌

state¹ n status; locus m; (political) civitas, respublica f; (pomp) magnificentia f; fig condicio f

state² vt narro; declaro, indico ③; perscribo ③

stately adj superbus; splendidus, lautus, augustus

statement n affirmatio f; testimonium, indicium nt

statesman n peritus qui in republica versatur m

station¹ n statio f; locus m

station² vt loco 🗌; dispono ③

stationary adj stabilis, loco fixus, immotus

stationer n chartarius m

□ ~'s **shop** taberna chartaria f

stationery n charta f; res chartariae fpl

statue n statua, imago, effigies f; signum, simulacrum nt

stature n statura f; habitus m

status n status m

statute n statutum; decretum nt; lex f

staunch¹ adj firmus, fidus, constans

staunch² vt sisto ③; cohibeo ②

stay¹ vi maneo ②; commoror; (loiter)

cunctor 1
■ ~ vt detineo 2; sisto 3; (curb) coerceo 2

stay² n (sojourn) commoratio, mansio; (delay) mora f; (prop) fulcrum nt; fig subsidium, columen nt

steadfast adj stabilis, firmus, constans
■ ~ly adv constanter, firmiter

steadiness n firmitas, stabilitas, constantia f

steady adj firmus, stabilis; constans; fig (serious) gravis

steal vt furor 1; (away) surripio 3
■ ~ vi repo, serpo 3; insinuo 1

stealth n (act) furtum nt
□ by ~ furtim, clam

stealthy adj furtivus

steam¹ n (aquae) vapor m

steam² vt&i vaporo; fumo 1

steel n chalybs m; fig ferrum nt

steep¹ adj praeceps, arduus, praeruptus

steep² vt madefacio 3; macero 1; imbuo, tingo 3

steeple n turris f

steeply adv in praeceps

steepness n acclivitas, declivitas f

steer vt&i guberno, moderor 1; dirigo, rego 3

stem¹ n (of a plant) stirps f

stem² vt obsisto, obnitor both + dat; reprimo 3

stench n fetor, odor m

step¹ n passus, gradus, gressus m
■ ~ by ~ adv gradatim, sensim, pedetentim

step² vi gradior 3

stepbrother n (of father's side) vitrici filius; (of mother's side)

novercae filius m

stepdaughter n privigna f

stepfather n vitricus m

stepmother n noverca f

stepson n privignus m

sterile adj sterilis, infecundus

sterility n sterilitas f

stern¹ adj durus, severus; torvus

stern² n puppis (navis) f

stethoscope n stethoscopium nt

steward n administrator, procurator; vilicus m

stick¹ n baculus, scipio, fustis m; baculum nt

stick² vt affigo 3
■ ~ vi haereo; adhaereo 2
□ ~ prominео 2

sticky adj lentus, tenax

stiff adj rigidus; fig severus; frigidus

stiffen vt rigidum facio 3
■ ~ vi rigesco, derigesco 3

stiffness n rigor m; fig pertinacia f; rigor m

stifle vt suffoco; strangulo 1; fig opprimo 3

stigma n nota, ignominia f

still¹ adj quietus, immotus, tacitus

still² adv nihilominus; (yet) adhuc; (however) tamen, attamen; (even now) etiam nunc; (always) semper

stillness n silentium nt; quies f

stilts npl grallae fpl

stimulant n irritamentum, irritamen nt; stimulus m

stimulate vt stimulo, exstimulo, excito 1

stimulus n ► **stimulant**

sting¹ n (of insects and plants) aculeus m; spiculum nt; (wound) ictus, morsus m; fig (of conscience) angor

sting | stow

conscientiae *m*

sting² *vt* pungo ③; mordeo ②; (as nettles) uro ③; fig excrucio ①

stingy *adj* sordidus, parcus

stink¹ *vi* feteo, male oleo ②

stink² *n* fetor *m*

stint *vt* moderor ①; coerceo ②; circumscribo, parco ③ + *dat*

stipulate *vt* paciscor ③; stipulor ①

stipulation *n* stipulatio; condicio *f*; pactum *nt*

stir *n* tumultus, motus *m*; turba *f*
■ ~ *vt* (arouse) excito ①; (move) moveo ②
■ ~ *vi* se movere ②

stitch *vt* suo ③

stoat *n* mustela *f*

stock¹ *n* (of a tree) caudex, truncus, stipes *m*; (handle) lignum *nt*; (race) genus *nt*; (of goods) copia, vis *f*; (cattle) pecus *nt*; stirps *f*; (of cattle) res pecuaria *f*

stock² *vt* instruo ③; orno, suppedito ①

stockade *n* vallum *nt*

stock-still *adj* immotus, immobilis

stoic *adj* (also **stoical**) stoicus; fig patiens

stoicism *n* Stoica disciplina *f*; fig patientia

stolen *adj* furtivus; clandestinus
□ ~ **goods** furta *ntpl*

stomach *n* stomachus, venter, ventriculus; (appetite) appetitus *m*
■ ~ *vt* (put up with) fero ③; tolero ①

stone¹ *n* lapis *m*; saxum *nt*; (med) calculus; (gem) gemma *f*; (of fruit) nucleus *m*
□ **leave no** ~ **unturned** nihil reliqui facio ③

stone² *vt* lapido ①

stone³ *adj* lapideus, saxeus

stony *adj* (full of stones) lapidosus; saxeus, saxosus

stool *n* scabellum, scamnum *nt*; sella *f*

stoop *vi* proclino ①; fig me summitto ③

stop¹ *vt* prohibeo ②; sisto ③; moror, tardo, retardo ①
■ ~ *vi* subsisto; (cease) desisto, desino, omitto ③; (remain) maneo ②; (sojourn) commoror ①
□ ~ **up** obturo ①; intercludo ③

stop² *n* (delay) mora *f*; impedimentum *nt*; pausa *f*; (end) finis *m/f*

stoppage *n* obstructio *f*

stopper *n* obturamentum *nt*

store *n* copia *f*; apparatus; (provisions) commeatus *m*
■ ~ *vt* coacervo ①; condo; (with) instruo ③

storehouse *n* cella *f*; promptuarium; (granary) horreum *nt*

storey *n* (of a house) tabulatum *nt*

stork *n* ciconia *f*

storm¹ *n* procella, tempestas; (mil) expugnatio *f*

storm² *vt* expugno ①
■ ~ *vi* saevio, desaevio ④

stormy *adj* turbidus; procellosus; fig tumultuosus

story *n* (tale) narratio; fabula; (history) historia *f*; (lie) mendacium *nt*

storyteller *n* narrator; (liar) mendax *m*

stout *adj* robustus; firmus; validus; (fat) pinguis; (brave) fortis

stove *n* fornax *f*; caminus *m*

stow *vt* condo, recondo, repono ③

straddle vi varico 🔢

straggle vi palor, vagor 🔢

straggler n vagus; erro m

straight adj rectus, directus
■ ~ adv (directly) recte, recta
□ ~ **away** statim, confestim, protinus

straighten vt rectum facio 🔢; corrigo 🔢

straightforward adj simplex, apertus, directus, sincerus

strain¹ vt (stretch) contendo 🔢; (a joint) luxo 🔢; (filter) percolo 🔢; (press out) exprimo 🔢
■ ~ vi percolor 🔢; enitor 🔢

strain² n contentio; vis; (nervorum) intentio f; (effort) conamen nt; nisus m

strainer n colum nt

strait n fretum nt; fig difficultas f; angustiae fpl

strand n (shore) litus nt; (thread) filum nt

strange adj peregrinus f; fig inusitatus; rarus; novus; mirus; mirificus

stranger n advena m/f; hospes; peregrinus m

strangle vt strangulo, suffoco 🔢

strangulation n strangulatio, suffocatio f; strangulatus m

strap n lorum nt; struppus m; amentum nt

strapping adj robustus

stratagem n insidiae fpl; fig dolus m

strategy n ars imperatoria f

straw¹ n stramentum, stramen nt; stipula f

straw² adj stramineus

strawberry n fragum nt

stray¹ vi erro, aberro, palor, vagor 🔢

stray² adj vagus; (sporadic) rarus

streak¹ n linea, virga f

streak² vt distinguo 🔢

streaky adj virgatus

stream¹ n flumen nt; amnis m

stream² vi fluo, curro, effundor 🔢; mano 🔢

street n via; (with houses) platea f; vicus m

strength n robur nt; firmitas; (power) potentia, potestas f; vires fpl

strengthen vt roboro, confirmo 🔢; munio 🔢

strenuous adj strenuus; fortis; acer
■ ~ly adv strenue, fortiter, acriter

stress n (anxiety) angor m; (chief point) summa f; caput nt; (emphasis) vis f; pondus nt

stretch¹ vt tendo; produco, extendo; distendo 🔢
■ ~ vi extendo; producor; distendor; (of country) patesco 🔢
□ ~ **out** porrigo 🔢; (oneself) pandicular 🔢

stretch² n (effort) intentio, contentio f; (expanse) spatium nt; tractus m

stretcher n lecticula f

strew vt spargo, conspergo, sterno, insterno 🔢

stricken adj vulneratus, afflictus

strict adj (precise) accuratus, exactus; (severe) rigidus, severus
■ ~ly adv accurate; rigide; severe

strictness n severitas f; rigor m

stride¹ vi varico 🔢

stride² n gradus m
□ **make** ~s fig proficio 🔢

strife n iurgium nt; lis; pugna; discordia, rixa f

strike vt ferio 4; pulso 1; percutio 3; (cudgel) verbero 1; (stamp) cudo 3; (the mind) subeo 4; succurro 3 + dat
□ **be struck** fig commoveor 2

string¹ n linea f; filum nt; (for a bow; sinew) nervus m; (for musical instruments) chorda; fig series f

string² vt persero 3

stringent adj severus

strip¹ vt (off) spolio; nudo; denudo 1; (clothes) exuo 3; (the rind, etc.) decortico 1

strip² n particula, lacinia f; (of paper) schida f

stripe n (mark of a blow) vibex f; (blow) ictus m; verbera ntpl; (for garments) virga f
■ **purple ~** n clavus m

striped adj virgatus

strive vi nitor, enitor 3; molior 4; conor 1; contendo 3; (after, for) annitor 3; sector 1; (against) obnitor 3 + dat

stroke¹ n ictus m; plaga f; (of an oar) pulsus m

stroke² vt mulceo, permulceo 2

stroll vi (about) perambulo, obambulo, spatior 1

stroll n ambulatio f

strong adj robustus; fortis; firmus, valens; (powerful) potens, validus; fig vehemens; gravis
■ **~ly** adv robuste; valide; firme; fortiter, vehementer; graviter

stronghold n arx f; castellum nt

structure n (construction) structura f; (building) aedificium nt

struggle vi contendo 3; certo,

luctor 1; nitor, obnitor 3; (fight) pugno 1
■ **~** n certamen nt; pugna; luctatio f; luctamen nt

strut vi spatior 1

stubble n stipula f; culmus m

stubborn adj obstinatus, pervicax, contumax
■ **~ly** adv pervicaciter, obstinate; contumaciter

stubbornness n pervicacia, contumacia f

stud n bulla f; clavus m

student n litterarum studiosus m

studious adj diligens, industrius, navus

study n studium; (room) umbraculum nt; bibliotheca f
■ **~** vt&i studeo 2 + dat, exploro, meditor 1

stuff¹ n (material) materia f; (furniture, etc.) supellex f; (cloth) pannus m; (things) res fpl; (woven ~) textile nt

stuff² vt farcio 4; sagino 1; (fill) expleo, repleo 2

stuffing n (in cookery) fartum; (for chairs, etc.) tomentum nt

stumble¹ vi offendo 3; (falter) haesito 1; (upon) incido 3 in + acc

stumble² n offensio f

stumbling-block n offensio f

stump n truncus, caudex, stipes m

stun vt obstupefacio, obtundo, stupefacio 3; perturbo 1; sopio 4

stunt vt incrementum (alicuius, etc.) impedio 4

stupefy vt obstupefacio 3; terreo 2; perturbo; hebeto 1; sopio 4

stupid adj stupidus, fatuus, stultus
■ **~ly** adv stulte

stupidity n stupiditas, fatuitas,

stultitia f

stupor n stupor; torpor m

sturdiness n firmitas f; robur nt

sturdy adj robustus, validus, firmus

stutter vi balbutio [4]

sty n hara f

style n sermo; modus m; genus nt

stylish adj nitidus, lautus

suave adj blandus

suavity n suavitas, dulcedo f; blanditia f

subdue vt subicio, subigo, vinco [3]; domo [1]

subject¹ adj subiectus; (liable to) obnoxious + dat

subject² n (member of population) subditus; civis m; (theme) materia f; argumentum nt

subject³ vt subicio, subigo [3]

subjection n servitus; patientia f

subjugate vt subigo [3]; domo [1]

sublime adj altus, celsus; fig excelsus, sublimis

submerge vt&i summergo [3]; inundo [1]

submersion n summersio f

submission n obsequium nt

submissive adj summissus; supplex

■ **~ly** adv summisse, suppliciter

submit vt summitto, subicio
■ **~** vi (condescend) subeo [3]; (endure) subeo [4]; (yield) cedo [3]

subordinate¹ vt posthabeo [2]

subordinate² adj & n inferior m

subscribe vt subscribo [3]; subsigno [1]; assentior [4]; (give money) pecuniam do [1]

subscriber n subscriptor m

subscription n (act) subscriptio, collecta f

subsequent adj sequens, posterior
■ **~ly** adv deinde, postea

subservient adj summissus

subside vi sido, consido, resido, subsido [3]

subsidiary adj subsidiarius

subsidize vt pecunias suppedito [1]

subsidy n collatio f; subsidium nt

subsistence n victus m; vita f

substance n substantia; materia, res f; (wealth) opes fpl

substantial adj solidus, firmus; (real) verus; (chief) praecipuus; (rich) opulentus
■ **~ly** adv solide; (truly) vere; (by nature) natura

substantiate vt confirmo [1]; ratum facio [3]

substitute¹ n vicarius m

substitute² vt substituo, suppono [3]

substitution n substitutio f

subterfuge n tergiversatio f; effugium nt; praetextus m

subtle adj subtilis; acutus, vafer

subtlety n subtilitas; tenuitas, astutia f; acumen nt

subtract vt subtraho, adimo, aufero [3]

suburb n suburbium nt

suburban adj suburbanus

subversion n excidium nt

subvert vt everto, subverto [3]

succeed vi succedo, sequor [3]; fig succedo [3]; prospere evenio [4]
□ **~ to** (take over) excipio [3]

success n bonus or felix exitus, successus m

successful adj fortunatus, prosperus, faustus, felix
■ ~**ly** adv fortunate, prospere, fauste, feliciter

succession n series, successio f

successive adj continuus
■ ~**ly** adv in ordine; continenter; deinceps

successor n successor m

succinct adj succinctus; brevis, concisus
■ ~**ly** adv succincte, brevi

succulent adj sucosus, suculentus

succumb vi succumbo, cado ③

such adj talis; eius modi
■ ~ adv sic, adeo, tam
□ ~ **as** qualis

suck vt sugo ③; (in, up) sorbeo ②; exsugo ③
■ ~ vi ubera duco ③

suckle vt ubera do, do mammam ①

suction n suctus m

sudden adj subitus, repentinus, inexspectatus; inopinatus, inopinus, necopinus
■ ~**ly** adv subito, repente

sue vt in ius voco ①
■ ~ vi oro, precor, flagito ①; posco, peto ③

suet n sebum nt; adeps m/f

suffer vt patior, fero ③; tolero ①; sustineo ②
■ ~ vi laboro ①

suffering n perpessio, toleratio f; (labours) labores mpl

suffice vi sufficio ③; satis sum ir

sufficiency n satias f

sufficient adj sufficiens
■ ~**ly** adv satis, affatim

suffocate vt suffoco ①

suffocation n suffocatio f

suffrage n suffragium nt

sugar n saccharon nt

suggest vt subicio, suggero ③; moneo ②

suggestion n admonitio f

suicide n mors voluntaria f
□ **commit** ~ mihi mortem consisco ③

suit[1] n (lawsuit) lis, causa f; (of clothes) vestimenta ntpl, synthesis f

suit[2] vt accommodo, apto ①
■ ~ vi convenio ④; congruo ③ both + dat

suitable adj aptus, idoneus, opportunus, congruus

suite n (of rooms) series f

suitor n (suppliant) supplex m/f; (wooer) procus m

sulky adv morosus

sullen adj taetricus; morosus

sullenness n morositas f

sulphur n sulpur nt

sultry adj aestuosus, torridus, fervidus

sum[1] n (total) summa; (money) pecunia f; fig caput nt

sum[2] vt (up) consummo ①; fig breviter repeto ③

summary[1] n epitome f; summarium nt

summary[2] adj brevis

summer n aestas f
■ ~**house** n umbraculum nt
■ ~ adj aestivus

summit n culmen, cacumen nt; apex, vertex m; fastigium nt

summon vt cito; (challenge) provoco ①; (send for) accio ④;

accesso ③; (up) **excito** ①; (animum) **erigo** ③

summons *n* accitus *m*; evocatio *f*

sumptuous *adj* sumptuosus; magnificus, lautus

sun¹ *n* sol *m*

sun² *vt* insolo ①

sunburnt *adj* adustus

sundial *n* solarium *nt*

sundry *adj* diversus, varius

sunny *adj* apricus

sunrise *n* solis ortus *m*

sunset *n* solis occasus *m*

sunshine *n* sol *m*; apricitas *f*

superb *adj* magnificus, speciosus, splendidus

supercilious *adj* arrogans, superbus, fastidiosus
■ **~ly** *adv* superbe, arroganter, fastidiose

superficial *adj* levis, indoctus
■ **~ly** *adv* leviter

superfluous *adj* supervacaneus; superfluus; supervacuus

superintend *vt* praesum *ir* + *dat*; administro ①

superintendent *n* praefectus; curator *m*

superior¹ *adj* superior, melior

superior² *n* praepositus *m*

superiority *n* praestantia *f*

superlative *adj* eximius

supersede *vt* aboleo ②; in locum (alicuius) succedo ③

superstition *n* superstitio *f*

superstitious *adj* superstitiosus
■ **~ly** *adv* superstitiose

supervise *vt* curo, procuro ①

supervision *n* cura, curatio *f*

supervisor *n* curator *m*

supper *n* cena *f*

supplant *vt* supplanto ①; per dolum deicio, praeverto ③

supple *adj* flexibilis, flexilis; mollis

supplement *n* supplementum *nt*; appendix *f*

suppleness *n* mollitia *f*

suppliant *n* supplex *m/f*

supplicate *vt* supplico, obsecro ①

supplication *n* obsecratio *f*; preces *fpl*

supply¹ *n* supplementum *nt*; copia, vis *f*; (supplies) commeatus *m*

supply² *vt* suppleo, praebeo ②; suppedito ①

support *n* (prop) fulcrum *nt*; fig subsidium *nt*; (favour) gratia *f*; favor *m*
■ **~** *vt* sustineo ②; (prop) fulcio ④; (maintain) alo ③; (aid) adiuvo ①; (favour) faveo ② + *dat*

supporter *n* adiutor; fautor *m*

suppose *vt* (imagine) opinor, puto ①; credo ③; reor ②; arbitror ①

supposition *n* opinio, coniectura *f*

suppress *vt* supprimo, comprimo ③; aboleo, coerceo ②

suppurate *vi* suppuro ①

supremacy *n* principatus *m*; imperium *nt*

supreme *adj* supremus, summus
■ **~ly** *adv* prae omnibus aliis, summe

sure *adj* certus; (reliable) fidus; (safe) tutus

surely *adv* certe; tuto; firme; profecto; (in questions) nonne
□ **~ not?** num

surf *n* fluctus *m*; unda *f*

surface *n* superficies *f*; aequor *nt*

surfeit n satietas f; taedium, fastidium nt

surge¹ n fluctus, aestus m

surge² vi tumesco ③; aestuo ①

surgeon n chirurgus m

surgery n chirurgia f

surgical adj chirurgicus

surly adj morosus, difficilis

surmise¹ n coniectura f

surmise² vt coniecto ①; conicio ③; suspicor ①

surmount vt supero ①; vinco ③

surname n cognomen nt

surpass vt supero ①; excedo, excello ③

surplus n reliquum, residuum nt

surprise¹ n admiratio f; (sudden attack) repens adventus hostium m

surprise² vt deprehendo ③

surprising adj mirus, mirabilis; inexpectatus; inopinatus
■ ~ly adv mirandum in modum

surrender¹ n (mil) deditio f; (law) cessio f

surrender² vt cedo; dedo; trado ③
■ ~ vi me dedo ③

surreptitious adj furtivus, clandestinus
□ ~ly clam, furtim

surround vt circumdo; circumsto ①; cingo ③; circumvallo ①

survey¹ n (act) inspectio; contemplatio; (measuring) mensura f

survey² vt inspicio ③; contemplor ①; (measure land) permetior ④

surveyor n mensor, metator, decempedator m

survive vi superstes sum, supersum ir; supero ①

survivor n superstes m/f

susceptible adj mollis; (capable) capax

suspect vt suspicor ①

suspend vt suspendo ③; fig intermitto ③; differo ir; abrogo ①

suspense n dubitatio f
□ in ~ incertus, dubius

suspicion n suspicio f

suspicious adj suspicax; suspiciosus; (suspected) suspectus; suspiciosus

sustain vt (prop) sustineo ②; sustento ①; fulcio ④; (bear, etc.) tolero ①; fero ③; (defend) defendo ③; (strengthen) corroboro ①

sustenance n victus m

swallow¹ n hirundo f

swallow² vt glutio ④; voro; devoro ①; haurio ④

swamp¹ n palus f

swamp² vt demergo ③; inundo ①

swampy adj paludosus, palustris, uliginosus

swan n cycnus m; olor m

swarm¹ n (of bees) examen nt; fig turba f

swarm² vi examino ①; confluo ③

swarthy adj fuscus, subniger

sway¹ n dicio f; imperium nt; (motion) aestus m

sway² vt rego ③
■ ~ vi aestuo, titubo ①

swear vi iuro; (curse) exsecror ①

sweat¹ n sudor m

sweat² vi sudo ①

sweep¹ n ambitus; iactus m

sweep² vt (brush, etc.) verro ③; purgo ①; (pass quickly over) percurro; verro ③

sweet *adj* dulcis, suavis; blandus; iucundus

sweeten *vt* dulcem facio *or* reddo ③; *fig* lenio ④; mulceo ②

sweetheart *n* deliciae *fpl*; amica f

sweetness *n* dulcedo; suavitas f

swell[1] *vt* inflo ①; tumefacio ③
■ ~ *vi* tumeo, turgeo ②; intumesco ③

swell[2] *n* aestus m

swelling *n* tumor m

swerve *vi* aberro, vagor; declino ①

swift *adj* celer, velox, rapidus, citus
■ ~**ly** *adv* celeriter, velociter, cito

swiftness *n* celeritas, velocitas f

swill *vt* haurio ④; ingurgito ①

swim *vi* nato, no; fluito ①; madeo ②

swimmer *n* natator m

swimming *n* natatio f

swindle *vt* fraudo ①; circumvenio ④

swindler *n* fraudator m

swing[1] *n* oscillatio f; impetus m

swing[2] *vt* huc illuc iacto, vibro ①
■ ~ *vi* fluito ①; pendeo ②; huc illuc iactor ①

swivel *n* verticula f

swoop *n* impulsus, impetus m

sword *n* ensis, gladius m; ferrum nt

sycamore *n* sycamorus f

sycophant *n* sycophanta; adulator m

syllable *n* syllaba f

symbol *n* signum, symbolum n

symmetrical *adj* symmetrus, concinnus

symmetry *n* symmetria, concinnitas f

sympathetic *adj* (gentle) lenis, mitis, humanus
■ ~**ally** *adv* humane

sympathize *vi* (pity) misereor ② + *gen*

sympathy *n* (agreement) consensus m; (fellow-feeling) sympathia f

symphony *n* symphonia f; concentus m

symptom *n* signum, indicium nt

synagogue *n* synagoga f

synonym *n* vocabulum idem declarans, synonymum nt

synonymous *adj* idem declarans

syntax *n* syntaxis f; constructio verborum f

synthesis *n* synthesis f

syringe *n* sipho m

system *n* systema nt; ratio, disciplina f

systematic *adj* ad certam disciplinam redactus, ordinatus

systematically *adv* ordinate

Tt

table *n* mensa f; (register) index m

tablecloth *n* mantele nt

tablet *n* tabula, tabella, tessera f

tacit *adj* tacitus
■ ~**ly** *adv* tacite

taciturn *adj* taciturnus

taciturnity *n* taciturnitas f

tack[1] *n* clavulus m

tack[2] *vt* assuo; affigo ③

tackle[1] *vt* tracto ①

tackle² n armamenta, arma ntpl

tact n dexteritas; prudentia f

tactful adj dexter

tactics n ars militaris, ratio f

tactless adj ineptus, insulsus, molestus

tadpole n ranunculus m; ranula f

tag n ligula f

tail n cauda f; (of a comet) crinis m

tailor n vestitor m

taint¹ vt inficio ③; contamino ①; polluo; fig corrumpo ③

taint² n contagio f; vitium nt; contactus m

take vt capio; sumo; accipio, recipio; rapio ③; (consider, etc.) interpretor ③; accipio ③
◼ ~ **vi** (be successful) efficax sum ir; bene succedo; (fire) accendor ③
□ ~ **after** similis sum ir + gen
□ ~ **away** adimo ③, aufero ir
□ ~ **back** recipio ③
□ ~ **down** demo ③
□ ~ **for** habeo ②; puto ①
□ ~ **in** percipio, intellego ③; fig decipio ③
□ ~ **off** exuo, demo ③; fig imitor ①
□ ~ **up** sumo ③

tale n narratio; fabula f
□ ~**bearer** famigerator m; delator m

talent n fig ingenium nt; facultas f

talented adj ingeniosus

talk¹ n sermo m; colloquium nt; (idle ~) fabulae fpl; (rumour) rumor m; fama f

talk² vi loquor, colloquor ③; confabulor ①

talkative adj loquax, garrulus

tall adj altus, celsus, procerus

tallness n proceritas; altitudo f

tally¹ n tessera f

tally² vi convenio ④

talon n unguis m; ungula f

tambourine n tympanum nt

tame¹ adj cicur; mansuefactus, mansuetus; fig frigidus, insulsus

tame² vt perdomo, domo ①; mansuefacio, subigo ③

tangible adj tractilis

tangle vt ▶ **entangle**

tangled adj irreligatus, incomptus

tank n cisterna; piscina f; lacus m

tankard n cantharus m

tantalize vt crucio ①

tantamount adj tantusdem, par

tap¹ n (blow) ictus m; (pipe) fistula f

tap² vt leviter pulso ①; (wine, etc.) relino ③

tape n taenia f

taper¹ n cereus m; funale nt

taper² vt&i fastigio; fastigor ①

tapestry n aulaeum, tapete nt

tapeworm n taenia f

tar¹ n pix f

tar² vt pice oblino ③

tardy adj tardus, lentus

target n parma f; (mark to aim at) scopus m

tarnish vt infusco; hebeto; fig obscuro ①
◼ ~ **vi** hebesco ③

tart¹ n scriblita f; crustulum nt; (girl) scortillum m

tart² adj acidus, acerbus; fig mordax
◼ ~**ly** adv acerbe; mordaciter

task n pensum, opus nt; labor m

tassel n cirrus m

taste¹ n (sense) gustatus; (flavour) gustus, sapor m; fig iudicium;

palatum *nt*

taste² *vt* gusto, degusto ①
■ ~ *vi* sapio ③

tasteful *adj* elegans
■ ~ly *adv* fig eleganter

tasteless *adj* insulsus; inelegans
■ ~ly *adv* insulse, inelegante, insulse

tasty *adj* sapidus, conditus

tatters *n* panni *mpl*

taunt¹ *n* convicium *nt*; contumelia *f*

taunt² *vt* exprobro ①

tavern *n* taberna, caupona *f*

tawdry *adj* speciosus

tawny *adj* fuscus, fulvus, ravus, flavus

tax¹ *n* vectigal; tributum, stipendium *nt*

tax² *vt* (financially) vectigal impono ③

taxable *adj* vectigali solvendo obnoxius

tax-collector *n* exactor *m*

teach *vt* doceo, perdoceo ②; instruo ③; erudio ④

teacher *n* magister, praeceptor *m*

teaching *n* doctrina, eruditio *f*

team *n* protelum *nt*; iugales *mpl*

tear¹ *n* lacrima; fig gutta *f*; (rent) scissura *f*

tear² *vt* scindo ③; (in pieces) lacero, dilacero, lanio, dilanio ①
■ ~ *vi* ▸ **rush**

tear³ *n* scissura *f*

tease *vt* vexo, crucio ①

technical *adj* artificialis; (word) arti proprium (verbum)

tedious *adj* tardus, lentus; longus; diuturnus, molestus
■ ~ly *adv* tarde; moleste

tedium *n* taedium *nt*; molestia *f*

teem *vi* scateo ②; redundo ①; abundo

teeming *adj* gravidus; fig frequens

tell *vt* (say) dico ③; (relate) narro ①; (inform) aliquem certiorem facio ③; (order) iubeo ③

temper¹ *vt* tempero ①; diluo ③; commisceo ②; (mitigate) mitigo ①; remitto ③

temper² *n* temperatio *f*; animus *m*; ingenium *nt*; (anger) iracundia *f*

temperament *n* temperamentum *nt*

temperate *adj* temperatus; sobrius; abstinens
■ ~ly *adv* temperanter, sobrie

temperature *n* temperatura, temperies *f*

temple *n* templum, fanum *nt*; aedes *f*; (of the head) tempora *ntpl*

temporary *adj* temporarius, ad tempus

tempt *vt* tento, sollicito ①; allicio ③

temptation *n* sollicitatio; illecebra *f*

tempter *n* tentator *m*

tempting *adj* illecebrosus

ten *adj* decem
□ ~ **times** decies

tenacious *adj* tenax
■ ~ly *adv* tenaciter

tenacity *n* tenacitas *f*

tenant *n* conductor; inquilinus *m*

tend *vt* curo ①
■ ~ *vi* tendo ③; specto ①

tendency *n* inclinatio *f*
□ **having a ~ to** proclivis ad + *acc*

tender¹ *adj* tener, mollis; fig misericors
■ ~ly *adv* tenere; molliter;

miseicorditer

tender² vt offero ③

tenderness n teneritas, mollitia; misericordia, bonitas f

tendon n nervus m

tendril n (of a vine) pampinus m/f; (of climbing plants) clavicula f

tenement n insula f

tenet n dogma, institutum nt; doctrina f

tense adj tensus, rigidus

tension n intentio f

tent n tentorium, tabernaculum nt
□ **general's ~** praetorium nt

tenterhook n
■ **on ~s** adj suspensus

tenth adj decimus
■ **~ n** decima pars f

tenure n possessio f

tepid adj tepidus

term¹ n (word) verbum nt; (limit) terminus m; (period) spatium nt; (condition) condicio, lex f

term² vt dico ③; appello, voco ①

terminate vt termino ①; finio ④; concludo ③
■ **~ vi** terminor ①; finem habeo ②

termination n terminatio f; finis m/f, exitus m

terrace n solarium nt

terrible adj terribilis, horribilis, dirus

terribly adv horrendum in modum

terrific adj terrificus, terribilis, formidabilis

terrify vt terreo, perterreo ②; territo ①

territory n regio; terra f; fines mpl; (around a town) territorium nt

terror n terror, metus, pavor m; formido f

terse adj (neat, polished) tersus; brevis; pressus

test¹ n (trial) tentamentum, tentamen, periculum nt

test² vt tento, exploro ①; experior ④; periclitor ①

testify vt testificor, testor ①

testimonial n litterae testimoniales fpl

testimony n testimonium, indicium nt

testy adj stomachosus, morosus

tetanus n tetanus m

tether¹ n retinaculum nt

tether² vt religo ①

text n verba scriptoris ntpl; contextus m

textile adj textilis

texture n textum nt; textura f

than conj quam

thank vt gratias ago ③ + dat
□ **~ you** tibi gratias ago

thankful adj gratus

thankless adj ingratus

thanks n gratia f; grates fpl

that¹ adj & pn ille, is, iste; (who, which) qui

that² conj ut (after verbs of fearing) ne

thatch¹ n stramentum nt

thatch² vt stramento tego ③

thaw vt solvo, dissolvo, liquefacio ③
■ **~ vi** regelo ①; solvor, liquesco ③

theatre n theatrum nt; scaena, cavea f

theatrical adj theatralis; scaenicus

theft n furtum nt

their adj (and **theirs** pn) suus, eorum, earum, illorum, illarum

theme n argumentum nt; materies f

themselves pn se, sese
□ **they ∼** illi ipsi, illae ipsae
□ **of ∼** sui

then adv (at that time) tum, tunc; (after that) deinde, inde; (therefore) igitur
□ **now and ∼** nonnunquam, interdum, aliquando

theologian n theologus m

theology n theologia f

theorem n theorema nt

theoretical adj theoreticus

theory n theoria, ratio, ars f

there adv ibi, illic; (thither) illo, illac, illuc
□ **∼abouts** circiter
□ **∼after** exinde
□ **∼by** inde
□ **∼fore** igitur, idcirco; propterea
□ **∼upon** exinde; deinde; tum

thesis n thesis f; propositum n

they pn ii, eae, illi, illae

thick adj densus, spissus; (gross) crassus; (fat) pinguis; (muddy) turbidus, lutosus; (crowded) frequens; creber

thicken vt denso; condenso; spisso ①
■ **∼** vi densor ①; spissor ③

thicket n dumetum nt; virgulta ntpl

thickness n densitas; crassitudo f

thief n fur m

thieve vt furor ①

thigh n femur nt

thin[1] adj tenuis; angustus; rarus; (lean) macer

thin[2] vt tenuo, attenuo, extenuo ①

thing n res f; (affair) negotium nt
■ **∼s** pl bona ntpl

think vt&i cogito ①; (imagine, believe, etc.) puto ①; credo ③; opinor ①; reor ②; arbitror ①

thinker n philosophus m

thinness n tenuitas; raritas f

third adj tertius
■ **∼** n tertia pars f
■ **∼ly** adv tertio

thirst n sitis f (also fig)

thirsty adj sitiens; aridus, siccus; bibulus
□ **be ∼** sitio ④

thirteen adj tredecim

thirteenth adj tertius decimus

thirtieth adj tricesimus

thirty adj triginta

this adj & pn hic

thistle n carduus m

thong n lorum, amentum nt

thorn n spina f; aculeus m

thorny adj spinosus; spineus; fig difficilis

thorough adj germanus, perfectus; accuratus
■ **∼ly** adv penitus, plane, prorsus, funditus

thoroughfare n pervium nt; via pervia f

though conj etsi, etiamsi, quamvis, quamquam, licet

thought n (thinking, idea, opinion) cogitatio, sententia, mens f

thoughtful adj cogitabundus; providus; humanus

thoughtless adj incuriosus, neglegens, inconsultus
■ **∼ly** adv temere

thousand adj mille

t

□ a ~ times millies
thousandth *adj* millesimus
thrash *vt* tero, tundo ③; *fig* verbero ①
thread *n* filum *nt*; linea *f*; *fig* tenor *m*
threadbare *adj* tritus, detritus
threat *n* minae *fpl*
threaten *vt* minor ①
■ ~ *vi* impendeo, immineo ② *all + dat*
three *adj* tres
□ ~ times ter
threefold *adj* triplex, triplus
thresh *vt* tero, tundo ③
□ ~-ing-floor area *f*
threshold *n* limen *nt*
thrift *n* frugalitas, parsimonia *f*
thrifty *adj* parcus, frugalior
thrill[1] *vt* percello
■ ~ *vi* percellor ③
thrill[2] *n* (excitement) animi concitatio *f*
thrilling *adj* periculosus
thrive *vi* vireo, floreo; valeo ②
thriving *adj* prosperus
throat *n* iugulum, guttur *nt*; gula *f*
throb[1] *vi* palpito ①
throb[2] *n* palpitatio *f*; pulsus *m*
throne *n* solium *nt*; *fig* regia dignitas *f*; (kingdom) regnum *nt*
throng[1] *n* multitudo, turba, frequentia *f*
throng[2] *vt&i* premo; circumfundor; confluo ③
throttle *vt* strangulo ①
through *prep* per, propter, ob *all + acc*
throughout *adv* penitus, prorsus
throw[1] *vt* iacio, conicio; mitto ③;

iaculor, iacto ①; (away) abicio; (down) deicio, sterno, everto ③; (oneself) me praecipito ①; (open) patefacio; (off) excutio; deicio; (clothes) exuo; (out) eicio; (together) conicio; (up) egero ③
throw[2] *n* iactus *m*; iaculatio *f*
thrush *n* turdus *m*
thrust[1] *vt* trudo, impello; (with a sword) perfodio ③
□ ~ out extrudo ③
thrust[2] *n* ictus; impetus *m*; petitio *f*
thumb[1] *n* pollex *m*
thumb[2] *vt* (a book) pollice verso ①
thump[1] *vt* contundo ③
thump[2] *n* ictus *m*; percussio *f*
thunder[1] *n* tonitrus; fragor *m*
thunder[2] *vt&i* tono, intono ①
thunderbolt *n* fulmen *nt*
thunderstruck *adj* attonitus; obstupefactus
thus *adv* ita, sic
□ and ~ itaque
thwart *vt* obsto + *dat*; frustror ①
thyme *n* thymum *nt*
tiara *n* tiara *f*; tiaras *m*
ticket *n* tessera *f*; titulus *m*
tickle *vt&i* titillo ①
ticklish *adj* difficilis, periculosus, lubricus
tide *n* aestus, *fig* cursus *m*
tidings *n* rumor *m*; (message) nuntius *m*; (news) novum *nt*
tidy *adj* mundus
tie[1] *vt* ligo, alligo; nodo ①; vincio ④
tie[2] *n* vinculum *nt*; nodus *m*; coniunctio, necessitas *f*
tier *n* ordo, gradus *m*
tiger *n* tigris *m/f*

tight *adj* artus, astrictus
■ **~ly** *adv* arte, stricte

tighten *vt* stringo, astringo ③

tightness *n* soliditas, firmitas *f*

tile¹ *n* tegula, imbrex *f*

tile² *vt* tegulis tego ③

till¹ *adv* (*prep*) usque ad + *acc*

till² *conj* dum, donec

tiller *n* (helm) gubernaculum *nt*;
clavus *m*

tilt¹ *n* (inclination) inclinatio *f*; (rush)
impetus *m*

tilt² *vt* proclino ①

timber *n* materia *f*; lignum *nt*;
tignum *nt*; trabs *f*

time *n* tempus *nt*; dies *m*; (age,
etc.) aetas *f*; aevum *nt*; (century)
saeculum *nt*; (leisure) otium *nt*;
(opportunity) occasio *f*; (hour) hora *f*
□ **at this ~** in praesenti
□ **at any ~** unquam
□ **if at any ~** siquando
□ **at a ~** una
□ **all the ~** continuo

timely *adj* tempestivus,
opportunus

timid *adj* timidus, anxius

timidity *n* timiditas *f*

tin *n* stannum, plumbum album *nt*

tinge *vt* tingo, imbuo, inficio ③

tinkle¹ *n* tinnitus *m*

tinkle² *vt* tinnio ④; crepito ①

tint¹ *vt* tingo ③

tint² *n* color *m*

tiny *adj* parvulus, exiguus

tip¹ *n* (top) cacumen; acumen *nt*;
apex *m*

tip² *vt* (attach to end of) praefigo;
(incline) inverto ③

tipsy *adj* ebrius, temulentus,

vinosus

tiptoe *adv*
□ **on ~** in digitos erectus

tire *vt* fatigo, lasso
■ **~** *vi* defatigor ①

tired *adj* fessus, defessus, lassus

tiresome *adj* laboriosus;
molestus; operosus

tissue *n* textum *nt*

titbit *n* cuppedia *ntpl*

title *n* titulus *m*; inscriptio *f*; (label)
index *m/f*; (name, etc.) appellatio,
dignitas *f*

titter *vi* subrideo ②

to¹ *prep* ad + *acc*; (in comparison with)
prae + *abl*; (until) usque ad + *acc*
□ **~ and fro** huc illuc

to² *conj* (in order to) ut

toad *n* bufo *m*

toadstool *n* fungus *m*

toast¹ *n* (health drunk) propinatio *f*

toast² *vt* torreo ②; (in drinking)
propino ①

today *adv* hodie

toe *n* digitus *m*

together *adv* simul, una;
coniunctim

toil¹ *n* labor *m*; opera *f*; sudor *m*

toil² *vi* laboro ①

toilet *n* cultus, ornatus *m*; (lavatory)
latrina *f*

token *n* signum, pignus *nt*

tolerable *adj* tolerabilis;
mediocris

tolerance *n* tolerantia, toleratio,
indulgentia *f*

tolerant *adj* tolerans, patiens;
indulgens

tolerate *vt* tolero ①; patior, fero ③

toleration *n* toleratio;

t

indulgentia f

toll n vectigal, tributum nt

tomb n sepulcrum, bustum nt; tumulus m

tomorrow n crastinus dies m
■ ~ adv cras
□ **the day after** ~ perendie

tone n sonus m; fig color m; vox f

tongs n forceps f

tongue n lingua f

tonight adv hac nocte

too adv nimis, nimium; (also) etiam, insuper

tool n instrumentum; (of iron) ferramentum nt; fig minister m

tooth n (also fig) dens m

toothache n dolor dentium m

toothless adj edentulus

top[1] n cacumen, culmen nt; apex m; (of a house) fastigium nt; (toy) trochus, turbo m

top[2] adj summus; (the top of the mountain) summus mons

topic n res f; argumentum nt; quaestio f

topical adj hodiernus

topmost adj summus

topsy-turvy adv sursum deorsum

torch n fax, taeda f; funale nt

torment[1] vt crucio, excrucio ①; torqueo ②

torment[2] n cruciatus m; tormentum nt

torrent n (also fig) torrens m

tortoise n testudo f
■ ~-shell n testudo f

torture[1] n tormentum nt; cruciatus m

torture[2] vt (also fig) torqueo ②

torturer n tortor m

toss[1] vt iacto; agito, verso ①
■ ~ vi iactor ①; aestuo ①

toss[2] n iactus m; iactatio f

total[1] adj totus, universus
■ ~ly adv omnino, prorsus

total[2] n summa f

totter vi vacillo, titubo, labo ①

touch[1] vt tango, attingo ③; fig moveo ②; afficio ③

touch[2] n tactus, contactus m; fig commotio f
□ **finishing** ~ fig manus extrema f

touchy adj offensioni pronior, stomachosus

tough adj tenax, lentus; durus; fig difficilis; (stout) strenuus

toughness n tenacitas f; lentor m; duritia; fig difficultas; (courage) fortitudo f

tour n circuitus m; peregrinatio f; iter nt

tourist n viator, peregrinator m

tournament n decursio equestris f; ludus equester m

tow vt (a ship) navem remulco trahere ③
■ ~-rope n remulcum nt

towards prep (also **toward**) adversus, ad, (of people) erga; contra, in; (of time) sub all + acc

towel n mantele, sudarium nt

tower[1] n turris, arx f; castellum nt

tower[2] vi emineo, supereminео ②

town n urbs f; oppidum, municipium nt
□ ~ **hall** curia f

toy n crepundia ntpl

trace n vestigium; indicium; signum; nt; (for horse) helcium nt

■ ~ vt delineo; (down) indago ⬜

track¹ n vestigium nt; (path) semita f

track² vt vestigo, investigo ⬜

tract n tractus m; regio f; (small treatise) tractatus m

trade¹ n mercatura f; commercium, negotium nt; (calling) ars f; quaestus m

trade² vi mercaturas facio ③; negotior ⬜; mercor ⬜

trader n mercator m

tradesman n negotiator; caupo m

tradition n fama f

traditional adj ab maioribus traditus; translaticius

traffic¹ n (in trade) commercium nt; mercatura f

traffic² vi negotior, mercor ⬜

tragedy n tragoedia f; cothurnus m

tragic adj tragicus
■ ~ally adv tragice

trail¹ vt traho, verro ③

trail² n vestigium nt; ductus m

train¹ n series f; ordo m; (of a robe) peniculamentum nt; (retinue) comitatus m

train² vt educo ⬜; instruo; fig assuefacio ③

trainer n exercitor m

training n disciplina; exercitatio f

traitor n proditor m

traitorous adj perfidus; perfidiosus
■ ~ly adv perfide, perfidiose

tramp n homo vagus m

trample vi (on, upon) conculco ⬜; opprimo, obtero ③

trance n animus a corpore abstractus m

tranquil adj tranquillus, placidus, aequus

tranquillity n tranquillitas, quies f; tranquillus animus m

transact vt transigo, gero, ago, perficio, fungor ③

transaction n negotium nt; res f

transcribe vt transcribo, exscribo ③

transcription n transcriptio f

transfer¹ vt transfero ir; transmitto ③

transfer² n translatio f

transform vt transformo, transfiguro ⬜; verto ③

transformation n mutatio f

transgress vt violo ⬜; contra leges facio ③

transient adj (fleeting) fragilis, fluxus, caducus

transition n transitus m

transitory adj ▶ **transient**

translate vt verto, transfero ③

translation n translatio f; liber translatus m

translator n interpres m/f

transmission n transmissio f

transmit vt transmitto ③

transparency n perspicuitas f

transparent adj pellucidus, perspicuus, translucidus
□ be ~ pelluceo, transluceo ②

transpire vi evenio ④; fio ir

transplant vt transfero ③

transport¹ vt transporto ⬜; transveho, transmitto ③; fig delecto ⬜

transport² n transvectio f; (ship)

t

navigium vectorium *nt*; fig elatio *f*

transpose *vt* transpono ③

transposition *n* traiectio *f*

transverse *adj* transversus

trap[1] *n* laqueus *m*; tendicula, pedica *f*; fig insidiae *fpl*

trap[2] *vt* irretio ④

trash *n* scruta *ntpl*; nugae, res vilissimae *fpl*

travel[1] *vi* iter facio ③; peregrinor ①

travel[2] *n* iter *nt*; (abroad) peregrinatio *f*

traveller *n* viator, peregrinator *m*

tray *n* repositorium *nt*

treacherous *adj* perfidus; perfidiosus; dolosus
  ■ ~**ly** *adv* perfide, perfidiose

treachery *n* perfidia *f*

tread[1] *vt* calco, conculco ①
  ■ ~ *vi* incedo ③

tread[2] *n* gradus, incessus *m*

treason *n* perduellio, proditio *f*

treasure[1] *n* thesaurus *m*; gaza *f*; opes *fpl*

treasure[2] *vt* (value) magni aestimo ①

treasurer *n* aerarii praefectus *m*

treasury *n* fiscus *m*; aerarium *f*; (building) thesaurus *m*

treat *vt* (handle) tracto ①; (use) utor ③ + *abl*; (entertain) convivio (aliquem) accipio ③

treatise *n* libellus *m*

treatment *n* tractatio; cura, curatio *f*

treaty *n* foedus; pactum *nt*

treble[1] *adj* triplex, triplus

treble[2] *vt* triplico ①

tree *n* arbor *f*

tremble *vi* tremo, contremisco

③; trepido ①

trembling *n* trepidatio *f*; tremor *m*

tremendous *adj* formidolosus, ingens, immanis

trench *n* fossa *f*; vallum *nt*; agger *m*

trespass *vi*
  □ ~ **on** ingredior ③

trial *n* tentatio *f*; (law) iudicium *nt*; (attempt) conatus *m*; periculum *nt*

triangle *n* triangulum *nt*

triangular *adj* triangulus, triquetrus

tribe *n* tribus, natio *f*

tribunal *n* tribunal; (court) iudicium *nt*

tribune *n* tribunus *m*

tributary *n* amnis in alium influens *m*

tribute *n* tributum; vectigal *nt*; fig
  □ **pay ~ to** laudo ①

trice *n*
  □ **in a ~** momento temporis *f*

trick[1] *n* dolus *m*; artificium *nt*; fraus *f*

trick[2] *vt* dolis illudo ③; circumvenio ④

trickery *n* fraus *f*; dolus *m*; ars *f*

trickle *vi* stillo, mano ①

trident *n* tridens *m*

trifle *n* res parvi momenti *f*; nugae *fpl*

trifling *adj* levis, exiguus, parvi momenti, frivolus

trim[1] *adj* nitidus, comptus, bellus

trim[2] *vt* (prune) puto ①; tondeo ②

trinket *n* gemma *f*

trip[1] *n* (stumble) pedis offensio *f*; (journey) iter *nt*

trip² *vt* supplanto ①
■ ~ *vi* pedem offendo ③; fig erro ①

triple *adj* triplex, triplus
■ ~ *vt* triplico ①

tripod *n* tripus *m*; cortina *f*

trireme *n* (navis) triremis *f*

trite *adj* tritus; pervulgatus

triumph¹ *n* triumphus *m*; ovatio;
fig victoria; exsultatio *f*

triumph² *vi* triumpho, ovo ①

triumphant *adj* triumphans,
victor

triumvirate *n* triumviratus *m*

trivial *adj* levis

triviality *n* levitas *f*; nugae,
ineptiae *fpl*

troop *n* turma, caterva *f*; grex;
globus *m*; manus *f*
■ ~**s** *pl* copiae *fpl*

trophy *n* tropaeum *nt*

tropical *adj* tropicus

trot¹ *n* gradus *m*

trot² *vi* tolutim eo *ir*

trouble¹ *n* (nuisance) molestia *f*;
incommodum; (business) negotium
nt; labor; (grief) dolor *m*; aerumna *f*

trouble² *vt* turbo; vexo ①; ango ③

troublesome *adj* molestus;
operosus; difficilis

trough *n* alveus *m*

trousers *n* feminalia *ntpl*; bracae *fpl*

trowel *n* trulla *f*

truant *adj* otiosus; vagus

truce *n* indutiae *fpl*

truck *n* carrus *m*

true *adj* verus; sincerus; germanus;
rectus

truly *adv* vere; sincere; profecto

trump *vi* (up) conflo ①; confingo ③;

machinor ①

trumpet¹ *n* tuba, bucina *f*; lituus
m; cornu *nt*

trumpet² *vt* fig praedico, vendito,
celebro ①

trumpeter *n* tubicen *m*

trundle *vt* volvo
■ ~ *vi* volvor ③

trunk *n* truncus *m*; (of an elephant)
proboscis; (chest) cista *f*

trust¹ *n* fiducia *f*; fides *f*

trust² *vt* fido; confido; credo ③
all + dat of person; (entrust) commendo
①; permitto ③

trustworthy *adj* ▶ **trusty**

trusty *adj* fidus, fidelis; constans

truth *n* veritas; fides *f*; verum *nt*

truthful *adj* verax
■ ~**ly** *adv* veraciter

try¹ *n* conatus *m*

try² *vt* tento, probo, periclitor ①;
experior ④; (law) cognosco ③; in
ius voco ①
■ ~ *vi* conor ①; nitor ③; tento ①;
molior ④

tub *n* labrum *nt*; lacus *m*

tube *n* tubulus, tubus *m*

tubular *adj* tubulatus

tuck *vt* succingo ③

tuft *n* (of hair) cirrus *m*

tug *vt* & *i* traho; nitor ③

tuition *n* disciplina *f*

tumble *vi* corruo, labor, collabor,
cado; volvor ③

tumour *n* tumor, tuber *m*

tumult *n* tumultus *m*; turba *f*

tumultuous *adj* tumultuosus,
turbulentus

tune *n* numeri, moduli *mpl*
■ **in** ~ *adj* consonus

■ **out of ~** *adj* dissonus

tuneful *adj* canorus

tunic *n* tunica *f*

tunnel *n* canalis *m*; cuniculum *nt*

turbid *adj* turbidus; (muddy) caenosus

turbulence *n* tumultus *m*; seditio *f*; animus turbulentus *m*

turbulent *adj* turbulentus

turf *n* caespes *m*; herba *f*

turgid *adj* turgidus, tumidus, inflatus

turmoil *n* turba, perturbatio *f*; tumultus *m*

turn¹ *n* (circuit) circuitus *m*; (bend) flexus *m*; (turning round) conversio *f*; circumactus *m*; (change, course) vicissitudo; (inclination) inclinatio *f*
□ **good ~** officium, beneficium *nt*
□ **by ~s** alternis, in vicem; vicissim

turn² *vt* (bend) flecto, verto; (~ round) volvo, circumago ③; (change) muto ①; converto ③; (on the lathe) torno ①
■ **~ vi** convertor; flector; volvor ③; torqueor ②; mutor ①; (become) fio ir; evado ③
□ **~ aside** deflecto ③; detorqueo ②
□ **~ away** *vt&i* averto ③
□ **~ back** reflecto ③; recurvo ①; *vi* reverto ③; redeo ④
□ **~ down** inverto ③, (reject) reicio ③
□ **~ off** averto ③; derivo ①; *vi* deflecto ③
□ **~ out** eicio ③; *vi* evenio ④; evado; contingo ③
□ **~ over** everto ③; (a page) verso ①; (cede) transfero ③
□ **~ round** *vt* circumago ③; contorqueo ②; *vi* versor ①;

circumagor ③
□ **~ up** recurvo ①; (come into view) appareo ②

turning-point *n* cardo *m*; momentum, discrimen *nt*

turnip *n* rapum *nt*

turret *n* turricula *f*

turtle *n* testudo *f*

turtle-dove *n* turtur *m*

tusk *n* dens *m*

tutor¹ *n* educator; praeceptor, paedagogus; grammaticus *m*

tutor² *vt* doceo ②

tweezers *n* volsella *f*

twelfth *adj* duodecimus
□ **for the ~ time** duodecimo

twelve *adj* duodecim
□ **~ times** duodecies

twentieth *adj* vicesimus

twenty *adj* viginti

twice *adv* bis

twig *n* surculus *m*; virga *f*

twilight *n* (evening) crepusculum; (dawn) diluculum *nt*

twin *adj & n* geminus, gemellus

twine *vt* circumvolvo ③; circumplico ①; contorqueo ②
■ **~ vi** circumvolvor, circumplector ③

twinge *n* dolor *m*

twinkle *vi* mico, corusco ①

twirl *vt* verso ①; circumago ③
■ **~ vi** verso ①

twist *vt* torqueo ②; flecto ③
■ **~ vi** torqueor ②; flector ③

two *adj* duo

twofold *adj* duplex, duplus

type *n* exemplar, exemplum *nt*; forma *f*

typical *adj* typicus

tyrannical *adj* tyrannicus
tyranny *n* tyrannis, dominatio *f*
tyrant *n* tyrannus *m*

Uu

udder *n* uber *nt*; mamma *f*
ugliness *n* deformitas, foeditas *f*
ugly *adj* deformis, foedus, turpis
ulcer *n* ulcus *nt*
ulterior *adj* ulterior
ultimate *adj* ultimus
■ **~ly** *adv* denique, tandem
umpire *n* arbiter, disceptator *m*
unable *adj* invalidus
■ **be ~** *vi* non possum, nequeo ④
unacceptable *adj* ingratus,
odiosus
unaccompanied *adj*
incomitatus, solus
unaccountable *adj*
inexplicabilis, inenodabilis
unaccountably *adv* praeter
opinionem; sine causa
unaccustomed *adj* insolitus,
insuetus, inexpertus
unadorned *adj* inornatus;
incomptus; simplex
unadulterated *adj* merus,
sincerus
unaided *adj* non adiutus, solus
unanimity *n* unanimitas,
consensio *f*; consensus *m*
unanimous *adj* unanimus,
concors
■ **~ly** *adv* consensu omnium,

omnium sententiis
unapproachable *adj* inaccessus
unarmed *adj* inermis, inermus
unassailable *adj* inexpugnabilis
unassuming *adj* modestus,
moderatus; demissus
unattainable *adj* arduus, quod
consequi non potest
unattempted *adj* intentatus,
inexpertus; inausus
unattended *adj* incomitatus
unauthorized *adj* inconcessus
unavailing *adj* inutilis, inanis
unavoidable *adj* inevitabilis
unaware *adj* inscius, nescius,
ignarus
unawares *adv* (de) improviso,
inopinato
unbearable *adj* intolerabilis
unbecoming *adj* indecorus,
indecens, indignus, inhonestus
unbelievable *adj* incredibilis
unbending *adj* inflexibilis, rigidus
unbiased *adj* incorruptus; integer;
sine ira et studio
unblemished *adj* purus, integer,
intactus
unborn *adj* nondum natus
unbreakable *adj* infragilis
unbroken *adj* irruptus; integer
unburden *vt* exonero ①
unburied *adj* inhumatus,
insepultus
uncanny *adj* inscitus
uncared *adj* (**~ for**) neglectus
unceasing *adj* perpetuus,
assiduus
■ **~ly** *adv* perpetuo, continenter
uncertain *adj* incertus, dubius;
ambiguus, anceps

t
u

uncertainty n quod incertum est; dubitatio f

unchangeable adj immutabilis; constans

unchanged adj immutatus, perpetuus

unchanging adj immutatus, perpetuus

uncharitable adj immisericors, iniquus, inhumanus

uncivilized adj incultus, barbarus

uncle n (on the father's side) patruus; (on the mother's side) avunculus m

uncombed adj impexus, incomptus

uncomfortable adj incommodus, molestus, gravis, anxius

uncommon adj rarus, insolitus; enormis; insignis; singularis
■ ~ly adv raro; praeter solitum, plus solito

unconcerned adj neglegens; incuriosus; securus

unconditional adj simplex

unconscious adj (unaware) inscius; nescius
■ ~ly adv nesciens

uncontrollable adj impotens, effrenatus

uncouth adj barbarus, impolitus, rudis; vastus

uncover vt detego, recludo, retego ③; revelo ①

undaunted adj impavidus, intrepidus

undecided adj incertus, dubius, sine exitu; par; integer

undeniable adj quod negari non potest

under prep sub, subter; infra all
+ acc; (in number) minor + abl

undercurrent n torrens subterfluens m

underdone adj minus percoctus, subcrudus

underestimate vt minoris aestimo ①

undergo vi&t subeo ④; patior ③; tolero ①; fero ③

underground adj subterraneus

undergrowth n virgulta ntpl

underhand adj clandestinus
■ ~ adv clam

underline vt subnoto ①

underling n administer m; assecla, satelles m/f

undermine vt suffodio ③; fig supplanto, labefacto ①

underneath adv subter, infra
+ acc

understand vt&i intellego; sapio ③; scio ④; (hear) audio ④

understanding[1] adj peritus; sapiens, prudens; (sympathetic) humanus

understanding[2] n mens f; intellectus m; intellegentia f

undertake vt&i suscipio; incipio; aggredior ③; conor ①

undertaker n (of funerals) libitinarius m

undertaking n ausum, inceptum; propositum nt

undervalue vt parvi facio ③; parvi aestimo ①

underworld n Tartarus m

undeserved adj immeritus; indignus; iniustus
■ ~ly adv immerito, indigne

undisciplined adj rudis, inexercitatus

undisputed adj indubitabilis, certus

undisturbed adj imperturbatus; immotus

undivided adj indivisus

undo vt solvo, dissolvo; resolvo; dissuo; irritum facio; (ruin) perdo ③

undone adj infectus; imperfectus; perditus

undoubted adj indubitatus; certus
∎ ~**ly** adv haud dubie

undress vt vestem exuo; (another) vestem detraho (alicui) ③

undue adj indebitus; iniquus

undulate vi undo, fluctuo; vibro ①

unduly adv iniuste, plus iusto

undying adj immortalis; sempiternus

unearth vt recludo; detego ③

unearthly adj humano maior; terribilis

uneasy adj anxius

unemployed adj otiosus

unencumbered adj liber, expeditus

unenviable adj haud invidiosus

unequal adj inaequalis, dispar, impar
∎ ~**ly** adv inaequaliter, impariter

unerring adj certus

uneven adj inaequalis; iniquus; (of ground) asper

unexpected adj inexpectatus, insperatus, improvisus, inopinatus, inopinus
∎ ~**ly** adv (ex) improviso

unfailing adj certus

unfair adj iniquus
∎ ~**ly** adv inique

unfaithful adj infidus, perfidus
∎ ~**ly** adv perfide

unfamiliar adj peregrinus; ignarus; ignotus

unfasten vt laxo ①; solvo, resolvo ③

unfathomable adj profundus

unfavourable adj sinister; adversus

unfeeling adj durus, inhumanus, crudelis
∎ ~**ly** adv dure, crudeliter, inhumane

unfinished adj imperfectus

unfit adj inhabilis, incommodus, inutilis; (not physically fit) impiger

unfold vt explico ①; aperio ④; pando ③
∎ ~ vi dehisco ③

unforeseen adj inexpectatus, insperatus

unforgiving adj inexorabilis

unfortunate adj infelix; infortunatus
∎ ~**ly** adv infeliciter

unfounded adj vanus; sine causa

unfriendly adj parum amicus

unfulfilled adj infectus, imperfectus

unfurl vt expando, solvo, (vela) facio ③

ungainly adj inhabilis, rusticus

ungovernable adj impotens, effrenatus

ungrateful adj ingratus

unguarded adj incustoditus; fig inconsultus

unhappiness n miseria, tristitia f

unhappy adj infelix, infortunatus, miser

u

unharmed adj incolumis, integer

unhealthiness n infirmitas; pestilentia, gravitas f

unhealthy adj ad aegrotandum proclivis; morbosus; (things) insalubris

unholy adj impius; profanus

unhoped adj (~ for) insperatus

unhurt adj inviolatus, illaesus

unicorn n monoceros m

uniform[1] adj uniformis, sibi constans

uniform[2] n ornatus, habitus m

uniformity n uniformitas f

unimaginable adj quod animo fingi non potest

unimportant adj levis, parvus

uninhabitable adj inhabitabilis, non habitabilis

uninhabited adj cultoribus inanis; desertus

uninjured adj incolumis, illaesus

unintelligent adj crassus

unintelligible adj obscurus

unintentional adj haud meditatus

uninterrupted adj continuus, perpetuus, inoffensus

uninvited adj invocatus

union n (act) coniunctio; (alliance) consociatio; consensio; societas f; (marriage) matrimonium nt

unique adj unicus, singularis

unison n concentus m

unite vt consocio [1]; coniungo
■ ~ vi coalesco [3]; coniuro [1]

unity n (oneness) unitas; fig concordia f

universal adj universus
■ ~ly adv universe; (everywhere)

undique, ubique

universe n mundus m

university n academia f

unjust adj iniustus, iniquus
□ ~ly adv iniuste, inique

unkempt adj incomptus

unkind adj inhumanus, parum officiosus
■ ~ly adv inhumane

unkindness n inhumanitas f

unknown adj ignotus, incognitus

unlawful adj illicitus; inconcessus
■ ~ly adv contra leges

unless conj nisi, ni, nisi si

unlike adj dissimilis, dispar, diversus

unlikely adj non verisimilis

unlimited adj infinitus, immensus

unload vt exonero [1]

unlock vt recludo [3]; resero [1]

unluckily adv infeliciter

unlucky adj infelix, infaustus

unman vt (castrate) castro; fig enervo [1]

unmanageable adv intractabilis; contumax

unmarried adj caelebs, innuptus, innubus

unmask vt detego [3]; nudo [1]

unmerciful adj immisericors

unmindful adj immemor; incuriosus; securus

unmistakable adj certus

unmixed adj merus, sincerus

unmoved adj (also fig) immotus

unnatural adj crudelis, monstruosus, immanis; (preternatural) praeter naturam

unnecessary adj haud necessarius

unnerve | unshaven

unnerve *vt* debilito, infirmo, enervo [1]

unnoticed *adj* praetermissus

unobserved *adj* inobservatus

unoccupied *adj* otiosus, vacuus; (of land) apertus

unpack *vt* expedio [4]; eximo [3]

unpaid *adj* (of debt) quod adhuc debetur; gratuitus

unpalatable *adj* molestus

unparalleled *adj* unicus; eximius

unpardonable *adj* non ignoscendus

unpatriotic *adj* patriae non amans

unpleasant *adj* iniucundus; incommodus; molestus
■ **~ly** *adv* iniucunde; incommode

unpleasing *adj* ingratus

unpopular *adj* populo ingratus, invidiosus

unpopularity *n* invidia *f*; odium *nt*

unprecedented *adj* novus, inauditus, unicus

unpremeditated *adj* subitus, non elaboratus

unprepared *adj* imparatus

unprincipled *adj* corruptis moribus, improbus

unproductive *adj* infecundus, infructuosus

unprofitable *adj* inutilis, vanus

unprotected *adj* indefensus

unpunished *adj* impunitus

unqualified *adj* haud idoneus, inhabilis; merus

unquestionable *adj* certus

unravel *vt* extrico, enodo [1]; expedio [4]

unreasonable *adj* contra rationem, rationis expers, absurdus; iniquus

unrelenting *adj* implacabilis, inexorabilis

unreliable *adj* infidus

unremitting *adj* continuus, perpetuus, assiduus

unrepentant *adj* impaenitens

unrequited *adj* non mutuus, sine mercede

unreserved *adj* apertus, candidus
■ **~ly** *adv* aperte, libere, candide

unrest *n* tumultus *m*

unripe *adj* immaturus, crudus

unrivalled *adj* singularis

unroll *vt* evolvo [3]; explico [1]; pando [3]; expedio [4]

unruffled *adj* tranquillus, immotus

unruly *adj* effrenatus; turbulentus; petulans

unsafe *adj* intutus; periculosus

unsatisfactory *adj* non idoneus; improbabilis

unsavoury *adj* insulsus, foedus

unscathed *adj* salvus

unseal *vt* resigno [1]; aperio [4]

unseemly *adj* indecorus, indecens

unseen *adj* invisus; invisitatus; inobservatus

unselfish *adj* suae utilitatis immemor

unselfishness *n* suarum utilitatum neglegentia *f*

unsettled *adj* dubius, instabilis, inconstans, inquietus

unshaven *adj* intonsus

unsheath vt e vagina educo; (gladium) destringo ③

unsightly adj deformis; turpis, foedus

unsociable adj insociabilis

unsolicited adj ultro oblatus

unsophisticated adj simplex, sincerus, incorruptus

unsought adj non quaesitus

unspeakable adj ineffabilis, infandus, inenarrabilis

unstable adj instabilis; fluxus; incertus

unsteadily adv infirme, instabiliter

unsteadiness n instabilitas; infirmitas; levitas, inconstantia f

unsteady adj instabilis; infirmus; tremulus; vagus, levis

unsuccessful adj improsper; infaustus; infelix; (vain) irritus, vanus
■ ~ly adv infeliciter, improspere; (in vain) frustra, re infecta

unsuitable adj incongruens, inhabilis, incommodus

unsuspecting adj minime suspicax

untamed adj indomitus, ferus

untidy adj immundus

untie vt solvo, resolvo ③; laxo ①

until conj dum; quoad; donec
■ ~ prep ad, in; usque ad all + acc

untimely adj immaturus; importunus; intempestivus

untold adj indictus; immemoratus; (vast) vastus

untouched adj intactus; integer; immotus

untoward adj adversus, contumax

untrained adj inexercitatus

untrodden adj non tritus; avius

untroubled adj placidus; aequus; securus, imperturbatus

untrue adj falsus, mendax

untruth n mendacium nt

unused adj inusitatus; novus, non tritus

unusual adj inusitatus, insuetus; insolitus, novus, rarus
■ ~ly adv praeter solitum, raro

unvarnished adj non fucatus; fig sincerus, nudus

unveil vt velamen detraho; fig patefacio ③

unwarlike adj imbellis

unwary adj imprudens, incautus, inconsultus, temerarius

unwelcome adj non acceptus, ingratus, iniucundus

unwell adj aeger, invalidus, infirmus

unwieldy adj inhabilis, pinguis

unwilling adj invitus; coactus
■ ~ly adv invite, non libenter

unwind vt revolvo, retexo ③

unwise adj imprudens; inconsultus; stultus
■ ~ly adv stulte; imprudenter, inconsulte

unwitting adj inscius

unwonted adj insolitus, insuetus, inusitatus

unworthy adj indignus; immeritus

unwrap vi explico ①; evolvo ③

unwritten adj non scriptus, inscriptus

unyielding adj obstinatus

unyoke vt abiungo, disiungo ③

up *adv & prep* sursum
□ ~ **to** tenus; (of time) usque ad
both + *acc*
□ ~ **and down** sursum
deorsum; huc illuc

uphill *adj* adverso colle *abl*

uphold *vt* sustineo ②; sustento
①; tueor ②

upland *adj* editus, montanus

upon *prep* super, supra; (of time) e,
ex; (on) in *all* + *abl*

upper *adj* superus; superior
□ ~**most** summus

upright *adj* erectus; rectus; *fig*
honestus; integer

uprising *n* tumultus *m*

uproar *n* tumultus *m*; turba *f*

uproot *vt* radicitus tollo, eruo ③

upset[1] *adj* sollicitatus, perculsus

upset[2] *vt* everto, subverto;
sterno ③

upshot *n* exitus, eventus *m*

upside *n*
□ ~ **down** sursum deorsum
■ **turn** ~ **down** *vt* misceo ②;
confundo ③

upstart *n* homo novus, terrae
filius *m*

upstream *adv* in adversum
flumen, adverso flumine

upwards *adv* sursum; sublime;
superne; (of number) plus

urban *adj* urbanus

urge[1] *n* incitamentum *nt*

urge[2] *vt* urgeo ②; impello ③; insto
①; suadeo ② *both* + *dat*; (on)
stimulo ①

urgent *adj* instans; vehemens;
gravis
■ ~**ly** *adv* vehementer

urine *n* urina *f*

urn *n* urna; (water-pot) hydria *f*

usage *n* mos *m*; consuetudo *f*;
usus *m*

use[1] *n* usus *m*; utilitas *f*;
commodum *nt*; consuetudo *f*;
(interest) faenus *nt*
□ **be of** ~ valeo ②; prosum *ir* + *dat*

use[2] *vt* utor ③ + *abl*; adhibeo ②; in
usum verto ③; (treat) tracto ①
□ ~ **up** consumo ③

used *vi*
□ **be** ~ **to** soleo ②; consuesco ③

useful *adj* utilis; aptus, commodus;
salutaris
■ ~**ly** *adv* utiliter; apte, commode

usefulness *n* utilitas;
commoditas *f*

useless *adj* inutilis; inhabilis;
irritus, vanus
■ ~**ly** *adv* inutiliter, nequicquam,
frustra

uselessness *n* inutilitas *f*

usher[1] *vt* praeeo ④; introduco ③

usher[2] *n* apparitor *m*

usual *adj* usitatus, solitus,
consuetus; cottidianus
□ ~**ly** *adv* usitate; vulgo; plerumque,
fere

usurp *vt* usurpo; vindico (mihi) ①;
assumo ③

usurper *n* usurpator *m*

utensils *npl* utensilia; vasa *ntpl*;
supellex *f*

utility *n* utilitas, commoditas *f*

utmost *adj* extremus; ultimus;
summus
□ **do one's** ~ summis viribus
contendo ③

utter[1] *adj* (total) totus
■ ~**ly** *adv* omnino, penitus;
funditus

u

utter² vt eloquor, dico, mitto, fundo, profero ③; pronuntio ①

utterance n elocutio; pronuntiatio f; dictum nt; vox f

. . . .

Vv

. . . .

vacancy n (emptiness) inanitas f; inane nt; (place) locus m

vacant adj vacuus, inanis; fig mentis vacuus

vacate vt vacuefacio; (leave) relinquo ③

vacation n (law) iustitium nt; (holidays) feriae fpl

vacillate vi vacillo, fluctuo ①

vacuum n inane, vacuum nt

vagabond n homo vagus, erro m

vagrant n homo vagus, erro m

vague adj dubius; ambiguus; incertus

vain adj (pointless) vanus; futtilis; inanis, irritus; (proud) superbus, arrogans; (boastful) gloriosus
 ■ in ~, ~ly adv frustra; nequicquam, incassum

valet n cubicularius, famulus m

valiant adj fortis; audax, animosus
 ■ ~ly adv fortiter; audacter, animose

valid adj validus; legitimus, ratus

validity n firmitas; auctoritas f

valley n vallis, convallis f

valour n fortitudo, virtus f; animus m

valuable adj pretiosus; carus

valuation n aestimatio f

value¹ n pretium nt; aestimatio f

value² vt aestimo ①; pendo ③
 □ ~ highly magni aestimo ①

valueless adj vilis, parvi pretii

valve n valvae fpl

vanguard n primum agmen nt

vanish vi vanesco, diffugio, evanesco ③; abeo, pereo ④

vanity n (pointlessness) vanitas; levitas f; nugae fpl; (boastfulness) iactatio, ostentatio f

vapour n vapor m; exhalatio f; halitus m

variable adj mutabilis; varius; levis, inconstans

variance n discordia; discrepantia, dissensio, simultas f
 ■ be at ~ vi discrepo ①; dissideo ②

variation n varietas; variatio; vicissitudo f

varied adj varius, diversus

variety n varietas; diversitas; multitudo f

various adj varius, diversus
 ■ ~ly adv varie, diverse

varnish¹ n atramentum nt; fig fucus m

varnish² vt coloro ①

vary vt vario ①; distinguo ③
 ■ ~ vi vario ①

vase n amphora f; urceus m; vas nt

vast adj vastus; ingens, immensus
 ■ ~ly adv vaste; valde; multum

vastness n immensitas f

vat n cupa f; dolium nt

vault¹ n fornix m; camera f; (underground) hypogeum nt; (leap) saltus m

vault[2] *vt* (cover with a vault) concamero [1]; (leap over) transilio [4]

vaunt *vt* iacto [1]; glorior [1], vendo [3]; ostento [1]

veal *n* vitulina *f*

veer *vi* vertor, vergo [3]

vegetable *n* holus *nt*

vegetation *n* herba *f*

vehemence *n* vehementia, vis *f*; fervor, impetus *m*

vehement *adj* vehemens, violentus; fervidus; acer
■ **~ly** *adv* vehementer; acriter

vehicle *n* vehiculum *nt*

veil[1] *n* velamen; flammeolum *nt*; amictus *m*; fig praetextus *m*; simulacrum *nt*; species *f*

veil[2] *vt* velo [1]; tego [3]

vein *n* vena *f* (also fig)

velocity *n* velocitas, celeritas *f*

veneer *n* ligni brattea *f*; fig species *f*

venerable *adj* venerabilis, reverendus

venerate *vt* veneror, adoro [1]; colo [3]

veneration *n* veneratio, adoratio *f*; cultus *m*

venereal *adj* venereus

vengeance *n* ultio; vindicta, poena *f*
□ **take** ~ ulciscor [3]
□ **with a** ~ valde

venison *n* caro ferina *f*

venom *n* venenum, virus *nt*

venomous *adj* venenosus, virulentus

vent[1] *n* spiramentum *nt*; exitus *m*; foramen *nt*
□ **give** ~ **to** (utter), fundo, promo

[3]; (exercise) exerceo [2]

vent[2] *vt* aperio [4]; per foramen emitto [3]
□ ~ **one's anger on** stomachum in aliquem effundo [3]

ventilate *vt* ventilo [1]; fig in medium profero [3]

ventilation *n* ventilatio; fig prolatio *f*

venture[1] *n* discrimen, periculum *nt*; (hazard) alea *f*; (deed of daring) ausum *nt*

venture[2] *vt* periclitor [1]
■ ~ *vi* (dare) audeo [2]

verandah *n* subdiale *nt*

verb *n* verbum *nt*

verbatim *adv* ad verbum

verbose *adj* verbosus
■ ~**ly** *adv* verbose

verbosity *n* loquacitas *f*

verdant *adj* viridis, virens; florens

verdict *n* (of a jury) iudicium *nt*; sententia *f*

verge[1] *n* (border) confinium *nt*; margo *m/f*; ora *f*; (limit) limes *m*
□ **on the** ~ **of** use future participle

verge[2] *vi* vergo [3]

verification *n* affirmatio *f*

verify *vt* ratum facio [3]; confirmo [1]

vermin *n* bestiolae molestae *fpl*

vernacular *adj* vernaculus

vernal *adj* vernus

versatile *adj* versatilis; versabilis; agilis; varius

versatility *n* agilitas *f*

verse *n* versus *m*; carmen *nt*

versed *adj* peritus, exercitatus

version *n* translatio *f*

vertebra *n* vertebra *f*

vertex *n* vertex *m*

v

vertical adj rectus, directus
■ **~ly** adv ad lineam; recta linea

vertigo n vertigo f

very adj verus
■ ~ adv valde, admodum; multum

vessel n vas; (ship) navigium nt

vest n vestimentum nt; tunica f; (of a charioteer) pannus m

vestal n (virgo) vestalis f

vestige n vestigium; indicium nt

veteran¹ adj veteranus

veteran² n veteranus miles m

veterinary adj veterinarius

veto¹ n intercessio f

veto² vt veto ①

vex vt vexo, inquieto ①

vexation n vexatio; offensio f; stomachus, dolor m

vibrate vi vibro ①; tremo ③

vibration n vibratus, motus, tremor m

vicarious adj vicarius

vice n vitium nt; turpitudo f; (instrument) forceps m

vicinity n vicinitas, vicinia f

vicious adj vitiosus; perditus; turpis

victim n victima, hostia f

victimize vt (fig) noceo ② + dat; laedo ①

victor n victor m; victrix f

victorious adj superior; victor (m), victrix (f)
■ **~ly** adv victoris instar

victory n victoria f; triumphus m; palma f

victuals npl cibaria ntpl; victus; (mil) commeatus m

vie vi (with) aemulor ①; contendo ③;

certo ①; both + dat or cum + abl

view¹ n (act) aspectus, conspectus m; oculi mpl; species f; spectaculum nt; (prospect) prospectus m; fig (opinion) sententia; opinio f
□ **have in ~** cogito ①

view² vt viso, inviso, conspicio; inspicio ③; contemplor; investigo; lustro ①; (regard, feel) sentio ④

vigil n vigilia, pervigilatio f; pervigilium nt

vigilance n vigilantia, cura f

vigilant adj vigil, vigilans
■ **~ly** adv vigilanter

vigorous adj vigens, validus, acer, fortis, strenuus
■ **~ly** adv strenue; acriter; fortiter

vigour n vigor m; robur nt; impetus m

vile adj vilis, abiectus; (wicked) perditus, flagitiosus; foedus

villa n villa f

village n vicus, pagus m

villager n vicanus, paganus, rusticus m

villain n scelus nt; scelestus; nequam m (indecl)

villainous adj sceleratus, scelestus, nefarius

villainy n improbitas, nequitia f; scelus nt

vindicate vt vindico ①; assero ③; (justify) purgo ①; (defend) defendo ③

vindication n defensio f

vindictive adj ultionis cupidus, acerbus

vine n vitis f

vinegar n acetum nt

vineyard n vinea f; vinetum nt

vintage n vindemia f

violate vt violo ①; rumpo, frango ③

violation n violatio f

violence n violentia; vis f; (energy) impetus m; (cruelty) saevitia f

violent adj violentus; furiosus; vehemens
■ ~ly adv violenter, vehementer

violet n (flower) viola f; (colour) viola f

viper n vipera f

virgin¹ n virgo f; puella f

virgin² adj virginalis, virgineus

virginity n virginitas f

virile adj virilis, masculus

virility n virilitas f

virtual adj insitus, innatus

virtue n virtus; probitas; fortitudo; (efficacy) vis, virtus f

virtuous adj virtute praeditus; probus; integer
■ ~ly adv cum virtute; integre

virulence n acerbitas, gravitas f

virulent adj virulentus; acerbus, gravis

virus n virus nt

viscous adj viscosus, lentus

visibility n visibilitas f

visible adj aspectabilis, conspicuus; manifestus

visibly adv fig aperte, manifesto

vision n (faculty of sight) visus m; fig visio f; visum; somnium nt

visit¹ n aditus m; salutatio f

visit² vt viso ③; visito ①; adeo ir

visitor n salutator m; salutatrix f

visor n (cheek-piece of helmet) buccula f

vital adj vitalis; fig necessarius

vitality n vitalitas f; vigor m

vivacious adj vivax; vividus, alacer

vivacity n vivacitas; alacritas f

vivid adj vividus; (plain) manifestus
■ ~ly adv vivide; (plainly) manifesto

vocabulary n vocabulorum index m

vocal adj vocalis; canorus
■ ~ly adv voce, ore

vocation n officium, munus nt

vociferous adj clamosus

vogue n mos m; fama, aestimatio f
□ be in ~ invalesco ③

voice n vox f; sonus m; (vote) suffragium nt

void¹ adj vacuus, inanis; fig sterilis; invalidus, irritus, cassus
□ be ~ vaco ①

void² n vacuum, inane nt

void³ vt vacuefacio ①; vacuo ①; fig irritum facio, rescindo ③

volatile adj volatilis; fig levis, volaticus, inconstans

volcano n mons igneus m

volley n nubes f

voluble adj volubilis, loquax, garrulus

volume n volumen nt; tomus m; (size) magnitudo f

voluntarily adv sponte, libenter

voluntary adj voluntarius

volunteer¹ n (miles) voluntarius m

volunteer² vi me offero ir; audeo ②

voluptuous adj voluptarius, voluptuosus

vomit¹ vt&i vomo, evomo ③; eructo ①

vomit² n vomitus m

voracious adj vorax, edax
■ ~ly adv voraciter

voracity n voracitas, edacitas, gula f

vortex n vertex, turbo, gurges m

vote¹ n suffragium nt; fig (judgment) sententia f

vote² vt censeo ②
■ ~ vi suffragium fero ③

voter n suffragator m

voting-tablet n tabella f

votive adj votivus
□ ~ **tablet** tabella f

vouch vt&i testificor, testor, affirmo ①

voucher n (ticket) tessera f

vow¹ n votum nt

vow² vt voveo, devoveo ②; spondeo ②; (promise) promitto ③

vowel n vocalis f

voyage¹ n navigatio f

voyage² vi navigo ①

voyager n navigator m

vulgar adj vulgaris, plebeius; inurbanus; rusticus
■ ~ly adv vulgo; rustice

vulgarity n mores vulgi mpl; rusticitas f

vulnerable adj quod vulnerari potest

vulture n vultur, vulturius m

Ww

wad n fasciculus m

waddle vi anatis in modum incedo ③

wade vi per vada eo ④

waft vt deduco, defero, fero; traicio ③

wag vt agito, vibro ①; (the tail) moveo ②

wager¹ n sponsio f; pignus nt

wager² vt&i spondeo ②; sponsione provoco ①; (pignore contendo ③

wages n merces f; stipendium nt

wagon n carrus m; plaustrum nt

waif n erro m

wail vt&i ploro ①; plango ③; fleo ②

wailing n ploratus, planctus m

waist n medium corpus nt

waistcoat n subcula f

wait vi (stay) maneo ②; (for) exspecto ①; (on) inservio ④ + dat

wait² n (delay) mora f
□ **lie in** ~ insidior ①

waiter n minister, pedisequus m

waive vt decedo de + abl, remitto ③

wake vt exsuscito, excito ①; expergefacio ③
■ ~ vi expergiscor ③

wakeful adj exsomnis, insomnis, vigil, vigilans

waken vt ▶ wake

walk¹ n (act) ambulatio f; (place) ambulacrum nt; ambulatio f; (manner of walking) incessus m

walk² vi incedo ③; ambulo ①;

gradior ③

walker n ambulans; pedes m

walking n ambulatio f
- □ **~ stick** baculum m

wall n paries; (of a town, etc.) murus m; (mil) moenia ntpl

wallet n pera; mantica f; saccus m

wallow vi volutor ①

walnut n iuglans, nux iuglans f

wan adj pallidus, exsanguis

wand n virga f; caduceus m

wander vi vagor, erro, palor; (about) pervagor; (over) pererro ①

wandering[1] adj errabundus; vagus; erraticus

wandering[2] n erratio f; error m

wane vi decresco; minuor; tabesco ③

want[1] n egestas, inopia, penuria, defectio f

want[2] vt (lack) careo, egeo, indigeo ② all + abl; desidero ①; (wish) volo ③; opto ①; cupio ③
- □ **~** vi deficio ③; desum, absum ir

wanting adj
- □ **be ~** deficio ③; desum ir

wanton adj petulans, procax; libidinosus; lascivus; protervus

war n bellum nt; Mars m; arma ntpl

warble vi cano ③; fritinnio ④

ward n (minor) pupillus m; pupilla f
- ■ **~** vt (off) arceo ②; averto ③; prohibeo ②

warden n custos m/f

warder n excubitor m; vigil; custos m/f

wardrobe n arca vestiaria f; vestiarium nt; (clothes) vestimenta ntpl

warehouse n mercium

receptaculum nt; cella f

wares n merces fpl

warfare n bellum nt; res militaris f

warily adv caute, circumspecte

wariness n cautio, circumspectio f

warlike adj militaris, bellicosus, bellicus, pugnax

warm[1] adj calidus; tepidus; fig acer; iracundus

warm[2] vt tepefacio, calefacio ③; foveo ②

warmth n calor, tepor m

warn vt moneo; praemoneo ②

warning n monitio f; monitum nt; monitus m; fig exemplum nt

warp vt perverto ③
- ■ **~** vi (as wood) curvor ①; fig pervertor ③

warrant[1] n cautio; auctoritas, fides; licentia, facultas f; mandatum nt

warrant[2] vt (securum) praesto ①; promitto ③; sancio ④; copiam do ① + dat; (excuse) excuso ①

warranty n satisdatio f

warrior n miles m; homo militaris, bellator m

wart n verruca f

wary adj cautus, providus; prudens, circumspectus

wash[1] vt lavo ①; abluo ③
- ■ **~** vi lavor ①; perluor ③

wash[2] n lavatio f; (colour) fucus m

washing n lavatio; lotura f

washtub n alveus m; labrum nt

wasp n vespa f

waste[1] n (laying waste) vastatio f; (loss) detrimentum; (financial) dispendium nt; (refuse) ramenta ntpl

w

waste[2] *vt* (lay waste) vasto ①; (spend) prodigo, profundo, consumo, absumo ③
■ ~ **away** *vi* tabesco ③

wasteful *adj* profusus, prodigus

wasteland *n* solitudo *f*; deserta *ntpl* (desert)

watch[1] *n* (guard) vigilia *f*; excubiae *fpl*; (clock) horologium *nt*

watch[2] *vt* custodio ④; observo ①
■ ~ *vi* vigilo ①

watchful *adj* vigilans; vigil, vigilax

watchman *n* vigil, excubitor, custos *m*

watch-tower *n* specula *f*

watchword *n* tessera *f*; signum *nt*

water[1] *n* aqua *f*; latex *m*; lympha *f*; (urine) urina *f*

water[2] *vt* rigo, irrigo ①; aqua misceo ②

watercress *n* nasturcium *nt*

waterfall *n* aqua desiliens *f*; cataracta *f*

water-mill *n* mola aquaria *f*

waterproof *adj* impervius

waterworks *n* aquarum ductus, aquaeductus *m*

watery *adj* aquaticus; aquosus; (in appearance) aquatilis

wave[1] *n* unda *f*; fluctus *m*

wave[2] *vi* fluctuo, undo, fluito ①
■ ~ *vt* moveo ②, agito ①

waver *vi* fluctuo; (vacillate) labo; fig dubito ①

wavering *adj* dubius, incertus

wavy *adj* undans; undosus; (curling) crispus

wax[1] *n* cera *f*

wax[2] *vt* cero, incero ①

wax[3] *vi* (grow) cresco ③; augeor ②

waxy *adj* cerosus

way *n* via *f*; iter *nt*; fig (manner, etc.) ratio *f*; modus; (custom) mos; (course) cursus *m*

wayfarer *n* viator *m*

waylay *vt* insidior ① + *dat*

wayward *adj* libidinosus; inconstans; levis; mutabilis

we *pn* nos
□ ~ **ourselves** nosmet ipsi

weak *adj* infirmus, debilis, enervatus, imbecillus, invalidus

weaken *vt* infirmo, debilito, enervo; (things) extenuo ①

weakness *n* infirmitas, debilitas, imbecillitas *f*; (failing) vitium *nt*

wealth *n* divitiae, opes *fpl*; opulentia; abundantia *f*

wealthy *adj* opulentus, dives; locuples; abundans

wean *vt* infantem ab ubere depello ③; fig dedoceo ②

weapon *n* telum *nt*; arma *ntpl*

wear *vt* (on the body) gero ③; gesto ①
■ ~ *vi* duro ①; (be worn out) atteror ③
□ ~ **out** tero, exedo, consumo ③

weariness *n* lassitudo, fatigatio *f*; languor *m*

weary[1] *adj* lassus, fessus, defessus, fatigatus; languidus; operosus

weary[2] *vt* lasso, fatigo, defatigo ①; conficio ③
■ ~ *vi* defatigor ①

weasel *n* mustela *f*

weather *n* caelum *nt*; tempestas *f*

weather-beaten *adj* adustus, tempestate iactatus

weave *vt* texo; necto ③

weaver n textor m

web n textura f; textum nt

□ **spider's ~** aranea f

web-footed adj palmipes

wedding n nuptiae fpl

wedding-day n dies nuptiarum m

wedge[1] n cuneus m

wedge[2] vt cuneo [1]

wedge-shaped adj cuneatus

wedlock n matrimonium nt

weed[1] n herba inutilis or noxia f

weed[2] vt runco, erunco [1]; sarrio [4]

week n hebdomas, septimana f

weekly adj hebdomadalis

weep vi fleo [2]; lacrimo [1]; (for) deploro [1]

weeping n ploratus, fletus m; lacrimae fpl

weigh vt pendo [3]; pondero; penso; fig meditor [1]; (down) gravo, degravo [1]; opprimo [3]

weight n pondus nt; (heaviness) gravitas f; (burden) onus nt; fig momentum, pondus nt

weighty adj ponderosus, onerosus, (heavy, important) gravis

welcome[1] adj gratus, acceptus

□ **~!** salve!

welcome[2] n gratulatio, salutatio f

welcome[3] vt salvere iubeo [2]; excipio [3]

weld vt ferrumino, conferrumino [1]

welfare n salus; utilitas, prosperitas f; bonum nt

well[1] n puteus, fons m

well[2] adj sanus, validus; integer

□ **be ~** valeo [2]

■ **~** adv bene; recte; scite, scienter; praeclare

□ **very ~** optime

well-being n salus f

well-born adj nobilis, nobili genere ortus

well-bred adj liberaliter educatus; comis

well-known adj pervulgatus; notus; celeber, nobilis

well-wisher n benevolus, amicus m

west n occidens, occasus m

■ **~ wind** n Favonius, Zephyrus m

westerly adj occidentalis, occiduus

western adj occidentalis, occiduus

westward(s) adv in occasum, occasum versus

wet[1] adj umidus, uvidus, madidus, udus

wet[2] vt madefacio [3]; rigo, umecto [1]

wetness n umor m

whale n balaena f; cetus m

what pn quod, quidnam, ecquid

■ **~** adj qualis, quantus; qui

whatever adj & pn quodcumque, quicquid

whatsoever adj & pn quodcumque, quicquid

wheat n triticum nt

wheedle vt blandior, delenio [4]; adulor [1]

wheel n rota f; (lathe) tornus m

■ **~** vt&i circumago(r) [3], roto(r) [1]; converto(r) [3]

wheelbarrow n pabo m

wheeze vi anhelo [1]

when adv & conj cum; ubi; ut; postquam; (interrog) quando?

w

whence *adv* unde

whenever *rel adv* quandocunque, quoties, quotiescunque

where *adv interrog* ubi? qua? (*rel*) qua, ubi
□ **~as** quoniam, quandoquidem, cum; quo
□ **~upon** quo facto

wherever *rel adv* quacunque, ubicumque

whet *vt* acuo; exacuo ③

whether *conj*:
□ **~ ... or** seu, sive; utrum ... an, -ne ... an

whey *n* serum *nt*

which *adj interrog* quis, qui? *m*; uter? (*rel*) qui, quae, quod
□ **~ever** quicunque, quisquis

whiff *n* halitus *m*

while¹ *n* tempus, spatium *nt*; mora *f*
□ **in a little ~** mox, brevi, postmodo
□ **for a ~** paullulum

while² *conj* dum, quoad; donec

whilst *conj* ▶ **while²**

whim *n* libido *f*

whimper *vi* vagio ④

whimsical *adj* ridiculus, absurdus

whine¹ *vi* vagio ④; queror ③

whine² *n* vagitus *m*; querela *f*

whip¹ *n* flagellum *nt*; scutica *f*

whip² *vt* flagello, verbero ①

whipping *n* verberatio *f*

whirl¹ *n* vertex, turbo *m*; (of a spindle) verticillus *m*; vertigo *f*

whirl² *vt* torqueo, intorqueo ②; roto ①
■ **~** *vi* rotor ①; torqueor ②

whirlpool *n* vertex, gurges *m*

whirlwind *n* turbo, typhon *m*

whisk¹ *n* scopula *f*

whisk² *vt* verro ③
■ **~** *vi* circumagor ③

whisper¹ *n* susurrus *m*; murmur *nt*

whisper² *vt&i* insusurro; susurro, murmuro ①

whistle¹ *vi* sibilo ①

whistle² *n* (pipe) fistula *f*; (sound) sibilus *m*; sibila *ntpl*; stridor *m*

white¹ *adj* albus, candidus; (of hair) canus

white² *n* album *nt*; candor *m*

whiten *vt* dealbo ①; candefacio ③
■ **~** *vi* albesco; candesco; canesco ③

whiteness *n* albitudo *f*; candor *m*; (of hair) canities *f*

whitewash *vt* dealbo ①

whither *adv & rel* quo; quorsum
□ **~soever** quocunque

whitish *adj* albidus, subalbus

who *pn interrog* quis? quae? quid? (*rel*) qui
□ **~ever** quicumque; quisquis

whole *adj* totus, omnis, cunctus; integer; plenus, solidus; (safe) salvus
■ **~** *n* summa *f*; omnia *ntpl*
□ **on the ~** plerumque

wholesome *n* salubris, salutaris

wholly *adv* omnino, prorsus

whoop¹ *n* ululatus, clamor *m*

whoop² *vi* clamo, vociferor ①

whore *n* meretrix *f*; scortum *nt*

whose *rel pn* cuius

why *adv* cur; quare? quamobrem?

wick *n* ellychnium *nt*

wicked *adj* impius, nefarius, flagitiosus; malus, scelestus, sceleratus

wickedness n nequitia, impietas f; scelus, flagitium nt

wicker n vimen nt
■ **of ~** vimineus

wide adj latus, amplus; spatiosus
□ **far and ~** late, passim, undique
■ **~ly** adv late, spatiose

widen vt&i dilato(r); laxo(r) ①; extendor ③; promoveor ②

widespread adj longe lateque diffusus, pervulgatus

widow n vidua f

widowed adj viduatus, viduus

widower n viduus vir m

width n latitudo; amplitudo; laxitas f

wield vt tracto; guberno ①; gero ③; exerceo ②

wife n coniunx; uxor, marita f

wig n capillamentum, caliendrum nt

wild adj ferus, silvestris; (of places) vastus; immanis; fig incultus; saevus; insanus

wilderness n locus desertus m; vastitas, solitudo f

wile n fraus f; dolus m; ars f

wilful adj pervicax, obstinatus
■ **~ly** adv pervicaciter; (deliberately) de industria

will¹ n voluntas; libido; auctoritas f; arbitrium nt; (purpose) propositum; (last ~) testamentum nt

will² vt volo ir, iubeo ②
□ **leave by ~** lego ①; relinquo ③

willing adj libens, facilis, promptus
■ **~ly** adv libenter; prompte

willow n salix f

wily adj vafer, astutus, callidus, dolosus, subdolus

win vt&i lucror ①; lucrifacio ③; (obtain) potior ④ + abl; consequor, adipiscor ③; fig expugno ①; (the battle, etc.) victoriam adipiscor ③; supero ①; vinco ③

wince vi abhorreo ②

winch n sucula f

wind¹ n ventus m; aura f; flatus m; flabra ntpl

wind² vt circumvolvo; circumverto ③; glomero ①; torqueo ②
■ **~ vi** sinuor, glomero ①; circumvolvor ③
□ **~ up** fig concludo ③

windfall n fig lucrum insperatum nt

winding adj flexuosus, sinuosus

windmill n mola f

window n fenestra f; specularia ntpl

windpipe n arteria f

windy adj ventosus

wine n vinum, merum nt
□ **~ cellar** apotheca f

wing n ala f; pennae fpl; fig cornu; latus nt

winged adj alatus, aliger, penniger, pennatus

wink¹ n nictus m

wink² vi nicto ①; coniveo ②
□ **~ at** ignosco, praetermitto ③

winner n victor; superior m

winter¹ n hiems, bruma f

winter² vt&i hiberno, hibernor ①

wintry adj hiemalis, hibernus

wipe vt tergeo, detergeo ②; (the nose) emungo ③; (dry) sicco ①; (out) deleo ②

w

wire | work

wire n filum metallicum nt

wisdom n sapientia, prudentia f

wise adj sapiens, prudens
■ ~ly adv sapienter; prudenter

wish¹ n optatio f; optatum nt; desiderium nt; voluntas f

wish² vt&i opto ①; cupio ③, volo ir; (long for) desidero ①

wisp n fasciculus, manipulus m

wistful adj desiderii plenus

wit n (intelligence) ingenium nt; (humour) facetiae fpl; sal, lepos m; (person) vir acerrimo ingenio m

witch n saga, venefica, maga f

witchcraft n ars magica f; veneficium nt

with prep cum + abl; apud, penes both + acc; in + abl

withdraw vt seduco ③; avoco ①
■ ~ vi recedo ③

wither vt torreo ②; sicco ①; uro, aduro ③
■ ~ vi marceo ②; aresco, languesco ③

withhold vt detineo, retineo; cohibeo ②

within adv intus, intro
■ ~ prep in + abl, intra + acc
□ ~ **a few days** paucis diebus

without prep sine, absque + abl

withstand vt obsisto, resisto ③ + dat

witness¹ n testis m/f; arbiter m; testimonium nt
■ **call to** ~ vt testor, obtestor

witness² vt&i testificor, testor ①

witticism n dictum nt; sales mpl

wittingly adv scienter; cogitate

witty adj argutus, lepidus; salsus; facetus; dicax

wizard n magus, veneficus m

wizened adj retorridus

woad n vitrum nt

wobble vi titubo ①

woe n dolor, luctus m; calamitas f

woeful adj tristis, luctuosus, miser; maestus

wolf n lupus m; (she ~) lupa f

woman n femina, mulier f

womanly adj muliebris

womb n uterus, venter m; alvus f

wonder¹ n miraculum; (astonishment) miratio f; stupor m

wonder² vi admiror; miror ①; stupeo ②; (would like to know) scire velim ir

wonderful adj mirabilis, mirus, mirificus, admirandus

wood n lignum nt; (timber) materies f; (forest) silva f

wooded adj silvosus; saltuosus

wooden adj ligneus

woodland n silvae fpl; nemora ntpl

wood-nymph n Dryas, Hamadryas f

woodpecker n picus m

woodworm n teredo, tinea f

woody adj silvosus; silvestris; saltuosus

wool n lana f

woollen adj laneus

woolly adj (of wool) laneus; (as sheep, etc.) lanatus, laniger

word¹ n verbum; vocabulum; nomen; dictum nt

word² vt verbis exprimo, describo ③

wordy adj verbosus

work¹ n opera f; opus; (task) pensum nt; (trouble) labor m

■ ~ *vi* laboro, operor ①

work² *vt* (handle) tracto ①; (ply) exerceo ②; (fashion) fabrico ①; (on) persuadeo ② + *dat*

work-basket *n* calathus *m*

worker *n* operarius *m*; opifex *m/f*

working *adj* operans
  □ ~ **day** negotiosus dies *m*

workman *n* opifex, artifex, faber, operarius *m*

workmanship *n* opus *nt*; ars *f*

workshop *n* officina, fabrica *f*

world *n* mundus, orbis, orbis terrarum *m*
  □ **the next** ~ vita futura *f*
  □ **where in the** ~ ubi gentium

worldly *adj* terrenus, humanus; saecularis, profanus

worm¹ *n* vermis, vermiculus *m*

worm² *vt* fig (out) extorqueo ②; expiscor ①

worried *adj* anxius

worry¹ *n* anxietas, sollicitudo, vexatio *f*

worry² *vt* dilacero; fig vexo, excrucio ①

worse *adj* peior, deterior
  ■ ~ *adv* peius
  □ **make** ~ corrumpo ③; depravo ①; exaspero ①
  □ **get** ~ ingravesco ③

worsen *vi* ingravesco ③

worship¹ *n* reverentia; adoratio *f*; cultus *m*

worship² *vt* veneror, adoro ①; colo ③

worst *adj* pessimus; extremus, ultimus
  ■ ~ *adv* pessime

worth¹ *n* pretium *nt*; dignitas *f*; (excellence) virtus *f*

work | wretched

worth² *adj* dignus
  □ **be** ~ valeo ②
  □ **it is** ~ **while** operae pretium est

worthiness *n* meritum *nt*; dignitas *f*

worthless *adj* vilis, levis; inutilis; nequam *indecl*

worthlessness *n* levitas *f*; inane *nt*

worthy *adj* dignus, condignus

wound *n* vulnus *nt*; plaga *f*
  ■ ~ *vt* vulnero, saucio ①; fig offendo, laedo ③

wounded *adj* saucius

wrangle¹ *n* rixa, altercatio *f*; iurgium *nt*

wrangle² *vi* rixor, altercor ①

wrap *vt* involvo, obvolvo ③; velo ①

wrapper *n* involucrum; tegmen *nt*

wrath *n* ira; iracundia *f*; furor *m*

wreath *n* (of flowers) sertum *nt*; corona *f*

wreathe *vt* torqueo ②; convolvo; necto ③

wreck¹ *n* (shipwreck) naufragium; fig damnum *nt*; ruina *f*

wreck² *vt* frango ③

wrecked *adj* (shipwrecked) naufragus; fig fractus

wrench *vt* detorqueo, contorqueo ②; luxo ①

wrestle *vi* luctor ①

wrestler *n* luctator *m*

wrestling *n* luctamen *nt*; luctatio *f*

wrestling-school *n* palaestra *f*

wretch *n* miser, perditus *m*, nequam *m indecl*

wretched *adj* miser, miserabilis,

infelix, malus, vilis

wriggle vi torqueor ②

wring vt torqueo ②

wrinkle[1] n ruga f

wrinkle[2] vt rugo, corrugo ①; (the brow) (frontem) contraho ③

wrinkled adj rugosus

wrist n carpus m

write vt&i scribo; perscribo; (a literary work) compono ③

writer n (author) auctor m

writhe vi torqueor ②

writing n (act) scriptio f; scriptum nt; scriptura; (hand) manus f; chirographum nt; (document) tabulae fpl

writing-desk n scrinium nt

wrong[1] adj pravus, perversus; vitiosus; fig falsus; iniustus, iniquus ■ ~**ly** adv falso; male, prave, perperam □ **be** ~ erro ①; fallor ③

wrong[2] n nefas nt indecl; iniuria f

wrong[3] vt laedo ③; violo ①; iniuriam infero ③

wrongful adj iniustus, iniuriosus

wry adj distortus, obliquus; curvus

Yy

yacht n celox f

yard n (court) area; (for poultry) cohors; (measure) ulna f

yarn n filum nt; lana f; linum nt; fig fabula, narratio f

yawn[1] vi oscito ①; fig hio ①; (gape open) hisco, dehisco ③

yawn[2] n oscitatio f

year n annus m

yearly adj annuus, anniversarius

yearn vi desidero ①; requiro; cupio ③

yearning n desiderium nt

yeast n fermentum nt

yell[1] vi ululo, clamo ①

yell[2] n ululatus, clamor m

yellow adj flavus, luteus, croceus

yellowish adj sufflavus, fulvus, gilvus

yelp vi gannio ④

yes adv ita, ita est; recte; immo; sane, certe

yesterday adv heri □ **of** ~ a hesternus m

yet conj nihilominus, quamquam; tamen; (of time) adhuc □ **even** ~ etiam nunc □ **not** ~ nondum

yew n taxus f

yield[1] n fructus m

yield[2] vt (bring forth) fero ir, pario ③; praebeo ②; (give up) cedo, concedo ③ ■ ~ vi cedo ③; manus do ①

yielding adj obsequiosus; fig mollis; lucrum afferens

yoke[1] n iugum nt; fig servitus f

yoke[2] vt iugum impono, iungo, coniungo ③

yolk n luteum nt; vitellus m

you pn (singular) tu; (plural) vos □ ~ **yourself** tu ipse

young[1] adj parvus, infans; fig novus

young[2] n adulescens, puer m; (offspring) progenies f; genus nt; fetus m; proles f

Zz

younger *adj* iunior, minor
youngster *n* adulescentulus *m*
your *prep* tuus; vester
yourself *pn* tu ipse, tute
□ **yourselves** vos ipsi
youth *n* (age) adulescentia;
iuventus, iuventa, iuventas;
(collectively) iuventus *f*; (young man)
adulescens, iuvenis *m*
youthful *adj* iuvenilis; puerilis

zeal *n* studium *nt*; fervor *m*;
alacritas *f*
zealous *adj* studiosus, alacer,
acer, ardens
zero *n* nihil *nt*
zest *n* sapor, gustus; fig gustatus;
impetus *m*; studium *nt*
zigzag[1] *n* anfractus *m*
zigzag[2] *adj* obliquus
zodiac *n* zodiacus, signifer orbis *m*
zone *n* (region of the earth) zona *f*
zoology *n* descriptio
animantium *f*

Historical and Mythological Names

A. = Aulus

Achaeī, ōrum the ruling nation among the Greeks in Homeric times

Achillēs, is son of Peleus and of Thetis

Ācis, idis son of Faunus loved by Galatea

Actaeōn, onis a huntsman torn to pieces by his own dogs for having seen Diana bathing

Adōnis, is & **idis** son of Cinyras, king of Cyprus, beloved by Venus; beautiful young man

Aegeus, ī father of Theseus

Aemilius Paullus, Lūcius victor over Perseus, king of Macedon, at Pydna in 168 BC

Aenēās, ae son of Anchises and Venus

Aeolus, ī god of the winds

Agamemnōn, onis king of Mycenae, commander-in-chief of the Greek forces at Troy

Agathoclēs, is (361–289 BC) king of Sicily, celebrated for his victory over the Carthaginians to win Sicily

Agricola, ae: Cn. Iūlius ~ (40–93 AD) governor of Britain for seven years (77–84 AD)

Aiāx, ācis one of two Greek heroes in the Trojan War, **Aiāx Telamōnius** and **Aiāx** son of Oileus, known together as the **Aiācēs**

Alexander, drī, Alexander (the Great) (356–23 BC), king of Macedon (336–23 BC)

Alcidēs, ae Hercules (*lit.* descendant of Alceus)

Alcmaeōn, ōnis son of Amphiaraüs, who killed his mother Eriphyle

Alcyonē, ēs wife of Ceÿx; she was changed into a kingfisher

Amāta, ae in Virgil's Aeneid, the wife of Latinus and mother of Lavinia

Amphitrītē, ēs wife of Neptune, goddess of the sea

Anchīsēs, ae father of Aeneas

Andromacha, ae (also **Andromachē, ēs**) wife of Hector

Andromeda, ae daughter of Cepheus and Cassiope; rescued by Perseus from a sea-monster

Anna, ae in Virgil's *Aeneid*, sister of Dido

Antōnius, Mārcus (Mark Antony) (83–30 BC) the lover of Cleopatra, defeated by Octavius Caesar at Actium in 31 BC

Anūbis, is & **idis** Egyptian dog-headed god

Apellēs, is renowned Greek painter

Apollō, inis god of the sun, prophecy, music and poetry, archery and medicine, son of Jupiter and Leto

Arachnē, ēs a Lydian woman who

challenged Athena to a contest of weaving and was turned into a spider

Archimēdēs, is mathematician and mechanical inventor at Syracuse in the 3rd century BC

Argō f. ship in which the Greek heroes under Jason sailed to Colchis to obtain the golden fleece

Argonautae, ārum m. pl. the heroes who sailed in the *Argo*

Argus, ī the hundred-eyed keeper of Io

Ariadnē, ēs daughter of Minos, king of Crete

Ascanius, iī son of Aeneas; founder of Alba Longa

Atalanta, ae (1) daughter of Iasias; took part in the hunt of the Calydonian boar; (2) daughter of Schoeneus; very swift of foot; engaged in a race with Hippomenes and was defeated by a ruse

Athēna, ae, patron goddess of Athens, war-goddess and goddess of spinning and weaving

Atlās, antis a giant who supported the heavens on his shoulders

Atreus, ī king of Mycenae, father of Agamemnon and Menelaüs

Augustus see OCTAVIUS; after Octavian the title was held by all emperors

Bacchus, ī god of wine, son of Jupiter and Semele

Bellerophōn, ontis slayer of the Chimaera; rode the winged horse Pegasus

Bellōna, ae goddess of war

Bona Dea a goddess worshipped by Roman women as goddess of Fertility and Chastity on 1st May

Boreās, ae the north wind

Boudicca, ae f. British leader (from East Anglia) of the famous, though doomed, revolt against the occupying Romans in 61 AD

Brūtus, M. Iūnius (85–42 BC) one of the assassins of Julius Caesar, defeated at and taking his own life at Philippi in 42 BC

C. = Gaius

Cācus, ī a giant, son of Vulcan, slain by Hercules

Cadmus, ī legendary founder of Thebes

Caesar, aris a Roman family name, borne by all the Roman emperors until Hadrian and thereafter by both the emperor and his heir; **C. Iūlius Caesar** (100–44 BC), one of the great military men of the ancient world, who became dictator and was assassinated on the Ides (15th) of March, 44 BC

Calypsō, ūs f. a nymph, daughter of Oceanus, ruling over the island Ogygia

Camēnae, ārum Roman goddesses identified with the Muses

Camilla, ae in Virgil's *Aeneid*, a maiden-warrior of the Volsci, an Italian tribe

Cassandra, ae prophetess, daughter of Priam and Hecuba

Cassius, C. Longīnus one of the assassins of Julius Caesar, defeated at and taking his own life at Philippi in 42 BC

Castor, oris twin-brother of Pollux, son of Tyndareus

Catilīna, ae: L. Sergius ~ supposedly a conspirator against the Roman state when Cicero was consul (63 BC), killed on the battlefield near Pistoria in 62 BC

Catō, ōnis (1) **M. Porcius ~** (234–149 BC) the censor, author of the phrase **dēlenda est Carthāgō** ('Carthage must be destroyed'); (2) **M. Porcius ~ Uticēnsis** an opponent of Caesar; committed suicide at Utica when his cause was defeated, 49 BC

Centaurī, ōrum m. pl. a wild race of Thessaly, half-man, half-horse

Cephalus, ī husband of Procris, beloved by Eos (Dawn); he accidentally killed his wife

Cerberus, ī three-headed dog, guarding the entrance to Hell

Charōn, ōnis ferryman of the Lower World

Chimaera, ae f. a fire-breathing monster with the head of a lion, body of a she-goat, and tail of a snake

Chīrō(n), ōnis a Centaur who tutored Aesculapius, Hercules and Achilles

Cicerō, ōnis: M. Tullius ~ (106–43 BC) one of the greatest politicians, writers and lawyers of the ancient world

Cincinnātus, ī Roman dictator (485 BC)

Circē, ēs & ae a famous sorceress

Cleopātra, ae queen of Egypt,

daughter of Ptolemy Auletes; loved by Mark Antony

Clīō, ūs f. the Muse of History

Clōthō, (acc. **ō**), f. one of the Fates (who span the thread of life)

Clytaemnēstra, ae wife of Agamemnon

Cn. = Gnaeus

Coriolānus surname of C. Marcius, who took Corioli; became an enemy of his countrymen, the Romans

Crassus, M. Licinius, a member (with Julius Caesar and Pompey) of the First Triumvirate; killed by the Parthians near Carrhae in 53 BC

Creūsa, -ae in Virgil's *Aeneid*, daughter of the Trojan king Priam and his wife Hecuba, and mother of Ascanius

Croesus, ī king of Lydia; a (proverbially) rich man

Cupīdō, inis the love god Cupid, son of Venus

Cybelē, ēs the great Phrygian mother goddess

Cyclōps, ōpos Cyclops; **Cyclōpes, um** m. pl. one-eyed giants, workmen in Vulcan's smithy

Cytherēa, ae f. Venus

D. = Decimus

Daedalus, ī legendary Athenian craftsman and inventor, creator of the labyrinth and father of Icarus

Danaē, ēs mother of Perseus

Daphnē, ēs daughter of the river god Peneus, loved by Apollo

Dardanus, ī ancestor of the

Trojan dynasty

Decius Mūs consul 340 BC; devoted himself to death to save his country

Dēiphobus, ī son of Priam who married Helen after the death of Paris

Deucaliōn, ōnis king of Phthia in Thessaly, son of Prometheus; with his wife Pyrrha was the only mortal saved from the flood

Diāna, ae goddess of hunting, sister of Apollo

Didō, ōnis foundress of Carthage

Dīs, Dītis Pluto

Drancēs, ae m. in Virgil's *Aeneid*, the Italian chief who taunts the Rutulian king Turnus

Dryades, um f. pl. wood-nymphs

Echidna, ae f. Lernaean hydra, killed by Hercules

Ēlectra, ae daughter of Agamemnon and Clytemnestra

Endymiōn, ōnis a beautiful youth, beloved by Diana

Epēus, ī constructor of the Wooden Horse at Troy

Epicūrus, ī Greek philosopher, originator of the Epicurean philosophy

Eratō f. one of the Muses, associated by Ovid with love poetry

Erebus, ī god of darkness; the Lower World

Eurōpa, ae (also **Eurōpē, ēs**) daughter of Agenor, king of Phoenicia; carried off by Jupiter in the form of a bull

Eurydicē, ēs wife of Orpheus

Euterpē, ēs f. a Muse, later associated with the reed-pipe

Evander, drī emigrated from Arcadia to Italy 60 years before the Trojan War

Fabius Maximus Verrūcōsus, Quīntus (died 203 BC) the Roman dictator whose famous policy of attrition rather than direct confrontation with Hannibal earned him the name **Cūnctātor** ('Delayer')

Faunī, ōrum m. pl. Fauns

Feretrius, iī an epithet of Jupiter as worshipped on the Capitol at Rome

Flōra, ae goddess of the flowers and spring

Fōrtūna, ae the Goddess Fortune

Galatēa, ae a sea-nymph, loved by Acis

Ganymēdēs, is Jupiter's cupbearer

Gēryōn, onis a mythical three-bodied monster who lived in Erythea, an island in the far west; his oxen were carried off by Hercules

Gigantes, um the Giants

Gorgō(n), onis the snake-haired daughter of Phorcus, Medusa, and her two sisters were called the Gorgons

Gracchus, ī: (1) **C. Semprōnius** ~ a radical tribune of the people and younger brother of Tiberius, killed in 121 BC; (2) **Ti. Semprōnius**

Historical and Mythological Names

~ a radical tribune of the people and older brother of Gaius, killed in 133 BC

Grādīvus, ī a title of Mars

Hamilcar, aris father of Hannibal

Hannibal, alis Punic surname; the great Carthaginian general during the Second Punic War, son of Hamilcar

Hannō, ōnis Punic surname; opponent of Hannibal

Harpyae, ārum f. pl. mythical rapacious monsters, half-bird, half-woman

Hasdrubal, alis (1) brother of Hannibal; (2) son-in-law of Hamilcar

Hēbē, ēs goddess of youth, cupbearer to the gods

Hecatē, ēs goddess of the Lower World, worshipped as goddess of spells and enchantments

Hector, oris son of Priam and Hecuba

Helena, ae (also **Helenē, ēs**) (1) daughter of Jupiter and Leda, wife of Menelaüs; (2) mother of Constantine the Great

Helenus, ī after the fall of Troy, husband of Hector's widow Andromache and king of Chaonia, a part of Epirus

Hellē, ēs f. daughter of Athamas, king of Boeotia, who was drowned in the narrow sea (Hellespont) called after her

Herculēs, is & (e)ī son of Jupiter and Alcmene, a demigod and divine hero

Hesperides, um f. pl. daughters of Erebus and the Night; they lived in an island garden beyond Mt Atlas and guarded the golden apples which Juno received on her wedding

Hesperus, ī son of Atlas, or of Cephalus, and Aurora; planet Venus as evening-star

Hōrae, ārum f. pl. the Hours, goddesses of the seasons

Hyacinthus, ī beautiful youth beloved by Apollo, and accidentally killed by him

Hȳdra, ae f. seven-headed serpent, killed by Hercules

Hylās, ae beautiful youth who accompanied Hercules on the Argonautic expedition

Hyperiōn, ōnis son of a Titan and the Earth; the Sun

Iacchus, ī Bacchus

Iāsōn, onis son of Aeson, king of Thessaly, Grecian hero

Īcarus, ī son of Daedalus; tried to fly from Crete and fell into the sea

Īlia, ae Rhea Silvia, mother of Romulus and Remus

Īō daughter of Inachus; beloved of Zeus, turned into a cow and pursued by Argus

Īphigenīa, ae daughter of Agamemnon and Clytemnestra

Īris, idis & is daughter of Thaumus and Electra, messenger of the gods and goddess of the rainbow

Īsis, idis & is Egyptian goddess, wife of Osiris

Itys, yos son of Tereus and Procne;

made into a stew and served up to his father

Iūlius *see* CAESAR

Iūlus, ī son of Aeneas, also called Ascanius

Iūnō, ōnis goddess and wife of Jupiter

Iuppiter, Iovis Jupiter, the chief Roman god

K. = Kaesō

L. = Lūcius

Lāocoōn, oontis a Trojan priest of Neptune

Lāodamīa wife of Protesilaus

Lāomedōn, ontis father of Priam, king of Troy, killed by Hercules

Latīnus, ī king of the Laurentians

Lātōna, ae mother of Apollo and Diana

Lausus, ī in Virgil's *Aeneid*, the son of the monstrous Mezentius

Lāvīnia, ae daughter of Latinus, wife of Aeneas

Lēander, drī the lover of Hero

Lēda, ae (also **Lēdē, ēs**) wife of Tyndareus, mother of Clytemnestra, Helen, Castor and Pollux

Līber, erī Bacchus

Lībera, ae Proserpine

Libitīna, ae goddess of funerals

Līvia Drūsilla (58 BC–29 AD) wife of the first Roman emperor Augustus and mother, by her first husband, of the second, Tiberius

Lūcifer, erī *m.* planet Venus as morning-star

Lūcīna, ae goddess of childbirth

Lucrētia, ae *f.* the rape victim of the son of the Etruscan king Tarquinius Superbus; she committed suicide and thus proved the catalyst for the expulsion of the Tarquins

Lūna, ae the goddess of the Moon

Lupercālia, ium *nt. pl.* festival of the god Lupercus on 15th February

Lycāōn, onis son of Pelasgus and king of Arcadia, who was transformed into a wolf

M. = Mārcus; M'. = Mānius

Maecēnās, Gaius (died 8 BC) a friend of Augustus and a great patron of the arts

Maeonidēs, ae Homer

Māia, ae mother of Mercury by Jupiter

Mam. = Māmercus

Marius name of a Roman gens; **C. ~** conquered Jugurtha; conquered the Cimbri and Teutons; consul in 107 BC and six times subsequently

Mārs, tis (also **Māvors, ortis**) the god of war

Mausōlus, ī king of Caria, died 353 BC; his tomb was a costly monument called the Mausoleum

Māvors, ortis *see* MARS

Maximus, Q. Fabius *see* FABIUS

Mēdēa, ae daughter of Aeëtes, king of Colchis; deserted by Jason, killed her own children

Medūsa, ae one of the three Gorgons; anyone who looked at her head, even after it had been cut off, was turned to stone

Meleager, grī son of Oeneus and Althaea, who took part in the Calydonian boar hunt; his survival depended on the continuing existence of a fire brand

Melpomenē, ēs f. one of the Muses, later associated with tragedy

Memnōn, onis son of Tithonus and Aurora, king of the Ethiopians

Menelāus, ī brother of Agamemnon

Mentor, ōris faithful friend of Ulysses

Mercurius, iī son of Jupiter and Maia, the messenger of the gods; the god of eloquence and of merchants and thieves

Mēzentius, iī in Virgil's *Aeneid*, a brutal tyrant of Caerē in Etruria

Midās, ae king of Phrygia; all he touched was turned into gold

Minerva, ae daughter of Zeus, goddess of wisdom, of the arts, of handicraft and women's works

Mīnōs, ōis son of Zeus and Europa, king of Crete

Mīnōtaurus, ī m. monster with the head of a bull in the Labyrinth of Crete

Mīsēnus, ī in Virgil's *Aeneid*, the Trojan trumpeter who roused the jealousy of the sea-god Triton and was drowned

Mnēmosynē, ēs f. Memory, the mother of the Muses

Morpheus, (acc. ea) god of dreams

Mūsa, ae f. Muse, one of the nine patron goddesses of the arts

Narcissus, ī son of Cephissus, enamoured of his own beauty and turned into a flower named after him

Nemesis, eōs goddess of retribution

Neoptolemus, ī (also called **Pyrrhus**) son of Achilles and Deidamia, the brutal killer of the Trojan king Priam

Neptūnus, ī the god of the sea

Nēreus, ei & eos a sea-god, son of Oceanus and Tethys

Nessus, ī m. a Centaur, killed by Hercules

Nestor, oris king of Pylos, one of the oldest of the Greek heroes at Troy

Nīsus, ī homosexual athlete in Virgil's *Aeneid*, partner of Euryalus, both of whom were killed in a sortie from the Trojan camp in Italy

Numitor, ōris king of Alba, father of Ilia, grandfather of Romulus and Remus

Octāvius a Roman family name; **C. Iūlius Caesar Octāviānus** (often also **Octāvius**) (63 BC–14 AD) great-nephew of Julius Caesar; victorious at Actium (31 BC); given the title **Augustus**; ruled as first Roman emperor

Olympia, ōrum nt. pl. the Olympic games at Olympia

Ops, Opis goddess of plenty, wife of Saturn

Orestēs, is son of Agamemnon killed his mother Clytemnestra

Ōrīōn, ōnis son of Hyrieus, a

hunter; the constellation of Orion

Orpheus, eī & eos legendary musician, son of Oeagrus and Calliope, husband of Eurydice

Osīris, is Egyptian god, husband of Isis

P. = Pūblius

Palēs, is f. or m. tutelary goddess of flocks and herds

Palinūrus, ī the pilot of Aeneas

Palladium, ī n. statue of Pallas in the citadel of Troy; captured by Ulysses and Diomedes

Pallas, adis & ados Minerva, Athena

Pān, Pānos son of Mercury, the god of woods and shepherds, half-man, half-goat

Parca, ae f. one of the Fates; **Parcae, ārum** pl. the Fates, three sisters

Paris, idis a son of Priam and Hecuba; carried off Helen, wife of Menelaüs

Pāsiphaē, ēs daughter of Helios, wife of Minos, and sister of Circe

Patroclus, ī friend of Achilles, slain by Hector

Pēgasus, ī a winged horse, sprung from the blood of the slain Medusa; with the aid of Pegasus, Bellerophon slew the Chimaera

Pēleus, eī & eos king of a part of Thessaly, husband of Thetis, father of Achilles

Pēnelopē, ēs (also **Pēnelopa, ae**) f. wife of Ulysses, king of Ithaca; famed for her fidelity

Pēnēus, ī m. god of a river flowing through the vale of Tempe in Thessaly

Pentheus, eī & eos king of Thebes, grandson of Cadmus; opposed the worship of Bacchus and was torn to pieces by his mother

Perseus, eī & eos son of Jupiter and Danaë, killer of Medusa, husband of Andromeda

Phaedra, ae daughter of Minos, and second wife of Theseus; fell in love with Hippolytus

Phaëthōn, ontis son of Helios and Clymene; tried to drive the chariot of the sun

Philomēla, ae daughter of Pandion, sister of Procne; turned into a nightingale

Phoebus, ī Apollo

Pīcus, ī the Italian god of agriculture, changed into a woodpecker

Plēiades, um the seven daughters of Atlas and Pleione

Plūtō(n), ōnis the god of the Underworld

Pollūx, ūcis son of Tyndareus and Leda, brother of Castor

Polyphēmus, ī a Cyclops; son of Neptune

Polyxena, ae daughter of Priam; sacrificed to Achilles after the Trojan War

Pōmōna, ae the goddess of fruits

Portūnus, ī tutelary god of harbours

Priamus, ī king of Troy, son of Laomedon

Priāpus, ī m. a god of procreation

Historical and Mythological Names

Procnē, ēs daughter of Pandion, wife of Tereus; she was turned into a swallow

Procrustēs, ae highwayman in Attica, slain by Theseus; had a bed which all his victims were made to fit

Prōmētheus, eī & eos son of Iapetus and Clymene; stole fire from heaven and gave it to mortals

Proserpina, ae daughter of Ceres, wife of Pluto

Prōtesilāus, ī husband of Laodamia; the first of the Greek expedition to land at Troy and the first to be killed

Psȳchē, ēs the mistress and eventually the wife of Cupid

Pygmalīōn, ōnis king of Cyprus; fell in love with a statue he had made himself; Venus then brought it to life

Pyladēs, is son of king Strophius, bosom-friend of Orestes

Pȳramus, ī the lover of Thisbe

Pyrrhus, ī see NEOPTOLEMUS

Pȳthōn, ōnis *m.* a serpent slain by Apollo near Delphi

Q. = Quīntus

Remus, ī brother of Romulus

Rhadamanthus, ī son of Jupiter, brother of Minos, judge in the Lower World

Rhēa Silvia daughter of Numitor, mother of Romulus and Remus

Rōmulus, ī founder and first king of Rome

S. (also Sex.) = Sextus

Sāturnia, ae Juno

Sāturnus, ī father of Jupiter, originally a mythical king of Latium

Satyrī, ōrum Satyrs; companions of Bacchus

Scīpiō, ōnis: P. Cornēlius ~ the conqueror of Hannibal at Zama in 202 BC, for which he received the cognomen **Āfricānus**

Scylla, ae *f.* a sea-monster; lived on the Italian side of the Straits of Messina, opposite Charybdis

Semelē, ēs daughter of Cadmus, mother of Bacchus, by Jupiter

Ser. = Servius

Serāpis, is & idis *m.* an Egyptian god

Sibylla, ae one of a class of prophetic females variously located

Sīlēnus, ī tutor of Bacchus, elderly, drunken, and bestial in character

Silvānus, ī *m.* god of the woods

Sp. = Spurius

Spartacus, ī a Thracian gladiator, leader of the gladiators in their war against Rome; killed 71 BC

Sulla, ae: L. Cornēlius ~ (c.138–79 BC) dictator of Rome and legislator

Sȳrinx, ingis *f.* a nymph changed into the reed from which Pan made his pipes

T. = Titus

Tantalus, ī son of Jupiter, father of Pelops and Niobe; divulged the secrets of the gods; was punished in the Underworld by a raging thirst which he could not quench

Tarpeia, ae Roman maiden, who treacherously opened the citadel to the Sabines

Tarquinius Superbus the last king of Rome

Tēreus, eī & eos king of Thrace, husband of Procne, and father of Itys; cut out the tongue of his wife's sister Philomela; Procne, in revenge, killed Itys and served him up to her husband in a stew

Terpsichorē, ēs f. a Muse, in later times associated with lyric poetry (dance)

Tēthys, yos a sea-goddess, wife of Oceanus

Thalēa (also **Thalīa**), **ae** f. the Muse of comedy or light verse

Themis, is goddess of justice and order

Thēseus, eī & eos king of Athens, son of Aegeus

Thespis, is a pioneer of Greek tragedy

Thetis, idis & idos a sea-nymph, daughter of Nereus, wife of Peleus, and mother of Achilles

Thisbē, ēs maiden of Babylon, loved by Pyramus

Ti. (also **Tib.**) = Tiberius

Tīresiās, ae a blind prophet of Thebes

Tīsiphonē, ēs f. a Fury

Tītān, ānos one of the Titans, a race of gods descended from Heaven and Earth, who preceded the

Olympians; the sun-god

Tīthōnus, ī son of Laomedon, husband of Aurora

Tityos, ī a giant punished in the Underworld for attempting, on Juno's orders, to rape Latona

Trītōn, ōnis m. one of a kind of supernatural marine beings, represented as blowing conches and attending on Neptune

Trītōnis, idis & idos Minerva, Athena

Turnus, ī king of the Rutuli, killed by Aeneas

Tyndaris, idis Helen, daughter of Tyndareus

Typhōeus, eos a giant, struck with lightning by Jupiter, and buried under Etna

Ulixēs, is & eī Ulysses, king of Ithaca, one of the Greek heroes at Troy, also known as Odysseus

Ūrania, ae f. the Muse of Astronomy

Venus, eris f. the goddess of Love

Verrēs, is governor of Sicily, 73–71 bc; denounced by Cicero for his rapacity

Vertumnus, ī god of the seasons

Vesta, ae daughter of Saturn and Rhea, goddess of the hearth-fire and of domestic life

Vulcānus, ī (also **Volcānus, ī**) lame son of Juno, god of fire

Zephyrus, ī the west wind

Geographical Names

Acadēmia, ae a gymnasium near Athens in which Plato taught

Achelōus, ī *m.* the largest river in Greece, rises in Mt Pindus and flows into the Ionian Sea

Acherōn, ontis *m.* river in the Underworld

Achīvus, a, um *adj.* Achaean, Grecian

Actium, ī *nt.* promontory and town in Epirus; celebrated for the victory of Augustus over Anthony in 31 BC

Aegyptius, a, um *adj.* Egyptian

Aegyptus, ī *f.* Egypt

Aetna (also **Aetnē, ēs**) *f.* Mt Etna, a volcano in Sicily

Āfrī, ōrum *m. pl.* Africans

Āfrica, ae *f.* Africa, Libya

Alba (Longa), ae *f.* mother city of Rome (between the Alban Lake and Mons Albanus)

Albānī, ōrum *m. pl.* inhabitants of Alba Longa

Alexandrīa, ae *f.* city on the north coast of Egypt, founded by Alexander the Great

Alpēs, ium *f. pl.* the Alps

Alpīnus, a, um *adj.* of the Alps

Āpennīnus, ī *m.* the Apennine mountains

Āpūlia, ae *f.* region of south-east Italy

Arabia, ae *f.* Arabia

Arabicus, Arabus, a, um *adj.* Arabian

Argīlētum, ī *nt.* quarter of the city of Rome which contained many booksellers' and cobblers' shops

Argīvus, a, um *adj.* of Argos; Greek

Asia, ae *f.* (1) Asia; (2) the Roman province of Asia Minor

Ātella, ae *f.* an Oscan town of Campania, the home of a particular kind of farce

Athēnae, ārum *f. pl.* Athens

Athēniēnsis, e *adj.* Athenian

Atlās, antis *m.* mountain range in the north-west of Africa

Attica, ae *f.* city state of Greece, the capital of which was Athens

Atticus, a, um *adj.* Attic, Athenian

Aulis, idis *f.* seaport town in Boeotia from which the Greek fleet sailed for Troy

Ausonia, ae *f.* Italy

Aventīnus, ī *m.* the Aventine (one of the seven hills of Rome); ~, **a, um** *adj.* relating to the Aventine

Avernus (lacus), ī *m.* Lago d'Averno, a lake near Naples that gave off mephitic vapours, considered to be the entrance to the Underworld

Belgae, ārum *m. pl.* the Belgians

Belgicus, a, um *adj.* Belgian, Belgic

Bēnācus, ī *m.* Lago di Garda, a lake

of northern Italy

Bīthȳnia, ae f. district of Asia Minor between the Propontis and the Black Sea

Bīthȳnicus, Bīthȳnus, a, um adj. Bithynian

Boeōtia, ae f. district of Greece, the capital of which was Thebes

Bosp(h)orus, ī m.: (1) ~ **Thrācius** the strait between the sea of Marmora and the Black Sea; (2) ~ **Cimmerius** the strait between the sea of Azof and the Black Sea

Britannia, ae f. Britain

Britannicus, Britannus, a, um adj. British

Brundisium, iī nt. Brindisi, a seaport of Calabria

Byzantium, iī nt. Istanbul

Caecubum, ī nt. marshy district in southern Latium (producing the most excellent kind of Roman wine)

Calabria, ae f. a district of south-east Italy

Calēdonia, ae f. northern part of Britain

Campānia, ae f. a district of Italy south of Latium

Cannae, ārum f. pl. village in Apulia; the scene of the defeat of the Romans by Hannibal in 216 BC

Cantium, iī nt. Kent

Cappadocia, ae f. province of Asia Minor, between Silicia and Pontus

Cāria, ae f. country in the south-west of Asia Minor

Carthāgō, inis f. Carthage; ~ **Nova**

the modern Cartagena on the south-east coast of Spain

Castalia, ae f. fountain on Mt Parnassus at Delphi sacred to Apollo and the Muses

Castalius, a, um adj. Castalian

Caucasus, ī m. chain of mountains between the Black and Caspian Seas

Caÿstros, ī m. river in Lydia noted for its swans

Celtae, ārum m. pl. the Celts

Celticus, a, um adj. Celtic

Charybdis, is f. dangerous whirlpool between Italy and Sicily opposite to Scylla

Chersonēsus (also **Cherronēsus**), **ī** f. Chersonese; (1) Thracian, Gallipoli peninsula; (2) Tauric, between the Black Sea and the Sea of Azof.

Cilices, um m. pl. Cilicians

Cilicia, ae f. province in the south-east of Asia Minor

Cōcȳtus, ī m. river in the Underworld

Colchis, idis f. country in Asia, east of the Black Sea

Colch(ic)us, a, um adj. of Colchis

Corinthi(ac)us, a, um adj. Corinthian

Corinthus, ī f. a city of Greece, on the Corinthian isthmus

Crēs, ētis m. Cretan

Crēta, ae f. Crete

Cūmae, ārum f. pl. city on the coast of Campania

Cynthius, a, um adj. relating to Cynthus

Geographical Names

Cynthus, ī m. mountain of Delos

Cyprius, a, um adj. of Cyprus

Cyprus, ī f. island in the Mediterranean Sea south of Cilicia

Dācī, ōrum m. pl. the Dacians

Dācia, ae f. country of the Dacians on the north of the Danube

Danaī, ōrum m. pl. the Greeks

Dānuvius, iī m. Danube

Dēlius, a, um adj. of Delos

Dēlos, ī f. the smallest of the Cyclades, famous for the worship of Apollo

Delphī, ōrum m. pl. Delphi (in Phocis), containing a famous oracle of Apollo; ~ inhabitants of Delphi

Delphicus, a, um adj. of Delphi

Dēva, ae f. Chester

Dīa, ae f. Naxos

Dictaeus, a, um adj. of Dicte

Dictē, ēs f. mountain in Crete

Dōdōna, ae f. town in Epirus with a famed oracle of Jupiter

Eborācum, ī nt. town in Britain, the modern York

Ēlysium, iī nt. the abode of the blessed in the Underworld

Ēlysius, a, um adj. Elysian

Ēmathia, ae f. district of Macedonia

Ēpīrōticus, a, um adj. of Epirus

Ēpīrus (also **Ēpīros**), **ī** f. country in the north-west of Greece

Erebus, ī m. the Underworld; the god of darkness

Eryx, ycis m. mountain in Sicily on which stood a temple of Venus

Esquiliae, ārum f. pl. the Esquiline (one of the seven hills of Rome)

Esquilīnus, a, um adj. of the Esquiline hill

Etrūria, ae f. country on the west coast of central Italy

Etruscus, a, um adj. Etrurian

Eurōpa, ae f. (the continent of) Europe

Euxīnus Pontus m. Black Sea

Gādēs, ium f. pl. Cadiz

Galatia, ae f. country of the Galatians; a district of Asia Minor

Gallī, ōrum m. pl. the Gauls

Gallia, ae f. Gaul

Gallic(ān)us, a, um adj. Gallic

Germānī, ōrum m. pl. the Germans

Germānia, ae f. Germany

Germān(ic)us, a, um adj. German

Glēvum, ī n. Gloucester

Graecī, ōrum m. pl. Greeks

Graecia, ae f. Greece

Graecus, a, um adj. Greek

Graiī, ōrum m. pl. Greeks

Hadria, ae m. Adriatic Sea

Helicōn, ōnis m. mountain in Boeotia (sacred to Apollo and the Muses)

Hellēspontus, ī m. the Dardanelles

Helvētiī, ōrum m. pl. a Gallic people, in modern Switzerland

Helvēti(c)us, a, um adj. Swiss

Geographical Names

Hibēria, ae f. Spain

Hibēricus, a, um adj. Spanish

Hibernia, ae f. Ireland

Hierosolyma, ōrum nt. pl. Jerusalem

Hippocrēnē, ēs f. a spring on Mt Helicon, made by Pegasus with a blow of his hoof

Hispānī, ōrum m. pl. the Spaniards

Hispānia, ae f. Spain

Hispāniēnsis, e, Hispān(ic)us, a, um adj. Spanish

Hymettus (also Hymettos), ī m. mountain near Athens, famous for its honey and marble

īda, ae (also īdē, ēs) f. (1) mountain in Crete; (2) mountain range near Troy

īlium (also īlion), iī nt., **īlios, ī** f. Troy

īlius, a, um adj. of Troy, Trojan

Ind(ic)us, a, um adj. Indian

Iōnium mare part of the Mediterranean between Italy and Greece

Ister, trī m. (lower part of the) Danube

Italia, ae f. Italy

Italicus, Italius, Italus, a, um adj. Italian

Ithaca, ae f. island in the Ionian Sea, the kingdom of Ulysses

Iūdaea, ae f. Judaea, the country of the Jews

Iūdaeus, iūdaicus, a, um adj. Jewish

Lacedaemonius, a, um adj. Spartan

Latium, iī n. a district of Italy in which Rome was situated

Latius, Latīnus, a, um adj. Latin

Lāvinium, iī n. a city of Latium

Lerna, ae (also Lernē, ēs) f. a forest and marsh near Argos, the haunt of the Hydra

Lēthē, ēs f. river of the Underworld which conferred oblivion on those who drank from it

Libya, ae (also Libyē, ēs) f. Lybia; North Africa

Lybicus, a, um adj. Lybian

Londinium, iī nt. London

Lupercal, ālis nt. grotto on the Palatine Hill, sacred to the god Lupercus

Lutētia, ae f. the modern Paris

Lycēum, ī nt. a gymnasium near Athens where Aristotle taught

Lycia, ae f. a country in the south of Asia Minor

Lycius, a, um adj. Lycian

Lȳdia, ae f. a country in western Asia Minor, the capital of which was Sardis

Macedones, um m. pl. the Macedonians

Macedonia, ae f. country of the Macedonians, a large district in the north of Greece

Macedoni(c)us, a, um adj. Macedonian

Massicus, ī m. Monte Massico, a mountain of Campania celebrated for its wine

Massilia, ae f. Marseilles

Maurī, ōrum *m. pl.* the Moors

Mauritānia, ae *f.* country of the Moors, Morocco

Mēdī, ōrum *m. pl.* the Medes

Mēdia, ae *f.* country of the Medes, situated between Armenia, Parthia, Hyrcania, and Assyria

Mēdicus, a, um *adj.* of the Medes

Mediōlānum, ī *nt.* Milan, a town of North Italy

Melita, ae (also **Melitē, ēs**) *f.* Malta, island in the Mediterranean

Mesopotamia, ae *f.* a country of Asia, between the Euphrates and Tigris

Milēsius, a, um *adj.* of Miletus

Milētus, ī *m.* city in Asia Minor

Mona, ae *f.* (1) Isle of Man; (2) Isle of Anglesey

Mycēnae, ārum *f. pl.*, **Mycēnē, ēs** *f. sg.* a city in Argolis, the city of Agamemnon

Myrmidones, um *m. pl.* a people of Thessaly, ruled by Achilles

Neāpolis, is *f.* Naples, a city of Campania

Neāpolītānus, a, um *a.* Neapolitan

Nīlus, ī *m.* the Nile

Nōricum, ī *nt.* a country between the Danube and the Alps, west of Pannonia

Nōricus, a, um *adj.* of Noricum

Numidae, ārum *m. pl.* a people of northern Africa

Numidia, ae *f.* country of the Numidians

Numidicus, a, um *adj.* Numidian

Olympia, ae *f.* the grove and shrine of Olympian Zeus in Elis where the Olympian games were held

Olympi(a)cus, a, um *adj.* Olympian, Olympic

Olympus, ī *m.* (1) a mountain on the boundary of Macedonia and Thessaly, dwelling of the gods; (2) a mountain in Mysia

Ōstia, ae *f.*, **Ōstia, ōrum** *nt. pl.* a seaport town in Latium, at the mouth of the Tiber

Padus, ī *m.* the Po

Palātium, iī *nt.* the Palatine, one of the seven hills of Rome

Pannonia, ae *f.* a country between the Danube and the Alps, east of Noricum

Paphlagonia, ae *f.* a province of Asia Minor on the Black Sea

Parnās(s)os (also **Parnās(s)us**), **ī** *m.* a mountain in Phocis sacred to Apollo and to the Muses

Paros, ī *f.* one of the Cyclades, noted for its marble

Parthī, ōrum *m. pl.* a Scythian people, the Parthians

Parthia, ae *f.* country of the Parthians

Parth(ic)us, a, um *adj.* Parthian

Patavīnus, a, um *adj.* of Padua

Patavium, iī *nt.* Padua

Pelasgī, ōrum *m. pl.* the oldest inhabitants of Greece; the Greeks

Pelion, iī *nt.* a mountain in eastern Thessaly

Pēnēus, ī *m.* river of Thessaly,

flowing through the valley of Tempe

Pergamum, ī *nt.*, **Pergamos**, ī *f.*, **Pergama**, ōrum *nt. pl.* the citadel of Troy; Troy

Persae, ārum *m. pl.* the Persians

Persis, idis *f.* Persia

Persicus, a, um *adj.* Persian

Pharsālos (also **Pharsālus**), ī *f.* a town in Thessaly, noted for the defeat of Pompey by Caesar, 48 BC

Pharus (also **Pharos**), ī *f.* an island near Alexandria, famous for its lighthouse

Philippī, ōrum *m. pl.* a city in Macedonia

Phlegethōn, ontis *m.* a river in the Underworld

Phoenissa, ae *f.* a Phoenician woman

Phryges, um *m. pl.* Phrygians; Trojans

Phrygia, ae *f.* Phrygia; Troy

Phrygius, a, um, **Phryx**, ygis *adj.* Phrygian; Trojan

Pieria, ae *f.* (1) a district of Macedonia, famous for the worship of the Muses; (2) a district of Syria

Pīraeus, ī *m.* the port at Athens

Pīrēnē, ēs *f.* a fountain in the citadel of Corinth

Pīsa, ae *f. sg.*, **Pīsae**, ārum *f. pl.* a city of Elis, near which the Olympic games were held

Poenī, ōrum *m. pl.* the Carthaginians

Pompeiī, ōrum *m. pl.* a maritime city in the south of Campania,

near Vesuvius

Ponticus, a, um *adj.* of the Pontus

Pontus, ī *m.* (1) the Black Sea; (2) north-eastern province of Asia Minor

Propontis, idos & idis *f.* the Sea of Marmara

Pūnicus, a, um *adj.* Punic, Carthaginian

Pȳrēnaeus, a, um *adj.* of the Pyrenees

Pȳthō(n), ōnis *f.* old name of Delphi

Rhēnus, ī *m.* the Rhine

Rhodanus, ī *m.* the Rhone

Rhodos (also **Rhodus**), ī *f.* Rhodes; town of the same name on the island of Rhodes

Rōma, ae *f.* Rome

Rōmānus, a, um *a.* Roman

Rubicō(n), ōnis *m.* a small boundary-stream between Italy and Cisalpine Gaul; the crossing of the Rubicon by Caesar, 49 BC, was the prelude to civil war

Rutulī, ōrum *m. pl.* a people of Latium, whose capital was Ardea

Sabell(ic)us, a, um *adj.* Sabine

Sabīnī, ōrum *m. pl.* the Sabines, an ancient Italian people

Samnium, iī *nt.* a country of central Italy, inhabited by the Samnites

Samnis, ītis *adj.* Samnite

Samnīticus, a, um *adj.* of the Samnites

Scamander, drī *m.* a river near Troy

Scylla, ae *f.* a rock between Italy and Sicily, opposite Charybdis

Scythae, ārum *m. pl.* the Scythians, people dwelling north and east of the Black Sea

Scythia, ae *f.* country inhabited by the Scythians

Scythicus, a, um *adj.* Scythian

Sēricus, a, um *adj.* Chinese; made of silk

Siculī, ōrum *m. pl.* Sicilians

Siculus, a, um *adj.* Sicilian

Sīdōn, ōnis & ōnos *f.* a Phoenician city, the mother-city of Tyre

Sīdōni(c)us, a, um *adj.* of or relating to Sidon

Simoīs, entis *m.* a river in Troas, which runs into the Scamander

Sirmiō, ōnis *f.* peninsula of Lake Garda

Sparta, ae *f.* the capital of Laconia, in the Peloponnese

Spartānus, Sparticus, a, um *adj.* Spartan

Stygius, a, um *adj.* of or belonging to the Styx

Stymphālus, ī *m.*, **Stymphālum, ī** *nt.* a district in Arcadia, with a town and lake of the same name; here lived the man-eating birds killed by Hercules

Styx, gis *f.* the principal river of the underworld

Sybaris, is *f.* a town of Lucania on the Gulf of Tarentum, proverbial for its luxury

Symplēgades, um *f. pl.* two floating islands at the entrance of the Euxine

Syrācūsae, ārum *f. pl.* Syracuse, the ancient capital of Sicily

Syrācūsānus, Syrācūsius, a, um *adj.* Syracusan

Syria, ae *f.* Syria

Syrius, Syrus, Syriacus, Syriscus, a, um *adj.* Syrian

Syrtēs, ium *f. pl.* two very dangerous sandy flats on the north coast of Africa

Tamesis, is *m* the Thames

Tempē *nt. indecl.* a valley in Thessaly, through which ran the River Peneus

Thēbae, ārum *f. pl.* (1) a city in upper Egypt; (2) the capital of Boeotia

Thēbānus, a, um *adj.* Theban

Thessalia, ae *f.* Thessaly, a district in the north of Greece

Thessal(ic)us, a, um *adj.* Thessalian, Thessalic

Thrāc(i)a, ae (also **Thrācē, ēs**) *f.* Thrace, a district of North Greece

Thrācius, a, um *adj.* Thracian

Thrāx, ācis *f.* a Thracian

Thūlē, ēs *f.* an island in the far north, usually in references to Iceland or Scandinavia

Tiberis, is *m.* a river of Latium, on which Rome stood, the Tiber

Tomis, is *f.*, **Tomī, ōrum** *m. pl.* a town of Moesia, on the Black Sea, to which Ovid was banished; modern Constanţa

Trīnacria, ae *f.* Sicily

Trīnacrius, a, um *adj.* Sicilian

Trōas, adis & ados *f.* a Trojan

woman; the region about Troy, the Troad

Trōi(c)us, Trōiānus, a, um a, Trojan

Trōia, ae *f.* Troy, city of Asia Minor

Trōiugena, ae *adj.* Trojan

Trōs, Trōis *m.* a Trojan

Tyrr(h)ēnia, ae *f.* Etruria

Tyrr(h)ēnus, a, um *adj.* Etrurian, Tuscan

Umber, bra, brum *adj.* Umbrian

Umbrī, ōrum *m. pl.* the people of Umbria

Umbria, ae *f.* country of the Umbri,

a district of Italy on the Adriatic, north of Picenum

Vāticānus (mōns, collis), ī *m.* the Vatican (one of the seven hills of Rome)

Venetī, ōrum *m. pl.* a people in the north-east of Italy; a people in the north-west of Gaul

Vesuvius, ī *m.* a volcano in Campania

Vīminālis collis *m.* the Viminal (one of the seven hills of Rome)

Volscī, ōrum *m. pl.* a people to the south of Latium

Volscus, a, um *adj.* of the Volsci

Summary of Grammar

This Summary of Grammar is intended to be a handy reference guide to the patterns of inflections (i.e. endings) found in the vast majority of Latin words. It thus concentrates on the regular patterns and the most important or frequent irregular exceptions. We do not, however, offer any guidance on the word order and constructions of Latin. For these, the reader is referred to the companion *Latin Grammar* (Oxford, 1999).

Nouns 601

Adjectives 604

Adverbs 608

Numerals 609

Pronouns 612

Verbs 616

Nouns

The declension of a noun can be worked out from the its endings in the nom. and/or gen. sg., as given in the Latin–English section of the dictionary. For example, **nauta** has gen. sg. **nautae** and thus declines like **domina**; all nouns that have gen. sg. in **-is** are third declension, and they form all their cases (except sometimes the nom. sg.) from the same stem as the gen. sg

	1st decl.	2nd decl.		3rd decl.	
	girl, f.	*master*, m.	*war*, n.	*king*, m.	*shore*, n.
singular					
nom.	puell-a	domin-us	bell-um	rēx	lītus
acc.	puell-am	domin-um	bell-um	rēg-em	lītus
gen.	puell-ae	domin-ī	bell-ī	rēg-is	lītor-is
dat.	puell-ae	domin-ō	bell-ō	rēg-ī	lītor-ī
abl.	puell-ā	domin-ō	bell-ō	rēg-e	lītor-e
plural					
nom.	puell-ae	domin-ī	bell-a	rēg-ēs	lītor-a
acc.	puell-ās	domin-ōs	bell-a	rēg-ēs	lītor-a
gen.	puell-ārum	domin-ōrum	bell-ōrum	rēg-um	lītor-um
dat.	puell-īs	domin-īs	bell-īs	rēg-ibus	lītor-ibus
abl.	puell-īs	domin-īs	bell-īs	rēg-ibus	lītor-ibus

Summary of Grammar

	3rd decl. cont.			
	ship, f.	*sea*, n.	*city*, f.	*animal*, n.
singular				
nom.	nāv-is	mare	urb-s	animal
acc.	nāv-em	mare	urb-em	animal
gen.	nāv-is	mar-is	urb-is	animāl-is
dat.	nāv-ī	mar-ī	urb-ī	animāl-ī
abl.	nāv-e	mar-ī	urb-e	animāl-e
plural				
nom.	nāv-ēs	mar-ia	urb-ēs	animāl-ia
acc.	nāv-ēs (-īs)	mar-ia	urb-ēs (-īs)	animāl-ia
gen.	nāv-ium	mar-ium	urb-ium	animāl-ium
dat.	nāv-ibus	mar-ibus	urb-ibus	animāl-ibus
abl.	nāv-ibus	mar-ibus	urb-ibus	animāl-ibus

	4th decl.		5th decl.	
	step, m.	*horn*, n.	*thing*, f.	*day*, m./f.
singular				
nom.	grad-us	corn-ū	r-ēs	di-ēs
acc.	grad-um	corn-ū	r-em	di-em
gen.	grad-ūs	corn-ūs	r-eī	di-ēī
dat.	grad-uī	corn-ū	r-eī	di-ēī
abl.	grad-ū	corn-ū	r-ē	di-ē
plural				
nom.	grad-ūs	cornu-a	r-ēs	di-ēs
acc.	grad-ūs	cornu-a	r-ēs	di-ēs
gen.	grad-uum	corn-uum	r-ērum	di-ērum
dat.	grad-ibus	corn-ibus	r-ēbus	di-ēbus
abl.	grad-ibus	corn-ibus	r-ēbus	di-ēbus

Notes

1 Neuter nouns of all declensions (viz. 2nd, 3rd, and 4th) always have the acc. identical to the nom. In their plural, the nom./acc. always ends in **-a**.

2 The vocative case is the same as the nominative for all nouns of all declensions, except that 2nd declension nouns ending in **-us** form vocative sg. in **-e** (e.g. **domine**) unless they end in **-ius**, when the vocative sg. is in **-ī** (e.g. **fīlī** from **fīlius**).

3 Some 2nd declension nouns have nom. sg. in **-er** (e.g. **puer, ager**). Of these, some keep their **-e-** in the other cases while others drop it (e.g. gen. sg. **puer-ī, agr-ī**).

4 Nouns of the second declension with nom. sg. in **-ius** or **-ium** often form a 'contracted' gen. sg. in **-ī** rather than **-iī** (e.g. **fīlī, ingenī**).

5 The 3rd declension includes nouns with stems ending in consonants (e.g. **rēx = rēg-s, lītus**) and those ending in **-i** (e.g. **nāvis** etc.). The two groups differ in their gen. pl.: a basic practical rule is that nouns with one more syllable in the gen. sg. than in the nom. sg. form their gen. pl. in **-um**, while the remainder have gen. pl. **-ium**; however, note that most nouns with a monosyllabic nom. sg. ending in two consonants (**-ns, -rs, -bs, -ps, -rx,** and **-lx**), together with neuters with nom. sg. in **-ar** or **-al** have gen. pl. **-ium**, while **canis, iuvenis, senex, pater, māter,** and **frāter** have gen. pl. in **-um**.

6 The locative case (expressing 'place at which') for the first and second declensions is identical to the gen. for place names that are singular in form, and to the dat./abl.

for names that are plural in form, e.g. **Rōma → Rōmae,
Athēnae → Athēnīs, Corinthus → Corinthī**. For the third
declension, the locative singular ends in **-ī** or **-e** while the
plural again is identical to the dat./abl., e.g. **Carthāgō →
Carthāginī, Gādēs → Gādibus**. Note also the locatives
domī, humī, and **rūrī**.

7 The following very common nouns have some irregular
forms: **dea, fīlia, deus, vir, vīs, domus**. These are detailed
in their dictionary entries. **Iuppiter** ('Jupiter, Jove') declines
Iuppiter, Iovem, Iovis, Iovī, Iove.

Adjectives

	2nd & 1st decl.		
	bonus *good*		
	m.	f.	n.
singular			
nom.	bon-us	bon-a	bon-um
acc.	bon-um	bon-am	bon-um
gen.	bon-ī	bon-ae	bon-ī
dat.	bon-ō	bon-ae	bon-ō
abl.	bon-ō	bon-ā	bon-ō
plural			
nom.	bon-ī	bon-ae	bon-a
acc.	bon-ōs	bon-ās	bon-a
gen.	bon-ōrum	bon-ārum	bon-ōrum
dat.	bon-īs	bon-īs	bon-īs
abl.	bon-īs	bon-īs	bon-īs

Summary of Grammar

Note

Like **bonus** decline some adjectives in **-er** such as **miser, misera, miserum** (keeping the **-e-** like **puer**) and **pulcher, pulchra, pulchrum** (dropping the **-e-** like **ager**).

	3rd decl.				
	ācer *swift*			ingēns *huge*	
	m.	f.	n.	m. & f.	n.
singular					
nom.	ācer	ācr-is	ācr-e	ingēns	ingēns
acc.	ācr-em	ācr-em	ācr-e	ingent-em	ingēns
gen.	ācr-is	ācr-is	ācr-is	ingent-is	
dat.	ācr-ī	ācr-ī	ācr-ī	ingent-ī	
abl.	ācr-ī	ācr-ī	ācr-ī	ingent-ī	
plural					
nom.	ācr-ēs	ācr-ēs	ācr-ia	ingent-ēs	ingent-ia
acc.	ācr-ēs	ācr-ēs	ācr-ia	ingent-ēs (-īs)	ingent-ia
gen.	ācr-ium	ācr-ium	ācr-ium	ingent-ium	
dat.	ācr-ibus	ācr-ibus	ācr-ibus	ingent-ibus	
abl.	ācr-ibus	ācr-ibus	ācr-ibus	ingent-ibus	

	3rd decl.			
	pauper *poor*		laetior *happier*	
	m. & f.	n.	m. & f.	n.
singular				
nom.	pauper	pauper	laetior	laetius
acc.	pauper-em	pauper	laetiōr-em	laetius
gen.		pauper-is	laetiōr-is	
dat.		pauper-ī	laetiōr-ī	
abl.		pauper-e	laetiōr-e	
plural				
nom.	pauper-ēs	pauper-a	laetiōr-ēs	laetiōr-a
acc.	pauper-ēs	pauper-a	laetiōr-ēs	laetiōr-a
gen.		pauper-um	laetiōr-um	
dat.		pauper-ibus	laetiōr-ibus	
abl.		pauper-ibus	laetiōr-ibus	

Notes

1 Many 3rd declension adjectives (e.g. **trīstis**, **fortis**, **omnis**) have nom. sg. m. & f. in **-is**, declining like **ācer** in all other forms.

Like **ingēns** decline all present participles and all adjectives with nom. sg. in **-x** (e.g. **audāx**, **ferōx**). The latter have a stem in **-c-** (so gen. sg. **audācis** etc.). Note that present participles have their abl. sg. in **-e** when used as participles (e.g. in the ablative absolute construction) but in **-ī** when used simply as adjectives.

2 There are very few consonant stem adjectives declining like **pauper**, but note that comparative adjectives with nom. sg. in **-ior**, **-ius** follow essentially the same pattern, except in the nom./acc. sg. n.

Comparison of adjectives

Most adjectives form their comparative and superlative by adding **-ior** and **-issimus** to their stem respectively. For example, **laetus** forms comparative **laetior** and superlative **laetissimus**. All comparatives decline like **laetior** and all superlatives like **bonus**.

Adjectives ending in **-er** (like **miser**, **pulcher**, and **ācer**) form their comparatives regularly (**miserior**, **pulchrior**, **ācrior**), but have superlatives in **-errimus** (**miserrimus**, **pulcherrimus**, **ācerrimus**). Note also the six superlatives in **-illimus**, from **facilis**, **difficilis**, **gracilis**, **humilis**, **similis**, and **dissimilis** (e.g. **facillimus**).

Adjectives that end in **-eus**, **-ius**, or **-uus** usually stay the same in the comparative and superlative, making use of the Latin words for 'more' or 'most', as, for example, **dubius**, **magis dubius**, **maximē dubius**.

Some common adjectives have irregular comparison:

	comparative	superlative
bonus *good*	melior *better*	optimus *best*
malus *bad*	peior	pessimus
magnus *great*	maior	maximus
multus *much*	(plūs)	plūrimus
parvus *small*	minor	minimus
senex *old man*	nātū maior	nātū maximus
iuvenis *young man*	iūnior *or* nātū minor	nātū minimus

Adverbs

Adverbs can be regularly formed from adjectives. From adjectives of the **bonus** type (though not **bonus** itself), adverbs are usually formed by adding **-ē** to the stem, e.g. **lentus → lentē**, **miser → miserē**. Some add **-ō**, for example **tūtō** from **tūtus**, **subitō** from **subitus**. From 3rd declension adjectives, the adverb is generally formed by adding **-ter** to the stem, so **ācer → ācriter**, **fortis → fortiter**; some, however, simply use the acc. sg. n., for example **facilis → facile**.

Comparison of adverbs

Comparative adverbs are the same as the acc. sg. n. of the corresponding adjective (and therefore usually end in **-(i)us**), while the superlative is formed by changing the corresponding adjective's nom. sg. m. from **-us** to **-ē**; for example, **fortiter** has comparative **fortius** and superlative **fortissimē**, and **ācriter** has **ācrius** and **ācerrimē**.

Some common adverbs have irregular comparison:

	adverb	comparative	superlative
bonus	bene *well*	melius	optimē
malus	male *badly*	peius	pessimē
magnus	magnopere *greatly*	magis	maximē
multus	multum *much*	plūs	plūrimum
parvus	paul(l)um *little*	minus	minimē
—	diū *for a long time*	diūtius	diūtissimē
—	[post *later*]	posterius	postrēmō
—	[prope *near*]	propius	proximē

Numerals

		cardinal	ordinal	adverb
		one	*first*	*once*
1	I	ūnus	prīmus	semel
2	II	duo	secundus, alter	bis
3	III	trēs	tertius	ter
4	IV	quattuor	quārtus	quater
5	V	quīnque	quīntus	quīnquiēns
6	VI	sex	sextus	sexiēns
7	VII	septem	septimus	septiēns
8	VIII	octō	octāvus	octiēns
9	IX	novem	nōnus	noviēns
10	X	decem	decimus	deciēns
11	XI	ūndecim	ūndecimus	ūndeciēns
12	XII	duodecim	duodecimus	duodeciēns
13	XIII	tredecim	tertius decimus	terdeciēns
14	XIV	quattuordecim	quārtus decimus	quattuordeciēns
15	XV	quīndecim	quīntus decimus	quīndeciēns
16	XVI	sēdecim	sextus decimus	sēdeciēns
17	XVII	septendecim	septimus decimus	septiēnsdeciēns
18	XVIII	duodēvīgintī	duodēvīcēnsimus	duodēviciēns
19	XIX	ūndēvīgintī	ūndēvīcēnsimus	ūndēviciēns
20	XX	vīgintī	vīcēnsimus	vīciēns
30	XXX	trīgintā	trīcēnsimus	trīciēns
40	XL	quadrāgintā	quadrāgēnsimus	quadrāgiēns

Summary of Grammar

50	L	quīnquāgintā		200	CC	ducentī
51	LI	ūnus et quīnquāgintā		300	CCC	trēcentī
60	LX	sexāgintā		400	CCCC	quadringentī
70	LXX	septuāgintā		500	D	quīngentī
80	LXXX	octāgintā		600	DC	sescentī
90	XC	nōnāgintā		700	DCC	septingentī
100	C	centum		800	DCCC	octingentī
101	CI	centum et ūnus		900	DCCCC	nōngentī
		1000	CD or M	mīlle		

Notes

1 The cardinal numbers 1 to 3 decline as follows:

	m.	f.	n.
nom.	ūnus	ūna	ūnum
acc.	ūnum	ūnam	ūnum
gen.	ūnĭus	ūnĭus	ūnĭus
dat.	ūnī	ūnī	ūnī
abl.	ūnō	ūnā	ūnō

	m.	f.	n.	m. & f.	n.
nom.	duo	duae	duo	trēs	tria
acc.	duŏs, duo	duās	duo	trēs	tria
gen.	duōrum	duārum	duōrum	trium	
dat./abl.	duōbus	duābus	duōbus	tribus	

2 The cardinal numbers 4 to 100 are indeclinable (except that where **ūnus**, **duo** and **trēs** appear as part of the form, they are declined). The cardinal numbers for hundreds from 200 to 900 decline like the plural of **bonus**.

3 The ordinal numbers all decline like **bonus**.

4 The endings **-ēns** and **-ēnsimus** are often found as **-ēs** and **-ēsimus**.

5 To form cardinal numbers between 20 and 99, the order is either that of 'twenty-four' (**vīgintī quattuor**) or 'four-and-twenty' (**quattuor et vīgintī**), though the latter is more usual if the number includes **ūnus** (e.g. **ūnus et trīgintā**). For numbers greater than 100, the order is usually that of English: hence, 752 is **septingentī quīnquāgintā duo**.

6 Cardinal numbers involving thousands can be expressed in two ways, either with the noun **mīlia** in the relevant case itself modified by a cardinal number and followed by a genitive noun dependent on it, or with the indeclinable adjective **mīlle** qualified by a numeral adverb and followed by the noun in the relevant case. For example, 'with three thousand sailors' is either **cum tribus mīlibus nautārum** or **cum ter mīlle nautīs**. A 'mile' is **mīlle passūs** ('a thousand paces') and so 'two miles' is **duo mīlia passuum** (lit. 'two thousands of paces').

Summary of Grammar

Pronouns

Personal pronouns

	I, we	*you*	*he, she, it, that*		
			m.	f.	n.
singular					
nom.	ego	tū	is	ea	id
acc.	mē	tū	eum	eam	id
gen.	meī	tuī	eius	eius	eius
dat.	mihĭ	tibĭ	eī	eī	eī
abl.	mē	tē	eō	eā	eō
plural					
nom.	nōs	vōs	iī (eī, ī)	eae	ea
acc.	nōs	vōs	eōs	eās	ea
gen.	nostrī (-um)	vestrī (-um)	eōrum	eārum	eōrum
dat.	nōbīs	vōbīs	eīs, iīs	eīs, iīs	eīs, iīs
abl.	nōbīs	vōbīs	eīs, iīs	eīs, iīs	eīs, iīs

Reflexive pronoun

	himself, herself, itself, themselves
acc.	sē, sēsē
gen.	suī
dat.	sibĭ
abl.	sē, sēsē

Notes

1 The possessive adjectives corresponding to **ego**, **tū**, **nōs**, **vōs**, and **sē** are respectively **meus**, **tuus**, **noster**, **vester**,

and **suus**. Possessives in **-us** decline like **bonus** (**meus** has voc. sg. masc. **mī**); **noster** and **vester** decline like **pulcher**. There is no adjective corresponding to **is**, whose genitive is used instead.

2 The dative of **ego** is sometimes **mī**.

3 The gen. forms **nostrum** and **vestrum** are used in partitive constructions, e.g. **ūnus vestrum** 'one of you'. The alternative forms **nostrī** and **vestrī** are used where the genitive expresses the object of an action, esp. with the gerund(ive); regardless of number and gender, **nostrī** and **vestrī** (likewise **suī**) always take the masc. gen. sg. of the gerund(ive), e.g. **vestrī irrīdendī causā** 'for the sake of mocking you'.

Demonstrative pronouns

	this			*that*		
	m.	f.	n.	m.	f.	n.
singular						
nom.	hic	haec	hoc	ille	illa	illud
acc.	hunc	hanc	hoc	illum	illam	illud
gen.	huius	huius	huius	illīus	illīus	illīus
dat.	huic	huic	huic	illī	illī	illī
abl.	hōc	hāc	hōc	illō	illā	illō
plural						
nom.	hī	hae	haec	illī	illae	illa
acc.	hōs	hās	haec	illōs	illās	illa
gen.	hōrum	hārum	hōrum	illōrum	illārum	illōrum
dat.	hīs	hīs	hīs	illīs	illīs	illīs
abl.	hīs	hīs	hīs	illīs	illīs	illīs

Summary of Grammar

Like **ille** declines **iste** ('that'), as does **ipse** ('self') except its nom./acc. sg. n. **ipsum**.

Relative pronoun

	the same			who, which	
m.	**f.**	**n.**	**m.**	**f.**	**n.**
singular					
nom.	īdem	eadem	idem	quī	quae	quod
acc.	eundem	eandem	idem	quem	quam	quod
gen.	eiusdem	eiusdem	eiusdem	cuius	cuius	cuius
dat.	eīdem	eīdem	eīdem	cui	cui	cui
abl.	eōdem	eādem	eōdem	quō	quā	quō
plural					
nom.	(e)īdem	eaedem	eadem	quī	quae	quae
acc.	eōsdem	eāsdem	eadem	quōs	quās	quae
gen.	eōrundem	eārundem	eōrundem	quōrum	quārum	quōrum
dat./abl.	eīsdem or īsdem			quibus or quīs		

The interrogative **quis** ('who?') declines exactly like **quī** except that the nom. sg. f. may be **quis** and the nom./acc. sg. n. is usually **quid**. The indefinite **quis** ('someone, anyone') declines in the same way as interrogative **quis** except that the nom./acc. pl. n. may be **qua**.

As well as being a relative pronoun, **quī** can also be interrogative or indefinite: distinguish **quis** and **quid** as (pro)nouns from **quī** and **quod** which can only be used as adjectives.

Pronominal adjectives

	the other (of two)		
	m.	f.	n.
singular			
nom.	alter	altera	alterum
acc.	alterum	alteram	alterum
gen.	alterīus	alterīus	alterīus
dat.	alterī	alterī	alterī
abl.	alterō	alterā	alterō
plural			
nom.	alterī	alterae	altera
acc.	alterōs	alterās	altera
gen.	alterōrum	alterārum	alterōrum
dat./abl.	alterīs	alterīs	alterīs

Among the other pronominal adjectives, **ūllus**, **nūllus**, **sōlus**, and **tōtus** are declined like **ūnus**; **alius** declines like **ille** (except with nom. sg. m. **alius**). Like **alter** decline both **uter** and **neuter**, though with stems **utr-** and **neutr-** in all forms except the nom. sg. m.

Verbs

Latin verbs take different endings according to person, number, tense, voice, and mood. There are four regular sets of inflections for verbs, known as conjugations. In this dictionary the conjugation of a verb is shown by a number in square brackets following the verb. The citation (headword) form of a Latin verb is usually its 1 sg. pres. ind. act., often followed by its principal parts, from which one can predict the rest of its forms: they are, in order, the infinitive, the 1 sg. perf. ind. act., and the supine.

There is also a mixed conjugation containing a small number of (common) verbs. These follow the 3rd conjugation for most forms, but have the endings of the 4th conjugation where the latter have two successive vowels.

A number of Latin verbs (some in each conjugation) are passive in form but active in meaning. These are called deponent verbs and their forms are identical to verbs of their conjugations in the passive. A very small number of verbs are semi-deponent: they are active in form and meaning in the present, future and imperfect, but deponent in the perfect, pluperfect, and future perfect.

Latin also has a number of irregular verbs, some of which are very common indeed. We give the irregular forms in full.

Regular Verbs

Active — Indicative

	paró 1	moneó 2	regó 3	audió 4
	I prepare	*I warn*	*I rule*	*I hear*
present				
sg 1	paró	moneó	regó	audió
2	parās	monēs	regis	audīs
3	parat	monet	regit	audit
pl 1	parāmus	monēmus	regimus	audīmus
2	parātis	monētis	regitis	audītis
3	parant	monent	regunt	audiunt
future				
sg 1	parābō	monēbō	regam	audiam
2	parābis	monēbis	regēs	audiēs
3	parābit	monēbit	reget	audiet
pl 1	parābimus	monēbimus	regēmus	audiēmus
2	parābitis	monēbitis	regētis	audiētis
3	parābunt	monēbunt	regent	audient
imperfect				
sg 1	parābam	monēbam	regēbam	audiēbam
2	parābās	monēbās	regēbās	audiēbās
3	parābat	monēbat	regēbat	audiēbat
pl 1	parābāmus	monēbāmus	regēbāmus	audiēbāmus
2	parābātis	monēbātis	regēbātis	audiēbātis
3	parābant	monēbant	regēbant	audiēbant

Imperative

sg 2	parā	monē	rege	audī
3	parātō	monētō	regitō	audītō
pl 2	parāte	monēte	regite	audīte
3	parantō	monentō	reguntō	audiuntō

Summary of Grammar

Participle

pres.	parāns	monēns	regēns	audiēns
fut.	parātūrus	monitūrus	rēctūrus	audītūrus

Gerund

parandum	monendum	regendum	audiendum

Active — Indicative

	1st conj.	2nd conj.	3rd conj.	4th conj.
perfect				
sg 1	parāvī	monuī	rēxī	audīvī
2	parāvistī	monuistī	rēxistī	audīvistī
3	parāvit	monuit	rēxit	audīvit
pl 1	parāvimus	monuimus	rēximus	audīvimus
2	parāvistis	monuistis	rēxistis	audīvistis
3	parāvērunt	monuērunt	rēxērunt	audīvērunt
future perfect				
sg 1	parāverō	monuerō	rēxerō	audīverō
2	parāveris	monueris	rēxeris	audīveris
3	parāverit	monuerit	rēxerit	audīverit
pl 1	parāverimus	monuerimus	rēxerimus	audīverimus
2	parāveritis	monueritis	rēxeritis	audīveritis
3	parāverint	monuerint	rēxerint	audīverint
pluperfect				
sg 1	parāveram	monueram	rēxeram	audīveram
2	parāverās	monuerās	rēxerās	audīverās
3	parāverat	monuerat	rēxerat	audīverat
pl 1	parāverāmus	monuerāmus	rēxerāmus	audīverāmus
2	parāverātis	monuerātis	rēxerātis	audīverātis
3	parāverant	monuerant	rēxerant	audīverant

Infinitive

pres.	parāre	monēre	regere	audīre
fut.	parātūrus esse	monitūrus esse	rēctūrus esse	audītūrus esse
perf.	parāvisse	monuisse	rēxisse	audīvisse

Supine

	parātum	monitum	rēctum	audītum

The 3 pl. perf. ind. act., particularly in verse, may also end in **-ēre** or sometimes **-erunt**.

Mixed conjugation

Verbs such as **faciō** and **capiō** follow the pattern of **regō** for all forms based on the present stem, but they take the endings of the 4th conjugation where the latter have two successive vowels: so **capiō** and **capiunt** vs. **capis** and **capit**, and likewise **capiam**, **capiēbam**, **capiēns** etc.

Summary of Grammar

Passive — Indicative

	1st conj.	2nd conj.	3rd conj.	4th conj.
present				
sg 1	paror	moneor	regor	audior
2	parāris	monēris	regeris	audīris
3	parātur	monētur	regitur	audītur
pl 1	parāmur	monēmur	regimur	audīmur
2	parāminī	monēminī	regiminī	audīminī
3	parantur	monentur	reguntur	audiuntur
future				
sg 1	parābor	monēbor	regar	audiar
2	parāberis	monēberis	regēris	audiēris
3	parābitur	monēbitur	regētur	audiētur
pl 1	parābimur	monēbimur	regēmur	audiēmur
2	parābiminī	monēbiminī	regēminī	audiēminī
3	parābuntur	monēbuntur	regentur	audientur
imperfect				
sg 1	parābar	monēbar	regēbar	audiēbar
2	parābā ris	monēbāris	regēbāris	audiēbāris
3	parābātur	monēbātur	regēbātur	audiēbātur
pl 1	parābāmur	monēbāmur	regēbāmur	audiēbāmur
2	parābāminī	monēbāminī	regēbāminī	audiēbāminī
3	parābantur	monēbantur	regēbantur	audiēbantur

Imperative

	1st conj.	2nd conj.	3rd conj.	4th conj.
sg 2	parāre	monēre	regere	audīre
3	parātor	monētor	regitor	audītor
pl 2	parāminī	monēminī	regiminī	audīminī
3	parantor	monentor	reguntor	audiuntor

Gerundive

| parandus | monendus | regendus | audiendus |

Passive — Indicative

	1st conj.	2nd conj.	3rd conj.	4th conj.
perfect				
sg 1	parātus sum	monitus sum	rēctus sum	audītus sum
	... es *etc.*	... es *etc.*	... es *etc.*	... es *etc.*
future perfect				
sg 1	parātus erō	monitus erō	rēctus erō	audītus erō
	... eris *etc.*	... eris *etc.*	... eris *etc.*	... eris *etc.*
pluperfect				
sg 1	parātus eram	monitus eram	rēctus eram	audītus eram
	... erās *etc.*	... erās *etc.*	... erās *etc.*	... erās *etc.*

Infinitive

pres.	parārī	monērī	regī	audīrī
fut.	parātum īrī	monitum īrī	rēctum īrī	audītum īrī
perf.	parātus esse	monitus esse	rēctus esse	audītus esse

Participle

perf.	parātus	monitus	rēctus	audītus

Notes

1 In those passive forms that include the perfect participle,
   the participle is adjectival and agrees with its subject, e.g.
   parātī erāmus. The same applies to passive subjunctives
   containing the participle.

2 The future infinitive is made up of the supine (not the perfect participle) with **īrī**; the supine does not change in this form.

3 Except in the present indicative, any passive 2 sg. form ending in **-ris** may instead end in **-re**; this applies equally to the subjunctive forms on pp. 623–4.

4 For verbs like **capiō** the principle given at the foot of p. 619 applies to the passive as to the active, thus **capior** and **capiuntur** beside **caperis** and **capitur**, similarly **capiar** and **capiēbar**.

Active — Subjunctive

	1st conj.	2nd conj.	3rd conj.	4th conj.
present				
sg 1	parem	moneam	regam	audiam
2	parēs	moneās	regās	audiās
3	paret	moneat	regat	audiat
pl 1	parēmus	moneāmus	regāmus	audiāmus
2	parētis	moneātis	regātis	audiātis
3	parent	moneant	regant	audiant
imperfect				
sg 1	parārem	monērem	regerem	audīrem
2	parārēs	monērēs	regerēs	audīrēs
3	parāret	monēret	regeret	audīret
pl 1	parārēmus	monērēmus	regerēmus	audīrēmus
2	parārētis	monērētis	regerētis	audīrētis
3	parārent	monērent	regerent	audīrent
perfect				
sg 1	parāverim	monuerim	rēxerim	audīverim
2	parāverīs	monuerīs	rēxerīs	audīverīs
3	parāverit	monuerit	rēxerit	audīverit
pl 1	parāverīmus	monuerīmus	rēxerīmus	audīverīmus
2	parāverītis	monuerītis	rēxerītis	audīverītis
3	parāverint	monuerint	rēxerint	audīverint
pluperfect				
sg 1	parāvissem	monuissem	rēxissem	audīvissem
2	parāvissēs	monuissēs	rēxissēs	audīvissēs
3	parāvisset	monuisset	rēxisset	audīvisset
pl 1	parāvissēmus	monuissēmus	rēxissēmus	audīvissēmus
2	parāvissētis	monuissētis	rēxissētis	audīvissētis
3	parāvissent	monuissent	rēxissent	audīvissent

Summary of Grammar

Passive — Subjunctive

	1st conj.	2nd conj.	3rd conj.	4th conj.
present				
sg 1	parer	monear	regar	audiar
2	parēris	moneāris	regāris	audiāris
3	parētur	moneātur	regātur	audiātur
pl 1	parēmur	moneāmur	regāmur	audiāmur
2	parēminī	moneāminī	regāminī	audiāminī
3	parentur	moneantur	regantur	audiantur
imperfect				
sg 1	parā rer	monērer	regerer	audīrer
2	parā rēris	monērēris	regerēris	audīrēris
3	parā rētur	monērētur	regerētur	audīrētur
pl 1	parā rēmur	monērēmur	regerēmur	audīrēmur
2	parā rēminī	monērēminī	regerēminī	audīrēminī
3	parā rentur	monērentur	regerentur	audīrentur
perfect				
sg 1	parātus sim	monitus sim	rē ctus sim	audītus sim
	... sīs *etc.*	... sīs *etc.*	... sīs *etc.*	... sīs *etc.*
pluperfect				
sg 1	parātus essem	monitus essem	rēctus essem	audītus essem
	... essēs *etc.*	... essēs *etc.*	... essēs *etc.*	... essēs *etc.*

Notes

1 As with the indicative, in those passive forms that include the perfect participle, the participle is adjectival and agrees with its subject, e.g. **parātī sīmus**.

2 There is no future subjunctive: in indirect questions, a future tense, if active, is reported with the future participle

(agreeing with its subject) and **sim** or **essem** *etc.* according to sequence.

3 Any subjunctive passive 2 sg. form ending in **-ris** may instead end in **-re**.

4 For verbs like **capiō** the principle given at the foot of p. 619 applies to the subjunctive as to the indicative; thus the present subjunctive **capiam** and **capiar** has the **-i-** throughout like **audiam** and **audiar** while **caperem** and **caperer** do not.

Irregular Verbs

	sum, esse, fuī I am, to be		possum, posse, potuī I can, to be able	
	indicative	subjunctive	indicative	subjunctive
present				
sg 1	sum	sim	possum	possim
2	es	sīs	potes	possīs
3	est	sit	potest	possit
pl 1	sumus	sīmus	possumus	possīmus
2	estis	sītis	potestis	possītis
3	sunt	sint	possunt	possint
future				
sg 1	erō		poterō	
2	eris		poteris	
3	erit		poterit	
pl 1	erimus		poterimus	
2	eritis		poteritis	
3	erunt		poterunt	
imperfect				
sg 1	eram	essem	poteram	possem
2	erās	essēs	poterās	possēs
3	erat	esset	poterat	posset
pl 1	erāmus	essēmus	poterāmus	possēmus
2	erātis	essētis	poterātis	possētis
3	erant	essent	poterant	possent

For these verbs, the tenses formed from the perfect stem are formed regularly, from the stems **fu-** and **potu-** (thus **fuī** and **potuī** as, for example, **monuī**). Neither verb has a present or perfect participle; the future participle of **esse** is **futūrus**. The imperatives from **esse** are **es** and **estō** in the singular, and **este** and **suntō** in the plural. The present and perfect infinitives are formed regularly; **esse** has a future infinitive which is either **futūrus esse** or **fore**.

	volō, velle, voluī *I want*		nōlō, nōlle, nōluī *I do not want*		mālō, mālle, māluī *I prefer*	
	indic.	subj.	indic.	subj.	indic.	subj.
present						
sg 1	volō	velim	nōlō	nōlim	mālō	mālim
2	vīs	velīs	nōn vīs	nōlīs	māvīs	mālīs
3	vult	velit	nōn vult	nōlit	māvult	mālit
pl 1	volumus	velīmus	nōlumus	nōlīmus	mālumus	mālīmus
2	vultis	velītis	nōn vultis	nōlītis	māvultis	mālītis
3	volunt	velint	nōlunt	nōlint	mālunt	malint
future						
sg 1	volam		nōlam		mālam	
2	volēs *etc.*		nōlēs *etc.*		mālēs *etc.*	
imperfect						
sg 1	volēbam	vellem	nōlēbam	nōllem	mālēbam	māllem
2	volēbās	vellēs	nōlēbās	nōllēs	mālēbās	māllēs
	etc.	*etc.*	*etc.*	*etc.*	*etc.*	*etc.*

Tenses formed from the perfect stem are formed regularly for all three verbs, from the stems **volu-**, **nōlu-**, and **mālu-**. Present participles are **volēns** and **nō lēns**; **mālō** has no participle. The only imperatives are from **nōlō**: **nōlī** and **nōlītō** in the singular, and **nōlīte** and **nōluntō** in the plural. There are no supines.

	eō, īre, iī, itum *I go*		fīō, fierī *I become; I am made*	
	indicative	subjunctive	indicative	subjunctive
present				
sg 1	eō	eam	fīō	fīam
2	īs	eās	fīs	fīās
3	it	eat	fit	fīat
pl 1	īmus	eāmus	(fīmus)	fīāmus
2	ītis	eātis	(fītis)	fīātis
3	eunt	eant	fīunt	fīant
future				
sg 1	ībō		fīam	
2	ībis *etc.*		fīēs *etc.*	
imperfect				
sg 1	ībam	īrem	fīēbam	fierem
2	ībās *etc.*	īrēs *etc.*	fīēbās *etc.*	fierēs *etc.*

Tenses formed from the perfect stem are formed regularly for **eō**, from the stem **i-**, although **ii-** before **-s-** usually becomes **ī-**; thus **iī, īstī, iit** *etc.* A perfect stem **īv-** is occasionally found. The present participle is **iēns** (gen. sg. **euntis**) and the future participle **itūrus**. The imperatives from **eō** are **ī** and **ītō** in the singular, and **īte** and **euntō** in the plural. The future and perfect infinitives are formed regularly; the gerund is **eundum**. The impersonal 3 sg. pres. indic. **ītur** is common.

fīō has no forms in tenses/moods other than those given. Note that **fīō** takes the place of the passive forms from the present stem of **faciō** and its compounds.